ACCLAIM FOR

Robert Hughes's

BARCELONA

"For those interested in epic storytelling, captivating characters, and authoritative insights, *Barcelona* has no real competition. . . . Hughes leads readers on an enlightening and sophisticated cultural journey that will illuminate the city's history."
—*San Francisco Chronicle*

"Lavish . . . Hughes sees deeply and meticulously [and] his feel for the texture of things [is] acute . . . a tribute that could hardly be better rendered."
—*Chicago Tribune*

"Hughes can move commandingly from a Miró canvas to transvestite hookers in the street without missing a beat—and bring to both the same kind of rigorous attention and full-bodied sensibility. . . . The text is enlivened at every turn by . . . mischievous erudition, rococo diction, and Augustan bite."
—*Time*

"Truly majestic . . . The city is lucky to be commemorated . . . by so formidable a chronicler. . . . [A] cornucopia of facts, evocations, interpretations and speculations, presented with a grand enthusiasm . . . immense range, variety, and exuberance."
—Jan Morris, *Los Angeles Times*

"Hughes is a writer of such virtuosity that he could make a mattress tag lively reading. . . . He has sketched a portrait of the city and its 2,000-year history with such brio that one comes to think of it as a person. . . . His writing is a species of engaging highbrow hip-hop—great fun in itself. . . . His kinetic prose is a performance."
—*Christian Science Monitor*

Also by Robert Hughes

Robert Hughes

BARCELONA

Robert Hughes was born in Australia in 1938 and has
lived in Europe and the United States since 1964. Since
1970 he has worked in New York as art critic for *Time*
magazine. His books include *The Art of Australia* (1966);
Heaven and Hell in Western Art (1969); *The Shock of the New*
(1981, 1991); *The Fatal Shore* (1987), winner of both the
W. H. Smith Prize and the Duff Cooper Award; a collection of essays on art and artists, *Nothing If Not Critical*
(1990); and *Frank Auerbach* (1990). He has twice received
the Franklin Jewett Mather Award for Distinguished
Criticism from the College Art Association of America,
and in 1991 was made an Officer in the Order of
Australia.

BARCELONA

Robert Hughes

VINTAGE BOOKS

A DIVISION OF RANDOM HOUSE, INC.

NEW YORK

FIRST VINTAGE BOOKS EDITION, MARCH 1993

Copyright © 1992 by Robert Hughes

All rights reserved under International and Pan-American
Copyright Conventions. Published in the United States by
Vintage Books, a division of Random House, Inc., New York,
and simultaneously in Canada by Random House of Canada
Limited, Toronto. Originally published in hardcover by
Alfred A. Knopf, Inc., New York, in 1992.

Library of Congress Cataloging-in-Publication Data
Hughes, Robert, 1938–
Barcelona / Robert Hughes.—1st Vintage Books ed.
p.   cm.
Includes bibliographical references and index.
ISBN 0-679-74383-9 (pbk.)
1. Barcelona (Spain)—Civilization.   2. Barcelona (Spain)—
Buidlings, structures, etc.   3. Arts, Spanish—Spain—Barcelona.
4. Architecture—Spain—Barcelona.   I. Title.
DP402.B265H86   1992
946'.72—dc20   92-56349
CIP

Designed by Barbara Balch

Author photograph © Joyce Ravid

Manufactured in the United States of America
10   9   8   7   6   5   4   3   2   1

For Xavier and Maria-Luisa Corberó

CONTENTS

This book was meant to be thinner. My original intent, in 1987, was to write an account of the *modernista* or Art Nouveau period (roughly, 1875–1910) in Barcelona, concentrating on its architecture, as a companion for visitors to the city.

This notion changed. It would have meant examining the foliage of the tree without considering its trunk and roots. So much of what was built in Barcelona in the late nineteenth century was grounded in a strong, even obsessive, sense of the Catalan past, in particular its medieval past, that there was little point in trying to describe the newer without the older. Moreover, the desire to revive the glories of the Catalan middle ages, felt so strongly by the architects of Barcelona's *fin de siècle*, was also shared by writers, painters, and sculptors, and deeply entwined with the issues of political independence from Madrid and a sense of cultural continuity expressed in the struggle for the Catalan language.

It is a truism that all cities are shaped by politics. But it is true nevertheless—and true, to a spectacular and insistent degree, of Barcelona. To take only the Catalan architect everyone has heard of, Antoni Gaudí: his work is hard to read until one grasps not only his sense of a specifically Catalan past, but his convictions about Catalan autonomy and his intense and patriarchal religious conservatism as well. In such matters lies the clue to why his rich patrons, notably Eusebi Güell, employed him: not just because he was an architect of genius, but because his ideology fitted theirs. The political and economic history of Barcelona is written all over its plan and buildings, and one cannot begin to understand Catalan architecture—particularly that of the nineteenth century, when it was such a forceful expression of national aspiration—

without the image bank of local identity that lay behind it and often makes sense of what the foreign visitor is apt, at first, to assign to "mere" fantasy.

The time span of the book is nearly two thousand years, from the emergence of Barcelona as a tiny Augustan colony in the first century A.D. to the death of Gaudí in 1926. It treats the Roman, Visigothic, Moorish, and Frankish periods of the city—say, to about 900 A.D.— very sketchily. Its period is the thousand years after that, and its main concentration is on the city in the second half of the nineteenth and the first quarter of the twentieth century. I refer to some of the urbanistic and cultural results of the Franco years (1939–75) in the first chapter, but I have made no attempt to deal with the Republic and the civil war at all, since it is the one decade in Barcelona's history that is exhaustively covered by non-Spanish historians—and it requires, in any case, skills I do not have.

The coming decade, it seems, will see the final winding-up of the model of cultural activity that served modernism so well, one that it inherited from papal Rome and seventeenth- to nineteenth-century Paris: the idea of the central city dictating its norms to the provinces and colonies. Probably the last city to assume that role in culture was New York, whose heyday lasted from about 1925 to 1975. In a postimperial world sundered by irrepressible nationalisms, and in a Europe where— irony of ironies—nationalist fervor, often of an ugly and racist kind, is once more on the rise even as the structures of European unification are bolted into place, the focus of cultural interest seems bound to follow the political shift and address itself to the local, the particular, the "non-mainstream." In writing about Barcelona, I wanted to write about a culture that was, from the point of view of the larger capitals, "provincial." (No doubt this was involved, on a none-too-subliminal level, with the fact that I am a provincial, an Australian.) Even though the issue of Catalan political separatism was repudiated by its own State government in September 1991 and now seems politically dead except among a few nostalgists and rhetoricians (it could hardly be expected to survive the real democratic changes of Spain after 1975), the sense of Catalunya as a distinct cultural entity within the larger Iberian body endures. It has been a source of great strength—and, occasionally, of self-delusion as well—for writers, architects, and artists, many of whom viewed their own creative efforts as rebuttals of centralism; and its results have often transcended centralist ideas of the "merely local."

There remains, however, one thing I must emphasize. This is not intended to be, in any sense, a "scholarly" work. It is a general introduction. It is written from secondary sources and makes no claim to academic rigor, though I have made every effort to get the facts right. Nothing in it is aimed at the specialist in Catalan history. This should be clear from the absence of footnotes. For those who wish to pursue the story of the city in more detail—and most of the pursuit must be done in Catalan and Spanish, since relatively little that is of value has been written on Barcelona in English—I have included a bibliography of the main sources consulted. It represents, as I hope will be apparent, quite a lot of looking, reading, and walking over the last twenty years, but it is aimed at the intelligent general reader: the person I kept writing for, I now realize, was my younger self when I first came under the spell of the city Joan Maragall called *la gran encisera*, "the great enchantress"—making his first visits to Barcelona, neither reading nor speaking the language, unfamiliar with the city, but extremely curious about it.

My main thanks for help with the book go to two people: Marcy Rudo, researcher, whose work on both the historical research and the finding of pictures in Barcelona archives was invaluable; and Xavier Corberó, for his generous friendship in letting me use his house so long, and so often, during the research and writing. Others favored me with guidance, information, and encouragement, though they are not to be blamed for the errors that inevitably arise when a non-Spanish writer attempts to tackle the intricacies of Catalan cultural history: Josep Acebillo, Oriol Bohigas, Victoria Combalía, Beth Galí, Lluís Goytisolo, Jordi Llovet, David Mackay, Margarita Obiols, Xavier Rubert de Ventós, and Maria-Luisa Tifón.

BARCELONA

CHAPTER ONE

The Color of a Dog Running Away

I

It is possible, some days, to see the whole of Barcelona with your feet on the ground. The vantage point is the old funfair on the Collserola massif behind the city, known as Tibidabo. Its odd name comes from the Latin phrase meaning "I will give you": words spoken by the devil to Jesus Christ when he took him up on a mountain and showed him the estates of the world in their entire and seductive vanity. Jesus refused the offer; the modern visitor need not. When the weather is wrong and a dome of heat hangs over Barcelona, pressing the exhaust gases of its cars down into a brown smog that stretches out to sea, with only a few modern skyscrapers and the towers of Antoni Gaudí's church of the Sagrada Família, like drippy wax candles, piercing the murk, it is a depressing sight. But then the next morning a wind will spring up and carry the smirched air away, and the whole city looks washed, virginal, new in the sunlight.

Barcelona is really three cities, sharply distinct in character, the newest enclosing the older, in which the oldest is set. On the perimeter, laced with ribbons of freeway, are the industrial suburbs that grew up in the post-1945 years of the Franco dictatorship; they are the products of unconstrained, unplanned growth in the 1950s and 1960s, stretching south to the Llobregat and north to the Besós rivers—a sprawl of factories and polygons, housing blocks for the hundreds of thousands of migrant workers who flooded Barcelona and decisively changed its social mix. Inside that is the big nineteenth-century grid of the Eixample, or Enlargement, which occupies the coastal plain where the massif breaks away and slopes down to the Mediterranean: the New City, a repetitive carpet of squares with chamfered corners, slit by larger avenues, all laid out on paper in 1859 and mostly filled in by 1910. Then, inside that, where the grid meets the bay, you see the regular march of units break up, bunch into confusion, and become an irregular cell cluster from which older-looking protrusions rise: old square towers, Gothic peaks. This is the Old City, the Barri Gòtic, or Gothic Quarter. To the right of it, the mountain of Montjuic rises. Beyond Montjuic lies the flat plane of the Mediterranean, silky, blue, and glittering. Inland ridge, plain, mountain, sea: the elements from which the city's life was shaped.

I became a Barcelona enthusiast, as near as I can recall, in the spring of 1966. I hardly knew a word of Spanish, let alone Catalan, but I went there for the oblique reason that I was fanatically keen on George Orwell and wanted to see the place to which he had paid his homage—the one city in Europe about which that insular Englishman felt moved to write with wholehearted affection. I did have one Catalan friend, met in London, who turned out to be my key to the city: one of the last of its dandies, the sculptor Xavier Corberó, a wiry bantam of a man with a bladelike gypsy nose, a sharp cackling sense of humor, and an aptitude for carving marble into refined shells, wings, and demilunes. Corberó's ambition, which he shared with a number of young Catalans—writers, economists, doctors, architects, embryo politicians—was to help Barcelona recapture some of the luster it had a half century before their birth, back in the 1880s: a moment forgotten, in 1966, by everyone but the Catalans themselves.

This seemed to deter neither Corberó nor his friends. He lived in a dark rambling *masia*, or farmhouse, preserved along with the rest of a rural lane, south of the city in Esplugües de Llobregat. *Esplugües* means "caves," and indeed the place seemed riddled with catacombs dating back to Roman times; Corberó kept thousands of bottles of excellent wine in them, not racked but dumped in heaps, the labels half-obliterated by mold and rats. In this labyrinth, one was apt to lose track of time and place alike, given the Spanish hours and a floating population of polyglot houseguests, but most mornings I would manage to lurch out into the white-gold coastal light like a disoriented bat and head for the city, there to study—if that was the mot juste—the works of Gaudí and his circle, to riffle through the boxes of prints and cards and old photos in the dark narrow bookshops in the Barri Gòtic, and then, at three in the afternoon, to have lunch.

The meals of my conversion took place in the fish restaurants that stuck like wooden fingers out to the beach at Barceloneta, the triangular grid of tenement blocks occupying the northern end of the port, built by an eighteenth-century engineer to house some of the fishermen and other workers left roofless after the Bourbon conquest of Barcelona in 1714. These restaurants are gone now, swept away by the socialist city government's redevelopment of the seashore. They were a popular institution then, and cheap. The best of them was called El Salmonete, but they all had much the same layout. One walked past the open kitchen, with its haze of smoke from the roaring grills and crackle of sea things dumped with a flourish in tubs of boiling oil, and past the gargantuan display of ingredients—the round trays of *cigalas*, each stiffly arched on the ice; the mounds of red shrimp; the arrays of dentex, sea bass, squid, minuscule sand dabs, sardines, and toad-headed anglerfish; the tanks of live rock lobsters (*Palinurus vulgaris*, named for Aeneas's drowned helmsman). One sat down as near the doors to the sea as possible. One struggled with the Catalan menu.

Fried baby eels arrived, like white spaghetti in boiling oil; raw gooseneck barnacles known as *percebes*; and *parrilladas*, oval steel platters crammed with six or eight kinds of grilled fish. The long noisy room was full of families, three generations represented at each trestle table, from elderly patriarchs with seamed faces and nailbrush mustaches, down to *allioli*-smeared infants gumming their first squid. Beyond the glass doors, it seemed that half the working population of Barcelona was spending its lunchtime on the beach. No matter that the sand was grayish brown and littered with plastic. This was a populist paradise, like Reginald Marsh's drawings of Coney Island in the 1930s or the Bondi Beach I had left behind in Sydney in 1964.

Barceloneta presented a spectacle of democratic pleasure very unlike other parts of the Mediterranean I had come to know. This, it dawned on me through the wine and the hubbub, was because the city around it was in essence a citizen's town. Barcelona has always been more a city of capital and labor than of nobility and commoners; its democratic roots are old and run very deep. Its medieval charter of citizens' rights, the Usatges, grew from a nucleus which antedated the Magna Carta by more than a hundred years. Its government, the Consell de Cent (Council of One Hundred), had been the oldest protodemocratic political body in Spain. On it, artisans and laborers had equal votes with landowners and bankers. Catalans were fervent trade unionists at a time when most other Spaniards were bowing to the throne, and repeatedly, from the Burning of the Convents in 1835, through its various revolts of the 1840s and 1850s, its anarchist bombings of the 1890s, the orgy of anticlerical violence called the Setmana Tragica in 1909, and, of course, its bitter resistance to Franco and its terrible internecine conflicts and betrayals among anarchists, republicans, and Stalinists during the civil war of

1936–39, the city tore or blew itself apart in spasms of class violence. This seemed (at least to a young and vaguely left-leaning writer in the 1960s) to confer on it a more romantic character than most other modern places in Spain. The independence of Barcelonese working-class character was summed up in a cabaret song about the girl from Sants, the quarter between Montjuic and the sea, where the big calico mills once were. *"Soc filla de Sants, / tinc les males sangs i les tares / de la llibertat"*:

> I am a daughter of Sants
> And I've got the bloodymindedness
> And the faults
> Of the freedom
> My parents gave me—
> The factory made me feel
> Whimsical . . .

I admired the signs of this spirit with the naïve intensity that (fortunately or not) is reserved for one's twenties. But what did foreigners, including juvenile art critics, know about Barcelona and its peculiar local culture twenty-five years ago? Almost nothing. The fifteen hundred years of the city's existence had produced only five names that came easily to mind: the cellist Pau Casals, the artist Joan Miró and his somewhat tarnished coeval Salvador Dalí, both of whom were still very much alive, and the dead architect Antoni Gaudí, whom most visitors supposed to have been some kind of a Surrealist as well. And Picasso, who had studied there as a youth and remained sentimentally attached to his memories of its fin de siècle bohemia. Barcelona was the springboard from which he dived into Paris. There were fragments of literary association too: Jean Genet, for instance, had reputedly based his play *The Balcony* on a seedily grand whorehouse that in the 1960s still existed in the Eixample. It boasted rooms of illusion whose tattiness echoed that of the preelectronic funfair up on Tibidabo. They included, apart from the usual dungeons and fairy grottoes, a room fixed up as the sleeping carriage on an imagined Orient Express. The bed shook and a crudely painted diorama of the Alps unrolled past the window, getting stuck now and again. But the house, far from being the theater of power imagined by Genet, was frequented mainly by sedate Catalan businessmen who played Parcheesi with the girls.

Apart from Gaudí's more visible buildings, such as the Sagrada Família or La Pedrera (the Stone Quarry, as everyone calls the undulating apartment block, formally known as the Casa Milà, on Passeig de

Gràcia), the rest of the city might as well have been created—to a foreigner's eye—by men from Mars. Barcelona had two great periods of building: the first in the Middle Ages, which created the Old City, and the second between 1870 and 1910, which formed the Eixample, the New City. Most of these buildings were in a recognizable Art Nouveau idiom, and in the mid-1960s the rehabilitation of Art Nouveau had not yet happened; for most people it was still an obsolete, unrevivable period style, an ornamental freak, liked mainly by hippies.

No guidebooks to Barcelonese architecture existed that were of any use. Who outside Catalunya had ever heard of such architects as Lluís Domènech i Montaner, for instance, or Josep Puig i Cadafalch? Or, for that matter, Ildefons Cerdà i Sunyer, the socialist civil engineer who in 1859 had designed the grid layout of the Eixample, the first of modernism's Utopian city plans and (in its original form) the only humane one? What foreign visitors, except a few specialists who knew Catalan, could read the verse of Barcelona's leading poets of the period from 1875 to 1925, Jacint Verdaguer, Joan Maragall, Josep Carner? Or the sinewy and idiomatic prose of its indefatigable chronicler, Josep Pla, the city's memory man? None that I knew, and certainly not me. Portable and untroubled by the opacities of foreign language, painting crossed the world's cultural frontiers easily. You might (indeed, you would) somewhat misunderstand Miró by not grasping the Catalanism that lies behind so many of his images and by missing the peculiarly local references in his work—hints that cannot be fully experienced without visiting Catalunya and knowing something about the special sentiments that, in the early 1900s, attached to its folklore and rural life. The same, mutatis mutandis, with Dali. But you could certainly tune in to what was general, rather than local, in their surrealism. This was not the case with other aspects of Catalan culture, and so the city remained largely illegible to the foreigner. And what kind of political history, earlier than the civil war, was inscribed on its stones? Nobody except the Catalans—and not all of them, either—seemed to know.

II

The sight of the present was disagreeable enough. In the late 1960s only a minority of Barcelonans had any adult memory of democratic government in Spain. Those born after 1925 had none whatsoever. Franco's dictatorship had begun in 1939 and it was to last until 1975: thirty-six years of uninterrupted one-man power, consolidated, at first, by vengeance and a ruthless settling of scores. The Caudillo had started off with a purge of all Catalan resistance. Thousands of left-wingers were shot without trial, beginning at the top with Lluís Companys, the last republican president of the Generalitat, the state government of Catalunya. Many of their bodies—nobody knows how many, since the Falange did not keep records—were cast into an abandoned quarry on the southern flank of Montjuic; twenty years later, if the ground of this mass grave was wet from rain, one could still smell the very faint but persistent odor of their decay in the air. Tens of thousands more Catalans, like other Spaniards, fled into exile or were deported.

Opposition parties continued to exist in Catalunya after 1939, tolerated, though barely, in order to diffuse the image of autocracy. There was, for instance, the National Front of Catalunya, a left-wing nationalist group, and the Liberty Front, consisting mainly of Marxists and anarcho-syndicalists, which was in effect a splinter off the POUM, or Partit Obrer d'Unificació Marxista, the party that had played so large a role in Catalunya during the civil war. But they were closely watched, tiny and completely ineffective. Though resentment of Franco simmered on among Barcelonese workers, the unions were too weak to provide any organized resistance; the postwar years had only one big strike, in 1951, in protest against a fare increase on Barcelona's soon-to-be-abolished tramway system. It was the last protest by the civil war generation of Catalan workers. The 1950s saw all vestiges of anti-Franco hopes extinguished, and even the forlorn expectation of moral pressure from abroad died when Franco signed accords with the Vatican and with the United States in 1953.

One of the key elements of Franco's ideology was centralism: the belief, to which no exceptions were allowed, that Spain was a unified body whose head was Madrid; that, in the celebrated phrase of José Ortega y Gasset, "Spain is a thing made by Castile." This concept had had a long history. It had lain at the core of the policies of the Hapsburg and then the Bourbon monarchs toward Catalunya. As long as it existed, Catalans resented it as an affront to their sense of political selfhood. That selfhood was definitively lost with the civil war. Barcelona had been the last bastion of resistance to Franco, and the dictator never forgave the city for it. After 1939 Catalunya was disbanded as an autonomous political region and split into four smaller provinces.

Now the Caudillo disliked Barcelona not only because it resisted him but because tsars, emperors, and dictators, right or left, are apt to distrust ports; in the days of shipping, port cities were too open to the influence of foreigners, to strange and nonnative ideas—shifting and labile places, offering an ease of entry and exit that a landlocked capital does not. The port is where the *ser autentic*, or "essence," of a country, as centralizing power imagines it, begins to fray. That is why Peter the Great's successors shifted the capital of Russia from Saint Petersburg to Moscow; why Kemal Atatürk, inheriting one of the world's great port capitals in Istanbul, chose to create a new administrative center in Ankara; why the absurd and artificial Brasília, not Rio de Janeiro, is the capital of Brazil. It may also help explain Franco's desire to make it clear to Barcelona that it no longer had any right to consider itself the capital of anywhere.

The retribution that Falangism visited on its defeated enemy was cultural. Freedom of thought, publication, and teaching were suppressed throughout Spain as a whole, but in Catalunya the target was language itself. The civil war had been a class struggle, but Franco saw very clearly that the Catalans were also animated by strong feelings of local, cultural nationalism and that this was bound up with the preservation and use of their language.

In 1714, as part of Catalunya's punishment for backing the wrong side in the War of the Spanish Succession, Felipe V banned the public use of Catalan in teaching, publishing, the press, and government. The logic was simple: deprived of their ancestral tongue, the Catalans would no longer be able to think separatist thoughts. This strategem failed, but after 1939 Franco renewed it, with much more efficiency and zeal. As a result, you could walk down the Ramblas in 1966 hearing Catalan spoken on every side and see newspapers, magazines, and books on the newsstands in all languages—Spanish, German, English, French, Dutch, Swedish—except one: Catalan. The official line was that Catalan was merely a dialect of Spanish and, as such, a source of internal division, a useless linguistic fossil. "It may be said," ran a state-sponsored textbook of the time, cast in question-and-answer form, "that in Spain only the Castilian language is spoken, for apart from it, only Basque is used, which is spoken as the only language in no more than a few Basque hamlets; it is reduced to the functions of a dialect by its linguistic and philological poverty. Q.—And what are the main dialects spoken in Spain? A.—They are four: Catalan, Valencian, Majorcan and Galician.

This was, in fact, false. Catalan is not a dialect of Castilian. Nevertheless, Franco's campaign against it was effective—in the short run. Writers might write in Catalan as a gesture of defiance, but their relation with the public was broken, since Catalan texts had only a small chance of publication. Nevertheless there were signs of relaxation of the ban in the 1960s. From 1959 onward intellectuals and academics had been petitioning the government to "normalize" the use of Catalan, but with scant success. Then in 1962 an indispensable publishing venture began: Editions 62, whose aim was to bring out, in paperback, as complete a set as possible of significant literary and historic texts written in Catalan, from the early chronicles of Jaume I and Bernat Desclot through to the present. In 1967 the regime reluctantly allowed the University of Barcelona to form a department of Catalan-language studies—Catalan was taught as though it were a foreign language like French or English. In 1970 the secondary schools were allowed to teach Catalan, but under the same conditions, though such courses were uncommon and did not become general until after 1975, the year of Franco's death.

In 1966 Catalan was still officially a proscribed language—even shop signs and street names had to be in Castilian—and the anti-Catalanist slogans of the Falange were still fresh in memory: "*Perro Catalan, habla en cristiano*" ("Catalan dog, speak Christian") or, a shade less offensively, "*No ladres! Habla la lengua del imperio!*" ("Don't bark! Speak the language of the empire!"). Most Catalans, particularly in the countryside and the provincial towns outside Barcelona, still spoke Catalan as a matter of course. But so long a campaign against the language had effects that are still felt today. Eleven years after Franco died, the 1986 census showed that while 89 percent of the residents of Catalunya between forty-five and sixty-four years of age (that is, the sector of the populace that had grown to adulthood during his dictatorship—1.36 million people) could *understand* Catalan when it was spoken to them, only 59 percent of them could actually speak it, 55 percent read it, and a mere 20 percent write it. By contrast, among the 1.39 million Catalans aged fifteen to twenty-nine—those who received their education after the Caudillo's death—95 percent could understand the spoken language, 73 percent speak it, 75 percent read it, and 48 percent write it. The language owed its survival to a tenacious oral tradition, but its increase since 1975 was also due to an aggressive program of education launched by the new democratic governments of both the state of Catalunya and the city of Barcelona. The "implantation" and "fomentation" of Catalan (two words favored by the new breed of sociologues) were a necessary prelude to Catalan *autodeterminació*—whatever *that* was going to mean.

The strongest spontaneous impulse toward the reinstatement of Catalan among the young in the 1960s came from popular folk and early rock music, which was almost automatically political. Pop singers who wrote and performed in Catalan saw themselves as the heirs of Carles Aribau i Farriols, the romantic poet whose "Oda a la Pàtria," written in Catalan in 1833, was the emblematic starting point of the nineteenth-century cultural separatist movement in Barcelona known as the Renaixença. The year 1959 saw the manifesto of the Nova Cançó (New Song) movement, an article by Lluís Serrahima arguing for the right to sing popular songs in the language of the people. New Song rapidly accumulated a nucleus of talent, and its best-known group was Els Setze Jutges, The Sixteen Judges, whose odd-sounding name came from a phrase used as a password by Catalan patriot troops during the rising against an occupation army in 1640 during the Reapers' War: "*Setze jutges d'un jutjat menjen fetge d'un penjat*" ("Sixteen judges on a tribunal eat the liver of a hanged man"). No lisping Castilian, it was believed, could pronounce this barrage of fricatives. New Song got popular fast. The state radio and television channels were opposed to giving it airtime—in 1968 there was a noisy confrontation with Spanish television when the singer Joan Manuel Serrat was chosen to represent Spain at the Eurovision Festival, insisted on singing in Catalan, and found his appearance canceled at the last minute—but despite continuous lawsuits and fines and prohibitions the records sold widely. Two songs in particular became symbols of anti-Franco sentiment among the young: "L'Estaca" ("The Stake") by Lluís Llach, and "Diguem No" ("Let's Say No") by Ramon Pelegro, who sang under the name of Raimon.

The sheer pervasiveness of Franco in the late 1960s—and, truth to tell, the general acquiescence to his regime shown by the ever-pragmatic Catalan middle classes, who cozied up to him after the civil war as quickly as, two hundred years before, they had to the occupying *regidors* of the Bourbon king Felipe V—gave the discontents of youth in Barcelona an air more symbolic than practical. Young Barcelona, as Manuel Vásquez Montalbán caustically wrote, fell into the habit of seeing itself wistfully as Beauty in the thrall of the Beast; the impotence of student "revolution" in France was no surprise to them, for they had metabolized it as style some time before:

At the end of the 1960s, the thin social layer of young, cultivated Barcelonans, who went to France to view the May Revolution, or to Perpignan to see the ass of Marlon Brando, or to Le Boulou to attend a marathon of films banned by Franquism, were still inexorably fated to return to the stable like Cinderella—before midnight, where the ogre was waiting. Clearly, the ogre was an added value. The sophisticated dialectic of the pair Marat and Sade, in Spain, in Catalunya, in Barcelona, turned itself into a picturesque *ménage à trois*: Marat, Sade, and Franco.

Radical chic was as current in Barcelona during the late 1960s and early 1970s as in New York or London. If its emblematic moment in Manhattan was Leonard Bernstein's fund-raiser for the Black Panthers, in Barcelona it was produced by Oriol Regás, the owner of its fashionable political disco, Boccaccio. Several terrorist leaders of ETA, the Basque separatist movement, had been condemned to death in Madrid, and Catalan leftists occupied part of the monastery of Montserrat in protest. In a gesture that combined the selflessness of the Jacobin with the aplomb of Marie Antoinette, Regás dispatched a small van full of Boccaccio's expensive smoked-salmon sandwiches to the holy mountain so that its occupiers would not go hungry in the expected police siege. (It never materialized: the radicals departed.)

In habits, in entertainment, in morals—disgracefully lax, by the puritan standards of Franquism, and getting laxer—and in the sense of style sustained by its *gauche divine*, or "divine left" (a play of words, of course, on the divine right of Spanish monarchs and, by extension, of Franco), in their bars and clubs along the Carrer Tuset, Barcelona in the 1960s was more clearly oriented toward Paris, London, and New York than toward Madrid. But it had also been very deeply marked by Franco, and in more areas than that of language. Particularly so in the composition, shape, and texture of the city itself.

III

Barcelona had a habit of getting and losing its mayors and city governments with bewildering speed. Between 1890 and 1900, for instance, it had no fewer than fifteen mayors. After Franco won the civil war, this turnover stopped. The longest mayoral office in Barcelona's history was held by Franco's appointee, Josep Maria de Porcioles i Colomer, who took over the Ajuntament, or city hall, in March 1957 and remained there for sixteen years straight, retiring only in 1973, two years before his patron's death. This period of one-party rule was also one of huge demographic change in the population and economy of Barcelona.

Between 1920 and 1930 the population of Barcelona had risen by 41 percent, reaching one million at the end of the decade and making it the most populous city in Spain. It was pulling in twenty-five thousand immigrants a year, mostly from the countryside of Catalunya itself. For obvious reasons, this growth ceased altogether during the civil war and hardly began to rise again until 1950. But then there was a wave of immigration to Catalunya from the miserably poor regions of southern Spain, Andalusia especially. By 1965, two million people, half the total population of Catalunya, were living in Barcelona. Today, there are nearly four million, the same population as Sydney or Los Angeles.

This growth continued, at a slightly less frantic pace, through the 1970s, and its effect on the fabric of the city was vast. It created the human fuel for Barcelona's new industrial expansion, which took place on a hitherto unimagined scale. It also began to dissolve the city's once-comprehensible shape—in the absence of any thoughtful or comprehensive planning by Porcioles's city government. Through the 1950s Barcelona sprawled outward into a formless periphery of factories, *terrains vagues*, and industrial slums. Just as the New City of the nineteenth-century, the Eixample, had gobbled up villages once considered remote and distinct from the Old City—Sants, Gracia, Sant Andreu—so the newer Barcelona of the late Franco years absorbed more than twenty neighboring towns and created an industrial belt that stretched as far as the Llobregat River to the south of the city. Between 1964 and 1977 alone, more than five hundred industrial companies pitched their factories on this growing periphery: auto factories, metal-processing plants, plastics, chemicals, synthetic fibers.

The first result of this expansion was a growth of industrial slums —mass cramming of existing buildings, with few effective laws or means of inspection to restrain it. Then, to house the new workers, enormous polygonal clusters of housing blocks were run up, bearing names the tourist never hears—Torrent Gornal, La Pedrosa, Bellvitge, La Guineneta, Verdum, Singuerlin. (The tourists, meanwhile, were also arriving in force in Catalunya from the late 1950s on, heading for Majorca and the semispoiled beaches of the Costa Brava north of Barcelona, the first fish-and-chip belt of the Mediterranean holiday industry—which needed migrant labor as well.) Some of Barcelona's outlying villages, such as Santa Coloma de Gramanet, multiplied their population sevenfold between 1950 and 1970. Fortunes were to be made in these new localities out of cinder blocks, cheap terra-cotta, electrical supplies, plumbing; and if you were in with the local authorities, you made them. "On earth, the God of Wealth was made / Sole Patron of the Building Trade." These were the Spanish cousins of the *grands ensembles* that were to cause such misery and alienation among French workers in the same period: termitaries built by speculators under license from the Caudillo's placemen, designed without paved roads, playgrounds for the kids, or other signs of thought for infrastructure or public space, quite often made of poor materials that started falling apart within a few years. They illustrated the truth that when public housing is at stake, there is not always much to choose from between left and right: Franco's Spain produced the same results as Brezhnev's Russia or Pompidou's France, because abstraction, incuriosity, and greed are among the common attributes of mankind. It is de rigueur today to blame Porcioles and, through him, Franquism itself for everything that went wrong with the urban structure and services of Barcelona between the end of the war and 1975, as though the Caudillo's ideology had some unique power to degrade a city that other political systems did not possess.

But the truth is that neither the capitalist nations (England, France, Italy, the United States, or Australia) nor the Marxist regimes (Russia and its European satellites) did much better than the ritually loathed Porcioles in the domain of urbanism. In those three decades few people in power anywhere in the world, right, left, or center, gave a hoot for the kind of historical, contextual, and environmental responsibilities that city planners must now, at the risk of citizen protest and press criticism, at least pay lip service to. A regard for city context, for planning in terms of large and small fabrics of use and life, in terms of preserving what was already in place and of value, was hardly even a gleam in the eye of civic authorities until the mid-1970s, and Porcioles was probably no worse than his counterparts in London, New York, or Rome. This, after all, was the period that occluded Saint Paul's with its mediocre jumble of institutional high rises, which saw the creation of urban horrors like Pruitt-Igoe in St. Louis, and choked the sea gate of downtown Sydney with its impacted skyscrapers.

So the visitor—locked in the roaring maw of traffic between the indifferent high-rise walls of the *autovía* that cuts north toward France and is called the Meridiana (1971), or gazing at the brutal gashes of the Via Augusta and the Avinguda General Mitre, Haussmann-like incisions that tore out so much of interest in the upper part of nineteenth-century Barcelona—may not think kindly of Porcioles; but in honesty one should reflect that he was no worse than many of his counterparts elsewhere and should not demonize him, as it is the custom to do among *bien-pensant* designers in Barcelona these days. Except for the Fundació Miró (Miró Foundation) and three or four others, most of the new buildings of "his" Barcelona lack distinction, and some are ugly solecisms—the worst being the office extension of the Ajuntament, a repellent concrete-and-glass multistory box, jammed into the Gothic environment of the Old City. But at least Porcioles did not tear down any Gaudí buildings the way New York destroyed the old McKim, Meade, and White Pennsylvania Station, one of the most beautiful Beaux-Arts spaces in the world, in the 1960s.

Sins of omission, as much as those of commission, were what depressed the urban fabric of Barcelona in the Franco years. The city had no coherent policy on maintenance and restoration of its historic pre–civil war buildings. Entropy ruled, in the midst of opportunistic speculation and official corruption. It was much costlier to convert a nineteenth-century palace into flats than to raze it and put up a seven-story block on the site; the new building would look like stained cardboard in ten years, but who cared? If the new periphery of Barcelona was chaos, the Eixample and the old center began to turn into grunge—one of the worst parts being the Ramblas, whose neoclassical essence all but disappeared behind honky-tonk placards. Here, policy seems to have reinforced neglect. The great square at the seaward end of the Ramblas, Plaça Reial, became a drug and prostitution market and the city council was quite content to leave it that way, since it tended to condense petty criminals and hippies in one spot, where they could be watched.

Many valuable *modernista* structures were demolished, or left to decay, or wrecked by intrusive "renovation." They were regarded as hopelessly old-fashioned and thus became fair game for whatever changes commercial interests saw fit to wreak on them. Of course, this had happened before; an egregious case from the days of the Republic was the demolition of the Café Torino at 18 Passeig de Gràcia, a building partly designed by Gaudí that was replaced by the boring glass-block Joyeria Roca by José-Lluís Sert. But now the tempo of loss accelerated, showing itself not only in dull new structures where fine old ones had been but also in decay and ugly renovations. One victim among many was Gaudí's Casa Milà on Passeig de Gràcia, which by the beginning of the 1980s was in pitiable shape. The frescoes on the entrance floor had decayed to illegibility, the mezzanine had become a bingo hall, neon signs disfigured the facade, rectangular metal-frame windows were jammed in at street level by shop owners who did not want to spend money on frames that would follow the curve of the openings. It was also filthy, the creamy-white Montjuic limestone of its facades dulled to dark brown.

Across the street one could see the even worse vandalism inflicted on Domènech i Montaner's Casa Lleó Morera by a luxury leather-goods firm named Loewe. These handbag makers tore out the whole street-level facade, destroying its sculptures by Eusebi Arnau, along with all the rest of its decorative detail, and stuck in plate glass instead. No one who cares for architecture should ever buy anything from Loewe, on principle.

There were some bright spots in *La Barcelona grisa*, "gray Barcelona," as the present city hall dubbed Porcioles's city in one of its many public-relations brochures. In the 1960s the gradual conversion and renovation of the fifteenth- and sixteenth-century merchants' town houses on Carrer Montcada began, and the Picasso Museum was created in two of them —a brilliant recycling of medieval architecture to accommodate Picasso's gift of a huge block of his earliest work to the city in which he had created much of it. Likewise, it was in 1970 that Joan Miró, the greatest artist Catalunya had produced since the twelfth century, created the Fundació Miró, endowed it with a mass of his work, and gave the money for José-Lluís Sert to create a home for it on Montjuic. At the time, both these small, concentrated one-man museums seemed very innovative. They suggested that, underneath the Franquist crust, a new Barcelona was preparing to emerge.

Over these decades, investment in the Eixample was piecemeal and in the Old City gradual; otherwise much more of the past would have been lost. As things were, good buildings merely decayed or else were hidden by the scurf of additions, renovations, chaotic signs, placards, neon. But because the Franco period was also a paradise of unregulation for small-scale Catalan speculators, it brought endless harm to the Eixample as a city plan. Its designer, Ildefons Cerdà, had intended that its chamfered blocks carry only a small density of housing, limited in height and each block with open garden space in the middle. The 1950s and 1960s brought the final collapse of this century-old ideal, whose regulations could no longer be enforced; by the time the Barcelonans had finished adding new attics to the blocks, closing them off, covering the internal patios with storage rooms, garages, and the like, the whole center of the Eixample had acquired the look of a dense, grimy, Brobdingnagian beehive.

One strikingly poetic Catalan phrase evokes the drabness of Barcelona twenty-five years ago: *"color de gos com fuig,"* "the color of a dog running away"—that is, no color, indeterminacy, mud, yet with something unquestionably there. Barcelona was culturally the most exciting city in Spain, filled with a potential for change that seemed absent (at least, to the visitor) in Madrid. And who could deny that there were pleasures in the city, in its apparently secret life and its artistic cliques, its cheap restaurants and ten-dollar-a-night hotels with big, slightly musty rooms, its entertainments—the broad infectious humor of the old music halls like El Molino on the Parallel—veiled from the foreigner by his ignorance of Catalan (all of which may be disappearing today under the stress of Barcelona's PoMo fixations, its concern with attitude and self-exposition)? Not to mention a kind of bohemian style, a dandyism that lingered on, whose roots lay in the nineteenth century among the tables of Els Quatre Gats café (and are now permanently withered by the deodorant-laden breath of Catalan yuppiedom)? A friend used to recount, as the quintessence of this attitude, the story of an elderly and impoverished poet named Albert Llanas, who was making his way down the Ramblas one morning, dressed in his last perfectly cut dove-gray Saturday suit but wondering where his next bite to eat would come from. He looked up and recognized the widow of a distant acquaintance on a balcony.

"Madam," he cried politely, fingering the lapel in which no boutonniere yet reposed, "do you have a pin?"

"I believe so, Senyor Llanas."

"Then would you be so kind as to stick it in a piece of bread and throw it down to me?"

You could still see traces of that ancient, tattered dandyism in Barcelona twenty-five years ago. Today, none remains. It lived at all levels. The Catalan gypsies of the Parallel had it in abundance. Corberó swears that he owes his conception of the dignity of his métier as an artist to three gypsy friends back in the early 1960s, old-clothes sellers who went under the nicknames of Puça (Flea), Flanél (Flannel), and Plàstic. They were brilliant salesmen. They sold the worst, the rattiest clothes as though they were the newest English tweeds from Bel on Passeig de Gràcia. They were so good that the artist, amazed, suggested that they go upscale. Why not put some of the take back into buying better merchandise, things that—compared with the coarse rubbish they now sold with such virtuoso effort—would walk out of the cart? Flea, Flannel, and Plastic listened to this suggestion gravely and with scorn. "You may be right about the pesetas," concluded Flannel, dismissively. "But what about art?"

IV

General Francisco Franco y Bahamonde died, after a long illness, on November 20, 1975. Fortunately for Spain, his expected successor, Admiral Luis Carrero Blanco, had already been blown to pieces by a Basque separatist bomb in 1973—one of the few terrorist actions of the 1970s that can be shown to have had unequivocally good results, since it left no one in power capable of preserving the ideology of Franquism. When the news of Franco's death was announced on radio and television, Barcelona went into ecstasy. Everyone except the Guardia Civil poured into the streets, danced, hollered, and got drunk. Red and yellow stripes waved everywhere: the four red bars, symbol of Catalunya. Within hours, not a case of *cava*, the local champagne, or even a bottle of Moët or Cliquot, remained in the city. Under the aegis of the new king, Juan Carlos I, the work of dismantling the institutions of Franquism and making a peaceful transfer to democracy—the *ruptura pactada*, or "negotiated break" with the old regime—now began. This task fell to the national government of Adolfo Suárez. In the first democratic general elections on June 15, 1977, the centrist UCD (Central Democratic Union) won by a handy majority throughout Spain, with the PSOE (Spanish Workers' Socialist Party, the oldest socialist political group in Spain, nearing its hundredth birthday) in second place. In Barcelona, however, the polls favored the "socialists of Catalunya," a coalition of local socialists and PSOE (28.5 percent) over the UCD (18.7 percent); the city's *obrerista* temper was clearly undiminished, although the Catalan countryside voted, as it always had in the far past, more conservatively.

These alignments came to dominate the provincial and municipal elections in Catalunya. There, in 1978, the PSOE merged with a newly formed local party, the PSC, or Partit Socialista de Catalunya. It went into the first municipal elections of the post-Franco period led by a brilliantly gifted young economist named Narcis Serra i Serra, a former student at the London School of Economics, who had been expelled from his teaching post at the University of Barcelona for siding with student protests against Franco in the early 1970s. The PSC-PSOE took 34 percent of the votes, almost twice the score of its nearest rival, the older and more radical-Marxist PSUC, or Partit Socialista Unificat de Catalunya. A few years later, the PSUC would go the way of many a European socialist party overloaded with old-style Leninists and pro-Soviet ideologues—down, into schism and irreconcilable squabbles, as the Soviet empire in central Europe began to break up. The PSC-PSOE, which was more moderate in its socialist inclinations and attracted the votes of the young, was unharmed by this and went on from strength to strength. In the general election of October 1982, which had an enormous voting turnout—almost 80 percent of the nationwide electorate went to the urns, for an attempted coup by a right-wing army officer in the Madrid parliament early in 1981 had raised the specter of the Caudillo again, reminding Spaniards how fragile their new democracy might be—the socialists picked up six million extra votes from people disenchanted with the far left and from the disintegration of the Central Democratic Union. In Barcelona alone the PSC-PSOE got one hundred thousand votes more than in any previous general election. A socialist government took power in Madrid, with Felipe González at its head.

In Catalunya, the surprise of the 1979 elections had been the growing success of a new moderate-conservative coalition party in the provincial government, the CiU (Convergència i Unió, or Convergence and Union), founded in 1974 and led by Jordí Pujol i Soley. Doctor and banker, Pujol (b. 1930) had a solid record of opposition to Franco—not as a Marxist but as a Catalanist, agitating for the political independence of the province against Madrid, for self-determination. In the 1950s nearly all Catalan business had to work through the local branches of Madrid banks to get its loans, but in 1959 Pujol had laid the cornerstone of an independent Catalan banking system by founding the Banca Catalana, the first such institution in the province. Naturally this endeared him to Catalan businessmen, and he earned a more general popularity the next year by his association with the so-called *fets del Palau* (deeds of the Palau). In May 1960 Franco made one of his rare visits to Barcelona, accompanied by his ministers. On May 19, the ministers attended a concert at the Palau de la Música Catalana, the sumptuous *modernista* concert hall built in 1905–8 by Domènech i Montaner as the home of Catalan choral music. The concert was given for the centenary of the Barcelonese poet Joan Maragall, and it included a musical setting of his patriotic poem "El Cant de la Senyera" ("The Song of the Flag"), the Catalanist anthem and, as such, banned by Franco. To the consternation of the Franquist dignitaries, a group of Catalan nationalists rose from the audience and sang along with the orchestra:

> *Oh, bandera catalana*
> *nostre cor t'es ben fidel.*
> *Volaràs com au galana*
> *per damunt del nostre anhel.*
> *Per mirar-te sobirana*
> *alçarem els ulls al cel.*

> O flag of Catalunya
> our hearts keep faith with you.
> You will fly like a brave bird
> above our desires.
> To see you reigning there
> we'll lift our eyes to the sky.

Scandalized, the Franquists started a wave of arrests and detentions; though he had not been in the *palau* that night, Pujol was sentenced to seven years in prison and served three of them. Released in 1963, he rapidly became the voice of conservative local interests: Pujol was, and is, a highly recognizable Catalan type of politician—the reincarnation of those Catalanist burghers who ran Barcelona in the late nineteenth century on a platform of industrial expansion and local patriotism, preaching self-determination for the province while constantly negotiating with Madrid. The socialists appealed to the idea of an internationalized Catalunya, open to the "mainstream" beyond the Pyrenees; Pujol invoked the local, the immemorial "deep Catalunya," while implying that it could become as fiscally solid as Switzerland or Japan if only Madrid would leave it to its own economic devices. This gave him and his party, the CiU, a solid base among the large stratum of Catalans, particularly outside Barcelona, who did not think of themselves as members of something diffuse, called Europe, and distrusted socialism anyway, even in the moderate and unideological form practiced by the PSC-PSOE. Thus, when Catalunya held "autonomous" elections as a province in March 1980 (the first elections of that kind in almost fifty years), Pujol's Convergence and Union party, running on a self-determination ticket against the socialists' platform of orientation to Europe, swept into the Generalitat with a large margin. The CiU, not the PSC-PSOE, was now the majority party of Catalunya, and Jordí Pujol has remained the president of the Generalitat down to the present day, just as the socialists—led first by Narcis Serra and since 1982 by Pasqual Maragall i Mira (b. 1941), grandson of the poet and a formidable politician himself—have been returned to power in the Ajuntament by the twelve districts of the city electorate without missing a beat.

Thus for the last ten years there has been a heads-and-tails face-off across Plaça Sant Jaume, the center of the Old City: Pujol's moderate conservatives in the Generalitat, Maragall's moderate socialists in the Ajuntament, each competing to be seen as more truly "Catalan" than the other. The difference is that, as the historian Felipe Fernández-Armesto recently wrote, "though the inhabitants of City Hall are all good Catalanists, they were put there by the votes of non-Catalan immigrant workers, mostly Andalusians, whose loyalty to Catalan identity, traditions and language is, at best, slight and secondary." In the eyes of the electorate, Pujol's party wins the more-Catalan-than-thou contest hands down, because the Generalitat's idea of Catalanism is reinforced with older images of Catalan identity than the Ajuntament's. One example on the cultural plane, and by no means a minor one, is the

Generalitat's policy of encouraging a statewide program in the study of Catalan folklore. (Curiously enough, the Catalan word for "folklore" is *folklore*. It used to be *cultura popular*, until pop culture heaved in sight, causing a tangle whose only exit lay through an Anglicism.) Thus, while Maragall's officials in the Ajuntament and on the Olympic Cultural Committee concern themselves with glorifying the city by restoring *modernista* buildings or choosing the right American architect to design a new museum of modern art, Pujol's officials set up congresses on the traditional art forms of Catalunya: rituals, *festes*, devil's dances, folk theater, *sardanas*, or *castells*—those peculiar images of the Catalan admiration for aplomb, phlegm, and cooperation, in which sixteen, twenty, or more husky young men, known as *castellers*, clamber on one another's shoulders to form a human tower.

The traditional love of folklore—naturally stronger in the country than in the city—connects to another long-standing Catalan trait, a fondness for special-interest groups, local cells, affinities of every kind from choral societies to pigeon-fancying clubs. These are details that no politician can afford to ignore, because they enable Catalans to feel like Catalans. In sport, the great bonding agent is, of course, *el fútbol*. Barcelona has two bullrings, one of them fallen into semipermanent disuse, the other largely kept alive by Andalusian migrants and foreign tourists. Tauromachy has never been an obsession in Catalunya, as it is farther south, and the only real Catalan aficionado I have ever met is a bullfight critic named Mariano de la Cruz, who also happens to be a leading Barcelonese psychiatrist, specializing—to judge from the large collection of inscribed drawings and prints on his walls—in the neuroses of local artists. Anywhere else in Spain, the idea of a shrink writing about a *corrida* would be unthinkable. But to see Catalan patriotism in full collective cry, go to the stadium one night when a big soccer game— Barça versus Madrid, ideally—is on, and 120,000 throats are bawling in chorus for the home team while the heraldic figures dash and dodge on the unnaturally green field and tiny frantic bats skitter through the arc-lighted air.

It would be an oversimplification to say that the Ajuntament looks out to Europe while the Generalitat looks inward to deep Catalunya, but there is some truth in it. Pujol, in particular, has no hesitation in venting rather rhetorical speculations on Catalan character and destiny. As he declaimed in one of his books (*Construir Catalunya*, 1980):

A people is a fact of mentality, of language, of feelings. It is a historic fact, and it is a fact of spiritual ethnicity. Finally it is a fact of will. In our case, however, it is in an important sense an achievement of language. The first characteristic of a people has to be the will to exist. It is this will, more than anything else, which assures the survival and, above all, the promotion, the blossoming of a people . . .

To be Catalan, in short, you may close your eyes and wish. The idea of "a people" is diluted to "spiritual ethnicity," whereas Catalanists a century ago spoke of a Catalan *race*. Since it is in your mentality, language, and "feelings," rather than your birthplace and inherited culture, Catalanism is acquired and does not have to be innate; it is something any immigrant can aspire to. Such rhetoric has general appeal, because it is pitched both at traditional Catalans, whose families have been there for generations, and at new or relatively new arrivals—the immigrants from Andalusia, their children, and (by now) their grandchildren. By 1980 these immigrants' families dominated the working class of Barcelona, and they knew that they had passed from Andalusia's misery and squalor into Catalunya's (relative) prosperity: a flat, a car for family outings, a television set. Hence they were impervious to the traditional calls of Marxism—let alone of anarchism, the ideology that dominated worker politics in Barcelona in the 1890s and has now vanished without a trace. The first wave of immigrant workers, once settled in Barcelona, supported the idea of Catalan autonomy because it was anti-Franco, not because they felt they had become Catalans. Their children, going to school after 1975, learned Catalan in school and from the television set. Most of them (72.6 percent of all residents of Catalunya between the ages of fifteen and twenty-nine, according to the 1986 census) could speak the Catalan tongue. But though they thought of themselves as Catalans the autochthonous Catalans did not necessarily accept them as such.

V

There cannot be many images of cardinal social virtue in modern art, but one of them was certainly painted by the Catalan artist Joan Miró. It is *The Farm, Montroig*, a portrait of the place where he spent much of his childhood and to which, for the rest of his life, his imagination would always return. He began to paint it in 1921, in the place itself: the family house, or *casa pairal*, in a small village near Tarragona, south of Barcelona. He then took the unfinished picture, along with a bunch of dried grass from the farm—a fetish of contact with the Catalunya he was about to lose—to Paris. Shifting between lodgings, he lost the grass but replaced it with some from the Bois de Boulogne; the picture was too advanced by then to lose any truth by the substitution. Miró finished it in Paris in 1922 and eventually sold it to Ernest Hemingway, who for the rest of his life revered it as *his* fetish of Iberian memory: "It has in it," he wrote, "all that you feel about Spain when you are there and all that you feel when you are away and cannot go there. No one else has been able to paint these two very opposing things."

He was right; *The Farm* is, above all, an expatriate's painting, combining in one image the intense pressure of immediate experience of one's homeland and an equally extreme longing for it. Everything on the farm, the leaves on the trees no less than each crack in the old wall and pebble in the red Tarragonese earth, is rendered with utter fidelity: the landscape is a palace of recollection, a mnemonic device in itself. Miró's sense of separation and longing is conveyed by a kind of visual accountancy, an exact toting up and tallying of everything that is (or was) the case on the family farm. It could be a pictorial form of the meticulous inventory that went with peasant marriage contracts. Each tool, pitcher, keg, press, cart, watering can, donkey, dog, chicken, goat, pigeon, and donkey's rump (just visible through the door of the *bestiar* on the ground floor of the farmhouse) is turned to the light, delineated, listed, fixed. The sharp focus, the hallucinated clarity of light, make the painting exquisitely frank. But they also produce the effect of looking down the wrong end of a telescope, so that the scene is remote as well. Hence *The Farm*'s power as an image of nostalgia for what is distant but vivid and dear, for the sights, smells, and sounds of childhood. Such longings are known in Catalan as *enyorança*.

Enyorança was the basic trope that suffused the nationalistic literature of Catalunya from Carles Aribau's "Oda a la Pàtria" (1833) right through the nineteenth century and into the early twentieth, when Miró was an art student on the top floor of the Llotja, or Lodge, the Barcelona stock exchange. Indeed, a suitable gloss on *The Farm* might have been the lines of Barcelona's poet-priest Jacint Verdaguer in his most popular short poem, "L'Emigrant," which every Barcelonese schoolboy was taught to recite as a matter of course:

> *Dolça Catalunya,*
> *patria del meu cor,*
> *quan de tu s'allunya,*
> *d'enyorança es mor.*

Sweet Catalunya
homeland of my heart
to be far from you
is to die of longing.

There are other elements behind *The Farm*: continuity, conservatism, precise craftsmanship, and something the Catalans untranslatably call *seny*.

By tradition, when Catalans reflect on themselves they get absorbed by the differences that set them off, individually and as a "nation," from the rest of Spain. Speculating about this *fet differential*, as Barcelona's great fin de siècle poet Joan Maragall called it, was a favorite intellectual sport in Miró's youth, filling countless essays. Usually the argument devolved, as such arguments will, into a play of stereotypes. Thus when Catalans looked at Castile, they saw sloth, privilege, and a morbid tendency to inwardness, bred of long years of aristocratic effeteness; a taste for oppressing others, particularly Catalans; a lack of practical sense. The image of the Castilian as occupying leech, taxing the lifeblood out of Catalunya, was standard in Barcelona from the seventeenth century to the death of Franco in the late twentieth.

When Castilians looked at Catalans, they had their say too. Catalans were dull. They were pedantic and resentful by turns, usually both; too addicted to material things to understand the classic austerities of Castile, let alone its spirituality; and inordinately self-satisfied with their patch of Mediterranean earth—a polity of grocers, barking at one another in a bastard language. No Catalan, in their view, could see beyond the pig in his yard, the fat angel sent to earth by God to supply Catalans with their daily viaticum of *butifarra* and ham.

When the Catalans observed themselves, it was a different story. Loyal, patriotic (as long as you understood that the *pàtria* was Catalunya, not the Iberian abstraction dear to Madrid centralists), practical, ingenious, innovative though respectful of their roots, the whole mass of virtues leavened with just a *xic* of humor—what a people! For once, the Lord got it right, and though Catalans might not take their piety to the edge of superstition (like the Sevillians, say, who were practically Arabs anyhow), they had every right to praise Him for placing them on earth, armed with the virtues for which they were justly famous: *continuitat, mesura, ironia,* and *seny*.

That *The Farm* is conceived in praise of *continuitat* is evident enough. The farm is old and goes back for generations; its tools are traditional; it represents an unchanging order of work, dictated by seasons and weather, by the fertility of the soil and the benignity of that strange, electric-blue sky. The same with *mesura*, for nothing in the painting lacks order, proportion, a sense of graded repetition. A clan that works steadfastly at the same task, down the generations, trusting in the work of the hand to make things tangible and spaces habitable, eschewing abstract speculation and fanciful enthusiasm—that family has *mesura*, and its members are the right kind of folk to belong on such a farm as this. *Ironia* is present in the copy of a French newspaper, *L'Intransigeant*, neatly folded and weighted down on the foreground by a watering can. It is the only foreign thing in the painting—a sign of Miró's destination, Paris, and of course a reference to cubism with its newsprint and cutoff headlines, but also a confession that he, in quitting the idealized Catalunya of his ancestors, is being "intransigent" (the word is the same in Catalan), a stubborn prodigal son, the *hereu*, or "heir," leaving his birthright. Put *continuitat*, *mesura*, and *ironia* together, and you are on the way to *seny*.

Seny signifies, approximately, "common sense"; it means what Samuel Johnson meant by "bottom," an instinctive and reliable sense of order, a refusal to go whoring after novelties. In traditional Catalan terms it comes close to "natural wisdom" and is treated almost as a theological virtue. When the fifteenth-century Catalan metaphysical poet Ausiàs March wanted words to sum up his devotion to the unnamed woman his verses address, he called her either *llir entre cards* (lily among thistles) or *plena de seny* (woman full of wisdom). Catalans suppose that *seny* is their main national trait. It is to them what *duende* (literally "goblin," and by extension a sense of fatality or tragic unpredictability) is to more southern Spaniards. It is a country virtue, rising from the settled routines and inflexible obligations of rural life. In *The Forms of Catalan Life* (1944) Josep Ferrater Mora gave a lengthy disquisition on *seny*. "The man with *seny* is, primordially, the well-tempered man; that is to say, the man who contemplates things and human actions with a serene vision." It was the mirror reverse of Castilian quixotism. It was opposed to intellectual overrefinement. Its inherent danger was being lowbrow. The pragmatic nature of *seny*, he thought, gave Catalans a markedly antispiritual stamp and set their collective temperament somewhere between the puritan and the Faustian: "Faustian man or Romantic man are those to whom salvation and morality matter little; Puritan man is only concerned with salvation and morals. The man of *seny* renounces neither salvation nor experience, and is always trying to set up a fruitful integration between both opposed, warring extremes."

Perhaps Catalan *seny* is, as Mora thought, antispiritual; this would seem to be borne out by the recent experience of a Catalan friend who went home for Christmas to his native village and attended midnight mass with his relatives. The church was packed. The priest and deacon brought forth the image of the Infant Jesus so that everyone in the congregation could kiss its wooden feet. A long line began to shuffle toward the communion rail; so long, the priest realized, that it would be three in the morning before he got to dinner. There was a whispered confabulation. The deacon scurried into the sacristy and emerged with another wooden Jesus; two lines formed, and the kissing was over in half the time. Perhaps only in Catalunya, the first industrial region of Spain, could time-and-motion study be so quickly and instinctively applied to piety.

The relief from *seny* is *rauxa*. *Rauxa* means "uncontrollable emotion, outburst." It applies to any kind of irrational or Dionysiac or (sometimes) just plain dumb activity—getting drunk, screwing around, burning churches, and disrupting the social consensus. The purpose of feast days is to give *rauxa* a sanctioned outlet: on Saint John's Night, in June, for instance, the whole of Catalunya is lighted by bonfires as its towns erupt in the continuous thunder of *petardes*, "fireworks," which go on until five or six in the morning. Not even in New York on the Fourth of July is the bombardment so intense. *Rauxa* and *seny* coexist like heads and tails on a coin; you cannot separate them, and the basic reason that Joan Miró is seen as so quintessentially a Catalan artist is that he displayed both at once in such abundance.

Probably the most pervasive cultural form of *rauxa* is an abiding taste for obscene humor: not so much sexual—or not more so, anyway, than in the United States and possibly rather less so than in the rest of Spain—as scatological. The Catalan preoccupation with shit would make Sigmund Freud proud; no society offers more frequent and shining confirmations of his theories of anal retention. In this respect, the Catalans resemble other highly mercantile people such as the Japanese and the Germans.

The pleasures of a good crap are considered in Catalunya on a level with those of a good meal; "*Menjar be i cagar fort / I no tingues por de la mort*," goes the folk saying: "Eat well, shit strongly, and you will have no fear of death."

The image of shit has a festive quality unknown in the rest of Europe. On the Feast of the Kings, January 6, children who have been good the previous year are given pretty sweetmeats; the bad ones get *caca i carbo*, "shit and coal," emblems of the hell that awaits them if they do not mend their childish ways. These days the *caca* consists of brown-marzipan turds made by confectioners, some elaborately embellished with spun-sugar flies. Then there is the *tio*, or "log," a cross between the French *bûche de Noël* and the Mexican piñata. This artificial piece of wood, filled with candy and trinkets, is produced at Christmas; the children whack it with sticks, exclaiming, "*Caga, tio, caga!*" ("Shit, log, shit!") until it breaks and disgorges its treasures.

If you find yourself in Barcelona just before Christmas, go to the Cathedral and browse the stalls that have been set up in front of its facade, where figures for the crèche are sold. They are what you expect: the shepherds, the Magi, Mary, Baby Jesus, the sheep, the oxen. But there is one who is a complete anomaly, met with nowhere else in the iconography of Christendom. A red Catalan cap, or *barretina*, flopping over his head, the fellow squats, breeches down, with a small brown cone of excrement connecting his bare buttocks to the earth. He is the immemorial fecundator, whom nature calls even as the Messiah arrives. Nothing can distract him from the archetypal task of giving back to the soil the nourishment that it supplied to him. He is known as the *caganer*, the "shitter," and he exists in scores of versions: some pop-eyed with effort, others rapt in calm meditation, but most with no expression at all; big papier-mâché ones three feet tall, minuscule terra-cotta ones with caca pyramids no bigger than mouse turds, and all sizes in between. During Christmas 1989, the Museum of Figueras held an exhibition of some five hundred *caganers*, borrowed from private collections all over Catalunya. (There are, of course, collectors who specialize in them.) It was solemnly and equably reviewed in the Barcelona papers, with close-up photos of one or two of the figures, just as one might wish to reproduce a David Smith totem or a nude by Josep Llimona. The origins of the *caganer* are veiled in antiquity and await the attentions of scholarship. Sixteenth-century sculptures of him exist, but he seems to be curiously absent from medieval painting. He is, essentially, a folk-art personage rather than a high-art one. His place is outside the manger, not inside the altarpiece. Yet he makes an unmistakable entrance into twentieth-century art in the work of that great and shit-obsessed son of Catalunya, Joan Miró. If you look closely at *The Farm, Montroig*, you will see a pale infant squatting in front of the cistern where his mother is doing the washing. This boy is none other than the *caganer* of Miró's childhood Christmases; it may also be Miró himself, the future painter of *Man and Woman in Front of a Pile of Excrement* (1935).

Nor can it be an accident that the other scatologist of modern painting, Salvador Dalí, was a Catalan. Other Surrealists might shock the

French bourgeoisie (at least in the 1920s) but it was Dalí's achievement to shock the Surrealists themselves, which he first did through his excremental imagery, profoundly offensive to the nostrils of André Breton: in 1929, when Dalí produced *The Lugubrious Game*, Breton and his colleagues felt obliged to hold a serious discussion on whether the stained shorts of the man holding a fishnet in the foreground were acceptable to the movement or not. I did not know Dalí well, but I remember a conversation with him in Paris twenty-five years ago, during which I asked him who, in his view, was *the* great unknown modernist artist (apart, of course, from himself). Joseph Pujol, he replied with a gust of carious breath and a flourish of the cane; only Joseph Pujol, Pujol forever. I had no idea who Joseph Pujol was. He turned out to be a forgotten, but in his time prodigious, star of the fin de siècle Parisian music hall: a Marseillais—but, as Dalí pointed out, with a Catalan name—who performed under the nickname of Le Petomane, the Fartomaniac. Pujol had a vast gas capacity and perfect control over his bowels and anal sphincter. Not only could he fart tunefully, but he could absorb a whole bowl of water on stage by sitting in it and drawing it up, like an Indian yogi. These, Dalí insisted, were not simply natural endowments, but the achievements of incessant practice and relentless discipline, like Raphael's ability to draw. With them, Pujol would keep packed houses rolling in the aisles with renditions of popular airs, "La Marseillaise" and even snatches of Verdi and Offenbach. He would also imitate the posterior sounds of animals—the deep bass elephant, the gibbon, the mouse—and do character sketches, such as the imperious fart of the president of the Republic or the nervous squeak of the *petite postulante de quatorze ans*.

Just as some Catalans collect *caganers*, so there has always been a vigorous strain of scatological humor in their folk songs, folk poetry, and educated verse. Its antiquity refutes all Marxist efforts to explain it as a product of postindustrial bourgeois repression. (There are, however, a few Catalan Marxists who still believe this, as one might believe in the tooth fairy or the dictatorship of the proletariat.) It is preindustrial; it belongs to the long epoch during which the emissions of Barcelona, instead of rising into the Mediterranean air to form a noxious smog, lay thick on its streets. Indeed, it almost predates the streets themselves. The earliest names for the two rivers that bordered the medieval city of Barcelona were the Merdança (shit stream) and the Cagallel (turd bearer), whose waters were totally unfit to drink by the fourteenth century and have remained so ever since. The first item in the invaluable collection of *Versos Bruts* (*Coarse Poems*, edited by Empar Pérez-Cors) was written in the early thirteenth century and takes the form of a discussion between two nobles, Arnaut Catalan and Ramon Berenguer V, count of Provence and Cerdanya, concerning a hundred noble ladies who went to sea in a boat and, becalmed, got back to shore by farting in chorus into its sails. One of the durable favorites of Catalan verse was Vicent Garcia (c. 1580–1623), rector of Vallfogona, who wrote sonnets in imitation of Luis de Góngora and Francisco Gómez de Quevedo, but whose real popularity depended on his burlesques, banned by the Inquisition. They included such works as *To a Monumental Latrine, Constructed by the Author in the Garden of his Rectory* and *On a Delicate Matter*, which roundly asserts that no person, however low, not even a Portuguese, could have anything bad to say about shit. Excrement, Garcia wrote in a Dalí-like transport of enthusiasm, is beneficial, the sign of our true nature, a kind of philosophers' stone that "the pharmacists of Sarrià / contemplate night and day." In doing so he evoked the peasant origins of the cult: shit as the great fertilizer, the farmer's friend, the emblem of root and place.

VI

"Real" Catalans—*Catalans de sempre*, as they sometimes call themselves, "Catalans since forever"—tend to be somewhat xenophobic, and the farther out in the country they are, the more they condescend to the foreigner. A Barcelonese friend of mine was recently driving past a tiny village in the Ampurdan in northern Catalunya—picturesque houses on a rocky hill, haystacks, a crumbling church—when she saw a peasant hoeing furrows by the side of the road: a weather-beaten figure straight out of the iconography of Catalan patriotism, wearing corduroy trousers, espadrilles, a *faixa*, or sash. She stopped, and they began to chat. How many other peasants lived in the village? Just him and his wife, said the peasant; all the other people had left. Then were the other houses empty? Most of the time—except on weekends. What happened on weekends? Foreigners came here in cars from the city, from the south. Did he know any of these weekenders? "Know them?" spat this emanation of folklore contemptuously. "How should I know them? *Son tots moros*—they're all Moors."

The key expression of xenophobia is violently loaded: *xarnego*. Originally, *xarnego* was fairly neutral and meant a Catalan whose parents came from different valleys. Then it shifted to "foreigner"; a peasant living in one valley of the Ampurdan, for instance, would use it of a peasant from the other side of the hill. But with immigration, it came to denote—in the most pejorative sense—any working-class person of non-Catalan Spanish origin living in Catalunya. Today it has the same power of insult as "nigger" does in America, and if you call someone a *xarnego* in a bar, you will get the fight you are asking for. Immigrants, however, may call themselves *xarnegos*, jokingly or in ironic self-assertion, like blacks talking to other blacks about "us niggers."

In fact, though "old" Catalans find it hard to imagine why a Spanish immigrant should not want to be a Catalan, not all of them do. The mere fact of being Catalan confers no legal rights, obligations, or privileges in Catalunya. The legal definition of a Catalan, written into the province's short-lived Statute of Autonomy in 1932 and reaffirmed in 1979, is very broad: "the political condition of Catalan" belongs to all Spanish citizens with "administrative residence" in any municipality of Catalunya. In the provincial and city elections of 1979–80, politicians representing migrant workers from Aragon and Andalusia demanded a new clause in the statute allowing immigrants to retain the political status of their region of birth. They did not get it.

Whatever the law may say, the popular definitions of a Catalan are all cultural and impossible to legislate. The basic one is language. Nobody can be considered Catalan unless he or she speaks Catalan naturally, as a first-string language. To be a *catalanoparlant* is not necessarily enough, however. Even in the unlikely event that the Spanish resident speaks perfect Catalan, he may not be accepted *as* Catalan by everyone—Catalan fundamentalists are just as likely to view him as a foreigner who, like a dancing bear, has mastered an unnatural feat.

A decade ago, in the wake of Franco's death and the return of democracy to Catalunya, Barcelona experienced an outburst of militant linguistic Catalanism. Agitators demanded that the university teach only texts written in (or translated into) Catalan—a sure recipe for academic disaster, since most of Spanish literature (let alone English, French, German, or Italian) would have been excluded by such a policy, while the chaos that Catalan exclusiveness would have produced in the study of the sciences hardly bears thinking about. Mostly the fuss came down to the public as inconvenience, particularly when enthusiasts spray painted street signs back into Catalan (*carrer* for *calle*) or scrawled "*No al bilingüisme*" across them, rendering them illegible to Catalans, Castilians, and foreigners alike.

This militancy seems to be spent now. It holds out on the margins of intellectual life, but its energy is clearly lost in a time of transition.

It is still possible to find curious superpatriotic anthologies, collections of uplifting Catalanist sentiments culled from the work of eighteenth- to twentieth-century writers. A durable paperback of nationalist poems and songs includes such ludicrous gems as an "Ode to the Fatherland, Sung by Its Unborn Sons," written in 1923 by one Oriol Casassas, whose muse smote him with a vision of serried ranks of Catalan fetuses chanting lustily in their wombs. *"Umbilicoses cintes,"* it begins,

> *ens lliguen a la mare*
> *i liquids amniòtics ens banyen a pleret:*
> *Oh Pàtria pressentida, desconeguda encara,*
> *fins que serem a terme i el claustre farà net!*

Umbilical cords link us to our mothers
and amniotic fluids softly bathe us:
Oh Fatherland we imagine, still unknown to us
until we come to term, and the womb will be empty!

This might go over well with the wife of Jordi Pujol, who is one of the leaders of the Catalan antiabortion movement, but otherwise it is hard to imagine anyone reading such stuff today, let alone writing it.

Or is it? Efforts by nationalists to impose Catalan on unwilling speakers do happen in the Generalitat. The most recent—a political embarrassment for Pujol and his party—occurred in January 1991, when the minister of social welfare, Antoni Comas, circulated a memo to his staff rebuking them for their habit of speaking Spanish to one another, even though they spoke Catalan to him. This unpatriotic custom, he warned, "must be rooted out." The document, leaked to the press, caused a scandal. Big Brother, it seemed, was alive and well on Plaça Sant Jaume. Comas then tried to blame the memo on bad shorthand by his secretary, claiming that he never said any such thing. Eventually Pujol had to step in and publicly disown the memo.

When the Statute of Autonomy declared Catalan to be the official language of Catalunya, it gave a tremendous boost to Catalan translation and publication. In 1939, the year Franco banned the language, not a single book was published in Catalan. In 1942 there were four and in 1950 thirteen. The year 1975 saw 611 titles, and then the figures began to zoom, reaching about 4,200 new titles in Catalan in 1988. Moreover, Barcelona publishes more new books in Spanish than Madrid does. Between them the two cities account for 80 percent of all publishing in Spain.

But especially in Catalan-language publishing, the number of book titles is misleading. The number of copies sold is what counts, and since the whole readership is bilingual, the actual market for books in Catalan is only a fraction of the demand for those in Spanish. And the majority of Spaniards, including Catalans, do not read much beyond the papers and magazines. They are passive television watchers, like Americans. Recent surveys indicate that six out of ten of them, in 1990, did not buy a single new book. Since about three and a half million of the six million *catalanoparlants* can actually read the language, the largest imaginable sales base for Catalan book publishing cannot be more than two million people; actually it is much less. Hence the paradox: there are enough people to make an audience for Catalan television as long as the government pays for it, but not enough to support a "national" Catalan literature. No serious imaginative writer can make a decent living from the sales of his or her books in Catalan alone, unsupported by journalism; none ever has. Barcelona's bookshops all have their Catalan and Spanish sections, side by side, reflecting the bilingualism of their clients; there is one big specialist Catalan bookshop on Gran Via, called Ona, which stocks a wide range of texts on Catalan history, sociology, literature, folklore, cooking, and erotica and of international writing translated into Catalan, but nothing at all in Spanish. Not a few of these books have been helped to press by government grants, but as the novelist Lluís Goytisolo pointed out, "In the long term, and even in the medium run, the existence of a literature founded on grants has to be mortally endangered."

Goytisolo's situation is perhaps an instructive one. He is one of a number of highly gifted Catalan writers in their fifties who grew up in the Franco period writing in Spanish. Others include his brother Juan, Jaime de Bledma, Eduardo Mendoza, Manuel Vásquez Montalbán, Carlos Barral, Ana María Matute, and José Agustin. All of them were strongly anti-Franco; Lluís Goytisolo suffered imprisonment for his ideas. They were all living in a city that, Goytisolo argued, had a very meager literary tradition in its own right until the nineteenth century. Only one of the classic medieval Catalan writers, Bernat Metge, actually came from Barcelona: Ramon Llull was Majorcan; Joanot Martorell and Ausiàs March were both from Valencia. Not until the late nineteenth century, with the emergence of the poets Jacint Verdaguer and Joan Maragall, did Catalanism in Barcelona find an important literary aspect, but at a time when the mere fact of writing in Catalan was regarded as a patriotic act, most "patriotic" poetry was exalted kitsch. Nevertheless, with the single exception of Josep Pla, most of the important writing in

Catalan between 1900 and the Second Republic (1931) was poetry by such writers as Guerau de Lliost, Josep Carner, Josep Sagarra, and, above all, Josep Foix. And Catalunya had never produced much literature in Spanish, except for the Renaissance poet Juan Boscán.

The Franco regime in Catalunya, therefore, not only gave the then-young writers of Goytisolo's generation a new subject matter of exile, loss, confrontation, and social change to deal with; by banning Catalan, it forced them into the mainstream of Spanish writing. Being a left-wing writer entailed the desire to reach a worker audience—and most of the industrial workers in Barcelona were immigrants who spoke Spanish, not Catalan. The Barcelonese middle class, a traditional audience for literature, was bilingual and, on the whole, preferred to read Spanish. This sudden irruption of Catalan writers into Spanish literature seemed, to Goytisolo, "a new phenomenon in the history of Spanish literature," one that coincided with the emergence of Barcelona as the capital of Spanish publishing. The Spanish minister of culture, a Catalan named Jordi Solé Tura, takes the reasonable view that "I have always believed that Catalan culture is what happens in Catalunya in Catalan *and* in Spanish. The reductionism of saying 'We only care about culture if it's in Catalan' strikes me as a grave mistake." On the other hand, pro-Pujolist Catalan fundamentalists like the JNC (Nationalist Youth of Catalunya) still fiercely support just this kind of reductionism. "We have to affirm," one of their manifestos ran in 1991, "that not all the culture one has in Catalunya is Catalan culture, and if we recognize writers like Goytisolo and Marsé as belonging to Catalan culture, we might as well do the same for Robert Graves, who wrote in English from Majorca." Intellectuals were always the first to abandon their ideals, the JNC complained, and "When a young writer announces that he has decided to create in Spanish . . . he does something more than make a personal choice; he sends society a message of abandonment, renunciation and materialism."

Catalan and Spanish coexist in print journalism and on television. Barcelona has three state-sponsored television channels, one broadcasting entirely in Catalan (TV3), one mostly in Spanish (TVE1), and one half-and-half (TVE2); the total of prime-time broadcasting hours divides almost equally between the two languages. It also has a commercial channel, Canal 33, broadcasting entirely in Catalan. Little Catalan TV3 carries ads but is subsidized by the Catalan government. It started in 1984—the David to big Spanish TVE's rather sclerotic Goliath. Before long TV3 showed itself to be livelier in editing, visually sharper, tougher in reporting and interviewing, and more acute in commentary than its rival. It is probably the best example of true regional television in Europe.

Its audience is attached to it for reasons that go beyond passive entertainment: a 1986 survey showed that more than half of TV3's watchers had a "patriotic attachment" to it, while 86 percent felt it was worth watching because it improved their grasp of Catalan; most concurred that its reports were more "politically objective" than those of TVE. With some hesitation, advertisers got behind TV3 in the 1980s, and the annual number of *espots*, or "commercials," in Catalan went from 5,468 in 1984 to more than 44,000 in 1988.

A similar pattern of choice exists among the newspapers. Of the five Barcelona dailies, three (*El Periódico*, *La Vanguardia*, and *El País*) are in Spanish, and two (*Avui* and *Diari de Barcelona*) in Catalan. The Spanish papers have about 1.3 million readers among them, the Catalan ones fewer than 250,000. But *El País* and *La Vanguardia* both publish regular cultural supplements—reviews of books, art, theater, movies—in Catalan, which suggests that as far as the press is concerned, Catalan in Barcelona is mainly a language for the upscale, the university educated, the cultivated.

But these are the very people who most need to communicate with the rest of Europe, and nobody can do that in Catalan. The hope that a uniquely Europe-oriented culture could be created around a minority language like Catalan worked as long as Barcelona was a nucleus of liberal ferment, the one spearhead of an open society in an otherwise black, inward-turning, authoritarian Spain. That long moment lasted from the mid-1960s to Franco's death. It is gone, for the general Europeanization of Spain, especially of Madrid, has been an accomplished fact for at least ten years. If immigration to Catalunya from the rest of Spain stabilizes at roughly its present level, and if local governments continue their policies of encouraging Catalan language use—in education and on television—Catalan will certainly remain the common vernacular of Catalunya and draw its strength, as it always has, from that. If not, not: it could slowly decompose, dropping out of use, as Latin did.

Moreover, it may be that the very idea of a language-based, political Catalan consciousness will slip gradually into the background in years to come, since the oppression that enabled it to define itself against Franco in the 1970s has gone forever. The sense of exclusion recedes as Catalan politicians acquire more influence on the national stage of Spain: at present, the second most powerful politician in Madrid, after Felipe González himself, is a Catalan—the vice-president, the former mayor of Barcelona, Narcis Serra. The man who succeeded him as socialist mayor of Barcelona in 1982, and is still in office after a ten-year term, is Pasqual Maragall.

VII

Maragall's administration is radically changing the physical form of Barcelona. It set out to undo the damage the Porcioles years had left on its fabric and, where possible, to make the city a more agreeable place to be; at the cost of a certain surrender to the public-relations zeitgeist of the 1980s, not to mention a loss of whatever meaning the word "socialist" might once have had, it succeeded.

In the mid-1980s, the hopes of Maragall's people in the Ajuntament, or city hall, were infectious. Coming from New York, a city that had begun resigning itself to entropy, I couldn't help envying them, feeling enchanted by their optimism. "This is the omphalos," Margarita Obiols, a city hall staffer who later became the head of the Olimpiada Cultural, said to me in 1985: "Barcelona is going to be the center of Mediterranean culture." Problems could be cut through, alliances forged, investment pulled in, the gray city renewed like the phoenix—all through urban renewal and its emblem, the public artwork. The last time Barcelona had flung itself into such a convulsion of replanning and sprucing up to feed its own self-confidence and attract the gaze of Europe had been a hundred years before, under its mayor Francesc de Paula Rius i Taulet, who orchestrated its 1888 Universal Exposition.

The visitor to Barcelona in late 1991, seeing the signs of hurry to get things in place for the 1992 Olympic Games, was apt to suppose that the city's whole renewal program had been keyed to that event. Not so: though Barcelona's role as host came as a huge civic boost when Maragall got back from Lausanne in 1986 with the games in his pocket, the policy of revamping the city itself was fixed several years before that and was expected even then to continue until the ominous year of the millennium, 2000. Essentially, the argument of Maragall, of his predecessor Narcis Serra, and of their political team—made up mainly of Catalan *soixante-huitards* in their thirties and forties, who had been excluded from the smallest access to the political levers until 1975 and were now determined to reverse everything the dictator's culture had done to the city—went as follows.

First, general matters of nationalism, both Catalan and Spanish. "A Catalan who claims to be a Catalanist but does not like nationalism," Maragall said in a speech at Saint Antony's College in Oxford in 1986, "finds himself in a somewhat difficult position. But it is my position." The minority call for a completely independent Catalan state—the *paisos Catalans*, embracing Valencia, the Balearic Islands, and even the Roussillon, or French Catalunya—was a romantic idea, popular among the young who needed some issue through which to contest the existing political system: "It is almost the only ideology that does not fit into the Spanish Constitution." But it was not going to come true. Catalunya was part of Spain. Maragall's grandfather, the poet, had written his "Oda a l'Espanya" in the aftermath of 1898 and the humiliating loss of Cuba and the Philippines to the United States. Rebuking centralist Spain for its neglect of its former peoples and for its ignorance of Catalunya, Joan Maragall wrote:

> On ets, Espanya?—No et veig enlloc.
> No sents la meva veu entronadora?
> No entens aquesta llengua—que et parla entre perills?
> Has desaprès d'entendre an els teus fills?
> Adéu, Espanya!

> Where are you, Spain?—nowhere in sight.
> Don't you hear my resounding voice?
> Don't you understand this language, speaking to you between risks?
> Have you left off listening to your sons?
> Farewell, Spain!

But nearly a century later, his grandson argued, Barcelona could not escape Spain or say farewell to it. After nearly forty years of Franco's insisting that *his* ideology was the essence of Spain, that everything else was foreign and un-Spanish, Spain must (as it were) re-Hispanicize itself, draw a self-definition that includes openness; Barcelona should lead the way in this not because of its Catalan "essence" but because of its orientation to a more liberal northern Europe. Moreover, young Maragall could not accept the Pujolist line that there was an immutable essence of Catalunya to which Barcelona was somehow foreign. Barcelona had created Catalunya, not the other way around. And it had a natural, competitive affinity with other cities in Europe: once Spain joined the Common Market, Barcelona was destined to be "the link that will attach the Iberian peninsula to the urban European axis that goes from London to Milan." Maragall saw Barcelona as the future capital of what he called "the north of the south of Europe," connected with Montpellier, Marseilles, Toulouse. Its connections would be industrial and cultural, not rural; the mayor and his colleagues in city hall were convinced, not surprisingly, of the primacy of cities. The Generalitat—like other governments in the European Economic Community, notably France's— taxed the city to subsidize the country; the Catalan parliamentary system, again like other European systems, gave an unfair weight to territorial representation over population. Hence the laws favored rural interests —paying for subsidized farm surpluses, for instance—at the city's expense, and were keyed to more conservative views than most people actually held. "In my opinion," said Maragall,

> Europe has to recover a certain urban militancy. Paying for food surpluses is expensive and has to be done every year. Paying for the cities is also expensive, but cities are already there: they are not produced yearly. A Europe, a world seen as a set of nations are slower, with more opposed languages, than a Europe and a world seen as a system of cities. Cities have no frontiers, no armies, no customs, no immigration officials. Cities are places for invention, for creativity, for freedom.

The first thing to be reinvented was the city itself, and no European capital in recent years has made such a point of reinventing itself as has Barcelona. However the bill is eventually paid, the scale of the work is pharaonic. In some ways it matches the rapid enlargement of the city into the grid plan designed by the engineer Ildefons Cerdà a hundred years before: the Eixample. Each time, Barcelona made a convulsive leap of growth after a long period of urban neglect and repression. Each time, it had to start from the ground up. No city gives its planners a clean slate, but sometimes a large chance of rethinking does come along, and that was what happened to Barcelona after the death of Franco.

For twenty years—and still today—one of the worst urban experiences Barcelona offers is that of leaving it: all traffic north has to go through the bottleneck of the Via Meridiana, and southbound traffic must exit by either the Diagonal or the Gran Via. At rush hours and during the *festes* that speckle the Spanish calendar, these become glaciers of simmering metal, and the main roads of the urban center are so jammed that cars and trucks move at an average speed of about five miles an hour. To relieve this, the city is constructing two beltways: one, the Ronda del Mar, carrying traffic (mostly underground) from the Llobregat to the Bésos on the seaward side of the city; the other, the Ronda de Muntanya, doing the same along the flank of the Collserola massif. If they are not ready for 1992, the Olympic Games will plunge Barcelona into previously unheard-of depths of traffic congestion; wisely, the Ajuntament's pamphlet on the subject of urban macrorenewal is entitled *La Barcelona del 93*.

If circulation in Barcelona is horrible, it is partly because parking is insufficient. The city has more than 600,000 cars but only 432,000 parking spaces, of which 4 in 10 are on public streets and the rest in private lots. This means that at any time of the day or night at least 160,000 vehicles in the metropolitan area are either illegally parked or looking for a slot. Those who have not driven in Barcelona (except, perhaps, those rash enough to try to keep a car in Manhattan) cannot imagine the vileness of civic temper that rises from this situation. Most public transport is by bus. The subway's main line finishes near the university on the Diagonal; thus half the work force enters the city by car. On weekdays, the average speed of motor traffic is twelve miles per hour. Given the wear and tear this inflicts on the central nervous system, it is not surprising that the accident rate in Barcelona increased in the 1980s. Catalan drivers are bad, impatient, and (it seems) getting worse. In 1980–86, the accident rate in downtown Barcelona shot up by 40 percent; in 1987 there were ten thousand vehicle accidents with thirteen thousand casualties.

There is only so much that the Ajuntament can do to cure this situation. The ring roads will certainly help, and so will the twenty-five new underground municipal *parkings* (at present, the city has forty) that will add fifteen thousand new parking places by 1993. Rather gingerly, the Ajuntament plans to install a computer-controlled system of traffic direction, governing the rhythm of traffic lights and showing information on such matters as parking density and traffic flow on luminous roadside panels; but if this is done, it will be completed by closer to 2000 than by 1992. In the meantime, the Ajuntament may be getting ready to ban traffic from the center (but which part of the center?) of Barcelona or charge a per-car fee to enter the city; in 1991 Maragall told a reporter from *La Vanguardia*, "The citizens would be happy if the politicians tried solutions of that sort." This seems unlikely.

All cities have a city below them—the infrastructure that carries sewage, electricity, phone lines, and other services. Barcelona's was inefficient and large: it included slightly more than six hundred miles of major drains and sewers, many of them dating back to the eighteenth century and some to the fifteenth. Ever since the days of Dr. Pedro Garcia Faria, the late-nineteenth-century Catalan sanitary engineer who mounted a campaign for public health in the face of the city's regular epidemics of cholera, typhoid, and malaria, the drains of Barcelona have been a difficult civic issue—property owners resented excavation for new ones, and the completion of a major sewer was regarded as such a political coup that a mayor once held a banquet for a hundred and fifty dignitaries, by the light of carbide lamps, in his newly finished underground collector. Perhaps because of the traditional Catalan penchant for the scatological, Barcelona's city administrations like to flaunt their sewer work,

and Maragall's is no exception: the Ajuntament recently filled the winter
garden of the Citadel Park with a large didactic exhibition called "Barcelona Sub," explaining in detail the new, visitable ducts, trunk collectors, and recycling plants, its catalog filled with archaeological,
hydrographic, and bacteriologic data and embellished with quotations
from T. S. Eliot's *Four Quartets*, rendered in Catalan ("Time present
and time past / Are both perhaps present in time future")—surely the
most recherché use of Old Possum's legacy ever devised, but one that
illustrates the Ajuntament's belief in the symbiosis of high and low
culture.

What was the frame of Barcelona? Land and sea. But the land behind
the city was the Collserola Hills, hardly used at all by the Barcelonans
themselves—except for the old funfair at Tibidabo—while the sea, curiously enough, was almost inaccessible to them. The city had sealed off
its own way of life from the sea by a cluttered industrial port with scant
marina facilities and the virtual annihilation of any kind of social use of
the coast that ran northeast to the mouth of the Besós River. Anywhere
else, this could have been prime recreational ground. In Barcelona it
was waste—the beaches fouled with industrial effluents, access to them
prevented by a tangle of obsolete factories, railroad tracks, yards, and
dumps around the nineteenth-century industrial area of Poblenou. The
Ajuntament's plan is to open up the Collserola Hills as parkland, and
reclaim the whole waterfront of Poblenou between the Citadel Park and
the Old Cemetery—about 250 acres, or the equivalent in area of fifty
blocks of the Eixample—as a sports, recreation, and housing area. It
would first be used as the Olympic Village (housing for fifteen thousand
athletes) at the 1992 games, and then—or so the mayor announced back
in 1986—sold at "low, competitive" prices as a housing development for
ten thousand people. In the process, five kilometers of public-access
beachfront north toward the Besós River would be created, along with
five seafront parks. The main business developments were two forty-
two-story skyscrapers overlooking the water, one for offices, the other
a hotel. Thus Poblenou would become Barcelona's new "maritime facade." It was, in short, the kind of urban-clearance project that in the
United States today would bog down in the courts for years, as one
special-interest group after another whittled away at it. In Barcelona it
was pushed through fast, with a large boost from private money. The
overseeing architects for the Olympic Village were the firm of Bohigas,
Martorell and Mackay. A year away from the Olympics, the immense
Poblenou project was so far from completion that its architectural quality
could hardly be judged, but as town planning, it looked admirable and

excited only one cavil. This concerns its name, Nova Icaria—New Icaria. Icaria was the name that nineteenth-century followers of the Utopian socialist Étienne Cabet, some of them Catalans, gave to the ideal workers' community of the future, which some of them tried—and abjectly failed—to found in the United States. The Olympic Village scheme has absolutely nothing to do with worker housing, for no blue-collar family could afford to buy one of its pricey apartments; you might as well call an upscale condo block in Berlin the Rosa Luxemburg Tower. The "low" prices Maragall spoke of in 1986 turned out, by 1991, to be quite high —about a quarter of a million pesetas per square meter, or $250 per square foot.

In all, by 1992 Barcelona will have spent about two hundred billion pesetas (some two billion dollars) on buildings and infrastructure associated with the Olympic Games. Parallel with the recovery of the coast goes the reclaiming of Montjuic, site of the Olympic Ring and the track and indoor events of the 1992 games. In 1929, the main ceremonial buildings of the Barcelona World's Fair decreed by the dictator Miguel Primo de Rivera, such as the huge Palau Nacional, which now houses the Museum of Catalan Art, were pitched on and near Montjuic—where their gross monumentality contrasted with the abstract, almost ethereal lines of Mies van der Rohe's German pavilion, which, after its demolition, remained one of the ruling ghosts or absent classics of modernism. In the mid-1980s the Ajuntament reconstructed Mies's building as accurately as it could from drawings and photos, and it restored that likable remnant of the 1929 Exposition, the light-show fountain on the downhill axis between the Palau Nacional and Plaça d'Espanya. But Montjuic still felt like no-man's-land, not exactly a park, nor in any satisfactory way an urban center. It has been pulled together by the Olympic Ring, the official name for the redesign of a large slice of the mountain, under the general control of the architects Federico Correa and Alfonso Milá. They carefully preserved the facade of the old oval stadium with its classicizing bronze sculptures by Pau Gargallo—one of the better examples of twentieth-century European dictatorial architecture—but lowered the level of the sports track by some thirty-five feet, thus giving more room for raked seats: enough for seventy thousand spectators. From this excellent conversion, one descends by stairs and plazas to the most distinguished new building associated with the Olympics: the Palau Sant Jordi, or Palace of Saint George, a roofed sports arena seating seventeen thousand spectators, designed by the Japanese architect Arata Isozaki.

From outside, the *palau*'s low profile and its dark gray-glazed ceramic roof pierced with porthole skylights give it the air of a grounded flying saucer. But inside, the ground-hugging effect is dramatically reversed: the vast roof, a curved metal space frame, soars over the arena, its structural daring turned into near weightlessness by the light pouring through the array of round holes above. Here, high tech turns into architectural poetry, as it does in Norman Foster's eight-hundred-foot telecommunications tower, rising like a lance from the Collserola Hills near Tibidabo.

None of the other stadiums, tracks, swimming pools, and offices built for the Olympics compare with Isozaki's arena, but in terms of urbanism the Olympic project was, from Barcelona's point of view, more a means of priming the pump than an end in itself. For Barcelona's sense of neighborhood and the fabric of its past has recently begun to change.

Porcioles's city had been based on zoning. The new city hall was persuaded by its chief urban theorist, the architect and historian Oriol Bohigas, that this was not the way to go. Instead—as Maragall put it in a speech to the Harvard Graduate School of Design in 1986—Barcelona should decentralize, even within the center of the city itself. "This meant," he said, "giving up zoning and looking for a city in which all activities coexisted." What this rather cloudy idea signified was not that the Ajuntament would put factories back in the Barri Gòtic, but that the center should not be exclusively showcased at the expense of the periphery and that run-down and shapeless areas all over town should be brought back with what Maragall termed "a set of urban spaces— parks, squares—of high urban and design quality throughout the city." Thus, the Ajuntament hoped, by thinking in terms of individual projects instead of a general plan, the city could be retuned. The idea was to reassert the claims of the *barri*, the "neighborhood," many of which were the remnants of a distinct village from Barcelona's far past, as the city's traditional social unit.

At first, this was done with the help of a public sculpture program, linked to restoration of the squares and arcades, the open spaces and gardens, which were the lungs of the neighborhood. No amount of new sculpture will tart up a socially dead space, and the day of the official monument was past—especially in Spain, where the very idea reeked of Franco. So city hall decided to approach sculptors and get them together with architects to work on spaces that needed invigoration, sometimes with the aim of provoking memory, but always with a view to engaging the people of the *barri*.

Barcelona's sculpture-in-public-space program was largely devised by a member of Maragall's staff at the Ajuntament, an energetic bear of a man named Josep Acebillo. It is the largest of any Western city's, a unique anthology, and it could only come about because the artists—some Spanish, others American or English or French—agreed to work for a fraction of their usual market price, with all costs of making and installing assumed by the Ajuntament. The scheme acquired such a cachet that there are now more than seventy such projects completed in the metropolitan area of Barcelona. A few are straight revival—the replacement of sculptures that had been dismantled for political reasons during the Franco period but fortunately not destroyed; one of these is the monument to the Catalanist mayor of Barcelona Bartolomeu Robert i Yarzábal, the base designed by Gaudí and the bronze figures by Josep Llimona, which now stands in Plaça de Tetuán; another is the bronze commemorating Rafael Casanova, a hero of the 1714 siege of Barcelona, which was found in storage and then reerected on the Ronda de Sant Pere. But most were made for their sites by, or to the design of, living artists, and they tend to eschew the oratorical distance and single-minded speech of official monuments. You must peer and puzzle at the giant still life of cubist shapes inside the glass box, streaming with water and rippling with reflection, that Antoni Tàpies raised as a monument to Picasso, next to the fern house of the Citadel Park. Xavier Corberó's array of carved marble blades and fins in the Plaça de Soller—a lake apparition with faint echoes of the Fontana di Trevi—is generously urbane, completing rather than dominating the square and the lake. Beverly Pepper got a whole park adjacent to the long-disused Estació del Nord and turned it into a huge earthwork on and around which children play: their favorite part of it is *Fallen Sky*, a whaleback hill rising from the green turf, sheathed in slabs of cobalt and turquoise ceramic. The most "monumental" of the projects so far, the last big work of Joan Miró, could not be less authoritarian: a lunar, massive torso with a horned cylinder of a head, ponderous but also silly in its dignity, a moon calf dropped from Brobdingnag. Its bovine appearance neatly refers to its urban context near the Arenas bullring. Sixty feet high, sheathed in the *trencadís*, or "broken tiles," that pay Miró's homage to Gaudí, it is best seen from the lower levels of the Parc de l'Escorxador, rising oneirically above the rows of palm trees planted by the project's designer, Beth Gali. Not every project works as well as these, and several are banal, like the incoherent *Homage to the Universal Exhibition of 1888* stuck on a prime site in the Citadel Park by Antoni Clavé, a painter without sculptural talent, but a Catalan.

One of the habits, almost a reflex, of Porcioles's planners was to prefer the car to the foot. Thus, without explanation, one of the city's most liked promenades, the Rambla de Sant Andreu, was closed to pedestrians in November 1969; all its trees were cut down and it became a highway. But Barcelona is a walker's city, despite its inflexible grid. Its "natural" patterns pertain to the square and the *barri*, not the beltway and the ramp. One of the things that strikes the foreigner there—behind the smog, the din, and the traffic—is the social importance assigned to strolling and the reality of its pedestrian etiquette. Passeig de Gràcia is one of the great promenades of the world, an expression of social consensus, as are the Ramblas and the Güell Park. It is a city in which one still sees things from eye level, on foot; where there is always a collective instinct to browse. Thus, recovering the street as promenade became a high priority in the 1980s. The Ajuntament restored the Rambla de Sant Andreu and brought back the generous axis of the Passeig Lluís Companys, between the Arch of Triumph built for the 1888 Exposition and the gates of the Citadel Park; it banished cars from the diagonal Avinguda de Gaudí that links those twin masterpieces of *modernisme*, Gaudí's Sagrada Família and the Hospital of the Holy Cross and Saint Paul by Domènech i Montaner. It began to repair plazas in the Old City, large and small, that had fallen into decay: Plaça dels Angels, Plaça de Sant Augustí Vell, and a dozen others. It recycled old buildings into new uses. The medieval Convent dels Angels, long since abandoned, became the new site of the Hemeroteca Municipal, Barcelona's archive of newspapers and journals. The neoclassical Casa de la Caritat, disused since 1956, is to be fixed up by the American architect Richard Meier as a center for contemporary art. The Editorial Montaner i Simón, designed by Domènech i Montaner, is recycled as a museum for the work of Barcelona's most famous living painter, Antoni Tàpies—a project that strikes some critics who are not Catalan as tinged by nationalistic piety. In 1989, the Ajuntament struck a deal with the monks of the great Gothic monastery of Pedralbes and began to convert their fourteenth-century dormitory into an exhibition space for part of the Thyssen Collection, lent but not given to Barcelona.

But for the returning visitor who may, perhaps, have come to the city a decade ago, the quickly visible change is not on the large scale of planning, or even in the conversion projects, but in the texture and detail of the streetscape. The work done to clean, restore, and strip false accretions from the historical facades of Barcelona has been long and resolute. This is especially true of buildings from the modernist decades, 1870–1910, ignored by Porcioles and his colleagues. Gaudí's Casa Milà is a pale golden sea cliff again, not the dark hulk it had become; the Monet-like mosaic facade of his Casa Batlló glitters, and its foyer is once

again a cool blue grotto; next door, every red-and-gold luster tile on the
stepped Dutch pediment of Puig i Cadafalch's Casa Amatller twinkles
in the oblique morning light. Unnoticed details spring out as you walk
around the Eixample and the Barri Gòtic: the whiplash frame of a 1900
doorway with its green mosaic inserts that had been too grimy to see;
a spitting iron dragon returned to its bracket; the clutter of neon and
plastic stripped from a neoclassical facade on the Ramblas. And then
there are larger projects, such as Oscar Tusquets's superbly informed
and sensitive remodeling of the Palau de la Música Catalana, which—
being a highly charged emblem of Catalan independence—had been left
to decay during the Franco years.

Not all of this is paid for by the Ajuntament: the Generalitat, for
instance, put in half a billion pesetas (five million dollars) toward the
Palau de la Música, the same amount for Gae Aulenti's remodeling of
the Museum of Catalan Art—which critics await with trepidation, remembering what an overwrought monster she made of the Musée d'Or-
say in Paris—and eight hundred million pesetas (eight million dollars)
for the Museum of Contemporary Art. But most of the impulse for
preservation came from Maragall's administration in the late 1980s, and
especially from Oriol Bohigas, the architect-historian whose essential
role was to supply what one might call the ideology of preservation, and
José Acevillo, his successor from 1985 on.

Taste cannot be legislated, but at least the integrity of the past can
be. With the guidance of Bohigas and other conservation-minded architects, Barcelona in the 1980s developed the strictest historical preservation code of any city in Europe.

The code specifically protects 860 "Buildings, Elements and Groups"
in Barcelona on the grounds of historical significance. Most of them (578,
or 67 percent) are in the Old City, while 134 more, or 15 percent, are
in the Eixample. The rest are split between the ten other electoral districts of Barcelona, from Sarrià (49 items, or nearly 6 percent) to the
industrial quarter of Sant Andreu, which has 4 items considered worth
protecting. What seems remarkable about the code, at least to the foreigner, is not just its rigor but its conceptual inclusiveness. It sets out
five levels for protected buildings. Those at level A are "of a singular
character, which, because of their great architectural value, are considered as monuments"—like Gaudí's Sagrada Família or Domènech's Palau
de la Música Catalana. For these, "protection is total," and no additions
of any kind may be made to them. At level B are buildings of type A
that have been altered in the past and must be brought back. Level C

—the commonest in the Eixample—are those "whose value lies mainly in their characteristic structure, outwardly expressed in the facade." Level D applies to structures of facade interest only; and the lowest, E, contains ones with isolated "elements of interest"—a fine staircase, a skylight, unusual molding.

Essentially, the new code puts the onus on the property holder. Before he can touch a brick, the owner of a building must prove to the Ajuntament's satisfaction that it is *not* of historical significance. He must provide "documentary evidence that the building in question does *not* possess the following characteristics," signs of possible value that are so broad as to make change all but impossible, such as these traits of a street facade:

> The surface of the facade generated by its alignment; vertical hierarchy with the lower floors and cornice or finial standing out; the existence of symmetrical axes subordinating the general composition. The predominance of solid wall over opening. The general layout of the openings according to vertical composition axes with the presence of projecting elements such as balconies . . .

Then the code moves to details, forbidding the developer to alter any building in the Historic Preservation District that shows, among other things,

> The presence . . . of decorative architectural elements, reliefs or sculptural forms, paintings, *sgraffito*, stucco, ceramics, carpentry, leaded lights, ironwork, and applied arts in general. The use of fine materials such as stone, marble, wood, etc. The presence of singular fixtures, such as screens . . .

> The existence of structural or building elements indicative of the period of technological transition which characterized the construction process of the historic *Eixample*, important both for the recovery of traditional techniques (vaults, brickwork, etc.) and for the introduction of new materials (cast-iron columns and the early use of iron).

The code works somewhat to the advantage of traditional Catalan crafts—ceramics, iron forging, high-grade joinery, glass—which were dying twenty years ago. But mainly, it protects the historic city not only from the greed of developers but from the zeal and hubris of designers. For Barcelona has a glut of design.

VIII

At two in the morning, on what its habitués call the Via Liturgica, an unnamed strip of orange-dirt road behind the University of Barcelona, near the football stadium west of the city, the transvestite hookers display themselves, waiting for clients while Catalans in cars look at them.

Unless they get into a cat fight, which sometimes happens, their dignity is vestal. They do not camp up and down, like models vogueing on a runway. They stand widely separated, like idealized statues carved from the gross and hairy male protein of their former selves, occasionally doing a circuit to mark off territory, the older ones stalking and the younger ones teetering slightly in their high heels on the rutted surface. This one looks like Carmen Miranda, that like the young Anita Ekberg, a third like Veruschka, and a fourth, with an Egyptian wedge of frizzy hair, resembles Sonia Braga. But for a cache-sexe and some accessories—a feather boa, a leather bustier, or mesh stockings—they are naked, some with magnificent breasts that possess the artificial perfection of hothouse fruit, achieved like the grace of Saint Theresa through patient devotional mortification and self-denial: hormones, surgery, and much saving up to pay the doctors. Sometimes one of them will snarl at a carload of useless gawking teenagers, all testosterone and zits but no pesetas, and spit. Most of the time they exhibit a regal indifference, a self-absorption within the strutting temple of the redesigned body that goes far beyond the ordinary narcissism of mannequins. "*Són arquitectes*," says my friend Corberó.

The cars drive slowly by, jouncing on the ruts; turn; cruise back. There are battered little Renaults and big Mercedes. Their wheels raise a yellow fog of dust that hangs in the air. The headlights burn through it, casting inky elongated shadows from the human statues. Very rarely a vehicle will stop, and one of the apparitions, after a minute's palaver, will get in. But most cars keep circulating. Their drivers are there to look, not buy. This is street theater of a curiously pure kind, a *tableau vivant* in which the audience moves but the actors do not. But it seems to go back beyond theater into ritual: in their fantastic incongruity, remade by pills and scalpels, shaved, wigged, depilated, creamed, rouged, kitted out like Marlene Dietrich, and then spotlighted on this stage of dirt and ratty concrete, the *travestits* of the Via Liturgica are like fantasies out of a pagan past as imagined by Beardsley illustrating the *Satyricon* of Petronius, haughty Messalinas, pre-Christian as well as postmodern.

They are also an extreme metaphor of their city's present obsession. They are on the cutting edge, so to speak, of Catalan design. In their sacrificial devotion to it, they are the real thing, representing the *ser autentic* of Barcelona's struggles to remake itself. If London has the changing of the guard as one of its emblems for mass tourism, Barcelona has the changing of the body. This has required a number of prolonged and sometimes painful operations, accompanied by an obstinate defiance of norms and a certain amount of rebuke from the conservative minded. The depth of the change is accompanied by a great deal of bitching, competition, and stylistic froufrou. In what other city could you find a bilingual guidebook rating bars, discos, and restaurants not by the quality of their food or service but entirely by their design ambience? Thus for a place called Network, on the Diagonal, the English text reads: "It's hard not to feel like Harrison Ford in *Blade Runner* in this disquieting setting, permeated by an aesthetic somewhere between 'destroy' and high-tech. However, the yuppies and would-bes eating by the light of the TV monitors bring you back to reality. . . . The unisex toilets are worth a look." Can't wait. Or try Flash-Flash, another restaurant: "In the purest 60s-meets-70s style . . . now a classic and an obligatory point of reference. An interesting democratic phenomenon takes place in this black-and-white setting in which voyeurism and exhibitionism play an important part . . . we suggest the hamburgers." One imagines flocks of design-crazed Japanese and Californians moving from one such place to the next like avid insects, picking up the ethereal pollen of interior-decoration ideas on their sticky palps, and staying thin. Those who want *serious* food can eat in their accustomed staid holes.

Barcelona moves into the 1990s obsessed with design. Designers are to it what young cigar-chomping art stars were to New York in the 1980s. Design consciousness pervades the city, in an irritated ecstasy of angular, spiky, spotted, jerry-built, post-Memphis, sub-Miróesque mannerism. Designer ashtrays, designer pencils, designer kitchen gear, designer food, and even designer chocolate in the form of Ionic capitals and miniature mastabas filled with liqueur: it's franchise heaven for Name Anyone. Even the children appear to have been designed—flocks of tots, garbed like medieval jesters in Day-Glo sneakers and parti-colored blouson jackets, with panels of saffron yellow, black, lime green, puce, orange, magenta. They look like models from a Benetton ad, especially when you see thirty of them sitting under the awning of a bank in Passeig de Gràcia, solemnly drawing Gaudí's Casa Batlló with crayons. They, too, will grow up to be designers, as their remote ancestors were encouraged to be Catalan secessionists. The men you see in Los Angeles restaurants and assume to be film producers or, at least, postulant scriptwriters—Armani shoulders and brilliantined hair, combed straight back and secured in a small ponytail with a rubber band; that is, half the clientele—may be assumed, in Barcelona, to be designers. And of what? Of a hotel that will not be open for the Olympics; of a wire-mesh ashtray; of some PoMo whatnot with a stepped Dutch top and black balls on its legs.

In truth, Barcelona has long had excellent designers: the upper-middle-class Catalan taste for luxury, solidity, and fantasy in the fin de siècle reached a climax in the work of men like Joan Busquets i Jané and Gaspar Homar i Mezquida, whose marquetry furniture attained a level of refinement comparable to anything made in Paris or Vienna. But this tradition died with *modernisme* itself; there were no outstanding Catalan designers of furniture and domestic objects in the Art Deco idiom, and no industrial base existed for the manufacture of "rationalist" material. Toward the end of Franquism, pioneering Barcelona designers in the 1960s such as André Ricard and Miguel Milà set up an axis of communication with Milan, studying the careful and rational "classics" of Italian designers like Magistretti, Scarpa, and Gardella. Italian prototypes continue to set the sense of quality for much serious Catalan design, including the work of Oscar Tusquets and Pep Bonet for Studio PER, and the brilliant industrial designer Ramón Benedito, who, with Lluís Morillas and Josep Puig, formed an experimental group in Barcelona called Transatlàntic. But in the 1980s Barcelona was also flooded with a peculiarly nitwitted and lighthearted mode of design, growing from a juncture among disco, comics, fashion, PoMo theory (or what passed for it), and Memphis mannerisms. This is the stuff with franchising clout and media appeal, and it ramps over the city like kudzu.

Its reductio ad absurdum, or locus classicus if you prefer, is a discotheque called the Torre d'Avila, built into the entrance rampart of the Poble Espanyol on Montjuic, the ever-popular fake village of buildings done in all the traditional architectural styles of Spain that was erected for the 1929 World's Fair. Elsewhere in Spain, real old buildings are converted into restaurants, discos, or art galleries. The Torre d'Avila is unique in being a fake old building, a medieval simulacrum, which some sixty years after its construction has been filled with an orgy of equally simulated postmodernism. The conversion is said to have cost its Catalan entrepreneurs half a billion pesetas, or five million dollars at the current rate of exchange, and nobody can deny that they got some bang for their buck. The Torre d'Avila has some claim, not to put too fine a point on it, to be considered the most seriously unenjoyable *boîte de nuit* in Spain, or maybe the world. This is not so much due to the price of its drinks (fourteen hundred pesetas, about fourteen dollars) or to its clientele (mostly the young Catalan equivalents of what, in New York, is dismissively called the BTC, or Bridge and Tunnel crowd—out-of-towners come in to look) as to its design or, rather, designiness. Its authors are Alfredo Arribas and Javier Mariscal, a comic-strip artist who lives in Barcelona and has become the official limner of the Olympic Games, creating its mascot, Cobi, a ubiquitous dog derived from George Herriman's immortal figure of Krazy Kat. (Cobi has a partner, Nosi, presumably a bitch. She has no arms and is the symbol of the Paralympics, the athletic competitions for the handicapped.) He is also the creator of a twenty-foot-long fiberglass prawn that was installed on top of Gambrinus, a snack bar on the newly renovated Moll de la Fusta, Barcelona's harbor esplanade, in the late 1980s. Mariscal comes from Valencia, a part of Spain noted for its *fallas*: straw-and-papier-mâché effigies used on feast days and then burned. Unfortunately this *falla* is incombustible, and much to the Ajuntament's taste.

Whether the Torre d'Avila will last is hard to predict. Its sheer awfulness may entitle it to preservation. Mariscal and Arribas set out to make your big night on the town an uninterrupted barrage of the clichés of PoMo irony—as though Philippe Starck at his most morbid teamed up with Peter Eisenman at his most hostile to do the sets for *Pee-wee's Playhouse*.

The Torre d'Avila is built on several levels, all linked by hanging steel staircases and a glass capsule elevator whose riders are spotlighted to make them feel like stars. The club's floors have holes in them, enabling those above to look down on those below, while those below gaze up the skirts of those above. The main lounge has a canopy that goes up and down on wires, and sharp spotlights that pick out mock-antique masks on the semicircular walls. The tables are tiny, the chairs penitential. More tables stick out of the curved wall, at which you may also sit; but below each of them hangs, on a wire, a small metal sputnik with more wires protruding from it, whose sole aim seems to be to snag and ladder the stockings of unwary women. On the floor below there is a circular billiard table, next to which is the gents' lavatory, a transparent glass enclosure. The urinal is top lighted by UV bulbs, which turn your piss a lurid green. If you turn around to zip your fly, you find yourself facing the billiard players through the glass. It is hard to be sure whether this frankness about bodily functions is designed to force the clientele to scorn false modesty, or to discourage it from cruising and snorting coke in the john.

Barcelona is a metropolis; it has long been an intensely provincial place as well. The obtrusive sense of Catalan specialness gives rise to nagging doubts about the value of new cultural endeavors (does this beat Madrid at its own game?) and to a defensive overrating of the vitality of local culture (who cares about Madrid anyway?). This syndrome is perfectly familiar to anyone who, like me, grew up in Australia. It leads to a mildly compulsive exaggeration of the merits of, among other things, local design. Not to believe completely in the regional culture hero is, in some degree, to let the side down. A striking example is the reputation of the architect Ricardo Bofill, whose name is so closely identified with the post-Franco resurgence in Barcelona. His most recent building is a mock-classical affair in the Olympic Ring on Montjuic, the National Institute of Physical Education. "Ricardo Bofill," one of the Ajunta-ment's brochures announces with a flourish, "has built practically noth-ing in Barcelona, the city where he was born. The Olympic Games have ensured that this anomalous situation should change."

Actually, Bofill does have a building history in Barcelona. But it is awkward, and one does not dwell on it. The "practically nothing" he built was one of the most discussed buildings of modern Spain.

Ricardo Bofill emerged in the late 1960s with large social theories. He was the right man for the Divine Left, with notions of collectivity overlaid by the authoritative pose of the Formgiver who knows what the People need. His first large building, a cobalt-blue array of modular flats on a hill above Sitges, looking like one of the blocks of niches in a cemetery, went up in 1966, and by 1969 it was officially a ruin, con-demned as structurally too dangerous to live in. But Sitges is a fair distance down the coast from Barcelona, and Bofill was soon immersed in a larger housing project, this time for workers, in the industrial suburb of Sant Just Desvern, a little way toward the airport past Esplugües de Llobregat. He named it Walden Seven, after the Utopia of social con-ditioning proposed by the American behavioral psychologist B. F. Skin-ner. It is a landmark: a hulking castlelike structure with half-cylinder balconies, all sheathed in terra-cotta tiles. When it opened in 1975, it was widely hailed as an emblem of Barcelona's renewal after Franco and Porcioles—look what the left can do for people oppressed by the mo-notony of the industrial polygons!

But the families who had to live in it loathed Walden Seven. It was poky; it leaked; its elevators and plumbing and electricity kept failing.

Naturally, neither its defects nor the discontent of its inhabitants showed up in the many photographs of Walden Seven that appeared in architectural magazines. Nor did they perturb the autocratic serenity of Bofill, who in 1978 declared in his own text *Architecture and Man* (published, perhaps wisely, in French and in Paris) that those lucky enough to dwell in Walden Seven were

> thrilled to take part in an original experience, because they feel different from others, because they now live in a place so extraordinary that they can feel proud of it. . . . The confrontation over Walden Seven is serious, because its inhabitants have only now become aware that they are, in a sense, the pioneers of an experience . . . they know that they can protest, object, shout, but that they can change nothing. They only have one choice: stay or go. They wanted to change the building to make it conventional. But they failed: the presence of the place, the spatial organization are too strong.

Take that, housewives! Perhaps the "original experience" was not so original; Spanish workers had been living in ill-heated buildings with defective elevators and fuses that kept blowing for quite some time before Walden Seven. But then a further hitch developed. It began to fall apart. The terra-cotta cladding on its external walls started peeling off, though if there is one thing Catalans traditionally know how to do, it is how to keep tiles on a wall. Now the whole perimeter of the building had to be strung with nets so that Bofill's falling tiles did not brain its inhabitants. Ten years later, the nets are still there, falling to pieces themselves. The fallen tiles are removed from time to time, which is just as well, since their accumulated weight would have collapsed the net scaffolding long ago. Today every side of the hulk, ground to roof, shows huge patches of raw mortar where hundreds of square feet of terra-cotta have come off. Restoring it is out of the question, but this seems not to worry the town hall of Sant Just Desvern, which has it on its list of local buildings of architectural interest. Bofill's offices remain in a converted cement factory right next to it.

This juxtaposition—as though a doctor had his surgery next to his patients' graveyard—seems to have troubled no one except the tenants of Walden Seven. Bofill was Catalan and therefore deserved patronage, even though another of his housing developments—the so-called Barri Gaudí in Reus—also became uninhabitable within a decade of completion. Meanwhile, in the 1980s, his work appealed to French officials, who gave him enormous projects to do outside Paris and in Montpellier.

These he carried out in a coarsely scenographic style, a parody of neo-classicism. (*Autres temps, autres moeurs*: bye-bye Skinner, hi Ledoux!) Few of his clients, in France or the United States, seem to have checked out his built buildings: that was not the way with postmodernism. One looked at photos in design magazines, not real buildings, just as collectors in the 1980s bought art from slides. Bofill's reputation in Barcelona came from being "international," while in New York it came from being Catalan. Thus it happened that Bofill was hired by Madrid to do the gateway to Barcelona for the Olympic year: a new main terminal for the airport of Barcelona at El Prat de Llobregat. It is a high, handsome steel-and-glass cube, floored with red marble, with palm trees growing inside it: a stylish job. But the marble is cracking into potholes and the palms are dying for lack of air, and it seems that neither Bofill nor his design-fuddled clients looked into the effect that such large planes of glass might have on radar signals received by the adjacent control tower. They generate so much radar interference that the flight traffic-control screens are plagued with ghost blips, which often cannot be distinguished from incoming or outgoing aircraft. One hopes a cure will be found, but in the meantime—as *La Vanguardia* sighed in the article that broke the unwelcome story in June 1991—"the terminal . . . has not escaped from a mass of unforeseen defects that may end by turning it into a permanent example of a national fiasco."

Such are the perils of the culture hero. Faced with the present design mania, even the foreigner may find himself mildly yearning for an older Catalunya—for the pitted moon-white wall of Miró's farmhouse, as it were, rather than the smirking reflexiveness of Catalan PoMo; for the solid culinary ground of Catalan "brown food"—the *butifarra amb mon-guetes* and the *rossejat de fideus*, the sweet-salty taste of the gunk in the head of a perfectly fresh grilled *gamba* or the weird, ancient, dark taste of a *mar i muntanya*, stew involving squid, lobster, rabbit, meatballs, and chocolate—rather than the latest frippery of Catalo-Californian cuisine. Is this the nostalgia of a middle-aged tourist? Perhaps, but one may stick with it anyway. The city, one is constantly told, is "in transition." So it is. Like all other great cities, it always has been. But without a sense of its traditions and its history, how can anyone know what "transition" means? Barcelona has a tradition of intense, wrenching civic change, of long-shot gambles and risky endeavors that consort oddly with its self-image of bourgeois *seny*. Such proclivities were not invented when the dictator died; they go far back, and to see them one should begin at the beginning.

PART I

The Old City

CHAPTER TWO

The Domain of the Hairy Hero

I

Barcelona starts with the Romans. There are traces of an earlier Bronze Age people, known to the Romans as the Laietani, scattered across the coastal plain and up the flanks of Montjuic. But they were an agricultural folk and did not make a city. They planted their grain on the long slope to the sea and raked their famously good oysters on the sandbanks of what, even then, was a poor and shallow port. The Laietani had the bad luck to be where Rome wanted to go, and they were in due course obliterated. The oysters remained—they are mentioned by the fourth-century Gallo-Roman writer Decimus Ausonius—peaceably spawning for another two millennia, until industrial effluvia did them in.

Though modern historians wish to favor the underdog, it is unlikely that the Laietani could have been of much interest to anyone but themselves. Catalans of a later day—eager to make their ancestry look as old and well rooted as possible, and imagining some parallel between the Roman erasure of the Laietani and the eighteenth-century Bourbon occupation of Barcelona, which was still their historical sore point—insisted on naming a new avenue cut through the city to the port in 1908 the Via Laietana. Alas, in the course of excavating the huge trench for it, little trace of the Laietani themselves was found. In the nineteenth century there were also claims that Barcelona had been founded by the Greeks or the Phoenicians, but there is no acceptable evidence for this. The Greeks did, in fact, colonize this coast: farther north toward the French border are the ruins of Emporion, a whole Greek city of the sixth century B.C., the westernmost of all known Phocaean settlements, which gave its name to the Catalan province of Empordà, or the Ampurdan. But the Greeks showed no interest in the site of Barcelona. Neither, at first, did the Romans.

Rome came to occupy Spain because it was at war with a North African power, Carthage, for control of the western Mediterranean. In the first Punic War (264–241 B.C.), Rome had defeated Carthage and stripped her of her island possessions in the Mediterranean: Sicily, Corsica, and eventually Sardinia; however, the Carthaginians continued to hold the Strait of Gibraltar and southeastern Spain. In 228–227 B.C. they established a colony there named Carthago Nova, or New Carthage—modern Cartagena—which gave them access to the rich silver mines in the hills behind the coast and a strategic command of the Mediterranean approaches to Gibraltar. Before long their influence was felt all the way up the eastern coast of Spain and even into what is now France, where the citizens of the Greek colony of Massilia (modern Marseilles) worried about Carthaginian power. A long negotiation with the Romans ended with a treaty that obliged the Carthaginians to stay south of the River Ebro.

But Carthage was not to be restrained by a piece of parchment. In 219 its general Hannibal besieged and conquered Saguntum (modern Sagunto), an Iberian city-state allied to Rome. Carthaginian reinforcements, in a daring march across southern France, started moving toward Italy. The Roman Senate voted for war, and in 218 an army of two legions led by the brothers Publius (Scipio Africanus Major) and Cnaeus Scipio landed at Emporion on what is now the Costa Brava, northeast of Barcelona; they met no resistance from the small Greek colony there, for it had been ravaged by Carthaginian raids earlier in the century. The object was to cut Hannibal's supply lines and then to roll his army back to Africa. Cnaeus Scipio moved south and set up headquarters at Tarraco (modern Tarragona), northeast of the Ebro.

From then on, Tarraco was the northern administrative capital of what the Roman colonists called Hispania Citerior, or Nearer Spain, comprising the Mediterranean coastal strip from the Pyrenees to modern Linares. Beyond that lay the richer province of Further Spain, Hispania Ulterior, whose capital was Corduba (modern Córdoba); it embraced most of modern Andalusia to the Baetis (modern Guadalquivir) River, from which the Roman province got its alternative name of Baetica.

All of Catalunya lay within Hispania Citerior, and the region was fully under Roman control by 210 B.C.—except for the occasional battle with fractious Iberian tribes, who allied with the Carthaginians against the Romans.

In 209 the young general Scipio Africanus Major marched south from Tarraco to Carthago Nova, the main Punic base, slaughtered its defenders, and enslaved its citizens. Within three years not a Punic stronghold was left on the whole Iberian peninsula.

In economic terms, southern Spain mattered far more to Rome than most of Hispania Citerior. The silver mines of Carthago Nova alone produced twenty-five thousand drachmas a day; and then there were copper and tin, for bronze making, and lead. The significance of the northern area was, at first, mainly strategic. It carried the road from the Ampurdan region south through Tarraco to the mines, and Tarraco, being then the chief port on the coast, evolved into the first capital of Roman Spain. (A curious survival of its former role is that the archbishop of Tarragona still carries the title Primate of the Spains.) It acquired full colonial status in 45 B.C., when Julius Caesar bestowed on it the title of Colonia Iulia Urbs Triumphalis Tarraconensis, and with its immense walls, its forum, its temples, its circus, and its amphitheater, it is still more richly endowed with surviving Roman buildings than any other Spanish city. At the height of its power, which came with the reign of Augustus (c. 27 B.C.), it had a population of thirty thousand people.

The economy that evolved in the general northern area of Hispania Citerior exerted a long subterranean and decisive influence on the traits of deep Catalunya. The people were a mix, the residue of earlier invasions from the north and the south. The Iberian tribes were of North African origin, related to the Berbers; centuries before they had crossed the Strait of Gibraltar and spread along the Mediterranean coast. Other, Celtic tribes had come down across the Pyrenees, interbred with the Iberians, and produced the people diffusely known to protohistorians as the Celtiberians, one of whose tribes was the Laietani. In general, these folk seem to have been stubborn and resistant fighters, but as time went by their men were enslaved and their women taken in marriage or concubinage by Roman settlers, so that their tribal structures eventually dissolved. But the settlers were generally army veterans—privates, centurions, minor line officers—who got a few acres of stony soil at the end of their service to the imperium. There was little free capital floating around, and certainly no chance of consolidating farms into giant latifundia along the lines of the slave plantations of Sicily. Farms and households were slave run, but by a servant or two, not lines of driven laborers. Olive oil, cereals, wine, goats, some chickens, perhaps a pig—the chestnut-fed hams of the Ampurdan were already famous by the first century as an esteemed export to Rome—and a fortified farmhouse: in its clusters of family-and-slave homes that anticipated the later groupings of the Catalan *poblet*, or village, the prototype of Catalunya's rural future was prepared. Even by the standards of the times, this economy was conservative and low tech. What its farms produced, its inhabitants consumed. If there was a surplus it was sold locally or, at the most, brought to market in Tarraco. Unlike Hispania Ulterior, Hispania Citerior had no export trade. The bond between the producing countryside and the consuming, administering city was strong, but Rome was very far away.

The way the Romans settled Catalunya also had linguistic results. Like Spanish and all other Romance languages, Catalan originated in Latin, the speech of the Roman occupation. As the process of subjugation and settlement went on, Latin was laid over and mingled with the substrata of tongues spoken by the indigenous Celts and Iberians. Since there are no written records of these earlier tongues, it is unlikely that anyone will ever figure out (especially to the satisfaction of other language historians) just how Latin imposed itself on them and absorbed traces of them. But one thing is quite sure: Spanish and Catalan developed, independently of each other, from a common root in Latin.

This happened because of the pattern of Roman settlement. Roman traders and financiers—the better class of conqueror—tended to gravitate to Hispania Ulterior, to Carthago Nova, Gades (modern Cádiz), and Hispalis (modern Seville), where the mines and the big trading opportunities were and where civilized life, thanks to the Phoenicians, had been going on for more than half a millennium before the Roman conquest. It was from the old, more formal, high-class Latin used by Romans who occupied Baetica, which spread north along the Baetis (modern Guadalquivir) River, that Spanish emerged.

Whereas in the north of Hispania Citerior, modern Catalunya, the situation was different. In the early years of occupation Hispania Citerior had little importance to Rome except as a gateway to the south, which had only to be secured and kept open by the legionaries. It had no industry or colonial trade, but there was a constant flow of traffic through it from Rome. Its Roman settlers, former footsloggers, spoke a demotic Latin, slangy and more modern than the official language of the south. This was the root of Catalan, and this, not the notion that Catalan is a degenerate form of Spanish or merely a dialect, accounts for the difference between the languages.

The dual origin—and the affinities between Catalan and other Romance languages that derive from later Latin—can be seen in a few common words. "Fear," in early Latin, is *metus*, whence the Spanish *miedo*; in later Latin usage, "fear" is *pavor*, which becomes *por* in Catalan, *peur* in French, and *paura* in Italian. Early Latin *comedere*, "to eat," becomes the Spanish *comer*; new Latin *manducare* turns into the Catalan *menjar*, the French *manger*, and the Italian *mangiare*. *Fabulare*, old Latin for "talk," gives the Spanish *hablar*; whereas the later Latin form, *parabolare*, produces *parlar* in Catalan, *parler* in French, and *parlare* in Italian.

Later still, innumerable mixtures and word transfers occurred between emergent Catalan and Provençal, also rooted in the newer Latin, when the Frankish kings for whom Provençal was the language of administration and court culture ruled Catalunya. For these reasons, Catalan is in some ways closer to Provençal than it is to Castilian Spanish.

The rough division—elite in the south, common in the north—extended from language to politics to literature. Indeed, from the south, Baetica, came the men who, among all those in the empire of provincial birth, had the greatest influence on Rome itself. Between about A.D. 90 and 150, a substantial bloc of Hispanic senators appeared in Rome, and one of them, Marcus Ulpius Traianus, was chosen by the emperor Nerva as his successor. He reigned as Trajan (A.D. 98–117), the first provincial to rule over the Roman world. His relative and successor was Hadrian (A.D. 117–138). During their reigns, Hispano-Romans accounted for nearly a quarter of all new admissions to the Roman Senate.

Roman Spain also produced at least two major Latin writers, one famous, the other infamous. The former was Lucius Annaeus Seneca, born to a wealthy equestrian family in Corduba around 4 B.C. Seneca wrote philosophical tracts arguing the Stoic ethic: indifference to money, self-containment, lofty disdain for power and politics, restraint of base appetite, and so forth. He was a gifted and sententious stylist, and his work had an immense influence on later European literature—especially in England, where he was a literary god to a succession of writers from Ben Jonson and John Dryden through to Alexander Pope and Joseph Addison. Senecan Stoicism had much to do with the formation of the stiff upper lip and *le phlegme anglais*, because it lay at the root of the ideology of the English public schools. He was probably the worst hypocrite in the history of literature, for as Dio Cassius would later put it:

> Though finding fault with the rich, [Seneca] himself acquired a fortune of 300,000,000 sesterces; and though he censured the extravagances of others, he had 500 tables of citrus wood with legs of ivory, all identically alike, and he served banquets on them. In stating this much I have also made clear what naturally went with it—the licentiousness in which he indulged at the very time that he contracted a most respectable

marriage, and the delight he took in boys past their prime, a practice which he also taught Nero to follow.

He wormed and pontificated his way to the heights of influence in Rome as tutor, and later adviser, to the young emperor Nero. Later his mad patron turned on Seneca and forced him to commit suicide, which he did—showing, for once in his life, a Stoic fortitude—by slitting his wrists in a warm bath.

The other writer came from the present-day territory of Catalunya. He was Seneca's exact opposite, a man who was born poor and remained so, but was incessantly criticized by the respectable for the license, viciousness, and general social nastiness of his work—which, of course, they eagerly read. He was, in other words, a satirist with an integral moral vision and a cruel though admirably realistic eye for social folly. This was the poet Marcus Valerius Martialis, or Martial (A.D. 40–104). He was born in Bilbilis, a few miles from modern Calatayud, lived in Tarragona, and reached Rome when he was in his early twenties. About his life and physical appearance, little is known: there are many portraits of Seneca but none of Martial, although he referred to his own "stiff Spanish hair"—one imagines him dark and hirsute, with the typical *cara de Català*, the thin-bladed, prominent Catalan nose. For most of his thirty-five years in Rome, Martial led the life of an indigent poet, in a third-floor garret, bitching about the need to dance attendance on patrons—"*Liber non potes et gulosus esse,*" he growled in one of his thousands of epigrams, "You can't be both independent and a glutton." He was the sharpest and least deceived spectator at the gross social feast of imperial Rome, whose pullulating life is skewered on his wit with a kind of entomological relish: here they all are, the servile placeman and the thug with equestrian ambitions, the parlor philosopher and the gourmet who flogs his cook for an underdone hare, the orators and hawkers, the fops and bores, the posturing new-rich senator and the clapped-out voluptuary—the whole empire of the gross and the self-satisfied:

> *Non est, Tucca, satis quod es gulosus:*
> *et dici cupis et cupis videri.*

> Tucca, it's not enough for you to *be* a glutton—
> you have to be called one, and to look like one.

> *Sic tamquam tabulas scyphosque, Paule,*
> *omnes archetypos habes amicos.*

Just like your pictures and your cups, Paulus,
all your friends are genuine antiques.

Triginta tibi sunt pueri totidemque puellae:
una est nec surgit mentula. Quid facies?

You have thirty boys and as many girls:
and one cock, and it won't stand. What will you do?

At times Martial's encyclopedic scorn seems to carry you forward
from late Rome to a later New York:

Et delator es et calumniator,
et fraudator es et negotiator,
et fellator es et lanista, miror
quare non habeas, Vacerra, nummos.

You're an informer and a backbiter,
a cheat and a pimp,
a cocksucker, a show-promoter—
it amazes me, Vacerra, you're not rich.

At other moments, one could be at the fashionable resort of Caldetas
outside Barcelona for a weekend:

At tu sub urbe possides famem mundam
et turre ab alta prospicis meras lauros,
furem Priapo non timente securus
et vinitorem farre pascis urbano
pictamque portas otiosus ad villam
holus, ova, pullos, poma, caseum . . .
rus hoc vocari debet, an domus longe?

But you, in the suburbs, have elegant starvation,
and see only evergreens from your high tower;
why worry? your Priapus fears no thief,
your gardener feeds you corn brought from the city,
at leisure, you bring to your art-filled villa
cabbages, eggs, chickens, fruit, cheese . . .
do you call this a farm, or a town house out of town?

With the street smarts of the acclimatized provincial, Martial could make himself at home in Rome and yet be the stranger at the feast: thin-skinned, glaring, but always *outside*. He was the great model for the eighteenth-century English satirist: in, strike, and out before the victim knows it. *"Postume, non bene olet qui bene semper olet"*—"Postumus, you don't smell right if you smell too good," or as famously rendered by an Augustan wit:

> Non amo te, Sabidi, nec possum dicere quare:
> hoc tantum possum dicere, non amo te.

> I do not like thee, Doctor Fell:
> Why it is so, I cannot tell,
> But this I know, and know full well:
> I do not like thee, Doctor Fell.

Yet he also dreamed, as provincials will, of getting back to where he had started from, to Catalunya, the ground of reality against which he judged the life of Rome; and in fact he did return there and died in some comfort:

> At cum December canus et bruma impotens
>   Aquilone rauco mugiet,
> aprica repetes Tarraconis litora
>   tuamque Laletaniam . . .
> lunata nusquam pellis et nusquam toga
>   olidaeque vestes murice;
> procul horridus Liburnus et querulus cliens,
>   imperia viduarum procul . . .
> mereatur alius grande et insanum sophos:
>   miserere tu felicium
> veroque fruere non superbus gaudio.

> But when frosty December and wild winter
>   shriek hoarsely from the north,
> then you will seek the shore of Tarragona,
>   your own Laietania . . .
> no more of the pointy shoe, no more togas,
>   or the clothes reeking of purple dye,
> far from the hateful messenger, the whining client,
>   far from arrogant, demanding widows . . .
> Let another man go after frantic *¡Olés!*
>   Keep your pity for the Big Successes,
> be truly happy, without pride.

This seems to be the first expression of that homesickness, yearning, *enyorança*, which would become a permanent trope of Catalan writing in the nineteenth century.

II

The main Roman road through Catalunya connected Emporion with Tarraco and then went south to Hispania Ulterior. It ran along the side of the Collserola Ridge, through Esplugües de Llobregat, and so on down the coast. It ignored the present site of Barcelona. Until late in the first century B.C. no town existed where Barcelona now stands, so there was no reason to make a detour down to the shallow bay.

Nevertheless, a harbor, however poor, was a harbor—and Barcelona's was the only one on the long stretch of coast between Narbonne and Tarraco. It attracted ships that beached themselves there and in the reed-fringed delta of the Llobregat River, looking for provisions and, perhaps, trade goods. A township, and presently a Roman city, grew up.

It began as a tiny settlement on Mont Tàber, a knoll between the two streams overlooking the harbor. There may have been a Celtiberian shrine on this spot, whose site became the core of the Roman forum. There was probably another on the big hill to the southeast, over which the Romans built their own shrine to thundering Jupiter, thus giving the eminence its name—Mons Iovis, which turned into Montjuic. (The other theory about the origin of Montjuic's name is that it held an early Jewish cemetery, which made it the Jews' hill, not Jove's; but there were enough small Jewish burial grounds in medieval Barcelona to make it unlikely that they would have troubled to bury their dead so far out of town.) But though Montjuic had obvious strategic advantages—confirmed a thousand and a half years later by the erection of a huge fort on its crest—it had one insuperable drawback, lack of water. It made more sense to pitch a village between the two streams, which were to become so extremely polluted that, as early as the twelfth century, they were known respectively as the Merdança and the Cagallel. In any case, nobody seemed likely to invade the flat ground there, for Rome had no powerful enemies left in this part of the Mediterranean. The place was recognized as an Augustan colony around 15 B.C., with the lengthy title of Faventia Julia Augusta Paterna Barcino, or Barcino for short. Thus Barcelona began as a cluster of huts,

Three columns from the Temple of Augustus, in the courtyard at 10 Carrer del Paradis; nineteenth-century drawing by F. J. Parecerisa

after Tarraco had been a walled capital for the best part of two centuries.

Historians who want to claim an earlier origin for Barcelona have pointed to Ausonius's phrase, "*Me punica laedit Barcino*"—"Punic Barcino annoys me"—but this would seem to have been meant as a joke, Barcino being "Punic" in the sense of "hustling"; evidently its citizens, then as now, had a fondness for the deal that irked this Gallo-Roman scholar. There is no evidence that Barcino was ever a Carthaginian settlement, still less (as has sometimes been claimed) a Greek or Phoenician one.

Probably its civic existence as an *urbs* began when the Roman authorities in Tarraco wanted to formalize an administrative center to control the locals—a mixed bag of Roman emigrants and semi-Romanized natives: army veterans; *libertini* (half-Spanish freemen); mercenaries; Laietani; and port riffraff. Now the surplus of local agriculture and fishing began to go seaward, onto the ships. It included wheat, woolen goods, amphorae of wine and oil, and pots of the fermented sauce made of anchovies or tuna called *garum*, to which the entire Roman world was partial.

Barcino was quite a small town, constructed in th
of the *oppidum*, or "fortified camp," thrown up by Roman
march. Its walls—part brick, part masonry, and part ceme
about 6 feet thick—had a circuit of about 1,350 yards; the)
site shaped like a fat coffin, about 25 acres in area. They we pierced
by four gates, and the avenues connecting these crossed at the ritual
center, where the forum lay. Streets and houses were laid out in square
blocks. Barcino was standard Roman bureaucratic issue, throughout.

Its establishment signified Roman power, and this required at least
one major ceremonial building, out of proportion, probably, to the size
of the town. This was the Temple of Augustus (peripteral hexastyle,
Corinthian order), three of whose columns stand at their original site in
the courtyard of 10 Carrer del Paradis, tucked away in a crook between
the Cathedral and the Plaça Sant Jaume in the Barri Gòtic.

Other, quite extensive traces of Roman Barcelona remain below the
Gothic center. The original forum is presumed to lie under the Plaça
Sant Jaume, between the Palau de la Generalitat and the Ajuntament.
The Cathedral is almost certainly built over the site of another temple
—and the flock of white geese that have been hissing and honking bossily
at visitors to its cloister for as long as records have existed may be the
descendants of Roman birds, colonial cousins of the Capitoline geese.
Vestiges of Roman houses are embedded in the crypts below most of
the ceremonial buildings of the Barri Gòtic—the Saló del Tinell, the
Arxiu de la Corona d'Aragó, the chapel of Santa Agada. A whole sub-
basement of the city has been meticulously excavated by archaeologists
and may be visited by a staircase that goes down to the original city
level from the sixteenth-century Museu de l'Historia de la Ciutat (in the
Casa Clariana-Padellàs, at the corner of Carrer del Veguer and Plaça del
Rei). It is no Pompeii, and its aesthetic interest is minimal, but it gives
a clear impression of the ordinary buildings of the time.

Apart from the Temple of Augustus and a bathhouse built by a rich
Barcelona-born Roman praetor named Lucius Minucius Natalis (its remains lie below Plaça Sant Miquel, behind the Town Hall), the only
monumental structure in ancient Barcelona that has survived is the city
walls. These were raised, strengthened, and given an array of seventy-
eight towers in the third century A.D. (The surviving towers were less
impressive then than they are now; their height was doubled, perhaps
tripled, by later medieval builders.) Their perimeter remained exactly
the same, which suggests that Barcelona was still a ceremonial and administrative center but not a residential one—its population had not
grown much because people still lived outside the walls, on their farms.

Roman walls in Barcelona

Yet traces of some substantial houses survive: a fine mosaic floor of a horse race in the Circus Maximus was found under the Carrer Comtessa de Sobradiel in the 1840s; another, depicting the Three Graces, came to light during excavations for the Passatge del Credit.

Large sections of the third-century walls survive, and their boot-heel outline is preserved in the jostling streets of the Barri Gòtic. One can walk around its perimeter. Start at the Plaça Nova outside the Cathedral: here, the walls are well preserved, the lower courses being made of large ashlar blocks interspersed with recycled stone from earlier buildings—tombstones, fragments of pediment, and the like. The upper sections are rubble and concrete with infiltrations of Gothic building. The lower sections of the twin semicircular towers of the Portal de l'Angel, crushing in the little slot of an entrance into Carrer del Bisbe, are Roman.

The line of the walls follows the Carrer de la Palla, which swings left into the Carrer dels Banys Nous. This becomes the Carrer d'Avinyo and leads toward the port. At the corner of Carrer Ample, turn left; left again at Carrer del Hostal d'En Sol; first right at Carrer Angel Baixeras;

Roman mosaic floor depicting the Three Graces, from an excavation under the Passatge del Credit

and promptly left again on Carrer del Sots-Tinent Navarro, which runs parallel to the Via Laietana and becomes the Carrer de la Tapineria where it crosses Carrer Jaume I; finally, swing left on Avinguda de la Catedral, and you have completed the circuit. Navarro and Tapineria, opposite and more or less parallel to Banys Nous and Avinyo, form one of the two long sides of the walls, and they contain another substantial run of surviving Roman masonry overbuilt with medieval stonework. But rough fragments of the old wall poke out in other unexpected places, such as the basement of the Museu Marés and inside a draper's shop.

So there it was: an undistinguished town, tiny in comparison with Tarraco or even Emporion, though perhaps more various in its people. The ancestors of Barcelona's large medieval Jewish community had begun to move there by the second century A.D., some time after Titus destroyed the Temple of Jerusalem in A.D. 70. Barcelona's ghetto, El Call, dates back to the late second century. When the name Montjuic gets attached to streets in the Barri Gòtic, like the Carrer Montjuic del Bisbe or the Carrer Montjuic del Carme, it probably commemorates a Jewish cemetery segregated from an existing Christian one. The first

Bartolomé Ordoñez, Martyrdom of Saint Eulalia, *sixteenth century, Cathedral, Barcelona*

synagogue may have been built there by the end of the second century; though it may have been earlier, if one takes literally Saint John Chrysostom's claim that Saint Paul visited Spain and met with resident Jews there.

Certainly the little city had a vibrant and polyglot population, though none of the claims to greatness that later Catalan writers would make for late Roman Barcelona has the slightest basis in fact. No sooner had it grown to a respectable size than the general decline of the Spanish Roman Empire began to overtake it. This seems to have first become clear in religion. Rome had always had the utmost difficulty in imposing its pantheon of personal gods and their cults on the Iberian tribespeople it conquered. It built temples and set up effigies, but, as the historian S. J. Keay pointed out, "Gods like Hercules, Mars and Jupiter rapidly merged with their local counterparts, ensuring the continuity of centuries of native belief beneath a Roman mask." And Roman emperor worship, however useful administratively, was not going to satisfy the craving for mystery and revelation that lay at the heart of the religious impulse. That repressed desire was slaked by the greatest and fastest-growing of all Eastern mystery religions, which began to spread in Spain by the end of the second century A.D.: Christianity, with its bizarre and yet infinitely attractive claims of eternal bliss for the dead in the company of a god who, as recently as the reign of Augustus, had walked the earth with the living.

Christianity competed with the official religion of the Roman state for close to two hundred years, and the last wave of Roman persecution, launched by the emperor Diocletian around 300 produced Barcelona's female patron saint and official martyr: the Christian virgin Saint Eulalia, done to death with fire, pincers, hooks, and a crucifix by a Roman procurator.

Her remains were buried and venerated on the site of Santa Maria del Mar until the late fourth century, when they were moved to another shrine where the Cathedral, dedicated to her cult, now stands. There is, nevertheless, some doubt about her existence; she may simply be a fictional clone of another Spanish saint, Eulalia of Mérida (naturally, some Catalan priests held that if there was any cloning done, it went the other way). And it is fairly certain that other things associated with her—the sites of her family house in Sarrià, her martyrdom on the Baixada de Santa Eulàlia and crucifixion on the Plaça del Pedró, and the story that her dry heart, as it was being carried from Santa Maria del Mar to the Cathedral shrine, miraculously became so heavy that its bearers were obliged to set it down and pray—are, to put it no more harshly, apocryphal. Nor do modern hagiographers accept the common seventeenth-century view that she was the daughter of two other martyrs, Saint Philet and Saint Leda. The trouble with early persecutions is that they overload the canon. Fortunately, not long after the time of Eulàlia's death (if she lived) an edict arrived from the emperor Constantine in A.D. 312 making Christianity the official religion of the empire, thus drying up what might otherwise have become a surplus of Catalan martyrs. The politically correct may note that Barcelona was not content with making a woman its first major saint. Its second, Saint Cugat, came from Africa and was probably black.

III

Pagan ways did not die quietly. Saint Pacianus, a late fourth-century bishop of Barcelona, complained that on New Year's Day its citizens would put on stags' heads and dance in the streets before abandoning themselves to frightful revelings—"All my invectives against such vileness, as mad as it is popular," he wailed, "only seem to have the effect of inflaming the debauchery."

The decline of Roman Barcelona was on its way, and it had more to do with its slave economy than with its festive habits. No such economy can work without a constant supply of new slaves, and this supply had been ensured by conquest. But in Roman Spain by 350 there were no tribes left to conquer. (The idea that the early Christians strove to enhance the "dignity of man" by abolishing slavery is a pious fiction. In Spain they wanted to enslave the Jews, and they did.) Hence there was a labor shortage, and the price of work rose steeply. Moreover, the cost of running the Spanish colonies—army, bureaucracy, public spectacles, and free food, the *panis et circenses* that were the Roman form of welfare—had once been offset by plunder, and in a static empire there was no more of that either. So public money had to come from increased taxes and monetary devaluation; the fourth century showed a continuous debasement of the silver denarius to the point where no one trusted the once-impeccable Roman currency. Bands of the poor began to attack villages and farms. In response, the rich dropped their political obligations to the city and set up their own fortified slave communities with private armies. In these self-contained and self-defending *fincas*, which reduced the tax base even further, one may see the remote seed of the feudal countships that came to dominate Catalan political life in the early Middle Ages.

This pattern had immediate economic consequences for the cities. Barcino, which had been a center of export, turned into a net importer. As the fortified community-farms of the rich were swollen by refugees from the city, they bypassed the Barcino market, preferring to barter their surplus goods left after taxation directly with other farms. More and more shut out of the economic cycle of the country, Barcino still had to feed its mouths; by the fifth century this city, whose *garum* Pliny had once extravagantly praised, and whose oil jars had been shipped to buyers as far away as Rhodes, had to import most of its olive oil and *garum* from North Africa.

Because the silver standard had collapsed, the mercenary guards who replaced the old imperial legions could no longer be relied on to defend the Pyrenees against the intruding Germanic tribes that had marched down through Gaul and seemed intent on taking all Europe. Some of the guards mutinied, and others simply deserted en masse. And so, beginning in A.D. 409, wave after wave of invaders came pouring through the high passes: a combined force of some two hundred thousand Vandals, Suevians, and Alani. Nothing opposed them. They took over northern Catalunya and kept moving south. "The irruption of these nations," wrote a Christian chronicler named Idatius, was followed by the most dreadful calamities, as the barbarians exercised their indiscriminate cruelty on the fortunes of the Romans and Spaniards, and ravaged with equal fury the cities and the open countryside. . . . Famine reduced the miserable inhabitants to feed on the flesh of their fellow-creatures, and even the wild beasts, which multiplied unchecked in the wilderness, were maddened by the taste of blood. . . . Pestilence soon appeared; a large proportion of the people were swept away; and the groans of the dying excited the envy of their surviving friends. At last the barbarians, satiated by carnage and rapine . . . fixed their permanent seats in the depopulated country.

In fact, the invaders did not stay in Catalunya: they went straight on through to the south. Within a year or two, fifty thousand Vandals had settled in Baetica, thirty thousand Alani in the provinces of Lusitania (modern Portugal) and Carthaginesis, and eighty thousand Suevians and forty thousand more Vandals in Galicia. The structure of Roman rule in northern Spain had now disintegrated so far that when the next invading army, consisting of somewhere between seventy thousand and three hundred thousand Visigoths, commanded by their king Ataulf (the vagueness of the number may reflect the panic of the observers), came over the eastern Pyrenees in A.D. 415, the Romans allied with them in the hope that they could somehow be used to get rid of the other blond beasts from the north.

Thus did the Visigoths march straight into Barcino and set up their court, no doubt to the relief of its residents, who had spent most of the last six years behind its walls waiting nervously to be raped, pillaged, and put to the sword.

Once the "barbarians" had arrived, they turned out not to be so barbarous as the Hispano-Romans feared. In a series of maneuvers too long and complicated to be described here, the Visigoths dislodged the Vandals from Baetica and the Alani from Lusitania, and won from the Franks at the battle of Vouillé (507) a swath of territory that lay across the eastern Pyrenees, part in what is now France and part in what is now Spain. This land, known as Septimania, or the kingdom of Tolosa (Toulouse), was the origin of the territory of medieval Catalunya, which spilled over the Pyrenees into the territory known in French as the Roussillon and in Catalan as the Rosselló; this is why Catalan—so similar to Provençal—is still spoken in the Languedoc region of southern France. Rome made desperate diplomatic and military attempts to win back some vestige of control in the Iberian peninsula. But they were all in vain, and by 476, when the feeble emperor Romulus Augustulus was deposed, the Roman Empire in the West had ceased to exist. The Visigoths were

Visigothic medallion in gold of Galla Placidia, daughter of the emperor Theodosius I, circa A.D. *420.*

masters of Catalunya and of most of the rest of Spain as well. In stages, they moved their capital south; having taken it from Narbonne to Barcino, they took it on to Seville, Mérida, and finally Toledo. This left Barcelona on the periphery of Gothic power.

One should not imagine that the Gothic occupation marked a sudden cultural change for Barcelona, as we may now call the post-Roman city. On the contrary: the process was one of absorbing and merging. Compared with the Vandals, the Visigoths were almost genteel, for quite a lot had rubbed off on them in the few years since they had devastated Greece and sacked Rome. During their occupation of Rome, Ataulf had carried off and married the twenty-year-old Galla Placidia, daughter of the emperor Theodosius I. (Later she married the emperor Constantius III and imperiously redecorated the city of Ravenna.) Her entry into Barcelona was inauspicious; she came in chains, in a group of other prisoners, walking in front of her husband's war-horse. But before long she helped convert Ataulf to Christianity—though he embraced Arianism, a heresy of which her father stonily disapproved—and this meant an easy transition for Barcelona.

The Visigoths did not destroy the Hispano-Roman aristocrats, though they were apt to confiscate a half or two-thirds of their possessions and country fiefs. One of Ataulf's successors, the Visigothic king Teudis (A.D. 531–48), married a local noblewoman who was so rich that her dowry paid for his additional private militia of two thousand men. In the late sixth century another monarch, Reccared, imposed Catholicism over Arianism as the official Visigothic religion. This ushered in a period of lavish church building, both in Barcelona and out of it. Much of the great Visigothic cathedral of Tarragona, built into what had been the shell of the Roman Temple of Augustus, survives, but Visigothic remains in Barcelona are only fragmentary—a few building foundations and carved screens, fonts, columns, and capitals, often of exquisite workmanship—because they were destroyed by medieval developers and clerics. Moreover, while they were enlarging primitive Christian chapels and shrines, the Visigoths implanted their own baronies over the top of existing ones in town and country. This reinforced the progress toward what would later become a feudal society in Catalunya. It was further helped by the great Visigothic law codes, one of the monuments of Western jurisprudence—though much confusion and dissent ensued when they were superimposed on the existing Roman laws—and by their kings, who were elected to the throne by virtue of their intelligence and bravery and did not simply succeed to it by birth. The growth of the Gothic baronies also spelled the end of whatever free peasantry survived. The poor had to depend on local autarchs, landowners, and warlords; they were being harried in the direction of medieval serfdom. At councils held in Toledo in 589, and again in 633, the Visigoth monarchs made clumsy efforts to reduce the independence of these barons, counts, and dukes. They were in vain. The new aristocracy was busy confirming its social control and collapsing the social classes of northern Spain. In 694, in the first of Spain's many convulsions of Catholic anti-Semitism, all Jews were decreed to be slaves. In 702 new laws were passed against "runaway slaves," which meant dissenters of any kind or peasants trying to escape serfdom. The control of a central Visigothic state was well on its way to disappearance in Catalunya by the beginning of the eighth century, just as the Arabs made their appearance in southern Spain.

IV

When in 711 the Arabs looked across the Bahr al-Rumi, or Sea of Rome, which is what they called the Mediterranean, they saw in Visigothic Spain what the Visigoths themselves had seen in Roman Spain three hundred years before: division and softness, an invitation to conquest.

The Gothic baronies were alienated from central command; the Christians were distracted by their efforts to get at the throats of Hispanic Jews. It may be that the sight of a Gothic Christian majority persecuting a tiny Jewish minority helped persuade the Arabs that Visigothic Spain was truly divided against itself, ripe for the taking. What is not true is the ancient canard, popular among old-school, anti-Semitic Spanish historians in the nineteenth and twentieth centuries, that the Jews secretly invited the Arabs in and became a fifth column for them. The Arabs needed no invitation. They swarmed across the western Mediterranean and went through the patchy Visigothic resistance like a tank through a cornfield.

Their arrival brought the collapse of the Goths' baronies in Catalunya. In the years between 712 and 718, all of southern Spain and most of Catalunya were occupied by the Saracens. In some places the Gothic aristocrats prudently surrendered and got to keep their possessions, laws, and customs, governing as satraps of the new occupying power. A few cities, notably Tarragona, held out—and were badly damaged. Barcelona does not seem to have resisted much, if at all. It was not in a position to: if Tarragona could not withstand the *sarrains*, it was futile to expect that a small coastal town, assailed by ships from the sea and an army on land, could do so. The pockets of resistance were all in the north, toward the Pyrenees.

The Saracen advance changed the demographics of Catalunya almost at once. Peasants fled from the flat, vulnerable plains, such as the Baix Camp de Tarragona, and made their way north to find shelter among the passes and granite wrinkles of the Pyrenean foothills. Having lost their manpower and their main source of wealth, the Hispano-Gothic nobles were stranded and exposed; but the displaced peasants, forming their tiny troglodytic settlements in the deep northern valleys where the rivers came winding down from the Pyrenees—the Ter, the Fluvia—found themselves free, isolated, and independent. The Saracens could not follow them. As the aristocracy of the plains declined, so the mountain peasantry from the eighth century onward rose. Economically, it could not rise far, but it soon attained a solid level of subsistence, hacking a hard living from the patches of soil between the stone. The peasants' endurance would have profound results for the iconography of Catalunya. The northern refuge of Catalunya Vella, or Old Catalunya, came to signify the *ser autentic* of the principate: a place where men did not knuckle under, populated by hard, resistant, sharp-eyed, and suspicious peasants whose social horizons were bounded by their valleys and who were, above all, free. As Roman slavery had flourished on the plains, so its vestiges died in the mountains. And although the Saracens pushed north over the Pyrenees in their drive to conquer southern France, they could not hold these remote Catalan villages: it was hardly worth their while to try. They went straight up the coast to Narbonne and took it in A.D. 719. By now, the Islamic empire extended from Portugal to the borders of China, with Damascus as its capital.

Only one obstacle to the Saracens remained in the western Mediterranean: the Franks, or "free people," a name assumed in the third century by a loose confederation of German tribes on the middle Rhine. They too invaded France, but fetched up against the mountain wall of the Pyrenees and went no farther. From the time of Dagobert III, who died in 716, the Frankish kings supplied the only strong military and political framework in southern France. It was his successor, Chilperic, who lost Narbonne; but in 732 Charles Martel, mayor of the Frankish court, turned back the Muslims at the battles of Tours and Poitiers, which marked the limit of the Arab advance into western Europe. Back they recoiled, across the coastal Pyrenees. For the next half century the efforts of the Frankish kings were bent on securing the Pyrenees and turning their southern foothills into a kind of buffer state against the possibility of another Saracen invasion. When Pepin the Short died in 768, the Frankish frontier still lay on the French side of the Pyrenees, but his son and successor, Charlemagne, drove the limits of his Holy Roman Empire across the mountains and down as far as the Ebro, with the aim of turning half of Spain into a *zona franca*.

In this, Charlemagne failed—or, at best, only partially succeeded. His expedition against Zaragoza in 778 finished with the crushing defeat of his Frankish army by the Saracens at Roncesvalles, where dying Roland blew his horn and entered the domain of epic memory. But Charlemagne was able to hold the north of the Iberian peninsula, because its inhabitants willingly placed their towns and villages under his protection. Girona ceded itself to the Franks in 785, and all the sub-Pyrenean *comarques* followed suit. In 801 the Franks under Charlemagne's son, Louis the Pious, drove the Saracens out of Barcelona. That was as far south as they could get; a Frankish army attacked Tortosa shortly afterward, hoping to get through to the Ebro, but was beaten back.

This defeat drew the southern line of Old Catalunya, which stretched from the Pyrenees to the Llobregat River just south of Barcelona. It was a mosaic of districts whose limits were fixed by mountain passes, rivers, massifs, coast. One district, Rosselló, was on what is now the French side of the maritime Pyrenees, and in modern France it is known as Le Roussillon. The rest were in modern Spanish territory: Osona, Cer-

danya, Urgell, Pellars, Ribagorça, and, most ancient of all, the spot
where the Carthaginians and then the Romans had landed, the Ampurdan. These *comarques* were ruled by counts created by Charlemagne and
his successors. Around 795, for instance, Charlemagne gave the town
of Fontjoncosa to a warrior, Joan by name, who arrived at his court with
a letter from Charlemagne's son Louis the Pious:

> I have read in this document that Joan took part in a great battle
> against the heretics and the Saracen infidels in the *pagus* [territory] of
> Barcelona, where they beat them in the place called The Bridge . . .
> because of these deeds [Joan] has received from our beloved son the
> best horse and the best armor and an oriental sword with a silver-
> mounted hilt. . . . The above mentioned, our loyal Joan, delivering
> himself into our hands, has asked us to make him a concession of the
> domains that our son gave him. In consequence whereof I have con-
> ceded to him this territory in its entirety. . . . I give it to him with-
> out any tax or condition so long as he remains loyal to Us and to our
> sons . . .

The mountain warlords ruled contingently, not absolutely. They
took on the primitive trappings of aristocracy and owed their allegiance
to the French king, who could (and sometimes did) unseat them at his
royal pleasure. But human ambition being what it is, some of these
counts did not wish to think of themselves as mere satraps. They wanted
power as their own inheritance, which they could pass on to their sons
without Frankish say-so. Thus in ninth-century Catalunya, there was a
centrifugal force. It was typical of the problem that defeated Charlemagne's successors and caused the Carolingian empire to break up: lack
of communication, at a time when news and orders could move across
the Pyrenees only at the speed of a clambering man. The political horizons of a ninth-century Catalan warrior were extremely close to his
feet. Hence the *comarques* began to crystallize into independent units, on
the whole deferential but no longer perfectly submissive to the Franks.
And within some of them the towns and villages had rapidly grown, as
the *pagesos*, or peasants, no longer menaced by the Saracens, began to
flow back to the lowlands, and dispossessed aristocrats began to recover
their lands. Deserted areas of Catalunya were repopulating fast. In 839,
when the cathedral of Urgell was consecrated, its deeds mentioned nearly
280 parish churches in Urgell, Bergueda, Cerdanya, and Ripoll—practically as many parishes as there were villages: underpopulation no longer
induced the Church to roll several villages together in one *parroquià*. By
the end of the first millennium, if one can judge from the declarations

of counts themselves, northern Catalunya thought of itself as a perfect haven of tranquillity, full of contented refugees and law-abiding folk. "When my father the count and marquis Guifré, of good memory, first built this castle," announced Count Borrell II to the inhabitants of Cardona in 986,

> he ordained . . . that all men who came here to live and arrived with their goods, should have and hold them forever, in peace. And if any evil person, scandalous and full of pride, should take or damage any part of the possessions of these inhabitants, then the injured party should receive double the value of the damage from the criminal who did the act: so that if he has lost a donkey, he should receive two better ones: and in the same way he ordained that in every case all men should be protected with double indemnity. Thus, too, he established that all crimes and injuries should be doubly punished . . . and that none should pay taxes, except what they owed to the holy Church. . . . And if a fugitive slave, man or woman, should arrive here, or any man with another man's wife, or even a cunning thief, or a forger, or any criminal, he might live safely here among the other inhabitants in complete peace.

This would change, and drastically, with the spread of the feudal regimes.

V

The "count and marquis Guifré, of good memory" was the strongman who became the great unifier of the Catalan Dark Ages—the warrior who emerged from the confused murk of Pyrenean history, established the political primacy of Barcelona once and for all, and was mythologized by Catalans for a thousand years after his death as the creator of national independence. His name was Guifré el Pelós: Wilfred the Hairy. He was born somewhere around the middle of the ninth century and died in about 898. About Guifré's character and tastes we know very little (beyond his obvious bellicosity), but he was certainly no fool, and he grasped the point that, to ensure the gratitude of history, the successful ruler should have the intellectuals on his side. In the ninth century, that meant the priests, who did most of the writing. Guifré was therefore an enthusiastic endower of monasteries and churches, and almost all the earliest church foundations of Catalunya were his doing: Santa Maria de Formiguera (873), Santa Maria de la Grassa (878), Sant Joan de Ripoll

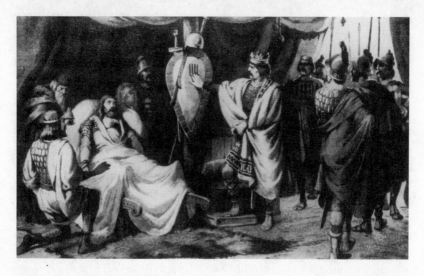

A nineteenth-century painting of Louis the Pious marking the four stripes on the shield with Guifré's blood

(885), Sant Joan de les Abadesses (887), Santa Maria de Ripoll (888), and Sant Pere de Ripoll (890). Sant Joan de Ripoll he built for his own sister, who was installed as abbess; Sant Joan de les Abadesses, for his daughter Emma. The size of his donations ensured him the praise of every monkish scribe who touched quill to chronicle. It is hardly surprising, therefore, that Guifré the Hairy emerges from their collective hosannas as a man of deep piety and unsurpassable valor.

Guifré, according to one monk's chronicle, the *History of Languedoc*, was the son of Count Sunifred of Urgell and the grandson of Count Borrell of Ausona. In less than a decade, from 870 to 878, he and his brother slugged and chopped their way to power over most of Old Catalunya—the *comarques* of Urgell, Cerdanya, Barcelona, Osona, Rosselló, and Girona. One would suppose that this would have put Wilfred the Hairy in direct conflict with the Carolingian monarch (who, by a nice coincidence, was Charles the Bald). No such thing occurred, because the man from whom Guifré wrested control of Catalunya was the son of Bernat of Septimania, a Frankish noble whom Charles had exiled to Spain under suspicion of tampering with his queen. To assail the house of Bernat did not seem inherently treasonous, and in any case Guifré el Pelòs made a point of conspicuously declaring his loyalty to the Carolingian empire, stressing that his authority over Catalunya came, ultimately, from Charlemagne's own heirs. In no sense was he what nineteenth-century Catalanists made him in their anachronistic way—

Reinard Fonoll, knight with the escutcheon of Catalunya, capital from cloister of the monastery of Santes Creus, circa 1330

a sort of Simón Bolívar in chain mail, the inspired leader of a Catalan secession from Carolingian rule. And yet he did achieve power by throwing out Frankish overlords and he was the last Catalan count to be invested with his title by the Carolingian emperor. After Guifré, the line of Catalan counts was self-generating, and the keystone of authority in this small country, with a disintegrating Frankish empire to the north and the constant threat of the Saracens to the south, was the city and the countship of Barcelona. The first and most honored of Guifré's titles, and the first among those of his descendants, was always Count of Barcelona.

It was really Louis the Pious, Charlemagne's son, the Frankish king of Aquitaine, who had given Wilfred the Hairy his chance to start this process, and he had done so more for empire than for piety. Barcelona until the end of the eighth century had been a town of minor importance—Tarragona was the key city of the territory between the Ebro and the Pyrenees. Saracens held Barcelona: a small place, albeit with a harbor, a wasp's nest of Moorish freebooters and land pirates who harassed the surrounding villages and plundered traffic on the road south to the Ebro. It was a great inconvenience to anyone who, like Louis, had plans to expel the Saracens from Spain, for it was difficult to take—its Roman walls were virtually intact, and they were strong and high. But in 801, Louis finally conquered the city and installed a

Wilfred the Hairy attacks the dragon with his oak branch, late fourteenth century, portal of Sant Iu, Cathedral, Barcelona

French regent there. Even so, Barcelona did not become the capital of Catalunya, because there was no single control over the *comarques* until Guifré the Hairy came along and rolled them all together. Once he had done so, and moved to Barcelona, the little city promptly and automatically became the administrative capital. It has remained so ever since.

Guifré comes down to us swathed in apocryphal deeds. He is as much a legend in Barcelona as are Romulus and Remus in Rome, and the known facts of his life are a good deal fewer than the legends that encrust it. The most famous of these is his role in the invention of the Catalan flag—the four crimson stripes on a gold field. The story goes that Guifré, fighting for Louis the Pious in his siege of Barcelona, was badly wounded by the Saracens. As he lay in his tent after the victory, the king came to visit him and noticed Guifré's shield, covered in gold leaf but without a blazon. What device could the king give his warrior? Louis dipped his fingers in Guifré's blood and dragged them down the shield, a gesture celebrated endlessly by Catalanist poets and occasionally by history painters. Obviously this stirring story cannot be true, since Louis died before Guifré was born, and Barcelona was conquered long before that. However, in terms of heraldry, politics, and myth, the idea of Catalan independence begins with Guifré el Pelós.

He was a hero born of heroes. And indeed, he sometimes got confused with his father; the two are apt to merge, in art if not in history.

If you walk down the Carrer dels Comtes along the flank of the Cathedral, you will come to the portal of Sant Iu (Saint Ives). High on the left, it has two late fourteenth-century carvings, each depicting a fight between an armed warrior and a *drac*, or dragon. One is in "modern" armor, chain mail. He carries a sword, and his shield is emblazoned with a cross. He is Saint George, the patron saint of Catalunya. But the other figure is archaic. He has no armor, only a pair of trews. His naked chest and legs are covered with a rippling pelt of hair. His weapon is not a sword, but a long wooden club. Who is this wild man, whose presence on the doorway invites the faithful to compare him with Saint George himself? None other than Hairy Willy, the primal count and political creator of Catalunya. Or perhaps (since the legends tended to shift, depending on who was telling them) it is Guifré's equally hairy father.

When the Cathedral was being built, its clergy wanted to illustrate a founding legend of their country: the supposed battle between Guifré's father (or Guifré himself, in some versions; the confusion is made worse by a tendency to call the father Guifré as well) and a dragon, which the Saracens had left in Catalunya. In this way Guifré's line takes on the heroic and saintly aura of Saint George.

Stripped of its accretions of fantastic detail—which were still current in monkish writings as late as 1600—the story goes like this. The Saracens, unable to beat the counts of Barcelona in war, decided to retreat. Before doing so, they sent an expedition to the mountains of Africa. Its purpose: to catch a young dragon. Moorish hunters snared the little monster, roped it up like a steer, bundled it (not, one presumes, without some fireproofing) into a ship, and sailed it to Catalunya. With fiendish ingenuity they unloaded it at the mouth of the Llobregat, carried it inland, and let it loose.

The dragon found itself a lair near Sant Llorenç del Munt, which is still known as the Cova del Drac, the Dragon's Cave. It adapted nicely to Catalan conditions. At first it satisfied its growing appetite with sheep. Then it took to eating peasants, and then knights, spitting out the armor like pistachio shells. Nobody—not even a Catalan knight named Espes, who had been to Africa and was used to dealing with dragons—could kill the brute. A cavalry squadron attacked it, but the dragon huffed fire and so terrified the horses that they stampeded over the lip of a gorge —a spot still known as the Salt dels Cavalls, or Horses' Leap. Eventually the Catalans set fire to the forest and smoked it out. It flew to Montserrat but then worked its way back to its cave in Sant Llorenç del Munt.

At this point Guifré's father stepped in. He approached the dragon's cave on foot, tore off a big oak branch, and went for the reptile hammer and tongs. It showed its Moorish deviousness by grabbing the branch, breaking it in half, and holding the two pieces up in its claws to make the sign of the cross; but undeceived, the hero stabbed the dragon over and over again with his lance and then transfixed it with his sword. The dragon flew up in the air and then crashed, shrieking and flapping, on the far side of the Creu Massif. The Catalans skinned it and stuffed the hide with straw, bringing it out on major feast days like a Chinatown dragon; its gigantic bones—actually, some historians now think, the ribs of a stranded whale—were exposed as relics.

So ended this primitive attempt at biological warfare. As its hands-down winner, Guifré's father was highly honored in Catalunya; but he fell victim (or so another part of his legend would have it) to the untrustworthy French.

An account written by an anonymous medieval monk of Ripoll, the *Gesta Comitum Barcinonensium* (*Deeds of the Counts of Barcelona*)—a propaganda manuscript meant to cover the line of Guifré with glory, in thanks for his support of monasteries—says that Guifré the Hairy's father was made count of Barcelona by the king of France, thus becoming one of the most important figures in the Spanish part of the kingdom of Languedoc. But then, the *Gesta* relates, when he was summoned to the French court across the Pyrenees, he fell into an affray with some French knights on the road and was killed. (One of the motifs of the glorification of the Catalan counts creeps in here: the perfidy of the French. It turned into a full-scale rewriting of Guifré and his line into anti-Gallic rulers, which they were not.) The knights took the son of this elder Guifré with them to the king of France, who put him under the protection of the count of Flanders. So little Guifré grew up in Flanders, side by side with the count's little daughter—with whom, in time, he fell violently in love. The countess abetted their youthful affair, but made Guifré swear that, after he had taken back the overlordship of Barcelona, he would marry the girl. So off young Guifré went to Barcelona, where—after sixteen years' absence—he found his mother again. And his mother identified him at once, because he had hair "on a part of the body where it should not have been." (Which part, the legend does not specify. The most popular version says it was the soles of his feet; if so, one can well believe Mama spotted him at once.) So the young inheritor of Catalunya was hailed as their lord by a circle of Catalan nobles and undertook to seize the countship of Barcelona himself, having first killed the Frankish pretender with his own hands.

This pious tale is, of course, the biblical story of Esau, the hairy brother done out of his birthright, retooled for Catalan purposes. It is mixed with the medieval image of the wild man, abundant in hair and machismo. Indeed, the imagery of hair would crop up again in what one might call Guifré's posthumous career. In the Museum of the City of Barcelona is a pair of small, dark, crude sixteenth-century sculptures relating the story of a wicked knight who violated and slew Guifré the Hairy's daughter Riquildis. Like Nebuchadnezzar, he went half-mad with remorse and expiated his sins by becoming Fray Garis, the first hermit of Montserrat. There, in a cave, he spent twenty years doing nothing but praying and growing his hair. One sees him as a block of writhing tarry curls surmounted by an anguished face; the companion sculpture depicts Guifré's grandson in the arms of his nurse. This infant (somewhat precociously, since he was only three months old) gave Fray Garis the glad news that God had finally pardoned him.

Despite these hirsute entanglements of legend, Guifré's hairiness is folklore. In addition to meaning "hairy," *pilosus*, the Latin root of *pelòs*, can mean "overgrown," and some modern scholars now think that Guifré got his nickname from the wildness of the territory he governed in northern Catalunya. Others see it deriving from *pilum*, the javelin used by Roman soldiers, so possibly Guifré the Hairy was really Guifré the Lancer. Still, folklore is not "mere" folklore, and Guifré's hairiness was an integral part of the Catalan belief—not restricted to Catalunya by any means, but extremely durable there—in hair as a signifier of prowess. The immense *bigotis* (mustaches) and *patillas* (muttonchop whiskers) sported by Barcelonese industrialists a thousand years later may, in their walruslike magnificence, have seemed to some of their owners to claim the virtues of the line of Guifré el Pelós.

VI

Guifré built himself a palace in Barcelona, but it has entirely vanished. He endowed churches there, of which hardly a trace remains. The usual explanation for the lack of Carolingian buildings in Barcelona is to blame the Moors, who retook the city almost two hundred years after Louis the Pious drove them out. In 985 the vizier of Córdoba, al-Mansur, conquered Barcelona. The day was July 6—the first accurately recorded date in Catalan history, and one that reflects the terrible panic and confusion that the Saracens' return spread among the city's clergy, who were also its record keepers. Al-Mansur's arrival has ever since been known, by a contemporary chronicler's phrase, as "the day the city died."

Symbols of two Evangelists and, center, the Hand of God from the portal of Sant Pau del Camp, Barcelona, twelfth century

In fact Barcelona did nothing of the sort, and although al-Mansur's troops certainly thinned its abundant population of priests and nuns a little and burned down a few religious foundations, such as the convent of Sant Pere de les Puelles, the monkish chroniclers had a vested interest in making the loss of life, of churches, and of saintly relics seem rather worse than it was. The economic life of Barcelona appears to have recovered quite rapidly. In fact the Carolingian buildings were knocked down long after the vizier died (in 1002) by early Catalan "developers" during Barcelona's first building boom in the twelfth century. If you want to see elements of Christian architecture from the first millennium in Catalunya, they are not to be found in Barcelona but in the northern countryside, especially in the Ampurdan—the Porta Ferrada, or Iron Doorway, of the monastery of San Feliu de Guixols on the Costa Brava, for instance, or the churches of Sant Esteve de Canapost in Vullpellac and Santa Maria in Vilanant. Whenever a pre-1000 fragment turns up in a Romanesque or an Early Gothic building in Barcelona, one can be sure that the structure was built on the cheap with recycled material excavated from the site. So it was with Sant Pau del Camp, in the Barri del Raval.

Sant Pau del Camp is the oldest church in Barcelona, in the sense that it displays the most ancient visible elements to the visitor. It is small, at least by the standards of other Romanesque buildings in Catalunya. With its squat octagonal tower and rough walls, it looks more like a country church than a city one—and that is what it was, for in the twelfth century it stood well out in the fields beyond the city walls. Its compact facade speaks of theological determination: the crude bas-reliefs of the Evangelists—Saint Mark as a lion, for instance—and the hand of God the Father sculpted in a roundel above them, his fingers pointing to indicate the world he has just made and the invisible world beyond the visible one; the weird little masks beneath the corbels, much eroded by time; and on either side of the portal, two columns made up of seventh- and eighth-century fragments (capitals, shafts, bases, none of them matching) that were all that survived of an earlier Christian chapel, dug out of its site.

The surviving buildings of Guifré and his early descendants are all to the north, in Catalunya Vella—especially, in the area around Ripoll and Sant Joan de les Abadesses, where the snow-fed Freses and Ter rivers come racing down the limestone gorges of the Pyrenean foothills, converging at Ripoll. This hill town likes to call itself the cradle of Catalunya, which, in an ecclesiastical sense, it is: the Benedictine monastery of Santa Maria de Ripoll was the largest and one of the earliest of the church foundations set up by Guifré the Hairy, whose bones— recovered from the ruins of its cloister in the nineteenth century—lie in a plain sarcophagus on the wall of its left transept. Only the bones are real. The rest of the church interior is total pastiche. Originally it had five naves: one imagines a gloomy, powerful, and dankly troglodytic structure of parallel tunnels with squat columns. But an earthquake demolished its roof system in 1428; it was rebuilt, only to suffer a disastrous restoration in the 1820s at the hands of a neoclassical architect named Josep Morato, who turned it into a conventional basilica with one high central nave and two aisles. Then came the 1830s and a whole-sale suppression of religious communities; the monks were thrown out and the monastery was soon a gutted ruin. (Fortunately, the abbot had already given the monastery's irreplaceable archive of documents and illuminated manuscripts to the archive of the Crown of Aragon, in Barcelona.)

What fire, vandalism, and neglect did not finish off, a new wave of pious restoration did. In the 1880s, Catalan nationalism required that the cradle of Catalunya should be glorified and reconsecrated. This job went to Elias Rogent i Amat, the supervising architect of Barcelona's 1888 Universal Exposition. It was done by 1893, complete with a large, pale, and saccharine mosaic altarpiece of a doe-eyed Madonna and Child—a present from Pope Leo XIII, made in the Vatican workshops. Since a number of Ripoll's finest illuminated codices, dating from the

Alabaster portal of Santa Maria de Ripoll

eleventh century, wound up in the Vatican Library, one could say that Rome got the better of the deal. Santa Maria would be closer to the depressing pietism of Lourdes than to the virile Catalunya of the early counts were it not for two features.

The first is its two-story cloister, a noble contemplative space begun in the late twelfth century by Ramon de Berga, who was abbot from 1171 to 1205. Its Romanesque arches (some of which were not actually finished until the fifteenth century) are raised on paired columns linked by carved capitals of the hard, dark local limestone. The echt-Romanesque ones are a marvel of invention and still in good condition. They embody the grotesque fecundity of twelfth-century dreaming at full pitch: vegetable motifs, demons and mermaids, hybrid monsters, signs and portents of every kind. Spend an hour with them, and you are ready for the main portal of the church.

Cracked by fire, spalled by weather, battered by iconoclastic *liberales*, and now, fortunately, protected by a glassed-in porch, the alabaster facade of Santa Maria de Ripoll is the greatest single work of Romanesque sculpture in Spain. Even in its degraded state it remains mesmerizing, not only for the aesthetic vividness of its figures and emblems but for its narrative completeness. There are more than a hundred separate scenes, and the better-preserved figures, such as the out-leaning, stocky, fiercely intense Pantocrator surrounded by angels above the doorway, are of the tersest formal beauty, every line as intent on its job as the curl of a whip or the forking of a twig. What is especially interesting about it, as storytelling, is its power as a political statement. This is the earliest surviving Catalan work of sculpture to set forth metaphors of the foundation of Catalunya itself—the retreat of its people to the mountains and valleys before the Saracen armies and then the vision of return and of the expulsion of the Moors. In the two bands of panels on either side of the entrance arch, one sees the Biblical story of Exodus: Moses guiding his people to the promised land, the rain of manna, the striking of water from the rock, the Israelites following the angel and the column of fire. Then there is the removal of the Ark of the Covenant and the founding of Jerusalem; Daniel's vision of the Jews set free by the Messiah; and much more besides. For "Jews," read "Catalans"; for "Egyptians," "Saracens"; for "Moses," by implication "Guifré the Hairy"; while the presence of stern stalwarts like Joshua (whose battle against Amalec at Rafidim takes up a large panel on the right of the door) could only have been understood by a twelfth-century viewer as prophetic of the noble valor of the counts of Barcelona. And, of course, one also sees the Catalans working at their promised land: the inner face of the doorway arch bears scenes of labor, month by month—casting bronze in January, tilling in March, picking fruit in May, pruning in June, harvesting in July, butchering a deer in November, and so on.

And so, although the inside of Santa Maria cannot be compared with any one of twoscore genuine Romanesque churches in northern Catalunya, its portal justifies its status in the order of Catalan memory. It is the Ur-temple of Catalunya, the archexample of the kind of church—remote, obdurate, provincial, and yet humming in its day with scholastic life—that evoked a founding myth for the poets and architects of the Renaixença. Such places represented the Romanesque root of national being that had been torn out of Barcelona itself by its own development as a medieval city, its volte-face from the plains and the Pyrenean valleys and out toward the Mediterranean.

To know what these inner spaces looked and felt like, one should consult Sant Joan de les Abadesses, the monastery that Guifré the Hairy founded for his daughter Emma in the valley of the Ter, not far from Ripoll. The church was consecrated in 898. Its physical drama is intense. But it does not come from verticality, as is the case with later Gothic. Rather, it emerges slowly from its cavelike power. To experience this, try asking the lay sacristan to turn off the electric lights for a while—he may do it if there are no other visitors in the church. In the darkness, the space swims into your mind, slowly developing, felt rather than seen. First, a high nave, whose barrel vault would have been all but lost

Sant Joan de les Abadesses, circa 890

in darkness, since the only daylight came (then as now) from windows glazed with thin parchment-colored sheets of resawn alabaster. Then, the apse, which closes down in a half dome behind the altar. Gravity and darkness combine; the stone piers and the thick chamfered embrasures of the windows seem to be built, not in defiance of gravity, but in acknowledgment of mass; it is architecture of the most primal kind, tactile for all its size—an unnaturally stretched cave, a place for troglodytes to seek transcendence. No wonder it resisted the earthquake of 1428 that knocked down its sister church in Ripoll.

But though there is so little Romanesque architecture in Barcelona, the great buildings of the period all lying to the north, most of the real masterpieces of eleventh- and twelfth-century Catalan fresco painting are in the city and not the country. This paradox is due to the zeal of preservers who in the 1920s began a program of salvaging Romanesque paintings from the rural churches of Old Catalunya—mostly abandoned or falling inexorably into decay—and bringing them to Barcelona, where they hang in the Museum of Catalan Art on Montjuic. When touring in the north, one may feel a sentimental twinge on seeing the walls which once they adorned now either bare or filled with lifeless replicas—but if these frescoes had not been removed and remounted, they would not exist today. The iconoclastic fury of Communists and anarchists in the civil war, plus routine vandalism over the next half century, would have destroyed whatever age and weather left. As they stand, they are the finest group of "primitive" (pre-Giotto) painted murals in Europe. It is scarcely an exaggeration that this part of the Museum of Catalan Art is to wall painting what Venice and Ravenna are to the art of mosaic.

The artists' names have not survived, but several of them were painters of real sophistication. Perhaps some of their borrowings were unconscious and came out of the cultural environment—including the relics of Roman occupation, which lay much closer to the surface, both physically and mentally, than they do today. Thus in their art, God and the Virgin are imperial figures; the semicircular opening of the church apse gets used as a kind of Roman triumphal arch; even the trompe l'oeil Greek key pattern of the decorative bands in the apse fresco from the twelfth-century monastic church of Sant Pere de Burgal are lifted from the borders of some Roman mosaic. (The donor of this fresco, Countess Lucy of Pallars, makes an appearance at the lower right side, below the order of the saints, this becoming the first known secular portrait in Catalan art—another Roman link.)

In any case, the word "primitive" hardly applies to artists who had such a close and even learned grip of the principles of Byzantine style, and it seems unlikely that these murals were painted by locals. More likely the artists traveled from one commission to another, just as troubadours did between the castles of the Languedoc and Catalunya, and they were able to bring the style's intricacies over the Pyrenees (or by sea) to these remote churches. The twelfth-century fresco of the parable of the wise and the foolish virgins by the Pedret Master, from the church of Sant Quirze de Pedret, is almost pure Ravenna. Facing out frontally, staring at you with their big black pupils, the eight women have a hieratic intensity that is not a whit diminished by the tiny, intimate size of the curved wall they inhabit; and the foolish virgins on the left show their extravagance (a trait not liked by the thrifty Catalans, which may be why this minor parable from the gospel of Saint Matthew found its own chapel) by wearing the rigid, pearled, and jeweled headdresses of Byzantine noblewomen.

These images are designed to fix you, to hold you in thrall. It is the art of maximum eye contact, sublimely confrontational: one thinks of the Spanish obsession with the *mirada fuerte*, the "strong look," the gaze of power and appropriation, with which Picasso's work would be saturated eight hundred years later. This reaches an almost crushing pitch of exaltation in the gaze of the Pantocrator from the apse of Sant Climent de Taull, painted in 1123. No expense was spared on the Taull murals—blue, made of lapis lazuli, was the costliest of all pigments, and there is enough of it here to ransom a shipload of Saracens. But it is his

Fresco of the Pantocrator from the apse of Sant Climent de Taull, 1123

gaze that one remembers. Framed in his mandala, a symbol of celestial power that derived from ancient (but then, not so ancient) Roman monumental sculpture, Christ sits on a curved band that represents the sphere of the universe, holding an open book inscribed with the words "*Ego sum lux mundi*"—"I am the Light of the World." His body is strangely proportioned. The bare feet are small, but the volume and grandeur of the drawing increase as your eye moves upward, reaching a climax in the curled folds of cloth on the god's gesturing arm and in his face, with its immense, dilated, hypnotic eyes. The effect of this, combined with the curve of the dome that holds the image, is to make Christ's whole body lean outward, toward and over you, so that his *mirada fuerte* cannot have been escaped at any point in the small parochial church of Sant Climent. It is a staggeringly direct image of the divine character of omnipresence. But this Christ, unlike Dr. Faustus's, is as far from anger as he is from pity. His calm is absolute. He is the Lawgiver, the direct pictorial descendant—in this land of ancient Roman occupation—of the incontrovertible emperor, lord of the triumphal arch. No wonder that the angels on either side of him seem to be tiptoeing anxiously away instead of holding up the mandala, as they do in other images of the same kind, as though they were there only on sufferance. No figure could compete with this Christ, and the theological existence of God the Father is indicated only by a disembodied hand, the same as the

Fresco of a seraph from the apse of Santa Maria d'Aneu, twelfth century

hand on the facade of Sant Pau del Camp, pointing out of a circle of white radiance: "This is my Son."

Elsewhere, more eyes proliferate. They reach a sort of optical mania in the figures of seraphim below the (now obliterated) Virgin and Child in the twelfth-century apse fresco from Santa Maria d'Aneu. Seraphim (one of the higher orders of angel) had six wings, and the Apocalypse of Saint John mentions eyes on those wings. So the painter, faithful to the text, endowed his seraphim with about three dozen eyes each— thirty on the wings, two on the head, and two more, for good measure, displayed on the palms of their hands. One of the arches in Sant Climent carries, as a painted keystone, the image of the Paschal Lamb as seen in Saint John's Apocalypse—not with its seven horns, which would have taxed the painter's powers and perhaps the viewer's credibility, but with seven eyes, four on one side of its face and three on the other. It does not look much like a lamb, but Catalan Romanesque lions, the attribute of the Evangelist Mark, do not look like lions either: they more resemble bears. No eleventh- or twelfth-century Spanish painter, one may assume, had ever seen a lion, any more than he had seen a dragon or a demon,

Fresco of the lion of Saint Mark as a bear from the apse of Santa Maria d'Aneu, twelfth century

except in his sleep; but there were bears in the Pyrenees, hairy, scary, and sharp in tooth and claw, which served perfectly well for the generic image of the savage beast. On the other hand, the Taull painter did very well—in a realist sense—with that familiar animal, the dog, one of which is busily licking the sores of poor woebegone Lazarus with a nervous, pointed tongue.

The frescoes, sculptures, and architectural detail of these early Pyrenean churches were, as we shall see later, a continuous inspiration to nineteenth-century Catalan architects: Puig i Cadafalch, Domènech i Montaner, and of course Antoni Gaudí. But almost from the time they were salvaged and brought to Barcelona, the frescoes exerted a peculiar fascination on more modern Catalan artists—notably Joan Miró, who never spent a year without long visits to the Museum of Catalan Art. And if you look at the details in works like the Sant Climent painter's, you see why. On one wall, David is killing Goliath. The giant is dressed in a sort of tube of chain mail, like a giant lugworm. He floats in the air. His hand sticks out—a wildly disproportionate flipper, a separate body part with a bizarre life of its own. One realizes that one has seen it before: in the disembodied hands and feet of the twentieth-century master of Montroig, those queer signs for human anatomy that take over the space of the painting. Miró always loved the metamorphic, the bestial, the fabulous. And then there are the more general formal properties.

Fresco of David slaying Goliath in the apse of Sant Climent de Taull, 1123

The hard wiry outlines in Catalan Romanesque painting, the flat declarative shapes silhouetted on clear background fields of color, the way that widely separated forms energize the flatness between them—all this seems deeply Miróesque. But of course it is better to say that Miró was deeply Romanesque, especially since Guifré the Hairy's brother was also named Miró, and Joan Miró was fascinated by hair, the more anal or genital the better.

VII

Guifré's medieval descendants, the count-kings of Barcelona, ruled as much by contract as by the threat of force. The independence and bloody-mindedness of Catalunya's Dark Age peasants, deeply resistant to absolute orders from foreign invader or local authority, got into the Catalan temper and stayed there from the tenth century on, becoming the source not only of its renowned litigiousness but of all its future disagreements with Castile. The feudal institutions of medieval Catalunya developed out of a healthy concern for the mutual rights and obligations of nobles, clerics, peasants, burghers, and workmen. And Catalunya's particular feudalism was the core of its national identity. It enabled Catalunya to think of itself as detached from the rest of Spain—from the absolute monarchy of Castile and its provinces. There were no similar states, no models of government, in Spain itself. Feudal structures in its neighbor state, Aragon, were weak; and in the south, controlled by the Saracens, they were, of course, nonexistent. Catalunya's natural political affinities were with states north of the Pyrenees, the polities of Provence and Burgundy. Feudalism, with its corporate loyalties and its belief in negotiation—"pactism" was the key word—would transform itself in the Catalan political world straight into modern capitalism: what happened in Catalunya was not unlike the conversion of Japan from a feudal, samurai society into a manufacturing one. But Catalunya was the only part of Spain in which this happened. Like France and Germany, Catalunya could industrialize without losing its particular local identity. Thus one might say that the origins of nineteenth-century industrial Catalunya lay deep inside its medieval system.

The complete reconquest of Catalunya from the Arabs, and its first stage of territorial expansion, had taken about a hundred years—from 850 to 950. The development of its feudal system took another century, more or less, from 950 to 1050, and that system was consolidated, within static frontiers, between 1050 and 1150. So for the best part of two hundred years a warrior caste whose supremacy was the basis for an entire culture's way of life and government had no big wars to fight; apart from the routine of crushing some fractious peasants or waging local conflicts over land with the noble a few valleys away, the Catalan knights had nothing military to do. Small wonder that so many of them turned into haughty landed drones, squabbling over precedents and privileges, staging ceremonial tourneys and finding relief from provincial ennui in the twanging of troubadours' lutes. The obsession with codes of chivalric honor tended to obscure the fact that feudalism in Catalunya grew through an activity that was not honorable: grinding the last penny in taxes and dues out of the landlocked lower classes and savagely punishing those who did not pay.

Privilege to the feudal lord meant virtual slavery to the peasants, who, at the end of the tenth century, made up about three-quarters (figures are naturally very inexact) of the population of Catalunya. Most of these people were small freeholders. Their plots of land may have been tiny, but their rights to them, under law and custom, were secure. When in the eleventh century local warlords and strongmen took the freeholders' land, either buying it or grabbing it, they turned the independent farmers into serfs or, at best, into leaseholders—sharecroppers who grew the wheat and olives and vines, pastured the herds, and paid a share of the profits (commonly half) along with various additional taxes to the lord in his manor. This flow of cash and kind enriched the nobles and enabled them to acquire more land, more dependencies.

The nobles inherited from the old structure of Roman and Visigothic law the rights of local fiscal and military authority (*mandamentum*) together with those of judgment and punishment (*districtum*). Because they controlled the law, they had arbitrary powers of extortion, which they tended to use without restraint. And because the technology of war was changing, the peasants could do nothing about it. In the days of Guifré el Pelós and his immediate successors, peasants had been the backbone of the army, and they kept their weapons with them at home; this meant that the local lord had to be on reasonably good terms with the peasantry in order to raise an effective army. But now the key to military efficiency became the horse, an animal no mere farmer could afford. The word "chivalric" comes from the French *cheval*. No gaggle of farm workers waving their billhooks could stand up to cavalry. Only a few people— the richer *noblesa*—could afford the cost of maintaining a war-horse and all the equipage that went with it, from stables to armor. The man in the saddle was the man who ruled. In this changed agrarian society, the difference between the equestrian and the pedestrian classes rapidly became fixed and absolute.

By the twelfth century the *noblesa* in Catalunya, like its counterpart in France, had an elaborate hierarchy—the order of chivalry. At the very top were the older patrician families and the slightly newer lineages of counts and viscounts, with huge estates and many castles. Beneath them were the deputies of power, the lesser nobles, the castle keepers (known as *varvassors*) and the knights. In return for unwavering military loyalty and the punctual remittance of taxes from the peasants under their control, these minor nobles received from their lords a guarantee known as the *feu*—their portion of income from the lands.

In theory, the greed of this *noblesa castral* (the country lords, the nobility of the castles) was somewhat restrained by the authority of the count-kings in Barcelona. But their moderating influence dropped in the early eleventh century and never quite recovered. When the count-king Ramon Borrell died in 1017 the title passed to his son, Berenguer Ramon I, who was only fifteen. For six years his mother, Ermessenda of Carcassonne, reigned in his place, and when the heir took the count's throne, he proved no better at keeping the warlords of deep Catalunya in line than his mother was. When he died in 1035 control of Catalunya was split between his two sons (one got the northern provinces, the other Tarragona); and not until 1049 did the elder of these sons, rather confusingly named Ramon Berenguer I, take the reins of Catalunya as a whole.

These thirty years created a power vacuum in which neither the house of Barcelona nor its city aristocracy could muster much influence over the *noblesa castral*, let alone prevent it from gouging and expropriating the peasants it ruled.

What was more, the violence of the country lords unleashed itself on the Church—on the monastic foundations, dependent on land income themselves, which took the farmers' side. The nobles devastated Church land, attacked monasteries, and violated the custom of sanctuary by pursuing fugitives into churches, sometimes even hewing them down before the monks' appalled gaze at the very altar where the Eucharist was displayed. The Catalan clergy, led by that formidable intellectual the abbot Oliba of Ripoll (971–1046), fought back with the weapons it had—anathema and excommunication. In 1027, at the Congress of Toluges held in the Roussillon, Oliba instituted the Pau i Treva de Déu, the Peace and Truce of God, which was to be accepted throughout Europe. Backed by the threat of excommunication—which was the gravest imaginable punishment, since it meant cutting the sinner off from the living body of the Church, denying him access to the sacraments, and thus, in effect, dooming his black soul and bellicose carcass to the eternal fires of hell after death—the Peace and Truce asserted the rights of fugitives from lordly violence and established periods during which all hostilities had to cease.

This was more of a brake than a solution, but it helped. Ramon Berenguer I, having emerged as the first feudal monarch of all Catalunya, realized that he must reconstruct the whole political space of the principate if it were to survive as a kingdom and not as a cockpit. He set out to construct a framework of law that would hold a balance among the throne, the court aristocracy, the *noblesa castral*, the emerging merchant classes, the tradesmen, and the peasants. Owing to him, Catalunya became the first realm in all Europe to acquire a written bill of rights. The Usatges, or Usages, first sketched in before Ramon Berenguer I's death in 1076, acquired full form in the early twelfth century, nearly a hundred years before England had its Magna Carta; and, in fact, they initiated an epoch of responsible feudalism in Catalunya.

The key to this bill of rights was the explicit recognition that all burghers—*ciutadans honrats*, "honored citizens" (which meant, in practice, any man who was not already reduced to mere serfdom)—stood on an equal legal footing with the nobility. When rights were in dispute, issues were not to be settled by rulings from above: they had to be thrashed out before an adjudicator, as between equals, on level ground. Instead of government by fiat and *mandamentum*, Ramon Berenguer I and his successors insisted on pacts: negotiated agreements between interested parties. Pactism among groups and individuals became the very soul of civic politics in Catalunya and—foreign conquests apart—the core of its external relations with other states as well.

Pactism did not turn Catalunya into an idyll of harmony. It did not free the serfs or restore land to peasants who had already lost it. Nor was it capable of quelling the forces of unrest, as later uprisings proved. From the late eleventh to the fourteenth centuries, Catalan peasants frequently staged revolts against the iniquitous feudal system of *remences*, which forced them to pay heavy taxes to the lords before they could be freed—in effect, compelling slaves to buy themselves. And in the fifteenth century, class struggles in Barcelona between its artisans and workers, called the Busca, and the patricians and big merchants, known as the Biga, brought the city more than once to the edge of civil war.

Nevertheless, having a bill of rights was certainly better than having none. The Usatges did, at least, tame the rapacity of the robber barons and create an atmosphere in which country farmers and city traders alike could defend their interests—against one another or against the *noblesa*. From this stemmed one of the main traits of the Catalan character: its litigiousness. "The early Catalans," wrote the historian Salvador Giner, "were already obsessed with covenants, lawsuits, contracts, claims, counterclaims and appeals to court and to higher authorities." They seem to have been almost as fond of throwing writs around as modern Americans.

VIII

The lessons of feudal greed sank deep into the free Catalan peasantry. They might not always have had the means to take their grievances to court; but they became resistant, jealous of their rights, and even more stubbornly conservative. They regarded themselves as the salt of the earth and wanted to keep their independence at any cost. The legal guarantee of this desire was the lease.

By the end of the twelfth century many peasants owned their land, but most leased it. In practice, two kinds of lease were in use. The first was hereditary emphyteusis, a system that prevailed in much of Europe going back to the tenth century, in which land-tenure agreements were passed down from father to son, jealously guarded by the tenants and nearly impossible for the landlord to revoke. Some leases of this kind, issued in the twelfth century, were still in force seven hundred years later. In Italy this was known as the *mezzadria* system and in Spain as the *censo*. It was a simple sharecropping lease: the peasant worked the land and paid the taxes; the cost of seed and equipment was shared; owner and tenant split the profits. The *censo* may have been a primitive system, but it worked well so long as owner and tenant trusted each other, the soil was good, and the tenant worked hard. Generally, all three tended to hold true in rural Catalunya.

The second kind of lease was created for wine production, which—even allowing for the slow growth of young vines—was by far the most profitable type of Catalan farming. Vine-growing leaseholders were known as *rabassaires*, and, as in the usual lease, owner and *rabassaire* split the costs and profits. But the length of the lease was geared to the life of the *ceps*, or "vines." When three-quarters of the vines had died—a situation known as *rabassa mort*—the land reverted to the vineyard owner who could then issue another lease, or not, as he pleased. Naturally, the wily Catalan *rabassaires* got very good at keeping vines alive. Their stock usually survived for fifty years, more than a man's working life.

But beyond the formal terms of the law—the *drets* (rights) and *furs* (charters and privileges) that came to enlace their relations with other classes once the house of Barcelona had tamed the robber barons—the farmers installed themselves at the core of Catalunya's self-image. In this respect they were like the yeomen of England. The knights and nobles had their architectural emblems—the castles that studded the countryside and stood for chivalric power. The Catalan yeomanry had its symbolic building type as well. It was a mixture of fort and farmhouse known as the *masia*, "farmhouse," or in a social sense as the *casa pairal*, "patriarchal house."

The imagery and ideology of the *casa pairal* have deep, winding roots in Catalan history. Its meaning has thinned out considerably in the late twentieth century, because most Catalans now live in cities, and the family-based structure of rural life that such houses represented is gone. But from the Middle Ages to the First World War, the *casa pairal* was a vital ingredient in Catalan life. In the nineteenth century, it ballooned into a social myth of large and somewhat obstructive proportions. By the 1880s it mattered as much to the secular imagination of Catalans as the Church did to their religious instincts. It was the key image of Catalan conservatism. It stood for attachment to the soil and to the tribe. The "father's house" was the primal, quasi-biblical symbol of property and inheritance. It evoked hard work, loyalty, patriotism. It meant continuity of customs, bloodline, and authentic being: the state of being a Catalan rather than some other kind of Spaniard, and a particular kind of Catalan at that, not an aristocrat but a *pagès*. Above all, it meant not being a foreigner and resisting anyone who was.

Since the 1970s, such houses have been bought and restored in quantity by city folk: the one you see from the car window is as likely to be owned by some Barcelonese artist or the vice-president of the Banco de Santander as by a real farmer. Their form has also inscribed itself in developers' building all over the Costa Brava, where multicondo spreads struggle gamely but hopelessly to reproduce the look in hollow terra-cotta brick-and-stucco skim. For though the Ur-house of Catalunya can be restored, it cannot be imitated, and the laws and customs it symbolized have gone forever. Improbably enough, a few are left in Barcelona itself, survivors from a time when the terrain around them was still *horts i vinyets*, "gardens and vineyards." The oldest of them is the Masia Torre Rondona, built in 1610 and now an annex to the Hotel Princesa Sofia. Another is the Masia Can Planas, at 2–14 Avinguda Papa Joan XIII, now the headquarters of the Barcelona Football Club. Others, such as the Masia Can Fargas (Passeig Maragall 383–389), were built in the eighteenth century or later. There is a magnificent seventeenth-century example, thick white walls, stone quoins, sundial, and all, in the obscure Carrer d'Esplugas, in Esplugues de Llobregat, south of the city, but it is closed to visitors. To find the really old ones, you must get out in the country.

Like the Tuscan *casa colonica* and the Provençal *mas*, both of which it closely resembles, the Catalan *masia* comes down to us from the Middle Ages. But its roots are much older than that and lie among the rustic *villae* (fortified farms) built by Roman settlers, with their heavy walls, attached wings for animals, and watchtowers. Some *masias* were actually built on the foundations of earlier Roman *villae* and thus reproduce their plan. Their design is not uniform by any means: there is no rubber-stamp *masia*, because they were completely functional, formed as inexorably as a bird's plumage or a mammal's digestive tract by local conditions of climate and social behavior. They are architecture by evolution.

A seventeenth-century casa pairal, *Esplugües de Llobregut, in Barcelona*

In the wet, cold Pyrenees, *masias* have high-pitched roofs to shed the snow, exterior stairs, stables and cattle pens right against the house (so that fermenting manure could add to the heating), tiny windows, and walls of a positively cyclopean thickness. In the foothills, the roofs flatten and the windows enlarge, though not by much; the stairs go inside, and there is a covered porch and perhaps a small *clos*, or "walled enclosure." On the plains of the Ampurdan, Vic, or Tarragona, the roof pitch is still less pronounced, and three or four attic windows sit right under the gable; sometimes there is an arcaded porch, and the wall openings are bigger, though still closed with massive oak doors and shutters. And on the coast, the *masia's* roof is flat, and its attic space disappears; it may have a watchtower, from which approaching Saracens or other strangers could be seen.

The kind of soil and the type of farming determined the form of houses as much as climate did. Thus in some districts—Girona, the plain of Vic, Selva, and Vallès—where crops were diverse, there would be many storage rooms to hold the different crops (fruit, beans, oil, wine, grain) and the tools used with them. Because farmers there did not have many animals (some chickens, a few pigs for the sacramental *butifarra*), large stables did not figure in the plan, whereas in the Ampurdan and around Tarragona, where there was more single-crop farming, cereals especially, the storage rooms were fewer and larger, while farmers with grazing herds built big stables attached to the *masia*.

Whatever the local variations, the basic imagery of the house remained much the same. Everything about it was thick and rooted. No screens, no curlicues (except the occasional rough capital or country-Gothic pierced arch on a fifteenth-century window, or painted scroll over an eighteenth-century opening). Heavy walls, commonly two feet thick and made of rubble gathered from the fields, mortared on both sides, whitewashed, and quoined with cut stone. Pantiles, double- or triple-layered and set in a mortar bed, for a cake of a roof that recalls thatch. Heavy ceiling beams of oak, often resting on rounded stone corbels, with smaller rafters between them to carry the brick or tile floor above. Massive iron hinges, locks, and bolts. Tiny squinting windows, armed with solid shutters. What mattered to the inhabitants of the *casa pairal* was not the view—they had enough view when they were working in the fields—but coziness, security, defense. Right up to the nineteenth century, rural Catalunya swarmed with foes: Saracens, hill pirates, posses of knights intent on conquest, footpads, *bandolers*, Carlists. The father's house stood foursquare against them.

Its core was the *llar de foc*. "Fireplace" translates this term only pallidly, since *llar* comes from the Latin *lares*, the "hearth gods," and suggests a sacramental space, not just a spot where a fire is built. The *llar* had a fireplace hood the size of a small room, under which a whole family could sit; a swinging crane of oak, from which a caldron hung on chains; a battery of grills, pokers, and spits; a row of pots and earthenware basins on the long mantelpiece; and straight-backed wooden chairs—with arms and a drawer under the seat for the *avi*, or "patriarch," of the clan and his wife, the *mestressa* or *padrina*, and plain ones for the rest of the family, starting with the *hereu* or heir, the oldest son, and the *pubilla*, or oldest daughter, and going down the fixed line of rank and seniority to the stools for youngest children and farmhands. The same undeviating order was observed in the bench seating around the table at meals. No Polynesian or African tribe had a more rigid hierarchy than the rural Catalan family as it existed through the Middle Ages and into the seventeenth century. It was a society of pure production that had to make everything it consumed, including its amusements: hence the role of the *llar* as the primal site of Catalan folk culture, music making, song, and the recitation of *rondalles* (stories and fables). Locked into the cycle of the seasons and the very slowly developing processes of craft and technique, the *pagesos* had no reason to change. The very thought of change made them suspicious. In the seventeenth century, when the Catalan countryside was afflicted by banditry and the social order seemed to be breaking up, the *casa pairal* became more of a fortress than ever. Such places, wrote a nostalgic eulogist named J. Gibert, were

> the last relics of a way of life inescapably condemned to death . . . a sign of what has been lost in the vanishing of the past, the sign of deep and concrete human feeling. They were the great family trunk, severe and patriarchal, in whose branches it was possible to capture a fragment of eternity, because in them the customs that were followed like liturgical rites, and the traditions—the good Catalan traditions, such as inheritance law—formed a chain from fathers to sons. Thus, when we seek the primal soul of our people, we must study it in these rural structures.

The less nostalgic may wonder if the "good Catalan traditions" of inheritance law were such a loss. But they certainly kept landholdings intact—through primogeniture. The *hereu* got everything when the patriarch died. If there was no son, the *pubilla* inherited; this fortune made her a more desirable mate. Marriage contracts in rural Catalunya were lengthy and highly specific: every last chicken and square foot of land were read out by lawyers in the presence of the engaged couple and both families. The younger sons got nothing, although a *hereu* might be expected to give them a leg up in their careers. Just as in England, the second son went into the army and the third into the Church. By the eighteenth century it was trade in Barcelona that beckoned, rather than a military or religious career. And so the growing Barcelonese bourgeoisie was full of *fadristerns*, or younger sons, left out of the inheritance system, nostalgic for the patriarchal house and apt to console their sense of deprivation with long descants on the special value and down-home truth of their own rural roots. This was probably why the *casa pairal* and all it stood for became such a fetish in the culture of the Barcelonese middle class by the 1830s.

Indeed, as we shall presently see, the full cult of the *casa pairal*—its rise to the terrain of nationalist ideology—did not occur until the nineteenth century. One does not find the troubadours of the fourteenth century singing about the family *masia*. They wrote to please the courts—the barons and count-kings who were emphatically not interested in identifying with farmers. Nowhere in Joanot Martorell's chivalric novel *Tirant lo Blanc* is there a trace of the worship of ancestral peasants and their ways that suffused the utterances of the Catalan Renaixença four centuries later. The Middle Ages did not make the *casa pairal* the fount and site of patriotism, or identify it with Catalunya itself, or conflate its inhabitants with the Holy Family. The nineteenth century did that. Before the Noble Peasant could become a literary trope, he had to be on the verge of extinction. To the actual rulers of the Middle Ages, the peasant was an economic necessity, a potential soldier, a reluctant taxpayer, and a stubborn negotiator. But he was not an object of sentiment, still less a symbol of national identity. That role was reserved for the count-king in Barcelona.

IX

Thanks to the royal house, the territory of Catalunya was expanding: not by conquest, but by civil agreement and marriage. As king, Ramon Berenguer I managed to consolidate the fealty of the counties south of the Pyrenees—Cerdanya, Besalú, the Ampurdan, Urgell, and Pallars—as well as the Roussillon to the north. Between 1067 and 1071 he expanded farther into Provençal territory by buying a large tract of it, the counties of Carcassonne and Rasès, for five thousand ounces of gold. His sons and grandsons continued the policy by marriage. Thus Ramon Berenguer III acquired another slice of Occitan territory in 1112 as a dowry, when he married its princess, Dolça of Provence.

But the crucial political event for twelfth-century Catalunya was its union with the neighboring kingdom of Aragon, which consolidated and immensely increased the power of the count-kings of Barcelona. In 1134 the Aragonese king, Alfons the Warrior, died without a direct male heir, leaving his kingdom to an order of knights. The Aragonese nobles rejected his will and chose as their king Alfons's brother, a bishop named Ramir. Aragon was under intense military and political pressure from Castile, and to secure its independence Ramir arranged a marriage of state between his daughter Petronella and the next Catalan monarch, Ramon Berenguer IV. Her dowry was the whole kingdom of Aragon. The aristocrats of Aragon supported this merger because they guessed, correctly, that their own interests and privileges would survive better under the system of pacts among clans and groups that Catalunya stood for than under the Castilian monarchy. Both Catalunya and Aragon were to keep their political character, their laws and rights and customs; and so they did. They formed a strong power bloc that, for the next several centuries, kept Castilian influence at bay and resisted the growing centralism of the kings in Madrid. Their economies reinforced each other. Most important of all, their armies combined. The union of Aragon and Catalunya created the armed manpower that went out into the Mediterranean in the thirteenth century and created a Catalan empire there. Beginning with Jaume I, who spectacularly deserved his sobriquet El Conqueridor, the kings of Aragon and Catalunya took a coastal city that until then had stubbornly faced in toward the hinterland, turned its gaze 180 degrees, and made Barcelona a great sea power of the Mediterranean: the only city in Spain, at that time, to possess an empire.

CHAPTER THREE

"If Not, Not"

I

The kingdom of Aragon and Catalunya (which Catalan history books prefer to call the kingdom of Catalunya and Aragon) had an empire by the beginning of the fourteenth century. It was run from Barcelona. It would not have existed if Catalunya had the same problem as the rest of Christian Spain—the effort of dislodging the Arabs, which in other parts of the peninsula took seven hundred years. But Catalunya's short *reconquista* was finished by the thirteenth century, and now it could start getting itself an empire. It did so with almost hallucinatory speed.

Two factors had previously stopped Barcelona from becoming a serious sea power. The first was the shallowness of her harbor, which kept silting up. Even in the nineteenth century, ships might get stuck in port for a month or more, and passengers on the larger vessels had to be disembarked, with great inconvenience and fuss, by lighter: no big steamship could tie up to a pier without the risk of grounding. In the thirteenth to fifteenth centuries vessels were smaller and more maneuverable, but the problem was still acute, especially for the deep-draft, high-pooped, potbellied caravels that became the workhorses of Mediterranean commercial transport.

The second and far worse problem for Barcelona up to the reign of Jaume I was that the Moors were in the way of its sea traffic. They had been driven out of the Catalan mainland, but they were firmly ensconced in the Balearic Islands—Majorca, Minorca, Ibiza. Large medieval vessels, unable to sail close to the wind, could not avoid these islands when they shaped their outward course from Barcelona. The currents and prevailing winds took a ship right to them, where it might be captured and plundered.

Jaume I

Even when relations with the Arab island ports were good—and the
Moorish authorities were certainly not averse to Catalan vessels docking
and trading there, for it meant a flow of customs imposts and transit
tax—Barcelona's outward trade through the Balearics toward the eastern
Mediterranean had in the past been further limited by its dependence
on galleys rather than sail. A galley, rowed by slaves, was a short-range
vessel: fast, but uneconomical. The fuel of galley slaves was water (you
dehydrate fast, pulling all day on the loom of a thirty-foot oar), and the
galleys could not carry enough of it for a long voyage. Their range was
a week at most. And galleys were poor cargo vessels. It was not for
purely humanitarian reasons that the Catalan fleet went over to sail in
the thirteenth century; but this in itself could not solve the problem of
the Balearics.

Arab corsairs, who swooped down in their fast lateen-rigged dhows
on any sea traffic that ventured within fifty miles of the Balearics, condemned Barcelona's sea trade to shore-hugging provinciality. This especially galled the Catalans, since, though they called the Arabs
"pirates," they knew quite well that they were actually traders: after five
centuries of Moorish occupation Majorca was the main staging point for
trade in the western Mediterranean, the center of a web of contracts that
ran from Venice and Genoa to Sicily and Tunis and embraced the
interests of Catholics and Muslims impartially. The Catalans longed to

break into this sewn-up business. In the thirteenth and fourteenth centuries they set out to capture a series of island bases that would open the eastern Mediterranean for them: stepping-stones, from the Balearics to Sardinia down to Sicily. Naturally, like every conquistador since, they did it in the name of God and gave their motives a religious veneer. To take an island was to drive out the Moor, if he was there, or keep him out, if he was not. They began with Majorca. "When I took Majorca," boasted Jaume I, count of Barcelona and king of Aragon, "God willed that I should do the best thing man has done in the past hundred years."

His expedition sailed in 1229. Barcelona was going to be the big winner if it won; but Jaume I was eager to make it clear that Barcelona was not alone in the venture, that it was a collective enterprise of many Christian interests, and he gathered a fleet from French as well as Catalan ports, including Marseilles. Barcelona did not have enough ships of its own, and an invasion force against island defenses, then as now, required enormous naval overkill. This was the first big military effort by the combined kingdoms of Aragon and Catalunya, and it took much orchestration. Jaume's negotiations over rights of conquest with other counts whose arms he needed were long and intense. But in the end, he assembled a fleet: five hundred ships, by the reckoning of one court poet; probably fewer, but still the most impressive naval force that had ever been seen in the western Mediterranean. Jaume I was then thirty-one years old—a fiery young King Harry, whose appearance the chronicler Bernat Desclot described with breathless enthusiasm:

> This King, Jaume of Aragon, was the handsomest man in the world; for he was four inches taller than any other man, very well shaped and endowed in all his members; he had an imposing ruddy face and a long perfectly straight nose, a large well-formed mouth, with fine teeth so white that they resembled pearls; sparkling eyes, and red hair that looked like gold thread; and wide shoulders . . . he burned with enthusiasm, and was skilled with weapons, and strong, and brave, and generous, and polite to all men, and easily moved to pity: and his whole heart's desire and will was to wage war upon the Saracens.

Jaume I was so hot to go down in history that, with help from court scribes, he later penned an autobiography (the only detailed one ever written by a medieval king) called the *Llibre dels Feits*, or *Book of Deeds*.

Not only did he write most of it himself, but he wrote it very well. Its high spirits, its sense of mission, are still stirring; its images flash out. "We set sail on Wednesday morning from Salou with the land-wind behind us . . . and when the men of Tarragona and Cambrils saw the fleet getting under way from Salou, they too made sail, and it was a fine thing both for those on the land and for us to watch, for all the sea seemed white with sails, so great was our fleet." He described the terrors of a storm—"the sea was so great that a third part of the galley, the prow, passed beneath the water when its great waves came. . . . And all the ships and the galleys that were around us and in the fleet were under bare spars. And a bad sea came from that gale from Provence. And no-one in our galley spoke or said a thing." The wrath of the deep, the will of God, the lamentation of kings and heroes, the conquest of a kingdom "in the midst of the sea, where God has seen fit to place it"— it is all there; the *Book of Deeds* has long been seen by Catalans, and with some reason, as the Homeric work of their early history.

One hand washes the other. Jaume I had wanted Majorca, and the Aragonese had helped him get it. Now Aragon wanted Valencia, and it was Jaume's turn to help. The conquest of Valencia by the Catalo-Aragonese forces was a bloody business that took sixteen years, from 1232 to 1248. In the end the Aragonese imposed their feudal rule on its inland counties, reorganizing their agriculture into serf-worked latifundia, while Barcelona took the coastal provinces and repopulated them with Catalans. The center of this enterprise was the city of Lleida, inland from Tarragona, which was soon completely Catalanized. The conquest of Valencia preempted Castile's own designs on the province, and in 1244 the king of Castile signed a nonexpansion pact with the Crown of Aragon.

Meanwhile it had taken Jaume I six years (until 1235) to consolidate his hold on Majorca, and once that was done there was no stopping Catalo-Aragonese expansion in the Mediterranean. Out the ships went, taking the Catalan language with them; its traces marked a linguistic rim around the sea, vivid in some places and faint elsewhere, recording the presence of Barcelonese sailors, traders, and administrators. By the end of the fifteenth century Catalan was probably more spoken around the Mediterranean ports than French, Spanish, Italian—or indeed any other tongue except Arabic.

First, Jaume's son Pere II, or Pere el Gran (the Great), 1240–1285, secured the throne of Sicily by marrying its princess, Constanza. Sicily was still the granary of southern Europe; it was the sea gate to the Levant, to Greece and Egypt and Constantinople; and an embassy had come from Palermo to Barcelona inviting the king to invade it. For the next two hundred and fifty years Catalan shared with Sicilian the status of

Pere III (the Ceremonious), from Pedro Serrar, Montserrate, *1742*

an official language, in the royal administration of Palermo and Messina. Nevertheless, Sicily was too large and too firmly populated to be culturally much affected by the Catalans, who married Sicilian women and were soon absorbed into Sicilian life. This was a peaceful annexation.

Not so the conquest of Sardinia. In 1324 Pere II's grandson Alfons III (the Benign) sailed against that rocky island to make it a colony of the Catalo-Aragonese throne. By taking Sardinia, the king hoped to dominate the Tyrrhenian Sea.

Even today, one reads tub-thumping *catalanistes* claiming that the mark of their medieval forefathers' power grab in the Mediterranean was its amiable pactism; that the armies did nobody any serious harm and respected local institutions, in contrast (of course) to the brutal imperial behavior of the Castilians. What happened in Sardinia and Minorca, however, was as bad as anything the Castilians inflicted on the Peruvians or Incas, and far worse than anything they later did to the Catalans themselves. It verged on cultural genocide. In 1287 the Catalan count-king Alfons II (the Liberal) invaded Minorca—Jaume I had been content to leave it as a Moorish vassal state after conquering its larger neighbor—and slaughtered most of its male population; the rest were sold as slaves, leaving the island in economic ruin for two hundred years. Sardinia fared almost as badly, though the Catalans had more difficulty imposing their rule on it. They viewed Sardinian commoners as sub-

Arnau de Vilanova

humans, fit only to be slaves—and sold they were, in the thousands. All the original inhabitants of Alghero, on the northwestern coast, were put to the sword or exiled without ceremony in 1354 by Pere III (the Ceremonious). He then repopulated the whole area with Catalan settlers, whose twentieth-century descendants continue to speak a recognizably Catalan patois. To this day, when a Sardinian wants to tell you that someone expresses himself poorly or not at all, he may say *"No sidi su gadalanu"*—literally, "He doesn't speak Catalan." But outside the coastal cities the Sardians fiercely resisted Catalan rule, as the Irish did English; the colony remained a wasteful and bloody place for the count-kings and an expensive one for the Barcelonese merchants, whose taxes and levies paid for the army of occupation there.

There was, indeed, a slightly irrational quality in the count-kings' determination to expand their empire. It seems to have issued from a prevailing strand of visionary mysticism in the official culture of medieval Barcelona—the ideas that reached and influenced its fourteenth-century count-kings and sustained their ideology of empire. Such ideas were summed up in the career of their main Catalan propagator, Arnau de Vilanova (1240–1311).

Vilanova was a strange junction of opposites: a man who preached holy poverty but (like Seneca) was an adviser to kings; an empirical scientist, a doctor by profession, who wrote valuable medical texts—yet embraced the most extreme forms of apocalyptic mysticism and prophesied the coming millennium and the end of the world. Born in Valencia, he had studied medicine at Montpellier. His medical works, based on Hippocrates and Galen, were (by the standards of their time) faultlessly scholastic in their adherence to Greek tradition. His religious ones were another matter. There, he was antirationalist. Faith and reason were not compatible; only direct illumination counted. Vilanova was, in fact, the chief Spanish exponent of the most powerful ideology to arise between Jesus Christ and Karl Marx—the teachings of the Italian mystic Joachim de Fiore (1145–1202), which were the root of charismatic Christianity, and much else besides.

Joachim, a Calabrian hermit-scholar, had come to believe that the Scriptures contained esoteric meanings that could be decoded. With the right key, the Old and New Testaments and especially the Book of Revelation would reveal the future. He imagined human history as consisting of three ages, each governed by one of the persons of the Trinity. The first age was that of the Father, marked by fear, servitude, and law. The second was that of the Son, brought by Jesus Christ and initiated by the New Testament: a period of relative enlightenment, but with many flaws. The third age was to be that of the Spirit, which would turn the world into one vast monastery, its inhabitants rapt in ecstatic contemplation of the divine. In this age all things would be shared; mine and thine would cease; every Jew, Arab, and pagan would embrace the Church, wars would end, and mankind would have reached a point beyond which no further evolution was possible. But before this happened, Antichrist would appear. He would come as a king and overthrow the corrupt Church; then he himself would be destroyed in a climactic battle between good and evil. This third age, Joachim calculated, was at hand. He predicted it happening somewhere between 1200 and 1260. He did not live to see it, but neither has anyone else.

As Norman Cohn has shown in *The Pursuit of the Millennium*, Joachim's fantasy of history lies behind an extraordinary range of later ideas, from the Anabaptist movements of the sixteenth century to Auguste Comte's theory of three-stage historical evolution, from Hutterites and Ranters to the most influential chimera of the twentieth century, the Marxist belief in world revolution followed by the dictatorship of the proletariat and the end of history. And in Barcelona, Arnau de Vilanova not only swallowed it whole but spent his life preaching it. He seems to have learned it in Montpellier, from the "spiritual" wing of the Franciscans, who were Joachim's main disciples and regarded themselves as the avant-garde of the coming millennium. And so the doctor, while still practicing medicine, became the fiercest anti-intellectual in Spain. "It is certain," he announced, "that by learning philosophy a man does not come to love God more; he becomes a worse quibbler, a bigger chatterbox . . . and beyond that, a bigger hypocrite." The official Church naturally took a dim view of him. "Busy yourself with medicine," Pope Boniface VIII told Vilanova, "and not with theology, and we will honor you."

However, the house of Barcelona viewed him with awe, as a savant whose powers bordered on the magical—for Vilanova's scientific interests spilled over into more arcane matters, alchemy, divination, and astrology—and in 1281 he became court physician to Pere II (the Great). He then helped with the education of the king's sons, who would ascend the throne of Catalunya-Aragon as Alfons II (the Liberal) and Jaume II (the Just). Nor was he just a tutor: Jaume II seems to have relied on him heavily, not only for political advice, but to interpret his dreams. As astrologer, shrink, physician, teacher, and ideological witch doctor to the count-kings for more than twenty years, Vilanova used his influence to shape their policy. He set it forth in two books: *De Tempore Adventus Antichristi* (*On the Time of the Coming of Antichrist*), 1297, and *De Mysterio Cymbalorum* (*On the Mystery of Symbols*), circa 1300. In these he argued that the house of Barcelona had to play a decisive role in accelerating the millennium. It must purify the Church, convert or kill the Jews, take back Jerusalem, stamp out Islam, and create a new Christian empire with dominion over the entire world, whose capital would be not corrupt Rome, but Sicily—ruled, now, by Pere II and his successors. Such ideas must have swollen the count-kings' heads with eschatological dreams of vast destiny, and Vilanova's writings and personal influence probably inflamed their expansionist policies in the Mediterranean as much as any "rational" hope of trade.

II

As Catalunya's imperial plans grew almost uncontrollably fast, its commercial empire followed right along. Before the end of the thirteenth century the count-kings had consulates in no fewer than 126 places across the Mediterranean, from Málaga to Constantinople, from Venice to Beirut, from Montpellier to Malta, from Famagusta to Tripoli.

Catalans being Catalans, a nationalistic and boastful lot then as now, this gave rise to some inflated claims of cultural hegemony. There was, for instance, a sizable Catalan colony doing business in the eastern Mediterranean out of Athens and the Peloponnese. Its presence led a jingoistic bishop of Barcelona to assure his parliament, during the reign of Joan II (the Faithless), 1398–1479, that "famed and ancient Athens, from which all the elegance, eloquence and doctrine of the Greeks once sprang, has been converted to the Catalan tongue." Nothing of the sort had happened, of course.

Barcelona's trade with the cities of the Levant (Constantinople, Beirut, Alexandria) was profitable, since it yielded the goods on which the growing luxury trades of a medieval surplus economy fed. Barcelona merchants exported woolen cloth and sheepskins, dried fruit, olive oil, coral, tin, and iron. They got back pepper, incense, cinnamon, and ginger (a mania for spices pervaded medieval Europe—strong flavors drowned the rancid tastes of meat in a time that had no refrigeration—and was particularly strong among the gourmandizing Catalans). They also imported alum and thousands of slaves. To their empire—the Balearics, Sardinia, Naples, and Sicily—they sent cloth, leather goods, saffron, and arms, in trade for Sicilian wheat, cotton, and slaves and Sardinian coral and salt fish. They even traded through the Atlantic, with Flanders, from which the finest of fine textiles came. And once Barcelona had secured the western Mediterranean, it developed an even more lucrative—and shorter-range—trade with northwestern Africa, through Tunis. The count-kings never did conquer the African coast, though they certainly dreamed of doing so: the work of chroniclers like Bernat Desclot and Ramon Muntaner is full of fantasies of such a dominion, and Muntaner—a fact-muddling knight who tended to make up his history in the interests of chivalric propaganda—blamed the pope for not giving his king, Pere III (the Ceremonious), the military help that would have enabled him to take Tunis. But what was not done by conquest was achieved by treaty. By the early fourteenth century Barcelona's caravels were bearing dried figs, Valencian rice, cheese, nuts, and miles of cloth to the Barbary Coast and returning with raw cotton, dyes—and, above all, Barbary gold.

The main dealers with North Africa were Catalan Jews, on whom, in the fifteenth century, the terrors of Spanish Christian anti-Semitism were to burst. But in the thirteenth and fourteenth centuries, in Barcelona at least, they were esteemed by the count-kings, not out of any religious sympathy but simply because they were so useful: a Jew could set up business as a trading agent in North African cities from which

A Catalan Jew marked by the red and yellow button, fourteenth century, Santa Lucia Chapel, Tarragona

---

Christian residents were excluded. Barcelona, like Venice, grew flushed with money. What was better than a merchant? Two merchants. Or so one might suppose, from the encomiums lavished on the new bourgeoisie by such figures as the Catalan theologian Francesc de Eiximenis (c. 1330–1409), whose Franciscan past did not make him require holy poverty from others. In 1383 or so he penned his *Regiment de la Cosa Publica* (*The Administration of Public Affairs*), part of a monumental work called *Lo Crestià* (*The Summary*). This was to be a thirteen-volume encyclopedia of Christian principles and practice, a heaven-and-earth-explaining monster. He only finished the first four volumes, which comprise more than 2,500 chapters. In the *Regiment*, Eiximenis condemned all warlords and tyrants, arguing that the best defense against them was a dominant middle class. The bourgeois, full of *seny* and public spirit, exemplified Catalan virtue at its height. The whole structure of pactism and negotiation depended on these people—and pactism was the glory of Catalan life. They should be a protected species. What is good for business is good for Catalunya:

The land where the market flourishes unimpeded is full, and fertile, and in the best of shape. And so . . . merchants should be favoured above all other lay people in the world . . . they are the life of the people, the treasure of public interest, they are the food of the poor, the arm of all good commerce, and the fulfilment of all business matters. Without merchants societies fall apart, princes become tyrants, the young are lost and the poor weep. For knights and citizens who live as *rentiers* do not take care of large charities. Only merchants are big givers and great fathers and brothers of the common good.

"Everything that's done, is done by cash," wrote the Majorcan poet Anselm Turmeda (1352?–1425?) in his *Elogi dels Diners* (*In Praise of Money*):

> Diners de tort fan veritat,
> e de jutge fan advocat
> savi fan tornar l'hom orat,
>   puix que d'ells haja.
>
> Diners fan bé, diners fan mal,
> diners fan l'home infernal
> e fan-lo sant celestial,
>   segons que els usa.
>
> Diners alegren los infants
> e fan cantar los capellans
> e los frares carmelitans
>   a les grans festes.
>
> Diners, doncs, vulles aplegar.
> Si els pots haver no els lleixs anar:
> si molts n'hauràs poràs tornar
>   papa de Roma.

> Money makes lies into truth
> it makes a judge a lawyer—
> a crackpot becomes a pundit
>   If he's got it.
>
> Money does good, it does evil,
> money makes a man a demon,
> or a heavenly saint—
>   Depends how he uses it.
>
> Money makes children dance
> it makes priests sing
> (Carmelite friars too)
>   on the big feast-days.

The Llotja, the Stock Exchange of Barcelona

> So you must get money!
> If you get it, don't let it go!
> If you have lots, you can become
> The Pope of Rome.

The Barcelonese merchants were highly conscious of their rank and importance. Their collective temple stood near the sea, at the foot of the present Via Laietana. It was the Llotja, or Lodge—the city's stock exchange, which faced the water from which so much of its business came.

You would not suspect, arriving at the Llotja today, that it was ever a medieval building. What you see on Pla del Palau is a heavy, freestanding, neoclassical shell, finished in 1802 for the Junta de Comerç, Barcelona's powerful chamber of commerce, whose offices were on the northeast side of its upper floors. Not even the courtyard, with its jam of stockbrokers' cars and its handsome curving stair, gives a hint of any Gothic past. The Llotja has had a hybrid life. For much of the nineteenth century half its top floor housed the main art academy of Barcelona, the School of Fine Arts: Picasso's father, a mediocre artist, taught there, and young Pablo studied there from 1895 to 1897, as did Joan Miró and a host of lesser-known nineteenth-century Catalan painters and sculptors.

The original Llotja was a mere pavilion, a seaside exchange mart, built by Pere Llobet—the architect of the Saló de Cent—in the 1350s. But a stormy sea flooded it and Pere III (the Ceremonious) decreed that it should be rebuilt as part of his redevelopment program for Barcelona in the late fourteenth century. The architect was Pere Arbei, and the work was done between 1380 and 1392. Arbei's new lodge somewhat resembles the Loggia dei Lanzi in Florence, but closed in: a single big arcaded room, with a flat beamed ceiling and a viewers' gallery at half height, the roof carried on three double bays of diaphragm arches that spring from pipe-cluster Gothic pillars, quatrefoil in section.

The Contract Room of the Llotja is the oldest continuously operating stock exchange in Europe; its seats are open desks with the brokers' names neatly labeled on stove-enamel plaques, arranged around a central bull pen with brass rails. On trading days there is a muted jabbering roar of bids underlaid by the soft chitter of computer keyboards; the medieval arches preside over this hubbub, dark and grimy from the smoke of millions of stockbrokers' cigars. The Llotja is not exactly open to the public but not altogether closed to it either, though tour parties are excluded.

If the Llotja suggests the gravity with which medieval Catalan merchants did their work, the end product of their acuity and self-esteem can be seen on Carrer Montcada, a well-preserved street of palaces built by the *alta burgesia* that runs up from Santa Maria al Mar, across Carrer de la Princesa, to Plaça Marcus, where the little twelfth-century Capilla Marcus stands—the spot from which, in the Middle Ages, all travelers started out on the road north to France.

One rarely knows when an old street began its existence, but Carrer Montcada is an exception: it was created from scratch, without any earlier buildings on it, by the last count of Barcelona before the union with Aragon, Ramon Berenguer IV, in 1148. He gave it to the seneschal of the city, a patrician merchant named Guillem Ramon de Montcada, as a reward for raising the financial support he needed to reconquer the city of Tortosa. Carrer Montcada is thus one of the earliest efforts at "urbanism" in Barcelona. Little remains of its original town houses. Most of them are fifteenth century or later, a museum of upper-crust housing—a museum, however, that always looks closed, because the burghers built their mansions right up to the property line on the street and were not in the least concerned with looking welcoming. These town houses, with their thick walls and squinting windows, were built to defend, and they look as rebarbative as any fifteenth-century Florentine palace.

The staircase of Casa Cervelló-Giudice, fifteenth century

This changes once you are inside. The typical *palau* was a four-sided affair, built between party walls and around an inner court, with storage and functional rooms on the ground floor and an arcaded staircase leading to the living space and ceremonial rooms above. It is a universal Mediterranean plan—one sees it from Gozo to Tangier—but in the houses of Carrer Montcada it takes on a particular amplitude, for the owners did not stint on space. Most of them are open to the public, having been recycled into museums and art galleries. But this conversion into public use is only the most recent of their many alterations. Relatively little fourteenth- or even fifteenth-century material remains, because the houses were constantly changed and added to with the changing fortunes of their owners. One of them, the Palau Dalmases (number 20, now the Omnium Cultural), has some fifteenth-century vaulting, but the main feature of its courtyard is the seventeenth-century staircase, with richly carved candy-stick columns and a balustrade whose panels bear baroque allegories of Catalan sea trade and naval triumph. Neptune, his nymphs, and sea horses go charging through the foam, but uphill, at an angle of thirty degrees—a layout enforced by the staircase, but one which, looking back on it, seems to fit Barcelona's eventual economic decadence.

The Casa Cervelló-Giudice (number 25, now the Galerie Maeght) was built by Catalans and acquired in the eighteenth century by the Guidice family, merchants from Genoa. It has the finest staircase of any, with vaults carried on fifteenth-century Gothic stone columns so slender that you would think they were cast iron. The Palau dels Marquesos de Lliò (number 12, now the Textile and Clothing Museum) has an almost-pure fourteenth-century courtyard, whose shallow, sloping stair arch plays beautifully against the massive flat planes of stone wall. Probably the oldest architectural vestiges on Carrer Montcada are in the Palau Berenguer d'Aguilar (number 15, and now, with the adjacent Palau del Baron de Castellet, the Picasso Museum). Some of its details go back to the late thirteenth century, and it seems likely that its fifteenth-century rebuilding was done by Marc Safont, the architect of the original Gothic facade of the Palau de la Generalitat.

At root, it was the growth of trade that shaped the political frame of Barcelona in the thirteenth and fourteenth centuries. The Usatges existed, but how did they apply in the larger political sphere? That was the business of the hybrid, protodemocratic form of government that medieval Barcelona evolved to suit its needs. It, too, was partly the handiwork of Jaume I.

III

The count-king in Barcelona did not rule Catalunya and Aragon absolutely. The citizens of the state, jealous of their liberties, would allow no such thing, and they had the financial clout to make sure it did not happen. "What people is there in the world," asked the last count-king, Martí I (the Humanist) of Aragon, in 1406, speaking to the Catalan government, the Corts, "enjoying as many freedoms and exemptions as you; and what people so generous?" To the Catalans this question would have seemed agreeably rhetorical. There could be no such people. Their sense of exception ran back to the ideal of the ancient Roman republic, of the head of state as *primus inter pares*, first among equals. To them, the count-king ruled by contract and not by divine right. This view was crystallized in the famous and unique Catalo-Aragonese oath of allegiance to the monarch: "We, who are as good as you, swear to you, who are no better than us, to accept you as our king and sovereign lord, provided you observe all our liberties and laws—but if not, not." Catalans have always waxed lyrical over medieval defiance of kingship. In the 1850s, when the neoclassical facade of the Ajuntament was being built, a statue of a fifteenth-century patrician merchant named Joan Fiveller was installed in a niche in place of a figure of Hercules, mainly because, as *conseller*, he had forced the retinue of the first Castilian king of Aragon and Catalunya to pay city taxes on the salt fish they ate.

The nature of those "liberties and laws" was determined by a legislative council called the Corts Catalanes, which represented the three slices of oligarchic power in the country: nobles, high clergy, and the superior sort of merchants, known as the *boni homines*, "good men." The Corts was set up in 1283. At first it met once a year, but after 1301 its sessions became less frequent and were held every three years. The Corts passed laws but required royal approval on each one. If the king wanted special economic help from the state fiscus—in time of war, for instance—that subsidy had to be approved by the Corts. Hence there was a certain amount of leverage on either side. Nevertheless the Corts was restricted to advice and consent. It could not compel the king to do anything against his sovereign will, but it did have some power of suasion. When not in session, it was permanently represented by a standing committee of twelve men, known as the Diputació del General, or Generalitat: three deputies from each arm, plus three *oidors*, or "auditors," of accounts.

This government of the principate met in what came to be known as the Palau de la Generalitat, which stands on the northwest side of the Plaça Sant Jaume, confronting the Ajuntament, the headquarters of Barcelona's city government. Because its functions have expanded over the centuries, the Palau de la Generalitat is a palimpsest—in places, a magnificent example of late Catalan Gothic. Its entrance off Carrer del Bisbe, and the early fifteenth-century courtyard beyond it, are by the architect Marc Safont; his ceremonial courtyard stair—a leaping, shallow segment of a catenary arch—takes you up to a gallery with ethereally slender-looking stone columns and, beyond that, to the Orange-Tree Patio, a formal *hortus conclusus* one floor above street level, done by Pere Mateu between 1532 and 1547. There is a subliminal match between the trunks of the orange trees, planted in their formal grid, and the columns of the courtyard you have just left. Lucky the politicians who can lobby one another in such a place, or pray for extra *seny* among the cusps and whiplash curls of Marc Safont's chapel of Saint George (c. 1430), a small masterpiece of local flamboyant Gothic.

The government of the city of Barcelona was run by another body, the Consell de Cent, or Council of One Hundred. This had a more democratic, or at least more populist, base than the rigidly elite Corts.

Consellers *receiving a copy of the Usatges de Catalunya in the presence of Queen Maria, wife of Alfons the Magnanimous, miniature by Bernat Martorell*

It began with an order of Jaume I's in 1249 to create a committee of "peers," twenty high-ranking citizens, also known as *probi homines* ("honest men" in Latin or, in the common Catalan word, *prohoms*) to advise on city management. This committee had the power to convene larger citizens' meetings. In 1258 the count-king broadened its base by appointing an electoral college of two hundred men, representing various interests, professions, and even trades, who were to appoint a council of twenty.

Finally in 1274 the system emerged that was to govern Barcelona until the Bourbons did away with it. Five *consellers*, the *batlle* (mayor), and the *veguer* (roughly, "chief magistrate") together chose a council of one hundred representative citizens. This figure was nominal; the Council of One Hundred might be ninety, or as many as a hundred and forty-four, depending on who could not be left out. At the end of each year the Council of One Hundred would name a new board of councillors, who would then nominate a new council. And so it went for nearly four hundred and fifty years.

The Council of One Hundred proved itself to be one of Europe's more durable political institutions, mainly because it was flexible: it let in "lower" people. There was usually one representative of the *artistes* (higher tradesmen) and quite often one of the *menestrals* (skilled workers in lower trades) among the five *consellers*, and many more, of course, within the ranks of the council itself. A leather worker, a tailor, a cooper, or a smith might sit in session with a trading banker or the biggest spice importer in Barcelona on terms of voting equality—although the larger voting bloc was certainly that of the upper mercantile orders, the professionals, and the *artistes*, because the latter two made their living purveying services and luxury goods to the former. And the lower presence did not meet with approval from everyone: this was not a true parliament and the patricians were apt to oppose the intrusion of common tradesmen into the quintet of *consellers*—"one might as well put *cabrós* [a particularly insulting term, meaning literally "billy goats"] in the place as men of vile condition," sniffed one fifteenth-century political scribe, Jaume Safont.

To defuse the class rivalries and the fierce lobbying that sometimes attended the election of *consellers*, the Council of One Hundred eventually adopted the curious, but supposedly influenceproof, practice of *insaculació* —"election by lottery." This was almost universal in Catalunya by the early fifteenth century. "Let them make five bags of green canvas," ran an electoral directive in Girona in 1457, "with two locks each. The first will be the bag for judges and *consellers* who live in the city and are considered sufficient and worthy . . . let each man's name be written on a small strip of parchment, let each strip be enclosed in a roll of wax all of the same color, and let all these rolls be placed in the said bag." This procedure was not adopted in Barcelona until 1455. Its defect was that the bag could not control what names went into it, and so the jockeying for representation between patricians and tradesmen shifted to the issue of who got chosen for the lottery.

The Saló de Cent (Room of the Hundred) remains the core, the heart, of the Casa de la Ciutat, the largely Gothic town-hall complex with the Renaissance facade on Plaça Sant Jaume that houses the offices and ceremonial rooms of the Ajuntament. The Saló de Cent was designed around 1360 by the architect Pere Llobet, inaugurated in 1373, badly damaged by bombardment during a workers' rising in 1842, and then remodeled in the 1880s by the patriot architect Lluís Domènech i Montaner. (Antoni Gaudí entered the competition for the job too, but not much is known of his design, which lost and was lost.) Some Neo-Gothic decor was slapped on in 1914, but it is still a noble space, drenched in history and aspiration. Its structure was designed to be economical: instead of roofing it with stone vaults, a costly system, Llobet opted for the simpler technique of spanning the room with diaphragm arches (four in all) and running wooden beams between them. This was exactly the same way that another architect, Guillem Carbonell, constructed the Great Hall, the Saló del Tinell, in the nearby complex of the Palau Reial Major at the same time. The Saló de Cent is smaller and shorter than the Saló del Tinell, but in its original plainness it vividly connects back to the ancient components of Catalan architecture, coming out of the Roman past and linking sideways to the structure of cloister and *casa pairal*—a fine metaphor, intentional or not, for the mixture of tradition and innovation it represented in the political sphere. It is keyed to human proportions and does not try to overwhelm you with the majesty of the abstract state.

However, architecture makes things seem stabler than they are. There is a limit to one's ability to intuit the political life of a city from its monuments, because monuments always speak a language of order, inheritance, and shelter. Little is known of civic unrest in the thirteenth-century Barcelona of Jaume I and his successor Pere II, although there was certainly a current of working-class animosity against Jews and the rich. A "revolutionary" charismatic named Berenguer d'Oller appeared in 1285, preaching holy poverty, the leveling of privilege, and the imminent arrival of Armageddon, but although he gathered a following and sparked some mob violence, he was soon hanged, and thirty of his followers with him. Gang warfare in the streets of the medieval city was continuous and seen as a normal condition of life. Even priests fomented it, and Catalan surgeons insisted on being allowed to bear arms if they went out at night. In 1358 factional thugs bashed the lieutenant governor of Minorca to death with a candlestick on the high altar of a church. With its continual background of random violence, city life in Barcelona then had a more than passing resemblance to that in the South Bronx today, and the ferocity of the Middle Ages left no room for the sentiments with which we are apt to gloss the beast in man. The versifier Jaume Roig, for instance, mentions the skinning alive of a witch with a casual vindictiveness whose reality cannot be doubted:

> *Porc ple de vicis,*
> *un mal matí son sanct Martí*
> *ella troba; la pell lleixà*
> *per far-ne bóts.*

> Pig full of vices,
> one bad morning she found
> her holy martyrdom; they left her skin
> to make boots with.

The court records of the city are filled with the sins of our own day, from wife beating to poisoning, from embezzlement to the rape of nine-year-old girls; and if one is to believe Roig (presumably his medieval readers got a moralizing thrill from doing so), Barcelona had its own early version of the legend of Sweeney Todd, the demon barber who made his clients into pies—a fiendish woman innkeeper and her two daughters, who ran a cannibals' delicatessen:

> *Dels que bi venien, alli bevien,*
> *alguns mataven; com capolaven*
> *feien pastells e dels budells,*
> *feien salsisses o longanisses*
> *del mon pus fines . . .*

> From those who came to drink there
> they killed some when they cut them up
> they made pies and tripe
> they made sausages and salamis
> the best in the world . . .

The taste for this kind of *guignol* was so widespread that courtesy books warned against it; one finds Francesc de Eiximenis advising his new-rich readers, the merchant class of Barcelona, how to act at the table. One should not clean one's teeth or nails between courses, nor do anything else that "might provoke or move another person to horror or vomit. Nor, for the same reason, should you talk about disgusting things, like shit or enemas or laxatives or repulsive diseases, or about hangings or judicial sentences, or anything else that might cause nausea or vomiting."

Above the raw level of street violence, the main factional division in Barcelona was between the Biga and the Busca. One would caricature this by calling it a pure class struggle, although it had some of the characteristics of one. The Biga (the word means "beam," suggesting structural permanence) consisted of established merchants, patricians, and their allies. The Busca (meaning "fragment" or "splinter") tended to be smaller businessmen—clothiers, lesser merchants, and artisans, who felt excluded from power by machinations of the establishment on the Consell de Cent and elsewhere. The Biga tended to be better off than the Busca. But the Busca was not a populist party, though it often pretended to be for the sake of rhetoric.

The Biga, for instance, wanted free trade, which favored luxury imports. The Busca wanted protectionism, claiming to represent little people who would be the first to get thrown out of work if Catalan cloth was undercut by imported goods. The Busca also wanted to devalue the currency, in order to stem the growing trade crisis and bring some realistic exchange value to the grossly overvalued Barcelonese *croat*. This, too, the Biga would not accept. All this ensured a constant level of nasty political infighting. In 1422 a *constitució*, or "general policy," on imports was handed down by the Council of One Hundred: a sumptuary law, forbidding citizens to wear imported woolen cloth or to make garments from anything but Catalan textiles. Naturally, this favored the smaller shopkeepers and home weavers to whom the Busca appealed. But, reported the minutes of the Generalitat in 1456, the *constitució* was never fully published. One of the *consellers*, Franci de Perarnau by name, kept half the ruling under wraps for thirty years,

> because he has a big store full of silk cloth, and he will not be able to sell any of it if he obeys the whole rule. So in fact they arranged for a part of the aforesaid rule to be published, the part forbidding the use of foreign woollen cloth, but they said nothing about cloth of gold or silk in order to oblige this councillor. So they published a false version of the law, since they should not have suppressed or changed anything or altered so much as a word or a letter.

IV

Meanwhile, the Catalan language was growing. It was a vernacular long before the twelfth century, but not a literary language—the first known writings in Catalan are translations of biblical texts embedded in sermons, called the *Homilies d'Organya*, eight frail pages dating from the late twelfth century.

But although priests might preach in Catalan, the learned did their formal exposition—their intellectual work—in Latin. There were excellent reasons for this. Latin was the only universal tongue in Europe, the sole medium through which a philosopher in Paris could readily communicate with his counterparts in England, Rome, or Spain. It represented the mainstream of scholarly thought, and Catalunya had gained a place in that stream in earlier times. Some of Europe's earliest translations from Arabic into Latin were made by Benedictine monks in Ripoll in the ninth century, and by the eleventh to thirteenth centuries a whole school of Arabists flourished in its scriptorium. And it was through Arabic redactions—the original texts being lost—that much of

Portrait of Ramon Llull, from a sixteenth-century altarpiece by Pedro Barceló, Palma, Majorca

the literature of the classical world worked its way back into European thought. But Barcelona's main claim to intellectual importance was in the work of Scholastic writers who flourished there in the thirteenth century.

Scholasticism was the main enterprise of medieval European philosophy, a vast effort to establish continuity and harmony between the ancient Greek past and the Christian present: to reconcile Aristotle with the Scriptures, and reason—through the dialectical method of argument, whose great exemplar was Plato—with faith. Its overarching concern was theology, the study of what we can know and say about God's nature and man's experience of it. All philosophical inquiry in the Middle Ages was theological at root. For Scholastic philosophers the methods of Plato and Aristotle led inexorably to the confirmation of Catholic faith. The massive bridge between the two pylons of Greek thought and the teachings of Christ was built by Saint Thomas Aquinas (c. 1227–74), "the Angelic Doctor," a Dominican friar who had been educated at Montecassino near Naples and had worked in Cologne and in Paris. Aquinas's *Summa Theologica* became and remains the basis of Catholic philosophy: a colossal work, unfinished (since he died at forty-seven) at some twenty volumes. But if Aquinas was the unquestioned leader of the Scholastics, there were other and hardly less redoubtable figures as well, and one of them—certainly the most important in Spain—was a Catalan, Ramon Llull (c. 1235–1316).

Some literary and intellectual careers appear to lack any precedent and to conform, in their abundance and obsessiveness, to no known prototype. Llull's was one. He created Catalan as a literary language, a gigantic task. In the eighty years of his life he wrote some 256 texts in Catalan, Latin, and Arabic, totaling about 27,000 pages, and the editorial work of achieving a definitive edition of Llull's *obres completes* is still going on today. He was the first man since antiquity to write philosophy in the language of his people. (He then translated it from Catalan into Latin, so that other neo-Aristotelians could read it.) He was by turns rake, love poet, scholar, mystic, philosopher, man of action, and missionary. He was certainly one of the best-read men of his time, in at least six languages—including Arabic, which he studied for nine years. Islamic philosophy permeated his thought; Islamic poetry colored it with an ecstatic richness of phrasing and metaphor. Llull's absorption of Sufism is one of many traits that distinguish his work from the routine Latinate productions of orthodox Scholastics.

His literary masterpiece is generally considered to be the *Llibre de Contemplació de Déu*, or *Book of the Contemplation of God* (1282), a poetic mingling of introspection and theology somewhat along the lines of Saint Augustine's *Confessions*. But his works cover an immense range, from knotty philosophical argument and theological speculation to exalted mystical outpourings such as the *Llibre d'Amic e Amat* (*Book of the Lover and the Beloved*); from autobiographical poetry of lost illusions—*Cant de Ramon* (*Ramon's Song*) and *Lo Desconhort*—to a treatise on the conduct and ethic of the Christian knight, *Llibre del orde de la Cavalyeria*, from which the entire Spanish tradition of chivalric literature stems. He also wrote, in Catalan, what are probably the first two novels in any Romance language after the French Arthurian romances: *Felix of the Miracles* and *Blanquerna*, a Utopian tale, rich in the social texture of thirteenth-century life, of a young man's progress from lover to monk to cardinal to pope and of his final rejection of high office to embrace the life of a hermit.

But Llull's main efforts were reserved for the encyclopedic works in which he attempted vast syntheses of existing knowledge under the sign of Aristotelian thought, in order to secure a theoretical ground for the heroic, impossible ambition of his life: to complete the Mediterranean conquests of his king, Jaume I, by converting the entire Islamic world to Christianity. Llull, immersed in Arabic thought, had doubts about the savage ideology of the Crusades. But he believed that Arabs—whose philosophers and archivists had, after all, preserved the whole corpus of Aristotle's writings and given them back to Europe—could be swayed by argument alone to acknowledge the superiority of Christianity over Islam. He composed the chief of these texts in a Cistercian monastery: it was the *Ars Magna*, or *Ars Compendiosa Inveniendi Veritatem—The Great Art*, or *The Complete Art of Discovering Truth*. He was determined to put its ideas into practice as a missionary. For this desire, Ramon Llull—called Ramon the Madman by himself, and *El Gran Fantástico* by others—paid with his life.

Llull was born in Palma de Mallorca of land-rich parents from Barcelona who had settled on the island right after Jaume I conquered it. He was, by his own say-so in *Lo Desconhort*, a dissolute youth:

> *Can fui gran e senti del món sa vanitat,*
> *comencé a far mal e entré en pecat,*
> *oblidant Déus gloriós, siguent carnalitat . . .*

> When I grew up and felt the world's vanities
> I began to do evil, I fell into sin,
> forgetting God's glory, following the flesh . . .

Legend has it that he wrote a mass of troubadour love poetry, much of it licentious, all of it destroyed by Llull's own hand after a series of visions in his thirtieth year. A beautiful woman appeared to him on horseback, and he followed her into a church where she turned around, stripped—and revealed breasts hideously eaten away by cancer. He was writing a love poem to another man's wife when Christ materialized before him, not once but five times, nailed and suffering on the cross.

Llull changed his life. He became a nomad. Around 1265, he renounced his possessions, set up trustees to look after his wife and family, and set off on a religious and literary pilgrimage that was to last fifty years. In this, his mentor was an older Catalan, a priest attached to the royal household in Barcelona, the future Saint Ramon de Penyafort. From now on Llull's existence would be divided between monasteries, the court, and the deep blue sea. He wrote and studied during periods of seclusion that lasted for years; at intervals he served as a tutor to the royal family, educating the future king Jaume II. The rest of the time he traveled. The range of his journeys and pilgrimages was immense. He went to Montpellier and Avignon, to Rome and Genoa and Paris, to Libya and Egypt and Cyprus, and far into Asia Minor. When in his early forties, he got a royal charter to create Miramar, a training college for missionaries in Majorca on a cliff above the sea. It failed, perhaps because its students were soon exhausted by Llull's own charismatic energies.

For the next fifteen years, until his sixtieth birthday, Llull was not to see Majorca again. He traced and retraced his journeys across the Mediterranean world, urging its kings and prelates to do something so contrary to their views of Islam that it seemed heretical, even insane. To convert the Arabs, Llull argued, you must understand them; therefore, the Church must establish a network of schools in which non-Christian philosophies and religions could be studied, along with Middle Eastern tongues. This excellent idea fell mostly on deaf ears. Moors were there to be killed, not learned about. Only the Crown of Aragon and its religious arm, the Dominican order, were receptive to the practical idea of teaching the living languages of the Middle East. Llull's friend and mentor Ramon de Penyafort had set up twin schools, in Tunis and Murcia, for teaching both Arabic and Hebrew; thanks to Llull's influence Catalunya acquired a number of learned clerics who carried on long, winding theological disputes with their opposite numbers in Marrakech and Baghdad. But Llull's dream of bringing the adherents of two great monotheistic religions, Islam and Judaism, into the fold of the third, Christianity, by force of exegesis and rhetoric alone was obviously doomed to fail; and late in his life it was failure that dogged him, as he wrote in his *Cant de Ramon*:

> *Sóm hom vell, pobre, menyspreat,*
> *no hai ajuda d'home nat*
> *e hai trop gran fait emperat.*
> *Gran res hai del món cercat,*
> *mant bon eximpli hai donat:*
> *poc són conegut e amat.*
>
> *Vull morir en pélag d'amor . . .*

> I am an old man, poor and ridiculed,
> No man that is born will help me
> and I have taken on too great a task.
> I have sought a vast project in this world
> and given many a good example:
> I am unloved and unknown.
>
> I want to die on the high seas of love . . .

In time, Llull would fulfill the pathos of that last line. He was more than eighty years old, a stringy, frail, iron-hard old man, annealed by decades of poverty and burning conviction, when he made his last voyage to North Africa in 1315 or so to preach to the Arabs. He was attacked by a fanatical mob and left for dead. The crew of a Genoese ship got him on board and sailed for Majorca. Llull died, it is said, within sight of its coast.

Can such an utterly singular man as Llull be considered typical of anything, least of all a period? Perhaps only in a metaphorical sense: his life and work exemplify the obsessive outward drive of his native Catalunya, at a time when Catalan arms and trade were covering the Mediterranean world. Llull had a mystical, imperialist imagination: he believed that literally everything in the world, all human experience of all God's works, material and immaterial, could be evoked, described, related, explained, and transferred into a limitlessly unfolding framework of conceptual knowledge compressed between the boards of his books. Open them, and out it sprang. At the core of all reality stood the word, the Apophantic Logos, the face of God and the seed of things. In the thirteenth century, to Llull as to Thomas Aquinas, such a project seemed imaginable. To us, of course, it is not, though one can see the last traces it left in an increasingly secularized world in such Renaissance figures as Rabelais, with his gigantic piles of descriptive minutiae, or Leonardo da Vinci. And perhaps, much later, in James Joyce and Jorge Luis Borges as well.

To work in Barcelona, so close to the intersection of the Arab and Christian worlds, was to be an eclectic, was to long for synthesis. One sees this not only in Llull but in another outstanding Catalan apologist of the time, the Dominican monk Ramon Martí (1230–86), a follower of Aquinas who, in searching for arguments with which to confute Judaism, picked up numerous ideas from Arab and Jewish philosophers (Avicenna, Averroës, and Moses Maimonides), from the Koran and the Talmud.

Among the troubadours, the poets of the Middle Ages, however, it took time to establish Catalan as a suitable language. None of the conventions of troubadour poetry were invented in the Catalan courts. The very idea of courtly love, which was the central theme of medieval lyric and epic poetry, sprang from French feudalism: the relation of the lover to the adored lady as a kind of spiritual vassalage, never physically consummated (for that would have destroyed the ideal tension of desire sublimated as spiritual fealty), bordering on religion, inexhaustible and ennobling. The models were French, and so was the language proper to them: Provençal. All the *maestres* of the courtly love lyric wrote and sang in Provençal, starting with Guilhem IX, the eleventh-century duke of Aquitaine, and continuing through the twelfth century with such admired and, in their time, canonical poets as Bernart de Ventadorn, Guiraut de Borneil, and Arnaut Daniel (whose work would be so brilliantly revived in the twentieth century by Ezra Pound's translations). It was as hard for a writer living outside France to imagine describing courtly love in a tongue other than Provençal as it would have been for a priest to imagine saying mass in the vernacular and not in Latin. Even in Italy, at least until Dante and Petrarch, one wrote in Provençal, and likewise in Spain.

Since Provençal was the palette of troubadour poetry, since the particular sound and rhythm of the language, the color and nuance of its words, were so much at the heart of the poetic impulse, Catalan troubadours not only wrote in Provençal but showed signs of anxiety when they stepped outside it; and yet, because Catalan was the common language of ordinary life, they also worried about making the little solecisms when writing in Provençal that betrayed the "provincial." In *Les Flors del Gay Saber*, a treatise on Provençal usage from around 1350, there is a note on their fluffs:

> Li catala son grand dictayre
> Pero d'aysso no sabon gayre
> car de petit fan plenier so . . .

which means, roughly, that the Catalans are fine poets, full of inspiration, but not *technically* good, because they are always mixing up open and closed vowels.

But the steady pressure of the Catalan vernacular from prose and everyday spoken use continued to act on its poets, and by the end of the fourteenth century Provençal was looking more like a formal, learned language analogous to Latin and somewhat less like an inspirational tongue. Probably the first note of Catalan linguistic independence, if one can so call it, was struck by the fourteenth-century poet Lluís d'Averco. Referring to his prose work *Torsimany*, he explained that he had felt no obligation to write prose in Provençal—and in any case, "the other reason is that if I use a language other than Catalan, my native tongue, I could be accused of presumption because, being Catalan, I ought to use no language except my own."

If we are used to thinking of medieval poets as pallid creatures serenading distant virgins—an image created largely by the medieval revivals of the nineteenth century—it comes as a surprise to read what they actually wrote. In Catalunya, chaste troubadour poetry was actually quite a restricted genre and not popular; it came from the mannered, High Gothic taste of the Consistori del Gau Saber, or Association of Joyous Knowledge, a group of mainly religious poets formed at the court of Toulouse in 1323. It tended to be acutely nostalgic, mincing, and bloodless. It was always conflating the poet's beloved with the Virgin Mary. No doubt this was enforced by the rules at this prudish court— the Toulouse school was influenced by the then-current French fear of heresy in literature. No troubadour was allowed to address a love poem to a married woman; on the other hand, if he wrote one to a maiden (especially if it possessed some sexual content, however vague) he had to marry her. Under the circumstances it is no surprise that divine love was preferred to all other kinds in Toulouse. Other tastes, especially in Barcelona, preferred stronger stuff and did not give, as the euphemism went, a fig for the Virgin. The Valencian knight Jordi de Sant Jordi (c. 1370–1424), who served Alfons IV (the Magnanimous) both as soldier and as court poet, found his metaphor for love in war: "My sighs," he declared in "El Setge d'Amor" ("The Siege of Love"),

> are catapults I loose
> because I have nothing better to use;
> my moans are bombards, fired
> against the One who battles to destroy me:
> such are the only arms that I possess
> to defend my heart, here in its redoubt:
> I tell you, I do not believe their strength
> will save me from this danger . . .

Jordi knew Ovid's verse line for line and was given to its tropes; indeed, he wrote a work of 154 lines entitled "The Passion of Love According to Ovid." The Roman poet's *Ars Amatoria* is one of the great prototypes of Catalan poetic gallantry. Andreu Febrer (1375–1444?) translated Dante's *Divine Comedy* into Catalan, but he also wrote a number of love poems in the troubadour style, including the passionate "Combas e Valhs, Puigs, Muntanyes e Colhs" ("Passes and Valleys, Peaks, Mountains and Hills"):

> . . . *e suy seus;*
> *e si bé.m dis fos de s.amors stramps*
> *no me'n destulh plus que de carn fay lops,*
> *ans ay sper qu.elha e.z yeu esemps*
> *jausirem tant lo joy d'amor, que drut*
> *me dirà sieu tota gen, si ver dits*
> *e.ns amarem tant com la carn e l'ungla.*

> . . . and I am hers;
> and though I say I am free from her love
> I can no more leave it than a wolf can leave his meat:
> May she and I find such ecstasy in love
> that all men, in truth, will call me her lover,
> and we will love each other as the claw loves flesh.

Even in the gentler and more stylized forms of troubadour verse, there is an undissimulated eroticism, as in a charming dance dialogue by Pere Alamany:

> *que.n veniats una nuyt foscha*
> *ab paubr'arnes descosuts*
>   *e romputs*
> *per co quom nuls no.us conoscha*
> *Direts: "Fay be al hom nuts,"*
>   *e Na Luts*
> *fara.ntrar vostre cos quets.*
> *Adonchs veyrets son cors quay*
> *e mays qu'eras no.us diray.*

> Come one dark night
> your clothes gone at the seams
>   your harness broken
> so none can recognize you.
> Say: "Be good to a naked man"—
>   and she, the Light,
> will let you in, silently.
> Then you will see her lovely body,
> more than that, I can't tell you.

If the poet's love was refused, then he might die from it—provided that his death led to some union with the beloved. Thus Joan Roìs de Cornella, on the linkage of love and death:

Si en lo mal temps la serena bé canta,
jo dec cantar, puix dolor me turmenta
en tant estrem, que ma pensa es contenta
de presta mort; de tot l'aldrê s'espanta.
Mas, si voleu que davall vostra manta
muira prop vós, hauran fi mes dolors;
seré l'ocell que en llit ple de odors
mor, ja content de sa vida ser tanta.

If the siren sings best in time of storms
then I must sing, now misery torments me
so fiercely, that my thoughts are taken up
with instant death; they cling to nothing else.
But if you let me die beneath your mantle,
close to you, my pains are at an end;
like a bird dying in a perfumed bed,
happy to know its life has come to that.

As for the women who are the objects of such devotion, their voices are rarely heard. The most beautiful love poem put in the mouth of a medieval Catalan woman may have been written by one, but it is anonymous. She lies awake at night, pining for her lover:

No puc dormir soleta, no.
¿Quê em faré, llassa,
si no mi es passa?
Tant mi turmenta l'amor!

Ai, amic, mon dolç amic!
Somiat vos he esta nit.
Quê em fare, llassa?

Somat vos he esta nit
que us tenia en mon llit.
Quê em fare, llassa?

Ai, amat, mon dolc amat!
anit vos he somiat.
Quê em fare, lassa?

Anit vos he somiat,
que us tenia en mon brac.
Que em faré, llassa?

No, I cannot sleep alone.
Poor girl, what can I do
if he does not come to me?
Love torments me so—

Ah lover, my sweet lover!
I dreamed of you tonight.
Poor girl, what can I do?

I dreamed of you tonight
that I had you in my bed.
Poor girl, what can I do?

Ah beloved, my sweet beloved!
I dreamed of you at night.
Poor girl, what can I do?

I dreamed of you at night
That I held you in my arms—
Poor girl, what can I do?

It is impossible to know, across so great a gulf of time and manners, how far the religious adoration of the beloved lady was really felt by her poetic vassal and how much of it was poetic convention. Quite a lot, one suspects, of the latter: the language of self-surrender to the dame was so general that it even penetrated cookery. When Joan I of Catalunya and Aragon married his fourth wife, Sibilla de Fortià, in 1381, there was of course a feast with many set pieces. One of these, a roast peacock with all its feathers stuck back in by the cook in the Burgundian style, was set before the bride; it had a poem on a card tied to its neck, which began *"A vós me dò, senyora de valor"*—"I give myself to you, lady of bravery."

What is quite certain is that Catalan literature developed a strand that mocked the high yearning sensibility of troubadour love and the obsessive religious vocation of knighthood. Part of this strand issues from the sort of exacerbated disgust for the body—its mortality, its role as a vessel of guilt—that lived in symbiosis with an excessive idealism, and when the lady fell in the poet's eyes she fell a long way. So with the poet Jaume Roig, around 1460, in "Espill de les Dones" ("The Mirror of Women"):

Si s'adormia
tantost roncava:

molt m'enjutava
cascuna nit.
Sovint, al llit
se orinava
e fressejava
(tant i sovint
lo llit podrint) . . .

If she fell asleep
she started snoring:
it drove me crazy
every night.
Often, in bed
she pissed herself
and tossed and turned
(so much, so often
the mattress stank) . . .

Realism eventually conquered the idealizing urge, with a harsh mis-
ogyny meant for masculine ears: dirty jokes in verse. A similar process
took place in prose. One of the things that distinguish Joanot Martorell's
late fifteenth-century novel *Tirant lo Blanc* from all other chivalric novels
is that, while it continues to take the virtues of knighthood seriously and
reverently, it comes bawdily to life on the subject of courtly love, taking
every opportunity to poke fun at it. The hero Tirant, invincible on the
field of honor, is naïve in the bedroom—he cannot struggle out of his
moral chain mail. The women are the realists (of course!), and when
they start talking among themselves they are as frank about sex as any
merchant about exchange. Stephanie, a lady of the court, undertakes to
tell her priggish adolescent princess a few home truths:

> God graced women with such natures that if men understood us, they
> would have far less trouble inducing us to do their bidding. We all
> possess three inborn qualities which, as I have them myself, I can
> recognize in others: first, we are greedy; second, we love sweets; and
> third, we are lustful. . . . There is something far better, however,
> which is that when married women fall in love, it is always with men
> lower than their husbands, though every woman is born with the word
> *Chastity* engraved on her brow in gold.

Later, Martorell comes right out with it: the days of *amour courtois*
are over; sexually, the fifteenth century is a new age with new rules.

The princess has asked Tirant's page Hippolytus to give his master three hairs from her head—a gesture that in more idealizing days would have sent the lover into raptures. Hippolytus disabuses her. "May God punish me," he cries,

> if I take them unless you tell me the significance of their being three instead of four, ten, or twenty. Really, my lady! Does your Highness think these are the old days, when people followed the laws of grace and a damsel who loved some suitor in extreme degree would give him a well-perfumed bouquet of flowers or a hair or two from her head, whereupon he considered himself exceedingly fortunate? No, my lady, no. That time is past. I know quite well what my lord Tirant desires: to see you in bed, either naked or in your nightdress, and if the bed is not perfumed he will be just as pleased.

Not only Dante, but the works of Petrarch, Boccaccio, and other Italian humanists found Catalan translation early and were eagerly read; they became literary models in Barcelona and had a wide influence on verse in the fifteenth century. The greatest humanist poet to write exclusively in Catalan—last of the troubadours, first of the "moderns"—was Ausiàs March (c. 1397–1459).

March was born in Gandiá, a town in Valencia, around 1397. His family was noble. His father, Pere March (1338?–1413), was a well-known poet, author of such religious strophes as "Al punt C'om Naix, Comença de Morir" ("When Man Is Born, He Starts at Once to Die"):

Al punt c'om naix	*comença de morir*
e, morin, creix	*e, crexen, mor tot dia.*
c'un pauch momen	*no sesa de far via*
ne per menjar	*ne jaser ne dormir*
tro per edat	*mor e descrex a massa,*
tant qu'aysi vay	*al terme ordenat,*
ab dol, ab gaug	*ab mal, ab sanitat,*
mas pus avant	*del terme nulh hom passa.*

When man is born	he starts at once to die
and dying, grows	and growing, dies each day.
Not for an instant	does he cease to travel
not for a meal	not to lie down or sleep
until with age	he dies and leaves his life:
and so he goes	to his appointed end,
in pain, in joy	in sickness and in health,
but beyond that	no living man can go.

It is hardly surprising that, given his father's apparent beliefs, Ausiàs March too should have been preoccupied with death and God. But if he wrote juvenile poetry, it is lost; like Jordi de Sant Jordi, March spent his early manhood as a knight, fighting for Alfons IV in Sicily, Corsica, and other parts of the Mediterranean. But he did not join Alfons's court in Naples; instead he returned to Spain, managed the royal falconry at Albufera, and in 1437 married the sister of Joanot Martorell. She died two years later, and in 1443 March married Joana Scorna, who was to die in her turn in 1454. But although March poured forth his grief at her loss in a number of *Cants de Mort* (Death Songs), his main inspiration—at any rate, the person to whom much of his poetry was addressed—was an unnamed married woman. The strict convention, necessary in those days of easily enraged honor, was that the troubadour should never name the married object of his devotion; thus we shall never know who the lady actually was that March apostrophized as *llir entre cards* (lily among thistles) and *plena de seny* (full of wisdom), but by the fact of her enclosure in the poems she became as vivid a personage in Late Gothic culture as the equally anonymous woman in the unicorn tapestries of the Musée de Cluny.

March was at times an intensely philosophical writer, and his *Cant Espiritual* (*Spiritual Song*) is one of the great expressions of religious crisis in European poetry, part of a long tradition that runs through Saint John of the Cross in Spanish and from John Donne to Gerard Manley Hopkins in English: he trembles before the loss of God, believing in him, but confessing that he fears him more than he loves him. Donne's "Batter my heart, three-person'd God" is predicted by the anguished apostrophe of the *Cant Espiritual*, where March wonders if his own free will, given him by God, prevents him from union with the divine:

> *Puix que sens Tu algú a Tu no basta,*
> *dóna'm la mà o pels cabells me lleva;*
> *si no estenc la mia envers la tua,*
> *quasi forcat a Tu mateix me tira.*
> *lo vull anar envers Tu a l'encontre:*
> *no sé per què no fac lo que volria,*
> *puix io són cert haver voluntat franca*
> *e no sé què aquest voler m'empatxa.*

> Because without You no man is fit for You,
> give me your hand or raise me by the hair;
> if I do not stretch out my hand to You,

then drag me to You by the force of yours.
I want to go, to meet You face to face,
I do not know why I do not obey You,
since I am certain that my will is free,
and do not know if my free will prevents me.

March's lapidary precision was allied to an intense interest in the multiplicity, the ambiguity, of the self, and this is what most sets him apart from earlier troubadour poets. He knew that the "I" of poetry was not a constant thing:

> *Aixi dispost, dolç me sembla l'amarg,*
> *tant es en mi afecionat lo gust!*
> *A temps he cor d'acer, de carn e fust:*
> *jo só aquest que'm dic Ausiàs March.*

> Made as I am, sweet seems bitter to me—
> so veering and inconstant is my taste!
> Sometimes my heart is steel, then flesh, then wood:
> I am the one who calls himself Ausiàs March.

March's "modernity" lay, partly, in mingling the cerebral with the suddenly colloquial. "Black flour won't give white dough, / and a knackered donkey won't race." Memories of love "grow inside my heart / like vermin gnawing it." But his originality also stems from what Catalan poets of the nineteenth century recognized as March's Byronism, his sense of being a wanderer on the earth—a Romantic poet emerging, against all expectation, from the ordered stratum of late medieval Scholasticism and finding no place to settle. "Where is the place where my thought may rest?" he wrote. "Where can my will find contentment?" Nowhere in the world, for this lost traveler impelled by guilt and love:

> *No.m pren axi com al petit vaylet*
> *qui va cerquant senyor qui festa.l faça,*
> *tenint-lo calt en lo temps de la glaça*
> *e fresch, d'estiu, com la calor se met;*
> *preant molt poch la valor del senyor*
> *e concebent desalt de sa manera,*
> *vehent mlt clar que té mala carrera,*
> *de cambiar son estat en major.*

> *?Com se farâ que visca sens dolor*
> *tenint perdut lo bé que posseya?*

Clar et molt bé ho veu, si no ha follia,
que may porà tenir estat milor.
?Donchs què farà, puix altre bé no.1 resta,
sino plorar lo bé del temps perdut?
Vehent molt clar per si ser decebut
may trobarà qui.il faça millor festa.

Yo són aquell qui.n temps de tempesta
quan les més gents festegen prop los fochs
e pusch haver ab ells los propis jochs,
vaig sobre neu, descalç, ab nua testa . . .

Do not take me for a little courtier
seeking a lord to keep him comfortable
warm in the ice of winter, and cool
throughout the summer, when the heat comes on,
caring but little for his patron's worth,
spurning his code of behavior,
and clearly seeing he will not succeed
in making something better of his life.

How can a man live without misery
once he has lost whatever good he has?
He plainly sees, if he is not deluded,
that he can never rise to better things.
So what can he do, if he has nothing left
but grieve for the good that now is past,
clearly aware that he has trapped himself:
to him, no man will give a better life.

I am the man who, in time of storms
when most people get cozy round their fires,
though he could join them in their natural games,
goes on in snow, barefoot, with a bared head . . .

V

The prosperity of Barcelona meant that the city grew in the medieval period—rapidly, almost explosively. It also got new fortifications. The old Roman walls could no longer contain the burgeoning, bustling Mediterranean hub it had become. And so Jaume I began to construct new ones, to protect the town that his outward push into the Mediterranean had created.

The new walls were a huge civic project. They took more than a hundred years to finish. The original line of Jaume I's wall enclosed the main districts of Barcelona: the parishes of Sant Pere, the Mercè, and Ribera. It ran inland from the waterfront along the north bank of the filthy stream of the Cagallel (later to become the track of the Ramblas) up to the present site of the Plaça de Catalunya. Then the wall turned north, following the route of today's Ronda de Sant Pere, crossed the dirty trickle of the Merdança (which had been partly rerouted as an irrigation ditch, and euphemistically renamed the Rec Comtal, or Creek of the Counts) and headed seaward again. It enclosed an area twenty times the size of the Roman precinct, and this became the medieval city—the Barri Gòtic, as it was later called. Then in the second half of the fourteenth century, Pere III (the Ceremonious) decided to add another wall, starting at the port on the south side of the Drassanes, the vitally important shipyards, and enclosing all the area that now lies between the Ramblas and the Parallel. This sector became known later as the Raval, or Suburb. In Pere III's time it was not a suburb, but farmland. His idea was to protect Barcelona's emergency food supply, in time of siege, from marauders who might try to destroy the crops. In effect, Pere III's wall was an enormous, and enormously expensive, garden fence that locked into the line of Jaume I's wall at Plaça de Catalunya. Nothing of the latter wall survives, but a section of Pere III's wall does, down at the corner of the Drassanes—the Muralla de Santa Madrona, with its massive battlemented watchtower.

Today, despite centuries of attrition and destruction, Barcelona's Barri Gòtic still contains the most concentrated array of thirteenth- to fifteenth-century buildings in Spain and, not discounting even Venice, the most complete in Europe. They are of every type: parish churches, town houses, government buildings, council halls, guild headquarters, industrial structures, and of course the Cathedral.

The remarkable thing about this building boom was its manic quality. It flew, at least part of the time, in the face of economic reality. Pere III was a choleric man, bloody in war, given to luxury and elaborate protocol in peace; he did not brook appeals to moderation, and he wanted his city to testify to his reign. He set this forth in one of his poems, for he was a poet too:

> *Lo loch me par sia pus degut*
> *noble ciutat, o vila gross'e gran,*
> *o.ls enamichs valentment garreian,*
> *tenent al puny lança e'l bras escut,*

o'n esglesia, on devota[men] sia,
e si.u fa'xi, no sera ja repres
per cavallers ne per null hom entes
qui'n nobles fayts met se pensa tot dia.

The worthiest of places, so I think
is a noble city, or a great fine town,
or to be bravely fighting enemies
with lance in hand and shield upon one's arm,
or at one's devotions in a church:
and if I do this, I shall not be scorned
by knights, or any other men of worth
who constantly reflect on noble deeds.

The king set a kind of precedent: much the same overreaching occurred in Barcelona's next two building spurts and real-estate booms—
the development of the Eixample at the end of the nineteenth century,
and the furious pace of new construction and restoration that preceded
the 1992 Olympic Games—except that the medieval boom unfolded
against the backdrop of social disaster: first famine, then the Black Death.

In 1333 the Catalan wheat crop failed, and ten thousand people in
Barcelona—about a quarter of the city's population—starved to death.
There was no real food surplus for another ten years, and the battered
city was just beginning a recovery when, in 1348, the bacillus *Yersina
pestis* was carried into it by lice riding on ships' rats. The terrible plague
that struck across all of Europe came to Majorca first, in March, and by
May it was raging in Barcelona; by October, it had spread through all
Catalunya. One chronicler reported the mortality in Majorca as fifteen
thousand people a month, but it was probably much more, and it soon
killed 80 percent of the island's population. For Barcelona the gross death
toll was larger, the proportion smaller, and the outcome still catastrophic.
Whole areas of the city were depopulated, and, since the plague spared
neither high nor low, government was nearly wiped out: four of the five
consellers died. Probably 40 percent of the entire population of Catalunya
perished, but the toll was uneven; some parts of the Pyrenean counties
were untouched by the Black Death, whereas the city of Vic and the
plains around it lost two-thirds of their inhabitants. This brought the
life of rural Catalunya to the point of collapse; farmers had died along
with their sons and heirs, leaving abandoned *masos* open to looters with
no one to work them or lay claim to them. The biggest looters of all
were the country aristocracy, who began a new predatory cycle against
the surviving peasants by grabbing any farm left unclaimed thirty days

after the owner's death. Resentment of this, combined with a simmering hatred of the system of *remences*—the extortionate cash and kind payments demanded by feudal lords from land-bound peasants who wanted to leave and seek work elsewhere—led to a succession of peasant risings and land wars that started in 1370 and flared bitterly on through the fifteenth century. Pere III's son, Martí I, the last of the direct line of the count-kings of Barcelona, tried to create new laws favoring the peasants but died in 1410 before they could be enforced.

In the cities, including Barcelona, plague bred chaos. What had caused it? A furious God; a malign planetary conjunction; a black cloud from Asia, or from hell; foreigners and other evildoers infecting wells with mysterious powders and poisons? Those of a millenarian turn of mind concluded that the plague announced the Last Days and the Final Judgment. Many blamed it on the Jews, for every Catalan, it seemed, knew someone who knew someone else who knew for certain that Jews threw putrefying corpses in the wells. Hundreds of people were seized and tortured with screws, hot irons, and the strappado until they confessed their role in spreading the plague or denounced others. The years 1362 to 1371 brought a new cycle of epidemics and famine. In 1391, pogroms were launched and El Call, the Barcelona ghetto, was sacked by frantic Christian lynch mobs. If there was ever a medieval polity in imminent danger of collapse, you might suppose it was Barcelona during the reign of Pere III.

And yet the fact is that Pere III built voluminously: not only the walls but some of the largest and most notable monuments inside them, including the Drassanes, the Llotja, the Casa de la Ciutat, the major part of the Cathedral and some of its canons' houses, and the Saló del Tinell. Some church projects (not underwritten by the king) were stalled or left unfinished because of the plague—the church of Sant Just and Sant Pastor, for instance, whose foundation stone was laid in 1342 only to have work on the fourth and last bay of the nave stop in 1362 and not resume for a hundred and thirty years. Others, like the great monastery of Santa Maria de Pedralbes on Sarrià, the hill above the city, were essentially completed before 1450. But the three major churches of Gothic Barcelona, Santa Maria del Pi, Santa Maria del Mar, and the Cathedral, were constructed during and just after the plague years and serve as a reminder that not even the worst disasters can always extinguish the urge to architectural transcendence.

As secular design, the Saló del Tinell is of special interest. When first you enter it from the Plaça del Rei it looks like a very grand Quonset hut, with its six semicircular diaphragm arches that spring from low

Saló del Tinell, 1359–70

engaged columns in the wall. These span more than fifty feet and are among the largest unreinforced masonry arches ever built in Europe. The simple repetition of these stone rainbows, down six bays, gives a gravely Cistercian effect. The Saló del Tinell was designed by Pere III's architect Guillem Carbonell and built over a demolished section of Ramon Berenguer IV's royal palace, the principal residence since the twelfth century of the counts of Barcelona. Its name means "banqueting chamber," but it was also used as a parliament in the 1370s. In 1493 Ferdinand and Isabella, the new monarchs of the alliance of Aragon and Castile, are said to have received the news of the New World from Christopher Columbus in the Saló del Tinell, although there is no real evidence that they did so.

In its severity and structural daring, the Saló del Tinell is one of the archetypes of Catalan design. High-Catalan Gothic, the building style of Barcelona in the fourteenth century, is wholly distinctive and quite unlike English or French Gothic structures of the same period. The style grows out of the plainness of the thirteenth-century Cistercian foundations of the Alt Camp de Tarragona—Poblet and Santes Creus. It prefers solids to voids. North of the Pyrenees, the architects of Ely, Wells, or Chartres focused their genius on dissecting the wall into a glass membrane held together with stone lace and propped up by flying buttresses. Not in Catalunya, where the wall remains earthbound, defined by mass. The mass counts for more than the opening. Mass is praised in severe, opaque, prismatic forms—square, cylindrical, hexagonal, or octagonal in plan, with cornices and stringcourses that stress their horizontality. Their surfaces are plain. Catalan architects did not want to imitate the organic profusion of detail in northern Gothic. They liked a wall. Their bell towers end in flat roofs, not in spires. Their buttresses are square counterforts that reach back into the church to form the walls of chapels. They have no pinnacles on top—only gargoyles that bristle out horizontally, like the lancing spikes on Catalan ironwork, as in the Cathedral, Santa Maria del Mar, or Santa Maria del Pi. Even the bell towers end in flat roofs, not in spires. No matter how secure Barcelona felt, no matter how impregnable it was, its church architects obdurately kept the image of the fortress at the back of their minds. No matter how high, long, or wide their buildings were, they retain a ghost memory of the cave, the stony troglodytic God-shelters of the Pyrenees, of Catalunya Vella.

The main fourteenth-century type of Catalan church has no aisles. It is one big nave with an apse at one end—polygonal rather than round—and a choir at the other. North of the Pyrenees, this form was rare. (One sees it in the Sainte-Chapelle in Paris and in the basilica of Assisi, but seldom elsewhere.) In Catalunya it is common, the great example in Barcelona being Santa Maria del Pi. Single-nave churches could be very wide indeed—the Pi's span is fifty-four feet, about a third of its length. English and French cathedrals of this period were high and long; Catalan ones, broad. They are Wide Gothic. "We look at the monuments of other countries and find them strange," wrote the Catalan art historian Alexandre Cirici i Pellicer in 1980, pointing out that the length of English cathedral naves, which could run to six hundred feet, was unthinkable in Barcelona or anywhere else in Catalunya. As for the French, Cirici i Pellicer wrote, "When a Catalan enters [Notre Dame] he feels a great disappointment: it has a splendid facade but the interior is like a corridor—narrow, anxiety-making, too long, a thing which does not hold space and cannot be compared with the best of our churches, which are much roomier." Cirici i Pellicer's anxiety has much to say about the subliminal Catalan desire for coziness, felt as much by critics as by architects. If, as conservative prelates in the nineteenth century used to say, the church was the *casa pairal de Déu*, it should not run too far from your eye; you ought to be able to gather around the altar like a family around the *llar de foc*—the cave, again.

But the passion for width produces its own virtuosity. The largest

Santa Maria del Pi, 1322–1486

square vaulted room in Europe, without intermediary columns, is that of the Castel Nuovo in Naples. It measures eighty-six by eighty-six feet and was built by a Catalan architect named Guillem Sagrera. The widest vaulted Gothic nave in Europe (seventy-eight feet, only five feet narrower than the gigantic barrel vault of Saint Peter's in Rome) is that of the Cathedral of Girona, built as a single-nave church in the fourteenth century.

Wide Gothic has its own external grandeur and internal drama. As you approach it down the curve of the Carrer del Pi, the church of Santa Maria del Pi appears like a cliff, sunless (except briefly in the afternoons) and flat—an incontrovertible plane, closing the small square in front of it. It must have looked more ornamented once; the twelve high niches around its portal lost their sculptures long ago. But still, its aspect was always severe. It is a single plane of stone stretched between two engaged octagonal towers. The only holes in it are the pointed portal, framed by a two-tier gallery—whose projection is so shallow that it accentuates, rather than diminishes, the sheetlike tightness of the wall—and the huge rose window. It has three strips of horizontal molding, running clear across. Frame, face, window, door: the "primitive" house of God. And an octagonal bell tower, a hundred and eighty feet high—a brown prism, finished somewhat later, around 1470.

Inside, the severity persists, but its effects rise. The Pi's single nave confronts you all at once, explicitly, not unfolding to view angle by angle as a nave-and-aisle basilica does, but in one spatial utterance without hidden corners. There are chapels—fourteen in all, one between each pair of buttresses—but they seem less like nooks than clear extensions of the nave. At one end, the wall of the great box folds around into an apse, half a dodecagon, plain sheer facets of stone pierced by a gallery of stained-glass windows. At the other end, below the solemn disk of the rose window, a choir is supported on a shallow stone arch that spans the width of the church with a rise of no more than six feet from its springing. It is almost flat, so flat that it seems impossible to build in stone segments; yet it has been, for by the fourteenth century Catalan masons had developed a unique skill in constructing shallow arches that seem to defy the ordinary laws of bending stress. They still had it in the nineteenth century, when the Pi's choir was rebuilt in its present form. No modern architect would attempt such forms in stone without concealed steel reinforcement today, and no builder could make them stand up.

This combination of surface plainness and bony structural daring also marks Barcelona's other prime urban church of the fourteenth century, Santa Maria del Mar. The Pi was begun in 1322. Santa Maria del Mar got under way seven years later and took a little more than a half century to build.

It was not far in from the beach, a biblical ark side-on to the harbor, looking as though it had come to rest there after the Flood. (One often hears it said that Santa Maria del Mar was actually *on* the beach and constructed in the sand. This is not true.) The site was in fact very old, and Christian worship had already been conducted there for a thousand years. Santa Maria del Mar is built over a burial site that dates back to the first century A.D., and the original church may have been the first episcopal seat in Barcelona at the time of Constantine, in the fourth century. This little chapel, being close to the beach, was called Santa Maria dels Arenys—Holy Mary of the Sands. Its cult was that of Saint Eulalia, patron saint of Barcelona, the virgin martyr who was supposedly buried there in 303. After her remains were moved to the shrine where the Cathedral of Barcelona now stands, the Catalans began a new church on the site of the old, dedicated to Christ's mother in her role as patroness of mariners—Mary, Stella Maris, Star of the Sea.

Carving of stevedores, Santa Maria del Mar

By now the Ribera quarter, where the shrine stood, was exceedingly prosperous. The growth of trade had been good to it. It was surrounded by streets occupied by workers in specific guilds—Carrer del Argenteria (silversmiths), Carrer dels Sombrerers (hatmakers). Being so close to the port, it was associated with haulers and porters. The guild of the *bastaixos*, or longshoremen, made heavy cash contributions to its building. On the massive oaken portal of the church are two small, easily overlooked fifteenth-century bronze figures of men carrying loads. Inside, at the foot of the main altar, are a pair of stone reliefs. One shows a man shoveling grain from a big pile into a bag, while the other depicts a pair of stevedores carrying a cask slung on a pole between their shoulders. The latter are the *macips de Ribera*, "freed slaves," whose job it was to load and unload cargo ships. These were the folk whose labor made up for the permanent deficiencies of the harbor. They also brought the stone from the Foixada quarry on Montjuic to build the church.

Bernat Llull, the parish priest, laid the foundation stone in 1329, and construction began with the apse, working down toward the front facade—four bays in the nave, flanked by aisles, without a transept, the classic Cistercian plan that descends, without interruption, from the primitive basilicas of the early Church. The first architects were Berenguer de Montagut and Ramon Despuig; later they were replaced by Guillem Metge, who died in 1381, three years before the church was consecrated. For more than fifty years, according to the chronicles, most of the able-bodied population of Barcelona worked on Santa Maria del Mar, which gave it a lasting reputation as a popular church, a building made by workers for workers—though this did not prevent the anarchists from starting a fire in it during the Spanish civil war, destroying most of its accumulated ornaments and fittings, including a huge eighteenth-century organ and an elaborate but incongruous baroque high altar; the fire raged for eleven days, consumed an untold quantity of furniture, sculpture, reliquaries, paintings, and textiles, and somewhat weakened the structure of the church itself. Consequently only the original bones of Santa Maria del Mar are left, but these bones are so beautiful that one finds it hard to regret the loss of the intrusive altar.

By 1379 the apse and three of the four main vaults of the nave were closed, and their circular keystones, each six feet in diameter, were in place. The third vault was finished just before Christmas that year, when the wooden support scaffolding under it caught fire and collapsed. By the time a new scaffolding could be set up, it was clear that the keystone—bearing a colored relief of Saint George, in Catalan red and yellow stripes, lancing the dragon—had been ruined, but it could not be taken out and replaced without destroying the vault itself. So it was patched up, and the fourth and last vault was at last closed with due ceremony on November 3, 1383. The first solemn high mass in Santa Maria del Mar was celebrated by Pere de Planella, bishop of Barcelona, nine months later.

Outside, to an eye used to the French or English pointed styles of the fourteenth century, Santa Maria del Mar hardly looks Gothic at all. Where are the sharp ogives, the spires, the filigree, the detached airiness of flying buttresses? Nowhere to be seen: the buttresses that sink the outward thrust of the roof in their mass are solid rectangular blocks, foursquare, and their only ornaments are the rainspouts that project like fierce black beaks from their summits. Its bell tower is octagonal, finished with three diminishing octagons, almost as simple as a basalt pipe. The doors are oak, massive and iron studded. Despite the rose window, it looks as opaque as the rock from which it was built, more a fortress than a church: Cistercian in its imagery of plainness and shelter. A sect could make its last stand here.

Inside, the scale is immense. There is no grander or more solemn architectural space in Spain than Santa Maria del Mar. Its plan is basilican, a central nave with two flanking aisles that swing around to form a semicircular apse; chapels, set between the solid counterfort stub walls that oppose the outward thrust of the roof in lieu of flying buttresses, open from the aisles. The measure of the church is given by its columns, plain octagons in section, which rise to a little more than half the total height of the nave; from their thin capitals, hardly more than rings of gilded molding, spring the ribs of the roof and the Gothic arches of the nave. These ribs are plain stone pipes, and their linear definition against the planes of wall and vault is intensely moving in its abstract purity. The columns of Santa Maria del Mar are very wide apart. In fact their spacing is the widest of any Gothic church in Europe—about forty-three feet apart, center to center. Four of these bays define the nave, and then the rhythm of spacing quickens as eight more columns are planted in a semicircle to define the presbytery, with its altar raised a few feet above the church floor: a grove of stone, whose upper ribs converge in diaphragm arches on the circular keystone. In the morning, the sun strikes in between these diaphragms and dapples them with scribbles and fish scales of color, lifting them in radiance.

The Cathedral of Barcelona presents—at least to this lapsed Catholic—fewer such epiphanies. It is an altogether gloomier building than Santa Maria del Mar; despite its undeniable grandeur, it seems heavier, more blackened, more cluttered. But this clutter contains sublime things, the impacted accumulation of hundreds of years of artistic energy in the service of devotion: if you look past the heavy glitter and foliation of gold leaf in its chapels, at the altarpieces they frame, it soon becomes clear that the Cathedral possesses the richest conspectus of High Gothic Catalan painting—apart from the collection of the Museum of Catalan Art up on Montjuic—in Barcelona. The building is the record of 1,500 years of continuous worship and construction, from the first Christian basilica (built on the heart of the Roman forum, probably in the fourth century, and dedicated to the cult of Saint Severus, a bishop martyred by the Romans in Trajan's time) through to the late nineteenth-century facade, designed by the architects Josep Oriol i Mestres and August Font in a spirit of highly pedantic, Viollet-le-Duc–style revival, based on drawings made in 1408 in Rouen by a French architect named Mestre Carlí (Charles Galtés). This facade, being essentially northern French rather than Catalan, is so predominantly vertical in its lines that it seems out of kilter with the rest of the Barri Gòtic. But it is certainly better than the absurd idea, mooted during the constitutionalist enthusiasms of 1820, of imposing on the Cathedral a neoclassical facade inscribed with texts from the Constitution and the Civil Code.

The first steps in the structure of the Cathedral were taken by the

Santa Maria del Mar, 1329–67

bishop Bernat Pelegri in 1298, during the reign of Jaume II (the Just). Its basic plan was laid down: three naves, each of four bays, and an apse with a half-circle ambulatory behind the high altar, roofed with ogival (pointed) stone vaults. But to stress the antiquity of the worship there, the crypt was strongly emphasized: it opens right in the center of the nave under the altar, a yawning portal with another of those supremely daring, wide, shallow Catalan vault systems to carry the floor above; one goes down a wide flight of steps into the gloom of Saint Eulalia's chapel below, where the remains of Barcelona's patron saint are venerated amid banks of votive candles.

Four chief architects worked on the Cathedral during the Middle Ages. The first was Jaume Fabre, a Majorcan who signed his contract in 1317 and created the apse, the ambulatory, and the great crypt, and perhaps the transept with its two octagonal towers—one over the entrance to the cloister, the other above the portal of Sant Iu (Saint Ives) on Carrer dels Comtes.

The second and major part of the construction was undertaken by Bernat Roca, who worked unremittingly on it for twenty-three years,

Cloister of the Cathedral, Barcelona, in an oil painting by J. Mestres

from 1365 to his death in 1388. He raised (and probably vaulted) the main nave and three out of the four bays of the side naves. He also began the cloister.

The third stage fell to Arnau Bargués, who had already designed the rigorously plain Gothic facade of the Casa de la Ciutat. Between 1397 and 1405 he added the Cathedral's Sala Capitular, now the chapel of Christ of Lepanto: a magnificently proportioned chamber with a star-vaulted roof that rises more than sixty-five feet from the floor. Its cult object is a life-size wooden sculpture of the crucified Christ, made around 1300, whose torso has the characteristic serpentine curve—obeying the natural formation of the tree trunk—of Early Gothic figure carving. This ancient icon was carried before the mast of Don Juan of Austria's flagship at the battle of Lepanto in 1571, during which, as a pious legend explained, it twisted its wooden body into an S shape to avoid a cannonball fired straight at it by the bow cannon of the impious Turk.

The fourth stage, under the supervision of Bartomeu Gual, lasted from 1413 to 1441. It saw the completion of the cloister, the last bay of the nave, and the aisles. But money was running short: Gual also designed (but could not build) the Cathedral's facade and the structure for a *cimbori*, or octagonal dome, that was to rise from the vaults of the first bay of the nave. Both these projects had to wait for completion until the nineteenth century, in a more flamboyant Gothic style than the rest of the building.

One's favorite part of the Cathedral is its cloister, a cool reflective space with its goose pond and fountain, which is the most delicious public haven in the Barri Gòtic. The cloister is tied closely into the folk life and work life of Barcelona. The worn tomb slabs in its floor commemorate dead guild masters, as well as odd figures such as Monsignor Borra, the court jester of Alfons IV (the Magnanimous). It has a fountain, with a battered stone figure of Saint George almost unrecognizable under a green mantle of algae and cresses; it was once the custom to put an empty eggshell on its water jet during the Feast of Corpus Christi so that it danced up and down, but the symbolism of *l'ou com balla* (as it has long been called) is now lost. The cloister's chapels are closed with fine screens and gates of forged iron that date back to the fourteenth century. One of them is dedicated to the patron saint of electricians, and it seems that the cloister has also enjoyed the protection of whichever saint attends to plumbing: it has a working public urinal, which is almost a miracle, given the usual absence of such amenities in Spanish churches.

The feast day on which the cloister came into its own was Corpus Christi, in June, the occasion for *entremesos*—elaborate set pieces and masques that went along with the huge ecclesiastical street procession. Because they were paid for and created by the city guilds, Corpus Christi was the feast that most vividly expressed the liaisons between guild and church. All the main churches of Barcelona had their *entremesos*, but those of the Cathedral were the most splendid and lavish of all. The custom of the procession began in 1320, only four years after Pope John XXII made Corpus Christi a major feast day.

The pavements of the cloister and the streets around the Cathedral were strewn with flowering broom, thyme, rosemary, carnations, and rose petals. Overhead, silk and brocade awnings were stretched from house to house to shield the clergy and maskers from the sun. Inside the cloister, there was a bustle of last-minute preparations, pinning, painting, the strapping on of wicker frames to sturdy shoulders. Then trumpeters issued from the west door of the Cathedral and blew a fanfare; out the procession came, led by the banner of Saint Eulalia and the gonfalons of the Cathedral and the various parishes, the bishop, the priests and vergers, the choir, and then, to the wonder and delight of the crowd, the *entremesos*. These changed from year to year but always mingled the sacred with the profane. In 1461, the program included the Creation of the world; hell, complete with four devils, Saint Michael and a dragon; a battle between twenty-four demons and twenty angels; Adam and Eve; Cain and Abel; Noah's ark, with animals; a dancing eagle with a man inside, symbol of John the Evangelist, that brandished a huge book; and a dozen more scenes from the Old and New Testaments. Then came the climax of the spectacle: the giants and giantesses. The Catalan giant may have been originally modeled on Goliath, but he soon acquired the legendary traits of Charlemagne, who was supposed to have been bearded, uncommonly tall, and invincibly strong. By the sixteenth century the giants of Corpus Christi were twenty feet high, made of canvas and papier-mâché on wooden frames, with gilded plate armor, articulated limbs, lances and cutlasses in their hands, and huge staring eyes that opened and closed. The children in the crowd, pop-eyed in wonder and sticky with sugar water, went into screaming fits when they approached. Their consorts were built on the same scale and robed at the height of fashion by the best modistes in Barcelona, who vied for the privilege of dressing a *gegantessa*. For she, like the rest of the Corpus Christi spectacle, was free advertising for the guilds.

VI

The *gremis*, or guilds, were the core of medieval Barcelona's economic life, the spine around which all productive work was organized. Without inscription in a guild, no man could learn or practice a trade. To be a *menestral*, or skilled craftsman, outside the guild system was inconceivable. The medieval guilds all over Europe determined the rights of workers, supervised their training, enforced quality control, and fixed prices. The idea of the anonymity of medieval craftsmen has more to do with nineteenth-century sentiment than fifteenth-century reality. Good workers knew very well who they were, and their guilds made doubly sure of it. But the guilds' influence went beyond the immediate sphere of work. They negotiated for privileges with the monarch, helped write the city's laws, and even organized its defense in times of crisis— the early citizen militia was drawn from the guilds and run by their officials.

People looking back on the Middle Ages suppose the guilds were quaint, merely because we have no equivalent for them today. Quaint they were not. One has to imagine a system of closed-shop unions with paramilitary powers, slight overtones of the Mafia (in its view of itself as a "family"), and ample connections to the Church, the Corts, and the Consell de Cent. The guild system was wily, powerful, resilient, and jealous of its rights and privileges. It lasted about six hundred years, from the thirteenth to the middle of the nineteenth century, when abstract capital overwhelmed family businesses and factory production began to kill handwork.

All work was done by hand until the end of the eighteenth century, and all workshops were small. Sometimes they were half on the street. They consisted, typically, of one skilled man, the *mestre*, and an apprentice or two, the *aprenents*. These little cells agglomerated. The natural sympathy among workers in the same trade created the intricate, durable *esprit de quartier* of Barcelona, as of other medieval cities. Like hangs out with like; tools need to be shared; if you need to buy a plank of chestnut or a roll of ribbon, and fast, it makes sense to be near other carpenters or upholsterers. Dyers had to be near running water; shoemakers tended to set up shop near tanners, and vice versa. A client wanted to be able to comparison shop among various craftsmen in the same place, rather than zigzag all over the city. It was said, with some truth, that a blind man could find his way around the Barri Gòtic by smell and sound, knowing where he was by the rasp of saws or the clink of hammers on the cooper's bands, the stink of tanning leather, the fresh-hay smell of drying esparto grass in the espadrille makers', or the fumes of forges. These sounds and smells were street signs, and the concentration of similar workers in the same places also enabled them to keep out competition.

In the process, the guilds helped name the city. Walking in the Barri Gòtic today, one comes across their names everywhere, street by street: Agullers (needle makers), Boters (cask makers), Brocaters (brocade makers), Corders (rope spinners), Cotoners (cotton weavers), Dagueria (knife grinders), Escudellers (shield makers), Espaseria (swordsmiths), Fusteria (carpenters), Mirallers (mirror makers), Semoleres (pasta makers), Vidre (glaziers), and many more. They carry on a kind of ghost life in the telephone book as well, because some of the commonest Catalan surnames were trade names—Sabater, for instance, meaning "shoemaker."

The guilds thought of themselves as family organizations. They were grouped in confraternities, of which the three principal ones were the *elois*, the *julians*, and the *esteves*, named after their patron saints, Saint Eloi, Saint Julian, and Saint Stephen. These had some of the functions

Reliquary box of the guild of vegetable gardeners depicting Saints Abdo and Senen, fifteenth century

---

of insurance companies; for instance, they would help out guildsmen who fell sick or lost their tools in a shop fire.

Guilds oversaw the relations between apprentice and master, stipulating what clothing and food and religious training the boy should have, as well as his length of service and the formal requirements of his craft. The ordinances of the guild had to be met. Before an apprentice could get into a guild he had to pass a strict examination, set up in a place open to the public by the guild's inspectors. There was no room for indulgence. Either you passed or you failed; the fetishes of "self-esteem" and "creativity," which bulk so large in art education today, were not in the jury's lexicon. The guild's interest lay in sustaining its own status and that of its members—the dignity of the craft. It enforced high standards of work by making sure that difficult skills were fully acquired before their owner was let loose in the market. The students' diploma designs for this certificate of aptitude were recorded in the *llibres de passantia*, "examination books." If you sought, for instance, to join the silversmiths' guild, which was established in 1381 and set up its exam system in 1471, you first did a design drawing for the "masterpiece"— a word that, before acquiring its loony modern overtones, simply meant a demonstration object that graduated a student into full *mestre* status. If the examiners approved it, you made the thing itself or several variants on it: the painters' guild, for instance, demanded that a would-be member show his skill by making "two paintings on panel, one on ivory, two on horn, one on silver and three on horn and tortoiseshell."

But the guild's interest did not stop at the threshold of membership.

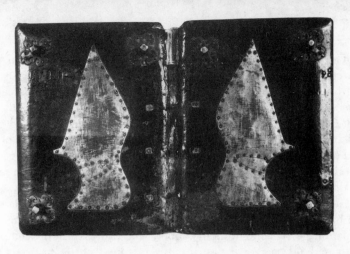

Book cover of Llibre Gremial dels Sabaters, *with brass silhouettes of pointed shoes, fifteenth century*

It kept strict control over the quality of the materials and work of each member, sending nosy inspectors known as *veedors* to make sure that there were no substitutions or shortcuts. If a casket or a shoe, a mantle or a caldron, did not meet their standards, they would destroy it on the spot and hang the mangled remains on the craftsman's door. From this awful public disgrace there was no appeal.

The records of the corporate life of artisans were known as the *llibres gremials*, "guild books": thick volumes kept in special boxes, elaborately bound, with the appropriate emblems, such as a brass silhouette of a pointed shoe for the Gremi dels Sabaters. These were semisacred objects, containing the complete chronological record of the privileges, rights, rules, and membership of each guild.

Though the guilds were not religious organizations, nevertheless they had an exalted sense of their own meaning within the framework of religious life in Barcelona, and for two reasons. The first was that productive work was one of the most common of religious metaphors. Ramon Llull, in his *Llibre de Contemplació de Déu*, had found metaphors of mystic intensity for the sacrifice of Christ in the day-to-day skills of cobblers, leather workers, barbers:

> We see cobblers take leather and stretch it and anoint it, to make it soft; and then we see them cut it and sew it. And so in my mind's eye, Lord, I see how your skin was stretched on the Cross, and bathed in blood and water, and torn and broken and pierced; and there was no man to heal and sew up your wounds.

The second reason was that each guild had close links to the Church—which was, not incidentally, a prime client—through ritual and the cult of patron saints. The Museum of the City of Barcelona preserves, among other guild paraphernalia, the busts of Saint Abdo and Saint Senen and a small piece of the former's leg bone in a sumptuous gold-and-crystal reliquary: these obscure saints were the patrons of the guild of *hortelanos*, or "market gardeners." Banners, masses, processions, ex-votos—all served to reinforce each guild's devotion to its patron saint, and thus its sense of corporate identity. Saint Peter, of course, was the saint of fishermen. Tanners fell under the aegis of Saint John the Baptist, who had worn a goatskin. Animal trainers and horse breakers enjoyed the patronage of Saint Anthony Abbot, who had lived in the company of a tame wild boar. Saint Eulalia, the patroness of the city, was also the saint of those who built it: stonecutters and bricklayers and, by extension, millstone makers. Sant Crist—Jesus himself, who had multiplied the fishes at the Sermon on the Mount—looked after herring salters. Doctors, surgeons, and barbers resorted to Saint Cosmas and Saint Damien, while the legal profession had a whole battery of heavenly advocates: Sant Ivo, Sant Ramon de Penyafort, Saint Andrew of Aveli, and the Madonna of the Mercè.

The most important of all the worker saints was Sant Eloi. He watched over the *mestres d'obra negra*, masters of black work—ironsmiths. Smiths were truculently proud of their profession, as well they might have been: every other trade depended on iron tools, and so did the defense of the state and the whole apparatus of chivalry. "*Per les lletres un noi de baves; / per picar ferro, un home amb barbes*": "For reading and writing, a puling boy / for hammering iron, a bearded man." Ironworking was associated with the origins of Catalunya; the forge and the church were its emblematic sites, and the Pyrenean villages in particular were places of iron:

> *Adéu, vila de Ripoll*
> *entremig de dues aigues:*
> *la meitat son traginers,*
> *l'altra meitat clavetairs.*

> Goodbye, Ripoll,
> between two streams:
> half of you are carters,
> the other half, nailmakers.

Eloi was the medieval John Henry, the Steel-Drivin' Man, and his sanctity was the metaphor of the worker's calling:

> *Sant Eloi—quan era petit era noi;*
> *de mitja—va esser manya;*
> *de mitjancer—va ésser ferrer;*
> *i de gran—va ésser sant.*

A natural evolution: "St. Eloi—when he was little, he was a boy; in youth, a workman; grown up, a blacksmith; and full size, he became a saint."

The iron tradition is fundamental to Catalan culture. In a primal way, iron—the stuff of keys, locks, latches, hinges, armor, and weapons—was the very symbol of Catalunya's collective interest in getting, keeping, and defending. Barcelona was not a great center for precious metals; its silversmiths and goldsmiths, though capable of fine and exact work, never rose to the creative heights of their counterparts in England, France, or Italy (though in the late nineteenth century, this gap closed). But nowhere in Europe was the art of creating direct and sharply expressive shapes from forged and welded metal brought to a higher pitch than in Barcelona between the fourteenth and nineteenth centuries. To visit the old iron collection in the Museu Frederic Marés, or the bewildering proliferation of objects from andirons to imbricated sword hilts and spike-tailed dragons that the *modernista* painter Santiago Rusinyol collected in the late nineteenth century and installed in his private museum in Sitges, is to realize how fantastically various is the language of form that an artisanal tradition can accumulate when it is driven by use and left to its own devices. The truth of the material comes out: its ductility, springiness, sharpness, weight, and fierce linearity. Catalan smiths were "drawing in space" centuries before Julio Gonzalez, who had been trained in their tradition, carried over its direct-welding technique into the domain of formal sculpture and created the syntax of Constructivism in the early twentieth century.

VII

Iron apart, the most vivid memories of any of the past métiers of Barcelona are those of the sea, its maritime essence; and they are preserved in the Drassanes, the ancient shipyards of the city that now house the Maritime Museum—a place as remarkable for its building as for its contents. The site, at the bottom of the Ramblas, gives a clear idea of

Replica of Don Juan of Austria's galley, displayed in the Drassanes

how far Barcelona has filled in its own waterfront in the last half millennium. When they were built in the fourteenth century, the slipways that ran the finished galleys into the harbor stood right on the water; today the Drassanes are landlocked, standing a couple of hundred yards back from the water's edge.

This is the most complete shipyard, and perhaps the most stirring ancient industrial space of any kind, that has survived from the Middle Ages: a masterpiece of civil engineering. The Barcelona shipyards were started in the thirteenth century by Pere II (the Great), and finished (at least in their essential outlines) by an architect named Arnau Ferré, working for Pere II's son Pere III (the Ceremonious), around 1378. In their time they were known as the new shipyards, since they replaced the older and smaller ones the Arabs had built on roughly the same site. To build a large ship you need a large covered space, and that is what the Drassanes afforded: a set of long parallel bays made of brick, their tiled roofs carried on great diaphragm arches. Catalunya had other flourishing shipyards along its coast, at San Feliu de Guixols, Mataró, Blanes, and Arenys de Mar, but none was on such a scale. In these rigorously plain and imposing spaces, the biggest vessels in the Mediterranean were

built. A facsimile of one of them, the *capitana*, or flagship, in which Don Juan of Austria led the Christians to victory over the Turks at Lepanto in 1571, occupies one entire bay, its high deck almost scraping the roof: a sleek baroque war machine encrusted with gilt and red lacquer, 195 feet long, displacing 237 tons, with fifty-eight oars as thick as telegraph poles, each worked by ten slaves.

All around the *capitana* are smaller craft, the workhorses of the Catalan coast; a jumble of *jabegas*, or "xebecs," share the space under its needle prow, and other bays contain a whole family of old fishing craft, whose main form—unchanged since the sixteenth century—is the *llaut*, from whose Catalan pronunciation one gets "yacht," a lateen-rigged, broad-beamed little craft with one jib and a sharply forward-raked mast that gives it an air of tubby eagerness. Its cousins, none of them more than twenty feet long and some as short as fifteen feet, include the sardine netter, the draggers, the day fishermen, and the line setters. Then there are the rowboats, from the minimal *bot* (dinghy) up to the heavy thirty-foot *xavega*, rowed by eight men and used for net hauling, brightly encrusted with red, white, and green paint, its gunwales grooved like an old wellhead by the friction of the net lines.

These basic craft convey the salty risk of Catalan maritime life. They are, so to speak, the common vernacular from which the formal utterances of exploration and conquest arose, symbolized by the bronze figure of Columbus on his pillar just across from the Drassanes. *"Es necessario navegar,"* proclaims a carved poop ornament, with fantastic arrogance, *"no es necessario vivir."* "You have to navigate; you do not have to live." The bravery of those who go down to the sea in ships is an unshakable component of the traditional Catalan self-image, provoking its writers to long dithyrambic flights. Joan Amades, in his immense compendium of Catalan folklore, wrote

> The mariner has a nobility, a marked elevation that make him highly sympathetic . . . to earn his daily bread, he must put his life in continuous danger. Whenever he sets out, he casts his body into a bottomless abyss and is delivered to the mood of the elements, which can be kind and gentle with him, or enraged and vicious; when he embarks, he never knows if he will disembark. The fact that he must constantly gamble with his life, often for nothing, gives him . . . a grandeur of soul which puts him far above the society around him.

No boat owner, of course, would dispute this sage judgment.

The Mediterranean fishery is a poor vestige of its former self today. It was inconceivably rich then. Never again will one see the sights that greeted the eyes of Joan Salvador i Riera, an early eighteenth-century observer who wrote the first treatise on Catalan fishing: the woven architecture (there is no other word for it) of the many-chambered nets hundreds of yards long, anchored to the bottom with rocks and buoyed up with chunks of cork to which shrub pines were lashed as marker buoys—gauzy forecourts and inner rooms hanging in the sea, into which whole schools of tuna would stray and be compressed to a frenzy of foam and chunky thrashing bodies as the walls were drawn closer around them and the *matanca*, the "killing time," approached. Tuna are all but gone from the Catalan seas, as is the red coral that commanded such huge prices in the Middle Ages (and appears, as a symbol of value, among the Virgin's attributes in many a Spanish altarpiece). Coral was sought blindly with undersea rams of curved wood slung fifty feet below the fishing boats, their beaks bumping into rock crevices and knocking off the precious twigs into bags of netting. The twentieth-century invention of scuba gear made them obsolete—and the coral all but extinct. But other devices survived into the nineteenth century and beyond: the intricately woven bell- or cylinder-shaped lobster pots, the purse seines, and even the *palangres*, anchored setlines with hundreds of snelled hooks. For fishing is an intensely conservative craft, and fishermen the most conservative of workers. The invention of plastics, electronics, power winches, and outboard motors changed it radically, but nothing in the repertory of nineteenth-century commercial fishing would have been unrecognizable to a fifteenth- or sixteenth-century fisherman: not the boats, not the gear, and especially not the customs, beliefs, and superstitions of the seamen themselves.

The Catalan mariner was, in many ways, as provincial as any farmer. As late as 1900 it was possible to meet a seaman from, say, Cadaqués near the French border who had been across the Atlantic several times—to Cuba or Venezuela or even New York—and yet had never set foot in Barcelona. Neither fishermen nor sailors took much interest in politics or in public affairs of any kind. In the Middle Ages fishermen were not represented on the Consell de Cent as farmers and merchant commoners were. They did not want to be. They were fixed on the sea, not the land; and their life at sea—each boat being, in some sense, a tiny state—was a rigorously fixed combination of absolutism and communism, sanctified by tradition and impervious to change. Absolutism, because the skipper's word at sea was law; communism, because the division of the catch and the profits among the crew at week's end were strictly equal—though the captain took two shares, one was for him and one for the maintenance of the boat and its gear. A new boy on board,

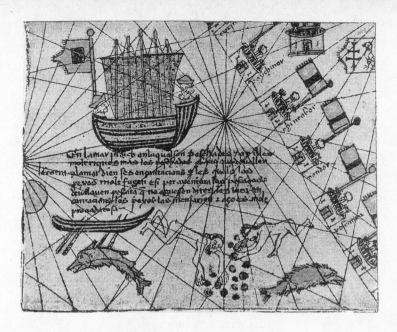

Pearl divers depicted in a Catalan atlas, 1375

even if he was the captain's son, had a two-year apprenticeship: for the first six months he drew a quarter share; for the next, a half; for the third, three-quarters; and then full pay. The rule of equality was symbolized whenever fishermen ate on board. None had an individual plate: each had his own spoon, with which he ate from a communal pot. Generally, the crew kept the best fish for themselves and sent the rest to market. It was a modest compensation for the hard work, danger, and low pay. The fiercely loyal bonding of shipmates was primitive communism because it confronted a common love, a common enemy, the great Giver and Taker. As a popular refrain put it:

> *A la mar*
> *no hi ha teu*
> *ni meu.*
> *A la mar*
> *tot es teu*
> *i tot es meu.*

> At sea
> There is no yours
> Or mine.

> At sea
> All is yours
> And all is mine.

The crew had one indispensable nonhuman member: the ship's cat
—or cats, the bigger and blacker the better. It was the custom to tempt
them on board with a piece of fish and thus shanghai them. The best
cats were always stolen, which gave rise to the saying

> *Farina del moliner*
> *gat del mariner*
> *i gallina di soldat,*
> *no preguntis que han costat.*

> A miller's flour
> a sailor's cat
> a soldier's chicken—
> don't ask what they cost.

Under the maritime law codified in the *Llibre del Consolat de Mar*, a
cargo ship's owner was penalized if he failed to provide a cat and the
vessel proved to be *gastat per rates*, "infested by rats"; the crew had to
have compensation. His only escape was to show that there had, indeed,
been a working cat on board but that it had died after the ship sailed;
its ability as a ratter, perhaps wisely, was not specified by law.

The boat, with its array of lines, pulleys, and other gear, was the most
complicated machine that existed in the Middle Ages, along with the mill.
Proverbially so: "*Per fer de mariner i moliner / Cal molt saber,*" runs one
saying—"To be a sailor or a miller / needs lots of know-how," or:

> There is always something going wrong
> With a mill, a boat and a woman.

And a boat required constant maintenance and respect. It was considered
a sacrilege to use the timber from an old boat for any nonmarine purpose,
and the *gats del mar*—"sea cats," the Catalan equivalents of English "sea
dogs"—used to burn their craft rather than let carpenters dismember
them:

> *La ventura de la barca:*
> *quan es jove, a treballar,*
> *i quan es vella, a cremar.*

A boat's fate:
to work when it is young,
and when old, to burn.

The sea was a field of superstitions, like the land. Never step off the ship with the right foot, only with the left. Carry a piece of coral for luck. Tuna carry drowned men to the beach and leave them there to be found and buried. A manatee skin, hoisted to the mast top, keeps lightning away. The souls of those lost at sea can be glimpsed at dusk, crewing a giant translucent caravel whose ghost captain directs them with blasts on a conch, lugubrious thutterings that can be heard from the horizon and freeze the blood of the living. The best time and place to catch a siren is Saint John's Night off the Costa Brava, and if you can seize her veil, you will be lucky and rich forever. If the *moixonet*, an imp in the form of a milk-white bird, rises from the sea and perches on the rigging, you will have good fishing for a year.

There was no charm or invocation that sailors would scorn; a vast body of apotropaic and prophetic devices is embedded in Catalan sea lore, from the Middle Ages through to the early twentieth century. The sea had its warlocks, known as *cridavents* (wind callers), who could raise a wind from a calm; some did it by shouting, others by singing, others still by waving their hats, and many fishing boats as late as the 1860s were still equipped with *cordes de vent*, "wind ropes"—a length of old blackened halyard with seven nicks cut in it that you swung in an arc, facing the direction from which you wanted the wind to blow. A variant had seven knots, each of which contained a wind: the captain would undo one to release the desired breeze. A prudent skipper would carry a spare, so as not to use up all the wind he had on board. They were very expensive and made by specialist witches, right down to the 1820s.

The worst storms of the year, those of October and November, were the work of demons. Surviving them required special prayers to Saint Francis, whose rope girdle was associated with the ropes of the sailor's craft and served to restrain the sea fiends. Or they were caused by an immense lion that lived in the deep, off Majorca—"*Voga de pressa, que el lleo dorm!*" ("Row quick, while the lion is asleep!").

Naturally, superstition shaded over into religion, with no clear boundary between them. This was true of sailors and fishermen all over Europe. In Catalunya, they would "confess" to the sea by throwing a pebble into it for each of their sins; if the water remained calm, it was a sign of forgiveness, but if the weather went bad, not. Others would throw twelve gourds—which were used as buoys—into the water and read the future in the patterns made by their movement. It was well known that to find the body of a man lost at sea, one took *panets d'ofegat*, or "drowned man's bread" (baked with a cross and a hole in it and blessed on the feast day of Saint Peter, chief patron saint of fishermen), stuck a lighted candle in the hole, and threw it overboard. The candle flame (the soul) would hiss out, but the bread (the body) would float to the spot where the corpse lay and remain there, like a marker buoy. Each family would have as many of these little loaves in readiness as it had fishermen. During the Saint Peter's Day ceremonies the officiating priest would swing his processional cross down to the water without actually touching it, but elsewhere (Sitges, for instance) the cross would be immersed, and there were other ways of blessing and thus controlling the sea: images of the saints were garlanded with every kind of fish, squid, and prawn (as they were with wheat or fruit, inland), and painted or carved Madonnas were taken down from the churches and solemnly dunked in the salt waves. The brotherhood of fishermen bought special bells for the churches: a large one called La Pescadora hung in Santa Maria del Mar, and its tolling was understood to say "Fishermen, to sea!" They would also whitewash the higher bell towers and spires, the better to see them from afar.

As Saint Peter looked after the supply of fish, so Saint Elmo, the other patron of seamen, was in charge of the ship's gear and the fortunes of the crew. Because he appeared as "Saint Elmo's fire"—static electricity glowing from the masthead during storms—his feast day (April 14) was celebrated with games and rituals associated with wood. The most popular was a horizontal variant on the greasy pole, in which a mast, well anointed with grease, would be lashed like a bridge between two anchored boats, and the first lad to walk across it without falling in won a prize. On Saint Elmo's Day the old salts would place pine trees in pots around their boats hauled onto the beach. But the main event was always the procession to Saint Elmo's well, a freshwater spring at the water's edge near the Portal del Mar, where the Nautical School now stands. The priests of Santa Maria del Mar went down to bless the spring each year, and a solemn file of clergy and fishermen issued from the other main church of mariners, the convent of Santa Clara in the Barri Ribera, to pay homage to Saint Elmo's water. (In the eighteenth century, when the convent was demolished on Felipe V's orders to build the Citadel, the cult shifted to the church of Sant Miquel in the newly built parish of Barceloneta.) After the procession reached the well, the sailors took its miraculous water in flasks and sprinkled it on their boats and gear with sprigs of rosemary. This custom began in the thirteenth century and lasted six hundred years; by 1850 it was extinct, victim of a growing liberal skepticism.

The third chief saint of seamen in general and Barcelona fishermen in particular was Saint Eulalia. For good fishing one was well advised to make thirteen visits to her sepulcher in the Cathedral on consecutive Fridays. And if you followed up by kneeling before the votive model of a war galley that hung on a wire from the roof of the chapel of Christ of Lepanto—the chapel with the holy image of the crucified Savior that Don Juan of Austria had carried on his flagship—then you could make doubly certain by noting which way the model pointed and laying the keel for your new boat accordingly. Later, the clergy spoiled this by hanging the little galley on two wires, so that it always pointed the same way.

God and the saints and the Madonna were there to be called on in moments of crisis. "If you want to learn to pray, learn to sail." The waterfront churches of Barcelona, especially Santa Maria del Mar, contained a forest of icons and ex-votos hung up by sailors, nearly all of which were lost in the various epidemics of anticlerical arson that swept Barcelona in the century between 1835, the year of convent burning, and the outbreak of the civil war in 1936. If things got really desperate at sea and the captain was unmarried, he could—as a last resort—swear loudly to God before his crew that if they got home to port he would marry the first woman he saw when he set foot on dry land, no matter how old, rachitic, or poor she was. Thus, especially after storms, spinsters and widows would go in unusual numbers to walk up and down the waterfront in the evenings, watching the sails approach. They gathered in a street off the Plaça de les Olles, which became known as the Carrer de les Dames.

The relation of women to seafaring was not an easy one. The sea was the widow maker and a stingy, dominating mistress in her own right. She kept your man away for weeks, months at a stretch, and condemned wives and sweethearts to fearful uncertainty. The folklore of Barcelona assigned few advantages to sailors' wives:

> *Els pescadors se'n van, se'n van*
> *Cap a la Mora, cap a la Mora,*
> *Els pescadors se'n van, se'n van,*
> *Cap a la Mora tot cantant.*
> *—Ai, mare, quin trico-traco!*

Ai, mare, quin xic tan guapo!
—No t'hi casis, filla, no,
que es un pobre pescador.

The fishermen they go, they go,
Up to Mora, up to Mora,
The fishermen they go, they go,
Up to Mora, all of them singing.
Ay, mother, what a to-do!
Ay, mother, what a handsome boy!
Don't get married, daughter, no,
Not to a poor fisherman.

But of course there were other views on this:

No et casis amb cap ferrer,
que sempre hauras de rentar:
casa't amb un mariner,
que ja va net de la mar.

Don't marry a smith
you'll always have to clean him:
marry a sailor
who comes clean from the sea.

The sea was jealous and it was death to let a woman step on board a boat: *La mar i la dona / no son cosa bona.* On the other hand, the sea could recognize its human sister and display what, five hundred years later, would be called gender solidarity: "*La mar es posa bona / si veu el cony d'una dona*" ("The sea calms down / if it sees a woman's cunt"). So it was not uncommon for fishermen's wives, or occasionally their sweethearts, to expose their privates to the water for luck—although woe betide everyone if a woman pissed in the waves, which brought on particularly violent tempests.

VIII

Folklore and customs change slowly, and endure; politics move faster. Barcelona moved through the fifteenth century like an angry invalid, badly sick, refusing to lie down.

The last member of the house of Barcelona to sit on the throne of Catalunya and Aragon was Martí I (the Humanist), who died in 1410 and left no legitimate heir. The task of finding one was taken on by the papal pretender in France, the antipope, Benedict XIII, who was spurned by most of Christian Europe but still accepted by Aragon. He summoned a conclave. After much debate on the merits of six candidates, it finally chose a Castilian to take the Crown of Aragon. He was Ferdinand of Antequera (1380–1416), son of Juan I of Castile and Elinor of Aragon. Some of the Barcelonese patriciate supported him, but the election was rigged. This choice became known as the Compromise of Casp, after the town where the antipope's committee sat. From now on, the kingdom of Aragon and Catalunya was ruled by Castilians.

The deadly plague epidemics, the collapse of the rural economy, the failure of banks: these were reducing the Crown of Aragon to impotence, even as the fortunes of Castile rose. Plague struck again and again through the fifteenth century, and by 1497 the population of Catalunya, which had stood at perhaps 600,000 before 1350 and 430,000 in 1365, was down to 278,000. All thought of Mediterranean empire was now fantasy. In trade, Genoese capital was beating the Barcelona merchants hands down in the eastern and western Mediterranean alike. Alfons IV of Catalunya (1396–1458) imitated his predecessors' dreams of imperial glory; he did manage to conquer Naples and even installed his court there, styling himself Master of the Mediterranean. But he was not master of Catalunya and Aragon, and the old sense of close compact between the monarch and his people, on which so much had rested, died before he did.

In Barcelona, the hostility of Busca to Biga cracked the civic consensus apart when, in 1453, the Busca finally managed to take over the Consell de Cent and expel most of the patricians from municipal office. In the country the nobles (and the big-city businessmen who owned land) were horrified to find that Alfons IV was earning his nickname, the Magnanimous, by siding with the peasants. Realizing that rural unrest had to be defused if Catalans were to eat, Alfons suspended the "six evil customs" of peasant taxation, the *remences*, in 1455. Such an outcry rose from the *prohoms* that he reinstated these taxes in 1456 and then, the year after that, canceled them again. By now the conservative patricians were ready to break with this vacillating do-gooder, but he died in 1458 and left the throne to his son, Joan II. Joan, however, was also soft on peasants, and the conservatives pinned their hopes to the son of his first marriage, Carles, prince of Viana. Father and son disliked each other so much that Joan II had Charles arrested and imprisoned in

King Ferdinand and Queen Isabella

1460. This grotesque mistake caused a constitutional crisis. What right had a Spanish king, who reigned by agreement with Catalan *consellers*, to imprison their favorite candidate—son or not? Then, most inopportunely, Carles died. The word got out that Joan II had poisoned him. The princeling was laid out in state in the Saló del Tinell, and a bizarre scene ensued: knights rode their war-horses up the steps and around the catafalque, roaring and sobbing, trailing their banners on the stone floor and flinging themselves from the saddle in transports of loyalty and grief.

In 1462, a civil war broke out that lasted ten years—a confused melee between the monarchy and the ruling class in the course of which most of the long-hoarded contractual bonds between throne, Generalitat, and Consell de Cent were ruptured. Joan II won, but it was a Pyrrhic victory. He died in 1479 and left the throne to his next son, Ferdinand II (the Catholic) (1452–1516). And it was Ferdinand who, by marrying the future Isabella I of Castile, brought Catalunya definitively under Castilian sway and wrote finis to the long independence of the principate that had begun, six hundred years before, with Guifré the Hairy. From then on, Catalunya was part of Spain and, with its trade shrinking and its empire in decline, a dependent part at that. By marrying Isabella, the prince of Aragon and Catalunya had created a supermerger of Aragon and Castile, with Catalunya thrown in. Starting with Ferdinand, the kings of Aragon and Castile distanced themselves from Catalunya and its local problems, which were of less weight—offensive, and well-nigh incredible, though this seemed to some Catalans—than those of Spain as a whole.

The symbol of this withdrawal was a new office: that of the viceroy or lieutenant general of Catalunya, whose fortified town house, prudently equipped with corbeled circular lookdowns at the corners of its roof for pouring oil on troubled Catalans, stands in Plaça del Rei and now houses the Archives of the Crown of Aragon. Next to the Palau del Lloctinent is a high arcaded watchtower, anachronistically called the Mirador del Rei Martí (it was built in 1555, nearly a century and a half after Martí the Humanist died). Presumably it received this name because the viceroy's men wanted it to seem the benign legacy of a Catalan king, rather than the observation post of a Castilian one.

In Barcelona, Ferdinand inherited a stagnant capital, plunged in financial gloom. "Today no trade at all is practiced in this city," ran a memorial from its councillors, "not a bolt of cloth is seen; the clothworkers are all unemployed and the other workers the same." Nevertheless one of Ferdinand's first acts was to install the Inquisition, that black tool of Castilian religious terror, in Barcelona. It was his invention; Pope Sixtus IV instituted it in 1478 at his and Isabella's request. The purpose of the Inquisition was to root out Muslims and Jews. Earlier Spanish monarchs had not worried too much about racial purity (*limpieza de sangre*, as it was called in Castile); high Christian families had intermarried with Jewish ones, and Catholic princes had formed pacts and alliances of convenience with Muslims throughout the Middle Ages, without incurring social odium or facing accusations of treason. Toward the end of the fifteenth century this changed dramatically. The Inquisition was a political as well as a religious instrument. Its range of terror was unbounded, since its controlling council, the Suprema, was directly appointed by the Crown and its powers overrode all regional governments and divisions. To be Jewish was heresy, to worship Allah a crime, and "pure blood" the sine qua non of any career. The Inquisition's task was to discover how much undesirable blood a person might have, to issue certificates of purity (without which no public office could be held), and to force Muslims and Jews to convert to Christianity. Those who abjured Islam and embraced the cross were known as *moriscos*, and Jewish converts were called *conversos* or *marranos*. The alternatives to conversion were flight or trial and death, usually by burning alive, in one of the spectacular autos-da-fé, or acts of faith, that the Inquisition staged to remind Spaniards of the impending terrors of the Last Judgment.

Few Muslims lived in Barcelona, but many Jews did, and they were part of the backbone of its financial life. Thus when the Inquisition arrived in Barcelona—its Tribunal sat in rooms of the Palau Reial that are now given over to the Museu Mares; in 1820 these were sacked and burned by indignant liberals—its immediate effect was to push the city's economy closer to the brink, because all the Jews in Barcelona who could afford to move did so rather than convert: they closed their businesses, packed what they could, and fled north to France, taking with them much of the liquid assets of the city's depleted business community.

Ferdinand died with the blood of Spanish Jewry on his hands, if not his conscience; the control of Catalunya was a minor aspect of the administrative problems of the great empire of Castile and Aragon, which now included the lands discovered in the New World by Christopher Columbus, and had devolved upon the Hapsburg emperor Charles V. Over the next two centuries the stream of gold and silver from the Spanish colonies in America would swell the economy of Castile. Catalunya was shut out of this immense plunder. Indeed, it is unlikely that it could have taken advantage of it had it been given the chance: its commercial fleet was now too feeble to sustain transatlantic trade. There were Catalan priests, soldiers, and freebooters among the conquistadores, but all the tons of treasure that were annually shipped back across the Atlantic went directly to Cádiz and thence to the Hapsburg coffers in Madrid.

Nevertheless Barcelona did benefit from the stream, derivatively, because it was now part of the greater state of Castile and Aragon. In any case its civic metabolism was too strong wholly to break down under economic crisis, and so was its belief in itself—however irrational that belief may sometimes have looked from Castile. Trade went on, the guilds flourished and even expanded, and industry, particularly the wool and cotton trades, continued to grow. The burghers enlarged their town houses and commissioned their altarpieces, now in a refined International Gothic style strongly influenced by Flemish prototypes, showing Barcelona glittering behind saints, Virgin, and themselves. The picture of absolute decrepitude is somewhat amended if one looks at the buildings: there was enough free money around in the late fifteenth and early sixteenth centuries, for instance, to build most of the Hospital of the Holy Cross in the Raval (Carrer de l'Hospital 56), one of the largest charitable foundations of its kind in Europe. The handsome sixteenth-century guildhalls—those of the shoemakers and the coppersmiths, which were dismantled to make way for the Via Laietana and rebuilt in Plaça de Sant Felip Neri—bear ample witness to the prosperity of their members. There is not much Renaissance architecture of distinction in Barcelona, compared with its immense fund of Gothic, but this does not mean that the city lacked a humanistic culture. Its literary side had been particularly strong since the fourteenth century. Gradually,

Catalans—some of them, anyway—came to entertain the idea that there was such a thing as a *noblesa* of letters, a sense of culture that descended along a literary tradition, rather than bloodlines; its prototypes lay in texts like Castiglione's *Book of the Courtier* and especially in Erasmus, whose works enjoyed a huge vogue throughout Spain in the 1530s.

You did not have to be born noble; you could *become* noble. This idea, of course, meshed well with the long-standing belief of patrician city families that they did, indeed, constitute an aristocracy, quite as much as the *noblesa castral*. And in some ways the roles of the groups were reversing. Country lords, through the sixteenth century, came in increasing numbers to the city, there to live off their rents under more sophisticated conditions than were afforded by some windy, cavernous, and isolated family fort surrounded by pigsties and muttering peasants in the Ampurdan. At the same time, country properties were being bought by the *ciutadans honrats*, "city burghers," to fulfill their own ideas of squirearchy.

This led to a curious revival of chivalric culture in Barcelona. Needless to say, the ancient orders of the Catalan knights no longer had much practical use by the 1560s: cannons and harquebuses had brought a new level of deadliness to warfare and rendered the man in the steel suit a ceremonial anachronism. In 1571, a fleet of galleys largely manned by Catalans under the command of Don Juan of Austria, bastard son of the Hapsburg emperor Charles V, had taught that lesson to the Turks at Lepanto. But in the age of gunpowder, chivalry returned to Barcelona in a decorative, *sportif* form. Annual tourneys were held from 1565 on —charges, armor, pennons, ladies looking on, and wooden-tipped lances. It was a preview of the nostalgic mania for chivalry that pervaded the culture of the Catalan Renaixença three centuries later. It was accompanied by the same jockeying for titles among the bourgeoisie.

The Catalans had always been interested in what the English were up to—there are, for instance, late-twelfth-century frescoes in the church of Santa Maria in Terrassa that depict the murder of Thomas à Becket in Canterbury in 1170. But now the desire to be *molt Anglès* gave Barcelona a new saint: the patron of Barcelona's perennial Anglophilia and, more generally, the result of the new interest with which Spain in general, having an emperor who reigned over the north as well, was looking at northern Europe.

This was Sant Jordí—Saint George, whose armored figure, spitting the dragon on his lance, came to infest the walls, altars, chimneypieces, ceilings, pediments, escutcheons, tiles, capitals, stained-glass windows, plumbing details, printed menus, and chocolate wrappers of Barcelona

Silver statue of Saint George, in the chapel of the Generalitat

from the late sixteenth century on. Probably he never existed (hagiographers have long been divided on this), but, if he did, he was martyred in the fourth century at what is now the Israeli town of Lod (ancient Lydda). Presumably no Catholics, and Catalan ones least of all, speculated that he might have been a Jew. His cult rose first in England and reached Barcelona later. He had been associated with Catalo-Aragonese chivalry quite early—Pere I (the Catholic) founded an order of the Knights of Saint George in 1201, and Pere III (the Ceremonious) favored devotion to him. But there were no relics of him in Barcelona, no church was dedicated to him, and he seems to have lacked a widespread cult until the late sixteenth century, when he came in, as warriors should, with a vengeance and took the city by storm. The chapel of the Generalitat enshrines a fine small silver figure of Saint George, a reminder that it was the Generalitat itself that promoted his cult: in 1574 it got Pope Gregory XIII to issue a plenary indulgence for prayers on his feast day, April 23, and in 1667 Clement IX made Saint George's Day a holiday throughout Catalunya.

It was this chivalry-obsessed city that Cervantes saw, recuperating after the battle of Lepanto. He wrote a litany of praise to it, which now seems to have had an ironic edge. If so, the Catalans have always ignored it. To them, it is obvious truth, though of course it is nice to hear it from a Castilian once in a while:

> Barcelona, honor of Spain, alarm and terror of enemies near and far, luxury and delight of its inhabitants, refuge of foreigners, school of chivalry, and epitome of all that a civilized and inquisitive taste could ask for in a great, famous, rich and well-founded city . . . school of courtesy, travelers' rest, protector of the poor, home of the brave, vengeance of the injured and happy meeting-place of close friendship.

Nevertheless, despite the sophistication, the later sixteenth and seventeenth centuries remain known to Catalans as La Decadencia. Partly this was because the culture of Barcelona was slack; it has no late Renaissance or baroque buildings to compare with what was being built in Italy or in other parts of Spain; when Castile was up, creating its Golden Age in the seventeenth century, Catalunya was down. In painting, it produced nothing but late, provincial reruns of what had been done better elsewhere; there was no Catalan equivalent to Velázquez, Ribera, Zurbarán, or El Greco.

But more fundamentally, there was the political question of rights. The decline of the institutions of Catalan independence was well under way by the seventeenth century. "If not, not" was a phrase no one dared use with Hapsburg viceroys, and Catalunya's absorption into the kingdom of Castile meant that its local *furs* and *drets*, however ancient, began to lose their primitive force. Rights, as far as the Hapsburg monarchs in Madrid were concerned, were issued at the royal will; there was nothing permanent or irrevocable about them. "Pactism" was not in their vocabulary. The past traditions and present desires of the provinces must bow before the interests of a united, integrated Spain, centered on Castile.

Such, in particular, was the view of Felipe IV's formidable minister of state, Gaspar de Guzmán, count-duke of Olivares (1587–1645). This brilliant, driven authoritarian, both quixotic imperialist and pragmatic organizer, had set out to transform the political face of Spain. His plan was to create a uniform system of laws, military levies, and taxation that would apply everywhere, no matter what the still-powerful local Corts of Aragon, Valencia, and Catalunya might say or want. Many realms, but one law. Olivares was not so naïve as to imagine that this could be done all at once, by fiat. More offices must be given to powerful men from the provinces; the closed shop of Madrid preferment must be opened, and the king must get out into the country, showing himself to his subjects, creating loyalty. There would be opposition, he realized, so the process must be done by stages. Olivares thought that a good way to start would be to create a kind of military bond among the various provinces of the Hapsburg empire—the Union of Arms, which would produce a tributary standing army of 140,000 men. For the Hapsburg realm was facing bankruptcy: the Thirty Years War, which broke out in 1618, was bleeding it white. In 1624 Olivares wrote down his quotas. The core of the new army would come from Castile and the Indies— 44,000 men. Valencia would raise 6,000, Milan 8,000, Aragon 10,000, and Portugal, Naples, and Catalunya most of all: 16,000 men apiece.

If this was meant to be the thin end of the wedge of unification, the Catalans received it as a hammer blow. Olivares apparently did think Catalunya could spare that many conscripts to fight in a foreign war. He had been badly misinformed by his own viceroys, who had shown nothing but arrogance and incompetence in dealing with Catalan problems and had given Olivares the impression that Catalunya had a population of one million, whereas the true figure was closer to three hundred thousand. The rural counties of the province were still depopulated and exhausted. Banditry, known as *bandolerisme*, was rampant; the country roads of Catalunya swarmed with rapacious footpads organized in gangs, some with the glimmerings of a political agenda, others just out for what they could steal from travelers and farms. *Bandolers* even raided the outskirts of Barcelona itself, and some city traders made a percentage laundering loot for them. One memorable day in 1613 a bandit named Barbeta, who had a Robin Hood–like renown, managed to hijack a whole mule train laden with silver on its way to the Hapsburg bankers—and stood there in the road, handing ingots to the peasants. The *bandolers*, like the early Mafia in Sicily, did a lot of dirty work that *ciutadans honrats* wanted done but would not touch. If Catalans were too weak to protect themselves against this epidemic of ruffians at home, why should they be rounded up to fight in Madrid's war abroad?

Felipe IV made a royal progress to Barcelona, staged-managed by Olivares. In his presence the Corts was assembled for the first time in twenty years. Carrots were dangled: Barcelona would have new Madrid-financed trading companies after it joined the Union of Arms. These blandishments failed. The Catalans would not cooperate. Felipe IV,

Pau Claris, in a nineteenth-century engraving

stiffly bemused by his subjects' mulishness, returned to Madrid; Olivares issued new orders to the viceroy to raise money and men by all means possible, however grinding.

In 1635 war broke out between France and the Hapsburg Austrian empire. A good part of the border between France and Spanish Hapsburg territory lay in Catalunya, and the Catalans seemed disinclined to fight; it was almost as though they welcomed the French (as indeed many of them did). Since Spain was more desperately short of money and men than ever, Olivares redoubled his efforts to squeeze the Catalans and proposed to launch his main attack on France from Catalan territory, thus leaving these fractious provincials no choice about which side they were on. But in 1639 the French moved first and captured the fortress of Salses in the Roussillon, Catalan territory. Olivares besieged it with a force largely made up of press-ganged Catalan troops, while his viceroy in Barcelona, the fuddled count of Santa Coloma—Catalan himself and a detested quisling—struggled to wring more taxes and military levies from the groaning province. All pretense of respect for Catalan autonomy went by the board as Olivares, through Santa Coloma, imposed what amounted to martial law on the province. The siege of Salses was a long, nightmarish bungle, although the French surrendered after six months. By the spring of 1640 everyone in Catalunya who had not hated Olivares before, this time including the *noblesa*— which had lost many sons and fathers under the walls of Salses—hated him now. Even the Catalan clergy, usually slow to protest, turned against Olivares and the king; their leader was Pau Claris (1586–1641), canon of Urgell, who had become president of the Generalitat in 1638.

Olivares was so pleased with the victory at Salses that he failed to see it had brought Catalunya to the verge of rebellion. He decided to go on with the Union of Arms. He would keep Castilian troops in Catalunya to force a meeting of the Corts, which (or so Olivares assured his monarch) would repeal the constitutions that impeded the full levying of Catalan troops to defend the Hapsburg empire. He therefore ordered that the Salses army should be billeted on Catalan farmers and townspeople until the Corts convened.

Francisco Maria de Melo, a Portuguese officer in Felipe IV's army —and not, one may assume, especially biased in favor of the Catalans —described the behavior of the *tercos*, or troops, once they were let loose on the countryside to forage for themselves. "There was no outrage that they did not consider licit," he noted,

> they ranged freely around the country without treating it any differently from occupied territory, trampling its crops, stealing its livestock, oppressing its villages . . . the officers of the royal troops, infected by the same lack of restraint and the same ambition, neither restrained the soldiers nor gave any compensation to the peasants. . . . All the outrage and discontent of noble and plebeian alike was centered on the oppression of their Fatherland; at times the mourning and unutterable sorrow bore witness to endless death and disaster.

This truly solipsistic error set off a general rising known (because its main force was the peasantry) as the Guerra dels Segadors, the Reapers' War, a patriotic bloodbath that lasted until 1652.

It was sparked by Santa Coloma's arrest of one of Pau Claris's fellow deputies on the Generalitat, Francesc de Tamarit. At once the countryside rose in arms; a band of enraged rebels marched straight into Barcelona, broke into the prison and freed him. Olivares, at last realizing that he had a revolution on his hands—another front in Castile's desperately overextended wars—tried to pacify the Catalans, but it was too late. In June 1640, Barcelona was full of casual laborers, sickles slung in their belts, hoping as usual to hire themselves out for harvest work at its central labor market. They began to riot. City workers joined them. Guards fled for their lives as the mob turned on the viceroy's palace and the ministers' houses, sacking and burning them. Santa Coloma, hoping to find a boat and sail to safety, hid in the shipyards of the Drassanes, but the crowd winkled him out, chased him down to the waterside, and bashed him to death on the rocky beach.

Over the next few years, most of the province dissolved in anarchy. The failure of Catalunya was that it could not make common cause with Aragon or Valencia. If the three states of the ancient kingdom of Aragon had combined against Castile at this point, they could probably have beaten back the enfeebled Hapsburg forces and re-created their old power bloc. But all three were rendered incapable of doing so by their deep-seated provinciality and mutual suspicions. Instead, Pau Claris, who had emerged as the charismatic leader of the Catalans in the first year of the war, pointed them toward an alliance with the French, who were only too happy to intervene. The Generalitat proclaimed a new count-king of Barcelona: Louis XIII of France. The French army marched into Barcelona and, with the Catalan forces, inflicted a severe defeat on the Hapsburg army upon the hill of Montjuic.

The Reapers' War was finally settled by compromise. Most of the French army withdrew from Catalunya by 1648, taking the province of Roussillon for their trouble; that was the end of Catalan territory north of the Pyrenees. Henceforth they were execrated by pious Catalans for "desertion." Felipe IV's forces starved Barcelona into surrender in the autumn of 1652—which was lucky for them, as they hardly had the strength to muster a direct assault on its walls. Felipe IV had no wish to take revenge on the defeated city: he still needed its allegiance and its taxes. So against the advice of counselors in Madrid he insisted on leaving the Corts and the constitutions in place, and there was a general amnesty. The *ciutadans honrats* went back to business, having learned one particularly important lesson from the war: that peasants, their social inferiors, were dangerous, unreachable, and needed to be repressed. The people who suffered most and gained least from the Reapers' War were the reapers themselves.

The Reapers' War is remembered as one of the archetypal struggles of Catalan independence, and so it was, but it was a dreadful time to live through, and the province emerged from it, inevitably, in even worse shape than it had been under Olivares, whose political career was destroyed by it. It left behind it a trail of devastation and one perennially popular anthem, "Els Segadors," which was, however, written in the late nineteenth century:

Ara és hora, segadors!
Ara és hora d'estar alerta!
Per quan vinqui an altre juny,
esmolem ben bé les eines!

Bon cop de falc!
Bon cop de falc,
si el blat ens volen prendre!
Bon cop de falc!

Now is the hour, reapers,
The time to be on your guard!
For when June comes round again,
we'll sharpen our tools well!

A good sickle-cut!
A good sickle-cut
if they want to take our wheat!
A good sickle-cut!

IX

The Catalans had defied the weak rule of the Hapsburgs and emerged, battered, with their basic institutions intact. They were not so lucky with the Bourbons, fifty years later.

It would be cruel and unusual punishment to immerse the reader deep in the details of the War of the Spanish Succession. But since it led directly to the conquest of Catalunya and the destruction of its political forms, it requires a brief sketch. Much simplified, what happened was this.

Carlos II, monarch of Spain and last king of the house of Hapsburg, died in 1700: a pathetic creature, half-mad, convulsed with fits and surrounded by charismatics and confessors. His two barren marriages had produced no Hapsburg heir. Four major powers, England, Holland, Austria, and France, were scheming well before his death to install their candidates on the Spanish throne.

England and Holland were set against an Austrian or a French successor. Accordingly, they backed a Bavarian prince, Joseph Ferdinand, grandson of the infanta Maria Teresa.

Austria wanted another of the infanta's grandsons, Archduke Charles, son of Holy Roman Emperor Leopold I.

France supported a prince from its house of Bourbon: Philippe d'Anjou, grandson of Louis XIV, the Sun King.

Carlos II himself favored the Bavarian Joseph Ferdinand, but his German queen—a termagant, who believed she could bully the ailing monarch as she chose—wanted the Austrian pretender, Archduke Charles.

There seemed to be no solution to this lock, and so, even before Carlos's death, the major powers signed a secret treaty to divide the Spanish realm among all three. But this was leaked to Carlos, who, whatever his deficiencies as a king, would not see his realm dismembered. He immediately flew into a rage and declared for his choice, the Bavarian candidate, Joseph Ferdinand. This was in 1698. But next year, with abominable timing, Joseph Ferdinand died. That left the Austrian and the Frenchman, and Carlos in 1700 willed his state to the latter. France was the most powerful state in Europe; a French king of Spain would unite the two realms and save the peninsula from political dissolution. Six months later the last Hapsburg monarch died. Philippe d'Anjou, first of the Spanish Bourbon dynasty, made his triumphal entry into Madrid in April 1701, taking the name of Felipe V.

England, Holland, Austria, and Savoy viewed his accession to the throne with horror. They saw the union of France and Spain producing a menacing superstate with instant hegemony over Europe. They declared war, meaning to throw Felipe V off the Spanish throne and replace him with Archduke Charles of Austria. Such was the War of the Spanish Succession that convulsed Europe from 1701 to 1714.

Catalunya backed the wrong side. It had its reasons, most of them bad. In effect, its ruling classes had been bought off by the Hapsburgs' relative magnanimity in the fifty years since the Reapers' War, and Catalunya, on one of its pendulum swings between obstinate revolt and nest-feathering obedience to external rule, had displayed an effusive loyalty to them. But more than that, a deep popular loathing of France now came to be shared by the *ciutadans honrats*, when they saw what Felipe V's political proclivities were. (The views of the Catalan aristocracy no longer mattered; in the past two centuries all its daughters had been married off to Castilian nobles like the dukes of Medinacoeli and taken the family estates as dowry, so that the *noblesa castral*, deprived of breeding power, was to all intents politically extinct.) Felipe IV and Olivares had been unable to impose centralized rule on the province— Madrid's coffers and army were too enfeebled for that—but Felipe V was an iron-willed centralist, born and bred. He had inherited his grandfather Louis XIV's near-religious passion for the centralized state, all its strings of power running straight back to the monarch and his ministries.

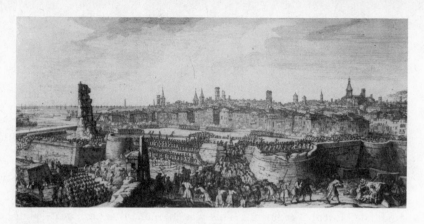

The siege of Barcelona, 1714

During thirteen years of war he steadily reconstructed Spain along centralist lines. Still, Felipe V wanted amicable relations with the Catalans if possible and was prepared to go a long way to gratify them: at first, anyway.

In 1702 he paid a state visit to Barcelona. The Catalan Corts was convened, for the first time in a generation, to swear allegiance to him —its last session had been thirty years before, and in indifference and complacency it had allowed itself to lapse. The king unfurled what amounted to a program of Catalan autonomy. He gave back to Catalunya the counties of Cerdanya and Roussillon, north of the Pyrenees. He described the principality as "free and independent" and spoke of a "Catalan nation," united by ancient custom and a common language with Valencia and the Balearics. He declared Barcelona to be a free port, whose ships might trade (on a restricted basis) with the Spanish colonies in the Caribbean.

The Catalans mulishly refused to believe a word of this, and so there is no way of knowing whether Felipe V would have honored his promises. Irked by the lack of response among his subjects, he tightened the ratchet of power by appointing, as viceroy, a singularly arrogant and stupid Castilian noble, Francisco Fernández de Velasco, the duke of Frías, whose blunders soon destroyed any disposition Catalunya had to believe Felipe V's promises.

The Catalans now wanted the Hapsburg pretender, the archduke Charles, more than ever. In a ceremony in Vienna in September 1703, Charles was proclaimed Charles III, king of Catalunya and Aragon as well as Castile. By 1705 he seemed to be winning the war, and the Catalans formally declared their loyalty to him. They also naïvely signed

Statue of Rafael Casanova, Barcelona

a treaty with England. Perfidious Albion promised to support their war against the Bourbons with its Mediterranean fleet, but (not for the first or last time) it was to renege on the deal. That November Charles III entered Barcelona with his composite multinational army, and at first things went well for him. He marched from Barcelona to Madrid, but the *madrileños* hated Charles as much as the Catalans loathed his rival, and his attempted coup failed. Felipe V counterattacked, drove Charles back to Valencia, and defeated his army there at the battle of Almansa in the spring of 1707. The badly mauled Charles recoiled to Barcelona, and Felipe showed Catalunya what lay in store for it by depriving Aragon and Valencia of all their liberties and rights.

This only stiffened the resolve of the Catalans, who, having so imprudently entered the war, fought on to its end with an almost kamikazelike heroism that transcended all questions of *seny* and self-interest. They had no one to turn to. Charles III beat a dignified retreat north from Barcelona in 1711, leaving his wife behind as regent. In 1713 the war-weary English government made peace with France and with Felipe

V, leaving Catalunya in the lurch. In March 1714 Charles (who had now, through the unexpected death of his brother, become Holy Roman Emperor Charles VI and could deal with the Bourbons as an equal) signed a peace treaty with Felipe V. Only Catalunya was left, fighting on without its big allies for a lost cause. And of Catalunya, by the summer of 1714, only Barcelona still held out against the Bourbon army, which, due to the disappearance of British ships, was supported by a naval blockade of the port as well.

The city had only about ten thousand soldiers, whose numbers were soon whittled down by gunfire, famine, and disease. But every citizen who could carry water to the walls or throw a rock was united with them in an agonized fanaticism that mounted during the months of the siege. Every male over the age of fourteen was issued arms by the Catalan commander, Antoni de Villaroel. The Bourbon army was led by the bastard son of James II of England, James Stuart, duke of Berwick (now duke of Liria as well, for his services in crushing the Hapsburg force at Almansa seven years before). Extraordinary moments of bravery were witnessed, particularly when the fifty-four-year-old Rafael de Casanova i Comes, a lawyer and the last *conseller en cap* of Barcelona, raised the standard of Saint Eulalia and led a last-moment counterattack from the walls on the last day of the siege. Villaroel repeatedly threatened to resign his command because the citizens of Barcelona refused to listen to any of Berwick's offers of clemency in return for surrender; and the Council of One Hundred—which now controlled all civil power in Barcelona, since the Diputació had just voted to dissolve itself—was so flown with religious exaltation that it issued a formal order making the statue of the Virgin of the Mercè commander in his stead. But although she had saved Catalunya from a plague of locusts in 1687, she could not produce the necessary miracle now.

CHAPTER FOUR

Under the Citadel

I

Barcelona surrendered to the Bourbons unconditionally on September 11, 1714, a date that incongruously remains the national day of Catalunya. Catalan nationalists from the nineteenth century on wrote about their eighteenth century as a period of repression, during which little that was good—in politics, economics, law, language, or the arts—happened in Barcelona. The legend of eighteenth-century "Bourbon tyranny" remains strong at all levels: not so long ago Catalan children, on their way to the lavatory, spoke of "going to visit Felipe," meaning Felipe V, the hated Bourbon monarch. But all this should be taken with a pinch of salt. Certainly there was no shortage of Castilian hotspurs who wanted to see the "treasonous" Catalans punished to the limit, and their city razed as Carthage had been by the Romans. But Felipe V did nothing of the kind, and once the immediate ceremonies and cruelties of Berwick's victory were over, the citizens of Barcelona —especially the middle classes—settled down quite comfortably with the Bourbon government for the next hundred years and prospered from the opportunities its policies gave them. To cast this occupation in twentieth-century terms—to imagine a ruthlessly exploited Catalunya groaning under the yoke of Madrid, as France suffered under the Nazis or Poland under the rule of Moscow—is wrong, however inspiring it has been to the rhetoric of Catalan separatism.

Nevertheless, war is war and conquest conquest. As marshal and ruler of the prostrate city, Berwick's orders from Felipe V were simple. The Catalans must learn what their bet on the wrong side now entailed.

He was to abolish the political framework of the Catalan state, so that the principate could be governed directly from Madrid. Any sign of rebellion—not that Barcelona, half-starved and worn out by the siege, had much stomach for resistance—was to be harshly put down.

Villaroel got away, and Casanova managed to hide on his property outside Barcelona. Berwick hanged one of the rebel leaders, Moragues, and his chief officers, quartered them, and set their heads up on poles at the main gates of the city. (Moragues's remained on view for twelve years.) A number of the resisters were buried in a mass grave next to Santa Maria del Mar—now marked by a monument erected in 1974, a low red granite wall toward which a fan-shaped plaza descends, inscribed with the words from a verse by the popular poet Serafí Pitarra:

> Al fossar de les Moreres
> no s'hi enterra cap traidor,
> fins perdent nostres banderes,
> sera l'urna de l'honor.

> In the Moreres cemetery
> no traitor is buried:
> even though we lose our flags
> this will be the urn of honor.

Some four thousand surviving Catalan troops were imprisoned or deported. It was death to try to leave Catalunya without a passport, although thousands managed to flee to Minorca and Majorca in fishing boats in the hope of getting even farther away on British vessels headed for other Mediterranean ports.

In Barcelona, all towers, magazines, barracks, fortifications, and redoubts that were not royal property were torn down, a demolition that prefigured the Bourbon razing of Catalan political institutions. The instrument for that was the Decree of the New Plan, promulgated by José Patiño, who in 1714 became the president of the Royal Committee of Justice and Government.

Patiño knew Catalunya well, and he knew what he was up against with the Catalans; he saw their stubbornness, their hardheadedness, their litigiousness, and their pride and was determined to beat them all down so that they would submit to the king "if not by allegiance and love, then through force of arms." Catalunya, he reported to Felipe, was

immensely fruitful in the hard work and concentration of its people; it is heavily populated, not in the number of its towns, but in the multitude of little villages, which are scarcely subjected at all to the rule of justice and education, bereft of teaching and politics, brought up without obedience and with few religious impulses. . . . The spirit of the natives lies in their love of liberty, their fondness for all kinds of weapons; they are quick to anger, touchy and vengeful. And one must never trust them, because they are always plotting and planning to evade the yoke of justice; they are full of self-interest.

So nothing of their laws and administration must remain. The New Plan abolished both the Diputació—which had already voted itself out of existence shortly before Berwick's troops came marching in—and the ancient Council of One Hundred. In future, the king in Madrid would rule Catalunya like the rest of Spain, through his appointed proconsuls, the much-hated *corregidors*. There were a dozen of these officials, none of them Catalan, each presiding over one of the twelve newly designated provinces of Catalunya. (These were Barcelona, Mataró, Tarragona, Cervera, Lleida, Vilafranca del Penedés, Manresa, Vic, Puigcerdá, Girona, Tortosa, and Talarn.) The New Plan took away whatever remained of the old Catalo-Aragonese territories in the Mediterranean: Minorca, Sicily, Sardinia, and Naples. It annulled all the *drets* and *furs*, or ancient entitlements, that had been jealously preserved since the Middle Ages and that Catalan patriots after 1830 constantly invoked in a mood of truculent nostalgia.

The New Plan imposed a new tax system, the Cadastre. Patiño knew how the stingy Catalans, who hated giving a penny in tax even to a state they called their own—let alone to a conquering foreign power—would receive this. For centuries, Catalans had been suing for tax relief through the Corts "and," Patiño noted, "there is nothing they resent so much as having taxes imposed on them by royal authority." It would not be so easy to find out their net worth, either: Catalans tended to look poorer than they were, not the other way around, as in Madrid.

So Patiño taxed them across the board. All private property in Catalunya was assessed for a 10 percent tax on its value. Workers had to pay 8.5 percent of their salary, based on a working year of one hundred days for peasants and day laborers and one hundred and eighty for artisans. Only the clergy, the nobility, children under fourteen, and men over sixty were exempt. If you were slow to pay, the Castilian troops came visiting. One taxpayer, Francesc Doblet, lamented that his own farm had to disgorge one hundred *lliures* in ten months—"and there are some peasant farms around here that have parted with 300 *lliures* in a year. They say that the whole province pays 15,000 *dobles* a day. I don't know where all the money comes from. . . . May Our Lord take pity on our labors, because otherwise I don't know what will happen."

The New Plan also set out a rather ineffectual program of cultural repression. Its main target was the Catalan language. Patiño saw clearly that language was the key to patriotic sentiment. "They feel the deepest love for their country, with such excess that it deranges their powers of reason and they speak only in their native tongue." Catalan was the speech of otherness, so Castilian must replace it; then, it was to be hoped, rebellious thoughts would wither and die.

So to ensure that the future elite of Catalunya would have no independent intellectual life, Felipe V issued a decree in May 1717 closing all the Catalan universities. In their place, he created the University of Cervera, in a paltry town of some two thousand inhabitants on the Madrid–Barcelona road that did not even have a library. But it was one of the few Catalan towns that sided with Berwick's troops, and as a mark of esteem large sums were lavished on its new college, known somewhat optimistically as the Bourbon Athens. It ran for one hundred and twenty-five years and was closed down in 1842, a victim of resurgent Spanish liberalism. In its lugubrious heyday, which lasted until Carlos III's expulsion of the Jesuits from Spain in 1767, Cervera was run by the Inquisition and the Society of Jesus. Lectures were given in Latin and Castilian. Its students were watched for heterodoxy and drilled in a ponderous curriculum that bore very little relation to the real world. Its faculty of medicine was probably the last in Europe to forbid the dissection of human bodies, and its courses consisted mainly of reading Galen, the "Father of Medicine," who had died in A.D. 199. Not surprisingly, the University of Cervera failed to cover itself with intellectual glory. It is remembered mainly for its chancellor's remark in an address to Ferdinand VII that marked the nadir of academic life in Spain. "*Lejos de nosotros,*" intoned that worthy, "*la funesta manía de pensar*"—"Far be from us the dangerous craze for thought." Intellectuals in Barcelona, meanwhile, used to say that the bells of Cervera sang a couplet: "*Tots ho som de botiflers, / La campana tambe ho es*"—"We are all traitors, and so is the bell."

In fact, neither the destruction of the Catalan universities nor the general ban on publication in Catalan—never a big business anyway—reduced the prevalence of the language. Most universities in Europe before the eighteenth century taught in Latin anyway, and at the College of Cordelles in Barcelona the Jesuits had been promoting Castilian over Catalan as the proper language of erudition for at least a century.

As a *literary* language, the tongue of formal public declamation,

Catalan seemed dead. But with a few exceptions, most "high" Catalan writing was moribund anyway—pompous and artificial, stuffed with florid *elegantiae*, bearing little relation to speech. Through the eighteenth century, Catalans liked to ridicule the priests who gave their Sunday sermons in Castilian, or new-rich people who spoke it to everyone but the servants because it sounded classier. Academic life, such as it was, was so insulated that it had little effect on the general culture, and most Catalans, like most people elsewhere in eighteenth-century Spain, could not read or write. They cared no more about what was going on in literary circles than Joe Sixpack cares about Jacques Derrida today. They just got on with speaking their vernacular. They had always spoken Catalan, and no edict could stop them. It named everything in their lives. The rhythm, syntax, resonance, and idioms of Catalan were all retained in speech: there was nothing Madrid could do about it. Catalan remained, not as some antiquarian fossil, but as a living vernacular, until the romantic writers of the nineteenth century turned it to literary uses once again.

II

Francesc Doblet noticed something apart from the Bourbon taxes. All his neighbors who had oak trees were losing them to logging parties of Berwick's soldiery. As the axes rang and the bullocks strained to drag the trunks down the rough roads to Barcelona, Doblet heard a rumor: the occupation army was building a huge fortress in Barcelona, in which it would stay forever.

This turned out to be true. Most of the tax was going, not to Madrid, but into the construction of the Ciutadella, the Citadel of Barcelona, designed by a Dutch military engineer named Prosper Verboom. Its girdling wall was finished by 1718 and the barracks, stores, and arsenals soon after. The whole complex remained a hated symbol of Castilian rule for a century and a half, and though it had been built in five years, it took the best part of twenty years' work to demolish. The huge pentagon, with a bastion at each of its five angles, enclosing some 150 acres, dominated the port and the city: Felipe V's army could simply ensconce itself behind its frowning walls and bombard Barcelona to rubble and splinters with their heavy mortars, which could throw a ball almost as far as Montjuic, on the far side of the harbor, and reach any target within

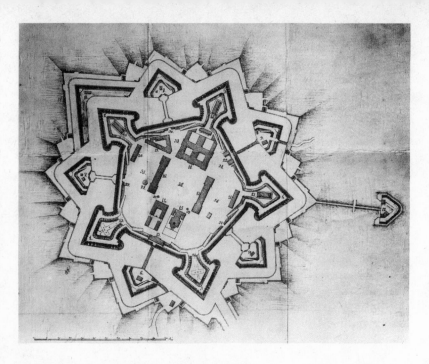

The Citadel of Barcelona and its exterior bastions, built in 1715–20

the city itself. By 1842, the military installations of Barcelona covered almost as much land as its civilian buildings. The city became one enormous fort.

In order to build the Citadel, the occupying army razed nearly all the old maritime quarter, the Ribera. Convents, hospitals, and some 1,200 houses were demolished without compensation to their owners. In the late 1880s, as the Citadel itself was at last razed to make a public park, the poet-priest Jacint Verdaguer would look back on these days of humiliation:

> Tenyit de sang encara, rugint com un fera,
> lo rei se'n baixa al barri famós de la Ribera
> davant sos granaders:
> —Deixau aqueixos glavis, preneu magalls i relles
> —los diu—, i enderrocau-les, aqueixes cases velles,
> catau de bandolers.
>
> Arreu arreu s'ajauen los grossos casalicis,
> los monestirs, escoles i emparadores hospicis,
> lo temple i l'hospital;

a rengles los tuguris s'aplanen en la sorra
i el mes joios dels barris barcelonins s'esborra
com xifra en un sorral.

Quan ja no en queda rastre com d'aigua escorreguda,
d'aquelles pedres, ossos de la ciutat volguda,
n'aixequen un castell,
lo de la malastruga i odible Ciutadela,
que naix a Barcelona com una erisipela,
enmig d'un rostre bell.

Boltered with blood, roaring like a wild beast,
the King goes down to the famous Ribera quarter
before his grenadiers:
"Drop your swords, take up hoes and ploughs,"
he says, "And tear down these old houses,
these bandits' lairs."

Around, around lie the great mansions,
the monasteries, the schools, the shelters,
the church and the hospital:
row by row the shacks are flattened into the sand
and the happiest quarter of Barcelona is erased
like a number drawn on the beach.

When, like water drained away, no trace remains
of these stones, the bones of the beloved city,
they build a fortress,
the ill-fated and hateful Citadel,
born in Barcelona like erysipelas
in the middle of a lovely face.

The destruction of Ribera settled down deep into popular memory.
Barcelona seemed to be crouching under the shadow of this symbol
of absolute Bourbon power, pincered between it and the fort on top of
Montjuic, which was enlarged and rebuilt as well. Popular songs, of
course, recorded its ominous presence in daily life:

He vist, he vist, he vist,
dalt de la Ciutadella,
com es gronxa el penjat
d'una creu greuxa.
El pare m'ha donat
una gran plantofada

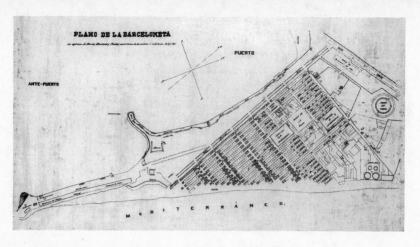

Verboom's plan for Barceloneta, 1753

perquè me'n recordi bé,
perquè la por em faci ser
bon hereu de casa.

I've seen, I've seen, I've seen
up on the Citadel
how the hanged man swung
from a crooked cross.
And father gave me
a great whack on the ear
so I'd remember the sight,
so I'd become, through fright,
his good little son and heir.

From the western face of the Citadel a high wall, fortified with more bastions and fronted by a moat, zigzagged up the north side of the city, around its back and down south again to the port, meeting the sea at the Drassanes. The result of this enormous military-engineering project was to enclose Barcelona in a rigid straitjacket of stone, preventing any further civic expansion. Felipe V's *muralles* in short order became the worst urban problem Barcelona had, and they were loathed as much as the Citadel itself. They were the Catalan bastille, and perhaps not until the construction of the Berlin Wall would another structure be so hated by a European city. In the nineteenth century the *muralles* freighted every town-planning decision with extra political meaning. Were you for democracy or for the military? Republican or Carlist? Church or state? Catalan independence or Madrid centralism? Privilege or benign public services? Your attitude toward the walls would tell. Separatists in the 1840s and 1850s used the image of urban space oppressed by Crown, Church, and army much as they used the issue of freedom to write and publish in Catalan: as an archsymbol of a general campaign for a free society. It was the key to "progressive" theories of social science. And this greatly affected the plan of the New City, once the walls of the old were razed.

Verboom, the Citadel's engineer, started another change in the shape of Barcelona that was more benign and has lasted: the area on the north side of the port known as Barceloneta, "little Barcelona." Originally it was meant to rehouse some of the displaced folk of the Ribera quarter, but it was not begun until 1753, a generation later. Verboom drew up his first plan in 1715, but the final work was actually done by another military engineer, Juan Martín Cermeño. Cermeño's construction of Barceloneta, followed by his creation of the Ramblas as an avenue, marked the beginning of recognizably modern urban planning in the city.

Barceloneta is a grid of narrow rectangular blocks standing on a triangle of land reclaimed from the sea. Only the tip of the triangle, the little Illa de Maians, now buried somewhere under the concrete of the esplanade, was once solid ground. Today, this is the only part of the city that still retains the working-class, maritime character of Barcelona's old waterfront. It is not automatically lovable, but it has a lot of juice. On first plunging into the human confusion of Barceloneta today—the cafés and cheap eateries with their clutter of signs along the Passeig Nacional, the jammed cars, the dilapidated houses, the fish smell and glittering scales running in the gutters when the tubs and baskets are hosed down, the yelling touts outside long hangarlike seafood restaurants that poke down to the grayish beach from the congested Passeig Marítim—one might not immediately guess that the place was conceived in a spirit of perfect abstraction by a military engineer, but so it was. The grid of Barceloneta (fifteen narrow streets cut across by five slightly broader "avenues," with a church square and—important, from the point of view of enforcing discipline by keeping the soldiers on view—a parade ground, all on a twenty-five-acre site) is purely abstract: cheap worker housing laid out in standard modules for future residents of whom Cermeño knew little and probably cared less. It was so abstract as to be proleptically modernist, a tiny sample of grids to come. The blocks were divided into lots, each twenty-eight feet square, on which uniform single-family two-story houses, each with two windows and a door on the ground floor and two windows and a balcony above, were to rise to a height of not more than twenty feet. This plan was ignored by later builders, who put upper floors and attics on the row houses, thus giving the narrow streets of Barceloneta the cramped and airless feel of small canyons.

III

Commercial life in Barcelona started up again after the Bourbon conquest almost without a hitch, except for the predictable resentments over the billeting of troops. Everyone, said one of the *consellers* of the now-extinct Diputació, should go straight back to work and forget about the siege. Merchants and *menestrals* were only too happy to comply, for, as the historian Felipe Fernandez-Armesto caustically pointed out, "Continuously underlying Madrid's policy towards Barcelona in the eighteenth century was the conviction that the obedience of the Barcelonese could be bought. Indeed, this was openly acknowledged in [Barcelona]." The city profited mightily from being hooked into the general Spanish economy, which continued to rise through the eighteenth century. Luxury trades—painted ceramics, silk weaving, ribbon making, rococo froufrous of every kind—began to boom, and there was a veritable cult of chocolate drinking, the craze imported from Mexico. One of the standard images of gallantry in Catalan popular art was the cavalier offering his lady a cup of the steaming brew. By 1770 six times as many *xocolaters* were plying their trade in Barcelona as had been forty years before.

Since the sixteenth century, Madrid had denied the kingdom of Aragon and Catalunya the right to dip into the river of gold and silver that had been flowing across the Atlantic from the Americas. Though Barcelona, in the days of its independence, had been frozen out of the plunder of the American colonies, its annexation by Madrid opened the Atlantic to its merchants, who in 1755 formed a trading syndicate, the Barcelona Company for West Indian Trade. Catalan ships began plying the ocean between Cádiz and the Spanish Caribbean colonies— Cuba, Santo Domingo, Puerto Rico. In 1778 restrictions on Catalan exports to Spain's American colonies were dropped. The merchants shipped goods that were costly for their bulk: spices, drugs, paper—but mainly brandy and textiles.

Firewater, *aguardiente*, was a potent colonial lubricant, and the Latin American thirst for it was unslakable. So, for the first time, Catalan vineyards acquired an export trade. It remained pointless to try to export wine to France (or anywhere else in Europe); the only Spanish wines that interested the rest of the Continent in the eighteenth century were Madeira, sherry, and port, but brandy, being distilled, was smaller in bulk and easier to ship. This began a trend in farming that crested a hundred years later—the conversion from cereal growing to viticulture. Much Catalan farmland was tucked away in valleys and pockets, remote from the main roads, almost out of touch with the great central market of Barcelona. Given the high price of transport, it was a losing proposition for such places to sell bulk crops like wheat in the city—or export them at all. But if the crop changed to vines, then the wine—poor, raw stuff as a rule—could be distilled where it was made and exported as *aguardiente*; distilling bulk wine into cheap brandy opened even the worst Catalan vineyards to the New World market. In eight years, between 1784 and 1792, the total of Catalan exports to the Spanish-American colonies quadrupled, zooming from fourteen million to fifty-six million reals.

But much of this was in textiles. After the War of Succession, the Bourbons no longer controlled the weaving mills of northern Italy and the Netherlands, which meant that the Catalan textile industry—still in its larval stage but growing quickly—was relatively secure from competition within the empire. By casting the Catalans back on their own ingenuity, Madrid turned them into manufacturers. They had to develop an industrial base, and they did. After 1730 both the prices of textiles and the international demand for them shot up, while labor in Barcelona remained cheap and plentiful, with Catalan peasants looking for work in the city mills, and foreign hands coming south across the Pyrenees. A boom resulted. Catalan industry kept growing, consolidating, drawing people in from the country to the city, and changing both. In 1750 Spain had only two bourgeois centers. One was Cádiz, a city of buyers and sellers, agents and traders. The other was Barcelona, a city of makers and, more and more, exporters.

The rest of Spain, sunk in its class-obsessed lethargy of privilege, tended to despise trade as ignoble: an activity for Jews and Englishmen —and Catalans, too, those money grubbers of dull lineage. But Barcelona's cotton and silk products transformed it into the Manchester of the Mediterranean.

The Catalan entrepreneurs plowed back their profits as capital reinvestment in their businesses. Technologically, they were backward— but not as backward as the rest of Spain. They built water mills and put in the first weaving machinery, primitive, clanking, and dangerous, but faster than the traditional *máquina bergadana*, or "hand spinner," used in every Catalan village since the sixteenth century. In 1785 Francisco

Gabriel Planella i Rodriguez, Interior of a Calico Cloth Shop, *early nineteenth century*

de Zamora, a visitor to Barcelona, looked across the city walls from the gallery of a church spire and saw "hamlets, farmhouses, fields full of cloth, trees, sown fields, vineyards and orchards." The "fields full of cloth" were the *prats d'indianes*, or "calico meadows," where the textile manufacturers spread out their bolts of fulled, bleached cotton to dry in long, colorful strips once their designs had been woodblock printed by hand in workshops within the walled city. At this stage, the scale of manufacture was small. Even the largest bleaching and dyeing shops, for instance, employed no more than forty hands. But there were many of them, all in fierce competition, forcing the survivors to the top—and to consolidation.

Most of the new capitalists were of humble origin: the cloth business enabled people to vault from obscurity to wealth in a generation or two. They began as artisans, members of the *menestralia*, whose values of thrift and family—along with a clannish indifference to foreigners, including most Spaniards other than Catalans—never left them. They were as like their counterparts in Lancashire as Latin Catholics could be: hardfisted, ruthlessly indifferent to the welfare of the proletariat their industries were creating, and loyal to the Bourbon regime, whose stability was good for their business. They wanted Madrid to protect them from foreign competition. Indeed, like their successors of the nineteenth century, they expected it. "To help the factories," wrote a Catalan named Josep Aparici in 1720, "one should ban foreign imports, or load them with strict imposts. . . . If textiles do not come from England, France and Holland, let us wear the ones made here, which are very good and will get better as we develop. . . . The king will get rich if his vassals do, and poor if they are poor."

Few of them were liberals and fewer still *ilustrados*, proponents of "soft" capitalism with time for airy speculations about social justice.

Nevertheless, the French Revolution, when it came, was a boon to them: suddenly there was lots of nervous émigré capital looking for an industrial home outside France and finding it in Barcelona, while Catalan textile manufacturers found they could take over a hefty slice of the French cloth industry's lost market. As cloth centers like Nîmes (from whose name comes "denim," originally *toile de Nîmes*) faltered in the late eighteenth century, so Barcelona began in earnest to prosper. "The Catalans are the most industrious people in Spain," wrote a Castilian named José Cadalso in 1789. They excelled, he said, in manufacture, fishing, navigation, commerce, finance, and the arts of war as well as those of peace:

> Cannon-founding, weapon manufacture, uniforms and harness for the army, use of artillery, munitions, the formation of high-quality light troops—all that comes from Catalunya. Fields are cultivated, the population increases, companies grow and, in fact, this nation seems to be a thousand leagues ahead of Galicia, Andalusia or Castile. But their talents are intractable, and solely dedicated to their own profit and interest; that is why some people call them the Dutch of Spain.

Though Barcelona went into a bad recession in the 1790s, it eventually recovered; though the Napoleonic wars of 1808–14 (the Peninsular Wars) damaged their factories and inflicted havoc on their workers, most manufacturers survived them. Another change, however—an ominous one for Barcelonese workers—came as the guild system withered away in the face of industrial capitalism. The guilds had been stripped of their political influence under Felipe V's New Plan, but they continued to direct and represent the interests of workers in a symbolic way up to the last decades of the eighteenth century. They were finally abolished by the votes of the liberal deputies at the Corts of Cádiz, in 1812. The guilds no longer had a practical function in a growing world of steam and mass labor. But this meant that Barcelona's working class had no protection either: the guilds were obsolete, but trade unions, as far as the *prohoms* of the industrializing city were concerned, were unthinkable.

IV

Two clear symbols of postwar prosperity stood near the waterfront. The first was the newly remodeled Llotja, Barcelona's stock exchange, whose medieval core was enclosed, between 1764 and 1802, in a neoclassical casing with Tuscan columns designed by Joan Soler i Faneca. It provided thousands of square feet of new office space for the Junta de Comerç, the city's rapidly expanding chamber of commerce. The second, somewhat less authentic—its marble and limestone facades were actually stucco—was a new Customs House (now the Palace of Civil Government) on the Avinguda del Marqués de l'Argentera, run up between 1790 and 1792 to replace an earlier building that had burned down twenty years before.

These new arrangements along the port marked the small beginnings of a deep change in the character of Barcelona: the entry of rational urbanism, that offspring of the Enlightenment. From now on there would be an increasing desire for clarity, order, the decisive marking out of urban spaces in terms of their different social functions. These signified a different way of envisaging cities that was becoming general throughout Europe. One saw the city, in the mind's eye, from above, in the abstracted form of a plan drawn to scale, whose elements could then be rectified. Partly this was owing to the needs of surveyors and military engineers like Cermeño, who thought in terms of exact spatial data about ranges, distances, slopes. In a more general way, it issued from the Enlightenment's love of generalization and abstraction. Nobody except God could see Barcelona (or any other city) from above: the town plan, drawn on paper, did not correspond to human experience in the way that a "view," a "prospect," taken from the eye level of a standing man, did. But it could carry vastly more *information* about the measurable physical layout of the city.

Up to the early eighteenth century the usual way of showing a city to the reader of a book was the topographical view, which conveyed a sense of looking at the town but did not say much—or not very clearly—about how the place was actually laid out. But a plan's power of abstraction made urbanism possible. It let you imagine the city as a whole system. Its malleability as a drawing made it easier to imagine big changes in it. If the plan was God's eye view, then revising it was God's act: a pencil slash abolished a *barri*, the aptly named ruler drove straight avenues through the ancient congestion of alleys. Blocks of people could be uprooted here and replanted there. Hidden patterns floated off the plan. Such was the habit of rationalization; and although its first modest monument in Barcelona was Barceloneta, its triumph was the creation of the great avenue known as the Ramblas, which would become to Barcelona what Piazza di San Marco is to Venice, or Regent Street to London. And like Haussmann's later eviscerations of old Paris, the straight line of the Ramblas carried a distinct message about power. The military mind likes straight lines—and Barcelona was an occupied city.

A sixteenth-century view of Barcelona, from Georgius Hoefragge, Civitates Orbis Terrarum, *1567*

You cannot fire a cannon around a corner or send cavalry charging through winding alleys. The Barri Gòtic was the natural home of the urban guerrilla—the tanner with his cobblestone, the carpenter with his blunderbuss—but the Ramblas implied the supremacy of the army.

In a city plan published in 1740 by the architect Francesc Renart i Closas, one can trace the first form of the Ramblas—a wide uneven street making a wobbly line clear across the city, running north–northeast from a point on the port next to the shipyards to a gate in the northern rampart of Felipe V's new *muralles*. It had bumps because it ran parallel with the older, medieval defense wall, built by Jaume I in the thirteenth century. And in fact, *rambla* in Arabic means "riverbed"; the embryo avenue was simply the filled-in gully of Barcelona's western stream, the Cagallel, which had become a moat as well as a sewer when Jaume's wall was built alongside it.

By the late eighteenth century this watercourse was so clogged with junk and ordure that you could hardly have called it a river at all. Bit by bit it was filled in, driven underground. (When the rain is really hard, the Cagallel will still glug up through the street gratings of the lower Ramblas.) The different names of the Ramblas on the way up from the port—Rambla de Santa Monica, Rambla dels Caputxins, Rambla de Sant Josep, Rambla dels Estudis, each recording the name of a convent, a church, or a foundation that the lengthening avenue passed —suggest how gradual this filling in was. Convents and churches had been built outside the wall, from the fifteenth century on, in the district between town and country on the far side of the Cagallel known as the Raval. These were the outriders of Barcelona's westward expansion and by the end of the seventeenth century the track of the Ramblas was regarded mainly as an access road to them.

The fact that the Ramblas preserved the line of the medieval edge

A view of the Ramblas, from Alexandre Laborde, Voyage Pittoresque et Historique in Espagne, *1812*

of the city explains the otherwise puzzling site of its great food market, the Boqueria (Ramblas 85–89). There had always been an open-air market on its approximate site just outside the medieval wall, the logical meeting spot between city shoppers and country vendors bringing their donkey carts of produce in from the farms and vineyards. After the 1720s the western space between the old and new walls soon filled with a tangle of narrow streets and tenements, but the market did not move to the new edge of the city: it obdurately stayed where it was, getting harder for the sellers to reach but, thanks to the increasing popularity of the Ramblas, easier for the buyers.

In 1775, the demolition of Jaume I's wall began—it was obsolete by then, an urban relic to which tenements clung like barnacles to a hulk. In 1776 the military engineer Cermeño, having finished Barceloneta, began the project of turning the riverbed into an avenue. One sees the result (in the abstract) in a plan and description of the city in Alexandre Laborde's *Voyage Pittoresque et Historique in Espagne* (1812). The new avenue slashed through the city, straight as a girder, studded with rivets—dots signifying the uniform plantation of trees in double file, the ancestors of the noble planes that shade the Ramblas today. It was, Laborde noted, a vast improvement over the old Ramblas, which had been "thronged with people, but ill-finished," choked with dust in summer and with mud in winter.

By then, however, palaces had already begun to rise along the Ramblas. One, in fact, was almost finished: the Palau de la Virreina (Ramblas 99) named after the widow of Felipe V's formidable and greedy officer Manuel d'Amat i de Junyent (1707–82), younger son of the first marquis of Castellbell.

Having served his king well in Felipe's Italian campaigns, d'Amat had been rewarded with the juiciest of colonial plums: he became captain general of Chile in 1755 and in 1761 viceroy of Peru, with virtually autocratic control over its resources—which included the most copious source of silver in the known world, the mines of Potosí.

A man, and especially a Catalan, would have needed a heart of lead to refuse these bounties of the Peruvian earth. The viceroy had no such inhibitions. He grafted and skimmed for ten years, and in 1771, feeling the onset of age and retirement, he sent back to Barcelona some sketches for a palace of epic proportions, twice as big as the actual site his agents procured on the Ramblas. His chosen architects, Josep Ausich and the sculptor Carles Grau, managed to bring the design down to actual size—a task which, one surmises, must have involved some tact in dealing with the viceroy's ego—and the palace was largely finished before its facade was found not to align with Cermeño's plan for the avenue. Today it still sits back some thirty feet from the facade line of the Ramblas, asserting its difference: a powerful, thickly modeled classical facade with baroque overtones, such as the heavy bracketed cornice and its urns. A central carriage arch admits you to an internal courtyard and to some ground-floor rooms converted into exhibition space, for the palace is now used as a cultural center. Beyond these the visitor cannot go: but it is no loss, since all the rooms of the palace were stripped of their decor and finishes over the years, reducing it to a shell. It was, reputedly, overdecorated to the point of stupefaction in 1778, when the viceroy moved in. But he had little time to enjoy his dream house; he died four years later, leaving the colossal pile—by far the largest private house in eighteenth-century Barcelona—to his wife, Maria Francesca Fivaller. Piqued by the thought of a single widow wandering in its cavernous and florid rooms, the Barcelonans renamed it the Vicereine's Palace.

D'Amat was the first of the new rich, whom Catalans came to call *indianos* or, more politely, *americanos*—people who made killings in the Spanish-American colonies, first by plunder and later through trade, and brought their wealth back to Barcelona. A few local financiers and

Josep Ausich and Carles Grau's Palau de la Virreina, 1773–77

officials could afford to build opulent palaces in Barcelona in the 1770s:
one was the Viceroy of Catalunya, Francisco Fernández de Córdoba,
the Duke of Sessa, who had d'Amat's architect Carles Grau design him
a smaller but equally severe town house, the Palau Sessa-Larrard (Carrer
Ample 28/Carrer de la Mercè 15) in 1772–78.

Within a year or two the vogue for neoclassical plainness was fully
risen, and Catalan architects embraced it with fervor. The best building
in this vein on the Ramblas is the four-story Casa March de Reus (Ramblas 8), constructed around 1780 for the head of the March family, a
strongly knit clan of businessmen who originated in the town of Reus,
near Tarragona. The architect, Joan Soler i Faneca, gave it a simple
plan—a square with a central courtyard, a garden behind, and the usual
main staircase to the formal rooms of the *pis noble*—and also the simplest
of facade treatments, an elegantly proportioned grid of windows and a
street wall that, rising from strongly jointed ashlar at the ground floor,
becomes hardly more than a stone membrane, with the smallest projection of unfluted pilasters and a subdued linear neatness in the ratios of
the bays.

Josep and Pau Mas i Dordal's Palau Moja, 1774–90

The March de Reus house set the standard of elegance for such noble domestic building as was done on the Ramblas in the 1780s, but it was surpassed farther up the avenue (Ramblas 118) by the Palau Moja (1774–90), designed by the brothers Josep and Pau Mas i Dordal. Its long facade on the Ramblas, a flat plane of stucco relieved with the minimum shadow lines of cornices, pilasters, and quoined corners, was raised on a ground-floor arcade and finished with a plain central pediment on top. It still bears traces of red-ocher decorative painting in the wall panels, but these give no hint of the sumptuous decor of the grand salon inside, a double-height room with an internal balcony running right around it, frescoed by El Vigata (Francesc Pla, a Catalan neoclassicist).

In the eighteenth century, within the larger context of town planning, such palaces meant little, and Barceloneta was only a stopgap. Twenty-five acres of extra housing could not relieve the pressures of the city's main social change in the eighteenth century: the entrance of industry, the increase of small shopkeepers and craftsmen, and the growth of population. In 1717, when the *muralles* were going up, Barcelona had only 37,000 people living and working in it. By 1798 there were more than three times that many, 130,000 or so, crammed into its constricted space. This was still a preindustrial city, but industrialization was just around the corner, and at no point in the eighteenth century did the government of Barcelona come up with a general housing code. Builders and speculators could do their worst—and did, higgledy-piggledy. The medieval center of Barcelona began to turn into a slum with monuments.

Hemmed in by the *muralles*, Barcelona could not spread out. It could only rise. In the last quarter of the eighteenth century 80 percent of construction in Barcelona consisted of making slums by clapping new floors on old buildings and chopping up the existing floors to make more rooms. In 1772 only 13 percent of its residential buildings went up four stories or more. By the 1790s, 72 percent of them did. And so the laboring poor of Barcelona, crammed into these warrens, toiling in dim basements and drawing their water from wells that bordered on communal cesspits, ravaged by unstemmable outbreaks of cholera and yellow fever, existed under sanitary conditions that were certainly no better and sometimes worse than those in London or Paris. Out of their discontent came the notorious instability of Barcelona's *patuleia*, the urban mob, quick to anger and revolt, easily swayed by rabble-rousers, a perpetual source of anxiety to the city's Bourbon regents, to its industrialists, and to anyone else who had a political or economic stake in keeping things exactly as they were. Before the early years of the nineteenth century were out, few observers of political life in Barcelona were willing to draw any hard-and-fast distinctions between the "mob" and the "people," as writers in London were prone to do; the city itself, not just a part of its citizenry, was quick to rise.

The French Revolution found no bloc of bourgeois Catalans who wished to imitate it in the 1790s. The city had no shortage of proletarian discontent, but this could only make riots, not a revolution. In 1789, the year the Revolution broke out in Paris, Barcelona too was racked by bread riots, the *rebomboris del pa*. But the war of 1793–95 between Spain and France was enthusiastically supported by all classes in Catalunya; as in the rest of Spain, committees were organized to marshal the defense of "Religion, Homeland, and King," and the Catalans saw the conflict as an opportunity to grab back their lost territory in the Roussillon—a hope that was soon dashed when the French, instead of letting that province go, seized the Catalan coastal area of Figueras. This inconclusive war sputtered to an end with the Treaty of Basle; even the Bourbons were capable of negotiating with the French Thermidoreans. In 1795 Spain entered an alliance with France, which turned out to be an economic disaster for Catalunya: now that Spain was in the Napoleonic wars on the French side, the British navy promptly blockaded its trade with America. In 1804 the value of Spanish (largely Catalan) exports to the American colonies totaled some twenty million pesetas. By 1807, they were down to fifty thousand pesetas. This violent slump did not altogether wreck the textile and wine industries of Catalunya, but it slowed them badly and caused widespread unemployment. This led to a distinctly Francophobe mood in Barcelona, all over again. It was shared in Madrid—"*Con todo el mundo guerra*," the Bourbon monarch Carlos IV reputedly exclaimed, "*y paz con Inglaterra*": "War with everyone else, but peace with England!" By 1808 Barcelona's leading *ilustrado* intellectual, the historian Antoni de Capmany i Montpalau (1742–1813)—a convinced liberal who wrote polemics against royal absolutism and the Inquisition and, in 1802, had set up the archive of the Royal Patrimony of Catalunya, a basic source for the culture's history: in short, a man whose public career had been a reflection of the ideals of the Enlightenment—was blowing the bugle for a jihad against the French:

> With war, we will open our doors. . . . With war, we will open our former trade and communications with England. . . . With war, that terrible but healing instrument of our eternal prosperity, we shall no longer absorb impious philosophising and the corruption of our way of life . . .

This collective Catalan animus against the French, fueled by memories of their "desertion" from the War of the Spanish Succession a hundred years before, was a rehearsal for Catalan resistance during the Peninsular War of 1808–14, when Napoleon's army—acting under the terms of the Franco-Spanish alliance—marched in, occupied the peninsula, and installed Joseph Bonaparte on the throne of Madrid. The Spanish resistance began with Madrid's rising against the intruder king, the *dos de Mayo* immortalized by Goya. It spread rapidly among the Catalans, who also refused to acknowledge the French pretender and hoped for the return of the Bourbon prince, El Deseado (the Desired One), Ferdinand VII. Was their resistance the first Catalan act of collective Spanishness, or a rising in the name of Catalan autonomy? Historians have spilled much ink over this question, and it is probably impossible to know, at this distance, what the Catalans believed they were fighting for: the nation, of course, but this was susceptible to many definitions, ranging from the "Catalan people" (as defined against Madrid) to the idea of Bourbon succession to a kind of ethnocultural-mystical agglomerate that included all persons of Hispanic origin and culture in both hemispheres, from Tenochtitlán to Montjuic. But it was very clear what they were fighting *against*: Napoleon and the French and Italian troops he had put on Catalan soil. In vain, the French tried to defuse the anger of the occupied. Napoleon's marshal in charge of Catalunya, Pierre-François-Charles Augereau, duke of Castiglione, strove to convince them that his occupation was really the fulfillment of Catalan patriotism. "Conquerors of Athens and Neopatria!" he proclaimed:

> The fatherland of Catalunya is to be reborn from its ashes. Your population, shrunk since the conquest of America, will be more numerous than it was in the days of its glory! Napoleon the Great will give you a new existence! His fatherly gaze is turned towards you! . . . In 1641, in your struggles for self-determination, you asked France to govern you, and remained for years beneath her protection. Your industry, activities and way of life are so like ours, that with every reason you are called the French of Spain.

Nobody in Catalunya appears to have believed this overture from the spider to the fly, and the resistance went on, forcing the French to lay siege to Girona (which lost half its population), Tarragona, and Tortosa. It was met with a savagery that struck even some Napoleonic officers as unspeakable: one of them would recall how thirty Catalan couriers might be buried at a crossroads each week, and remember seeing, in the yard of a farmhouse near the spot where ten French soldiers had been ambushed and garroted by Catalan irregulars, a tree from whose branches hung a white-bearded father, his five sons, a Dominican priest, an Englishman, and a Jew.

The French could control the cities but not the countryside. The Catalan resistance was badly armed and often ill led but capable of astonishing feats of courage and supported by a wide consensus—farmers, tradesmen, clergy, hill bandits, and city proletariat. This was the war that gave the word *guerrilla* to the languages of Europe. Its engagements with the French were hit-and-run affairs, nothing like the great pitched battles Napoleon was fighting elsewhere. The mystique of Catalan nationalism would later turn some of them into mythic events hardly inferior to the encounters of Hector and Ajax on the windy plains of Troy. The most famous (locally so, anyway) was the battle of Bruc in June 1808, in which one or two thousand Catalan irregulars surprised a column of four thousand French troops on the side of the Montserrat Massif and routed them. This victory, legend insisted, was due in part to the energetic work of a little drummer boy, whose rolls and rat-tat-tats echoed from the ancient rocks of the holy mountain and led the French to believe they were surrounded by a much larger force.

Salvador Mallol, Popular Scenes on the Ramblas, *early nineteenth century*

Though the Catalan fighting forces were provisionally raised, they continued to affect civil life in the principate long after the French retreated in disarray from Spain in 1814, and in fact had existed there long before. They were known, broadly, as *sometents*—"citizen volunteers," whose form of mobilization to confront communal threats or breakdowns of discipline dated back to the reign of Jaume I in the thirteenth century. The *sometents* were one of the Catalan institutions dissolved by the Bourbons in 1715, but culturally they were ineradicable. Raising and combining them was a task that fell to the various juntas of defense that sprang up in Catalunya and throughout Spain to oppose the French threat. They included the *miquelets*, an equally irregular force that corresponded, roughly, to the French Revolution's Garde Nationale. In the cities, especially Barcelona, they produced the civic militia, a group of permanently armed civilians who took extreme pride in their role as a free-lance urban police force.

Beyond their common opposition to Napoleon, it is impossible to generalize about these guerrilla groups, especially through the combined fogs of war and patriotic legend. Nobody even knows how many of them were in the field: estimates run from 30,000 to 150,000. Some were extreme rural reactionaries under the guidance of armed priests—the prototypes of the Carlists who would cause such trouble in the Catalan countryside later in the nineteenth century. Some were bandits, pure and simple. Some were outraged patriots of a middling political persuasion, fighting for a Spain united under Ferdinand VII; others, Catalans who dreamed of secession from Madrid. The National Militia in Barcelona, however, was of a progressive, left-wing–liberal cast. It was created by the short-lived Constitution of Cádiz in 1812. One of the first actions of Ferdinand VII, when that monarch returned from exile in the wake of Napoleon's defeat, was to abolish that Constitution altogether; but the National Militia, though it was driven underground, did not dissolve. During Barcelona's periods of conservatism in the nineteenth century, it would sink from view: it was officially disbanded from 1814 to 1820, only to reappear during the Liberal Triennial of 1820–23; dissolved again in 1823–34, it regrouped again under a different name, the Urban Militia, from 1834 to 1843. Once more repressed after the risings of the 1843 Jamancia, it popped up ten years later only to sink yet again in 1856. Finally, with the fall and exile of the Bourbon monarch in the Glorious Revolution of 1868, it reappeared in Barcelona as the Volunteers of Liberty and, lastly, as the Volunteers of the Republic, before vanishing definitively and for the last time in 1875. Through the first half of the nineteenth century, the militia held the key to a significant amount of political power in Barcelona, playing a crucial role in the implantation of constitutional monarchy between 1834 and 1843. It was not intrinsically a working-class force; but its sympathies lay with radicals, and sometimes radicals commanded it. For this reason alone, it would help to form the city.

V

Industrial development shaped Barcelona in the first half of the nineteenth century, but so did ideological violence. Between the Napoleonic Wars and the Setmana Tragica, or Tragic Week, of 1909, the Catalans repeatedly turned on their own city with frenzied vindictiveness, burning the symbols of absolutism and the Church. Moreover, in the name of town planning, liberal politicians erased even more of old Barcelona than the mob.

Architectural losses from the six-year French occupation (1808–14) were bearable. Convents and monasteries were emptied—sometimes they were trashed by being used as barracks, stores, and stables for Napoleon's troops—but the only major religious building that the French actually razed was the Convent of Jesus, which, with its attendant church, stood outside the *muralles* in what is now the Eixample, on a site between the Via Laietana and Passeig de Gràcia. The fourteenth-century Convent of Jonqueres (which gave its name to the Carrer Jonqueres near the western *muralla*), became a military hospital; its Benedictine nuns never reoccupied it after the war, and it was torn down almost a century later to make way for the Via Laietana.

The first of the big nineteenth-century losses in the Barri Gòtic began as a result of the Liberal Triennial—the brief, exalted constitutional interlude during the reign of Ferdinand VII. Once back in the saddle after the departure of the French, the Desired One had proved obstinately, fanatically opposed to any form of constitutional interference with his rule. One of his first acts in 1814 had been to repeal the Constitution drawn up in 1812 by the moderates in Cádiz. Then in 1820 this royal hatred of democracy led to a classic *pronunciamiento*, or "declaration," by the army under the young liberal officer Rafael de Riego, in which the king was given a choice: swear by the 1812 Constitution, or get out. Pallid with rage and fear, Ferdinand had sworn by it in 1820, ushering in a brief, illusory period of liberalism.

The *liberales* in Madrid—the word, like *guerrilla*, was another artifact of the Napoleonic occupation of Spain and came out of the views expressed by deputies at the Cádiz Corts as they were debating the form of the 1812 Constitution—now set about dismantling the apparatus of the Bourbon regime. The civic government of Barcelona was also dominated by moderate liberals. One of their projects was to give more importance to the buildings in the Barri Gòtic that housed the Ajuntament and the Generalitat: to "rationalize" the tangle of streets, churches, and convents around them with two fine squares, one residential (the Plaça Reial, just off the Ramblas), the other ceremonial (the Plaça Sant Jaume, across which the buildings of the Generalitat and the Ajuntament stare at each other). Between them would run a transverse street cutting northeast across the Barri Gòtic and given the Catalan form of Ferdinand VII's name: the Carrer de Ferran.

By the future standards of a Baron Haussmann or a Le Corbusier this was a modest incision, but several buildings stood in its way. The site of the future Plaça Reial was occupied by the large Capuchin convent of Santa Madrona, built in the eighteenth century, which probably was not much of a loss—not, at least, compared with the palpable urban gain registered by the creation of Plaça Reial itself. But to enlarge Plaça Sant Jaume, the construction gangs had to tear down one of the finest Romanesque churches in Barcelona, the parish church of Sant Jaume, saving nothing of it—not even the fourteenth-century porch with its celebrated carvings, of which no accurate record now exists. It was razed in 1823. And now that the planners had developed a taste for the sound of collapsing vaults, they began to look elsewhere for church foundations whose disappearance might provide the sullenly crammed city with new space: at the convents of the Mercè and of Santa Caterina and, most magnificent of all, at the Carme, the thirteenth-century church and convent of the Carmelites, south of the Ramblas. As a polemical gesture, the liberals even ordered the sixteenth-century statue and obelisk of Saint Eulalia, Barcelona's patron saint, to be removed from the site of her martyrdom in the Plaça del Pedró. But there was such a furious popular outcry against the idea that they contented themselves with shifting it to a corner of the square. Shortly afterward it was moved back to the middle. A century later, in 1936, the anarchists toppled the poor virgin from her obelisk; this time only her head survived. (Finally, in 1951, the whole monument was rebuilt by Frederic Marés i Deulovol, from photographs.)

Through the 1820s and 1830s Barcelona would see little civic building of importance. Nothing is built when politics are convulsed. The city was going broke, and its government was distracted by foreign occupation and civil war. The Carrer de Ferran, begun at the Ramblas, reached the Carrer d'Avinyo by 1826—about half its intended length—and then stalled for lack of money.

When the constitutional interlude came to an end in 1823, the seesaw of Spanish power once again tipped to the right: a French force with the high-flown name of the Hundred Thousand Sons of Saint Louis, commanded by the duke of Angoulême under the terms of the Holy Alliance between Austria, Prussia, and Russia, marched across the Pyrenees to put an end to the Triennial and reinstall Ferdinand VII in all his absolutist powers. There was some sharp resistance from the Catalan militia, commanded by the moderate regent of Catalunya, General Espoz i Mina. But it did not last long; one by one the Catalan cities fell—Tarragona, Lleida, Vic. Barcelona finally surrendered in November 1823 and was occupied by the French army until 1827. The Sons of Saint Louis marched on south and took Cádiz. Ferdinand, the last and in many ways the worst of the Bourbon absolutists, was back on the throne; he reigned until his death in 1833.

Barcelona was lucky to be occupied by a French army. It was a neutral peacekeeping force, its officers were relatively moderate, and the city was spared at least some of the fratricidal terrors that Spanish ultraroyalists visited on liberals in other cities. Some, but not all. A royal amnesty came for those who had "committed excesses against the persons and property of liberals." In Barcelona between October and December 1824, about two thousand people were murdered by far-right secret societies like the one that styled itself the "Exterminating Angel." Many Catalan progressives scooted for the border and found temporary exile in France or England. But most of the liberals and constitutionalists, along with manufacturers, bankers, and practically the whole middle class of Barcelona, chose to stay and rebuild their institutions—and their capital base.

Catalunya was nearly bankrupt. Its state revenues in 1823–25 were lower than they had been thirty years before. The liberation movement led by Simón Bolívar had swept the South American mainland—Venezuela won its nationhood in 1821, Peru in 1824—and the colonial markets on which Catalan industry had depended were shrunk: now only the island colonies of Cuba and Puerto Rico were left, and Catalan exports to America in 1827 were a tenth of what they had been in 1792. Agriculture was in deep recession, likewise the wine industry, and most of the olive trees of Catalunya were killed in a black spring frost in 1825. And Ferdinand, whose treasury in Madrid was nearly empty, kept ratcheting up the taxes on basics like meat and salt cod.

The Barcelona moderates were safe, however, because of Ferdinand VII's inscrutable decision in 1824 to appoint the Marquis of Campo Sagrado, an Asturian liberal who had served on the anti-Napoleonic Supreme Central Junta, as the new captain general of Catalunya. He took care to protect those of like mind. Thus Barcelona was largely spared the vengeance of the Inquisition and the ultraroyalists' Commissions of Purification, whose witch-hunts and murders had free rein elsewhere in the Iberian peninsula over the next few years.

Hence the nodes of unrepentant liberal power in Barcelona—in government, local city bureaucracy, teaching, publishing, and even the army—remained in place, much to the anger of the Church and the royalists. Like it or not, export manufacture now had to deal more and more with French and other European businessmen, who may not have been paragons of liberalism but certainly had little time for the fanatic ideologies of Ferdinand VII's Spanish supporters. This reinforced the already moderate tone of the Catalan burghers, who sensed which way the rest of Europe was going.

Yet Catalunya continued to be racked with unrest in 1823–34, the so-called Ominous Decade. The militia had been disbanded, but the principate still had two armies, one regular, consisting mainly of officers and troops who preferred the liberal Constitution to absolute rule, and another made up of irregular royalist volunteers who had taken up arms against the Liberal Triennial and stayed organized after Ferdinand's return. These latter were increasingly angry that the king seemed unable to impose absolute rule on the liberals and the moderate businessmen who, thanks to Campo Sagrado (whom they detested) still held so much of the real power in Barcelona. The city gave them no patronage, no official plums. They blamed this on the liberals, but also on Ferdinand.

They came to believe that the king had betrayed his own royalist coun-
terrevolution. Most of them were country people who, seeing their economy falling to shreds, like gut conservatives anywhere in time of crisis,
blamed the machinations of the left and the indifference of the corrupt
city to the "true, grass-roots" values of the land. Being Catalans, they
looked back to an earlier and "purer" form of monarchy, that of Aragon
and Catalunya, the sort for which their ancestors had rebelled against
Felipe IV in the Reapers' War of 1640.

The result was the brief Guerra dels Agraviats, or Malcontents' War,
which broke out in 1827 and, abetted by the Church, ravaged much of
the Catalan countryside in the name of Catalan patriotism. Bands of
ultraroyalists, chanting their slogans—"Long live the Absolute King,
Death to the Frenchies, long live Religion, Death to Politics, long live
the Inquisition!"—burned the farms and shops of suspected liberals all
across Catalunya, until they were put down by the regular army, whose
general, Espoz i Mina, gave no quarter to the royalists. He liked to make
examples. One was the village of Castellfollit, near Girona, a royalist
stronghold. Espoz i Mina razed it completely and set up an inscription:
"Here stood Castellfollit. Citizens! Take notice! Do not shelter the enemies of your Fatherland." The Malcontents' leaders, who bore picturesque nicknames, such as the Snail, were hanged; the French consul in
Barcelona noted sardonically that they received both the news of their
execution and the last sacraments from the very priests who had incited
them to rebellion in the first place. Ferdinand VII then condescended
to make a triumphal progress along the royal road from Madrid to Barcelona, where—to the immense relief of its worried and groveling business community—he affirmed a policy of state protectionism for the
Catalan textile industry and was given a cash present of one million reals
by its leaders. The French occupation forces were withdrawn.

Then came the bad news. Ferdinand, declaring that he had "a stick
for the white ass and a stick for the black one" (meaning both liberals
and ultras) recalled the Marquis of Campo Sagrado and replaced him
with a mad incompetent. This new captain general of Catalunya was
Charles, count of Spain, born in France in 1775 and destined to be
assassinated by a Catalan patriot in Organya in 1839. His father had
been guillotined in the French Revolution, which did not dispose the
count to look favorably on either rebellious peasants or city liberals. In
fact his loathing for the former was matched only by his hatred of the
latter, and during his five years in office he dispatched a great many of
both with noose, garrote, and firing squad. Inflamed by paranoia, he
saw plots everywhere, left, right, and center, and in his flailing efforts

to repress them with terror he managed to alienate not only liberals of all shades and every ultra in the city but also (because of his lack of any kind of rational economic policy) the middle-class establishment as well. He once had his wife arrested on suspicion of treason and posted his daughter with a broom as a guard on the palace balcony; he was given to prostrating himself on church floors, and once, in full gala uniform before his assembled troops, he danced a jig during the execution of some liberals. The count's decrees on censorship enjoyed a lugubrious sort of fame. When the editor of *El Diario de Barcelona* submitted an obsequiously flattering ode on his regime to him for its last publication clearance (it had already been passed by the civil and Church censors), permission was refused: "In its place," came the personal directive from the count of Spain, "you will insert an article on agriculture, with remedies for piles, toothache, corns and other human infirmities . . . and not moral issues."

All in all, the count was as demented a tyrant as ever afflicted a Spanish city, and as the historian Jaume Vicens Vives remarked, his rule created more Catalan liberals in five years than the constitutionalists had in twenty. He was Barcelona's final inoculation against royal absolutism. From now on, however reactionary politics in the Catalan countryside might be, the great capital remained democratic, dissenting, and reflexively at odds with Madrid. In reality, by the 1830s, liberalism had won in Catalunya as in the rest of Spain. The Church continued endlessly to plot and machinate against it, and nostalgic conservative landowners ground their teeth. But the power lay with the middle classes and, for the future, with the young. Both knew that there was no combining absolutism with capitalism; both put their faith in a Europe whose approaching changes were shown by the outcome of the July Revolution of 1830, when the constitutional monarchy of Louis Philippe and the Orleanists replaced the reactionary government of Charles X.

This did not mean that reaction tactfully vanished from Catalunya in the 1830s. On the contrary: liberal, industrial values had difficulty spreading outside Barcelona and could hardly penetrate at all into deep Catalunya, Valencia, or the Balearic Islands. The countryside remained legitimist, conservative, suspicious of innovation. In it, the discontents of the *agraviats* continued to smolder, and they flared out again after Ferdinand's death, in the form of the First Carlist War.

The monarch died in 1833. "Spain is a bottle of beer," he had once remarked, "and I am the cork; the moment it pops all the liquid will spurt out, and God knows where I will fall." No such thing happened. Instead, there was a brief period of political vacillation under the un-

An anti-Carlist print, 1835

certain hand of Ferdinand's prime minister, Cean Bermudez, followed in 1834 by a royal statute modeled on Louis XVIII's charter of democratic concessions. And then, in 1837, the moderates and liberals took over and framed a new constitution.

Ferdinand left, as heir, a daughter: Isabel II, a pure-minded creature who had the political disadvantage of being only three years old. So at first Spain was ruled by her two regents: her mother, María Cristina de Borbón and María Cristina's favored liberal general, Joaquín Espartero Baldomero. The seven years of this regency, 1833–40, transformed Spanish politics. "We thought we were crowning a queen," wrote one astute commentator, Mariano José de Larra, in 1836, "while in reality we were starting a revolution."

A liberal revolution: and it did not appeal to the late king's brother, Carlos María Isidro de Borbón, who was as extreme a reactionary as Ferdinand had been. Spain, Carlos and his followers believed, should not and could not be ruled by a woman, let alone by a baby girl. He claimed the throne for himself. Supporters rallied to him: ultraroyalists of every stripe, from peasants to aristocrats. And so a bitter conflict over the legitimacy of the Bourbon succession broke out in 1833 and raged across Catalunya, Navarre, and the Basque country for seven years.

Supported and egged on by the Church, the Carlists sought a return to absolute male monarchy under the motto "Religio, rei i furs"—the *furs* being the traditional rights of rural Catalunya, the old law of village

A pro-Carlist print, 1874

---

and valley. Carlism was rooted in the countryside. Like the rebels of the 1820s, the Carlists defined themselves mainly by what they opposed: all liberals and innovations of any kind, including technology. They had no following in Barcelona and little in other Catalan towns, but in the mountains they kept up a tenacious guerrilla campaign, marked on both sides by all the horrors of the Napoleónic Wars—scorched earth, terror, the slaughter of unarmed civilians, the shooting of hostages. Since anything industrial was by now a symbol of city liberalism, the Carlists destroyed any factory they could find outside the walls of Barcelona. Meanwhile, more and more peasants, fleeing from farms and villages that had become battlefields, came streaming into Barcelona to find work in the mills.

Barcelona, at least, was a haven. In 1832 Ferdinand had replaced the detested count of Spain as captain general of Catalunya with the more moderate (and, above all, clinically sane) general Manuel de Llauder. Llauder was a Catalan, born in Mataró. He had fought for Bourbon absolutism against the French. But he knew the peculiarities of Catalunya well, and although he was no liberal, his appointment had been greeted with rejoicing in the streets of Barcelona. Still, his job remained all but

The Burning of the Convents in Barcelona, 1835

impossible: he had to crush the Carlists in the country by building up a liberal army, while putting down liberal agitators in the city. In the course of juggling the two, he revived the militia, rearmed it to fight the Carlists, and set in train a number of cautious reforms designed to defuse the threat of an immediate liberal rising in the city. Against the Carlists, Llauder had some success, although his army remained too small (twenty thousand recruits) and ill armed to finish them off. To those of the far left, he offered too little, too late. But with businessmen, great and small, Llauder was an outstanding success, for his regime promised the stability and order without which business could not prosper. As a Catalan factory commission reported at the time, "Work cannot go on either in the tyranny of despotism, or in the disorders of anarchy." Llauder paved the way for the triumph of the moderate bourgeoisie in Barcelona. But the street people, the extremist liberals, the *exaltats* who wanted nothing less than a complete fulfillment of the Constitution of 1812—they were not so happy. Moreover, Llauder's resuscitation of the militia had an unforeseen result. The militia sided with the progressives. Three years into Llauder's term of office the *exaltats*, with the militia's none-too-covert approval, tried to tear the city apart.

The summer of 1835 brought a sudden flare-up of anticlericalism to the streets of Barcelona. Revolutionary mobs, inflamed by liberal agitators, began the Burning of the Convents, an orgy whose like would not be seen again until the Setmana Tragica of 1909. The wave of arson started in the city of Reus, in revenge for the assassination of several liberals by a gang of Carlists. It spread rapidly through the Catalan countryside, wrecking—among other foundations—the great Cistercian abbey of Poblet, the Benedictine monastery of Sant Cugat del Valles, and the Carthusian convents of Scala Dei and Montalegre. And it raged uncontrollably in Barcelona, gutting scores of Church buildings, among which, most tragically of all, was the thirteenth-century church and convent of the Carme, a building that ranked in architectural importance with Santa Maria del Mar. A street ditty attributed the fury of its mobs to their disappointment at a bad bullfight:

> *La nit de Sant Jaume*
> *de l'any trenta-cinc*
> *hi va haver gran broma*
> *dintre del Torin.*
> *Van sortir tres braus,*
> *tots van ser dolents:*
> *aixo fou la causa*
> *de cremar convents.*

> On the night of St James
> In the year '35
> There was a big dust-up
> Inside the bull-ring.
> Out came three bulls,
> every one of them bad:
> and that was the reason
> for burning the convents.

What actually happened was akin to a modern soccer riot, with politics added. On the evening of July 26, the authorities staged a bull-fight to celebrate the queen's birthday. By then the city was hot with rumors of an impending coup by Carlist forces. The crowd at the corrida in the Barcelona bullring, incensed by the torpid performance of the bulls, started throwing benches and rubbish into the arena. People vaulted the barrier; someone found a rope and tied it to the horns of a dying bull. The beast was dragged out of the ring and through the streets, finishing up in the Ramblas outside the Capuchin convent. By then the riot had turned political; stones were flying, and orators were whipping up indignation with speeches about the betrayal of liberalism and the vile plots of priests. This was the flash point. The motive for burning

Sacking and burning of the Convent of Santa Caterina, July 26, 1835

the convents lay far back, deep inside the hatred cherished by liberals and the Catalan poor for the absolutists and their patrons in reaction, the clergy. There can hardly have been a non-Catholic among the arsonists, but every torch held to a pile of pews and wooden saints was also a blow against the detested party the Church had fostered. Barcelona lay under a dense pall of smoke for weeks. The crowd's rage spilled over from the Church to industry: on August 6 a mob of Luddite demonstrators, seeking revenge for unemployment among small handworkers in the textile trade, forced its way into the new Bonaplata works—Spain's first steam factory and the pride of Catalan industry—and burned it.

Perhaps the Church might have been able to rebuild its ruined establishments, after a fashion; but the coup de grace came in 1837, with the Mendizábal Laws. Juan Álvarez Mendizábal (1790–1853) had been one of Riego's comrades in the 1820 *pronunciamiento*. When the constitutional Triennial collapsed and Ferdinand VII returned to autocratic power in 1823, Mendizábal fled to England, where he stayed for twelve years, creating a new life for himself as a businessman and becoming a firm believer in the market-driven virtues of classic English liberalism. Prosperity and circulation would, he believed, create freedom in Spain, as they had in England. In 1835 he returned from his long exile, and

Josep Arrau i Barba, The Mob, *depicting the onset of riots on the Ramblas, August 5, 1835*

Isabel II's regents welcomed him into her government as minister of finance. How was he to open the stagnant economy of Spain and get its wealth moving from hand to hand? There was an obvious target: the entailed estates of the nobility and the landed property of the Church. These, together with common lands, covered most of the surface of Spain. Because they were frozen, the country had scarcely any real-estate market to speak of.

So Mendizábal took an extraordinary step, so radical that no Western government could even contemplate it today. He confiscated the property of the Catholic Church and sold it to raise state money—for the army had to be enlarged if the Carlists were to be crushed—and, more generally, to prime the bourgeois pump. His long sojourn in England had shown him how feeble the Spanish middle classes were in comparison with those of northern Europe. To have a broad-based bourgeoisie in Spain, there must first be a land market. In July 1837 the Mendizábal Laws were enacted: they declared that all Church land and property (with certain exceptions) was now state property, to be sold at auction as soon as possible. Before long, 80 percent of the Church lands inside the walls of Barcelona had been auctioned off. This wholesale divestment of Church land was known as the *desamortació*. Its impact on

Juan Álvarez Mendizábel

Catalunya in general, and the urban fabric of Barcelona in particular, was prompt, deep, and lasting.

At the end of the eighteenth century about 46 percent of the arable surface of Catalunya belonged to secular owners (including the nobility), 27 percent to the Church, and 28 percent to the king. But the profits from aristocratic estates were falling—between 1800 and 1819, for instance, the land income of the largest noble house of Catalunya, the dukes of Medinacoeli, dropped by a quarter, and it fell by another 32 percent from 1820 to 1826. In part this was owing to a drop in agricultural prices, but it was also caused by the peasants' reluctance to keep paying the various seigneurial taxes and tithes with which they were saddled.

Naturally this made the nobility less eager to hold on to its land; and when the seigneurial regime was finally abolished in 1837 and noble estates ceased to be entailed, the aristocrats sold. The same happened with Church land. Under the Mendizábal Laws the Church's town and country properties throughout Catalunya (apart from the churches themselves) were appraised at about 122 million reals. Between 1837 and 1845 three-quarters of them were forced onto the government's auction block, where they brought more than twice their appraised value—228.1 million reals.

Where was this money coming from? Not the peasantry, obviously. Not from the aristocrats, either. The newly rich bourgeoisie of Barcelona and the big provincial towns—Tarragona, Lleida, Vic—were the new landholders. In one auction of Church land in Tarragona, though three-quarters of the buyers were local, half the acreage on sale was bought by fifteen businessmen from Barcelona.

In the countryside Mendizábal's forced sales were meant to stimulate farming, and they did. They produced recapitalization of the country-side: an injection of new techniques, more advanced machinery, and fertilizers (large amounts of guano, for instance, were imported from Chile on the ships owned by the new landholders), and an increase of rural building occurred.

But ensuing changes in traditional crops brought the stirrings of social conflict. The "natural" model for these new owners was industry, in the country as in the town. They looked on land as a commodity that could be bought and sold like any other, and they saw the ancient rights of emphyteusis and *rabassa morta* as obstacles to be eventually cleared away. In fact, they did not succeed in getting rid of them—not yet, at least—because the peasants were extremely cunning and tenacious in defense of their archaic contracts. (When one bought expropriated Church land in the big sell-off of the 1830s, it came with all leases intact.) This slowed the conversion of the peasantry into a landless proletariat of day workers. And indeed the new owners often issued new leases to day workers, turning them into peasants. But as one Catalan historian mordantly remarked, that was due not to some tender nostalgia for the splendors of medieval Catalan land law, but to the fact that sharecropping was more efficient than salaried labor—it gave the worker incentives. With his knowledge of the severe agricultural decay of southern Spain, even an inexperienced town trader could see that peasant sharecropping was more productive than the kind of latifundia farming prevalent in Andalusia. But it could not stop the general trend toward consolidation of property in big farms or the shift to high-profit winegrowing. This would cause chaos in the rural economy when the vines were wiped out by phylloxera later in the century.

In Barcelona itself, four-fifths of the Church's land was auctioned off. And what could you do with a church or a convent that you had just bought? Demolish it; clear the space for housing, offices, a theater, a square, or a marketplace. In the process, some great buildings were destroyed along with a number of mediocre ones, and irreparable damage was done to the aesthetic fabric of the city. It would go on for years: in 1844, for instance, the Royal Chapel of Saint Agatha, begun in 1302 by

Jaume II, was sold for factory space, and not long afterward there was a move to put the entire complex of the medieval Hospital of the Holy Cross on the market as well. But there is no question that, from the broader viewpoint of urbanism, the Mendizábal Laws were also a blessing to Barcelona. They created public space in a city that was strangling for want of it.

The Boqueria market, on the Ramblas, occupies the sites of the sixteenth-century convent of Saint Joseph and the fourteenth-century convent of Saint Mary of Jerusalem—whose name alone survives in a narrow one-way street at the back of the Boqueria, smelling of fish and old fruit: the Carrer de Jerusalem. A nearby Augustinian convent suffered, so to speak, a double disappearance. First it was knocked down, and the street that ran across its site was called the Carrer Mendizábal. Then, in 1942, the Franco regime (not wishing to irritate the Church further by reminding it of its liberal nemesis) changed its name to the Calle de Junta DeComercio (now the Carrer del Junta del Comerç). But one workers' bar in the street, the Bar Mendizábal, obstinately held out and is still in business today—the only commemoration of Mendizábal's name in the whole of the city that owed so many changes to his famous, or infamous, laws.

The Gothic church of Santa Caterina, the third largest in Barcelona, was burned in 1835 and torn down in 1837; it bequeathed its site and its name to the long hangars and arcades of the Mercat Santa Caterina. The Teatre del Liceu, the glittering opera house that was to become the center of the city's middle-class cultural life, rose on the Ramblas in 1847 where a convent of barefoot Trinitarian friars had been, and on the other side of the Old City the Palau de la Música Catalana was eventually built on the site of the church of Saint Vincent de Paul, whose gutted ruins were not razed until 1902. If you stray into the Hotel Oriente, which is on the Rambla dels Caputxins opposite the debouchment of the Carrer de Ferran, you will find its gloomy banquet room is contained within an arched cloister—all that remains of the seventeenth-century Capuchin College of Saint Bonaventure, from which that part of the Ramblas took its name.

In a city short of fine small squares, one of the best—though, until lately, most run-down—is the little Plaça del Duc de Medinaceli, looking out across the Moll de la Fusta to the harbor at the foot of the Barri Gòtic. It, too, owes its existence to the fires of 1835 and the *desamortació*. Before then, its space was filled by a late-thirteenth-century convent of Minorite Franciscans. But the duke of Medinacoeli, the largest lay landowner in nineteenth-century Catalunya and a shrewd businessman, made

X. *Parcerisa*, Partisan soldiers of Isabel II Occupy the Cloister of the Convent of San Francisco, *1839*

a case to the liberals in the Ajuntament that, since his remote ancestors had originally given all the land around it to Jaume I, and the king in turn had given it to the monks, it should now revert to him. After some bargaining, the city government did give him a small piece, and the duke developed it as a residential square, designed by Francesc Daniel Molina i Casamajo in 1849. The column and fountain in the middle of the square, the work of a sculptor named Josep Santigosa i Vestraten, is the first iron monument in Barcelona. In its day it was viewed ambiguously as a technical triumph but a rather vulgar one: Surely bronze would have been more fitting than mere iron? Already, in 1849, the spread of iron in Barcelona was becoming a subject for cartoons and satirical albums. In a certain sense, this statue begins the use of iron in formal, declamatory sculpture, which would become such a feature of Catalan practice in the early twentieth century, with the work of Julio Gonzalez, who taught Picasso to weld. It was also, strangely enough, the only commemorative sculpture of a historic figure in the whole city; there had been a statue of Ferdinand VII on the street that bears his name, but the mobs of 1835 had toppled it. Its remote inspiration was the Vendôme Column (1830) in Paris, and there was a wrangle over whose effigy should go on top of it,

Daniel Molina i Casamajo's Plaça Reial, with Gaudí's lamp on the right

looking out to sea. One faction wanted Christopher Columbus, whom the Catalans thought was Catalan; another wanted Blasco de Garay, a now-forgotten inventor once believed, by some Catalan nationalists, to have discovered the motive power of steam—a rebuke to the perfidious English. Finally the city settled on Galceran Marquet, a vice-admiral who had led the Catalan fleet to victory against the Genoese in 1331.

Molina's masterpiece, however, is to be entered from the Ramblas a few minutes' walk away: it is the Plaça Reial. This noble square was one of the main elements in Barcelona's first major urban-renewal project since the 1820s. For at last, there was money to finish the transverse cut of the Carrer de Ferran—much narrower than the Ramblas, not even wide enough to qualify as an avenue, but still an expensive project—straight from the Ramblas to the seats of government in Plaça Sant Jaume. Abandoned in 1826 at the corner of Carrer d'Avinyo, the Carrer de Ferran reached the central square by 1849 and by 1853 joined up with the Carrer de la Princesa, forming an axis clear across the city from the Ramblas to the future Parc de la Ciutadella: an urban metaphor of great depth and symbolic weight, uniting Mont Tàber, the ancient Roman center that lay buried under Plaça Sant Jaume, with the two mightiest civic projects Barcelona had so far acquired, its hated Citadel and its beloved Ramblas.

The key to the new street was the Plaça Reial, a tranquil precinct tied to Carrer de Ferran and the Ramblas by three handsome pedestrian links—the Passatge Madoz, the Carrer Colom, and the glass-roofed Passatge Bacardi. The Plaça Reial is the only square in Barcelona that was designed as a complete unit, buildings and all. It is modeled on the planned residential squares of Napoleonic France, with elements of John Nash's London residential projects—though Molina had never been to England. Two high-windowed floors, tied together vertically by white pilasters, rise above the arcades; then comes a heavy, emphatic cornice and, above that, attics. The bays are uniform on all four sides, and the square radiates an uncommon feeling of secure enclosure and solid grace.

An iron fountain in the middle is decorated with conventional figures of the Three Graces; in 1879 the very young Antoni Gaudí designed the square's elaborate six-torch lamp standards, surmounted by the attributes of Hermes—a caduceus (two serpents twined around a staff) and a winged helmet. Hermes, trickster and dealer, had long before been adopted as the patron god of the Catalan business community. However, his protection did not save Plaça Reial from decline. The bankers and merchants for whom it was designed deserted the Ramblas for the Eixample after 1880. The big apartments with their fifteen-foot ceilings fell empty, were subdivided, and turned into warrens. During the 1960s and 1970s Plaça Reial acquired a vile reputation as the central drug market of Barcelona. It was taken over by other, less socially desirable, hierophants of Hermes—colonized by every species of manky street life, from dead-eyed pubescent whores to harmless rouged old *maricones*, with a thick and dangerous stratum of muggers, addicts, dealers, and cutpurses in between. The most authoritative (if that's the word) of the various gay guides to Barcelona marks its entry for Plaça Reial with the emphatic letters *AYOR*, meaning "at your own risk," and no doubt it is true that by the time a rent boy fell to hustling there he would be at the bottom of the heap. On Saturday nights in Plaça Reial you can almost hear the viruses mutating. But it is not simply a crack mall or an open-air meat rack. Its life is more complex than that. Gentrification has begun; families stroll, kids bounce soccer balls off Gaudí's tense black lamp standards, the iron fountain dribbles; and since the respectful restoration of the square begun earlier in the 1980s by the architects Correa and Milá, it has recovered the architectural dignity it used to have. The work involved a lot of repaving, the planting of dozens of mature palms—which flourish mightily and reinforce the square's meaning as an urban oasis—and the cleaning and fixing of the facades. "Too yellow," grumps another architect of their painted stucco, but this is carping: in the sun, the yellow-ocher walls suffuse the whole space with a stately glow, heightened by the crisp framing of the pilasters and stringcourses:

Josep Buixareu and Francesc Vila's Porxos d'en Xifré

surely this fulfills Molina's intention. Personally, I can attest that since I first sat down in one of its cafés in 1966, nothing bad has ever happened to me in Plaça Reial, but what is true for bulky Australians does not necessarily apply to every size or sex of visitor. Hang on to your purse, and do not let your camera swing from a strap.

Apart from Molina's great square, Barcelona's only memorable building of the 1830s was the Porxos d'en Xifré, Mr. Xifré's Porches, built on a site just inside the seaward rampart of the port near the Llotja. (Its ground floor has been occupied for several decades by one of Barcelona's more popular restaurants, the 7 Portes—a Catalan version of Sardi's, though luckily with better food, sporting brass plaques above its banquettes to commemorate the celebrities, Picasso, Einstein, and Hemingway included, who have sat there.) Josep Xifré i Casas (1777–1856) was an *indiano* who made one fortune in Cuba, exporting slave-grown sugar to the United States; later he moved to New York, multiplied his money, and came back to Barcelona in 1831, where he spread his funds in banking and real estate, becoming the biggest property owner in the city.

In 1835, as a gesture of confidence in the violence-torn capital, he began to erect two blocks facing the Llotja on one side and the sea on the other—the combined sources of his wealth. Designed by Josep Buixareu and Francesc Vila, they had arcades on the ground floor with three

Damia Campeny, Allegory of Cuban Trade, *terra-cotta plaque on a corner of Porxos d'en Xifré*

substantial floors and an attic above—a neoclassical scheme, with elegant pilasters on the central block and a Latin inscription on the pediment: "Urania [Muse of astronomy, hence of navigation] observes the motion of the sky and the stars." The arcades below are embellished with cartouches and reliefs by Barcelonese sculptors. These are an anthology of praise for Spanish conquest in the New World and, in particular, for the work of Catalan *indianos* like Xifré himself. Because the Porxos twin blocks have come down in the world and are scruffy tenement flats now, it is easy to overlook the bas-reliefs, but they have a certain iconographic interest. On the pilasters of the central block are medallion portraits of the explorers and conquistadores who opened the way to Xifré and his ilk—Columbus, Magellan, Cortés, Pizarro. Between the arcade arches of the flanking wings are carved trophies suggesting the wealth of the New World: a cornucopia full of bananas and breadfruit, an anchor with account books and a fish trap, a slave's head. And finally, at the corners of the building, there are terra-cotta plaques by Damià Campeny, a Catalan sculptor who trained in Rome under the influence of Antonio Canova, supported by a bursary from the Barcelona Junta de Comerç. These symbolize Xifré's own trading interests as the work of cherubs: fat putti loading sugarcane, imperiously pointing to horizons, humping sacks of coffee (stenciled with the owner's initials, *JX*), pushing slaves around, and doing whatever else Catalan *indianos* did to get rich.

VI

But the *indianos* were not little angels, and neither were their employees. The first sign of awareness that new Catalan classes presented new Catalan problems appeared in the work of a priest from Vic, Jaume Balmes i Urpia (1810–48). Balmes was one of those transitional thinkers who, not uncommonly, arise when new ideologies—in this case, French liberalism and the first mutterings of socialism—pour from abroad into a fixed, deeply conservative society. He was not, in any sense, a renegade from his Church. And yet his literary hero and role model, on the other side of the Pyrenees, had been the target of two disapproving papal encyclicals—the French Catholic priest Felicité-Robert de Lamennais (1782–1854), whose ideas also exerted a great influence on Hugo, Lamartine, and Sainte-Beuve.

In a nutshell, Lamennais was pro-Church but antiroyalist. He thought the state should leave all spiritual authority to the Catholic Church, but that the people should unite in a liberal democracy to free themselves of monarchism. However much the pope might agree with the former, the latter was unthinkable—with the result that Lamennais, driven further left by the Church's denunciations, penned his *Paroles d'un Croyant* (*A Believer's Sayings*), a fervent semibiblical tract asserting the purity of his Christian faith. All democracy, he argued, was latent in the Gospels; Jesus Christ himself was the first republican.

The appeal of Lamennais's radicalized Christianity was felt by young Catholics all over Europe, including Balmes, who was ordained to the priesthood in 1834, the year *Paroles* was published. It was excoriated by Catholic conservatives, including Spanish ones, and appearing at the start of the First Carlist War it was seized on by the Catalan right as a fine example of the democratic cancer against which Spain must be defended. So although Balmes's views, a milder echo of Lammenais's, may seem conservative or even reactionary today, they did not then.

Balmes never wavered from his belief that Catholic dogma was the only base of social order. He saw Roman Catholicism as dynamic, a stimulus to "civilization": the industrial revolution was not inherently Protestant. And he had a nostalgia for *pairalisme*, the Catalan sentiment based on rural patriarchy and feeling for the land, which was also one of the strong cards of Carlist reaction. But like Lamennais, he wanted to clear the ideology of the Church away from that of the throne. The Bourbon obsession with centrality, he argued, had always been ineffi-

Jaume Balmes i Urpia

cient and imperfect, and never more so than now. The "traditional unity" of Spain was a myth, "not attained until the eighteenth century, and even then very incompletely." In four articles he wrote for the periodical he started in Barcelona in 1843, *La Sociedad*—in Spanish, since Catalan was so little used as the language of argument that, like most writers of the day, he could not feel sure of reaching an intelligent audience with it—Balmes reflected on Catalunya and Madrid's policies.

Here was Spain's nascent industrial region, its one area of capital development that resembled northern Europe. Beside it, Madrid was inert, "a center without life," and the rest of the peninsula utterly backward. Catalan manufacture was England's only rival in the Spanish market. Thus, only Catalunya could save Spain from becoming an economic colony of England. The key was state protection of Catalan industry—not the free trade favored by liberal politicians in Madrid. What was good for Catalan cloth mills was good for Spain. Catalan business could go forward, favored by Madrid, without "dreaming up absurd projects of independence." Seen in economic terms, this *causa de Catalunya* crossed all party lines; it should not even be a party issue; both liberals and conservatives could get on board.

But just as Catalunya was the only part of Spain to take part in the industrial movement of the north, so it was the only area where the new social problems of industry appeared. None of the old rural harmonies between landowner and peasant survived in the cloth mills. And this made industry and its owners terribly vulnerable to mistaken policy:

> If Catalan industry receives the blow it fears, if an economic treaty or an unwise change in import duties should wipe out in one day the result of so much sweat and crush so many hopeful expectations; if, as a result, Catalunya goes into a sudden recession, not knowing what work to give to thousands of hands or how to help innumerable families condemned to perish from hunger, we will undergo a tremendous crisis.

Conservative Catalanism, as it developed later in the nineteenth century, flowed out of Balmes's ideas. But by the 1840s Catalan politics had a distinct, unofficial left wing, a radical olla podrida of idealism, plots, manifestos, magazines hatched and suppressed, insurrection, prison, exile. When the cautious Jaume Balmes warned of the likely alternative to his ideas about enlightened, Church-guided capitalism, he wrote darkly of *descabelladas doctrinas* and *absurdos proyectos de independencia*: "irrational doctrines," "absurd projects of independence." What he had in mind was the gathering movement toward democratic radicalism in Catalunya. We may look briefly at its main currents.

Probably the first radical democrat in Catalunya—certainly the first to write in Catalan—was Pere-Felip Monlau i Roca (1808–71), who edited three short-lived but influential magazines: *El Vapor* (1833–36), *El Propagador de la Libertad* (1835–38), and *El Nuevo Vapor* (1836–38). None of these promoted a strictly Catalan separatist line. Precisely because he was a socialist, Monlau's ideas predicted the cleavage in Catalan politics for the rest of the nineteenth century—Catalanism being a capitalist, middle-class movement, while socialism (and, later, anarchism) sought an *internationale*.

Monlau admired the French socialist Henri de Saint-Simon (whose dictum "To each man according to his capacity, to each capacity according to his work" was to be appropriated by Marx). He looked forward to a world without class and hereditary rights; one where social equality, disarmament, and a belief in work would bring fraternity to Europe. "Men are not equal," he wrote, "but they have equal *rights* to intellectual development and to the benefits and pay to which this development entitles them. . . . We do not wish to perpetuate the degrading abuses heaped on our species." He had no time for Catalan nationalism, since Catalunya (or any other state, actual or possible) was "only a fraction of one unity, human society." But since he disliked Madrid rule, Monlau advocated an independent Catalunya divided into four federal republics.

Abdo Terrades i Puli

His coeditor, Pere Mata i Fontanet (1811–77), took this somewhat further. Mata, an admirer of Giuseppe Mazzini, was the most Catalanist of the early republicans of the 1830s. The rule of Madrid, he wrote in *El Vapor* in 1836, made progress in Catalunya impossible. The country was sapped by the reactionary horrors of the First Carlist War and mired in the bureaucracy of the "indolent Castilians," imposed on Catalunya as on a foreign country by "this bunch of whores who only think of raking in their salaries."

So largely because of Mata's influence, the Catalan left grew more nationalistic, more anti-Madrid—and hence less tolerant of moderate liberals—during the 1830s. After the convent burning in 1835 it formed a revolutionary junta that proposed a Catalan federation modeled on the old Crown of Aragon and Catalunya. In 1836 a republican manifesto, *La Bandera* (*The Flag*), tried to incite the workers to proclaim the independence of Catalunya. The next year, a secret society called simply The Federation—nucleus of the future Democratic party—formed in Barcelona, and with it Catalan federalism became part of the republican platform. Its first public voice, a short-lived one, belonged to an *exaltat* named Ramon Xaudaro i Fabregas.

Xaudaro had gone into French exile after Ferdinand VII returned to power in 1823. In Paris he had published a treatise on republican

The Jamancia of 1843, with protesters attacking the Citadel

government for Spain (1832), which was not, however, translated into his native tongue for another thirty-five years. He came back to Catalunya when the king died in 1833 and immediately fell foul of the moderate liberals, who shut down the republican paper he started, pursued him with agents and spies, exiled him briefly to the Canaries in 1836, and at last, for leading a rising against them in May 1837, had him shot in the Citadel.

The next figure in the growth of Catalan socialism was Abdo Terradas i Puli (1812–56). Terradas came from Figueras, where in his twenties he wrote a number of political satires against royal absolutism—*El Rei Micomico*, a farce modeled on the short comedies of Cervantes, lampooned Ferdinand VII. For such impertinences the authorities banished him to France, where he struck up a friendship with Étienne Cabet. Returning to Barcelona in 1840 he started a radical paper, *El Republicano*, in which he set forth his "Plan for Revolution," an effusion half in prose and half in verse that included the anthem "La Campana," promptly taken up as the hymn of Catalan republicanism:

> *Ja la campana sona*
> *ja lo cano retrona*
> *anem, republicans, anem!*
> *A la victoria anem!*

Now the bell tolls
Now the cannon thunders
Forward, Republicans, let's go!
Onward to victory!

A firebrand, Terradas believed in revolution by force of arms. He justified this with an appeal to old Catalan rights; in a pamphlet titled *What We Were and What We Are*, he argued that the Catalan habit of forming workers' associations, which ran back to the medieval guilds, should be harnessed and radicalized so that "the levelling blade of democracy" could sweep through town and country. He joined the militia, quickly got control of it, and had gone some way toward converting it into a socialist, antiliberal army by 1843—"the people in arms," as he put it, "for the defence of its rights." And so he helped lead the militia into the futile but celebrated Jamancia of 1843, when the Barcelonese radicals rose against General Espartero, the liberal Bourbon regent of Catalunya, a strongman who prided himself on his political *cojones*.

The Jamancia began as a workers' and small shopkeepers' protest against city tax—hence its derisive nickname, the Pastrycooks' Revolt. Then came a rumor that Madrid was about to sign a trade treaty with England that would have opened the Spanish market to duty-free English cotton goods, thus kicking the economic props from beneath Catalan textile workers. As soon as the mobs came out, Espartero jailed Terradas and any other radicals he could lay hands on.

But his soldiers proved unable to hold the streets. The insurgents pushed them back to the fortress atop Montjuic and even managed to demolish part of the Citadel before Espartero's troops started shelling the city from their redoubt. The bombardment damaged or destroyed some 460 buildings. The Museum of the City of Barcelona preserves a curious relic of this incident: a funereal iron candelabrum containing one of Espartero's unexploded mortar bombs, surmounted by an owl, the bird of night, death, and wisdom. It has thirteen candlesticks on top, one for each night of Espartero's bombardment. Nineteen of the republican leaders (but not Terradas) went to the firing squad, and Madrid imposed a fine of twelve million pesetas on Barcelona. Terradas was fated to spend the last thirteen years of his short life between jail and, rather surprisingly, the town hall of Figueras, where he was elected mayor no fewer than four times—the town was aboil with republican sentiment—before dying in exile in Andalusia.

The dream of socialism, and eventually of anarchism, remained deeply ingrained in the substance of Catalan politics from the 1840s

Commemorative candelabrum cast from bombs that fell on the Palau de la Virreina during Esparteros's bombardment

onward; and through its impact on the town planner Ildefons Cerdà it had, as we will see, an immense effect on the developing shape of the city. And it became entwined with a wider civic obsession, the removal of the Bourbon walls, the hated *muralles*, so that the city could grow. Liberals wanted them destroyed in the name of justice and hygiene; patriotic businessmen, in the name of Catalunya and real-estate opportunities. In 1840 the liberal Ajuntament held a conference on the question, "What advantages would Barcelona, and especially its industry, derive from the demolition of the walls that enclose the city?" Every possible advantage, it concluded: health, prosperity, self-esteem. But the Crown-appointed authorities would not budge. To them, volatile and rebellious Barcelona was still a garrison city, and the walls were essential to discipline. Demolition seemed so far away that Felip Monlau in *El Vapor* urged the people of Barcelona to vote with their feet—get out and live somewhere else, perhaps in Gracia. Bureaucrats could stay and stifle in the Old City. "But those who live from their work, profession or industry, the manufacturing and industrious Barcelona, can and must breathe with freedom and independence. So to the country, and let us found a NEW BARCELONA!"

Not only the people but the machines had to spread out: there was no choice about that. The city within the Bourbon walls was too crowded to absorb them. In 1846 the Ajuntament passed a law explicitly banning the construction of any new factories inside the *muralles*. But by then the pressure of industry had already descended on three districts outside Barcelona: Sants, on the ancient Roman road south to the Llobregat, and Sant Andreu and Sant Martí de Provençals to the north. The logic of manufacture meant moving the spinning and weaving factories to where the cloth was bleached and dried, in the *prats d'indianes*. Neither Sants nor Sant Martí had strong municipal governments or anything in the way of zoning laws. They did, however, have plenty of water— next to labor and raw cotton, the most necessary ingredient in textile making; and the agricultural value of the land around them was small. Both were close to the sea and, before long, to railroad tracks. By 1860 the once-empty pastures of Sant Martí housed some ten thousand industrial workers (the figure would rise to thirty-five thousand by 1888); Sants, the largest of the three centers, was built up so early that it was annexed and absorbed by Barcelona in 1839.

Naturally, this all but wiped out the economic power of home manufacture: in the textile industry, the work of the *menestralia* took a far second place to the interests of the large companies. And there were few names on the roster of Barcelona's "good families," the industrial oligarchy that controlled banking, manufacture, and real estate in Catalunya, whose money was not based on the textile industry or tied into it. Arnus, Bonaplata, Batlló, Clavé, Ferrer, Girona, Güell, Juncadella, Montadas, Pons, Puig, Ricart, Tintoré—all of them owed their fortunes, in whole or in part, to King Cotton.

The textile industry fluctuated, to be sure. It had seen hard times in the 1830s as a result of the First Carlist War; the ultraconservatives' guerrilla raids on factories outside the walls of Barcelona had hurt it. It would have worse troubles in 1862–65, when the sudden shortage of raw cotton caused by the American Civil War sent the Catalan textile business into a recession.

Hence Barcelona's cotton magnates were never quite free from the boll weevil of insecurity. Because the rest of Spain had no industrial bourgeoisie that matched Catalunya's, Catalan entrepreneurs had no natural allies in Madrid. Rich as they became, they were less powerful on the national stage than they would have hoped to be. They were stuck in the role of lobbyists and petitioners, trying as best they could to influence the central government—where agrarian and banking interests, not manufacturing ones, held sway—and keep state policy on industry going their way. Their obsessive concern was protecting Catalan industry against the liberal ideology of free trade—*lliurecanvisme*, to give this bogey its Catalan name.

Where could Catalunya sell its textiles? Mainly in Spain and its colonies: the rest of the European market was sewn up by England and France. But by the 1850s, the Spanish market was fairly static and, even as Britain's empire was growing, Spain's colonial market had shrunk to Cuba, the Antilles, and the Philippines, "the hope and future," as Catalans incessantly pointed out, of Catalan industry. If the bigger textile nations were given a foothold in the Spanish market, if the protectionist walls favoring local manufacture were not maintained as vigilantly as the dikes of Holland against the sea, Catalunya would be ruined. This issue lay right on the surface of Catalan life. It was obsessive and by no means confined to the factory owners; workers feared it just as much as bosses, or more. The threat of an opening to English imports had touched off Barcelona's risings against General Espartero in 1843, and Catalan workers were quick to riot whenever they saw (or thought they saw) a free-trade threat to their jobs.

And so the Catalan industrialists, for all their local power, were timid when it came to confronting Madrid. They were afraid of wasting their ammo; every shred of influence had to be kept for the sole issue of defending protectionism. And though they were fighting a losing battle, they managed to drag it out for decades. Protectionism had become policy in 1825 under Ferdinand VII, when his minister of finance imposed a tariff law meant to cosset the Spanish economy, battered by the recent loss of the major South American colonies and by the invasion of the Hundred Thousand Sons of Saint Louis. It listed no fewer than 657 forbidden products. This was too much even for Catalan protectionists, but in 1841 a milder tariff law was passed by Madrid, reducing the banned items to 83. It reflected the liberals' belief in free trade, spurred by a visit to Madrid by the paladin of English free-market theory, Richard Cobden.

Feeling the wind, the Catalans got organized and founded, in 1848, the Industrial Institute, a protectionist committee headed by Joan Güell, the powerful boss of the company that came to be called Maquinista Terrestre. It was not very successful. The 1849 tariff law cut the eighty-three forbidden articles to fourteen, although the pressure of Güell and his colleagues in the Industrial Institute did manage to retain prohibitive import duties on foreign textiles. This kept the lid on the problem for the next twenty years, until the Glorious Revolution of 1868 brought the complete triumph of the free traders—a victory that would not be rolled back until 1874, with the return of the monarchy. Even so, Madrid's condescending attitude to Catalan petitions can be judged from the fact that Güell's Maquinista Terrestre, which was by far the largest machine-assembly business in Spain and specialized in rolling stock, received no contracts for railroad cars from the Spanish state until 1882.

Since no other part of Spain was urging protectionism—there being so little Spanish industry to protect, outside of Catalunya—the struggle over tariffs became inextricably bound up with the question of Catalan rights in general. Protectionism and Catalanism were seen, in Catalunya and out of it, as one and the same thing. In Madrid, free traders derided the "provincialism" of the Catalans; in Barcelona, bigwigs inveighed across the snowy cloth at municipal banquets against the "torpidity" of the rest of Spain. The tariff issue would become the biggest economic factor in Catalanist politics in the last third of the nineteenth century; it produced a middle-class mind-set peculiar to Catalunya, by which manufacturers—who, one might normally think, would have shown a natural bent toward internationalism—became vigorous and even rabid apostles of the local, the provincial, the traditional, leery of foreign influences in culture (other than machines), and given to outpourings of sentiment about the old values of Catalunya Vella, which their own business practices were obliterating.

VII

A patriotic middle class, feeling its oats, aware of its economic power, rooted in a sense of place, will want to express itself. If its language is different from that of its political rulers, it will seek to legitimize its mother tongue. This, basically, is why the struggle for the Catalan language became such a large issue in the nineteenth century, and why the question of its legitimacy went beyond the narrow frame of literature into the greater one of politics. In Catalunya language and politics are entwined, interwoven, inseparable.

This process was set off, of course, by the Enlightenment, which came to Spain fifty years late: Bourbon autocracy and the Inquisition had barred its way, but they could not seal the peninsula off from the great current of northern European ideas, especially not in Barcelona,

Bonaventura Carles Aribau i Farriols

so close to France. The Catalan language began to turn back into a subject of cultural interest at the end of the eighteenth century. Castilian *ilustrados* saw no reason to repress the use of any local tongue, and Catalan ones began moving toward it to show their sympathy with the people and to assert their rights to independence and deep cultural memory.

Some of the impetus came from the Catalan politician and historian Antoni de Capmany i Montpalau, whose main work, *The Historical Memorials*, to give its full title, *of the Shipping, Trade and Arts of the Ancient City of Barcelona*, published in several tomes between 1779 and 1792, was the masterpiece of eighteenth-century Catalan history writing; Capmany, one might say, was the father of all subsequent efforts by Catalans to treat their culture as distinct and unique. It also embodied a paradox: to reach a wide, educated audience, Capmany had to write it in Spanish, not Catalan.

But after 1814, linguists as well as historians were arguing for a renewal of the language: inflamed by the sufferings of the whole peninsula, local patriotism went hand in hand with patriotism of the more generalized Spanish sort. The most vocal of these linguists of the 1820s was Josep Pau Ballot. He argued that Catalan was not, as Castilians routinely insisted, merely a local dialect. Rather, it had been "a court language for many years, spoken in the palace and much valued by

Jaume I and by the Aragonese kings." It was still the mother tongue, spoken at home, in the marketplace, and in church. It deserved "the utmost esteem, and we prize it for its smoothness, sweetness, acuity, grace, variety and abundance." It had room for every subtlety, every cultural twist and coding. "If the learned . . . were to cultivate [Catalan] and use it in their writings . . . they would smooth and polish it until one saw what art and diligence can do. Then, I have no doubt that it would return from death to life; it would equal or surpass other languages." But Ballot, too, was writing this in Castilian. Conscious of the bind, he compared himself to "a grindstone, which does not cut but sharpens other tools."

To assume its former dignity and autonomy as a language, what Catalan most needed was not linguists and historians, but poets—the "unacknowledged legislators" who would breathe imaginative fire back into it. And these emerged. It may be that the grateful Catalans overjudged their qualities as writers (which happens to most Great National Poets anyhow, once their reputations have entered the pantheon of patriotic aspiration); but, by the end of the 1830s, there they were, complete with laurels and Phrygian cap—Carles Aribau and Rubió i Ors. Catalan scholars have long wrangled over the intellectual scope of the Catalan Renaixença, how different it was from other forms of European romanticism, what it meant. But none of them disagree about the emblematic work of art with which the movement, however one might narrowly define its nature, began.

It was on August 24, 1833, when the Barcelona literary-political weekly *El Vapor* carried an ode, "La Pàtria" ("The Fatherland"), written in Catalan by Bonaventura Carles Aribau i Farriols (1798–1862). Aribau was a middle-class romantic poet, born thirty-five years before in Barcelona; in the 1820s he had launched a short-lived weekly called *El Europeo* that, as its name implied, looked eagerly beyond the Pyrenees to the romantic movement that was surging through French, German, and English writing. He had dreams of being a Chateaubriand, a Byron, exhorting the *paisos Catalans* to reclaim their ancient liberties. In between dreams, he worked for a financier in Madrid and cut his literary teeth on such projects as a lengthy didactic poem in praise of free trade—not a popular theme among his fellow Catalans.

His mentor and patron, Gaspar de Remisa (1784–1847), another Catalan, got rich from smuggled foodstuffs in Barcelona during the Napoleonic War and then, after 1814, invested in coach lines. Because transport in Spain was so bad—the worst in Europe—Remisa prospered. Before he turned forty he had his own bank in Barcelona. In 1826 he became secretary of the Royal Treasury in Madrid. He watched over Aribau and coaxed the younger man along. By the 1840s Aribau's own career as an economic bureaucrat had taken off: he took charge of the treasury and then the state mint, mines, and holdings. All this latter part of Aribau's career is forgotten, like Wallace Stevens's contributions to the insurance business—whatever they may have been. He is remembered for this one poem, written in his youth and dedicated to Gaspar de Remisa. But it is perhaps worth keeping in mind that "La Pàtria," like most of the cultural upsurge that followed it, came straight out of the environment of plush and tassels and gold-backed bank accounts of the conquering Catalan bourgeoisie. The Renaixença made a tremendous fuss over ancient peasant traditions, folklore, and popular language, but it was in no sense a workers' movement. It came from somewhere near the top of the new Catalunya, the industrial and banking society that was forging its own image. In this respect it was no different from French romanticism: Victor Hugo's father was a general, Alphonse de Lamartine's a landowner, Alfred de Musset's a high government official, Alfred de Vigny's a royalist rentier.

Aribau's ode begins with a long panning shot, a slow, nostalgic invocation of the Montseny Massif:

> *Adéu-siau, turons, per sempre adéu-siau,*
> *oh serres desiguals, que allí, en la pàtria mia,*
> *dels nuvols e del cel de lluny vos distingia,*
> *per lo repos etern, per lo color més blau.*
> *Adéu tu, vell Montseny, que des ton alt palau,*
> *com guarda vigilant, cobert de boira e neu,*
> *guaites per un forat la tomba del Jueu,*
> *e al mig del mar immens la mallorquina nau.*

> Farewell, hills, forever goodbye,
> O jagged ranges, there in my native land
> ranges that stand out from clouds and distant sky
> in their eternal peace, by their bluer color.
> Farewell, old Montseny, like a sentinel
> on a high rampart, wreathed in fog and hail
> watching, through a cleft, the tomb of the Jew
> and the Majorcan fishing-smack in the huge sea.

The mountain is the emblem of Catalunya, a landscape that signifies the family: "Once I knew your proud brow, as I could recognize the faces of my parents; I knew the sound of your torrents as well as my mother's voice, or the cries of my son. But torn away in time of persecution, I do not know or feel it as I did in better times, just as a tree transplanted to a different land loses the taste of its fruit and the odor of its flowers." In Madrid, he is pining away—the banker posing as prisoner. (Nothing except business, one should remember, was keeping Aribau in Madrid.) "What is it worth to me if bad luck has taken me away to see, close up, the towers of Castile, if my ear can no longer hear the troubadours' song, and no generous memories awaken in my breast?" It is the language—*la llengua llemosina*, or Catalan—that lies at the heart of belonging, of identity itself. From "exile" in Madrid, the blue ridge of Montseny has become a mirage: but the concreteness of the language remains.

> *Plau-me encara parlar la llengua d'aquells savis*
> *que ompliren l'univers de llurs costums e lleis,*
> *la llengua d'aquells forts que acataren los reis,*
> *defengueren llurs drets, venjaren llurs agravis.*
> *Muira, muira l'ingrat que, al sonar en sos llavis*
> *per estranya regió l'accent natiu, no plora,*
> *que, al pensar en sos llars, no es consum ni s'enyora,*
> *ni cull del mur sagrat la lira dels seus avis!*

> Let me speak again the tongue of those wise men
> who filled the world with their customs and laws,
> the tongue of the strong men who served the kings,
> defended their rights, avenged their insults.
> Beware, beware the ungrateful man whose lips utter
> his native accent in a far country and does not weep,
> who thinks of his origins without pangs of yearning,
> nor takes his fathers' lyre from the holy wall!

This array of patriotic images pervaded the writings of the Renaixença for the next half century: an idealized feudal past, a lost strength and wisdom buried, like the sword in the stone, in Catalan history; the *llar*, or "hearth," and the ancestral lyre, which must be taken down—it is nothing other than language itself—to contend with other languages, hanging on its "holy wall." Aribau's language forms an obsessive matrix through which all experience is refracted. Only in Catalan can he think straight:

> My first infant wail was in Catalan
> when I sucked the sweet milk from my mother's nipple;

I prayed to God in Catalan each day
and dreamed Catalan songs every night.
When I find myself alone, I talk with my soul,
it speaks Catalan, it knows no other tongue,
and then my mouth does not lie, or know how to lie,
and my words well up from the center of my breast.

If Aribau gave Catalanism its emblematic cri de coeur, Joaquim Rubió i Ors (1818–99) took it up and turned it into a linguistic crusade. In 1841, he published a small collection of his poems under the title *Lo Gayter de Llobregat*, (*The Bagpiper of Llobregat*). It became the first manifesto of the Catalan Renaixença, not so much for the poems themselves (none of which attained the fame of Aribau's ode) as for Rubió's introduction.

In it, he argued passionately for the recovery of Catalan, "our ancient, melodious and abundant tongue, which to our shame is vanishing from day to day," as a literary language. Perhaps it had been "an extravagance, an absurd anachronism" to bother with poetry amid the horrors of the Carlist civil war. Perhaps the poet who did so was a mere escapist, like "a heartless, disloyal sailor who, fleeing the storm, ends up singing on a rock on the beach while his brothers battle the waves and vanish in the depths." And yet the effort must be made, he wrote, since the future of Catalunya depends on its sense of its own past, and language is the link between them.

Rubió saw a long tradition of poets, from William of Aquitaine to "modest Aribau"—some anonymous or forgotten, and some gloriously remembered—bringing their gifts to the language, "this venerable and immense monument of past ages, of which one could say, as of the pyramid the Mexicans built in the center of their country, to which every passer-by brought a stone, 'all have raised it but none has signed it.' "

Is it hard to write poetry in a language "whose grammar is hardly even fixed"? No doubt. But can "our ancient glories and the achievements of our forebears" be conveyed in Spanish? Who can lay his hand on his heart and say that Spanish is the right instrument for so quintessentially Catalan a task? Against these rhetorical questions, Rubió posed another: Is Catalan so mean and sparse a language that it cannot repay the trouble of studying it? Surely not. Catalunya's chronicles are as abundant and various as any other nation's; we have "an immense gallery of troubadors, the fathers of modern popular poetry," and their work once influenced all Europe, lovesick Petrarch as well as *lo terrible Dante*. When the Bourbons conquered Barcelona a century and a quarter before, Rubió reminded his reader, our ancestors battled . . . in defence of their ancient rights, spilling rivers of blood on the walls, squares and churches of this city, so that they could pass on to their grandchildren the legacy and language that their parents left them; and though so little time has passed, not only have their descendants forgotten this sacrifice but some of them, ungrateful to their country, are ashamed to be caught speaking Catalan, like criminals surprised in the act.

Who can assess the merits of the language? Only writers: "Nobody can judge the richness of a mine better than those who work in it . . . who have gone down far enough to touch the seam." The Catalan language can, must, and will be brought back by generations later than his (he was twenty-three at the time), and those who resuscitate it will become one with the medieval past.

This past, as happened more and more in Catalunya as the decades of the Renaixença rolled by, ballooned into the stuff of myth: compared with Catalan fancies about their Middle Ages, the romances of Sir Walter Scott or Tennyson's *Idylls of the King* are almost social realism. The audience of the future, Rubió thought, would be the descendants of

those sons of the harp who went from castle to castle to assuage the melancholy of the barons in times of peace, and who exchanged the Phrygian cap [*gorra*] for the helmet in times of war . . . the poet-knights who came to lay at the feet of their Lady the silver rose won in a poetry-contest, as eagerly as they offered her the ribbons given them for bravery by the queen of a tourney . . . who spent their lives singing of love, religion and chivalry.

Rubió believed that though Catalunya could not hope for political independence, because it lacked economic and military power, *cultural* independence was something it could make for itself, on its own terms. We need institutions to foster Catalan writing, as in the Middle Ages: so bring back the poetry contests of the Jocs Florals! Reestablish the Consistori del Gay Saber! Astonish the world with sonnets, love songs, and aubades! Win back from the Castilians and their colonizing tongue "the crown of poetry that our country shamefully let fall from its forehead"!

It goes almost without saying that Rubió i Ors's argument was a pure emanation of romanticism in its yearning for the primitive essence of Catalunya, its trust in the instincts of youth and patriotism. Perhaps if it had been less measured it would have been less successful, but as it stood, it found an instant audience. *Lo Gayter de Llobregat* sold out; when every copy was gone, young men laboriously penned it, as in samizdat, and passed Rubió i Ors's introduction from hand to hand; it was declaimed in schools, in taverns, and even in military barracks, to pump up the ardor of Catalan militiamen in their struggles against the Carlists. But there was no immediate answer to *Lo Gayter*'s call for the revival of the Jocs Florals; almost eighteen years passed before this peculiar institution was set up again.

VIII

Before it could be reinstated, the body of Catalan poetry—both courtly and folk—had to be disinterred and revived. The first collections of Catalan folk literature, inspired by the romantic cult of sincerity and authenticity, belong to the same period as Aribau and Rubió i Ors. The main ones were made by two men who, though very different in character, had in common an unquenchable thirst for research: Manuel Milà i Fontanals and Pau Piferrer i Fàbregas, both born in the same year, 1818.

Piferrer was, by all accounts, a charismatic young man, red-hot with patriotism, and a hard worker. His literary hero was Victor Hugo. Born into a *menestral* family in Barcelona, he began his career writing drama criticism and, in 1838, became editor of an ambitious series of illustrated albums published in Barcelona under the general title *Recuerdos y Bellezas de España* (*Souvenirs and Beauties of Spain*), modeled on the "picturesque atlases" that were such a popular form in France. Over the next ten years he wrote the first of two lavish volumes on Catalunya and a good part of the second (it was finished after his death by the future politician Francesc Pi i Margall), along with a third on Majorca and the Balearic Islands. Their main focus was folk culture—songs, sayings, poems, costumes, vernacular buildings, rituals, and festivities—and Romanesque-Gothic architecture: everything that preserved some trace of what he called "the popular and religious genius of the Middle Ages, which is the true and only poetic past of modern nations." Most of the folk poetry and song that Piferrer collected came from the mountainous region around the inland village of Sant Felíu de Codines, where he and his family went in the summer to escape the heat of Barcelona; his romantic enthusiasms hardly had the chance to deepen into methodical scholarship, for he died of a fever in 1848, aged only thirty.

Manuel Milà i Fontanals

His friend Manuel Milà i Fontanals (1818–84) was his opposite in
every way: slow, measured, conservative, and a stickler for method. The
son of a farmer in Penedés, raised in the family *casa pairal*, he studied
law and letters at the universities of Barcelona and Cervera, took his
doctorate in 1844, and three years later won the chair of literature at the
University of Barcelona, where for decades he reigned ponderously over
its literary curriculum, half Moses, half absentminded professor. The
memoirs of the Barcelona playwright Josep de Sagarra recorded his own
father's impressions of Milà, which were indelible:

> The glory of our Renaixença was so asthmatic, wheezing and scan-
> dalously fat that his pupils called him "The Literary Whale." His voice
> was like the lowest note of an organ during the office of Tenebrae. He
> spoke with many pauses: a profound effect, which almost put the flies
> that impertinently circled his bald head to sleep. . . . The great man
> lived in an attic on University Square, amid a chaotic disorder of onion-
> forks and cakes from Vilafranca, his birthplace. My father described
> him sitting there one June afternoon, clad in tight pants that gave his
> belly the look of a bomb about to burst. He wore a peasant's shirt with
> big blue-and-white checks, and a pair of wide sweaty braces. . . . Don
> Manuel once lent my father a textbook which had a salted anchovy
> stuck between its pages, as a bookmark.

He had begun as a fervent romantic, an internationalist and something of a freethinker, whose literary pantheon included Goethe, Dumas, Byron, and Chateaubriand. But in his early twenties his views began to change. His brother Pau Milà i Fontanals had been living in Rome, in whose expatriate artists' colony he had come to know some of the German Nazarenes, including their ideological leader Johann Friedrich Overbeck. The Nazarenes represented the Catholic as distinct from the Lutheran strain of German romanticism; Overbeck had converted to Rome and fervently believed that a revival of Catholic orthodoxy, allied to a close study of past painting—early Raphael and his master Perugino, Fra Angelico, Masaccio, and, of course, Dürer—would lead art back to the one true way from which "pagan" neoclassicism had distracted it: a union of innocent faith, Latin grace, and German *einfuhlung*, "inwardness." He exhorted his juniors "to follow the old masters, particularly the earliest ones, assiduously imitating what is just and naïve in their works."

"Just and naïve": the phrase recalls Friedrich Schiller, a great influence on the Nazarenes through his disciple August Schlegel, and eventually on Milà i Fontanals too. For Schiller, there were two kinds of artist, the naïve and the sentimental. (Neither of these words had the disparaging overtones they do in English today. They were simply descriptive.) Schiller's sentimental poet is the man of culture who experiences things through a scrim of existing images: for him, direct contact with reality and direct apprehension of nature is only an ideal, and the task of poetry is to represent that ideal in all its elusiveness. He "*reflects* upon the impression that objects make on him, and only in that reflection is the emotion grounded which he himself experiences." Like Horace, his Roman prototype, the sentimental poet watches himself imagining the world and imagines himself watching it. The naïve poet, on the other hand, whose ancestor is Homer, need do no such thing. He "only follows simple nature and feeling . . . there is for him no choice in his treatment." Naïveté, in Schiller's sense, is the common denominator of all art that is direct, rugged, epic, and impersonally noble, in which the character of a people or a nation takes precedence over a single man's feelings. Naïveté is nature; sentimentality is culture.

The impact of Overbeck, Schiller, and Schlegel, coupled with the devout preachings of his newly Romanized brother, changed Milà's thinking. Indeed it seems to have sparked in him a deep inner crisis, as his desire for Catholic assurance wrestled with the secular subjectivity of the romantic heroes of his youth. He emerged from it stricter, more papal, far more of a conservative. But if anything, it increased his energies as a researcher and classifier, and from then on Milà i Fontanals never rested from his self-imposed task of seeking what he conceived to be the authentic purity of Catalan amid its popular roots. Here, he argued, was one of the world's great tongues, perhaps the oldest to spring directly from Latin: and once it was restored, so would be the "genius" of Catalan independence. It was, he wrote, the language

> that for nine centuries now has produced heroic, romantic and historic poems that rank with the best of the Middle Ages; that Guillem of Aquitaine used when the "talent de cantar" seized him; listened to and applauded not only by the Courts of Provence and Aragon, but by those of Castile, England and Italy as well; cultivated by Dante and Petrarch, and the mother-tongue of the Kings of Aragon; the language in which the early maps were written, as well as scholarly and respected codices and incomparable chronicles; a language that possessed a rich vein of folk-poetry . . .

Folk poetry was the irreplaceable model, the source of linguistic purity. The elements of its subject matter—religion, laws, customs—had to be winnowed out and preserved as models of thought. Like a roofless church, it was the ruin of an ancient, epic edifice, greatly changed in the course of oral transmission. The seal of its authenticity was tradition, slowly passed down along the generations. Tradition stood in contrast to the "vacuous artifice" and mere subjectivity of "modern" poetry (by which Milà meant romanticism). The zeitgeist was reflected in it, the feelings and the records of Catalunya, the air of the homeland. It was Milà, more than anyone else, who gave the Renaixença its search for poetic roots, its historicist slant—and its weakness for pedantry.

One catches the spirit of Milà's sense of the past, elegiac and powerfully conservative, in such verses as "Un Temple Antic" ("An Ancient Church"), where the sight of a Romanesque chapel in Old Catalunya becomes a metaphor of the natural order of traditional Catalan society: shelter, endurance, the manifestation of myth, and an organic closeness to the landscape:

> *Sos nobles murs han combatut set segles*
> *amb pluges, vents i llamps*
> *jamai vençut, a cada nova lluita*
> *més bell se n'és tornat.*
>
> *Avui pareix cobert al peu de boira,*

mes alça triomfant
arcs a dins d'arcs, historiades faixes,
cloquer enfinestrat.

Que bé colora l'alba son aspecte,
ensems joiós i gran!
Com s'avenen ses pedres envellides
i els arbres verdejants!

L'obra de l'home al camp belleses dóna,
i en pren ella del camp,
i maridats art i natura engendren
vida i amor i pau.

Riu d'oblidança, l'esperit neteja
de pensaments amargs:
plers somniats per un instant li porta
l'alè de l'Ideal.

Its noble walls have fought off seven centuries
of rain, wind and thunderbolts
Unconquered, and with each new struggle
becoming more beautiful.

Today, with its base shrouded in fog
it rises in triumph
Arch within arch, storied cornices,
a window-pierced spire.

How the dawn floods it with color
joyous and grand!
How its ancient stones harmonize
with the leafing trees!

The work of man gives the fields beauty
and receives it from the fields,
Art joins nature to engender
life, love and peace.

The stream of forgetfulness washes the soul
Clean of embittered thoughts;
Drowsy pleasures bring, for a moment,
The breath of the Ideal.

Rubió i Ors's introduction was the node around which a new patriotic sensibility formed: nostalgic, idealizing, full of pent-up energy. The energy came from obsession, and before the 1880s it decayed—at least in poetry—into the mincing medievalism of the late Jocs Florals. But while it worked, the prime object of that obsession was to turn fictions into myths and symbols into archetypes. In this respect, the project of nineteenth-century Catalan culture—in poetry, prose, the evocation of history, and, before long, in architecture and the decorative arts—was not dissimilar to that of other European countries facing rapid and sometimes revolutionary social change. It wanted to find, and if need be invent, a stable sense of identity through which it could define itself against other parts of Europe (including, in Catalunya's case, the rest of Spain itself). By going back to the Middle Ages and beyond, by plunging into archaism and folklore, Catalunya could show how different was its essential being, its *ser autentic*, from any other country's. And by reviving medieval forms under the sign of a pure, linking language, it could also show that something older and deeper was at work in these new times than steam jennies and capital development. Thus, though the Catalans shared the new industrial reality with other countries in Europe—the processes of investment banking and machine production being much the same everywhere—they could assuage the anxiety this homogenization caused by constantly pointing to what was old and uniquely theirs. Industrial capitalism might make them different from the rest of Spain, but the revival of their own Middle Ages would distinguish them from the rest of Europe.

This kind of national thinking, this enthusiastic construction of imagery, was going on in other countries too, whereas in Catalunya it had risen out of the eighteenth-century reverence for the primitive, the epic, the nobly authentic. But that taste was immensely amplified by the process that the English historian Eric Hobsbawm has dubbed "the invention of tradition." Wales had its bards and harps; Ireland, its Celtic twilight, "old Ireland," populated by the shades of kings and heroes, Finn MacCool and Cuchulain; Scotland its myth of the Highland tribes, its Caledonian chieftains "glowing," as Edward Gibbon put it, "with the warm virtues of nature" while the braw northern air circulated beneath their kilts. The cult of Ossian, that fictitious Gaelic bard invented by James Macpherson, spread all over Europe, endorsed by the outstanding minds of the age: Klopstock, Schiller, Goethe. Germany had Arminius, the warrior of the Teutoburg Forest, who, in A.D. 9, beat back the Roman legions of Publius Varus; the deeds of this primal hero-liberator gave rise to the Siegfried legend. The French looked back to the ancient Gauls as a relief from the ancient Romans. In the nineteenth century, reverence for the mythic or, at best, cloudily historical ancestor merged with an increasing cult of Gothic architecture as the style of "true," native building—as opposed to classical styles, which reminded people that they had once been Roman slaves. These impulses were general, if not universal; but it is no surprise that they were particularly felt in Ireland and in Catalunya, since both, with reason, felt themselves to be the victims of history, colonies whose power of cultural self-expression was always at risk of being obliterated not only by larger powers, London or Madrid, but by their own amnesia—the loss of Gaelic and of Catalan as languages of the high, uniting imagination. There is a melancholy stanza by W. B. Yeats that seems as true of the Catalan predicament in the 1840s as of the Irish in the 1890s:

> We were the last romantics—chose for theme
> Traditional sanctity and loveliness;
> Whatever's written in what poets name
> The book of the people; whatever most can bless
> The mind of man or elevate a rhyme;
> But all is changed, that high horse riderless,
> Though mounted in the saddle Homer rode
> Where the swan drifts upon a darkening flood.

PART II

The New City

CHAPTER FIVE

Blind with Love
for a Language

I

One of the peculiarities of Spanish history is how far and how often its rhythms were out of sync with those of northern European states. Nowhere is this clearer than in the mid-nineteenth century. In 1848 Europe seemed aflame with radical change. In that "year of revolutions" all autocracies, for a hopeful moment, appeared to be tottering, their worm-eaten cores exposed. The events of 1830 had marked the transition of power from the aristocracy to the middle classes in Europe—and, in the United States, from its propertied oligarchs to its small traders, its frontier farmers, and even its urban poor under the sweeping impetus of Jacksonian democracy, whose sight filled Alexis de Tocqueville with such doubt and foreboding. But the events of 1848 were still more vivid. Nationalism was grafted onto the model of insurrection created in 1789 and passed through the frontiers. Revolutions broke out in France and across Italy, in Germany, through much of the Hapsburg empire, and even in Switzerland. The Hapsburg emperor had to flee from Vienna to Innsbruck; Pope Pius IX decamped from Rome to Gaeta; in Paris, Louis Philippe abdicated; Lajos Kossuth rose in Hungary; the Czechs took to the streets after the pan-Slav conference in Prague; even the small island of Sardinia managed to declare war on Austria—and beat its army at the battles of Goito and Pastrengo. As Eric Hobsbawm put it, "There has never been anything closer to the world-revolution of which the insurrectionaries of the period dreamed than this spontaneous and general conflagration."

Below the Pyrenees, there was no aftershock from these convulsions except in the minds of a tiny minority of *ilustrados* and progressive liberals. Spain had no occupying power to rebel against. The spectacle of Europe in turmoil certainly hardened the policies of Isabel II, her ministers, and her supporting generals against the dangers of unbridled democracy. It did nothing to change the framework of monarchical government: Spain's cabinet was not elected, but appointed by Isabel II and endowed by her with the power to dissolve the parliament—thus effectively keeping progressives out of power. The lessons of 1848 in other countries only confirmed the Spanish Church's loathing of change and had no impact at all on the vast illiterate, conservative majority of the Spanish poor, for whom Europe was hardly even a figment of the imagination.

Between the 1840s and the liberal revolution of 1868, which shoved Isabel II off her throne in Madrid and into exile in France, the merchants, manufacturers, and bankers of Catalunya prepared their own triumph, their role in the Europe-wide victory of the bourgeoisie that would expand after 1851. It increased Catalunya's sense of apartness—its distance from Madrid, its proximity to Europe—not because Catalan businessmen sympathized with the events of 1848 (on the contrary, they viewed them with horror) but because their hopes lay with technological growth, whose models were outside Spain.

Yet the effects of industrialization in Catalunya seemed less radical than in northern Europe. The Catalans got industry without getting an industrial revolution. The rural and feudal imagery of Old Catalunya drifted into the domain of myth. But by treating it as myth—their own Gothic, their own Celtic Twilight—middle-class Catalans found comfort and gentility in it, an escape from the anxieties of the age. This longing for conservative refuge lay at the heart of the Catalan Renaixença.

By the mid-1850s Catalunya as a whole had 1.67 million people, of whom 189,000 lived in Barcelona. Since 1834 the population of the city had risen by 56,000—a gain of 40 percent in twenty years. The countryside and provincial towns grew slowly, but Barcelona, jammed tight against Felipe V's walls, had entered a period of explosive growth, based on industry.

By the mid-1850s more than a quarter of Spain's industrial gross national product came from Catalunya. The principate earned twice as much on manufacture, and half as much on agriculture, as the rest of the country. Apart from the Basque territory, it was Spain's sole industrial belt.

Still, Catalan industrial development was very spotty. Heavy industry in the nineteenth century was based on coal and iron: Catalunya's coal was scarce and bad, its iron nonexistent. Both had to be imported.

The poverty of local roads made matters worse. In 1848 Barcelona set up a committee to supervise the building of highways—"highway," in this context, meaning anything paved and wide enough for two wagons to pass each other—with the funds coming not from Madrid but from regional taxes. It achieved so little that by the end of the nineteenth century, Catalan roads were carrying five times the traffic volume of Castilian ones with only a third as many miles per citizen. Catalan businessmen wanted to keep their money for themselves, not spend it on public services, and this primitive reflex cost them dearly. So, too, with railways. The first passenger rail line in France had opened in 1828, but Catalunya's (and Spain's) first one, eighteen miles of track from Barcelona to Mataró, had to wait until 1848; by then, France had 1,140 miles of working track. Railroads from Barcelona snaked out to Zaragoza in 1861, Girona in 1862, Tarragona in 1865, and Valencia in 1867, but no track reached the French frontier (less than a hundred miles away) until 1878—almost ten years after a North American railroad linked the Pacific to the Atlantic coasts.

Nevertheless, the general framework of Catalan business grew rapidly after 1850. Its clearest signs were an expansion of long-term credit through new banks and a rush to form joint-stock companies. The first of these corporations had been set up in Barcelona in 1840; by 1849, eight more were registered; by 1852, another six. In an economy that had been focused on small family-owned businesses, the abstractness of the *societats anonimes* looked new and rather scary. But then came an explosion: sixty-two new companies went on the register between 1853 and 1857, and the trend was encouraged by a succession of new banks that specialized in long-term credit for industrial floats, the first of which—the Banco de Barcelona, founded by Manuel Girona i Agrafel —had appeared back in 1844. Catalans were not fond of mergers and takeovers: the ideal was the big family business, like a *casa pairal*. But sometimes families would pool their resources when the capital needs were too great for one clan. So it was with the powerful ironworking and machine-production firm known as the Maquinista Terrestre i Marítima, launched in 1855 by Joan Güell from a merger of several Barcelonese metal-founding factories and subscribed by many small investors.

In some ways this growth sounds more impressive than it was: no Catalan factory could produce a machine loom, a spinning jenny, or a locomotive to rival an English import. The boom in railroad shares that flushed the Llotja in the 1860s (more than half the investment total of 416 million pesetas there in 1866 went on railway speculation) soon faltered and died. In 1856 a third of Spain's heavy metal was made in

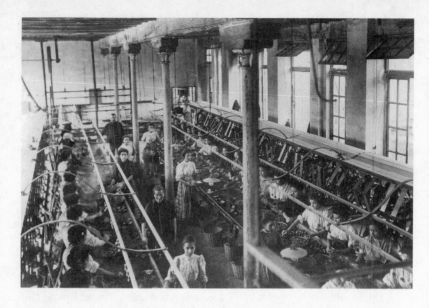

A mid-nineteenth-century spinning shop in Catalunya

Catalunya, but its output was only a little more than 3 percent of Catalunya's own gross industrial product; at the end of the nineteenth
century, Catalunya's heavy-metal mills were producing a quarter of the
output of Spain's entire metallurgical industry—but their output was a
mere speck beside the iron-smelting titans of the Ruhr or the Midlands
and still tiny compared with the rest of Catalan industry.

The ruling industry was textiles. Catalunya was by midcentury
the world's fourth largest producer of cotton goods, after England,
France, and the United States. Cloth manufacture—spinning, weaving,
dyeing—was largely mechanized, and it accounted for 61 percent of all
Catalan industrial output. Like ideas, technology had been slow in crossing the Pyrenees, but the shortage of manpower caused by the Napoleonic Wars meant that the cloth industry had to mechanize or perish.
Catalan industrial spies had gone north to England to glean what they
could in the Midlands factories. Some firms bought machinery in England, there being none in Spain. By 1831 Barcelona already had five
hundred spinning jennies of the Crompton pattern, running sixty thousand spindles to turn out the thread. The first *selfactina*, or "machine
loom" (its odd name came from the English manufacturer's claim that
it was automatic, or "self-acting"), was imported to Barcelona in 1832
by Josep Bonaplata (?–1839), who had spent several years in England

studying the use of steam power. It arrived just fifty years after the first such machine came into use in England. It could run five hundred spindles, and later models drove a thousand at a time. Controlled by one or two workers, it could turn out thousands of yards of cloth in a day. By 1861 there were 9,695 such looms in Catalunya, and the firm of Bonaplata, Vilagerut and Rull had seven hundred machine workers and its own machine shop for development and repairs. In this way the textile industry fostered the beginnings of Barcelona's second industry, engineering. By the end of the 1840s the big cotton and silk companies of Barcelona included La Fabril Igualadina (1847); the Muntadas brothers' firm, La España Industrial (1847); Güell, Ramis and Cia (1848); the Batlló brothers (1849); and La Fabril Algodonera. In 1862, the steam engines of the Catalan textile industry accounted for 35 percent of the entire steam power capacity of Spain. Raw cotton was Catalunya's biggest import, rising from 3,750 tons a year in 1834 to 22,000 in 1860.

II

If the 1850s and 1860s saw the consolidation of the Catalan upper-middle class, they also created the Catalan proletariat. And whatever the frustrations of industry, the life of its employees in Barcelona was infinitely worse.

Barcelonese workers had no writer to bear vivid witness to their lives, as Engels did to the proletariat of Manchester. But their memorials survive in the reporting of three men: Jaume Salarich, a doctor who concerned himself with their health; Ramón Simó i Badia, a self-educated foreman from Sants who went into national politics; and Ildefons Cerdà, the engineer who designed the Eixample, the great grid of the nineteenth-century city. A dreadful picture emerges from their testimony, the obverse of the successes of "heroic" Catalan capitalism, which, struggling against larger foreign competitors, had so little will to give its workers even the semblance of decent lives.

The prospects of the Barcelonese worker remained the same throughout the nineteenth century: grinding, brutish, and without much hope of change. Statistics altered and demographic shifts were seen: for instance, the more machines were used in the mills, the more demand there was for women to run them, since the machinery did not require as much physical strength, and women could be paid far less. But the

Gabriel Planella i Rodriguez, The Weaver, *showing a young girl operating a selfactina*

vile calculus of human misery was unaltered. Industrial workers were, in the literal sense of the cliché, wage slaves, scratching a precarious existence from a system that debased every part of their lives.

They lived crammed in garrets and basements, without heat or light or air. Midcentury Barcelona made Dickensian London look almost tolerable; Cerdà found that its population density was 350 people per acre, twice that of Paris, and that workers had a living space of about ninety square feet per person. Epidemics ravaged them: cholera, typhoid, dysentery, along with a range of work-induced disorders from spinal deformation to systemic poisoning from noxious dyes and chemical fumes. Salaried workers could expect to live to age fifty; *jornalers*, or "day workers," to forty. Their water was foul, their diet wretched; the working family spent 54 percent of its income on food and got only vegetables, rice, beans, a few sardines, and, occasionally, a slice of salt bacon, known as *carn de dissabte*, "Saturday meat." Contraception was unknown, and abortion, for most women, unthinkable. Public education did not exist, beyond a smattering of literacy imparted by priests and nuns so that some of the pale rachitic children of the poor might be able to follow the catechism and grasp how Jesus loved them. No laws governed such

Cartoon by M. Texero showing a Catalan being lured into a trap labeled "National Independence" by the emblematic figure of "English Cotton," from a Barcelona newspaper, June 22, 1842

matters as industrial safety or the exploitation of child labor. Wages were low—they plunged 11 percent between 1849 and 1862—and there was no job security; when the market dropped, factories would fire their workers, knowing that others could easily be hired when demand picked up. Few Catalan workers could buy what they made. The normal workday was twelve hours, but men would commonly labor for fourteen or even sixteen to feed their families. The working year was interrupted by a plethora of official and religious holidays, one hundred and twenty in all, four accumulated months of idleness in which no work could be done and no money earned. Obligatory religious observance accounted for seventy-five of these days per year—fifty-two Sundays and twenty-three other feasts, which did not improve the Catalan worker's tolerance of the Church. But then, the Catholic Church in Barcelona, as in the rest of Spain, was not the party of the dispossessed. The mill owner left his conscience to his bishop and his confessor, who obligingly left it intact.

Ramón Simó i Badia thought such a life was simply unimaginable to the rich:

> Those who, having wasted the day in amusements and the night in theaters and dances, slumber on a well-stuffed feather-bed in warm, comfortable rooms until ten in the morning, cannot grasp the physical and moral suffering of a proletarian who lives in some foul damp attic; who, at five in the morning, rises from the wretched straw palliasse he shares with his wife (and often with his children too); who grabs, by way of clothing, the coat which serves as their only blanket. . . . This man, this human creature made by God in His image, who thinks and

feels as other men do, leaves his miserable pigsty with cold in his body and ice in his soul. He arrives at the factory, and takes up his tools or sits down at his machine or at his office desk at 6.30 in the morning, and from then until 8 in the evening he is fixed to it except for half an hour or fifteen minutes for breakfast, an hour or so for lunch . . . does all this not brutalize men to the point of torture?

The struggle for the rights of these "mere laboring machines" was mainly theoretical at first.

Socialist ideas were slow in reaching Spain in the first half of the nineteenth century. There was a host of reasons for this: the power of the throne, the opposition of the Church, the low level of literacy, and—over and above all these—a general distrust, born of the Napoleonic Wars, of anything French. The Pyrenees were not some kind of hermetic gasket, sealing the peninsula off. Nevertheless, socialism was only a dream in Barcelona of the 1850s and 1860s, and one shared by a tiny minority of enthusiasts.

The main inspirer of Catalan republican socialism had never been to Spain. He was a Frenchman, Étienne Cabet (1785–1856). A child of worker parents in Dijon, trained as a lawyer, he did a brief stint as Louis Philippe's *procureur-général* in Corsica and then started a socialist sheet called *Le Populaire*, full of invective against the monarchy. Under prosecution, Cabet fled to England in 1834, where he met that benign Utopian manufacturer Robert Owen, prophet of socialist cooperation in industry. And like Marx in years to come, Cabet settled down to work in the British Museum Reading Room, devouring every blueprint for the future from Campanella and Sir Thomas More's *Utopia*, through the republican socialists of a generation earlier than his own (François-Emile Babeuf, Filippo Buonarotti) to Owen's *A New View of Society*. He was much influenced by that egregious crackpot Charles Fourier (1772–1837), whose ideal building block of social reorganization was the phalanstery, a group of 1,700 souls, more or less, who would live communally (shared profit, free love) in barracks. Each block would be self-sufficient, a minisociety in itself. By means of perfect mutual help, Fourier thought, phalansteries would cover the earth and paradise would return. The world would have thirty-seven million musical geniuses, each the equal of Mozart, and thirty-seven million mathematicians the equal of Newton. The very sea would turn to lemonade.

Cabet was not that crazy. His eccentricity was to have seen the Sermon on the Mount for what it was: a radical tract that, if literally applied, would have unseated every king and bigwig who ruled men in

Étienne Cabet in 1848

the name of Christ. "Anyone who closely examines the Gospel of Jesus Christ," he wrote, "will see that it sets forth the principles of a new social order based on the Brotherhood of Man, on gentleness and charity . . . we find in it the source of all the modern systems that now shake the world . . . there is no gulf between the social teachings of the Gospels and those of socialism."

He wanted to create "a veritable treatise on social and political morals, philosophy and economics . . . inspired by the purest and most ardent love for humanity." The result was *A Voyage to Icaria* (1839). It was pure communism—of an idiosyncratic kind, part practical decency and part cloud-cuckoo land.

A Voyage to Icaria is cast as a series of dialogues between an English aristocrat (based on Owen) and a young exiled artist (Cabet), who together dream up an ideal society: Icaria, where law is the only king. Since law is the product of philosophy, it cannot be changed by the ballot box. Everything in Icaria, from housing to the publication of books, is controlled by the state: "Naturally, the Republic . . . will print only those works which it considers useful to maintain the social harmony of Icaria." No irritants, and especially no trace of elitism, hated by-product of the competitive instinct, will be allowed in Icaria: benignly, inflexibly, the tall poppy will be cut down. Thus one sees the glare of the twentieth century in the mild eyes of the idealist in the British Museum. He was a prophet of the Marxist condition of total state hegemony, and his plan of the apparatus of power—a grand assembly of two thousand deputies deliberating in a hall, an executive body of a president and fifteen ministers, and so forth—bears its likeness to the political arrangements of Stalin and his heirs. Nor is his vision of intellectual life in Icaria so very distant from the vogue for "political correctness" on American campuses in the 1990s.

Cabet's ideas were largely ignored in France, but they fell on prepared ground in Barcelona. Progressive liberals, the *exaltats* of the 1830s and 1840s, had read him; and the failure of the Jamancia turned some of these radicals back toward ideals of peaceful republicanism, to Utopian fantasies, and to Icaria. Cabet's chief disciple among the Catalans in the late 1840s and 1850s was a singular and attractive figure: Narcis Monturiol i Estarriol, socialist, editor, inventor, and pioneer of the submarine.

Monturiol (1819–85) was born in the northern Catalan village of Figueres, near the sea. He was the second son of a *menestral* family; his father, like Cabet's, was a cooper, whose trade of making cylinders to keep wine in may have contributed, on some unconscious level, to his son's obsession with making hulls to keep salt water out. He studied at the University of Cervera and completed his law degree in Barcelona. Monturiol was twenty-four in 1843 when he joined the staff of *El Republicano* and took part in the Jamancia. But he was already, in essence, a pacifist. From then on, he would remain deeply involved with other Cabetians in Barcelona. In 1847 he and a few other earnest progressives—writers, printers, doctors, and a young musician named Josep Anselm Clavé, later to become the guiding spirit of the Catalan musical revival—formed an Icarian group in Barcelona and started a weekly sheet whose motto was "Vamos a Icaria!" Its anthem ran:

> *Desde hoy todos los hombres son hermanos*
> *ni siervo se conoce, ni señor.*
> *Marchemos, oh marchemos Icarianos,*
> *tendiendo el estandarte del Amor!*

> From today, all men are brothers,
> there will be no slave or master.
> Let us march, O march onward, Icarians,
> holding up the banner of Love!

It reached all of 340 subscribers, which did not discourage its band of editorial brothers' fantasizing about the New Jerusalem: "The Unversal Era," an editorial declared, "begins with the foundation of Icaria. January 20 1848 is the moment fixed for the regeneration of the World."

On that date, Étienne Cabet had departed for America. At last, he was going to put his dream into practice. He would take it to the great tabula rasa of the New World, where Icaria would at last be born. Monturiol joyously opined that twenty thousand Icarians would go. Sixty-nine actually did. Among them were three Catalans—a young doctor named Joan Rovira, his wife, and a friend. Rovira's comrades in Barcelona collected six hundred francs to pay his fare to Paris.

The Icarians filed on board an American steamer at Le Havre and set off for New Orleans. They struggled inland and reached the chosen spot on Red River north of Shreveport (which Cabet had bought unseen and in advance from some astute land shark) by the beginning of April.

There, Icaria was founded.

It failed immediately: nobody in the area seemed interested in universal brotherhood. Puzzlingly, it seemed not to exist on the American frontier. Besides, the ground was sand and swamp. Nothing but mosquitoes, rattlers, and water moccasins flourished there. Rovira, who had set out with a wide white sombrero and a double-barreled gun—"New surprises every minute! I believe that Icaria will be the center of all knowledge and understanding!" he wrote to Monturiol—shot himself dead in New Orleans in 1849. The rest of the Icarians trekked north to Nauvoo, Illinois, and founded a new settlement there, which lasted a few more years. In 1853 Monturiol wrote to Cabet and asked permission to join the settlement. Cabet did not answer for a year; Icaria II was breaking up. Harried by his resentful disciples, Cabet died of heartbreak in Illinois in 1856.

Only in Catalunya did Icaria survive as a figment of the radical imagination, fed by Monturiol's earnest fancies and by lying reports of the settlement's success. It bequeathed its name to an industrial slum, part of the workers' housing district of Sant Martí de Provençals in Barcelona. By the turn of the century the city fathers, not wishing to have a place-name with such plainly socialist memories attached to it, renamed the area Poblenou (New Town). But Cabet's dream stuck to a broad street, the Avinguda d'Icaria, which runs—not inappropriately, perhaps, since Poblenou with its crammed population of factory workers had a bad name as "the *barri* where most people are born old"—around the bottom of the zoo and stops dead at the gates of the local cemetery. The new Olympic Village for the 1992 games is absurdly named Nova Icaria.

Monturiol's dream of brotherhood was undamped by the loss of Icaria. He continued to edit magazines, which tended to fold under the pressure of censorship soon after they appeared: *La Madre de la Familia*, 1846, ran articles advocating equal rights for men and women; in its successor, *El Padre de la Familia*, 1849–50, Monturiol called for workers' rights, defended unionism, and wrote exposés of factory labor conditions. "Laborers want only bread, morality and education." The magazine collapsed under a censor's fine of 12,500 pesetas.

III

By the 1850s Monturiol's ambitions shifted to a new field: submarining. If humanity was to improve itself with education, it must press against scientific frontiers, for socialist man was Prometheus, too. Monturiol was no Luddite. To him, the machine was good. He was a complete positivist. He believed in the romance of human betterment through technology. "The poles of the Earth, the depths of the oceans, the upper regions of the air: these three conquests are undoubtedly reserved for the near future. To work to bring the time of these conquests closer—such is the task I have taken on."

Monturiol had seen a coral diver drown at Cadaqués, and in 1857 he and some friends formed a society at Figueras whose aim was to make coral gathering safer. Submarines would play a role in this. But their real use was scientific, not commercial—probing an unknown, sparsely imagined world. Such was the obsession on which Monturiol spent his life. Submarines were the spacecraft of the 1860s.

Europeans had dreamed of sailing the depths of the sea since the time of the Greeks. The first controlled underwater voyage was taken by an intrepid Dutchman named Cornelius Jacobszoon Drebbel (1572–1633), who to the astonishment of the Stuart court managed to go nearly three miles down the Thames, ten feet underwater, in a sort of wooden cask with oars. Sporadic experiments were made through the seventeenth and eighteenth centuries, culminating in 1801 with the *Nautilus* (whose name Jules Verne would take for Captain Nemo's submarine), in which the American inventor Robert Fulton made a five-hour descent to a depth of 160 feet into the sea off Brest. It was driven by a helical screw, turned by hand.

In Russia during the Crimean War, a German, Wilhelm Bauer, built an iron-hulled submarine, the *Sea-Devil*, likewise moved by human mus-

Narcis Monturiol, inventor of the Catalan submarine, in 1861

cles and propeller. It was launched off Kronstadt in 1856 and made 134 dives—during one of which Bauer actually succeeded in taking the world's first undersea photograph with carbide lights and a camera fixed to the inside of a porthole. It showed mud and some fuzzy rocks.

But the Russian admiralty cut off his funds, and he could find none elsewhere. No Western naval command between 1800 and 1860 showed much interest in submarines or put real money in the way of the various French, Spanish, German, and American inventors who approached them with their contraptions. Granted, subs were more dangerous to their own crews than to any imaginable enemy; they leaked, flooded, turned turtle, or got stuck on the bottom. But the underlying reason was that they raised a prospect of stealthy, invisible warfare that seemed uncivilized, deeply out of key with the chivalry of the sea.

Monturiol certainly knew about Bauer's work. The German inventor died, a bedridden pauper, in 1856, and the very next year Monturiol began work on his own submarine, which he christened the *Ictíneo* (from the Greek words for "fish" and "ship"). She was smaller, only 23 feet long, half the length of Bauer's *Sea-Devil*. She displaced eight tonnes and had an internal volume of 260 cubic feet—cramped quarters for the skipper and the four men who had to turn the cranks that drove its horizontal and vertical screws. She had two hulls, the inner cylindrical, the outer fish shaped. Between them were four ballast tanks, two fore

Monturiol's submarine Ictíneo

and two aft, that could be flooded to make a dive. You gazed out on the wonders of the deep through fish-eye portholes amidships and in the bow. To build her, Monturiol formed a public-subscription company. Much of the capital came from his fellow Icarians. He raised the considerable sum of 73,900 *rals*, nearly 20,000 pesetas. (Four *rals* equaled one peseta; five pesetas equaled one duro. The cost of *Ictíneo* was counted in *rals* so that Catalan workers, who could not afford to give a whole peseta, could contribute something to the birth of the socialist submarine.) Monturiol had her built in the Nuevo Vulcano shipyards in Barcelona, with the help of two naval designers, Joan Monjo i Pons and Josep Missé. In the end she cost one hundred thousand pesetas and left Monturiol with a load of debt from which he never escaped. It was, perhaps, his devoted wife who embroidered the flag for *Ictíneo*, now preserved in the Maritime Museum: a branch of red coral enclosing the blue waves of the sea, on which a gold star is shedding its rays, with the Latin motto *"Plus intra, plus extra,"* which means (more or less) "Far down! Far out!"

And the submarine worked. There were a few glitches and leaks, caused by damage from a botched launching in June 1859. But that September, *Ictíneo* made her first public trials in Barcelona harbor, followed by a flotilla of excursion boats with hundreds of people on board: deputies, professors, scientists, journalists, and the merely curious. She swam in a stately manner along the surface, filled her tanks, dived, surfaced, dived again. Her descents were short, because she carried no air supply beyond what was in her small hull at normal pressure. But by the end of the day she was a success, and Narcis Monturiol was a local hero, acclaimed as a veritable Catalan Leonardo da Vinci. General Leopoldo O'Donnell, the lover of Isabel II ("You love the institution of monarchy," the queen once said to her minister Narváez, "but O'Donnell loves me for myself"), also watched the trials. He promised Monturiol that his sovereign would come in person to see him put the submarine through its paces. She never did, but over the next couple of years Monturiol took *Ictíneo* and her sweating propeller turners down fifty more times. Sometimes he invited his more intrepid friends along. One of these, the popular poet Antoni Altadill, penned the world's first submarine poem, which began:

> *De tu monstruo en el seno*
> *yo he descendido a tu ignorado mundo,*
> *de audacia el pecho lleno,*
> *porque alli estabas tu, firme, sereno,*
> *porque alli estaba tu saber profundo.*
>
> *Tu fuiste, Monturiol, tu el escogido;*
> *el Genio te llamo; a su voz potente*
> *alzaste la cabeza*
> *y al leventarla de la tierra humilde*
> *polvo de estrella salpico tu frente!*

> In the body of your monster
> I went down into your unknown world,
> my breast filled with courage
> because you were there, firm, calm,
> because your deep knowledge was there.
>
> You, Monturiol, you were the chosen one;
> Genius called you; at his powerful voice
> you raised your head
> and as you lifted it from the lowly earth
> stardust sprinkled your forehead!

Another of Monturiol's diving buddies, Josep de Letamandi, a scholarly doctor, responded with the first prose description of a submarine descent ever written by a passenger:

The silence that accompanies the dives; the gradual vanishing of sunlight; the great mass of water, which sight pierces with difficulty; the pallor that light gives to the faces, the lessening of movement in the *Ictíneo*, the fishes passing outside the portholes—all this helps stir the imaginative faculties, and shows itself in the shortened breath and the utterances of the crew . . . there are times when nothing can be seen outside by natural light. All noise and movement stops. It seems as though nature is dead, and the *Ictíneo* is a tomb.

To Catalans, Narcis Monturiol was a hero. The success of *Ictíneo* in Barcelona was a nineteenth-century premonition of the emotions that gripped Americans a century later at the sight of their NASA astronauts. Now the argonaut of the coral depths was inundated with banquets, congratulations, poems, and florid letters of encouragement. His native coast shared the glory with the capital. The towns of Figueras and Cadaqués named him their favorite son. Catalan patriotism fused with a rapturous belief in can-do technology. The impenetrable frontier had been breached; a new world, an unexplored zone of physics and zoology, lay open to the man in the submarine. It would be hard to exaggerate the boost, however short-lived it turned out to be, that *Ictíneo* gave to Catalan self-confidence: to the belief that Barcelona was destined to be the site of a special modernity.

Madrid was less impressed. In 1861 Monturiol shipped his little sub to Alicante, where he demonstrated her to the ministers of the navy and of economic development; despite adverse weather, she sailed through the test course perfectly. But when a commission of Catalan deputies asked the government for research and development money for Monturiol, all they got was an offer to put *Ictíneo* on display as a maritime curiosity. Monturiol's friend and fellow Icarian, the musician Josep Anselm Clavé, wrote an indignant ode:

> Steadfastness, praise God, completes the work
> though rulers turn a deaf ear—
> if you do not find their favor, take heart,
> for the whole people will give you its hand.

And so Monturiol plunged ahead with his plans for a bigger and better submarine. The construction of *Ictíneo II* started in 1862, with a capital of nearly three hundred thousand pesetas, a third of it raised from Catalan speculators in Cuba. Her builder, once again, was the naval architect Joan Monjo i Pons. He liked Monturiol but had difficulties with him. The inventor had a maddening habit of disrupting the shipyard by preaching socialism to the men who were building the vessel, and accusing the foremen of severity. "If Monturiol's purpose was to mortify me," wrote Monjo in a plaintive manuscript entitled "Moral Sufferings the *Ictíneo* Caused Me," "he certainly picked the right way to do it."

Ictíneo II was more than twice the length of the first submarine (seventeen meters) and carried four times the crew (twenty men). She was designed to dive to a hundred feet and stay down for seven and a half hours. Like her prototype, she was built with a double hull, ballast tanks, and weights that could be jettisoned to give emergency buoyancy. But the rest of her design was new, and brilliantly innovative. Monturiol was the first designer to deal effectively with the two basic problems of human life undersea on extended dives: air supply and mechanical power.

Originally, sixteen of the crew were meant to turn the cranks that drove the propeller—a veritable underwater galley, signifying socialist cooperation rather than slavery. Clearly, it would be better if a submarine could have a steam engine, like a surface ship. And for surface running, Monturiol decided to save the muscles of his crew and install a six-horsepower steam engine. But you could not run a steam engine underwater: it would use up all the oxygen and turn the hull into an oven.

Monturiol had to find another way to raise heat, and thus steam. After prolonged experiment he came up with a form of chemical reaction between potassium chlorate, zinc, and manganese dioxide. It produced more than enough heat to boil water and (as a bonus) oxygen as well, which was purified and piped back into the air in the hull. This chemical furnace could not raise enough power to drive the main engine, so Monturiol linked it to a smaller, two-horsepower steam motor for underwater running.

This elegant system required much research, and Monturiol (who had not yet finished paying for his first submarine) found himself endlessly struggling for cash and credit. Nevertheless, *Ictíneo II* slid down the launching way in October 1864. She was a cluttered ship—in the end there was scarcely room for two men to move around inside her hull, what with the large and small steam engines, the carbide lamps, the cumbersome air purifier, the ventilating pumps, the boiler, and the chemical furnace. Monturiol and his socialist comrades shoehorned themselves into her and made more than a dozen demonstration dives over the next couple of years. She worked; of that there was no doubt. She was the most advanced submarine in the world. Like her predecessor, she got a lot of press, with illustrations of *Ictíneo*s hunting for coral, probing the depths, ramming men-of-war, and engaging in combat with other, hostile submarines. But she attracted no money. The torpid ministry of the navy penned its compliments and did nothing. The mill owners and iron magnates of Barcelona eyed the big fish with curiosity but saw no future in it. Monturiol was undoubtedly a genius, but also a socialist and the friend of revolutionaries: if *Ictíneo II* could somehow pay for herself they might be interested, but if not, not. In 1868 the shipyard, tired of waiting to be paid some twenty thousand pesetas that were still owing, foreclosed on Monturiol and seized *Ictíneo II*. Having no commercial value as a ship, she was broken up and sold for scrap. Her hot clanking heart—the six-horsepower steam engine—was sold to a farmer on the outskirts of Barcelona, who used it to grind flour: "Eyeless in Gaza, at the mill, with slaves."

As for Monturiol's own heart, it broke.

He lived on for another seventeen years, bearing his disappointments without any outward sign of embitterment. "Weak, poor and obscure, we have done something that nobody dared to expect of the great and powerful," he wrote. "If we fail, our honor remains intact. If we succeed, we will have done a great good." He busied himself with other inventions, including a cigarette-rolling machine and a sixteen-pound mountain howitzer that, he hoped, would put an end to the hated, reactionary Carlists, who in 1872 launched their third war in Catalunya against Spain's constitutional government, this time on behalf of the new Bourbon pretender Carlos VII.

None of these projects earned Monturiol anything. Family losses piled on business failures; two of his daughters died, and then his wife. Debt ridden and depressed, he was reduced to living in the spare room of his son-in-law's house at Sant Martí de Provençals, where he died in 1885. "Time flies," he wrote a couple of years before his death, "and I reach the end of my career leaving to others the things I should have accomplished myself. So many, many years miserably lost! Since 1869, everything has been hope, nothing reality."

When he died, Monturiol was a forgotten man in Catalunya, and yet it may be that his fame took a literary form and moved to France. In the 1860s Jules Verne was doing the research for *Twenty Thousand Leagues Under the Sea*. Was Captain Nemo inspired, if only in part, by Monturiol? One cannot be sure, but it seems at least possible. Verne plowed through as many scientific reports and treatises on underwater exploration as he could lay his hands on. In 1867 he even sailed on the *Great Eastern* to America; she had just finished laying the first transatlantic cable, and one of his fellow passengers was the American entrepreneur who had conceived this project, Cyrus Field, whom he interviewed at length about the ocean deeps.

Given Verne's passion for research—whose results, unwieldy homilies on hydrostatics, fish, and botany, clog his narrative—it seems unlikely that he would *not* have heard of Monturiol. Granted, Captain Nemo, an enigmatic creature of Hugoesque will and Byronic *terribilità* who bears his inward wound through the depths of the sea, is not very like the mild Catalan. Or not, as it were, on the surface. Nemo was immeasurably rich, Monturiol hopelessly poor; Nemo bent on vengeance, Monturiol on world brotherhood. And of course the *Nautilus*, with its plush and crystal salon lined with thousands of books and hung with "thirty first-rate pictures," including works by Leonardo, Raphael, Titian, Rubens, and Velázquez, is a far cry from the cramped hull of the *Ictíneo*.

And yet there are intriguing traces of similarity. Nemo is a Utopian. "The world," he announces, "does not want new continents, but new men." On rescuing a pearl diver from an immense shark, he remarks that the poor Indian "is an inhabitant of an oppressed country; and I am still, and shall be, to my last breath, one of them!" When the narrator delicately raises the thought that Nemo might be too rich, the captain rounds on him: "Who told you that I did not make a good use of it? Do you think I am ignorant that there are suffering beings and oppressed races on this earth, miserable creatures to console, victims to avenge? Do you not *understand*?" From which Professor Aronnax hastily concludes that "whatever the motive which had forced him to seek independence under the sea . . . his heart still beat for the sufferings of humanity." The *Nautilus*, ranging unconfined beyond the reach of land governments, free from the contamination of political dealings, is of course a country in itself and may be seen as a parallel to self-sustaining ideal states like Icaria. Utopia, as the Beatles as well as Monturiol and Nemo knew, wants to live in a yellow submarine.

IV

Monturiol's project, with its promise of benign technological possibility, was one of the key images of Barcelona in the 1860s. There were others, rich with social meaning. Two involved a large scale of planning: the overthrow of the Bourbon walls, signaling—or so *catalanistes* hoped—the symbolic defeat of Madrid centralism; and the design for the enlargement of Barcelona. Two were more narrowly cultural: the rebirth of choral music as a means of creating pride and mutual support among

Catalan workers and the re-creation of the Jocs Florals, an annual contest for nationalist writing, mainly poetry, which came to enshrine the approved values of the Catalan middle class.

The demolition of the walls was an event of great emblematic power, but it could not have happened if only the left had wanted it. In fact, every Barcelonan did—especially the merchants and manufacturers who sat on the powerful Junta de Comerç, the chamber of commerce that had been founded back in 1758 to promote the city's economic growth. Once it had happened, the design of the new Barcelona was handed over, not to an architect, but to a civil engineer with Utopian socialist ideas: Ildefons Cerdà. This man, who had more influence on the shape of Barcelona than any single person before or since, was a friend of Monturiol's and deeply influenced by the ideas of Saint-Simon and Étienne Cabet. He devised the most perfectly thought-out theoretical plan that anyone, in the course of the nineteenth century, got the chance to create for a great European city. To see its origins, we must go back a little.

In the 1820s the urban form of Barcelona was still fixed and frozen by the walls, but a tentative finger of urban development had poked out of the city. It was an extension of the line of the Ramblas into the old Camí de Jesús, a dirt road that led to the outlying village of Gracia. A proper paved highway linking the top of the Ramblas with Gracia was designed by a military engineer in 1821. It got the go-ahead in the flush of Catalan optimism caused by the Liberal Triennial. Work began the next year, and stopped when the fortunes of the liberals fell in 1823. Then it began again in 1827 as a public project to make work for men thrown out of their jobs by the terrible depression of the 1820s.

Thus the Passeig de Gràcia was born, the parade ground of Barcelona's upper-middle class, new wealth's answer to the demotic Ramblas. In the 1830s and 1840s, however, it was not much more than a street between two towns, with fields on either side. Nor did it run directly into the Ramblas; it started outside the obstructive ramparts, at the Portal de l'Angel. But its downhill parts, nearest the walls, soon became a place where people liked to stroll and take the air. Until the late 1840s, Barcelona's favorite pleasure had been on the port, where Passeig de Colom now runs—a formal esplanade park by the Bourbon seawall known as the Jardí del General, started in 1815 under the auspices of the then captain general of Barcelona, Francisco Javier Castaños y Aragorri, a benign aristocrat who would also play a considerable role in importing fine music to the city. But then its popularity began to decline, even as Passeig de Gràcia's rose. In 1853 the architect Josep Oriol i Mestres

Amusements on the Camps Elisis of the Passeig de Gràcia, circa 1860

imposed a design on a section of the Gracia highway above what is now the Carrer d'Aragó. It became Barcelona's Luxembourg Gardens, its Prater. Decked out with fountains and gardens and raree-shows, inns and dance halls, a switchback railway and an open-air concert theater complete with a statue of Euterpe, it was known as the Camps Elisis— the Elysian Fields. It made Passeig de Gràcia, wrote the poet Victor Balaguer, "the place with the most life":

> Fashion had chosen it, elegance had accepted it. . . . The Ramblas and the rampart of the port went into mourning. Passeig de Gràcia triumphed, and its victory does not seem a passing one—on the contrary, it was most durable. The day when this oppressive belt of stone that calls itself the *muralles* falls, never to rise again, will be the day when Passeig de Gràcia will be without any rivals.

In 1834 the Junta de Comerç proposed that the botanical gardens, which occupied what was by now prime real-estate space inside the *muralles* near the Portal de Sant Antoni, should be moved outside the walls to the open ground next to the Passeig de Gràcia. But buried in this was something much more consequential—noted merely as an aside. "For the greater convenience of the public," the junta remarked, "it is

General Espartero Baldomero

---

proposed to open a gate in the present Artillery Barracks to get access to the Ramblas."

This juncture of the Ramblas and Passeig de Gràcia was to become the first breach in the wall. The artillery barracks were in a medieval building at the north end of the Ramblas, taken over by Bourbon troops in 1714. They stood at the reentrant angle of the *muralles*, between the frowning bastions of Jonqueres (now Plaça Urquinaona) and Tallers (now the site of the University of Barcelona). A line between these bastions, together with the walls, makes a shallow triangle (today, defined by the Ronda de l'Universitat and the Ronda de Sant Pere, the Carrer de Pelai and the Carrer Fontanella) that encloses what is now Plaça de Catalunya, where the Ramblas awkwardly connects to Passeig de Gràcia. The problem of how to develop that triangle, the first "enlargement" of the city, was much disputed between civil interests (who wanted it for housing) and military ones (who were concerned with defense). Their squabble was never truly resolved. Hence the chaotic jump between the Old City and the New City that one always feels when crossing Plaça de Catalunya (which was not finished until the 1920s).

The issue of the walls kept seesawing in the political turbulence of the 1840s. Madrid and the army were determined to keep them up;

Queen Isabel II

Barcelona and its civil government fervently wished them down. In 1843, after the fall of General Espartero, the civil authorities ordered the Canaletes and Jonqueres bastions demolished. So they were—partially; but Espartero's successor had them repaired a few months later. The barracks that blocked the north end of the Ramblas were gone, but the walls would remain until the civil government of Barcelona got an edge over the military arm of Madrid.

That did not happen until 1854, after a long campaign by the Ajuntament and the Catalan press, at the start of the so-called Bienni Progressista—a two-year period of reforms set in train by Espartero and Isabel II. General Espartero came to power in Madrid through a *pronunciamiento* in favor of the progressives, in 1854. Most radical Catalan liberals were overjoyed. Others viewed Espartero's putsch with extreme suspicion: this was the man who had shelled the city from Montjuic eleven years before, in the Jamancia. But the more militant workers took Espartero's success as the green light for a rising. In July 1854, Luddite mobs converged on half a dozen textile factories and tried to incinerate them. It seemed that 1848 had finally come to Barcelona, six years late. The textile workers, who had formed the city's first trade union fourteen years before and were well organized, set forth a list of demands for collective bargaining, shorter hours, and higher wages. They threatened a general strike. Isabel II's captain general showed his mettle by fleeing

General Juan Zapatero

the city, and bargaining went on between workers and bosses. Then the momentum of revolt slowed: God, taking the side of capital, sent a cholera epidemic to Barcelona. As it ran its course through the late summer and autumn of 1854, the new captain general managed to negotiate new employment terms for the textile industry, along with promises of improved conditions. He also found a scapegoat against which some of the accumulated social rage could be turned—the *muralles*, whose demolition, one observer noted, remained "the most ardent desire of every Barcelonan, the most popular and discussed idea in the country."

A deputation from the Ajuntament and a provisional trades junta went to Madrid and finally, on August 12, got its royal demolition order—with one big string attached: the Citadel itself must stay. There was general rejoicing in the city, and its shops were emptied of pickaxes and crowbars overnight. Through the fall and winter of 1854, every citizen of Barcelona who could wield a tool (together with quite a few who could not, but contented themselves with oratory) was out on the ramparts.

The walls did not come down immediately. They were too big, too resistant; and in any case, more political turmoil was in store. Isabel II had no intention of putting up with strikes or allowing a workers' junta

Demolition of the Citadel

---

to keep negotiating on equal terms with established interests. To make sure that the insurrectionaries were put in their place, the monarch in May 1855 appointed yet another captain general, General Juan Zapatero y Navas (1810–81).

Thickset, hirsute, immensely strong and brutishly authoritarian, Zapatero's repressive talents earned his nickname: the Tiger of Catalunya. He was such a stickler for discipline that when one of his officers committed suicide to escape the humiliation of public execution after he had been convicted of a *crime passionel*, Zapatero had his corpse hauled to the scaffold on the Citadel and garroted. If one could make an example of the dead, the living would not escape. Zapatero arranged for the show trial and execution of one of the workers' leaders, Josep Barceló, on a trumped-up murder charge. He drove all labor groups underground, imprisoning their leaders or banishing them to Andalusia. He sent his troops against strikers and demonstrators and harried them back to the factories at bayonet point. He disarmed the citizen militia, which showed dangerous signs of alliance with the strikers; and he completely alienated most of the factory owners and their foremen, many of whom had sincerely looked forward to a negotiated settlement of their labor disputes. None of the progressives whose government had been installed in Madrid by Espartero's *pronunciamiento* lifted a finger to stop the Tiger, and in the hot July of 1856 Barcelona, driven beyond endurance by Zapatero's regime, exploded on receiving the news that General Leopoldo O'Donnell's conservative *pronunciamiento* had dismissed them. It took Zapatero's troops only three days to destroy the rising, and when they had finished, the streets were piled with corpses: few prisoners were taken. That was the end, for the moment, of labor agitation in Barcelona. But at least the *muralles*, those implacable stone compressors of misery, kept coming down. The demolition took a decade, but by 1865 the only signs of them left were the heaps of scarred limestone piled higgledy-piggledy around the city, waiting to be carted off as fill for Passeig de Gràcia and the new Barcelona. Whole sections of the Roman wall of ancient Barcelona have survived to this day; so have parts of the medieval wall, but of the Bourbon walls, nothing remains. And the New City that was opened by their demolition was very much the offspring of that crisis of 1854–56: an acknowledgment that the discontent of industrial Barcelona had to be solved, if possible, by planning and not by grapeshot.

V

The Cerdà plan, a grid layout of squares that encloses Barcelona's Old City like a walnut in an enormous slab of stamped chocolate, was the largest urban-planning project of nineteenth-century Spain, but its origins were in part French.

As the Catalan writer Josep Pla pointed out seventy years ago, nobody would have thought of planning on this scale or with such regularity without the prototype of Napoleon III's Paris before his eyes. After 1848, Baron Haussmann had driven his broad apartment-lined boulevards through Paris's old congested center, creating vast new axes of circulation and organization. He had gutted the city and, in terms of space and class, restructured it. Never in the previous history of Europe had a capital undergone such radical change in the course of one generation as Paris did between 1848 and 1870.

But there was a vast difference between Haussmann's and Cerdà's projects. Haussmann had to destroy the old Paris; it was in his way. Cerdà had only to build, for in Barcelona in 1860 nothing stood in the way of the grid. Most of the districts that have since been incorporated into the larger urban fabric of Barcelona—Sarrià, Sant Gervasi, Horta, Les Corts, Gràcia—were still independent villages with their own local governments, physically separated from the Old City by tracts of open countryside. The terrain between, except for Passeig de Gràcia and a few monasteries, farms, and patches of shantytown, was still a blank page: the Utopian designer's dream.

Here lay the second difference: Ildefons Cerdà i Sunyer (1815–1876) was a socialist. He came from the same ideological basket as Felip Monlau and Narcis Monturiol. He was deeply affected by French ideas of ideal community. If Baron Haussmann's ghost hovers over the Eixample today, so do the lost egalitarian fantasies of Étienne Cabet.

The clockwork of state control, which fascinated Cabet, was reflected in the plan of his Icaria—a territory divided into a hundred exactly equal departments, with a provincial capital in the exact geometric center of each. The general capital, seat of all administration, is a circular city called Icara. Its broad avenues, lined with trees and bordered by canals, radiate from a central point. Ring roads divide it into sixty equal *quartiers*, each of which is a sort of theme park, built in the architectural style of one of the "sixty principal nations of world history." Despite this concession to variety, none of the houses shows the smallest sign of superiority to its neighbor. Space is allotted by need, depending on the size of the family. Equality, mother of harmony, is the nurse of housing.

This Cabetian city of equal cells is the ideological ancestor of Cerdà's grid. Cerdà thought of each block in that grid as representing a social cross section, with *menestrals* and bourgeois, the merchant and the baker and the candlestick maker, all living next to one another: there would be no "good" and no "bad" end of town, no hierarchy. Of course, it did not turn out that way—some parts of Cerdà's Eixample, when built, at once became more desirable and expensive than others. The division between them, in the early years of building, was the railroad built in 1863 straight uphill between Plaça de Catalunya and Sarrià, along the Rambla de Catalunya. Property on the right side of the track—looking up toward Sarrià from the Old City—was dearest, most of all on Passeig de Gràcia. Plots on the left were cheaper. Since most *modernista* architecture clamored for prestige and show, few of the Eixample's important buildings by Gaudí, Montaner, Puig i Cadafalch, and other star architects of 1875–1910 rose on the wrong side of the tracks.

Naturally, Cerdà did not foresee this. He believed, with a sort of religious faith, that the grid was inherently pacifying. Here, he was a singularly prophetic figure. In his work two main images of reformers' urbanism, the garden city and the *ville radieuse*, are predicted; but in the Eixample both were degraded, as beautiful ideas for the betterment of mankind tend to be when the real world tramps greedily across them.

Cerdà was a Catalan, born at Centelles in 1815. He had studied civil engineering—roads, canals, and ports—in Madrid from 1835 to 1841, and in 1849 he moved to Barcelona to make a comprehensive study of the city. In 1855, the year after demolition of the walls began, he drew up the first accurately surveyed plan of Barcelona and its surroundings. It became the basis for all city-planning projects over the next few decades, including his own.

Cerdà soon got to know the progressives of the city. His earliest writings were Monlau-style philippics against the Bourbon walls, the overcrowding of the city, the sufferings of its workers. He also went into politics as a partisan of autonomy, a Catalanist. As such he was elected a deputy in 1851, and in 1855 he went to Madrid with some of his progressive colleagues to present a report on the growing crisis of the Catalan working class. He enlarged this into his first book: *A Statistical Monograph on the Working Class of Barcelona in 1856*. This highly detailed work, laden with tables and lists, entirely based on Cerdà's own fact gathering, was the cornerstone of Barcelona's urbanism—the first serious attempt to study the living space of the city and its patterns of movement and transport, its services, health, and the general working conditions of its trades. It was also a dense catalog of social suffering. While the bards of the early Renaixença were warbling nostalgically about the need to bring back the glories of the Catalan Middle Ages, it was clear that in some areas—mainly hygiene and social services—the ordinary people of Barcelona had never escaped them.

Nobody in Barcelona had given such matters a *statistical* basis before. Cerdà lacked the anecdotal genius of a Henry Mayhew, but he had some of his persistence, and his findings could only radicalize him further. "Architecture or Revolution!" Le Corbusier was to exclaim in the early 1920s, and the motto could well have been Cerdà's.

How to make the miserable life of industrial man better, before society exploded? This was the theme of Cerdà's next book, *General Theory of Urbanization, and the Application of Its Principles and Doctrines to the Reform and Expansion of Barcelona*, eventually published in 1867.

Cerdà's *General Theory* was a pure work of optimism: testimony to the excitement with which the liberal intelligentsia of Barcelona—and the progressives in Madrid—viewed the coming of steam, gas, and electricity. Under the sign of technology, human suffering could be

Ildefons Cerdà

abolished and all conservative instincts unmasked as the irrational reflexes of a historically doomed system. A new world was coming, Cerdà declared: to be alive in 1860 was to belong to "a new generation, furnished with new means and resources, powerful, irresistible, and not to be compared with those of the generations before us: we lead a new life, functioning in a new way; old cities are no more than an obstacle."

In April 1859, the Ajuntament of Barcelona held a competition for a new town plan. One candidate was the Ajuntament's own municipal architect, Antoni Rovira i Trias. Rovira's design—presented under the cannily unradical motto, "The plan of a city is more time's work than an architect's"—deferred as much as possible to the Old City. It prolonged the axis of the Ramblas into a new ceremonial square, to be called the Forum of Isabel II. From this square radiated several avenues, dividing the New City into five wedges, whose outer perimeters were to be closed by a canal and a railroad. It looked like a fan, and its radiating layout was presumably based on Haussmann's Place de l'Étoile in Paris. The central avenue was to follow the existing track of Passeig de Gràcia. Its radial scheme drew attention to the Old City as the heart and origin of Barcelona.

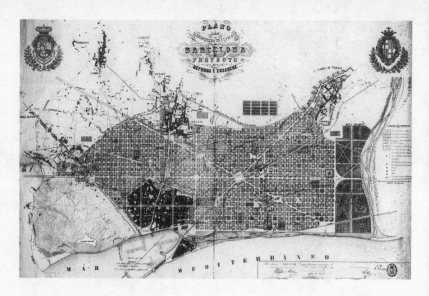

Cerdà's plan for the Eixample

Cerdà also drew up a plan. It made no such concessions: its abstractness was so absolute that it showed no sign of thought as to how the Old City might be integrated into the New City—it was simply absorbed by the march of grid blocks. To the extent that it had a focus at all, that focus was shifted far away from the Old City. It was produced by the crossing of the three great avenues that slice across the Eixample today: the Gran Via, the Diagonal, and the Meridiana, which intersect in what is now called the Plaça de les Glories Catalanes, a space to which, despite its resonant name, nobody attaches the slightest symbolic meaning. Cerdà's plan suggests that he intended it to mean something, perhaps to function as a new center, but it has done nothing of the kind. (Today, the Ajuntament plans to convert it into a nucleus of theaters and other cultural structures.) In effect, he dreamed up his grid without any manifest center of power and without the least relationship or concession to the long history of the city it enclosed. Nothing more alien to the spirit of the Catalan Renaixença, fixated on the Middle Ages as the source of modern cultural integrity, could have been put on a drawing board.

So there they were: Rovira's hierarchical fan of civic space, versus Cerdà's undifferentiated fabric of blocks. In November 1859 the Ajuntament chose Rovira. And then a most surprising thing happened: eight months later an order came from Madrid, reversing the decision. The job would be Cerdà's.

This caused much resentment and a flurry of pamphlets. Here was Madrid centralism sticking its thumb into Catalan politics again. Actually, to this day nobody really knows why Madrid decided to impose Cerdà on Barcelona. He was not a Castilian, but a Catalan, like Rovira—so he had no presumptive advantage in Madrid. He had lived and studied there, but he seems to have had no special strings to pull in the upper regions of its bureaucracy. Probably the explanation is the one that has been suggested by Jaume Fabre and Josep Huertas in *Barcelona: La Construccio d'Una Ciutat*: either it was simple arbitrariness, or, more likely, Cerdà—an engineer, whereas Rovira was an architect—had friends among the government engineers in Madrid, who formed "a very influential 'progressive' pressure group that Cerdà knew how to use." To the Madrid liberals Cerdà's plan, with its equality of space, would have looked more progressive than Rovira's. To the Catalan conservatives who were the patrons of the Renaixença and whose influence counted with the Ajuntament—specifically, the city real-estate investors whose capital was going to fill the plan with real bricks and mortar—this was not a virtue. They would have preferred something more Haussmann-like, with clear gradations, ceremonial axes, and points of convergence. Their objections were irritably summarized in Josep Pla's *Un Senyor de Barcelona*, when Rafael Puget complained that

> I often think about the enlargement of Barcelona, the Eixample, and the surprise is permanent: I mean the surprise of its total monotony, its lack of grace, its inability to understand that life can be pleasant. Maybe no capital city in Europe could have offered a generation of architects more land, more beautifully situated on a slope going down to the sea, a magnificent site for work and relaxation, and got more feeble and counterproductive results. . . . The great Expansion of Barcelona is a disaster of gigantic proportions.

An architect of the generation after Cerdà's, Josep Puig i Cadafalch, detested the plan of the Eixample. Cerdà, the *funest autor* (baleful designer), had left no room for human variety. "His plan's defenders," wrote Puig, "had the oddest ideas about urbanism. They believed, for instance, that the Ideal City was the one in which all citizens had the sensation of living under exactly identical urban conditions. Hence their mania for making all the streets the same width, all straight; hence their aversion to plazas that might break the sacred monotony of the whole." The Eixample was put on a Procrustean bed of abstract equality, "without so much as a glance at more complicated reality," so that

Cerdà responded to his historic moment, and wanted to organize the city the way men wished to organize the government—without reference to what man actually is, according to an *a priori* formula, based on a fictional history that referred to no concrete facts, and using simplistic arguments to solve very complex questions.

In 1900 and 1901, Puig i Cadafalch railed intemperately against Cerdà in a series of articles in the newspaper *La Veu de Catalunya (The Voice of Catalunya)*. His cellular city, he wrote, "is one of the biggest horrors of the world; certainly nothing equals it, except in the most vulgar cities of South America." The regularity of its blocks put him in mind of "slaves' quarters." Without modulations or spatial climaxes, the Eixample had "the monotony of an American city in the middle of the Pampas . . . destined for a pretentious tribe with no more civic aspiration than to run up houses in which to eat, drink and sleep." There was much more in this vein. Everything that would be said against the Eixample's heirs, from Le Corbusier's *ville radieuse* to Oscar Niemeyer's Brasília, was already said, with far less justice, about the Eixample itself. And all its critics concurred that the basic mistake was to have left the planning of a city in the hands of a socialist.

Not everyone, by any means, has thought so. But one also has to realize that the Eixample as it exists today—and as it had become by the 1890s—is not, except in broad outline, the place that Ildefons Cerdà had in mind.

He had envisioned 550 blocks covering a land surface of nearly nine square kilometers. But this grid was absolute; it bore no relation to the site; it could be expanded forever, a purely modular city. On the large social plan, each district of four hundred blocks (twenty square) would have its own hospital, large park, and so forth. Each of these districts would be further divided into four units of a hundred blocks (ten by ten), each unit with its own subsidiary services—a general market, for instance. And each of these hundred-block units would further break down into four *barris*, each of twenty-five blocks (five by five), with its own schools and day-care centers. Only about a third of each block (five thousand square meters) was to be covered by buildings, and the corridors of open space between the apartments were to be patio gardens lined with plane trees. Some blocks were to be entirely open and left as small parks. Every block would have at least a hundred trees, some on the sidewalks and the rest inside.

Every block would be 113.3 meters square, and the streets between them 20 meters wide; three blocks plus three street widths thus equaled exactly 400 meters. But each block would have its corners chamfered at forty-five degrees, forming little diagonally set open squares at the intersections. This simple feature was a happy stroke of the pen, designed to leave turning space for public transport—steam trams, the newest of the new—and to afford room for loading and unloading goods. Cerdà's *xamfrans* remain a saving grace in the now car-choked city. They enable the driver, harried by Barcelona's appalling traffic, to see around corners, and they open up the grid of the Eixample to more space and sunlight.

Both are badly needed, because all Cerdà's original provisions for the blocks went by the board, traduced by a century or more of developers' and landlords' greed. One could never guess from the fortresslike character of the blocks of the Eixample that Cerdà actually meant them to be open; many of Cerdà's sidewalk trees are still there on the streets of his grid, but the internal ones, along with the patio gardens themselves, have vanished altogether. First, the Ajuntament let developers deepen the blocks, thus narrowing the gardens. Then it became the custom to ignore the gardens and cover the whole inside of a block with a single-story structure for storage and rentable offices. The next developer would close off both open ends of the block with multistory buildings, the same height as the existing ones. And then, once the block was 80 to 100 percent "utilized," the push for more height began. Originally, the height of all buildings in the Eixample was limited to 57 feet. By 1891 a rewritten building code increased this to 65 feet, and the figure kept creeping up as fast as owners could push it, secure in the knowledge that a word in the right ear or, for the less well connected, an envelope in the right hand could always square things with the Ajuntament. A rash of attics was added to existing buildings all over the Eixample during the Franco years, so today it is far denser and higher, more chaotic in texture, and generally more oppressive than Ildefons Cerdà ever could have imagined. Cerdà designed his standard block with 710,000 square feet of built floor space. Over the next century, developers were able to increase this, in many cases, to three million square feet per block: an urbanistic disaster, and a travesty of Cerdà's plan.

Probably the only variation on Cerdà's plan that added something to the quality of life in the Eixample—and then, only for a very few—was the building of *passatges*, private streets lined with houses, some of great charm and a sort of cottagey opulence, with blue-tiled steps, palms, and orange trees in their front gardens. These cut across some of the blocks and provide oases of intimate scale in the grid: Passatge Permanyer—the handsomest—and Passatge Mendez Vico near Passeig de Gracia, Passatge Bocabella and Passatge de Pages near Plaça de Tetuán, and half a

J. Gaspar, aerial photograph of the Eixample, 1925

dozen others. They are the only blocks of the Eixample that preserve something like the ratio between open and built space that Cerdà meant all the residents of Barcelona to enjoy, and their houses cost a fortune today.

And yet because of the architecture it contains, the Eixample is also one of the most interesting urban areas in Europe. No one could find it, considered solely as a plan, as picturesque as the intestinal windings, crooked alleys, and sudden explosive vistas of the Barri Gòtic; our romantic instincts tacitly agree with William Blake—"Improvement makes strait roads; but the crooked roads without Improvement are roads of Genius." But is one to judge a city just on picturesqueness? The Eixample is irreplaceable though mangled evidence of the social consciousness of a single, visionary designer; if Cerdà's ideas had prevailed, it would be a far more agreeable place, but if the framework of the plan had not been so strong, one shudders to think what an intolerable mess the New City of Barcelona would now be. Everything that went wrong with it was the result of uncontrolled developers' greed. And despite its monotony, nowhere else can one see such a mass of the daring, generously over-wrought, sublimely mannered structures of Catalan *modernisme*. The implantation of such works is so strong that one is apt to suppose it was always there—that it was somehow designed into the Cerdà plan. Not

47 Carrer Roger de Llúria, one of the first buildings of the Eixample, designed by Beltramini, 1864

so. The building of the Eixample was under way before most of the designers one associates with it had finished architecture school.

On October 4, 1860, Isabel II laid the first stone of the Eixample, and the long task of filling the grid with real buildings officially began. The first were on the four corners of the intersection of Carrers Consell de Cent and Roger de Llúria, put up in 1863–64 by an investor named Josep Cerdà (no relation) and decorated with sgraffito work by an Italian artist, Beltramini. Three of them were demolished or hopelessly mutilated in the Franco years, and the only one that survives is on the corner corresponding to Consell de Cent 340/Roger de Llúria 49.

One would like to think that the tempo of building went on with a Haussmannlike efficiency through the 1860s, but it did not: it was sluggish, spotty, and—being entirely done with speculative money—notable less for the architectural merits of the results than for the bald indifference the owners and builders showed to the ordinances of Cerdà's plan. Nor did it produce one building of genuine interest. By 1870 the only grand thing about the Eixample was its street names.

The task of choosing these devolved in 1863 upon one of the literary stars of the newly revived Jocs Florals, the poet Victor Balaguer. What other poet in history has had the chance to name all the streets of a new city, thereby riveting a permanent narrative of myth on its plan? None, and Balaguer launched into it with zest. His street names are a palace of memory, a mnemonic device for recalling the Renaixença version of the glories of Catalunya—a highly edited and "inspiring" version, needless to add. Not a single Castilian person or non-Catalan event figured among them. (Indeed, eighty years later, when the victorious Falangists ordered the renaming of some of the major avenues after the civil war, the new names did not stick. No "real" Catalan would have put his mouth around the Avenida del Generalisimo Francisco Franco; it was the Diagonal, and if an unwary tourist called it anything else he got a glare from the taxi driver.)

So Balaguer's triumphalist lexicon includes Catalan conquerors (Roger de Llúria, Bernat de Rocafort); medieval dynasties (Borrell, Comte d'Urgell); the countries of Catalunya's lost Mediterranean empire (Corsega, Calabria, Napols, Sardenya, Sicilia); its ancient political institutions (Consell de Cent, Diputació, Corts Catalanes); the three kingdoms of the Crown of Aragon (Aragó, Mallorca, and València); political heroes (Pau Claris, Rafael Casanova); emblematic sites of the Catalan resistance to Napoleon (Bruc, Girona, Bailen); and a whole array of poets and writers, from the Middle Ages (Ausiàs March) to figureheads of the Renaixença (Balmes and Aribau). Curiously, no street in Barcelona is named after Balaguer himself, which seems a trifle unfair.

However good these names looked on the map at the end of the 1860s, the streets themselves were a different matter: strips of dust and rubble, unlighted, undrained, and mostly without buildings to which name plaques could be fixed. By 1872 there were about a thousand residential structures in the Eixample, whose most concentrated area was the twenty blocks bounded by Gràcia, Consell de Cent, Casp, and Bailen. Some forty thousand people had moved to these new apartments. Nevertheless the building of the Eixample did not take off until the mid-1870s, when the Catalan economy entered the boom decade known as the *febre d'or*, or "gold fever." But because there were so many millions of free *duros* swashing about in the Catalan economy, and so few teeth in the laws that were supposed to govern building in the Eixample, Cerdà's dream turned more and more into its opposite—a gigantic cellular slum for the proletariat and *menestralia*, punctuated with sumptuous trophy buildings for the new rich.

In 1888, a doctor and sanitary engineer named Pere Garcia Faria submitted a report to a medical congress held in Barcelona, which made it plain that the Eixample, far from inducting the common people of the city into a new environment of light, space, gardens, and Utopian hope, was just as bad as the Old City and possibly even worse. "These houses," he reported, "with two stories and a basement that the engineer Cerdà designed to be enclosed by gardens, set out in pleasant and smiling perspectives built on only two sides of each block, meant for one family at a time—today they have become veritable slums, in which the Barcelonan family is imprisoned." They were built far higher than the codes allowed, sometimes five or six stories, but to preserve a semblance of conformity, the developers had dropped the internal ceiling height and made them into warrens, "often lacking light and direct ventilation, or else getting it from mean and ill-constructed balconies. As a result, some floors are so damp as to be uninhabitable. As if that were not bad enough, people have taken to living in ground floors and basements, despite the [zoning laws], which are only obeyed when a landlord has no profit to make from evading them." The gardens were closed off or built over; and none of Cerdà's provisions for public parks had been respected. (This remains largely true today: Cerdà planned four big parks, but only one such park, the Parc de l'Escorxador, built over the site of an old slaughter-yard and lately renamed in honor of Joan Miró, near the Sants railway station, came into being.)

One of the main arguments for the demolition of the *muralles* had been health: the Old City was regularly swept by epidemics of cholera and typhoid. But so was the Eixample thirty years later, because the city had not required the developers to equip it with decent drainage or even an adequate water supply. Dr. Faria reported that typhoid, scrofula, anemia, and tuberculosis caused "havoc . . . in what should have been the handsomest and healthiest of cities," and that "the problem of waste disposal flouts [Cerdà's] design. The toilets and sinks often connect the house directly to the drain network, failing the most elementary standards of hygiene and often finishing in cess-pits. This appalling system . . . is the cause of the contamination of air and water from which the inhabitants suffer."

As a bonus, the Eixample harbored epidemic malaria, caused by the lack of storm-water drainage. In summer, swarms of anopheles mosquitoes bred in standing pools on its vacant lots.

VI

The three decades between the Burning of the Convents in 1835 and the Revolution of 1868 were, in the main, difficult times for Barcelona. The sites of razed convents stayed empty, and there was rarely enough money to build new public structures in spots confiscated from the Church under the Mendizábal Laws. The Old City was choked. The Eixample filled slowly; a full momentum of building was not reached until the 1880s. In any case, the only part of Barcelona that had been developed in the previous half century was the Ramblas, its social spine. So it is not altogether surprising that almost the only building of major social impact that rose in Barcelona in midcentury was on the Ramblas too, not far from Plaça Reial. This was the Liceu, the opera house, and to grasp what it meant to Barcelona one must understand something of the vagaries of nineteenth-century Catalan musical culture.

Catalans are very proud of their musical traditions and apt to go on at length about how old, enthusiastic, and knowing musical taste in Barcelona has been. This claim requires its pinch of salt, and for most of the eighteenth and nineteenth centuries it was true in only one area of "high" music: Italian opera.

From the end of the Napoleonic Wars to the Wagner craze of the 1880s and 1890s, the middle-class Barcelona public was fixated on Italian opera at the expense of almost every other kind of music. This had begun with the patronage of Castaños y Aragorri (1758–1852), the duke of Bailen, a music-loving soldier who served as Ferdinand VII's captain general of Catalunya in 1815–20. He had constructed the Jardí del General on the port; and now, with a view to improving the musical life of Barcelona, he imported an Italian opera company and installed its director, Pietro Generali, as the maestro of the Teatre de la Santa Creu on the Ramblas, which had staged a production of Mozart's *Cosi Fan Tutte* back in 1798. The new company's first effort was Gioacchino Rossini's *L'Italiana in Algeri* (*The Italian Girl in Algiers*), 1813, and for the next two decades Rossini's example exerted an iron control over Catalan operatic taste. He had various Catalan followers, chiefly Ramon Carnicer (1789–1855) and Baltasar Saldoni (1807–89). The works of Rossini, Donizetti, Verdi, and, later, Puccini were seen as the summation, the very quintessence, of elevated taste. Woe betide the musician who wanted to play anything else, no matter if he had written it himself. Even Franz Liszt, when he visited Barcelona in 1845, had to give four concerts without playing a single piece of his own. He was a virtuoso on the keyboard? Then let him show it by playing piano transcriptions of Italian opera. This audience thought of the arias from those operas as its own; it felt their composers were in some cloudy but meaningful way Catalan at heart. Instrumental pieces sent the audience into fidgets or deep sleep from which it could be roused only by the appearance of a soprano, hastily summoned to belt out "Vissi d'Arte."

Much the same held true for German music. *Bon gust* in Barcelona

for most of the nineteenth century was so indifferent to it (and to symphonic music in general) that Beethoven's Fifth Symphony, written in
1808, was not performed there until 1881. During rehearsals the Catalan
players warned their German conductor that its sounds were so harsh
and novel that the audience would walk out, and some people actually
did. Barcelona succumbed to a fever of Wagnerism in the 1890s, but
before Wagner's death (1883) practically no Catalan outside professional
music circles had heard his music or even, one may surmise, his name.

By the 1870s the Italian obsession began to change, though with gla-
cial slowness. Many well-off Catalans had French as their third language,
after Spanish—as well they might, since the French border lay not too far
north of Passeig de Gràcia. An acquaintance with French was considered
a mark of refinement in Barcelona as elsewhere in Europe. Nevertheless it
was the custom, when French operas at last made their appearance at the
Liceu—Gounod's *Faust* or works by Meyerbeer—to translate them into
Italian: the Barcelona public was still loath to believe that an opera in
French was really an opera at all. Even the names of the conductor and
instrumentalists on the Liceu's concert programs were printed in Italian
form—every Josep becoming a Giuseppe, every Pere a Pietro. It lent an
air and kept at bay the fear of seeming provincial or unprofessional.

Barcelona's two main musical institutions were obviously dedicated
to opera. The first of these was the Teatre Principal (Ramblas 27–29),
which had been built by the military engineer Francisco Cabrer in 1778.
(The rather stiff and heavy neoclassical facade with its three bays is a
much later addition, begun in 1847 by Francesc Molina i Casamajó.) It
replaced the old Teatre de la Santa Creu, inheriting its charter of monopoly bestowed by Felipe II in 1579. For nearly three centuries this
theater—which had acquired its site on the embryonic Ramblas at the
end of the sixteenth century—was literally the only one in Barcelona,
though at first it was a humble wooden structure nicknamed the Corral
dels Comedies (Drama Farmyard). Greenrooms, bleachers, and other
additions were stuck higgledy-piggledy onto it over the years, and the
first Italian operas were given there in 1750. Finally it was demolished
in 1775 to make way for Cermeño's straightening of the Ramblas, rebuilt
by Cabrer, and renamed the Teatre Principal. By the 1860s, when
Molina had finished modifying Cabrer's structure, enlarging it and building its massive facade, it could hold two thousand people.

However, the Principal was cramped, stuffy, ill-lighted, and a fire-
trap. It had nowhere to go but down. By the 1890s it was a seedily grand
vaudeville house that presented magicians and zarzuelas, and after 1930 it
suffered the last indignity and became a cinema. (Happily, it was restored

Ramón Casas, The Liceu, *circa 1898*

by the Ajuntament in the late 1980s.) At midcentury, Barcelona's new focus of musical interest, indeed the main cultural emblem of the city, had risen a few blocks farther up the Ramblas, at numbers 61–65.

This was the Gran Teatre del Liceu, which in short order became the cathedral of taste, display, and pretension of all the *bones famílies* of Barcelona, together with all those who aspired to their company—in short, of the city's upper bourgeoisie. It was founded in 1844 by a society resoundingly named the Barcelona Philharmonic and Dramatic Lyceum of Her Majesty the Queen Dona Isabel II. This group actually consisted of members of the Seventh Battalion of the Barcelona Militia, who in 1837 had quartered themselves in the ancient monastery of Montsió (whose monks had been thrown out during the convent burnings of 1835). Not being paid by Madrid—or Barcelona either—the militiamen had no money to buy guns or uniforms, so they started giving theatrical evenings in the monastery to raise funds. These were a success, and before long the Sunday soldiers had institutionalized themselves as the Philodramatic Society of Barcelona. Then they added a music school, offering classes in song, declamation, and instrumental technique. Shortly afterward they brought in the composer Marià Obiols, a fervent

Catalanist, as their director. The Liceu Filharmònico-Dramàtic Barcelones, as it now called itself, asked for and in 1844 was given a site on the Ramblas where another convent had stood. It hunted up subscriptions and donors; it engaged the architect Miquel Garriga i Roca to draw designs for an opera house of maximum splendor, rivaling La Scala, with space (counting standing room) for four thousand people.

The Teatre del Liceu opened with great pomp in the spring of 1847 with Donizetti's *Anna Bolena*—a safe choice, since it had already been given several times at the Santa Creu. The first unfamiliar opera it produced came that summer: Verdi's *Giovanna d'Arco*, which had premiered at La Scala only two years before. It then played a solid diet of Italian opera to packed houses and boxes for fourteen years, until it caught fire (fortunately, between performances) in 1861. Undeterred, the Liceu opened a subscription fund, and within a year, without a peseta of government money, the opera house was playing again. Its reconstruction was by Garriga i Roca's former assistant Josep Oriol i Mestres, and its near-incredible speed says much about the anxiety with which Barcelona's opera addicts viewed the stark prospect of a life without arias. Oriol Mestres's reconstruction was, if possible, even more splendiferous than Garriga i Roca's original, featuring acres of yellow and white marble, gilt, stucco, and bronze and a ceiling aswirl with painted cartouches in a whorish, elevated *pompier* style somewhere between Giambattista Tiepolo and César Ritz. The most ornate parts of all, the boxes, were completed in 1883 by Pere Falqués.

To discuss opera—or at least to make the right approbatory sounds about it—was de rigueur in Barcelona's polite society. But one cannot make the facile assumption that, merely because Catalan opera buffs were well off, they did not know what they were hearing. By the 1880s a serious and patient audience had precipitated itself around the Liceu. As Cristina and Eduardo Mendoza have put it, its fanatic partisanship in musical issues was a sublimation of political debate, and this gave the general melomania its urgency. One knew that in practical terms Spanish politics were decided in Madrid, not Barcelona. One also knew that none of the Madrid parties represented Catalan interests. And so,

> Barcelonans chose to direct the currents of thought of their time into symbolic but local areas, to channel their passions into them and, as best they could, solve their dilemmas there. Thus for several decades the opera, with all its emotional content, offered the Barcelonans a convenient, agreeable duelling-ground. Through opera they could stage a confrontation . . . between two ideas of life that the time presented

294 THE NEW CITY

as opposites: the prosaic, sensual life of the Mediterranean, to which they were bound by geography, and the militant idealism of feeling of a vaguely conceived North . . . to which they felt ineluctably drawn.

The force of this would become most vividly apparent in the late 1880s, when Wagnerianism swept Barcelona.

Nevertheless, though nobody could doubt the devotion to music felt by the Liceu's public, one may surmise that when heads of the *bones families* put on their *fracs* and white ties, while their better halves were laced into their stays and submitted their white bosoms to the chilly if gratifying touch of the diamond parure, they were at least partly impelled by something other than the pure love of organized sound. That something was, of course, social prestige: one went to the Liceu not only to hear this or that performance, but to enjoy the exacting social ceremony known as "going to the opera." Programs changed, but the abiding show at the Liceu was the mapping of class and the display of wealth as carriages disgorged their brilliantly caparisoned human freight at the porte cochere on the Ramblas and the crowds pressed sluggishly up the staircase into the ambient gold fudge of the auditorium, the wives clattering their tortoiseshell-and-vellum fans and perspiring slightly under the layers of powder, an Arnus nodding to a Girona, a López stiffly favoring a Comas with the minimal inclination of the trunk. The Liceu was nominally a public place, but its attachment, the Club del Liceu, which one could enter directly from the upper foyer, was entirely private: the inner sanctum of privilege for box holders, their wives, their mistresses, and their friends, complete with a ground-floor mirador from which one could watch the passing parade on the Ramblas, the distant theater of common life, the street as aquarium. The Liceu was the one public place in Barcelona where you could fire a cannon and never hit a worker.

If the Liceu was Barcelona's quintessential symbol of high-bourgeois culture, the ornate knob on the cane of capital, its musical programs created a degree of resentment among some Catalan musicians. The question was not their quality, but rather their content. The small scope given to purely orchestral work and the fixation on Italian opera, the reluctance of its directors to step beyond the taste of its private sponsors, were irksome. And such attitudes leaked into the conservatory attached to the Liceu, Barcelona's main music school. They reinforced the idea that Catalunya was a province—that the only "real" music came from abroad. This was made more offensive by the ceaseless harping on the superiority of Mediterranean music to more northern forms—German,

Belgian, even French. But the sticking point was the Liceu's implicit assumption that music—good, "cultivated" music—belonged only to one class, the rich. Inevitably, such attitudes were bound to collide with the more radical ideologies of Catalanism and socialism, brewing together at the edge of the Renaixença. This conflict came to a head over *cançó popular*, traditional Catalan folk music. The man who made it do so, and in the process set off a grass-roots revival of choral singing in Catalunya during the 1860s, a revival which was to deeply alter the cultural imagery of the Renaixença, was Josep Anselm Clavé i Camps (1824–75).

VII

Clavé was a musician, song collector, and politician. His ideas about the social role of music and society had been formed by Catalan republican thought during the 1850s. He was considered, by himself and others, a fervent revolutionary, one of the young men of the 1840s who would pay harsh dues for his beliefs. He had demonstrated in the Jamancia in 1843. played an important role in convincing the Barcelonese textile workers not to burn more factories during the rising of 1854, and had remonstrated with Zapatero—for which offense the frightful general lunged across the desk, grabbed him by the throat, and shook him "like a rat." He had suffered imprisonment and exile.

Clavé was friendly with Narcis Monturiol, but his closest mentor was Abdo Terradas. Terradas left a vivid mark on Catalan socialists, and not least on Clavé. He believed that the democracy he so passionately desired, and in a sense died for, could come only through a broad class rising: its motor would be not the proletariat alone but a general alliance between artisans, small shopkeepers, cottage-industry pieceworkers, factory hands, and, of course, professional liberals like himself. Only this broad band, galvanized by intellectuals and reaching from the *menestralia* to worse-exploited laborers, could resist the power of capital and the army. No "mob"—his word, *patuleia*—could do so.

And the key to this alliance was education. If people did not cooperate in gaining knowledge, Terradas argued, they would be slaves forever. But they must take charge of their own learning, or else they would merely imbibe the values, the all-pervasive social propaganda, of the bosses and the Church. So they must have alternatives to the official schooling system, 90 percent of which, even in Catalunya, was reserved for children of the well-off. Adult education, that invaluable tool of

Josep Anselm Clavé i Camps

socialist self-awareness, hardly existed in Spain. The solution, as Ter-radas and his comrades saw it, lay in the Catalans' own gregarious nature. In clubs and self-help societies, ordinary workingmen would convene in a spirit of sober endeavor, to read, to inquire, to debate, to learn. What would transform Spain, in the end, would be not the musket and the barricade, but the creation of an educated working class through a net-work of voluntary associations.

Anselm Clavé shared this belief, and he acted on it in the realm of music. His particular cultural interest lay in Catalan folk literature—*rondalles* (stories and fables)—and, especially, folk song. He had studied musical theory and composition. In his twenties he had traveled all over Catalunya, writing down the words of songs and transcribing their tunes.

Like his predecessors Milà i Fontanals and Pau Piferrer in the 1840s, Clavé was a man of huge taxonomic energy, inspired by the belief that *cançó popular*—still despised as naïve, provincial stuff by most Catalan literati—held the uncorrupted oral root of Catalan language and litera-ture. In popular song, insulated from change by the native conservatism of the *pagesos* and the remoteness of their farms and hamlets, handed down from generation to generation with very slow accretions or none at all, one heard the true model of national poetry and music, an ancient lyrical voice untouched by the preciosity of modern verse. But it could not be allowed to languish on the printed page in a scholars' limbo. It must be returned to the people and sung by them. And in singing, people would be put in mind of an older and freer Catalunya, the independent country that had existed for six hundred years before the rule of Madrid, whose administrative torque only made the miseries of capitalism worse. As a bonus, the choral societies Clavé had in mind would give—or so he hoped—a fresh aspect to the leisure time of city workers, weaning them away from the "sordid ambience" of their taverns, from drunken binges, wife beating, and child abuse. "Do you dare ask," Simó i Badia asked his middle-class readers, "that these degraded creatures should show good education, refined manners, decent dress, proper speech? What sarcasm could be more horrible? And what is more: How can you expect beings who have been turned into mere laboring machines, without stimulus or hope, to take pride in the work that destroys their bodies and kills their souls?" Clavé believed you could, through the healing power of music.

He started one Philharmonic society in Barcelona, the Aurora, in 1845; another in 1850, the Fraternity, renamed itself the Euterpe Society in 1857—Euterpe being the Muse of flute playing. By the mid-1860s a network of similar groups had sprung up in the major towns of Catalunya, not only Barcelona but Tarragona, Lleida, Vic and Reus as well. They were known as *cors de Clavé*, "Clavé's choirs." He arranged their programs, recruited singers and conductors, trained them, supplied them with sheet music and old songs—and new ones as well. Clavé's own songs were very popular. The best known of them, a perennial hit with Catalan choristers, was "Els Flors de Maig" ("The Flowers of May"), 1859. He also wrote work songs and hymns to labor, such as "Els Pescadors" ("The Fishermen"), 1861, and "La Maquinista" ("The Seamstress"), 1867; and songs in praise of folk culture and popular festivals, such as "Els Xiquets dels Valls" ("The Valley Lads"), 1867, and "Pasqua Florida" ("Flowering Easter"), 1868. On occasion he would turn out a patriotic anthem; he rewrote the "Marseillaise" in Catalan and celebrated General Prim's victory over the Moroccan army at the battle of Tetuán in 1860 with a song called "Els Nets dels Almogàvers" ("The Grandchildren of the Catalan Mercenaries")—the *almogàvers* being a much-mythologized force of Catalans used by the medieval kings of Aragon and Catalunya in their wars against the Muslims.

Clavé never quit politics, but his career on the hustings did not have a tenth of the political effect of his musical work. A new generation of writers, musicians, artists, and architects born around 1850, who were to carry the Renaixença to its full fruition—the generation of Domènech i Montaner, Gaudí, Joan Maragall—looked back on him with affection and a degree of awe, as one who had resuscitated the native voice of Catalunya: the Aribau of *cançó popular*.

VIII

The strangest instrument of cultural Catalanism—and one that had nothing whatsoever to do with the workers—was a poetry contest known as the Jocs Florals, or Floral Games. Its object was to confirm that a "great," patriotic, national literature was being written in Catalan. Catalan writers, acting on a belief in the power of poetry that was indissolubly part of romanticism, and under the influence of Aribau's ode, persuaded themselves that their verses could mobilize large numbers of their fellow Catalans into separatist fervor. To do this, one had to be archaic. As the Majorcan poet Marià Aguilo put it in the 1850s,

> *Cec d'amor per un llenguatge*
> *que no tinc prou dominat*
> *emprenc el pelerinatge*
> *pel fossar del temps passat.*

> Blind with love for a language
> All too powerless today,
> I set out on a pilgrimage
> Through the graveyard of olden times.

Thus it came about that every year, from 1859 on, a literary elite of Catalans would gather in Barcelona to recite their fulsome and stereotyped praises of Catalan virtue and Catalan history in verses so precious and old-fashioned that few other people could understand them. Each poet believed that he (or she) was thus striking a blow for Catalanism, and much windy rhetoric was expended to show why this was so. Few of their productions are read today. And yet the Jocs Florals were far more than just a literary game with prizes. Until well into the 1880s they were the binding institution, the "spinal column," as one critic put it, of the Catalan Renaixença; they were the yearly proof that the Catalan language was the conduit of elevated national sentiment, and their decline marked the transition between the Renaixença and the wider, more international and aestheticized interests of Catalan *modernisme*. The Jocs were a medieval revival, institutionally stronger, in some ways, than the original—though emphatically not in terms of poetic merit.

The original Jocs Florals—an outgrowth of troubadour poetry, a joust in verse, where poets would compete for prizes judged and given by the court—do not seem to have been held often, or for long. They began (or so the story goes) on All Saints' Day in 1324, when seven young nobles met in a garden in Toulouse and decided to invite poets and troubadours from the country around to recite their work the following May. Invitations went out to all the towns of the Languedoc, and replies supposedly poured in from ambitious Provençal bards. This eisteddfod offered a violet made of gold as its first prize, and it continued for sixty years until Violante de Bar, queen of Catalunya and Aragon and wife to Joan I, brought it and some members of its jury to Barcelona in 1388. The court officially adopted the Jocs Florals in 1393 and celebrated them with much pomp thereafter; they became a symbol of the High Gothic extravagances of Joan I, "the Lover of Refinement," as he was nicknamed.

By the early fifteenth century the Jocs Florals in Barcelona offered three trophies. The third prize was a violet made of silver; the second was a golden rose—an elaborate replica of the eglantine, which was also, in England, the emblem of the Tudors; the first prize, however, was a *flor natural*, a real rose. Nothing a jeweler made could surpass nature; and although the runners-up would need permanent proof of their success, the winner, it was assumed, would not—the rose would fade, but his poem would last.

The Jocs Florals died with the Middle Ages and were soon a memory, not a living tradition. The first call to revive them came from Rubió i Ors in 1841, but they did not actually start again for another eighteen years. During that time the practice of writing poetry in Catalan, inspired by Aribau and Rubió, began to consolidate. A reading public for Catalan verse was forming. Poets writing in the vernacular found a new proponent, Antoni de Bofarull i de Broca (1821–92), the nephew of Prosper de Bofarull, an archivist who had written profusely on the Middle Ages and assembled a sixteen-volume source collection on Catalan history. Being thus steeped in the annals of medieval Catalunya, Antoni de Bofarull was seized by the desire to bring back its glories. Their natural form, he believed, was troubadour poetry. In 1858 he brought out a collection of the work of thirty-five poets, mainly young but all writing in Catalan, entitled *Los Trobadors Nous* (*The New Troubadors*). It was popular enough to produce a prompt sequel, containing some Catalan writers Bofarull had left out: *Los Trobadors Moderns* (1859), edited by the fiery young romantic and cultural nationalist who later played a strong role in the politics of Catalan separatism, Victor Balaguer i Cirera (1824–1901). Balaguer was a chronic fabulist, a man for whom the ascertainable facts of history were merely the fodder of nationalist saga. "Modern troubadours": the very title now seems to epitomize the Janus-faced nature of the Catalan Renaixença, looking nostalgically back and eagerly forward at the same time.

Clearly, poets were at work in Catalan all over the principate—not only in Barcelona, but in Tarragona, Lleida, Reus, Vic, and Majorca as well. Because Rubió i Ors had called himself the Bagpiper of Llobregat, they broke out in a picturesque variety of imitative pseudonyms: the Drummer of the Bésos, the Fluter of the Ter, the Troubadour of Penedés, the Tambourine Player of the Fluvia, the Minstrel of Majorca, and so on. But scattered writers do not make a movement. For that, a common knot is needed: some institution to which the work can gravitate, through which it, and the ideas around it, can be refracted and promoted. Later in the nineteenth and through the twentieth centuries, little magazines (some of them not so little) performed that office, in Barcelona as in Paris, London, or New York. But the public for Catalan writing in the mid-nineteenth century, despite the success of Bofarull's anthology, was too small to support such magazines.

Thus Bofarull and his friends hit on the idea of an annual prize, sponsored by the Ajuntament. It would remind Catalans of their bonding past, bring new poets out of obscurity, confirm the importance of established ones, provoke argument, and, in general, whip up publicity for Catalan writing. Hence the Jocs Florals. The first prize, as in Joan I's time, would be a real rose, awarded for a poem on any subject—although it was expected that the theme should relate to the institution's motto, "Patria, Fides, Amor" ("Fatherland, Faith, Love"), and that the form should be narrative, "a romance, ballad or legend." The second prize was the *eglantina d'or*, or "gold rose," given for verses on Catalan customs or Catalan history. The third prize was a gold-and-silver violet, for a poem on a religious or moral theme. The absolute sine qua non was that entries should be written in Catalan. Bofarull, with an enthusiasm not untouched by the pleasure of organizing a costume party, threw himself into the task of researching—or, sometimes, simply inventing—the regulations of this literary tourney. One rule was that if a writer won three prizes, he would be given the medieval title Mestre

The emblem of the new Jocs Florals, 1862

---

en Gay Saber, Master of the Joyous Knowledge. Several Catalan writers were to win this distinction, among them Jacint Verdaguer, Josep Carner, Joan Maragall, and that barbed popular wit Josep Maria de Sagarra.

The prizes were given by a *consistori*, or "jury committee," which elected a president each year; on him fell the onus of delivering the ceremonial address, which was published in all its prolixity in the Barcelonese press and scanned with minute attention—like the honking of the white geese in the pond of the Cathedral cloister, one neglected poet griped—for signs of change in official views of the relations among verse, language, and politics.

The first meeting of the revived Jocs Florals was held on May 1, 1859, in the Saló de Cent of Barcelona. A portrait of Joan I hung above the dais and the room was draped with banners. (Next year, the venue shifted to the Llotja.) The literary scholar Milà i Fontanals had been elected the first president of the Jocs, and, one of his colleagues reverently exclaimed afterward, "He spoke for three hours in Catalan and nobody laughed." This may have been less of a sally than one might think, since the only declamatory use of Catalan up to then had been in the theater, where it was spoken by actors in comic vernacular parts like the "low" speech of porters and soldiers in Shakespeare. But perhaps the audience was indeed paralyzed by its own sense of august occasion. Either way, Milà i Fontanals struck the theme of this and most subsequent Jocs Florals in the first few minutes: it was not so much a poetry competition as a

festival of language, a site of memory, a refuge for the Catalan tongue
in all its purity:

> To those who remind us of the advantages of forgetting [Catalan], we
> say that we would rather keep a feeling in a corner of our breasts—
> and if anyone wishes to detect peril and conflict in this feeling, or a
> cooling of love for the communal fatherland . . . we can repeat an
> aphorism once applied to Antoni de Capmany, one of the best Catalans
> and most ardent Spaniards that ever lived: "No-one can love his nation
> that does not love his province."

None of the writers, apparently, wanted the Jocs Florals to be seen
as an instrument of Catalan political rebellion against Madrid: that would
have been going too far, although Victor Balaguer, in the course of his
speech that day, praised the long-abolished Council of One Hundred as
"an ardent protector of our country's literature, as of the liberties of its
people," and by "country" he meant Catalunya, not Spain. All in all,
the speeches and readings that May Day took about six hours, and the
quality of the prizewinning poems hardly made up for it. The first *flor
natural* was won by a woman, Isabel de Villamartin, with half a yard
of genteel doggerel that began:

> *Nobles senyors del Consistori Gai,*
> *el geni catala de la victoria*
> *noves regions li obriu i nou espai.*
> *Pus feu reviure l'oblidada història,*
> *tot revivint del trobador lo lai*
> *al patri i sant amor: Déu vos do gloria*
> *nobles senyors del Consistori Gai.*

> Noble gentlemen of the Joyous Committee,
> The Catalan genius of victory
> opens new regions to you, and a new space.
> You can make forgotten history live again,
> reviving the troubadour's song of praise
> to his country and to holy love; God give you glory,
> Noble gentlemen of the Joyous Committee.

Anyone could enter the Jocs, and increasing numbers of writers,
new and established, did. There were only 39 entries in 1859, but by
1869 there were ten times as many, and by 1875, 466. Along the way

The consistory of the Jocs Florals, 1900, at the home of Eusebi Güell, including Enric Morera (second from left) and Güell (seated at desk)

the Jocs, having begun a new life as a poetry contest, soon expanded to include all forms of writing: history, drama, essays, novels.

But the prestige of the institution rested on poetry. This may seem hard to square with the merits of the general run of the verse it fostered—what the Catalan critic Joan Fuster called "the mediocre mass of the poets of the Jocs Florals." In truth, the new Jocs Florals handed out its eglantines and violets for nearly a quarter century before it rewarded an authentic masterpiece—Jacint Verdaguer's epic poem *L'Atlàntida*, in 1879. But there was a strong patriotic tendency to look at quantity rather than quality. Patriotism was to the Renaixença what feminism and ecological virtue are to American poetry workshops today: it produced a flood of conventional sentiment, and "correct" political rhetoric, all written with the deepest conviction by poetasters who wished only to express what was in their Catalan hearts. Most of the verse of the Renaixença was proof that neither sincerity nor patriotism, however desirable in life, are quite enough in art.

Because the Jocs Florals aimed to stimulate regional literature in a broad way, its committee had connections with the French *Félibres*, or Doctors of the Law, the group of seven poets led by Frédéric Mistral who, in 1854, had begun their campaign for the restoration of Provençal, Catalan's sister language, as a living writers' tongue. Mistral himself struck up a friendship and an abundant correspondence with Victor Balaguer; in 1868, they both headed a pilgrimage of Catalan and Provençal poets to the monastery of Montserrat. But although the poets of the Languedoc sometimes entered the Jocs Florals, the Catalan judges rarely gave them a prize.

Since the overarching project of the Jocs Florals was to confirm the Catalan language rather than to explore this or that literary tendency, the same themes recur again and again—mainly, nostalgia (*enyoranca*, one of the favorite words of the period) followed by argumentative defiance. Nostalgia was attached to standard key images. In nature, the main one was the landscape of Catalunya itself (preferably one's rural birthplace, if one was not born in Barcelona) and its holy peaks, Montseny, Montjuic, and especially Montserrat—"*I sempre tindrem patria els fills de Catalunya,*" wrote Jaume Collell in the poem that won the *flor natural* in 1870, "*mentre al cel s'aixequin els pics de Montserrat*": "And we sons of Catalunya will hold our fatherland forever, / as long as the peaks of Montserrat reach to the sky." One invoked its spring flower carpets in the valleys and torrents of melting snow in the mountains, symbols of the awakening of Catalunya and its language after Bourbon repression. Its rocks betokened permanence and induced swooning raptures, mixed with romantic death wishes; thus Pere Talric, pining for his native Pyrenees:

> *Vallespir!*
> *dolc sospir!*
> *quina alegria!*
> *Mon cor somnia*
> *que un dia haure per darrer llit*
> *quatre lloses del teu granit.*
> *Si em nega Deu eixa esperanca,*
> *si sota un altre cel de Franca*
> *mon jorn suprem ha de venir*
> *de mi conserva est souvenir;*
> *no morire pas de vellesa,*
> *ai, no! morire de tristesa . . .*

> Vallespir!
> Sweet sigh!
> what happiness!
> My heart dreams
> that one day it will have, for its last bed

four slabs of your granite.
If God denies me this hope,
if my last day must come
beneath another sky of France
I will keep this memory:
I will not die of age,
Ah, no! I will die of sorrow . . .

On the whole, the poetic productions of the Jocs Florals had as little relation to the ascertainable facts of Catalan medieval life as English Pre-Raphaelitism, with its nostalgic fustian of blessed damozels, flowery meads, and proto-Rupert-Brooke Saint Georges in shining armor, had to the English Middle Ages. Practically nowhere in *floréaliste* verse does one find the muscularity, sharpness, and flashes of hard social acuity of the original Catalan troubadours. And of course the stink of the Middle Ages, its coarseness and animal side, was left out altogether. When scholars of the Renaixença came up against this kind of material, it made them deeply queasy; the worst case was perhaps an anonymous fifteenth-century verse fragment called "Coloqui de Dames" ("Ladies Talking"), which describes the buzz of amused outrage in a group of (presumably well-born) women in the cathedral of Valencia when an old man suddenly flashes his genitals at them:

> *"Oh del vell podrit vila!"*
>   *digueren elles.*
> *"Per com[m]oure eixam de abelles*
>   *molt sou feixuc;*
> *be mostrau tenir lo buc*
>   *granment rugat!*
>
>   . . . .
>
> *fred sou com a raim de parra*
>   *i sec com faig;*
> *llenyos, gipo de saig,*
>   *castrat, potros,*
> *brut, suat e gargallos,*
>   *i de tot foll!*
> *Ja us fariem torcer lo coll*
>   *com a colom!*
> *I graiu-ho al lloc on som,*
>   *que hom vos dara*
> *tapinades per la cara*

mes que fulles.
Fastig n'han les parafulles
  del teginat
vos hajau aixi gosat
  manar callar
al qui us pot, sens pecat, cagar
  enmig la barba!"

"O you dirty old man!"
  they say.
"You are so clapped-out
  you have to show your cock
wrinkled and old
  to make a swarm of bees buzz!

. . . .

You're as cold as a grape on a vine
  dry as a beech-twig,
rheumy-eyed, dressed like a beggar,
  castrated, herniated,
dirty, sweaty, drivelling,
  and crazy too!
We'll wring your neck
  like a pigeon!
Thank your stars we're in church
  or we'd hit you on the face
more times with our spike-heels
  than there are leaves on a tree.
Even the rafters
  in the roof detest you
because you managed
  to stop our talk—
nobody would blame us
  if we shat in your beard!"

When the devout Milà i Fontanals discovered this tidbit in some
Catalan archive, he copied it out and then, overwhelmed with guilt at
the sins of his ancestors, made a beeline for the confessional.

CHAPTER SIX

Going to the Fair

I

The Glorious Revolution of September 1868, which got rid of the Bourbon monarchy for six brief years, divides the old history of Spain from the new. It was a liberal coup carried out by the army. That alone made it unlike other European revolutions. We tend to think of armies as instruments of antidemocratic reaction. Not so in Spain, where throughout the nineteenth century and especially during the reign of Isabel II it was the custom for politicians to call in the generals when they needed help. The reason for this was put in a nutshell by the historian Raymond Carr. "In nations where civil society is weak . . . the army possesses, not merely a monopoly of physical force, but a disciplined cohesion and *esprit de corps* which no other social group can rival . . . thus the *pronunciamiento* replaced elections as a mechanism for political change."

The *pronunciamiento* was the act of declaring the army's loyalty to a political group. Since the defeat of Napoleon, every progressive regime in Spain had been installed by the military, not by votes. In 1854 General Joaquín Espartero Baldomero declared for Isabel II and the progressives. In 1856 General Leopoldo O'Donnell brought the moderates and conservatives back to parliamentary power by the same gesture. In 1868 yet another declared for the moderate liberals who felt excluded from cabinet power by the increasingly conservative sympathies of Isabel II. He was a Catalan, General Joan Prim i Prats (1814–70). Prim was joined in the act by General Francisco Serrano, a Castilian, somewhat to the right of him. The combination of these two generals and their political groups was known as the September Coalition. Their bloodless putsch toppled Isabel's government and sent her packing to France, where for

General Prim addressing the people from the balcony of the Casa de la Ciutat, October 4, 1868

the next six years she was sheltered by Napoleon III. During that time, the Glorious Revolution turned out to be no kind of revolution at all.

It did, however, produce a new constitution, drawn up in 1869, which created "universal" suffrage in Spain—not universal, of course, being limited to males over the age of twenty-one, but still a great step in the direction of democracy. Apart from this, the 1869 Constitution was inherently conservative. The republicans trained their special fire on Article Twenty-one, which confirmed Catholicism as the state religion, and Article Thirty-three, which reestablished monarchy as the form of government. The religious issue brought forth magnificent rhetoric on both sides, especially from the young republican José Echegaray (future winner of the Nobel Prize for literature) who invited his fellow deputies to think of what lay beneath the old site of the Inquisition's autos-da-fé in Calle Carranza in Madrid: "Layers of ashes soaked in human fat, then calcined bones, then a layer of sand thrown down to cover them, then another stratum of ashes, another of bones, another of sand, and so the horrible heap goes on." But the conservatives and moderates carried the day. The problem was to find a monarch, and here Prim's views were crucial.

General Prim, being Catalan, was genuinely popular in Barcelona. He had made all the right moves. In 1843 he had led an insurrection in Reus against the liberal general Espartero, who was detested by progressives and moderates alike for bombarding Barcelona from Montjuic during the Jamancia; after the fall of Espartero, and with a liberal-moderate consensus behind him, Prim was appointed military governor of Barcelona. Its *exaltats* and citizen militia refused to give up their arms, and this time it was Prim who gave the city a whiff of grapeshot; it won him the wholehearted approval of its business leaders. Having thus destroyed the short-lived Jamancia, Prim returned to foreign service, in Puerto Rico, the Crimean War, and, in 1860, at the head of a force of five hundred Catalan volunteers against the Arabs of Spanish Morocco at Tetuán. In reality, this "famous victory" achieved nothing, but it evoked memories of the *almogàvers* and excited the imperial fantasies of the Catalan bourgeois so much that Barcelona commissioned an enormous painting of the battle from the painter Marià Fortuny.

In 1862 Prim led the French-English-Spanish expedition to Mexico and then pleased all Spanish republicans by opposing the French decision to put the deposed Emperor Maximilian back on his throne. But for Spain, after his *pronunciamiento*, he wanted a constitutional monarchy— so long as it was not headed by Isabel II. There was a frantic search for a candidate. The fear that a Hohenzollern might become king of Spain became the pretext for the Franco-Prussian War of 1870–71. Prim's candidate for king was Amadeo, duke of Savoy. Though Prim was assassinated in Madrid in 1870, Amadeo was installed on the throne in 1871. He could not hold power and soon abdicated. In 1873 the First Spanish Republic was proclaimed, with the Catalan socialist Francesc Pi i Margall at its head. It was not to last long.

Though Spain was now technically a federal republic, its politicians were all but incapable of governing. Since 1870 there had been a huge increase in organized labor movements: the first Spanish Workers' Congress, held in Barcelona in 1870 under the aegis of the Communist International, refused to cooperate with the more moderate federalists, for labor believed in its mission to win an international class struggle and did not care particularly about state politics. Thus the image of consensus that the First Republic tried to present in 1873 was cardboard. It was rent by cantonal riots of all kinds, rightist to Communist—from Cartagena in the south to the Basque territories up in the Pyrenees. This had evil results for Catalunya, not least because it encouraged its ultra-conservatives who had been waiting in the wings: the Carlists, who—having tried and failed to install Bourbon pretenders in two previous civil wars, in 1833–40 and 1846–49— now started burning villages and shooting democrats in the name of yet another Bourbon pretender, Carlos Maria.

The Carlists, as one liberal general lamented, "swam like fish in the sea" among the conservative peasantry of Catalunya. In the Third Carlist War (1872–75) they got more support than ever, because as Spain became more "modern" its alienations of town from country increased. In rural Catalunya, Carlism was the duct into which all the spill off of conservative frustration from the First Republic, and the economic changes that surrounded it, was drawn. Over the centuries the Catalan *pagèsos* had shown an almost limitless capacity for stubborn resistance to anyone, Catalan or not, who wanted to do anything to disrupt their modest well-being and habits of work, and after 1874 they felt as threatened by Antonio Cánovas del Castillo (1828–97), the conservative architect of the First Republic's new Constitution, as their ancestors had by Olivares. Their priests, still nursing deep grudges after the *desamortació*, the sale of Church land, knew how to fan their anxieties. Who, they demanded from the pulpit, had been buying the land? Nobody from around here. City folk. People who took away the profits, who cared nothing about your ways and customs—"constitutionals" who would sell the land out from underneath you, pry your feet and fingers from it, tip you into the maw of the city. Meanwhile, the Carlists presented themselves as the sole guarantors of whatever was old, good, and preindustrial in Catalunya. Putting a male Bourbon back on the throne, they trumpeted, would re-create Catalan freedom from the oppressive, liberal center. Incorporate Catalunya with the rest of its ancient confederacy—the kingdom of Aragon, Majorca, Valencia—under the Crown of Castile, and the principality would "find its ancient nature again," said Francesc Savalls i Massot, baron of Vidra, marquis of Alpens, veteran of the last Carlist war and supreme commander of the Carlist forces in the 1870s. The state religion, his program went on, could only be Roman Catholic. "All inhabitants are soldiers of their country and when it is in danger they must take arms, whether against a foreign invader or a threat to their rights and privileges."

To fight the Carlist guerrillas the government had to rely on its generals, who tended to be antirepublican. Commanders like Pavia and Martínez Campos made short work of the left-wing risings, but they were not so eager to crush the Carlists, who were, in any case, better organized and much harder to handle. It took four years, from 1872 to 1876, to finish them off. At one point the Carlists had 9,000 men in the field, facing only 7,350 government troops, of whom 2,400 were stationed in Barcelona. The generals' rule was to put down the republican risings first and then think—preferably at leisure—about the Carlist ones. At the beginning of 1874 General Pavia, fed up with radicals, marched a detachment of troops into the Madrid parliament and set up a more conservative republic.

This *pronunciamiento* was the first of a number of such independent military efforts, down to the time of Franco: instead of acting as the military arm of a political party, Pavia intervened purely in the name of his own conception of Spain. But the new government, run by the Isabelist General Serrano, was inherently unstable, hated by the progressives, but not conservative enough for the conservatives. It took the great moderate politician Antonio Cánovas del Castillo to see a way out. He decided to bring back a constitutional monarchy, under Isabel's son, Alfonso XII. Before he could do so, General Martínez Campos made his own *pronunciamiento* for Alfonso, which settled the matter. In 1874 the young king, a Sandhurst cadet still wet behind the ears, ascended the throne. The Bourbon Restoration was an accomplished fact. It was, as the historian Albert Balcells wrote, "nothing more than the corrective second act of the pseudo-revolution of 1868."

II

In the first ten years of the Restoration, Catalanism, mainly a literary movement until then, became political. Actually, one cannot speak of Catalanism as if it were a united movement with a single program. In the broadest sense, late-nineteenth-century Catalanism can be defined as a political doctrine that sought to affirm the personality of Catalunya —in language, law, history, and culture—and to distinguish it from the rest of Spain. But under this wide, vague rubric, at least four main lines sheltered, crossing and recrossing.

The first, and earliest, was summed up in the literary culture of the Renaixença; despite the general level of mediocrity at which the patriotic verse encouraged by the Jocs Florals ran, it reached a peak of significance when the poet Jacint Verdaguer won the rose of the Jocs Florals with his epic *L'Atlantida*, in 1879. The Renaixença provided many of the emblems, catchphrases, and crystallized sentiments for Catalanism, but—except in that indirect sense—it had little real political effect and reached only a small cultivated elite.

The second was really populist: Carlism. But it only won allies in deep Catalunya and was seen by Barcelonans as a bogey of reaction.

The third was the extreme opposite of Carlism—republican or federalist Catalanism. Catalanist republicans of the 1870s, such as Narcis Roca i Farreras (1830–91), took the extreme view that Catalunya should be a self-governing republic, a state within a state. They hoped to see the political structure of Spain remade as a group of such states, buffering (if not eliminating) the central authority of Madrid. Their politics had many links to the socialist ideas that had circulated in Barcelona since the 1840s. They believed they could create a popular base for their movement among industrial workers. Members of the federalist movement disagreed, often quite sharply, about how to do this, but the outstanding figure among them was the Barcelonese politician, editor, and lawyer Valentí Almirall i Llozer (1841–1904), whose 1886 book *Lo Catalanisme* was the basic text of the movement. It was through Almirall that the "hard" republicanism of Narcis Roca and his allies mellowed into what the federalists later called particularism, meaning a recognition of the special qualities, culture, and so forth of Catalunya. This was merely a euphemism, designed not to annoy Madrid.

The fourth, and eventual winner, was regional conservatism—the Catalanism of the bosses: moderate, obsessively concerned with state protectionism for Catalan products, and hence chary of alienating or even irritating Madrid. Its conservatism, and its blood-and-soil imagery, gave it some points of contact with Carlism (at least early on)—it talked a great deal about ancient virtues, rights, and privileges, but it was fundamentally a movement of the city's industrial upper classes and of those who wanted to join them. Its main ideologues were a cleric, Josep Torras i Bagès, and a newspaper editor named Joan Mañé i Flaquer. Many writers, artists, and architects were active in its ranks, and it led to the formation of the first Catalanist political groups: the Centre Català (an alliance with the federalists) in 1882, followed by the Unió Catalanista (Catalanist Union) in 1891, and a full-fledged political party, the Lliga Regionalista (Regionalist League), created in 1901 by the union of the former two.

We may look at both the federalists and the conservatives in a little more detail. How did they see each other?

In 1873, Narcis Roca published a slashing attack on the conservatives in the daily Catalan-language newspaper *La Renaixença*, edited by the poet and playwright Àngel Guimerà. Their brand of conciliatory Catalanism, he wrote, was

platonic, inconsequential, self-cancelling; a static or reactionary Catalanism from which the rights of restoration can expect nothing . . . terrified of democracy, of revolution, of a republic, of the masses, and of the people—and, I fear, only moved by the interests of the upper classes, of the *gent conforme* who have a lot to lose—a matter of pride and egoism, to speak clearly and with Catalan frankness.

Conservative Catalanism betrays "all the historic deeds . . . of our country, puts itself with Madrid's Hispanicism, on the side of centralism, reaction, all that is most repugnant to the real right provincial spirit." And what did the progressives believe in? The Corts, not the court; anticlericalism, not monasteries and churches; the common man, not the *ciutadan honrat*; the peasant and the man in the *barretina* (the distinctive, floppy red cap of the Catalan working class), not the castled aristocrat. And, above all, three things:

First, the justice and reason of revolutionary, reforming hopes, carried forward by the common people . . . second, the impotence of the conservatives—timid, self-absorbed, decadent, dithering—to save the cause of Catalunya . . . and third, the need to look to the future. The ordinary people . . . are right in wanting to free themselves, become equal, come out from under the yoke. If the middle class, if the bourgeois have shaken off the yoke of aristocracy, monarchism and Catholic exclusivism, why shouldn't ordinary men emerge from the yoke of the middle classes, a control which is as much material as moral? The conservative spirit offers no guarantees against the centralist impulse. Actually, it favors centralism [by aligning] the material interests of the owning classes against the outbreak of revolution. The conservative spirit will sacrifice . . . all hope of autonomy.

There was a lot of truth in this. Besides Roca, the tone of radical Catalanist federalism in the 1870s was set by Francesc Pi i Margall (1824–1901). Pi i Margall had been one of the founders of the Spanish Democratic party in the 1840s, and by 1854 he was a convinced republican federalist: he wanted all Spain, and not, of course, just Catalunya, to

Francesc Pi i Margall   *Valentí Almirall*

be remade as a pattern of semi-independent states. Exiled to Paris for political agitation in 1866 (it was an unalterable habit of the Spanish authorities to banish radicals to places where they would only get more radical), Pi fell under the spell of Pierre-Joseph Proudhon's disciples and, by his return to Catalunya in 1869, had added a dash of anarchism to his federalism. In 1873 Pi i Margall became president of Spain's First Republic. His government—regionalist and pro-labor—had collapsed in two months, before it could set up any federal administrations, even in Catalunya.

As a Catalanist, the unfortunate Pi i Margall found a natural ally in the younger Valentí Almirall. However, the two men were very different. Almirall was the more moderate. He saw the middle class as the key to Catalanist success, since it had most of the power in Barcelona and the big country towns. He saw how, in 1873, the republican-federalist movement in the rest of Spain had instantly broken down into cantonal squabbling. With the bourgeoisie, Catalanism might not bring about the reign of social justice, but without it, nothing would happen at all. No broad Catalanist party could come into existence unless it brought the middle class and the peasants under its wing. Hence he pitched the first level of his Catalanist appeal at the accumulated resentment of taxpayers—a reliable stratum, then as now.

In 1879 he started a Catalan-language paper in Barcelona, *El Diari Catalá.* (Nothing is more alien to modern journalism, a game in which only corporate behemoths own daily presses, than the relative ease with which nonmillionaires could start local dailies a hundred years ago; certainly Almirall had little money.) This was the voice of political Catalanism; its arm would be the Centre Català, which Almirall helped to found in 1882. The Centre tried to embrace all shades of Catalanism, from left to right, for Almirall's dream was to forge a united party. He was also the moving spirit behind two Catalanist congresses: the first, in Barcelona in 1880, set up an organizational structure for the Catalanist movement, while the second, in 1883, agreed on a general platform that was written into the "Memorial dels Greuges" ("Memo of Complaints") the Centre Català submitted to the king two years later.

Here was Catalunya, Almirall argued in *El Diari* in 1881, with its practical temper, its love of work, and its *seny*, all of which had made it "the savings-bank of Spain . . . the wealth of Catalunya, which is by no means negligible in absolute terms, is extraordinary in relative ones. Compare our middle class with its counterparts in other countries, and one sees that ours spends the least." But what is the reward of this frugality? To be taxed mercilessly by Madrid:

> We know how to make money, but the folk in Madrid have the knack of making it jump out of our pockets, and all the savings accumulated in Catalunya go directly or indirectly to prop up a spendthrift court . . . if in the last fifty years we had been able to reinvest even a tenth of our wealth in improving [public services in] Catalunya, we would be the envy of more advanced countries today.

Such investment, and much else besides, was not going to happen without self-government.

As drafted by Almirall, the Centre Català's memo of gripes to Alfonso XII was less stridently phrased than this, but it covered much the same ground. He put the case for Catalan autonomy in terms of Spanish, not merely Catalan, self-interest. "We do not aim, Your Majesty, to weaken the glorious unity of the Spanish Fatherland, still less to attack it; rather, we want to sustain and consolidate it; but we know that to stifle and destroy regional life in order to substitute that of the center is not a good course." What was bad for the provinces, particularly for Catalunya, was bad for Spain in toto. But the best thing for Catalunya was what Almirall called "particularism," a regional monarchy under Alfonso's benign eye, in which Catalan language, law, local culture, and tax base would be respected, and Catalan industry protected. This industry—textiles and all the trades that hung on the cotton business—was now menaced by Madrid's trade treaties with France and "the project for a *modus vivendi* with England": in short, the reduction of tariffs on competing foreign imports. Free trade must go. "How can our industry, weak and thwarted, compete with the ever-growing, more than robust industrial might of England? God grant that our hardworking nation may regenerate itself through particularism."

There was an undoubtedly emotional appeal here. Anyone who knew Spanish industry in the 1880s also knew how big the sell-off of assets to foreign business had been since the liberal free traders in Madrid won in 1868. Only a tenth of the iron ore from the Basque mines in Vizcaya was smelted in Spain; the rest was shipped straight to England. The great open-cut Río Tinto copper mines, the largest producers of their kind in Europe, were entirely British controlled and policed by mounted Scots guards in white jackets and pith helmets. Wherever Spain was industrially developed, it was an economic colony too—except in Catalunya. And the Catalan economy was plunged in Stygian gloom. Its paladins felt like victims.

Unfortunately, the "Memorial dels Greuges" fell on deaf ears. Alfonso XII, though genuinely popular in many parts of Spain—he had raised, for instance, a national subscription to help the victims of a catastrophic earthquake in Granada and Almeria in 1884—was not deeply interested in the complaints of Catalan industry. He was, in any case, extremely ill with respiratory disease, and at the end of 1885 he died of it, at the age of twenty-eight, leaving the throne of Spain to his unborn son Alfonso XIII, thus guaranteeing Spain a prolonged regency under his queen, María Cristina of Hapsburg-Lorena. Catalan matters did not rate high with her, either.

III

Owing to the preponderance of bourgeois interests in the Centre Català, the federalists were edged aside, the main subject of Catalanism became trade protection, and then the Centre itself split. Its conservative wing took off on its own in 1887 and presently formed the Lliga Regionalista, whose leading lights were the lawyer-politicians Narcis Verdaguer, Enric Prat de la Riba i Sarrà, and Lluís Duran i Ventosa, and the architect Josep Puig i Cadafalch. But its main ideologues, the creators and propagandists of conservative Catalanism, were two: the newspaper editor

Joan Mañé i Flaquer (1823–1901), a sworn enemy of both Carlism and federalism, who ran the widest-circulating city newspaper, *El Diario de Barcelona*, for thirty-five years, and the formidable right-wing cleric Josep Torras i Bagès (1846–1916).

Mañé i Flaquer was the oracle of Barcelona's middle class. He shared, and formed, their collective views. For bourgeois Catalanism, at least until the Lliga Regionalista was formed in 1901, did not exactly have an ideology; it consisted of attitudes and responses. It viewed Catalunya as a special case, of course, and believed strongly in various kinds of *fets differentials*, starting with language, law, and business, that set it apart from Spain. It had no confidence in the centralized state that had replaced the Bourbon autocracy or in the *pronunciamientos* that heralded changes of power. It feared Madrid liberalism—the ideas that had cost Barcelona so much in riots and arson. It assumed Madrid politics were corrupt, but that Catalan politicians were more likely to be honest. All this was repeated, at length, in *El Diario*'s editorials. And if anyone in Madrid attacked the sacred personality of Catalunya, its ineffable, mystical, superior otherness—as the poet-politician Núñez del Arce did, in a much-resented speech in 1886—*El Diario* could be relied on for pages of rolling thunder in rebuttal, because its editor believed that the boundaries between Catalunya and the rest of Spain were something more than an artifact of human politics. No "caprice of a king or a conqueror" had put them there; "they are a work of Nature, or rather of Providence, and so they have resisted the vain attempts of men to destroy them."

Influential as Mañé was, Torras i Bages was even more so, because he spoke with the weight of the Church behind him. Apart from his vast influence on the Catalan clergy and faithful, he moved in most of the other circles of Catalan life, from art, architecture, and poetry to finance and regional politics. His views were as eagerly sought by Antoni Gaudí and the poet Joan Maragall as they were by the Gironas, Güells, Cambos, and Arnuses. He wrote voluminously; his *obres completes* run to seven thick volumes of allocutions, literary criticism, philosophical reflections, and nationalist theorizing on subjects from the mystery of the Trinity and the works of Ramon Llull to a sermon for Boy Scouts on "Jesus Christ, the Ultimate Athlete." Torras's career and writings illustrate, perhaps better than anyone else's, how futile it was to draw fixed lines between politics, culture, and religion at a time when the Catalanist movement enclosed all three.

Tall, corpulent, and as blind as a bat without his glasses, endowed with a deep resonant preacher's voice, Torras cut an imposing figure—

Josep Torras i Bagès

---

in Joan Llimona's fresco in the church of the Mother of God in Montserrat, the glare from his pebble lenses would make a liberal quake, a Protestant collapse.

Like Gaudí, he was born and raised in the country, the son of a farmer in Vilafranca de Penedés. His brothers died young, his mother sank under the loss, and his father, whom Torras revered, lived on to a great though enfeebled age.

Torras's devotion to his suffering parents combined with the ideology of the *casa pairal* to underpin the social beliefs of his adult life. The only basis on which Catalan independence could be raised was the values of traditional, rural Catalunya, which could apply to the industrial society of Barcelona. The patriarchal family was the proper model for Catalan society, old or new. The *casa pairal* was the secular metaphor of the Church, holding its members together in a seamless, authoritarian web of doctrine and dogma. Only the Church could raise the deep currents that lay beneath the political surface and thus give meaning to Catalan selfhood.

Torras preached transcendence and submission. But he was no ranting charismatic—he had taken his doctorate in philosophy under Milà i Fontanals himself. He wrote in a persuasive, heavy rhetorical style, full of generalizations and appeals to eternity, law, and nature. His thought, cast in the mold of Thomas Aquinas, proceeded with steady logic from one term to the next and seemed flawless if, at the beginning, you accepted its axioms and premises. But if Aquinas provided the framework for Torras i Bagès's ideas, their immediate Catalan precursor was the work of that other cleric of Vic, Jaume Balmes, to whose vision of a Catalan theocratic state he gave an even more authoritarian cast.

Torras summed up his version of Catalan independence in *The Catalan Tradition* (1892). In it he argued for an organic, traditional state whose value system had the same structure at every level: individual, family, town, Church, government. "All social or political construction claims tradition as its base." He distinguished between real right tradition and what he called "*Atavism*, which the moderns have so used and abused, [which] is nothing other than the ancient principle of tradition pushed to extremes, thus becoming monstrous and destructive of the free human personality." (Its guilty purveyors, Torras believed, were Nietzsche and Ibsen.) The Church is the sole guarantor of our intellectual heritage; reject her teachings and the common well is defiled. The sign of tradition at work is that famous attribute of Catalans, *seny*—a natural levelheadedness. The sign of its weakness or disappearance, which we see all around us, is a mania for novelty: "All outward exuberance is dangerous. In literature, in art, and in politics as well, periods of exuberance generally finish in times of excess, imbalance, corruption and death." Catalunya is "pre-eminent among all the Iberic peoples," because of "her ancient seeds hidden in the earth, in the Catalan humus made of our tradition . . . love and steady work, modesty of life, a practical and alert spirit not given to fantasy, a respect for family hierarchy." These are the models of industrial production and government, but their source is family life:

> The family is the substance and base of social organization. Social decadence supposes decay in the family. Social regeneration, social reconstruction, must begin with the reconstruction of the family. We turn our eyes to Spain, and we see that the spirit is strongest in those nationalities [*països*] that have the strongest regional spirit. Love for the homestead, the *casa pairal*, the desire to conserve the patrimony, the order of the family hierarchy . . . all is superior where regional life has been maintained . . . as opposed to those areas which are confused with that great mass, the nation.

Nationalism deludes and enslaves people by treating them as abstractions. Regionalism sets them free by reinforcing their nature, their collective selves—by letting them know who they are. Here, the Church also presides: "Catalunya and Church are two things in our past history which cannot be separated . . . if anyone wishes to reject the Church, have no doubt that at the same time he must reject the Fatherland along with it." The Church, like the region, represents the law of nature, not just culture. So in politics, too. For Torras, "Caesarism and liberalism are in essence the same: man, not Divine Providence, is lord of society." Take away the Church and tyranny rushes in. "The liberal state is constructed from the top down, that is to say, in an unnatural fashion; thus we see that constitutions are made in a council of ministers, or by a central Junta; but regionalist nations begin at the base, that is, from the foundations." Regional politics are deep-rooted as oak trees; liberal ones can be toppled by a gust. As for revolution, what could be more detestable, less natural? Obviously, those of 1868, 1848, and 1789 were disasters. (The problem of the American Revolution—the United States being much admired by Torras's high-bourgeois audience, at least before the Spanish-American War of 1898—was resolved with a little casuistry. We may *think* George Washington was a revolutionary, Torras wrote, but that is a vulgar slur. In fact, "He did no more than harmonize and set a seal on what the nature of things set before him: it was not Washington but God Himself who formed these peoples.")

Torras's bugbear was the French Revolution, which he saw as the ghastly result of the death of healthy regionalism. In writing about it, Torras liked to cite the two French writers most admired by conservatives across the Pyrenees. One was the philosopher and historian Hippolyte Taine, whose theories of historical evolution governed by race and environment (*la race, le milieu*) also inspired the work of extreme French conservatives like Paul Bourget and Maurice Barrès, whose mystico-nationalist notions bore more than a passing resemblance to Torras's own. (Barrès's vicious anti-Semitism has no echo in Torras's work, probably because the latter did not think Jews were even worth discussing, as Catalunya had so few left.) The other was the man whose profoundly authoritarian ideas lay (as Isaiah Berlin has shown) at the root of twentieth-century fascism: the archconservative Joseph de Maistre (1753–1821), whose ideal of government was an absolute monarchy subservient only to the pope. Torras compared him to "an eagle [who], from the sky, sees the utter falsity of the gigantic construction raised by human pride."

Sardana *dancers at Tibidabo, circa 1900, photograph by Ballell*

In cultural matters Torras i Bagès took an equally hard line. He was for folk culture, festivals, whatever rose from "the people"; against modernism, internationalism, and what we might now see as early pop culture. Village-square dancing, good; dance-hall dancing, bad. All is vanity: "Empty fashion contrives to corrupt natural good taste . . . today Catalunya is stuffed with Castilian songs, and the beautiful straightforward Catalan songs are forgotten." In particular he loathed the growing popular taste for flamenco, which had spread up from its origins in Andalusia. Flamenco dancing was charged with sexual passion and melancholy, with the *duende* of the south—"Nothing could be more antithetical to the Catalan character, or be more damaging to the severity and restraint of our race." Catalans should stick to their traditional *sardana*, a dance that expressed the social cooperation of the group, the village. Even worse were more distant imports, brought in from parts of the world that no Catalan, in the normal course of events, would choose to visit:

We throw away money bringing in foreigners . . . [instead of] the bagpipes, flutes, tambourines and other instruments that suit our feast-days, we summon . . . half-savage Filipinos to perform their writhings and play their cumbersome instruments; we view whatever typifies our own race with indifference, but are fascinated by whatever comes from Japan and China; and the *castells de xiquets* (human towers), those manly symbols of the strength and aplomb of our people, are losing ground to the *corridas de toros*—the symbolic expression of the daring and agility of a noble race, but one which is basically different to ours.

In "high" culture, Torras i Bagès was more active than any Spanish cleric of the time. It is hardly a surprise, given his commitment to Catalan regionalism, that he should have been made the president of the Jocs Florals in 1899, the year that he became bishop of Vic. But the choice of Torras as president confirmed that the Jocs would take an anti-*modernista* line and remain a megaphone of deep-Catalanist propaganda. In his presidential address, Torras did what conservative intellectuals so often do: he disclaimed any political intention as being beneath the interests of art and then defined his own political views—shared, of course, by all present—as "nature." "It's not that I want to talk of politics today . . . especially since the issues I want to raise emerge from the very nature of things, they are a manifestation of the essence of Catalan poetry. . . . *In order that there should be a Catalan poetry, there must be a Catalunya and . . . Catalunya must be Catalan.* Poetry is the perfume, the emanation, of the very substance of the Fatherland." If this was not a political utterance, what could "politics" mean? The Jocs Florals, Torras i Bagès said, were not a "loose" element in "the concert of elements we call the Fatherland"; they were bound into its essence. Poetry was "the incarnation of the Catalan spirit."

In uttering these heavy prescriptions, Torras (and others like him) were giving the Church's answer to what they perceived as an increasing frivolity of civic life in Barcelona—and something worse: its endemic political instability. For Barcelona was subject to violent swings of mood. "The unfolding of these [recent] great events," remarked the city's chronicler, Josep Pla, some years later,

represented a long stage of disquietude, with a riot every week, a revolution complete with barricades every three months, an enormous and pointless expenditure of ammunition and the creation of a citizenry that was fractious, bloody-minded and sarcastic. Just as Barcelona and the industrial area got rich and respectable, so the city heightened its own radical liberalism and created this refined product: the image of the good bourgeois, the family man, prosperous and rich, defending his liberty with a gun in his fist, dressed as a militiaman . . .

Barcelona was doing well. There was no shortage of work. Yet its mood was cynical and marked by indifference: "*No em dona la gana*"—roughly speaking, "I'm not in the mood for it"—was the universal phrase on the street. A taste for trivial demonstration, for amassing cobblestones and upended carts in the narrow alleys of the Barri Gòtic on little or no pretext, had been fostered by the ineffectual rule of the First Republic. Catalans, right and left, saw democracy but no continuity. It gave ample ground to their sarcastic humor—and little basis for anything else, except making money. "In Barcelona," Pla remarked, "nearly the whole nineteenth century was a time of facetiousness, but in [1865–75] it reached a point of delirium." Among artists and writers, this period fostered a taste for Parisian-style *blague*, the aggressive humor of the put-on and the put-down. It produced little writing of consequence, except from a few who went against its grain, as Jacint Verdaguer did when writing his romantic and superbly integrative poems *L'Atlàntida* and *Canigo*. What populist Barcelona loved were shows—fountains on Montjuic and mass barbecues on Mont Pelat, or Bald Mountain, above Gracia, street fairs of every kind, singsongs, habaneras, sugary love ditties, and the endless swollen Carnival, which, as Pla observed, "carried the hint of fatal consequences, whether of tuberculosis or matrimony." And always, because of the political simmer that lay just beneath the surface of Barcelona at play, there was the hint of violence: the person rubbing shoulders with you at the marionette show on the Ramblas could so easily be Carlist or an *exaltat*.

The city seemed a self-contained world. But no city really is. Barcelona had always faced back inland as well as out to sea, drawing a sense of place and origins from its countryside. It still did so, underneath the cosmopolitan surface; it was not built on a sandbank, like Venice; it was largely run by men who were nostalgic for the land. Partly as a result of their nostalgia, the changes that were to overtake the great port city in the last quarter of the nineteenth century began deep in Catalunya, among its vineyards.

IV

Throughout the nineteenth century, farming in Catalunya had a pattern very different from agriculture in the center and south of Spain.

Taken as a whole, Spain is the least fertile country in Europe. In its hot south (Murcia, Almeria, parts of Andalusia) droughts can last for years. And there is a Spanish proverb: "The worse the land, the more

The Boqueria market

nobles on it." After the Arabs were expelled, farming in central and southern Spain under Castilian rule went into a long decline. Absentee landlords rarely visited their estates. For most of the Castilian aristocracy, their estates might as well have been in Libya—which, indeed, they came to resemble. Once-fertile regions became depopulated heaths and deserts, and districts already cursed by poor soil and low rainfall were as empty as the moon. Southern Spanish farming ran on the latifundia system—huge estates worked by slaves or, later, by *braceros* (landless day laborers) all miserably unproductive. When landowners did allow peasants to farm on a sharecropping basis, they made sure that the leases were short, unfair, and easily broken. Consequently, throughout the nineteenth century—a period that, in most parts of Castile, Andalusia, Murcia, and Extremadura, actually lasted until after the Second World War—most of the rural population of central and southern Spain grubbed out its existence at a level of poverty, wretchedness, and insecurity that had no parallel elsewhere in southern Europe.

But in Catalunya, farming life was much better. The valleys of Catalunya Vella got up to forty-five inches of rain a year, along with the runoff from the Pyrenees. Though the soil was poor in some places, like the plains around Tarragona, in others it was as rich as Umbria's. Even today, one can easily get an impression of its bounty by visiting the Boqueria market on the Ramblas, with its seemingly endless succession of stalls under the iron vaults crammed with local fruits and vegetables in their season: ranks of fat fresh lettuces and lacy escarole, tight bundles of radishes, floppy bouquets of white-ribbed chard, bins of jade-colored peas and neat fagots of tiny green beans, soft cannonball peaches and russet pears, mountains of tomatoes, zucchini, melons, beets—and everywhere, in the fall, an orange glow and thick telluric perfume rising from the trays of *bolets*, or wild mushrooms.

In the early nineteenth century the agricultural bounty of Catalunya—not only vegetables, but wheat, barley, oats, and wine as well—was grown almost entirely by sharecropping farmers. But Catalan and southern sharecropping were very different. In Catalunya, farmers' rights were still protected by the remains of medieval custom; as we have seen, the word "feudal" in Catalunya implied a regard for the small man's rights. Relations between landowner and tenant tended to be good, whereas the latifundias of the south bred nothing but cruelty, misery, and sparse crops. In Catalunya most of the growing and reaping was done by the *pagesos*, not day laborers but sharecropping peasants, those conservative and clannish folk in their *cases pairales*, endowed with a deep attachment to the patch of soil that, even if they did not own it, had been turned and manured and sown and reaped by their forefathers for generations.

This system might have kept working nicely through the nineteenth century and into the twentieth, but it was irreversibly changed by investment from the city. Industrialists began to invest in farmland—particularly in the land that became available through the *desamortació*, the sell off of Church property. Partly, no doubt, they did so to make themselves look like landed gentry. But it turned out to be profitable. Gradually, but faster and faster, the peasant patchwork changed into agribusiness, and its focus shifted from extensive farming—cereals and vegetables—to intensive, high-profit cultivation of vines. Industrial capital financed the big Catalan wine businesses that grew after the Restoration. While the price of wheat and corn dropped steadily in the late nineteenth century, that of wine boomed by some 40 percent.

Wine and brandy pulled the whole Catalan industrial economy along behind them after 1865—a proof, if anything, of its lability. The growth in the wine market meant more business for coopers and transport workers; more railroads, trucks, locomotives; more work on the carriage roads. By 1875 foreign investors looked more kindly at a restored Spanish monarchy than at the liberal Republic of 1868. After a recession in the mid-1860s, the cotton industry was booming. Whereas the Barcelonese mills had been importing twenty-five thousand tons of raw cotton a year in the 1860s, they were using fifty-seven thousand tons a year in 1888–91, and production of cotton goods rose by more than a third between 1876 and 1883. Barcelonese cotton goods completely dominated the Spanish textile market, but their reign was artificially sustained by protectionism—in fact, they cost twice the price of comparable English cloth.

The main new product of Catalan finance was an unrestrained credit binge—known ever since as the *febre d'or*, Barcelona's "gold fever"—that lasted from 1875 to 1882. On a smaller scale it had much the same blind, manic character as the 1980s in the United States, sustained by a similar blend of folly and cynicism and ending in a painful crash.

Nothing was better than a banker in the eyes of the Catalan burghers. In 1881–82, sixteen new banks were started in Barcelona (and a dozen more in the regional capitals of Catalunya). The holdings of established banks shot up: between 1875 and 1881 the capital of the Credito Mercantil went from 2.5 to 15 million pesetas, that of the Banco de Barcelona from 7.5 to 12.8 million. The biggest player of all was the first investment bank in Barcelona, the Banco Hispano-Colonial, founded in 1876 by Antonio López and Manuel Girona. It financed railroads, shipping lines, mines, machine works: any enterprise that needed underwriting. Most of them ended up with Girona or López, or sometimes both, and usually some of their relatives and friends, on their boards.

Much of the starting capital for these schemes came from Cuba, Puerto Rico, and other Spanish colonies, brought back and invested by the new breed of Catalan businessmen. These *indianos*, in the course of reinventing themselves as merchant princes, transformed both the society and the physical appearance of Barcelona.

Some of the *indianos* were fairly rough diamonds. They had been too busy with business to pick up the social graces of the metropolis. The Liceu had given rise to a flock of opera stories, and one of them concerned the *indiano* who, after his triumphal return from Cuba in the early 1880s, was seized upon by fund-raisers for the opera and taken to the Liceu for the first time in his life, to see a performance of *Siegfried*. He lasted through the overture and the first act, but some way into act two the swarthy head lolled forward on the snowy boiled shirt; the *indiano* was deeply asleep, and the fund-raisers debated sotto voce whether they should rouse him or not. Then came the sound of conflict, as Siegfried's encounter with Fafnir began. The *indiano* sat up with a jerk and stared pop-eyed at the stage, where Wagner's heroic nitwit was battling the dragon. His hand flew to his absent machete. *"Carajo, cai-manes!"* he exclaimed—"Fuck, crocodiles!"

But sneer as you might at the *indianos*, they had the money, and Barcelona needed it. They learned fast, and their offspring even faster. Just as, in East Hampton or Hollywood, the corporate raider or the new-rich producer will soon blossom with every appurtenance of the gentleman, from Lobb polo boots to a trophy wife and a Botero bronze by the swimming pool, so the Catalan new rich in the period that cul-minated in the *febre d'or* set out to acquire as much patina as possible while exuberantly displaying the signs of wealth and power.

Among the early *indianos* was Josep Xifré i Casas, he of the porches, whom we have met before. Miquel Biada i Bunyol (1789–1848) set out to trade arms in Venezuela, turned his profits from the partial exter-mination of the local tribes into an early steam-driven cloth mill in his native Mataró, and then got the concession to build the first railroad in Spain—a single-tracker between Barcelona and Mataró, which opened a few months after his death in 1848. If you were not a rich *indiano* like these two you could still marry the daughter of one; by the 1870s, they had much the same value on the Catalan marriage market as American heiresses on the matrimonial bourse of Paris. The "good families," *indiano* or not, reinforced one another through a strong net of dynastic marriages and interlocking business partnerships. There were perhaps twenty of these clans. The most powerful names among them were Girona, López, and Güell.

Manuel Girona i Agrafel (1818–1905) was a Catalan banker. He married the *pubilla* of the Quadras family, an *indiano* clan whose sump-tuous house on the Diagonal, designed by Puig i Cadafalch, now houses the Music Museum. Nobody could have called Girona a man of vision—he seems to have maintained, until the end of his life, that Cerdà's enlargement of Barcelona was a mistake, a mere novelty, and he never bought property there—but he greatly expanded the bank he inherited from his father and became the mayor of the city in 1875. Mainly he was known for his parsimony, which even by Catalan stan-dards of peasant thrift was extreme. His house on the Ronda de Sant Pere carried on its facade the portentous motto "Faith strengthens you. Hope gives you life. Charity ennobles you. Work dignifies you." Girona, said the wits, had left out the fifth and most important maxim: "Women weaken you." When a cabdriver complained about his tiny tip, com-paring it unfavorably with the peseta he normally got from Girona's son, the merchant prince entered the folklore of Barcelona by pointing out

Manuel Girona i Agrafel

that such gestures were all very well for the boy, since he had a rich father; but he, Girona, did not. He once told his butler, as an economy measure, to light only half the dining room candelabra before a dinner for his chief political ally, Antonio Cánovas, the prime minister of Spain. When one of his elderly clerks asked for a small bonus so that he could buy a set of false teeth, Girona gave him a sermon instead. Didn't he know that false teeth run counter to the divine plan? Was it for him to alter the course of nature? "You must remember," Girona declared, warming to his theme, "that if our teeth fall out it shows our system needs greens, soups, a simple diet. You want to have teeth so that you can go back to eating meat. But how can you not understand that if your system needed meat, your teeth wouldn't have fallen out? Do as I do: submit yourself to God's designs and His will."

Where buildings were concerned, Girona put his money—and, eventually, his body, for he is buried in the Cathedral—into the Barri Gòtic. Never the Eixample, for he hated Cerdà's plan; his one town-planning suggestion for the Eixample was a fantasy of destruction. Like every other big capitalist in Barcelona, Girona had firm opinions on how to get rid of the city's deficit. So he proposed to the Ajuntament that it take the Gran Via—after the Diagonal and Passeig de Gràcia, the widest

Joan Güell i Ferrer   *Eusebi Güell i Bacigalupi*

avenue in Barcelona—and make it cost-effective by running a line of tenements down the middle, leaving a traffic lane on either side. The sale of these flats, a giant divider on a slim ribbon of city land, would put Barcelona in the black once more. To their credit, the mayor and councilmen did not adopt this absurdly cheapskate plan.

Girona was not wholly without philanthropic impulses. His main gift to Barcelona was the facade of its Cathedral, which had been a plain brick-and-stone front since the fifteenth century. Girona paid for a new one, which the architect Josep Oriol i Mestres erected between 1887 and 1890. Today, despite its coarse detailing and the general banality of its sculpture, few visitors realize that it is, in fact, a Gothic Revival skin tacked onto a genuine Gothic building.

Another *indiano* dynasty, Joan Güell i Ferrer (1800–72), founder of the preeminent Catalan textile dynasty and father of Gaudí's patron, Eusebi Güell i Bacigalupi, had made his first fortune in Cuba in the 1830s. His own father, Pau Güell i Roig, had been an artisan in Torredembara, a village on the coast south of Barcelona. Pau Güell took the teenage Joan across the Atlantic with him to look for business opportunities in Santo Domingo. They chose just the wrong moment, for revolution broke out in this Caribbean island colony of Spain soon after they arrived; Güell had to close shop, and he sent his boy back to Barcelona to study for his captain's ticket at the naval academy.

But young Joan Güell was determined to go into trade, and he returned to the Caribbean, this time to Cuba, where he found himself a job in a Havana textile company. Before long he worked his way up to manager and started his own textile firm. In 1835 he made a long trip up the East Coast of North America and then through England, France, Switzerland, Italy, and Belgium, boning up on mill machinery and techniques. He bought a cargo ship and loaded it with goods for Cuba, but it sank uninsured in the mid-Atlantic.

Undeterred, Joan Güell started a cotton mill in the booming industrial district of Sants. His studies paid off. By 1840 this plant—El Vapor Vell, it came to be called, or Old Steam—had a total steam capacity of eighty horsepower, big for its day, running 114 looms for smooth cloth and 165 for cotton velvets and corduroys. He was on his way, and in 1845 he married Francisca Bacigalupi i Dulcet, the daughter of a middling Italian merchant banker who did business in Barcelona. Her brother had a cloth mill too. Joan Güell bought a share in it and soon acquired complete control.

Francisca Bacigalupi died soon after giving birth to their only son, Eusebi, in 1847. Her husband, with a dynastic phlegm not uncommon in the rising middle classes of nineteenth-century Catalunya, promptly married her sister Camila. She died in 1853, having produced a daughter, Josefina. Joan Güell did not marry again. He concentrated on the firm and his other interests. By 1855 the capital of Güell, Ramis and Cia stood at more than 2 million pesetas (about $390,000 at the then rate of exchange), and he owned two-thirds of it.

Figuring that it made more sense to build industrial machinery than import it from England or France, Güell had started a foundry that, after merging with a number of smaller firms in 1855, became the Maquinista Terrestre i Marítima, making most of the factory and railroad machinery for northern Spain. He was also a partner in Catalunya's first inland canal project, the Canal d'Urgell, and a director of its biggest savings and loan bank, the Caixa d'Estalvis. He became an alderman, then a national deputy, and finally, in 1862, a senator. In his political life he was a "paladin of protectionism," determined to hold whatever monopolies on the Spanish and colonial market Catalan industry could secure from foreign competition. He died worth 7.55 million pesetas, a gigantic fortune.

As was the Catalan custom, two-thirds of it went to his *hereu*, the oldest son and heir. Eusebi Güell i Bacigalupi inherited, among other things, a 1.35-million-peseta share in the family company in Sants, a big house at Rambla dels Caputxins 30, an estate south of Barcelona at Santa Coloma de Cervello, and that precious emblem of social standing, an opera box in the Liceu—which even then was valued at 50,000 pesetas.

Antoni López y López, first marquis of Comillas

Eusebi Güell received all the refinements money could buy. He gained the bloom of travel not just checking out factories, but learning French in Paris and English in London and immersing himself in architecture, art, political history, poetry, and theology. Because of its old connections with the cotton trade, he had part of his schooling in Nîmes, where his teacher was Cardinal de Cabrieres, bishop of Montpellier and a member of the Académie Française. (The Güell Park, which Gaudí was to design for him half a century later, owed much to young Eusebi's perambulations in the park of Nîmes.)

Launched from the top of the Barcelonese elite, Eusebi inherited his father's business drive along with his money. Under his direction the family business prospered hugely. By 1895 its main company, Güell Parellada, had a capital of 2.23 million pesetas (about $431,000). Eusebi Güell had fingers in almost every area of Catalan industrial expansion: shipping, railroads, steel, portland cement, domestic gas, the Caixa and the Banco Hispano-Colonial. He owned a flour mill, bakeries, and a large wine business and was a director of the Philippine Tobacco Company, the main supplier of cigarettes and cheap cigars in Spain. (Better-off Catalans, of course, got their *puros* from Cuba.)

He married into a rich and recently ennobled family. His wife, Isabel López i Bru, was the daughter of a hardfisted shipping magnate and financier named Antonio López y López, who in 1878 was made the first marquis of Comillas, his family's point of origin, a fishing village on the Bay of Biscay near Santander.

The marquis's father, Antonio López, was a self-made Castilian who went to Cuba in the 1840s and made his money in shipping, trade, and slaves; he married a Catalan woman, Luisa Bru i Lassus, and brought his fortune back to Barcelona in 1849, reinvesting it in more trade with Cuba and the Philippines. Like father, like son: the first marquis of Comillas turned out to be in every way as tough as his *indiano* sire, so much so that his brother-in-law Francesc Bru was roused to accuse him of bastardy, embezzlement, fraud, and attempted murder, none of it proven. In any case, *"Poderoso caballero es Don Dinero"* ("Mr. Money is a mighty gentleman"), and by the time the marquis gave his daughter's hand to Güell, and with it the assurance of a third of his fortune, the *pubilla*'s share, the López family was at the very pinnacle of Catalan plutocracy. Even their natal village had been transformed into a private summer resort by the magnetism of their name and had become a kind of Newport for the *transatlanticos*—a code word for their social circle that punned on the fact that one of López's more lucrative companies, in which his friends held directorships, was the shipping firm Companyia Transatlàntica.

Such people were the Caesars—or perhaps more accurately, given their combination of wealth, Spanishness, and sententious moral hypocrisy, the Senecas—of Barcelona's mercantile society. But the tone of the *febre d'or* was not entirely defined by them; they preceded and outlasted it. Rather, the spirit of that long moment lay in a frenzied hope, a collective dream of speculation that was shared by thousands. People opened their savings and poured them into the Llotja. Schemes rose like thistledown, like bubbles, like balloons. The destiny of everything was to rise. For several years, the Catalans lost whatever claim they might have had to their supposed cardinal virtue of *seny*.

V

The mood of the time has been captured better by fiction than by history: by Eduardo Mendoza's saturnine and brilliant novel *The City of Marvels* (1988), with its unspeakable hero Onofre Bouvila, a beast of will whose rise from petty crook to merchant prince parallels that of late-nineteenth-century Barcelona itself; and, a century earlier, by Narcís Oller's *Gold Fever*, an acidulous novel of manners written in the hangover from the boom in 1890–93.

Narcís Oller i Moragas (1846–1930) was the first realist novelist to write in Catalan, and his model for *Gold Fever* was undoubtedly Émile Zola. (Zola wrote a preface for Oller's first novel, *The Butterfly*, and both men had been much influenced by the philosophy of Hippolyte Taine, well known to Catalan intellectuals of the time.) And yet *Gold Fever* is very much more than a "provincial" response to a Paris original. Oller's characters are drawn with astringent clarity and variety, as fully rounded creatures moving in their bizarre social space; yet his eventual purpose, like that of all satirists, is a moral one. "The study of lightly idealized characters passing through a very precise environment," Zola's remark in the preface to *The Butterfly*, was true of *Gold Fever* as well.

The story of *Gold Fever* is the rise of the new-rich speculator, seen in the late 1880s against the twilight of the Barcelonese nobility and the fading of the old, more tradition-minded bourgeoisie. Its setting is the Llotja, the promenades of the Eixample, and the lavish new villas of Sarrià, above the city. Its hero, if that is the word, is Gil Foix, a Catalan businessman of humble origins, obsessed with The Deal and with social climbing, tough and energetic but ridiculously vain and vulnerable to flattery. He is the archetypal nouveau riche, and around him, like planets round a vulgar sun with a strong gravitational field, move his family and friends: his shrewd, loyal, house-proud wife; his mediocre dreamer of a brother, "the inventor," stuffed with pseudophilosophical and amateur scientific notions; his brother-in-law Francesc, an intelligent and sardonic painter who finds himself ever more alienated by the push and shove of Barcelonese social life and who is in love with Delfineta, Foix's delicate and instinctively refined daughter, equally stifled by Barcelona's plush and passementerie.

Gold Fever begins with a protocinematic scene of stock trading in the Llotja, whose Gothic arches are subtly transformed into the cathedral of money worship. It ends with the emaciated and sweating Foix, who has suffered a nervous breakdown and reverts to his boyhood origins as a carpenter, glimpsed by his family obsessively and pointlessly sawing a plank into laths—"He's gone back to where he started," says one of them, in the last line of the novel. "He began as a carpenter; he's become one again. Let him breathe; perhaps that will cure him." Finis. In a sense, the whole novel is about the difficulty of "breathing." Its characters move in a space stuffed to the point of nausea by the growth of *things*, a landscape of suffocating acquisition layered over the "old" Barcelona. Foix and his family attend a reception in Sarrià given by another *nou ric*, Giro, who runs down the history of his villa, which was

> created by a Marquis thirty years before, sold by court order to a rich salt-cod merchant, and bought later, again at public auction, by the new owner. . . . Giro threw out his arm and, pirouetting on his heels, started showing them the boundaries of his estate, talking about the improvements he had made. "I got it cheap; I did the walls over, replanted the gardens, and then I put in the statues, pavilions and games—cost a bundle, as you see."
>
> And so they wandered through the entire property, praising the dripping basins, the artificial caverns and grottoes with their stalactites of plaster and pumice; Chinese aviaries of jigsawed wood; bas-relief Mercuries, Minervas and Venuses in oldish marble; tubs of begonias and a vast assortment of gardenias, camellias and cacti in the winter-garden; the coach-houses and the stables, truly luxurious; and the riding-ring for the children . . .

In the drawing rooms of the Eixample, too, the middle-class interior reaches a delirium of fullness:

> The family was smothering for want of air, among all the curtains, tapestries and rugs, and especially from the excess of plush that covered the walls, the beds, the tables and armchairs. Catarina kept bumping into all these pouffes, all these tables and chairs and pedestals; she felt assailed by the profusion of china flowers, little pictures and fragile bibelots which, scattered everywhere, constricted her natural movements and were a daily source of irritation and a cause of grumbling and tears for the servants.

This world of consumer objects seems more real and resistant than the economy that brought it into being. Oller was eloquent on the dreamlike quality of the *febre d'or*:

> [The banks] sprang up like mushrooms. . . . More and more, there seemed to be one for every daring entrepreneur. People created them on the pretext of carrying out reforms or great public works that existed solely in their promoters' minds. . . . The citizen of Barcelona began to feel sorry about the crowdedness of the old city, the unfinished state of the Eixample, the sorry neglected look of the streets, the lack of modern amenities, great monuments, squares and statues; the gold-

fever at once came up with projects to transform everything, there and then. Public bodies and authorities were showered with plans and more new plans every day, accompanied by long memos whose hypocritical motives of speculation were disguised as burning patriotism, as far-sighted and fatherly solicitude.

It took an insect, no more, to burst this bubble.

VI

Phylloxera vastatrix, so named for its devastating effects, was a kind of aphid that preyed on vines. It came from California, whose vines were immune to it. Those of Europe were not. The aphid made its first appearance in France in 1863 and quickly killed most of its vineyards. This catastrophe provoked joy in Catalunya, because it sent wine prices through the roof. Indeed it was the main reason that city financiers bought so much land and converted it to the grape during the 1860s. They had sixteen years of profits before their schadenfreude turned sour. The aphids took those sixteen years to cross the Pyrenees.

The Madrid authorities, seeing that the spread of the aphid plague into Spain was only a matter of time, ordered a quarantine: there should be a *cordon sanitaire* cleared at the foot of the Pyrenees—a zone fifteen miles wide with no vines in it, so that the insects could not advance southward. Naturally the Catalan growers, stubborn and myopically provincial, refused to obey a central government command to cut down their own vines. They would rather have cut off their own toes. The vines were pure gold. So in 1879 the aphids made their first appearance in the northern Ampurdan, in a district named Sant Quirc de Colera. By 1881 all the vineyards of Garrotxa and the Ampurdan were dead; six years later the phylloxera had killed the vineyards of Penedés south of Barcelona, and by 1890 the Catalan wine industry was facing extinction. Phylloxera wiped out nearly a million acres of vineyards in the four Catalan provinces of Barcelona, Tarragona, Lleida, and Girona. By 1900, despite frantic replanting, there were only half a million acres under vines in all Catalunya. Vast tracts were left to revert to scrub or were replanted as forest.

Just as wine speculation had set up the dominoes for Barcelona's stock-market and real-estate boom, so the aphid knocked them flat. The pernicious insect was helped by a severe crisis on the Paris stock exchange in 1882, which shook the Llotja in Barcelona. The Catalan boom became a bust, and the economy dived into a depression from which it did not start to recover until 1890. In 1883 five banks collapsed, seven more followed in 1884, and a further eight by the end of 1889.

As the credit system failed, so industry faltered, and this created eddies that were felt all over the mercantile system of Catalunya—and of Spain. Catalan merchants in Cuba, led by the marquis of Comillas, were enthusiastic defenders of slave labor, and twenty-five years after the American Civil War almost all Cuba's cane sugar was produced by slaves. In 1886 slavery was abolished in Cuba, just as the price of Cuban cane sugar in Europe was being forced down by French and Belgian beet sugar. The Cuban growers therefore had to sell their sugar in the United States, and they cut costs by purchasing American rather than Catalan machinery. The Spaniards tried to prevent, or at least reduce, these stirrings of free trade in Cuba—egged on, of course, by the ardently protectionist Catalans, who wanted nothing more than a controlled and subservient market in Cuba for their cheaper cotton goods. This all but throttled the island's economy and provoked a nationalist revolt there in 1895.

The end of the *febre d'or* was not just a bourgeois disaster. Plenty of businessmen and companies survived it. But for the men in the field, the rural workers, the impact of phylloxera was catastrophic. Viticulture is a labor-intensive, capital-heavy, slow-growth business. It takes four years for a vine to mature and bear, whereas the same land can be sown with two cereal crops a year. Vineyards stricken with phylloxera, therefore, even if they were immediately replanted with new vines, would be unproductive wasteland for at least four to five years. No small farm could survive that, and relatively few of the big ones (owned, more and more, by city capital) managed to do so. Thousands of winegrowing peasants went broke and drifted, with their families, into the maw of Barcelona to find what work they could and swell the ranks of the city proletariat.

Moreover, phylloxera struck at the very basis of the lease system around which the *rabassaires'* land rights had been organized, based on the life of the vines. In killing the vines, it killed the leases too. If the landlord did not want to renew the lease, and many did not, the peasant and his family would be left with no choice but to gravitate to the big city. If you had the capital to survive, which few peasants did, you could replant—with clean stock, imported from California and Australia. But it turned out that these imported vines, though productive, needed much more care and work than the old and lived only half as long. Hence even if his lease was renewed, no winegrowing *rabassaire* felt as secure as he had been before phylloxera. Mass evictions loomed; there was a mounting wave of rural protest, as the *rabassaires* closed ranks and began to stand up to their landlords. In some areas the Guardia Civil (that much-feared national armed force founded by the duke of Ahumada in 1844 to repress agrarian unrest, which by the 1880s had also become the state's weapon against city anarchists and strikers) was called in to extract the landlords' money and the government's taxes from the turbulent peasants. This severely wounded the image of traditional class harmony that big-city wine-owning clans like the Güells had cultivated as part of their own claims to be the "natural aristocracy," heirs to the feudal barons. It also led to the formation of the Unió de Rabassaires, which began in 1891 among the sharecroppers of Penedés, Valles, and Tarragona and was to become the biggest agrarian trade union in Catalunya, until Franco suppressed it in 1939.

In Barcelona, the population figures told their own story. For at least a century, its industrial proletariat had grown steadily, but the ratio between the population of all Catalunya and that of Barcelona had stayed much the same. In 1787, Barcelona with its 111,400 residents held about one out of every seven Catalans; in 1834, when the population of Catalunya passed a million, Barcelona had 135,500 people, still fewer than one in eight; by 1887 it had risen to one in almost seven, 272,500 people out of 1,843,000. But thereafter, the proportion zoomed. Thirteen years later, in 1900, more than half a million of Catalunya's 1,942,000 citizens lived and worked in Barcelona—one person in four, and the trend continued. Meanwhile, after phylloxera, the fertile plains around Tarragona lost fully 20 percent of their population to Barcelona; many villages of northern Catalunya were deserted as impoverished peasants made their way to the city. Some victims of phylloxera and gold fever went even farther abroad—to Cuba, Mexico, Argentina, or even to New York, where there was already enough of a Catalan community to support a monthly newspaper called *La Llumanera* (*The Lamp*), full of news from home, patriotic verses, silly riddles, advice to the migrant about the impossibility of spoken English, and advertisements for bulk lard. Even before the bust of 1882, *La Llumanera* was advising its readers against emigration—a pointless gesture, perhaps, since one had to be in New York to read its editorials. "*No vingueu als Estats Units*," intoned its front page in December 1879—"Do not come to the United States . . . we must counsel all our countrymen who are thinking of coming, or sending

Lluís Vermell, ivory miniature of the Famades family, an idealized group in their casa pairal, *1856*

a son, a parent or a friend to this country, that they must not do so unless they want to undergo black torment [*la pena negra*]." The reasons, it added, would take too long to explain.

Even in faraway Manhattan, *La Llumanera* was full of engravings depicting the lost pleasures of the *casa pairal*: the family round the hearth, the chickens pecking on the kitchen floor, the reapers' picnic, the baby getting his first dribble of wine from the *porró*. It was hardly surprising that Catalans should feel homesick when overseas. But they managed to do so when at home—a truly startling feat. The other boom in the 1870s and 1880s was in the literature of *enyorança*. It was as though no Catalan poet worth his or her bays could take a train to Madrid, or even sail fifty yards out of Barcelona harbor, without being assailed by uncontrollable yearnings for childhood, farm, and *pàtria*. Every versifier succumbed to them, but so did Barcelona's greatest poet of the period, Jacint Verdaguer, in laments like "L'Emigrant."

This was largely a political convention, of course—which is not to say that it was not, at least occasionally, felt. The derangement of the peasant economy caused by agribusiness and phylloxera only strengthened the nostalgia for peasant life that was part and parcel of the imagery of bourgeois, conservative Catalanism. Like the American Indian, the Catalan *pagès* looked noblest when he seemed headed for the margins. Even as the farmers were losing their land and fleeing to the cities, the burghers of Barcelona stepped up their efforts to claim that they, too, were sons (or at least grandsons, as some actually were) of the soil; that the ancestral virtues of the *casa pairal* had migrated to the town house in the Eixample and the factory in Sants. Much rhetoric was expended to make this illusory point, and the poets of the Jocs Florals and the orators of the Ajuntament reserved their windiest tropes for it. Whatever was folkish was good. The bourgeois revolution, from this aspect, was nothing other than a big *casa pairal* with steam engines out the back. The means of production had changed but the Catalan *race* was simply being itself with other tools. This uplifting argument might not have made much sense to the ex-peasants laboring in the mills, but then, since most of them could not read, it is unlikely that they knew about it. The sentimental ideology of Catalanism became a bulwark against the frightful uncertainties engendered by the *febre d'or*.

Thus in 1882, the dramatist and poet Frederic Soler rose to deliver the presidential address at the ceremonies of the Jocs Florals. He unfurled a picture of traditional Catalan life:

> Twenty years ago, on a day like this, we assembled here . . . or in some other place which, like this, brought memories of the homeland to our minds and feelings of love to our hearts.
>
> It looked like the hearth of the *casa pairal* to me. Imagination carried me away. I saw the flared hood of the chimney-nook, bearing its shield, like the throne of the patriarchal Catalan family. Seated within it were the grandparents, the mistress of the house, her husband the heir, and their children, with shepherds and farm-boys in between them; their traditional costumes, typical of the genius of our land, completed the image.
>
> Simplicity and strength were joined there. Against the invisible power of the sky, the palm cross and the laurel-branch blessed on Palm Sunday, which—as peasants believe—shield us from thunderbolts and hail. Against the forest wolves, mastiffs with nailed collars. Against the invading stranger, the blunderbuss charged to the muzzle—not with buckshot, but with the angular shards of iron that tore through the imperial cuirasses at Bruc.
>
> And all was peace and love. The roundelay or the innocent recitation of the Rosary were the entertainments of these sweet evenings . . .

This, one might say, is the double-distilled essence of the rural myth of the Catalan Renaixença. Soler's audience—poets and politicians, novelists and academics, musicians, clergy, businessmen, few of whom had much practical connection to real rural life—are imagined as a peasant family, united around the hearth of culture. He spins this out in detail, starting with the architectural frame—the *llar de foc* of the traditional farmhouse, more a room than a fireplace, with the tribe ensconced within it, in order of age. It carries a shield because nobility is the attribute of plain folk, not just aristocrats. Soler invokes the simple faith of the peasants, their dress—so different from the frock coats and cravats he and his audience were wearing that day—and their harmless, perhaps efficacious, charms and superstitions. The sanctity of the hearth entails the sanctity of property: hence the guard dog, an emblem of another Catalan tradition, self-defense. Xenophobia and patriotism are one, and even the ammunition in the ever-loaded family blunderbuss is of the rough, folksy type (no store-bought pellets here) that the peasant volunteers of Bruc let fly at Napoleon's troops from their *trabucs* in the famous battle in 1808. The mention of Bruc would instantly have warmed Soler's listeners with their own nursery-book memories of the drummer boy of Bruc, who was by now a folkloric figure, like Dick Whittington or the little Dutch boy with his finger in the dike.

It is a picture as perfectly conventionalized as the other patriotic images that northern European countries were turning out, under the psychic stress of industrialization, in the 1880s: the Welsh family melodiously singing to the harp, the Highland Scots family eating porridge in their tartan kilts, the Swiss peasant with his crossbow and flügelhorn. It would be propagated by the conservative Catalanist press led by Mañé i Flaquer and by militant Church intellectuals like Torras i Bagès. No workers believed it, and more astute Catalanists like Valentí Almirall treated it with reserve. Nevertheless it had a long life—so long that traces of it survive in the speeches of the president of today's conservative Catalan government, Jordí Pujol. It was the myth that enabled the conquering bourgeoisie to tamp down the anxieties of industry, not for others' sakes, but for their own. But ideally it needed a poet, not just propagandists: a figure who, by his writings, would raise the myth of Catalanism into full imaginative life and place it firmly within the precincts of the major European literature of the nineteenth century. The Catalan right found this man in a young priest from Vic named Jacint Verdaguer, whose poetry was to mark the climax of the Renaixença, and whose life—in its tragic denouement—would equally mark its end.

Jacint Verdaguer was born in the village of Folgueroles on the plain of Vic in May 1845. His parents were unusually literate sharecropping peasants; his father wrote correct Catalan, and his mother loved to read. They sent their son away to study for the priesthood in the seminary of Vic when he was only ten: the Church represented the best chance a poor, intelligent rural boy had for advancement. By his twentieth birthday Jacint Verdaguer was winning mentions at the Jocs Florals in Barcelona, and at twenty-two he started a literary society with other seminarians in Vic. By 1870 his work was known to the Provençal poet, Frédéric Mistral, and the two became fast friends. In that year Verdaguer was ordained a priest and sent to a rural parish, where he developed an ill-diagnosed cerebral disease, characterized by wasting and fevers. To put him near better medical care, his superiors moved him to Barcelona, where in 1874 Verdaguer was introduced to Claudi López i Bru, the son of the marquis of Comillas. The López clan, impressed by Verdaguer's piety and lyric talents, installed him as chaplain on the vessels of the Companyia Transatlàntica, plying the Atlantic. "For two years," he wrote later, "I passed from Spain to Cuba and from Cuba to Spain, like a shuttle going from one side of a wide, grandiose textile to the other." In all, he made nine voyages. These formed the basis of his epic poem *L'Atlàntida*.

The story of *L'Atlàntida* defies any attempt at a brief summary. It resembles a congested dream with mythological origins, populated with indistinct and titanic figures: a poem about a primal ocean, the sinking of Atlantis, the rising of Europe, the creation and burning of the Pyrenees, the founding of Barcelona by Hercules, the hero's passage across the Atlantic to the Garden of the Hesperides in the West, his slaying of the dragon that guards the golden apples, and much, much more besides. It is an epic of cosmic fermentation, told by an ancient hermit to a young Genoese mariner, shipwrecked on his remote island. At the end of the poem this youth turns out to be none other than Christopher Columbus, now inspired by the sage to repeat Hercules' discovery and conquest of the western isles. Thus the cosmic order, deranged by the loss of Atlantis, is restored by the "discovery" of the New World.

The language of *L'Atlàntida* is rich, sonorous, imbued not only with rhetorical grandeur but with intimate precision of observation and feeling. It has some of the qualities of Victor Hugo's diction in its accumulative force and its sweeping romantic imagery. Though there are passages of fustian, its atmospheric and geologic effects are frequently indelible, like the alexandrine describing a wall of fire advancing across

Jacint Verdaguer

---

the Pyrenees, *"cremant com teranyines els núvols de l'hivern"*—"burning up
the winter clouds like spider-webs"—or the vision of Teide, the volcanic
peak of the Canaries rising from the abyss:

> *restant-li sols lo Teide, dit de sa mà de ferre*
> *que sembla dir als homes:—L'Atlàntida era ací!*

> only Teide remains there, finger of that iron hand
> that seems to say to men: Atlantis was here!

Most important of all, from the viewpoint of Verdaguer's Catalan
readers, was the beauty of his language and the fact of his epic ambitions.
Catalan literature had been silent for centuries. No long poem of origins,
of the mythic transformation of a people, or of the quest had ever been
written in Catalan. Thus the Catalan language had not passed through
an epic phase; it had no *Paradise Lost*, no *Os Lusiades*, no *Odyssey* or *Aeneid*.
Yet here, suddenly, was a young man in his thirties with a complete
foundation myth, a heterodox fantasy with Christian imagery jammed
on top of Celtic and classical mythology, cloudy and craggy, malformed
in parts, but challenging the assumption that heroic literature *could*

not be written in Catalan because it *had* not been. This, clearly, was the man sent to affirm the most optimistic values of the Renaixença: a priest, a poet, a peasant's son, a Catalanist. When *L'Atlàntida* won first prize at the 1879 Jocs Florals, the jury believed that the long-awaited rebirth of the Catalan language as an instrument of national self-definition had come at last. Verdaguer was received almost as a literary messiah by the clergy and by middle-class Catalan nationalists. Later, they would brutally abandon him.

VII

Although building went on in the Eixample in the 1870s, its tempo was slow, and the results generally mediocre. Most of the new buildings were speculative blocks, unimaginative in design, and many were torn down in the 1890s. Some very large private houses were built in the immediate area of Passeig de Gràcia, but they, too, tended to be demolished later in favor of apartment blocks. Most of the ornate new villas for the new rich were built in Sarrià—as far from Barcelona as one could get while still being part of the city. Few of these were of pronounced architectural quality, either: the generation of architects—Gaudí, Domènech i Montaner, Puig i Cadafalch—that took command of Barcelonese building in the 1890s would be far more ambitious and talented. The better new buildings in Barcelona in the 1870s were functional, not ceremonial, and among them were two public markets: the Mercat del Born (1873–76) by Josep Fontseré i Mestres and the Mercat de Sant Antoni (1876–82) by Antoni Rovira i Trias, both designed with the help of the engineer Josep Cornet i Mas, Barcelona's specialist in static iron-truss structures.

The Mercat del Born stands between the Citadel Park and Santa Maria del Mar. Like the Boqueria (which was also roofed over, in 1870) the site had been an open-air market since the eighteenth century. The Ajuntament now decided to cover this traditional spot with the largest iron structure in Spain—a shed with a central nave, four aisles, and an octagonal ciborium in the middle. It measured 450 by 188 feet and was meant to show what Catalan industry could do; indeed, it may have been designed with an eye to surpassing the immense prefabricated iron tobacco warehouse that the American architect James Bogardus had shipped to Havana in the 1850s. The Catalans felt that they were locked in a technology race with the *yankis*; in 1879, when a pair of Catalan

Josep Fontseré's Mercat del Born, 1873–76

inventors came up with a means of splitting electrical current, *La Llumanera* headlined it

¡¡Important descubriment!!
¡DIVISIO PRACTICA DE LA LLUM ELÉCTRICA!
«¡¡EDISON ECLIPSAT PER DOS CATALANS!!»

In any case, the technical problem with the Mercat del Born was how to cover 185,000 square feet of site with a tile roof, get rid of the water runoff it gathered on rainy days, and provide the cavernous interior with enough natural light to function as a market. Iron framing was the only solution, and Cornet i Mas designed a modular system for its serial prefabrication. All its elements—columns, trusses, beams, arches—were made by Joan Güell's metalworks, the Maquinista Terrestre i Marítima. The cast-iron columns were also drains to carry the rainwater away. The architect, the engineer, and their client, the city, all wanted the Born market to be a demonstration piece of the industrial use of two materials in which Catalan artisans had always excelled: iron and tile. And so it is: the visual effect of this vast roof, which seems to hover free of obstacles above the ground, penetrated by shafts of light from the windows framed in the merest filaments of iron, is as poetic and impressive today as it must have been a hundred years ago. El Born is

The interior of the Mercat del Born

a plain building; its only decoration comes from the change of color in the roof tiles, whose diaper pattern marks the basic module of the bays and columns. But that geometric shift is enough.

The Mercat de Sant Antoni was built later and is slightly more ornate. The exceptional thing about this structure of Rovira's is the lucidity and thoughtfulness of its plan. The only market in the Eixample built on a site originally designated in Cerdà's plan, it has a plan that rethinks the site—a block defined by Carrers Urgell, Tamarit, Borrell, and Manso—in terms of orientation toward the corners rather than the sides. This makes sense, since the little squares formed by the chamfers of Cerdà's blocks created natural eddies in the traffic stream where transport wagons could park: it was easier to load and unload goods from the corners than the edges. So Rovira planned the market with two high, glazed naves set in the block like a diagonal *X*, each nave as wide as the whole chamfered face of the block. These were the goods and service entrances. Shoppers used entrances on the four sides, directly off the streets. Above the crossing of the *X*, there was an octagonal lantern, with tall, arched Romanesque windows, five to a side, to light the cathedrallike interior. It covers an area exactly the same size as the street squares generated in the open air outside by Cerdà's *xamfrans*. The closed space repeats the open space, positive against negative. One cannot but experience the building as a crystallization of the city plan in which it is embedded. No other industrial structure in Barcelona has such a clear, reinforced relation to its site.

It is also, like the Boqueria, a node of life and detail; its restrained iron decoration—cast scrolls in the panels around the slender windows and elegant molding of the metal framework of the huge, almost ecclesiastical windows above the corner entrances—acts as a foil to the structural conception of the naves and a transition to the pullulating mass of the market's life, the human chatter and roar, the colors of the goods and the glare of the lights.

The outstanding architects of the Restoration period were Josep Fontseré and Elias Rogent i Amat. Rogent (1821–97) had studied in Barcelona and later traveled quite widely in Europe, visiting Paris, Berlin, and Munich. His early taste, which he never abandoned, ran to romantic architecture: while still a student he made the splendid gesture of burning a copy of Vignola's famous sixteenth-century manual of classical style, *La Regola degli Cinque Ordini d'Architettura*. Not that he was opposed to neoclassicism per se—in fact he was greatly influenced by Leo von Klenze (1784–1864), the court architect of Ludwig I of Bavaria, whose twenty or so buildings in a neoclassical vein gave Munich its architectural idiom as a major court city. But he also liked Klenze's associate in Munich, Friedrich von Gärtner, whose work contained discreet romantic quotations from Gothic and Romanesque. He had studied (though not met) Viollet-le-Duc, the great French rationalist who laid down the canon of Gothic architecture through the criteria of function and structure rather than picturesque appeal. And he would have seen Henri Labrouste's Sainte-Genevieve Library in Paris (1838–40), with its unadorned iron structure of columns and trusses within a stone shell— the first use of an exposed iron frame in a monumental building.

Rogent was a friend of Ildefons Cerdà's, and in 1860 he was given the commission to design the first monumental structure in the Eixample—the new University of Barcelona, which was to replace the old Estudis Generals at the head of the Ramblas. The building took eight years to design and four to build; it was not finished (because of spotty funding) until 1872. It is a curious but dignified hybrid. The exterior lines of the university are Romanesque: wide planes of wall with very restrained decoration, slender stringcourses and elegant engaged arches, like eyebrows, over the windows. Rogent, who had made many

Elias Rogent's University of Barcelona, 1872

field trips into the Pyrenean villages of northern Catalunya, chose to quote Catalan Romanesque (rather than Barcelonese Gothic, which was nearer to hand) because he saw it as the *archetypal* style, the root of nationalist sensibility. Then, to pay his respects to the Islamic occupation of Spain, Rogent added Mozarabic details (of a more fanciful sort) and even Byzantine elements to the interior decoration. Finally, he decided as another polemical gesture to follow the lead of Labrouste, some forty years later, and leave the iron columns in the library plain and unsheathed.

Other architects took other directions: when Josep Fontseré designed Barcelona's Dipòsit d'Aigues, or Water Reservoir (1874–80), essentially a vast tank of water carried on thick rectangular brick piers connected by diaphragm arches, he created a homage to the plain prismatic grandeur of the thirteenth-century Cistercian foundations of Poblet and Santes Creus near Tarragona. Few nineteenth-century secular buildings—in Spain, at least—bear such a freight of awe as this reservoir (carefully recycled as an exhibition space in 1988 by the architects Ignacio Parisio, Lluís Clotet, and Joan Sabater). On the other hand, Joan Martorell i Montells (1833–1906), a mediocre Gothic Revivalist, stuck firmly to

Gothic as the one and only sanctified form of Barcelonese building, producing overwrought and stodgy efforts like the College of the German Marist Brothers (1882–85) at the corner of Passeig de Sant Joan and Carrer València.

But Rogent stuck with his Romanesque idiom; indeed, he acquired the reputation of a Catalan Viollet-le-Duc, thanks to his restoration— usually fanciful and often abusive—of old churches in the "cradle of Catalunya," the most famous (or notorious) of which was his work on the monastery Santa Maria de Ripoll. He believed, he said, in "patriotic reconstruction." This phrase would congeal the blood of a modern architectural restorer, but it meshed with the cultural spirit of the Renaixença. All Catalan culture had to be recovered. The Romanesque and Gothic monuments stood as much in need of revival, study, and use as the Catalan language itself. The practice around which the work of memory revolved was called "excursionism," and it tapped a deep vein of patriotic feeling.

Excursionism was not simply tourism. Tourism, in any organized sense, did not exist in Spain then. Rather, excursionism meant purposeful, educated travel with the aim of discovering one's own country and learning to value it. It brought poets together with intellectuals, botanists with architects, antiquarians with geologists. It was Ruskinian adventure—active, inquisitive, melding scientific curiosity about plants, weather, rocks, and ecology with aesthetic appreciation of old buildings, folk art, frescoes, and crafts. One did not set out to reach a few climactic sights. One noted everything along the way, and the reward for one's efforts was not only knowledge but a kind of historicist rapture, an ecstatic dreaming about the lost cultural past. Every ruin was a shrine, and the holiest of them was Ripoll. Here is the young artist Santiago Rusinyol approaching it in a small group led by an architectural-historian friend named Pellicer, down the valley of the Ter and through a thicket of exclamation points, in the summer of 1880:

> Ripoll!!! What sweet inspirations and great memories crowd on the mind when we hear the echo of your glorious name among the mountains!! How the hearts of true Catalans beat when we hear it uttered! Ah! At last we are near you, jewel of the Middle Ages! Soon we will be in your humble monastery! We come to breathe the same air that hundreds upon hundreds of Benedictines have breathed here; we come to rest on the same slabs of stone beneath which the crusaders and templars rest, worn out, on their return from the Holy Land. We are entering an unknown land, dreamed of a thousand times. Now we do

Excursionists painting a sign, 1900

not walk, we fly. Sweat streams down our faces and we are short of breath. Now there are no more slopes, screes and cliffs, and danger no longer exists for us . . . I reach the cloister, I enter the church, I run to the portal and . . . Ruins, all around!

Such ruins invited—no, *demanded*—restoration. They must be fortified, renewed, to bear the ever-increasing weight of romantic sentiment that the Renaixença exuded. Excursionism was not a hobby, but a cult, and practically every Catalan artist, architect, writer, and academic was bound up in it. If you wanted to grasp the true origins of Catalunya you had to be an excursionist, since there were so few signs of the "primitive" glories of Catalan architecture (let alone of their relation to nature) left in Barcelona. With their penchant for clubs and groups, the Catalans were quick to form excursionists' societies. The first, in 1876, was the Catalanist Association for Scientific Excursions, from which a splinter group broke off in 1878 to make the Catalan Excursionists' Association. Then they reknit in 1890 as the Excursionist Center of Catalunya. The ECC published guidebooks, built mountain refuge huts, promoted mountain climbing and skiing along Swiss lines; it even had a band of spelunkers who, in their tweed knickers, intrepidly descended into the limestone caves of the Pyrenees with pine torches and carbide lamps. Excursionism drew Gaudí to the monastery of Poblet, and took Domènech i Montaner through a score of crumbling Romanesque chapels with his measuring tape and sketchbook.

It also inspired many writers with visions of Catalunya that they might not otherwise have had—or not so concretely. Travel offered Jacint Verdaguer the raw material for *Canigó*, his epic about Catalan identity, whose images welled up in the course of several long journeys through the "Pyrenean sanctuaries." For Verdaguer, as the critic Josep Miracle has pointed out, the Pyrenees were not a frontier: they were the core of Catalunya. He imagined them as an immense cedar tree, their ridges its roots, their forests its leaves, where

> *com los aucells, los pobles fan niu a sa brancada.*
> *d'on cap voltor de races desllotjar-los pot.*

> like birds, villages nest in its branches—
> no high-bred vulture can harry them out of there.

All the excursionist needed, to have his national faith restored, was to ascend the Pyrenees:

> *los catalans que hi munten estimen més llur terra,*
> *veient totes les serres vassalles de llur serra,*
> *veient totes les testes al peu de llur tità;*
> *los estrangers que obiren de lluny eixa muntanya,*
> *—Aquell gegant—exclamen—és un gegant d'Espanya,*
> *d'Espanya i català.*

> Catalans who climb here love their land more,
> They see all the ranges, vassals to their range,
> They see all the peaks at the foot of their titan:
> And foreigners who bow down, from afar, before this mountain,
> Cry "This giant is a giant of Spain,
> Spanish—and Catalan."

The excursionist frame of mind was particularly important as raw material to two architects a generation younger than Rogent, who in the 1870s were both assistant professors at the Barcelona School of Architecture, where Rogent taught. These were Josep Vilaseca i Casanovas

(1848–1910) and Lluís Domènech i Montaner (1849–1923). However, they wanted to go beyond Rogent. What concerned them was not so much literal revival of past architectural styles, in the manner of Rogent's Romanesque or Viollet-le-Duc's Gothic, as a somewhat more complicated synthesis of structure and decoration that would lead to a "higher" eclecticism, more imaginative than reproductory, and closely tied not only to a craft base (bound to be relatively static and traditional) but to a continuously evolving technology of structure. Thus the old would be continuously infused by the new and made to point to the future.

The architect they most looked to as a model was Gottfried Semper (1803–79). They admired Semper's *Europeanness*, as young Catalans looking north of the Pyrenees well might. Semper had studied for three years in Italy and Greece and practiced—not just traveled, but taught, worked, and built buildings—in Switzerland, England, and Austria as well as his native Germany. And he had built on a grand scale, as Vienna's Burgtheater and the Museums of Art History and Natural History attested: these buildings were being finished when Domènech and Vilaseca were turning thirty.

But Semper's most influential creation was not his own building but a two-volume book: *Style in the Industrial and Structural Arts, or Practical Aesthetics*, 1860–63. In this, he sought to construct a typology of building based on the patient, "botanical" analysis of functional elements and social use, covering all manner of styles from the wigwam and the Caribbean hut through to the works of nineteenth-century Europeans. In particular he stressed the way these types changed in response to social use. (There is an analogy here to Darwin studying the beaks of Galápagos finches, but one need not press it too far: Semper was not a Darwinian evolutionist.) Without attempting to condense the intricacies of Semper's work, an impossible task, one can say that it rested on a genuinely new division of the elements of building. In his view, there were four: the hearth—the fire, generator of all social use of architecture; the platform, on which the fire burns; the roof—which includes the structural frame and columns that keep it up; and, fourth, the enclosure or wall, load bearing or not, which keeps out the weather.

Was there anything radical about this? Emphatically, yes: Semper's treatment of the roof and columns as a single unit, and his discussion of the wall as a screen that did not have to bear load to be a wall, are the root of all thinking about structural-frame buildings, the Ur-type of modernist architecture. And one may guess, incidentally, that what Semper had to say about the fundamental nature of the hearth rang a deep subliminal bell with the young Catalan architects, immersed since childhood in the peculiarly intense social imagery of the *casa pairal* and its *llar de foc*.

Beside him, Viollet-le-Duc and his literal Catalan followers must have seemed inescapably provincial. Vilaseca and Domènech marked the southern boundary, so to speak, of Semper's immense influence, which at its height extended as far west as California in the work of Bernard Maybeck and included such devotees as (to name only the big names) Walter Gropius, Otto Wagner, Bruno Taut, and Louis Sullivan. When Vilaseca inscribed the names of the great architects of the past on the cornice of a house he built on Plaça d'Urquinaona (1874–77), he ignored all the medieval revivalists of the nineteenth century but put Semper up there, right along with Ictinus (the Parthenon's designer), Michelangelo, Wren, and Mansart.

Domènech's views on the possible relations between modernity and tradition were put together in a manifesto he published in 1878, when he was just thirty: *En Busca de una Arquitectura Nacional* (*In Search of a National Architecture*). "The last word of every conversation about architecture," it begins, "the basic question of all criticism, turns involuntarily back to a single idea—that of a modern, national architecture. . . . Today, for today, can we have a real national architecture? Will we get one in the near future?" He summarizes, briefly and Semperwise, the social traits of the great styles of the past, the Hindu stupas that speak of "grandiose religious and cosmogonic ideas," the despotic monuments of the Euphrates, the theocratic order implicit in Egypt, the "republican" spirit of the Acropolis, the authoritarianism of Rome and the "fanatical, warrior-sensualist genius" of Islam. "Only societies without firm, fixed ideas, which fluctuate between today's thinking and yesterday's without faith in tomorrow—only these societies fail to inscribe their history in durable monuments." (He meant Spain in 1878, but he could just as well have been writing of postmodernist America a century later.) Today we have an immense accumulation of artistic forms and prototypes, gathered from all over the world, exhumed from a limitless past. But where is the myth around which it can crystallize? Domènech finds it in the Promethean moment of technology, in

> those immense edifices that industrial genius, in its delirium, raises in a day only to raze them the next morning; at will, the hand of a weak being, helped by electricity and chemistry, flattens the gigantic mountain of marble; iron melts in the furnace, is twisted on itself, and passes to the rolling-mill, to surrender its strength to us; already, mechanical

science determines the rudiments of architectonic form. . . . The nations open their treasures to the artist, so that he can raise his ideal concepts to the plane of reality. Everything heralds the appearance of a new era for architecture.

Architecture cannot adequately respond to this changed world by merely imitating classical or Gothic forms in the manner of Viollet-le-Duc—if it does, it becomes "a corpse or, rather, a repulsive mummy." And the less pedantic eclecticism of Germany may not be of much help in the long run either, because its menu is too stereotyped—"For it, a cemetery must be Egyptian in style, a museum Greek, a congress-hall Roman, a convent Byzantine or Romanesque, a church Gothic, a university Renaissance, and a theater part-Roman, part-Baroque . . . this school is learned, scholarly, but we don't believe we have to support it. Antique forms do not match our present needs nor our means of construction." Hence the academics get in difficulties when they use iron, for instance (an oblique reference to Elias Rogent and his university, where Domènech taught).

Spain (and Domènech is talking about Spain as a whole, not just Catalunya) has two wells, two great repositories, of ancient architectural style: Islamic in the south, Romanesque and Gothic in the north. Somehow a truly national architecture must draw strength from these, refer to them, use them. But it will get nowhere by merely copying them, and it must remember the structural origins of forms that, in the late nineteenth century, often sink into a sort of atrophied decor. "Let us subject decorative forms to the principles of structure, as the classic periods did," cried Domènech: let us extract, from Oriental architecture, the majesty of horizontal lines and polished plane surfaces in their contrast with huge decorative forms; let us find the "principle of solids" in Egyptian architecture, the "secrets of the grandeur of formal distribution and construction" in Augustan Rome, the "idealization of the material" in Gothic, the "system of linked, multiple ornamentation" in Arabic buildings. And then,

with these principles strictly absorbed, let us openly apply the forms that new experiences and needs impose on us, enriching them and giving them expressive strength with the treasures of ornament offered us by the monuments of all periods and by Nature. . . . Maybe people will say that this is only a new kind of eclecticism. If to seek the practice of all good doctrines, (which, since they are good, cannot contradict one another) . . . is to be eclectic; if to assimilate the elements one needs to live a healthy life, as a plant draws nourishment from air, water and earth, is to make "eclecticism"; if to believe that all generations have left us something worth learning, studying and applying is to fall into that sin—well, we declare ourselves guilty of eclecticism.

Domènech's manifesto indicated the course not only of his own work (at the time he had built very little) but of his generation's, of early Gaudí no less than Vilaseca or Puig i Cadafalch—the men whose best work unfolded to maturity in the period 1888–1908. Eclecticism, as Domènech conceived it, is the way to a "nationalist" architecture—but it also dissolves the supposed tensions between national and international by appealing to a higher order of structure while confirming the value of local cultural traditions and particular syntaxes. It fitted the mood of the late Catalan Renaixença to perfection, by evoking the industrial self-image of modern Catalunya while proclaiming the availability of its Gothic and Romanesque heritage, along with the utility of its still-enormous artisan base. But though he got to build the headquarters for his father's publishing business in 1879—the Editorial Montaner i Simón (Carrer d'Aragó 255, now the Tapiès Foundation)—Domènech's real emergence as an architect did not begin until the end of the 1880s. It happened as a result of the Universal Exposition of 1888, which was held in a public park built over the site of the much-loathed Bourbon Citadel. This park—the Parc de la Ciutadella—had its own importance for a city in transition.

VIII

Having unseated Isabel II, General Prim, a Catalan, wished to give something concrete to Barcelona before the Glorious Revolution of 1868 began to look less glorious. Not money, but space. The Eixample had created a huge amount of private space: sites on which to build houses, shops, apartments. But public space, shared space, was still short. The city had no parks, and with the building along Passeig de Gràcia it was being deprived even of the former waste ground that had been turned into a promenade, spontaneously, by Barcelonans in the 1850s. And so in 1869, in the second year of the revolution, this military man decided to turn over to civilian use Barcelona's big emblem of Bourbon military rule: the Citadel.

Though the Bourbon *muralles* had been demolished, the Citadel had stayed. Pulling it down seemed likely to cost more than putting it up, and the monarchy did not want to lose face by admitting its superfluity. Its site was enormous—some 270 acres, three-quarters the size of the Old City itself. Some of the structures on it were also gigantic: the military barracks, for instance, which could house eight thousand men. In fact, in October almost as soon as the 1868 Revolution began, the revolutionary junta of Barcelona had started demolishing the Citadel without asking anyone in Madrid—but their largely symbolic efforts, accompanied by much flag wagging and oratory for the curious crowd, soon ran out of steam because there was not enough money in hand to pay the workers. Prim now withdrew all vestiges of a garrison from the Citadel and gave the city some 150 acres of its site to be turned into a public park, leaving another 120 or so to be turned into the private housing whose sale would underwrite the park's construction cost. This was a canny political move: Prim knew only too well how hated the Citadel was, how impacted with memories of imprisonment, execution, and repression. He would be seen as a liberator, freeing Barcelona from its besmirched history. And he duly was. He also stipulated that the heirs of the original owners of property in the Ribera quarter that had been expropriated by Felipe V for the Citadel should now be compensated—a popular move, but one that so entangled the construction of the park in lawsuits and pleas and claims that it took years to get going.

The Ajuntament held a competition for the design of the new park. It came down to two finalists, an architect named Macchiachini and Josep Fontseré i Mestres (1829–97). Fontseré won and at once began to assemble a team of gifted young designers. One of them was the twenty-one-year-old Antoni Gaudí, just out of architecture school. Another was Domènech i Montaner, also still in his twenties. A few things were spared demolition: the arsenal designed by Prosper Verboom, which Pere Falques (1857–1916) remodeled into a palace for visiting royalty and which is now the seat of the Catalan parliament; the neoclassical chapel; the parade ground, known as the Plaça d'Armes. But the rest was to be razed and rebuilt. Fontseré declared his motto on one of the drawings: "Do not demolish to destroy; demolish to make things beautiful." And like Frederick Law Olmsted, the designer of Central Park in New York and nineteen others in the United States, he subscribed to the key maxim of late-nineteenth-century park design: "Gardens," he said, "are to the city what lungs are to a man." He envisaged the Citadel

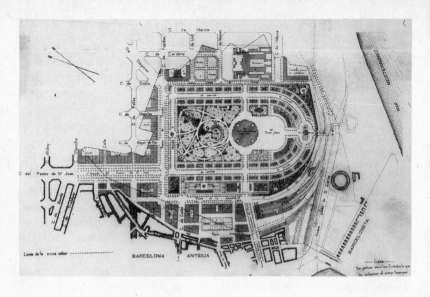

Fontseré's plan for the Citadel Park

Park completing the symmetry implicit in an earlier transformation of the Old City, the cutting of the transversal of Carrer Ferran and Carrer de la Princesa from the Ramblas to the Citadel, through the Plaça Sant Jaume. On one side, beyond the Ramblas, industrial Barcelona; on this side, where the Citadel had been, the relief from the stresses of work, the park balancing the factories.

Moreover, it seems that Fontseré and his team thought they should create the park as symbol of renascent Catalanism—a garden extended, as it were, over the buried bones of the Citadel, the corpse of imperial Bourbonism. The outline of the park would not "respect," "defer to," or even mention Verboom's Citadel plan. It would be a big horseshoe with another horseshoe inside it—an avenue that prolonged the line of one of the main avenues of Cerdà's plan, the Passeig de Sant Joan, then swept around in a semicircle and returned to the base of the horseshoe, which was the present Carrer Pujades. Parterres and mazes, fountains and ponds, a winter garden, a botanical museum and a shade house, palaces of industry and fine arts in the middle, and statues commemorating the great men of Catalunya scattered didactically about. Much later, a zoo was added, with an elephant, to be called, as Catalan elephants should be, L'Avi, the Ancestor. The original Avi, a gift from a rich Catalan whose private menagerie it had outgrown, died in 1915. He left behind him a verse by some unknown, disillusioned democrat:

Mirando el Avi del Parque
encuentra la democracia
una distracción honesta
buena, bonita y barata.

Behold the Elephant in the Park,
and meet Democracy:
an honest diversion,
good, attractive and dirt-cheap.

The Avi's fossil, so to speak, remains in the form of a ferroconcrete mastodon, life-size, with mighty recurved tusks, installed next to the duck pond. His place in the affections of Barcelona's children now belongs to Snowball, a seigneurial and torpid albino gorilla, the only one in the world.

In sum, the layout of the park would salute the Old City and the New City at once. Its most spectacular, not to say peculiar, feature is the Cascade, an enormous allegorical fountain designed by Fontseré and his team. It is an imitation of an earlier fountain in Marseilles, built in the 1860s in the Parc Longchamps by a Second Empire architect named Henri Espérandieu—which was in turn an imitation of those older fountains, such as the Fontana di Trevi, with which Rome celebrated the point of arrival of water from an aqueduct into the city. The water that the Cascade brings to the park comes from the Dipòsit d'Aigues on Carrer Wellington, also designed by Fontseré. This cannot be claimed for the Cascade. With its triumphal arch and steps, its quadriga and its water-spouting griffins, its Neptune and Leda and Amphitrite and Danaë, its river gods and its central group of a chastely draped marine Venus in a flamenco posture, standing on a shell on top of what appears to be a mass of artificial lava dragged, against friction, by four sea horses, the Cascade is a work of almost unsurpassable ugliness, pomposity, and eclectic confusion. It was also a benison for the academic sculptors of 1870s Barcelona, no less than seven of whom worked on it. So, it is thought, did the very young Gaudí, who may have contributed the design for the Cascade's central element, a *rocaillerie* grotto with seven entrances meant to serve as an aquarium. If so, this was the first expression of the Gaudínian mania for rock work that attained its apogee, some forty years later, in the Güell Park. Probably, Gaudí's posthumous fame has grossly exaggerated his actual contributions to the Citadel Park; is it really likely that a boy straight out of architecture school would have been given much to do? He was Gaudí the Gofer then, not Gaudí the

The Cascade in the Citadel Park

Genius. It may be, however, that Gaudí collaborated with Fontseré on the cast-iron entrance gates of the park, which, with their multiple gasoliers, shields of Catalunya, and heavy, spiky helmets, may well be from the same hand that did the lamp standards in Plaça Reial.

Though the Cascade blotted up much of the sculptural libido available in Barcelona at the time of the Restoration, the rest of the park does not lack emblems and statuary, most of them added later. Someone—it is not clear who—designed an artificial hill, its peaks shaped like the Catalan Fuji, the holy mountain of Montserrat; this semidevotional earthwork, which in surviving photographs looks like something one might encounter on a too-ambitious miniature-golf course, has happily disappeared. Allegorical figures of agriculture and the sea, industry and commerce, stood on the park's massive gate pillars; within, statues and busts of Aribau, Aguiló, Balaguer, and other heroes of the Renaixença rose on their herms, pedestals, and plinths amid the new boscage, together with a large equestrian bronze of General Prim. Apart from the clutter of allegorical maidens, there is only one sculpture commemorating a

Roig i Soler, Lady with the Parasol, *in the Citadel Park, 1884*

woman. She was a Catalan painter named Pepita Teixidor (1875–1914), whose marble bust by Manuel Fuxà was set up in 1917 by a Barcelonese feminist group.

Barcelona's favorite public sculpture is also here in the park: the *Lady with the Parasol*, alias *The Fountain*, alias *Josefina*, alias (more intimately) *Pepita*. Created by Joan Roig i Soler in 1884, this is the perfect boulevardier sculpture, charming, funny, and utterly within the spirit of its time: a young girl dressed at the height of fashion in a bustle skirt, glancing at the sky and holding out her hand to feel the raindrops. She has opened her umbrella, whose handle is the pipe of the fountain; water cascades over it. The novelist Manuel Vásquez Montalban thought this *concetto* made her the stone realization of the passing girl in Josep Carner's ditty, which begins

Dama del rostre sufocat
i amb lleu ombrel.la!

Fontseré, Umbracle in the Citadel Park, 1883–84

Feia la llum, de tant d'esclat,
com una fumarel.la.

Lady with the blushing face
and the light umbrella!
The sun bursts around you
like a cloud of vapor.

Fontseré's park project also contributed two large horticultural buildings, the Hivernacle (Winter Garden) and the Umbracle (Shade House), which flank the avenue now known as the Passeig de Picasso. The Hivernacle (1884) is a soaring, iron-framed glass greenhouse by Josep Amargós. The Umbracle (1883–84), the more interesting of the two, designed by Fontseré himself, is also a cast-iron structure, but its roof is open to the air, being made of parallel laths of wood. These cast a delightful and varying play of striped shadows on the shade-loving plants and subtropical palms inside. It consists of a single large tunnel of a nave, flanked by two half-arched "aisles" on either side—in section, an arch and four lobes—each end closed by a heavily detailed brick·wall that is pierced by a two-story archway, screened with more wooden lattice.

Fontseré's ideas about the park did not stop at its boundaries. The arcaded five-story apartment buildings that overlook the park from the other side of Passeig de Picasso were part of his plan too, and there can be no doubt that he wanted people to bear in mind his design for the great Mercat del Born, a five-minute walk away, when they were looking at other iron-frame structures, including the Umbracle, within the park. Of special importance was the antechamber park, then known as the Saló de Sant Joan and now as the Passeig de Lluís Companys, a "room" meant to lead pedestrians from the end of the Passeig de Sant Joan to the park entrance. It was defined by a cast-iron balustrade with massive urns cast in the Bonaplata works (again, some believe Gaudí had a hand in their design); originally it also had seven bronze statues of Catalan heroes on plinths. Five of them, including Guifré the Hairy, Ramon Berenguer I, and the chronicler Bernat Desclot, were toppled in 1937, melted down by the Franco authorities, and used to cast a huge Virgin atop the new church of the Mercè: as neat an allegory of the fate of Catalanism at the hands of centralism as any home ruler could have asked for. Only the statue of Rafael Casanova i Comes remains, and it was moved to a spot on the Ronda de Sant Pere.

Nobody could say that the Citadel Park, as it exists today, shows a very unified conception. It is more like a collection of emblems surrounded by greenery, containing elements of the *jardin anglais*, the didactic grove, the French formal garden, and the funfair—a hotchpotch, but a pleasant one. Its collection of plants is not of great botanical interest, but this does not matter to the bright flocks of children who scatter like wild budgerigars on the gravel, or to the lovers who wander, hands enlaced, by its ponds. In the autumn, especially, it has a De Chirican charm, eccentric and tinged with melancholy, which seems not to have altered much since Josep Pla described it in a memoir of his youth:

> The park seemed empty, although one or two people were passing at the end of an avenue: a depressed, homesick soldier, a gentleman going nowhere in particular, a couple. I sat down on a bench. Under the sweet, gentle leakage of the afternoon, the muffled din of the city went by like a slow, sleepy river. I had a book in my pocket. *Werther*, by Goethe. . . . Down the main avenue rolled a horsedrawn carriage; inside it, I saw a very old lady, anachronistically dressed, covered with powder, with tiny eyes. After a long time, a young man with tangled hair sat on the bench opposite mine. He was untidily dressed, stooped, pensive. I assumed he was an anarchist. In those days anyone who looked like that was taken for an anarchist. He started to read a book.

Without much difficulty I saw that it was a copy of *Werther*, by Goethe, in the same edition (0.60 pesetas) as mine. We looked at each other, but found nothing to say. It no longer seemed plausible to think him an anarchist.

In the late 1880s, the Citadel Park was abruptly transformed. It was chosen as the site of Barcelona's 1888 Universal Exposition, which changed the city's waterfront along with the park—and much else. The politician responsible for this event, the prototype of 1929 and possibly of 1992, which nearly sank the city administration under a load of debt while putting Barcelona (up to a point) on the European map, was the mayor, a liberal monarchist named Francesc de Paula Rius i Taulet (1833–89).

IX

Rius i Taulet was in some ways the ideal mayor to launch the bootstrap, populist operation that the Exposition of 1888 became. He was a conservative opportunist, full of enthusiasm, fire, and convictions of gravity; he had, in the expressive Texan phrase, "more hat than land." But he had four terms as mayor of Barcelona: once in 1872–73 (dismissed by the First Republic), again in 1874 (after the Restoration), a third time in 1881–84, and finally from 1885 to 1889. Rius i Taulet was a political survivor, though he did not survive his own exposition. With his portly body and enormous muttonchop side-whiskers, so large that they were said to impede his entrances and exits from closed carriages, he was a cartoonist's dream. Rius was persuasive and, like many good persuaders, susceptible to flattery; above all, he loved big schemes and longed to put his own permanent stamp on the city. He was the living incarnation of the pushy, confident, *m'as-tu-vu* spirit of Barcelona.

The idea for the Universal Exposition was not his, though he quickly made it so. It came from a Galician operator, Eugenio Serrano de Casanova. Serrano de Casanova was a former soldier and a failed priest, who had fought with the Carlists and then, once their cause had collapsed, had gone to Paris and set up as a promoter of spas. He attached himself to the Spanish contingent at the 1876 Philadelphia Exposition and hooked up with an architect who designed some of the temporary structures for the 1884 Universal Exposition in Antwerp.

Left, Francesc de Paula Rius i Taulet; right, cartoon from L'Esquella de la Torratxa, *May 5, 1888*

His disadvantage was that he had no roots in Catalunya. (One would have thought that his Carlist past would have counted against him, too, but it apparently did not: a small instance of the way in which the good Catalanist burghers of Barcelona could forgive almost anything if it was in their interests to do so. In fact, he had the backing of a powerful Carlist business family in Olot, the Vayredas, who had many connections in the capital. Thus it came about that a mayor appointed by a progressive and freemason in Madrid, Práxedes Sagasta, the president of the council of ministers, found himself working with a Carlist.) Serrano de Casanova's trump card was that no Catalans had any experience in organizing industrial fairs. And he realized that, at a time when the European and American public had come to believe that a city's potency was to be measured by these extravagant potlatches, wads of money could be made from a fair that gave Catalans a chance to show themselves off to the world and prove that Barcelona was, indeed, a European city and not merely a Spanish one.

It was, by any reasonable standards, an absurdly unpropitious time to launch such a public-relations foofaraw in Barcelona—in the hangover from the *febre d'or*, with banks stricken or collapsed, credit short, industry enfeebled. But that, in the eyes of Serrano de Casanova and Rius i Taulet, was just why it should be done. Barcelona needed autohypnosis, a total-immersion course in civic boosterism. The city lacked self-esteem, and

Rius would give it some, even if it meant strapping the patient down. It would be good for foreign investment. It would also strengthen Barcelona's hand against Madrid. All eyes would be on her. She would become the Queen City of the Mediterranean.

In 1885 Serrano offered his plan to the Ajuntament: he would set up the fair, without a peseta of city money up front, in return for a cut of the gate and the *drets d'explotació*, or concessions. It would open in September 1887 and run for six months.

In 1886 an executive committee was formed, led by Rius i Taulet —a cross section of the city's industrialists and conservative politicians. It soon appeared that Serrano was not having much luck raising the money: he asked for an advance of half a million pesetas, saying that he was going to build an iron wonder of the world six hundred feet higher than the Eiffel Tower, which was rising in Paris. Shortly thereafter Serrano was ditched, and Rius i Taulet boarded a train for Madrid where, after much lobbying and many petitions, he marshaled enough political support to get state underwriting for the scheme, minus the tower. The mayor returned to Catalunya in triumph and announced the new opening date of the International Exposition. It would be in May 1888—eleven months away. And it would be held in the Citadel Park. Josep Fontseré, fearing the ruin of the work he had immersed himself in for the past fifteen years, protested and was fired. The designated *mestre d'obres* for the fair would be Elias Rogent.

An uproar ensued. Many respected Catalanists, led by Valentí Almirall, denounced the scheme as lunacy. "For anyone who knows the facts," thundered Almirall in the *Bulletin of the Catalan Center*, "it is as clear and obvious as the light of day that the Universal Exposition of Barcelona, in the form that it has been dreamed up by its backers, either will not be finished or else will get done in a way that will bring ridicule on Barcelona and on Catalunya in general, producing the complete ruin of our Municipality."

Yet the fact was that, despite the ridicule of half the city and the resistance of its journalists, Rius i Taulet was able to bully the exposition through. Conceived in the giddy atmosphere of the *febre d'or*, it had to be brought into existence during the slump. But a great deal of civic building and rebuilding had got under way before the banks started failing, and it, too, was part of the background to the exposition. It seemed as though half of the city was being remade for it. The 1888 Exposition was a preview of the frantic and even larger-scale last-minute ceremonial building that would precede the Olympic Games a century later.

The Columbus monument, under construction, 1882

The first symbol of this "new" Barcelona was the statue of Christopher Columbus, atop its enormous pillar in the Plaça del Portal de la Pau, where the Ramblas meets the waterfront. It is by no means the only major public monument to Columbus in the world: at last count (in 1991, on the eve of the Columbian half millennium, which, now that the term "discovery of" has been erased in favor of the more accurate "encounter with" the New World, is unlikely to add any more to the list) there were twenty-eight in the United States, ten in the Caribbean, two in Mexico, five in South America, three in France, seven in Italy, and nine in Spain—a grand total of sixty-four Columbuses, of which the one in Barcelona, measuring 187 feet from the ground to the Discoverer's (or Encounterer's) bronze pate, is far and away the biggest. The presence of Columbus—Colom, to give his Catalan name—requires some explanation today, but in 1882, the year Rius i Taulet commissioned the monument, it was self-evident. Columbus did have connec-

The top of the Columbus monument

tions with Barcelona: he recuperated from his first voyage there and was received by Ferdinand and Isabella, who bestowed on him the plangent title of Almirante del Mar Oceano—Admiral of the Ocean Sea. But that was not the point of the monument—not all of it, anyway. Late-nineteenth-century Catalans were convinced, as an article of patriotic faith, that Columbus was a Catalan himself. (He was in fact Genoese.) Not only that: he was the Catalan who discovered the New World from whose subsequent plunder by Castile all future Catalans, at least until the time of the *indianos*, were excluded. It has never been lost on Barcelona that Columbus, up there on his monument, slightly higher than Nelson Stylites in Trafalgar Square, is pointing out to sea with his back toward Castile. Because of the inconvenient configuration of the coast, he is pointing in the general direction of Libya, not America, but the *sea* is Catalan. In order to reinforce Columbus's incipient *catalanisme*, the designer (an engineer named Gaietà Buigas i Monravà) covered the plinth with an iconographic program, much of it as obscure as it was elaborate, of bas-reliefs and figures symbolizing the role played by other Catalans in the discovery of America—the Blanes family, for instance, or the priest Bernat de Bol, who went on the Discoverer's second voyage and became the first apostolic vicar of the West Indies. Despite its elaboration, the Columbus monument was built hastily and badly to the mayor's deadline, and within a century it was in real danger of collapse: the internal iron structure was rusting away. It has now been repaired within and restored without.

From the area of the Columbus monument, three major streets branch away. The first is the Ramblas, but the other two owe their existence—or at least their "urbanization"—to Rius i Taulet and the exposition. One, running exactly due west to Plaça d'Espanya, following the line of Pere III's Raval wall as far as the corner of Ronda de Sant Pere, is the Avinguda del Parallel. This mystifying name—the Parallel is not actually parallel to anything else in the city—is explained by the fact that it happens to run along the parallel 41°44′ north latitude. Whoever was naming streets for the Ajuntament had a moment of writer's block. The Parallel was meant to become a fine ceremonial avenue like the Diagonal or the Gran Via, but it has always refused to: it became, instead, the spine of Barcelona's sleazy-to-populist nightlife, whose temples are such music halls as El Molino.

The other street, which runs along the waterfront north–northeast to the Citadel Park, is the Passeig de Colom. It was widened (there was plenty of room, now that the seaward rampart of the *muralles* was razed), and its prolongation, the Avinguda del Marquès de l'Argentera, was driven through to the southeastern boundary of the park. And in 1882, amid great public curiosity, it became the first street in Barcelona to get electric light. (The houses of the rich waited another two decades for this novelty.) Edison's fairy also made possible the exposition's big bravura piece of crash-schedule building: the construction of the Hotel Internacional, at the juncture of Passeig de Colom and Avinguda de l'Argentera.

Barcelona, then as now, was short of visitors' rooms and had no hotels that even a fervent patriot could call first-class by the standards of Paris, London, or Rome. Domènech i Montaner was given the commission to build one at the beginning of 1888. And (incredibly, by current standards of delay and cost overrun) he succeeded, on time and within budget. The Hotel Internacional, an iron-frame structure clad in brick and terra-cotta, had five stories and 1,600 rooms; its street facades were 500 feet long; and three months after the ground for it was broken,

Lluís Domènech i Montaner's Hotel Internacional: the façade on Passeig de Colom and the inner courtyard

the first guests were checking in. This feat would be unimaginable today. It was achieved by working the nonunion builders like galley slaves— twelve-hour days were not unusual—and running round-the-clock construction shifts under electric lights. Even more, it was the result of Domènech's phenomenal powers of conceptual organization—of gearing the rhythm of building to the use of prefabricated modules. We shall never know how many corners were cut, or how well the Hotel Internacional would have stood the test of time, because it was razed at the end of the exposition. Satirical papers like *L'Esquella de la Torratxa* (*The Balcony Bell*) drew cartoons of it sinking in the waterfront sands, like a liner going down. Certainly, Domènech had not designed it as an ephemeral structure, and there was much regret from the press when it was torn down to redevelop its site in 1889. "Property is theft—" wrote one indignant journalist, in the well-worn words of Proudhon, "of the rights of beauty and the interests of art."

With the exceptions of Domènech's other contribution, the Café-Restaurant, and the Arc de Triomf by Josep Vilaseca that still stands in the Passeig de Lluís Companys, none of the other World's Fair buildings evoked the same sympathy and admiration, and they have all been demolished too. The main one, which lingered on in a partially ruinous state until 1929, was the Palace of Industry, which Rogent's team had designed as a semicircular structure, a thick half ring of iron and glass naves to which the world's wonders would be brought. But there were also the Gallery of Machines, the Palace of Sciences, the Pavilion of Agriculture, the Palace of Fine Arts—and a tangled scrub of private pavilions as well, all hustling their own products, from soda syphons to steam-driven threshing machines. Was a six-foot-high model of a castle made of *manchego* cheese to be classified as an agricultural exhibit or a work of art? The problem of figuring out which exhibits to put where became a nightmare, especially since few of the participating nations said in advance what they were sending; often the nature of the exhibits remained a mystery until they were uncrated in the staging warehouses. The cornucopia of late-nineteenth-century capitalism tipped up and disgorged into the park a plethora of objects so unutterably confusing that the organizers—never mind the public—could hardly make sense of them. This, perhaps as much as the mania for object overload, accounts for the impenetrable clutter recorded in the surviving photographs of the bays of the Palace of Industry. The rate of pilferage was high, but even the thieves, if one can go by Eduardo Mendoza's hilarious treatment of the World's Fair in *City of Marvels*, were dumbfounded by the volume. The two budding villains, Onofre Bouvila and his giant stooge Efrén

Castells, specialize in stealing timepieces—not from fob pockets, but by the crate:

> There were pocket watches, clocks for towers and public buildings, repeater watches, watches with second hands, navy chronometers, pendulums, astral watches, chronometers for astronomical and scientific observations, clepsydras, hour glasses, regulators, clocks that showed the solar and lunar cycles, electric clocks, clocks for gnomonic applications, equinoctial, polar, horizontal, azimuthal, right ascension, and declination clocks. . . . "Unless we get rid of these clocks," said the giant, "we'll be driven out of our minds by the tick-tocking and chiming."

The Palace of Science was a temple of nostalgia, a museum of failure, for here, it seemed, the prospectuses, drawings, and models for every cockamamy scheme that Catalan inventors and con men had dreamed up during the high years of the *febre d'or* got their last viewing before being consigned, forever, to the junk pile. "How the years have flown!" wrote Narcís Oller's close friend the journalist Joan Sardà in *La Vanguardia* that summer of 1888:

> That year '81 was the year of fatted calves for the promoters. It will not come back, O poets of public works, premature Rothschilds, would-be Lessepses, promoters of railroads, tramways, canals, highways, concessionaires of impossible mines, inventors of perpetual motion, squarers of the circle . . . helpless, gasping, shipwrecked schemes, clinging to flotsam in the hope that some boat will pick them up, shelter them and bring them to safety.

As for foreign participation in the World's Fair—the rest of the world, that is to say—it was fairly disappointing. Spain did not have the diplomatic clout to turn it into a spectacle to rival London in 1851, Philadelphia in 1876, or, more to the point, the World's Fair with which Paris was about to celebrate the centenary of the French Revolution. The great industrial nations did not put their cutting-edge technology on view; they were keeping that for Paris in 1889. Instead they sent what they thought Spaniards (a backward and romantic folk, in their opinion) would like. The one exception was railroad engineering, which was booming in Spain: here, manufacturers saw a market.

But for all that, the Universal Exposition of Barcelona did open on schedule, on May 20, 1888. Not all of it was ready: Vilaseca's triumphal arch was still shrouded in scaffolding, and Domènech i Montaner's Café-Restaurant unfinished—in fact it did not sell a glass of wine or a slice of *pà amb tomaquet* all year. But the regent, María Cristina of Hapsburg-Lorena, arrived with the future Alfonso XIII to find warships of eight nations anchored off Barcelona harbor; to the delight (one presumes) of the two-year-old monarch, they blasted off a twenty-one-gun salute as the duke of Edinburgh, representing Great Britain, informed his mother that "In honor of Your Majesty, the fleets of the world have expended their powder in salvos. Peace is saved in Europe!" The opening ceremony was held in the Palace of Fine Arts. Rius i Taulet gave a short speech about progress, brotherhood, and pacifism. Manuel Girona, the banker, gave a long one about the difficulties of fund-raising. On behalf of María Cristina, the president of her council of ministers, Práxedes Sagasta, declared the show open. A procession moved to the Palace of Industry, where the regent seemed most attracted by the Austrian display. Later she was proclaimed the queen of the Jocs Florals, whose consistory of writers inflicted on her a long, florid address, groveling but with a faint undertone of pugnacity, about her role as defender of their ancestral Catalan rights and customs. Manufacturers showered her with presents, of which the best was undoubtedly a pure-white corset made by the firm of one Don J. Cardona Baldrich, which bore on the bodice a row of the shields of Spain embroidered in gold, with two round medallions set in the appropriate places, one depicting (in watercolor) her late husband Alfonso XII, the other her son Alfonso XIII. On the hips were embroidered six white doves, each holding in its wee beak a flower symbolizing charity, purity of feeling, constancy, wisdom, virtue, and greatness of soul. After twenty days of opening hospitals, unveiling statues, and listening to stuffed shirts enlarging on how Catalunya was filled with *un ardiente e inteligente amor al progreso, una valerosa tendencia hacia el perfecciónamiento material e intelectual de la actividad humana en todas sus manifestaciónes*, the regent, consumed with regret, found it was time to leave for Madrid.

The crowds loved the switchback railway, the Magic Fountain, and the sideshows, but a sense of anticlimax presently settled over the Citadel Park. In the hot months, nothing much moved, though attendance picked up in September. Given the saturation of hype that surrounded everything in the Universal Exposition, one could say that its true emblem was not the Palace of Industry. It was a balloon, in whose wicker basket the very daring would make short ascents over the Citadel Park, tethered by a hawser. Along the top of the enclosure that led to this *globo cautivo* was a sign with three-foot letters:

DO YOU WANT SONS??? PEDRELL PLASTERS!!
They prevent sterility, miscarriages and kidney-pains.

The Universal Exposition of 1888 remained open for thirty-five weeks. A million and a half people visited it, at an average rate of about six thousand a day. Most of them were Spaniards; the show attracted a healthy influx of foreign visitors, but the predicted flood of them did not come. When its doors closed on December 9, 1888, the books showed a deficit of six million pesetas, which surprised nobody. Rius i Taulet, it seemed, had a simple stratagem when money looked tight: he asked Madrid for money, got none, and spent it anyway. A cartoon published early in 1889 in the satirical sheet *La Campana de Gràcia* summed up the general feeling: the stout mayor festooned in new medals and orders, capering on a table in front of a cake shaped like the Palace of Industry, surrounded by his committee of municipal bigwigs and architects, all raising goblets of champagne and framed in two curving spouts of foam from bottles marked "Moët Municipal" and "Champagne Taulet." *"Un any que no s'ha fet res sólit,"* ran the caption, *"y en cambi s'ha gastat molt líquit"*—"A year when nothing solid was done, but lots of liquidity was wasted."

So it took the city another ten years to pay off the debt, but that was in no way exceptional—though it happened just in time for the depression that walloped Barcelona after Spain lost its last colonies in 1898. The real problem was that the city fathers could not bear to confront the need for tax reforms: the whole city debt in the late 1880s had risen so fast that the expense of the Universal Exposition was merely a fraction of the whole, six million out of twenty-four million pesetas. The financial ineptitude of the men in city hall was such that they proposed defraying this with a tax on brothels, which, fortunately for the sexual equilibrium of the city, was not imposed. By 1897 the nominal value of the Ajuntament's funded debt amounted to 59,821,000 pesetas, and the blame for this could not be laid at Rius i Taulet's door.

In general, the effect of the exposition on labor in Barcelona had been good. It created jobs and helped to palliate a severe labor crisis the city had been suffering through 1887–88. Its construction had employed two thousand workers, and its running had involved about three thousand more. Only a small group of extreme socialists had denounced some

Cartoon of visitors to the 1888 Exposition sleeping on a billiard table for lack of hotel rooms, from L'Esquella de la Torratxa, *October 27, 1888*

of its aspects: that beggars had been rounded up and taken off the streets to make the city look good to foreigners, for instance, and that the haste of construction had caused a high level of industrial accidents. The more moderate unions were behind the exposition; indeed, at the end of 1887 they even agreed to call off a general strike whose main issue was the introduction of an eight-hour day so that the reconstruction of the Citadel Park could be finished on time and the honor of Barcelona upheld. "Yes, we are going back to work!" one of the union leaders had declared. "Barcelona won't go without its Universal Exposition through any fault of ours; but the banner of the eight-hour day, raised for the first time by the bricklayers of Barcelona . . . will never again be furled."

The main benefit of the fair was what Rius i Taulet hoped it would be. It put the city on the map of industrial Europe and pumped up the self-confidence of its citizens. It encouraged optimism. But the mayor himself did not live to see the results, which unfolded in the 1890s. His one reward was to join the swelling ranks of the new Barcelonese nobility: he was made, to his delight, marquis of his native village of Olèrdola. Recuperating from his exhaustion there in 1889, he was struck by an apoplectic fit, keeled over, and died. "One more corpse and one less spendthrift," snarled an editorial in *El Diluvio*, one of the opposition newspapers. But in the long term, his critics were proven wrong.

CHAPTER SEVEN

The Feast of Modernity

I

Barcelona, in the last dozen years of the nineteenth century, was a bourgeois paradise. An atmosphere of boom returned, somewhat chastened by the memory of the *febre d'or* but unmistakably optimistic and flushed with money. For the middle classes, however, this paradise was not complete: the 1890s also brought escalating strikes and anarchist bombs. The resentments of the have-nots were fed by the exuberance of the haves, and the Catalan rich were sluggish and myopic in responding to the long-stored anger of the poor. They believed in "firm measures." Barcelona was *their* city; *they* had built it; and it was the swollen head of Catalunya. From the *gent de bé*—the fine folk of the Eixample—down to the factory hands, it contained nearly half a million people by 1890; the next largest city in Catalunya was Reus, with a population of twenty-eight thousand.

The Barcelonese bourgeoisie felt that it had a monopoly on civic and patriotic virtue, and Catalanism was mainly a middle-class movement. Most working-class immigration to Barcelona had come from rural Catalunya, but now more immigrants streamed in from Aragon, Valencia, and the Balearic Islands. Still, most of these people spoke Catalan, not Spanish; probably 80 to 90 percent of Barcelona's working class was basically of Catalan origin. Such homogeneity would neither last nor come again—for after 1900 the lure of Barcelona's industries started pulling in poor workers and their families from Andalusia and Murcia in the south—but at the turn of the century, a "republican" left-wing proletarian Catalanism was still theoretically possible. In reality, it had no chance of prevailing against the conservative Catalanism of the bosses.

And the more conservative Catalanism became, the more powerful it was.

However, the wealthiest Catalans, the real financial elite of Barcelona, were not out to reject Madrid. They were Spanish; the market for their textiles and machinery, which Catalunya alone produced, lay in Spain and its colonies. Without Madrid's protection, Catalan industry would wither. These *gent de bé*—such families as Güell, Arnus, Girona, Bosch i Alsina, Comillas—knew which side of their bread the tomato was on. They controlled Catalunya's major mercantile society, the Foment del Treball Nacional, to which more than two thousand Catalan businesses belonged; they ran the Junta de Comerç. Their fortunes, and in their opinion the future of Spain, lay with the architect of the Restoration, Antonio Cánovas, whose entire policy as Prime Minister of the Spanish government was to lead his exhausted country by prudence and conservatism out of the bog of failed hopes, Carlist wars, cantonal risings, military *pronunciamientos*, and repressive liberalism in which it had floundered for decades. The last straw, for them as for him, was the failure of the national government formed by the Catalan Pi i Margall in 1873, with its federalist program that was going to abolish Madrid centralism, put an end to the hated *quinta* (compulsory military service), bring in an eight-hour day, and much more besides; this "Utopian" government crashed in flames in only two months.

Back, then, to Madrid! The wealthy Catalans spoke Spanish and larded their Catalan with *castellanismes* to show that they were people of the better sort—thus earning much satire in Barcelona, but they could ignore the scribblers. They prefaced each mention of Catalan autonomy with disclaimers about their higher Spanish patriotism. Through the corrupt networks of Spanish government, they cultivated Madrid for all they were worth. They knew Madrid centralism was in their interests.

They tended to be ardent royalists. They thirsted after titles, and Madrid was happy to oblige them: a title cost nothing to bestow and bought much gratitude. Alfonso XII and Alfonso XIII were shrewd about creating new Catalan titles. They seem never to have given any to Catalanists, only to those conservative burghers—industrialists like Güell or newspaper proprietors like Antoni Brusi, owner of the strongly monarchist *El Diario de Barcelona*—whose support of the throne and Cánovas's government was unwavering. Thus a powerful nucleus of anti-Catalanist, procentralist opinion formed at the top of Barcelona's hierarchy, where it interlaced with that of the Church. Between 1880 and the early 1900s, more *noblesse* was created over the dining tables of the

Hotel Continental (the restaurant most favored by Catalan industrialists and politicians) than had been seen on the field of war since Wilfred the Hairy's time: Godo, Sert, Güell, Cabanes, Masnou, and dozens of others. The ancient battle cry of the counts of Barcelona as they drew their swords and charged—*"Desperta ferro!"* ("Iron, awake!")—came down to the rustle of a checkbook. One such new noble, Pere Grau Maristany, became the count of Lavern and soon afterward ran into another *gent de bé* named Forgas, newly ennobled as a viscount, in the Continental's dining room. Forgas looked pale. What was the matter? Maristany inquired. "To tell the truth, I'm feeling a bit off color," said Forgas. "Don't worry," said Maristany, "it was the same for me. It's the change of blood."

The real strength of conservative Catalanism lay elsewhere: among the ranks of the professional classes and across the wide stratum of smaller businessmen and larger shopkeepers. Doctors, architects, engineers, and especially lawyers formed the spearhead of the movement. Many of them came from outside Barcelona; they were the sons (typically, the *fadristerns*, or second sons) of well-off farmers who migrated to the city to take their degrees and then stayed on to practice. The architect Puig i Cadafalch, for instance, was raised in the Maresme; Enric Prat de la Riba, known as the *seny ordenador* (shaping intelligence) of Catalanist politics up to his premature death in 1917, was a lawyer from Castell-terçol; Francesc Cambó, the lawyer and financier who succeeded him as head of the Lliga Regionalista, hailed from Verges. Being of provincial origins, such men had absorbed the conservative, anti-Madrid values of deep Catalunya. One of the few exceptions was the architect Domènech i Montaner, who was born in Barcelona—but he had aesthetic as well as political reasons for holding strong Catalan convictions.

The charter of conservative Catalanism was drawn up in the spring of 1892, when delegates from the Unió Catalanista, under Domènech i Montaner's presidency, assembled in the provincial city of Manresa to draft a regional Catalan constitution. This document was called the Bases de Manresa. Catalunya alone, it announced, should manage its internal government as a state; it would take care of its own "organic laws," whether civil, penal, or mercantile (Article 6a); only Catalans could pursue public careers in Catalunya (Article 4a); all "conservation of public order and internal security" would be in the hands of a force responsible only to the Catalan regional government (Article 13a); public education must be geared to "the needs and character of the civilization of Catalunya" (Article 16a); and so on. Madrid did not grant any of this, of course—but the Bases became the political platform for the Lliga Re-

Enric Prat de la Riba

gionalista, the conservative Catalanist party led by Prat de la Riba, which won four seats out of seven from Barcelona in the national elections of May 1901, thus marking the emergence of Catalanism as a force in national Spanish politics.

Enric Prat de la Riba i Sarrà (1870–1917) was a remarkably astute politician. The Good Families of Barcelona accepted him as their spokesman because, more than anyone else in the political arena, his ideas gave ideological form to their desires and beliefs. He and Torras i Bagès made formidable allies. For Prat de la Riba, a right-wing Catholic, the necessary model of social organization was patriarchal—the *casa pairal*. Industry, he said, was "an immense family," in which boss and worker were bound by the same strands of reciprocal "duty and love" that had united Catalunya in the days of its medieval glory, their conscience kept by the Church. The industrial "house" was the rural "house" written large and mechanized. In an influential work called *The Law of Industry* (1893), Prat argued that its control must pass down the line from eldest son to eldest son, never going into the hands of the workers: "The heir, continuation of the personality of the father and of the unit of the family, is the patron par excellence—who maintains the House, saving it from that dissolution which is . . . synonymous with death."

The expression of the industrial family would be the *colonia industrial*, the self-contained industrial colony or mill town. It would look back to the medieval guilds and feudal hamlets of old Catalunya. The boss would take care of his workers' housing, food, education, medical and spiritual needs; in return, he would get obedience, as the counts of Catalunya had received fealty from their vassals. Prat de la Riba made no bones about the boss's paternal rights. He could expect

> to forbid in his *casa* anything other than certain fixed practices and customs, and to expel from the house those who deviate from them. He can prohibit the entrance of persons and things—newspapers, for instance—that do not agree with him. . . . On entering the industrial family, workers voluntarily accept this regime. If they tire of it, they can leave.

Nothing would be left to chance in the *colonia industrial*. Get them out of the corrupting city, and the workers would become as docile and productive as bees.

Several industrialists tried this experiment. The best known of the *colonias*—because Antoni Gaudí designed its unfinished church—was a cloth factory started by Eusebi Güell at Santa Coloma del Cervelló, one of his estates south of Barcelona. One of Güell's gestures of paternalism entered the industrial folklore of Barcelona. Child labor was still the norm in Catalan industry, and Güell was not going to do without it. In 1905 a boy fell into one of the vats of boiling dye and was hideously scalded. Large skin grafts were needed. Güell ordered his two sons Claudio and Santiago to give their skin. Claudio, the *hereu*, submitted to the surgeons first; then twenty volunteers from among the workers; and last, Santiago. For this self-sacrifice the Güell boys were given titles. The twenty workmen were not.

In religion, the upper-middle class tended to extremes of moral unction, which they mistook for a social salve. They imagined, quite wrongly, that the growing unrest in their factories might be quelled by a form of Catholic syndicalism—trade unions guided by the Church and run in accordance with the precepts of the 1891 papal encyclical on workers' rights, *Rerum Novarum*. This idea was eagerly promoted by priests all over Europe and especially in France, but in Barcelona, as we shall presently see, it had no chance against anarchist ideas.

Its main Catalan spokesman was a Jesuit, Antoni Vincent, whose backing came from the second marquis of Comillas, Claudi López Bru. Comillas's sire had died in 1883, passing on the title and the industrial, shipping, railway, and banking empire to his thirty-year-old *hereu*, who now proceeded to finance a series of Catholic Workers' Circles, hoping to defuse the class struggle by re-creating the conditions of the medieval workers' guilds. Since it was industry that killed the guild system, and most workers were anticlerical anyway, the project failed. Nevertheless, Comillas and Father Vincent pressed on. They organized events to win workers over—a pilgrimage to Rome in 1894 (by train: Comillas owned a large stake in the Spanish railroad system) and a series of "social weeks" given over to processions and pious discussion. Vincent had a degree of success among peasants, the most conservative part of the Catalan work force. But in Barcelona he had none, and by 1904 the Church's failure to win converts to "social Catholicism" was so complete that only 4 percent of Catalan workers had joined the Catholic syndicates. Most of the rest continued, stubbornly and with every reason, to treat the Church as their class enemy.

Thus the Catholic-worker movement fizzled out, and by the turn of the century its aristocratic patrons went back to more trivial forms of moral improvement. Comillas struck a blow for worker morality by keeping "questionable" publications out of the bookstalls of Spanish railway stations; he also managed to have a sexy dancer called La Bella Chiquita banned in Madrid. But apart from such exercises in sanctimony, he was the most powerful layman in Catalunya in the matter of ecclesiastical preferment. So strong were the links between Church and business that the marquis was always consulted when a new bishop was to be appointed, and his candidate always got the miter. Thus Torras i Bagès, Comillas's candidate, became bishop of Vic in 1899. Comillas's abiding dream was to create a new form of canonical feudalism in Spain. His efforts were mercilessly guyed by the left-wing press, which once cartooned him on his Cuban sugar plantations, leading a line of black slaves festooned in rosaries and scapulars instead of chains.

Ostentatious piety was a social requirement among the rich. A private chapel in one's town house was always a good sign. Gaudí designed one for the Casa Batlló on Passeig de Gràcia and another in the gloomy salon of the palace on Carrer Nou de la Rambla that he built, between 1885 and 1890, for Eusebi Güell. Most of these shrines were destroyed by anticlericals in 1936, but one has been preserved in the Museum of Modern Art of Barcelona: an astoundingly rich piece of virtuoso craftsmanship in carved and inlaid wood, copper, enamel, iron, and stained glass by Joan Busquets i Jané (1874–1949) for the Casa Cerdoya on Passeig de Gràcia.

The wives prayed; they spent long hours with the visiting priest; they immersed themselves in Good Works. Their idea of charity was like their husbands' and, as Raymond Carr put it, "morbidly puritanical

Joan Busquets' oratory from Casa Cendoya, Barcelona

and, like many contemporary religious movements . . . much concerned with fallen women." It also acquired a pseudofeminist slant from an upper-class Catalan bluestocking named Dolors Monserdà de Macià, who in 1910 tried to organize women pieceworkers—who worked at home without even the minimal protection afforded by the communal workplace of the factory—into a "syndicate of the needle." "The movement called 'feminist,' " she explained, "is a humanitarian act for the rich woman and an urgent need for the woman of the people." This genteel version had nothing to do, of course, with the struggle for rights and votes that northern European feminism, especially in England, had already been waging for several decades.

Relations between piety and living culture were rarely benign, and in literature they could be disastrous. Some artists and architects, such as Antoni Gaudí and the sculptor Josep Llimona, continued to believe that the Church could inspire creation, and they formed a group called the Artistic Circle of Saint Luke to propagate this idea. But literature was less apt to endure (or to receive) Church patronage in an age of sanctimony. In the 1890s Catalunya had one major religious poet, Jacint Verdaguer, and the Church destroyed him—with help from the marquis of Comillas.

Since the appearance of *L'Atlàntida* in 1878 and *Canigó* in 1885—his second epic, this time on the legendary origins of Catalunya—Verdaguer had almost become part of the Comillas family, its resident chaplain and chief cultural trophy. He lived in Palau Moja, the Comillas palace on the Ramblas, and moved in high society. Having dedicated *L'Atlàntida* to the first marquis of Comillas, he continued to enjoy the protection of Claudi López Bru, the second marquis, who kept him on as almoner in Palau Moja and paid for some overseas travel—to Germany, France, and Russia in 1884 and to the Holy Land in 1886. In that year he was also crowned and blessed by the bishop of Vic, Morgades by name, as the national poet of Catalunya. This ceremony took place in the ancient abbey of Ripoll, and it seems to have induced an acute slippage of self-confidence in Verdaguer. He was a humble man whose peasant origins meant a great deal to him; they kept him tethered to the ground of his imagination, and all the pomp and ceremony was now fraying the cord. In the summer of 1886 Verdaguer slid into a severe depression. "I have seen my forty years pass one by one," he wrote to a friend, "and I am ashamed of them all."

Verdaguer's malaise did not pass; as a priest he became increasingly convinced that, as a poet, he had not served God with enough humility. He began to show embarrassing signs of zeal. As almoner, he was expected to give alms to the poor on Comillas's behalf; now his handouts of the marquis's money became so large and frequent that long lines of the poor and ragged, flocking in from the slums of the Barri Xinó, were always waiting at the back door of Palau Moja. Then Verdaguer developed an obsession with exorcism. Toward 1889 he fell under the influence of a Paulist priest who haunted the Barri Gòtic, Joaquim Pinyol. This charismatic quack became his confessor and spiritual adviser. He convinced the poet that the street people of lower Barcelona were infested with demons, and that it was their combined mission to exorcise them. Before long Verdaguer was spending every moment he could find reciting the orders of exorcism over writhing epileptics and mumbling crones, with Pinyol showing him the needles and pieces of glass they had vomited up. Then Pinyol was joined by a family of morbid *illuminats* called Duran, whose daughter, Deseada, appears to have convinced poor Verdaguer that the Virgin Mary's voice spoke through her.

Comillas, seeing his poet turn from the Catalan Tennyson into an imp-hunting obsessive with writer's block and an unassuageable *crise de*

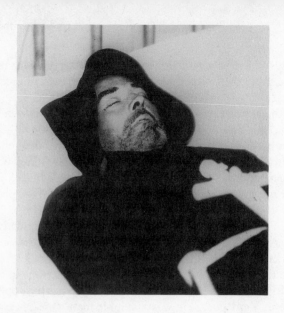

Jacint Verdaguer on his deathbed

---

nerfs, consulted the higher clergy. A succession of prelates and bishops, headed by Torras i Bagès, tried to talk sense into Verdaguer, with little result. At last, in 1893, Bishop Morgades ordered him to leave Barcelona for a rest cure in Vic. Verdaguer stayed there two years, but then in 1895 he vanished back to Barcelona and his demons, taking refuge in the Durans' house. In 1896 he sold them the rights on his entire literary estate for the derisory sum of two thousand pesetas. Then came the heaviest possible blow: Morgades suspended his priesthood, forbidding him to celebrate mass. Verdaguer, at the end of his tether, appealed to the public with a series of newspaper articles entitled "In My Own Defense." He had only been struggling to help the poor, he argued; everything he had done was dictated by Christian charity. He had been spied on, whispered about, persecuted, and abused by Comillas and the higher clergy—"Throughout my long and dreadful shipwreck, they put guards around me to keep the lifeboats far away." Comillas said he was deluded, but "The Marquis' gold has deluded many people about my case." Verdaguer's self-defense was by turns heartrending and sarcastic; excited discussion of it filled the cafés. Thus a priest who was also the doyen of Catalan poetry committed the unheard-of breach of publicly attacking his superiors.

The scandal split Barcelona in two and was soon politicized. Each side had its own Verdaguer: the left, a great national poet persecuted

by the establishment, a man who sacrificed his own precarious security
to care for the poor; the right, a former genius who had destroyed his
gifts, despite the benign interventions of patrons and hierarchy. From
now on, there would be no possibility of a truce between literary *modernisme* and the Church in Barcelona. Meanwhile, in exhaustion, Verdaguer recanted. He only wanted to retreat from the dreadful limelight
and to say mass. "They have shut me in a circle of iron," he told another
writer, Apelles Mestres, "and I keep turning and turning, with no way
out." In 1898 he was allowed to celebrate mass again, in the church of
Betlem in the Raval, across from Palau Moja. "Now you see," he said
to a friend. "So much work, hardship, suffering—just to get from one
side of the Ramblas to the other." He died in 1902, at the age of fifty-
seven, having written nothing for years; and ten thousand sympathizers
and admirers followed his coffin to the grave.

II

Such deep tremors in the culture of Barcelona were not, however, often
felt in the well-upholstered purlieus of the Eixample, among its risen
middle-class families. There, all social effort was dedicated to the cult
of tranquillity, not modernist anxiety. The head of the household, whom
we may call Senyor Puig, ruled the domestic roost absolutely. Even in
urban Barcelona, reverent nostalgia for the ways of the *casa pairal* remained strong, and the *pare*'s word was heavy, backed up by the injunctions of Saint Paul and the Church. The home was the metaphor
and seat of Catalan conservatism, an island deeply resistant to change.
Its running was of course delegated to the wife in her sacred function
as mother, nurse, and God's policewoman, moving within cultural con-
fines that approached the condition of purdah, with her horizons limited
to the home, the children, the Church, and the little theater of formal
society. Only proletarian women, by definition, worked. Women had
one natural destiny: marriage and the production of heirs. Most marriages
within the *gent de bé* were arranged; romantic love was more for novels
than for real life, divorce impossible, and premarital virginity jealously
guarded. Girls were married off early, to men twice their age or more.
As in China, love could grow later—or not, as the case might be. Once
a woman was past thirty she was, to all intents, unmarriageable. To
suitors Papa became a whiskered Cerberus, fiercely alert to the menace
of the rake and the fortune hunter. Senyor Puig's ideal was to move his
pubilla, that pure and defenseless vessel of a third of his fortune, from

Baroness Quadras and her daughter in the salon of Casa Vidal-Quadras

---

the parental household to the matrimonial one with as little delay as possible. Until that happened she was protected under glass. In 1907, when a magazine called *L'Illustració Català* ran a photograph of Baron Quadras's wife and daughter posed in the main salón of their new house on the Diagonal designed by Puig i Cadafalch, the caption dilated without the slightest irony upon "the charming Maria de Quadras, a living and palpitating flower, preserved among so many other flowers both living and petrified, next to her amiable mother the Baroness, illuminating with smiles all the magnificence of this place where Catalan art vibrates in all its forms."

Nevertheless there were signs of change, particularly in the status of women—slow, small, probably easy to overrate, but real. The Exposition of 1888 absorbed a lot of female labor and helped to defuse the moral odium that bourgeois society attached to working women (though it certainly did nothing for their pay, which remained far below that of men). At least, the more liberal moralists pointed out, a woman earning her own money behind a draper's counter was less likely to resort to prostitution. Their better-off sisters also looked outward—a little. They interested themselves in charitable work, which made them feel in touch with the real world, even though their efforts did little to improve its conditions. They went to concerts. Their mothers may have been self-effacing and submissive, content to spend their lives indoors with children and servants, and to dress up in crinolines and farthingales, like constricted effigies or pieces of furniture, when they were taken out to formal balls and to the opera. But Senyora Puig was a little more mobile. She began to buy ready-to-wear clothes of a clearer line; her three-piece city costume (jacket, blouse, and skirt), however cumbersome it may look to a modern eye, was simpler than the handmade affairs of an earlier generation. It was, moreover, machine cut and could be purchased in a shop. Thus, rather timidly and always in carriages, the middle-class ladies of the Eixample began to enter the throng of boulevard life along Passeig de Gràcia. They did not sit in cafés, but they did shop. To protect themselves from too brusque a contact with the outside environment, they wrapped up heavily. Even in summer, recalled Rafael Puget, whose memories of the city in the 1890s were transcribed by Josep Pla in *Un Senyor de Barcelona*, "they looked like perambulating sentry-boxes."

But the home was all consuming. Its running depended on a troupe of overworked and underpaid servants, whose management absorbed much of Senyora Puig's time. The rest was taken up by children (who, thanks to the drains of the Eixample, were always succumbing to scarlet fever and other juvenile afflictions) and by social obligations. This produced an imposing flow of traffic. The bourgeois home was not considered to be the intimate refuge it is today. It was far more public. There were no telephones, and so people visited more. But it was not only one's equals who came calling. So did the children's tutor (the *gent de bé* liked to educate the young at home, and the boarding school was not one of the English institutions the Spanish admired—they associated them with orphanages); the dancing master and the teachers of singing, piano, and sketching; the elocutionist (for one had to learn proper Castilian); the tailor for Papa and his older sons, the modiste for Mama and her daughters, the doctor, the lawyer, the notary; and eventually, since people died at home and the formal rites of death and mourning were always conducted there, the undertaker. The jeweler—a representative from one of the great Barcelonese designers of the time, such as Lluís Masriera—would arrive with his morocco bag, containing a velvet roll of exquisite brooches, pendants, and rings in which the whiplash lines of Art Nouveau and the enamel techniques of Limoges were married to the exacting traditional craftsmanship of Catalan gold work, the larger pieces cunningly hinged and articulated to conform to the wearer's skin.

Today, the best way to sense the texture of this way of life is to visit the Museu Sentimental of the Museu Frederic Marés, housed in a medieval palace next to the Cathedral. Frederic Marés i Deulovol, born toward the end of the nineteenth century, was the most singular collector that Barcelona—or possibly Spain, for that matter—ever produced. A sculptor who taught for decades at the Barcelona Academy, and never rich, he managed to accumulate an immense collection of Spanish religious sculpture from the twelfth to the eighteenth centuries. But he was also obsessed by junk, or what seemed junk to everyone else—the flotsam that filled the flea markets of Catalunya after *modernisme* went out of style. He wanted everything his parents' and grandparents' generations had used. He pursued this unfulfillable desire, the dream of total possession, for sixty years. The result, occupying sixteen rooms on the top floor of the palace, is a Don Giovanni's catalog of the past, a paean to repetition. Thousands of tiny conquests amount to a victory over Lost Time: 1,295 books of cigarette paper; 108 snuffboxes; 73 floral bouquets made of tiny seashells under glass cloches; 379 pipes and cigar holders in clay, bone, meerschaum, amber, briar, and porcelain; innumerable canes and pocket watches; and 158 pairs of opera glasses ranging from pearl-sheathed binoculars to the little telescopes known as *impertinents*. The museum catalog allows itself to be carried away on its warm current of recollection. "In this room," one reads, approaching Sala XXXV (Ladies' Apparel),

> an evocative feminine perfume, intensely romantic, surprises the visitor and prepares him for the enjoyment of the great and refined intimacy of the past. Curious and interesting collections of the most diverse pieces of women's ornament: fans, umbrellas, diadems, gloves, scissors, candle-snuffers, jewels, earrings, buckles, clasps, needle-cases, teething-rings, chromos, purses, card-cases—in short, a whole world of romantic suggestions, of feminine subtleties and grace-notes, of innocent idylls and sometimes dark dramas of passion, love and jealousy.

The original owners' sources of entertainment were, by modern standards, meager; or do they only seem so to us because we cannot imagine a life in which amusement could not be produced at the press of a button? No television, radio, cinema: instead, the decorous sound of the piano, as Senyora Puig and her daughter tinkled out a four-handed piece for Papa. Parcheesi was played, and whist. Increasingly, middle-class women read; mainly sentimental novels, but the menu widened a

Lluís Masriera's pendant

little as the Church began (slightly) to relax its all-encompassing injunctions against anything foreign or, especially, French. As for open-air sports, wives did not play them, though some rode a little and even accompanied their husbands to shoots on properties like Eusebi Güell's at Garraf, south of Barcelona. Athletics consorted badly with the dignity of women, and even worse with the imposing waistlines of their husbands. Life was essentially sedentary, ruminant, and processional. The only opportunity to work up a sweat was in bed or at one of the enormous formal balls that were the seasonal delight of the bourgeoisie. Nor were spectator sports popular in turn-of-the-century Barcelona. Football clubs had only just begun to come into existence, and the bullfight lacked the mystique and ritual popularity it enjoyed in the rest of Spain. The lower classes had their bars and cabarets and dance halls, a seamy and raucous nightlife concentrated in the Barri Xinó and along the demotic spine of the Parallel. Their betters had the café, the club, the promenade, and better brothels.

Senyor Puig spent most of his daylight hours away from home, in the office or in the handsome establishments that had sprouted everywhere in the Eixample, along Passeig de Gràcia and down the Ramblas, that catered to the boulevardier with time on his hands. The life of the cafés moved Josep Pla to ecstasies of recollection.

> A cup of coffee cost twenty-five *centims*. The cafés were grand, com-modious, with large mirrors and ample banquettes upholstered in red plush, on which one lounged at ease. . . . The Café Novetats, run by a Mr Elias, was a palace of dry noises; the domino tiles on the marble tables made their clean sounds; the click of billiard balls was dry, and the coffee-spoons rang like crystal. The smoke of Carunchos, of Murias, of Havana pipe-tobacco, was bluish, deliciously perfumed and of a pale elegance. Six lumps of sugar came with the coffee. The rum and the *canya* were authentic and exquisite. . . . The cafés were places of relaxation, stock exchanges and information centers . . . [their] decline signified the twilight of an entire civilization.

In the evening Senyor Puig would imitate his foreign ideal, the *milord Angles*, and make for his club. The best one was the Circol del Liceu, attached to the opera house on the Ramblas. One wall of its foyer was filled with stained-glass renderings of scenes from Wagner's *Ring*. It had a whole salon decorated with paintings by Barcelona's star "impression-ist," Ramón Casas i Carbó. They showed scenes of upper Barcelonese life, including one of a De Dion–Panhard driven straight at you by one of Casas's fresh Gibson girls; when a servant pulled a switch, the painted car's headlights lighted up. The elevator was all wood swirls and mar-quetry, with a boatlike ceiling and mirror-mosaic pendentives. On the ground floor was a luxurious mirador through whose picture window, as through the glass of an aquarium, one could observe the passing parade on the Ramblas. Upstairs were the dining rooms and a series of salons and smoking rooms furnished in the heavy, mock-ecclesiastical Neo-Gothic with overtones of Byzantium and Cairo favored by Catalan burghers. Above those were billiard rooms, whose tables had no pockets (one scored entirely from cannons, unlike the English game), and gaming rooms, where baccarat and *trente-et-quarante* were played far into the night. The Circol, too, was paradise from lunchtime on, a place where the political lion lay down with the lamb. At the Liceu in 1894, Puget remembered,

> the hours slipped by imperceptibly. Life in the city was placid and tranquil. All one's headaches were bearable. All was solid. Everyone knew everyone else. [Here was] Collaso, the mayor, dozing; in the next room, the President of the Diputació snoozed beatifically, in a black

shiny alpaca suit. Nearby, Emili Junoy, very much a radical, was also nodding off with a cigar in his mouth. The waiters tiptoed by. An agreeable drowsiness reigned. At the far end of the corridor one saw the light from the Ramblas, green and soft, tremulous, under the branches of the plane-trees.

Such was the sleep that would be brusquely disturbed by anarchist bombs.

In the club, at home, or on the street, the clothing style for middle-class men in Barcelona was firmly fixed, and it scarcely differed at all from that of Turin, Berlin, or Paris. A suit should be *molt Anglès* in cut, and Catalan tailors vied to imitate Savile Row. The basic units of male day dress were the *levita*, or "frock coat," the morning coat, and the less formal *americana*, origin of the modern two-piece suit. To go out at night, one donned the invariable *frac*: under no circumstances was *el smoking*, the dark tuxedo jacket newly fashionable for public wear in the United States, to be worn anywhere but at home.

Jackets had tiny lapels and buttoned up to a point just below the sternum. Trousers were tight and tubular; the trouser crease lay far in the future. Soft shirts were worn during the day, but with celluloid collars, whose edge fretted the neck, secured at the front with a stud that, Rafael Puget remembered, left a tiny long-lasting spot of rust or verdigris on one's Adam's apple. The favored cravat was green, with an enormous knot, ancestor of the Windsor, tied over a gutta-percha form to give it bulk. Evening shirts, starched rigid and pressed smooth by the fierce irons of laundresses, encased the masculine chest like white body armor. The favorite day hat was a hard derby with a narrow brim, and at night there was the topper. Shoes tended to be long, narrow, and of patent leather.

In sharp contrast to this sartorial constriction, the bourgeois head carried great masses of hair, signifying vitality, masculine energy, leonine vim. On some unconscious level the Catalans had never forgotten that their political identity had been created by Wilfred the Hairy. "*Donde hay pel hay alegria*," ran the proverb: "Where there is hair, there is happiness." Thus, at the hour of promenades, the Ramblas seemed infested by tightly buttoned corsairs and Old Testament patriarchs.

The mustache followed the same law of copiousness. Every man had one, often so large as to seem false. The mustache took three basic forms. If it grew horizontally, it was encouraged to puff out in volutes, a soufflé of hair. If the mustache had an upright habit of growth, it would be combed and twiddled into two vertical spikes, sculpted with wax—a stumpier version of the royal antennae sported by Felipe IV, which would be revived, after 1920, by Salvador Dalí. But if the hairs on one's upper lip were flaccid or aimless, the result was simply a drooping *bigoti*, which, if grown long enough, suggested melancholy and soulfulness—a misleading impression if its owner was actually a banker or an engineer, as he often turned out to be. Ildefons Cerdà, for instance, had a mustache of this kind.

The most famous mustache in nineteenth-century Barcelona belonged to the king of the local gypsies, who was known simply as En Bigotis—Mr. Mustaches. He was a tall, robust man, whose whiskers (his fans claimed) brushed against both walls of certain alleys in the Old City when he walked down them. The Carrer de Sant Pau, which runs from the Parallel (the quarter favored by gypsies) into the Ramblas at the Liceu, was said to mark their width, but this seems hardly possible, since the street in question is at least six yards wide.

Next in order of priority, for facial hair, was the beard. The popular model was French, Napoleon III's, which was copied by Catalan generals and descended from the military to the drawing rooms of the Eixample. Dandies paid close attention to the *mosca*, the little tuft of hair beneath the lower lip. The founding fathers of Catalan anarchism preferred the frank and manly facial bush. But the size of one's beard proved nothing about one's ideology. Some of the worst Gradgrinds in Catalan industry looked like Father Christmas. Politicians were apt to be more moderate. For public display, conservative Catalanists favored a beard type known as the *madrilenya*, square and parted in the middle. The ideal *madrilenya* had exactly the same number of hairs on each side of the parting. And finally there was *la patilla*—"sideburns," expanding into full-fledged muttonchop whiskers. The most famous and incessantly caricatured *patilla* in Barcelona belonged to its mayor, Rius i Taulet, whose whiskers stood straight out from his cheeks in the frontal plane of his face, thus giving it the air, someone unkindly remarked, of a whole *bacallà*, a split and salted cod.

The beards and whiskers are gone, though their likenesses are preserved in magazine illustrations, in photos, in bronze, and in stone, like Rius i Taulet's *patilles* on his monument facing the gates of the Citadel Park, or those of the philanthropic Pau Gil i Serra on his herm in front of the immense hospital for whose initial construction he paid. And yet their spirit of copiousness, symbolic precision, and stylistic punch has lived on, in a magnified form, in the buildings that were commissioned, designed, and engineered by their growers.

III

Modernisme—"modernism"—was the word Catalans used to denote the architectural style, and more broadly the whole literary, musical, and visual-arts culture, of the period 1890–1910. It implied an opening to Europe. The literary language of Catalan *modernisme* is stuffed with French phrases and French feelings. If *enyoranca*, longing for the homeland or childhood, was the key word of the Renaixença, then *somni*, "dream," was that of the new generation. The secret garden, the nodding lily, the gray hush of twilight, the floating swan, the pale hand of the mysterious maiden: these were the stage properties. The mood of persistent melancholy was condensed in Joan Alcover's "La Reliquia" ("The Relic"):

> *Trenta anys de ma vida volaren de pressa,*
> *i encara no manca*
> *penjat a la branca*
> *un tros de corda de l'engronsadora*
> *com trista penyora,*
> *despulla podrida d'un mon esbucat . . .*
> *Faune mutilat,*
> *brollador eixut,*
> *jardí desolat*
> *de ma joventut.*

Thirty years of my life have flown by
   and still there is left
   hanging from the branch
a piece of cord from my cradle
   like a sad pledge,
a decayed remnant of a vanished world . . .
   Mutilated faun,
   dry fountain,
   deserted garden
   of my youth.

The *modernistes* reacted against what seemed to them the moribund literature of national identity summed up in the Jocs Florals, the poetry of their bourgeois fathers (though the exception, too great to be cast off, was "Mossen Cinto"—Jacint Verdaguer). They focused not on the idea of a hereditary self, but on the self that is created daily out of anxiety and feeling and has nothing to do with the all-encumbering Catalan virtue of *seny*. They disparaged realism: Zola and Flaubert were out and so were their own realist writers of the Restoration years, such as Narcís Oller. To be a *modernista* in Barcelona was to be aware of Huysmans, Verhaeren, D'Annunzio, Hauptmann, and Wilde, and of the currents —poorly understood as yet—of idealism and symbolism in Paris, especially the poetry of Stephane Mallarmé. (Paul Verlaine, by contrast, was not much admired in Barcelona.) The Belgian playwright Maurice Maeterlinck was an idol, and so was Henrik Ibsen. Nietzsche's vitalism became a literary model: Joan Maragall, Barcelona's outstanding poet of the period, was also its spokesman for German literature, translating *Thus Spake Zarathustra* along with Goethe's *Roman Elegies* and fragments of *Faust* for the Catalan literary press. *Modernisme* liked the American transcendentalists, especially Ralph Waldo Emerson; poems by Walt Whitman were translated into Catalan during the 1890s. Above all, it adored Wagner.

Modernisme observed the butterfly's wing or the cosmic void, and not much in between. It could be insufferably pretentious about its scope and as snobbishly detached from real life as only rentiers can be. One example will do for all. In 1893 the critic Ramón Casellas penned a lengthy paean to the first play by Maeterlinck ever produced in Catalan, *La Intrusa* (*The Intruder*). The challenge of the modernist, the "decadent," he wrote, was

> to pluck from human life not direct and limited spectacles, not banal vernacular phrases . . . but gleaming, wild, paroxysmic, hallucinatory visions; to translate eternal verities into deranged paradox; to live by the abnormal and the unheard; to tally the horrors of reason, leaning on the very edge of the abyss. . . . Such is the formula of this nebulous and shining art, chaotic and radiant, prosaic and sublime, sensuous and mystical, refined and barbaric, modern and mediaeval . . .

A little of this goes a long way, and Barcelona produced a lot of it. One cannot avoid the feeling that the claims made for *modernisme* by its advocates were more thrilling than the works themselves and promised more than they could possibly deliver. It is, in any case, misleading to imagine that literary *modernisme* had a fixed program or a theoretical core. It wanted to be wistful, sensitive, and up-to-date and to shock the bourgeoisie; but *modernisme* was really a blanket word rather than a stylistic definition.

In architecture it gets especially confusing to the foreigner, because the Catalans' "modernism" bears little relation to any sense of the word elsewhere. For anyone from England, France, or the United States, modernism in art is wider reaching; it means practically anything between Georges Seurat and Andy Warhol, including all the constituent movements you can think of—Fauvism, Cubism, Surrealism, the Bauhaus, and so on through to Abstract Expressionism and Pop Art. In Catalunya, however, *modernisme* is the local branch of an international movement that was known in France and England as Art Nouveau; in Italy, as *lo stile Liberty*, after the English furniture store; in Austria as Secessionism, and in Germany as *Jugendstil*, "the style of youth." And though it certainly was used of every art, the special strength and glory of Catalan *modernisme* was architecture and its associated handcrafts: ceramics, iron forging, stained glass, fine woodwork, and the virtuoso use of brick. In these it was not excelled. Catalunya had symbolist poets, too, but not of genius and originality comparable to Mallarmé, Verlaine, or Rimbaud. It had composers, but no Debussy or Wagner; and among its turn-of-the-century painters there was no one who could cast more than a pale shadow of the sublime French fire of the nineteenth century. (The obvious exception was Picasso, but he was very young when he was in Barcelona, and in any case he was not a Catalan—just passing through.)

But architecture told a different story. By 1900 writers and critics were abandoning the word *modernisme*, because it had been so completely taken over by architecture and decorative arts and so internalized by their bourgeois patrons. Barcelona had at least two architects of genius, Antoni Gaudí and Lluís Domènech i Montaner, and a third who was close to it, Josep Puig i Cadafalch. There were several more of exuberant talent, such as Josep Marià Jujol, Josep Vilaseca, Enric Sagnier, Josep Fontseré, and Joan Rubio i Bellvé; and a rich stratum of skilled craftsmen, their skills honed by competition and not yet eroded by mass production, on whose collaborative talents they could call. Not only did the city have architects, but the architects had clients—rich people and ambitious institutions that wanted to leave a big mark on its material culture.

The exact time frame of an architectural movement can rarely be fixed. Does the architecture of Catalan *modernisme* begin and end with Gaudí? One can make a case for this, starting with one of Gaudí's immature works, the Casa Vicens (1883–88) and finishing with the Sagrada Família as it stood in 1926, just after Gaudí's death but before later architects took over its long stumbling march toward its still-distant completion. But it is obvious that the *modernista* impulse had exhausted itself in Catalunya long before that; for the last fifteen years of his life Gaudí himself was seen by most Catalans as a living anachronism, clinging to an obsolete style, and even his younger contemporaries like Puig i Cadafalch had gone over to a more Mediterranean idiom full of classical quotations. It might be truer to the architectural spirit of *modernisme* to start it in 1888–89, with the completion of Vilaseca's and Domènech's work for the Universal Exposition, and finish it around 1910 with the completion of Domènech's Palau de la Música Catalana (1905–8) and Gaudí's Casa Milà. But Gaudí is such a looming hulk, such a Melville-like mass of contradictions and jostling rhetoric, such an irksome and fundamentalist genius, that I have kept him for the next chapter, which he has to himself. In certain important respects Gaudí was not a *modernista* architect at all; his religious obsessions, for instance, separate him from the generally secular character of *modernisme*. Gaudí did not believe in modernity. He wanted to find radically new ways of being radically old: a fiercer project altogether.

Catalan *modernisme* was eclectic architecture that looked to the past for inspiration: mainly Gothic, and Arabic too. But its attitude was one of transformation, not passive copying and "correct" quotation. At its best, it was highly adventurous, open to new structural techniques—and capable of using old ones with a daring and precision that rivaled or even surpassed their original uses. To see the kind of craft base it could draw on, one may reflect on the work of a family of tilers and bricklayers, the Guastavinos. The Guastavinos distilled centuries of brick-and-tile know-how into their work; they knew all the empirical secrets of the wide-span, flat Catalan medieval arch. They emigrated to the United States at the end of the 1870s, and two of their three publicly accessible masterpieces are in New York City. These are the ceiling of the Oyster Bar in Grand Central Terminal and the arched vault of what is arguably the grandest single space in New York, the reception hall of Ellis Island. Both are done by the system of Catalan vaulting, whereby three layers of tile are woven together in such a way that a self-supporting tile membrane grows outward from the walls. This sort of structure depends entirely on the craftsman. Any fribbler can draw a flat vault—the problem is to build it. The Guastavinos and their American tile makers were so good that in the mid-1980s, when restoration of the great laminated Ellis Island vault began after decades of neglect, it was found that the structure was in such perfect shape that only seventeen of its twenty-nine thousand tiles needed to be replaced.

The Guastavinos' third chef d'oeuvre, which is in Barcelona, is an industrial structure, the brick chimney of the Batlló ceramics factory, standing within the present site of the Industrial University: a high octagonal pipe that rises from a flaring base, tapering slightly toward the top, and finished with a small cornice. It has a breathtaking simplicity and the beauty of ancient Persian prayer towers. But its virtues become most apparent when you hunker down at the base and squint upward along the corner lines where the plane faces of the octagon meet. Ground to cornice, they are absolutely straight. The bricks are laid to the tolerance of marquetry, thousands of courses without accumulated error. The tower is a perfect crystal. Though we have lasers instead of the plumb bobs the Guastavinos had, we do not have their hands, and such brickwork will never be done again. Neither will the kind of iron forging that went into the decorations of Gaudí's Palau Güell, or the level of ceramic production responsible for the fat fish-scale roof tiles and interior-vault mosaics of Domènech's Hospital de Sant Pau. Access to such a craft base is now irrevocably lost to the architect. This access is what makes Catalan *modernisme* look so rich and strange, for mere fantasy is never enough: fantasy has to be made concrete, and carry the empiricism of its making in every outward inch, before it becomes believable as architecture.

IV

Amid the confused panoply of buildings put up in Citadel Park for the Universal Exposition of 1888, one stood out as a suggestion of things to come: the Café-Restaurant by Domènech i Montaner. It looks medieval, with its crenellations and shields; in part, it is a witty parody of medievalism. But it is made of unadorned brick and industrial iron. The span between its medievality and its modernity—the former being part of the latter—is what makes the Café-Restaurant such an early *modernista* landmark.

To use plain brick in 1888 was close to a violation of etiquette. In fact most of the new buildings in the Eixample up to then were constructed of brick, but they were covered with stucco to imitate stone or faced with terra-cotta. Brick was considered a dumb material; the very word for "brick," *totxo*, meant "ugly, stupid." The idea of constructing a *festive* building of unadorned brick was unheard-of in Barcelona. But Domènech, from his study of Gottfried Semper, was concerned with the origins of architecture. To achieve "originality" was, precisely, to be involved with origins. Here, he says in effect, is a material whose

Domènech i Montaner's Café-Restaurant for the 1888 Exposition

---

expressive powers are disparaged and not explored, yet the brick is, or ought to be, the molecule of Catalan architecture. A brick building does not just sit on the surface of *la pàtria*: it is literally made from the earth of the homeland. To use a phrase that both he and his younger colleague Josep Puig i Cadafalch rejoiced in, brick was *clar i català*—"clear and Catalan." The sun strikes a brick wall in this way; the corbels and projections, the facets and planes, that can be done in brick have their own unused power and plasticity, their own capacity to create a play of light and shadow. You can do flat Catalan arches, like the entrance to the Café-Restaurant, and big engulfing Roman windows, like the three-bay Palladian opening above it that lights the interior, and Moorish arches and cogging and diapers and tricky reveals that draw razor lines in the plane. None of this is outside the vocabulary of brick. The same with iron, about which the young Domènech was just as explicit. His iron beams show. No effort is made to dissemble the iron window frames and door surrounds of the Café-Restaurant.

Of course, Domènech used "classier" materials too—with striking effect in the pale ocher–glazed ceramic "crowns" that finish each battlement, and especially in the band of ceramic escutcheons painted, in blue on white, by his friend Alexandre de Riquer i Inglada, that runs just below the battlements along the wall of the Café-Restaurant. These are a parody of Domènech's own interest in chivalric history, a subject on which he spent much time and energy, collecting and classifying and redrawing the shields and armorial bearings of Old Catalunya. But they have no chivalric meaning. They are more like an early Catalan form of pop art. Some of them depict flowers and herbal plants, others animals (a night heron, a squid, a snake), others the drinks one might expect to buy inside the café, and so forth.

They also announce one of the main decorative resources of *modernisme* in general and Domènech's work in particular—stylized nature. Catalan artists and architects, like their Art Nouveau equivalents in France, were much influenced by seventeenth- and eighteenth-century Japanese scroll painting, *tsuba* (sword hilts), lacquer, and pottery. From late Momoyama and early Edo art there grew a perfect myopic world of close focus on leaves, bugs, birds, and butterflies, in which a fish scale and the profile of Fuji could have the same degree of meaning. Art Nouveau drew deep on this reservoir of natural forms, not only as decorative and symbolic motifs, but as sources of abstraction—its prime formal element, the whiplash recurving line, is an abstraction from nature, a visual synonym for "vitality." Domènech's use of floral ornament was always meant to counterpoint the aggressive "rationality" of the architectural frame—a habit of mind that reaches a climax in the thick blossoming of ceramic and mosaic roses across the structural grid of the Palau de la Musica Catalana.

Domènech's originality lay in his rationalism, his scrupulous but daring use of historical elements, and his brilliant interfusion of Catalan craft traditions with the desire for new forms. Unlike the solitary and obsessive Gaudí, he was immersed in the society of his time, not frivolously—though he certainly liked dinner parties and the waspish wit of the *tertulias* (conversation groups)—but as a man moving among the obligations of practical and academic work, family and politics, the theory of architecture and its real effects on the real world. The son of a Barcelonese bookbinder, he was a protean figure: a gifted draftsman (unlike Gaudí), an architectural historian addicted to fieldwork, a publisher whose firm, Editorial Montaner i Simón, was one of the most ambitious creators of *éditions de luxe* in Spain, a designer of book jackets and heraldic emblems, a critic, an inspiring teacher, and, through the

Domènech's Casa Lleó Morera, 1905, with ground-floor sculptures by Eusebi Arnau, before the building was altered

1890s and into his later years, an active and influential Catalanist politician. In this area Domènech was, in the full and proper sense, a public man. He presided over the meeting of the Unió Catalanista that drew up the Bases de Manresa in 1892. In 1901 he was one of the four Catalans elected to the Madrid parliament by the electoral success of Prat de la Riba's Lliga Regionalista—though he left the Lliga three years later, finding it too conservative. He served six terms as president of the Barcelona Athenaeum. Through all this, he continued to build and to do the archaeological fieldwork and restoration that fed his inspiration as an architect. For Domènech's idea of *modernisme* was global—it entailed bringing the past forward into the present, as well as speculating about the future.

Domènech built nothing outside Catalunya, but he traveled widely in Europe, reading English, German, and French. He had a large German library. He loved Shakespeare but denied himself the pleasure of reciting the bard aloud to his friends, because he would lose control in the more emotional passages, break down, and weep. Yet he never got flustered on the job. Domènech was the paragon of the architect as master of works. His friends compared him to an orchestral conductor. Under his baton, you got to do well what you did best: Domènech understood the modern materials of architecture—iron rebars, trusses, concrete, sheet glass—as well as any engineer of his time and better than some, and his grasp of the traditional materials of finish and decoration, from fine joinery to tile, stone carving and iron forging, was encyclopedic.

If any architect can properly be called the *uomo universale* or Renaissance man of Catalan modernism, that person was Lluís Domènech i Montaner. But this antique image is misleading. Domènech was working in a wider industrial field than any Renaissance architect had to master. For him, even more than it was in the time of Alberti or Michelozzo, the question of the work team was central. He was not only a high-craft architect but, by the standards of his time, an extremely high-tech one as well, and this meant that he had constantly to delegate responsibility to others.

This may not have been a difficult issue in Domènech's projects for private houses or offices in Barcelona, such as the early Editorial Montaner i Simón (1881–86), the Casa Tomàs (1895–98), or the Casa Fuster (1908–10), because they did not present large problems of structure or function. Their work teams were mainly decorators.

The most highly embellished of Domènech's Barcelonese houses was the Casa Lleó Morera, 1905 (Passeig de Gràcia 35), which, though its exterior was mutilated in 1943 and its internal decor was mostly stripped, can be reimagined through photographs and through the furniture and decorative plaques preserved in the Museum of Modern Art in Barcelona. Domènech hired Eusebi Arnau, the most gifted decorative sculptor in Barcelona, to do the exterior sculptures for the ground floor, which housed the studios of a fashionable photographer named Pau Audouard. They included two exquisite, life-size *modernista* damsels clinging to fonts, more nymphs on the circular tribune that projected from the corner of the building, and a set of bas-reliefs symbolizing electric light, photography, the telephone, and the phonograph. (The maidens holding the camera and the light bulb, which are on the second floor of the facade and so were spared destruction by the renovators, are especially fetching.) Inside, Domènech commissioned the decorator Gaspar Homar i Mezquida (1870–1953) to create a series of domestic objects: lamps, tables, chairs, decorative panels, and a giant sofa-cabinet with marquetry panels designed by Josep Pey and executed by Joan Segarra—part of a suite for the main salon of the house that is probably the finest surviving set of Catalan *modernista* furniture.

Marquetry sofa-cabinet by Gasper Homar, designed for the Casa Lleó Morera

A number of interior designers in Barcelona sought to integrate the decorative arts—furniture, mural painting, screens, lighting, metalwork, glass, pottery—in a single ensemble. They had workshops, sometimes long-established family ones; but they were no strangers to Paris and Munich, and sometimes contributed theoretical articles to the small cultural magazines of the day, such as *Joventut*. Homar was one; another was Francesc Vidal; a third was the cabinetmaking firm founded by the Busquets brothers. They considered their field to be the decorative arts, custom design for a specific architectural context, rather than the industrial arts, the production of context-free objects for general sale, off the shelf. They were designers rather than cabinetmakers, and this facilitated a free and level exchange with other artists who would never have thought of themselves as "risen" artisans, such as Alexandre de Riquer, an aristocrat by birth, or the painter-lithographer-playwright Adrià Gual i Queralt. The prestige of such designers was hardly inferior to that of the architects themselves, and this helps to account for the very high level of conception and execution in the best decorative schemes of Barcelona *modernisme*. It also helps to explain why ideas and motifs spread so rapidly between the Catalan arts at the time, turning up impartially in posters, in weavings, on marquetry panels, in jewelry, and in mosaic.

Nevertheless, the architect carried the heaviest load of synthesis, and nowhere does this show more vividly than in Domènech's biggest project, the Hospital de La Santa Creu i Sant Pau, or Hospital of the Holy Cross

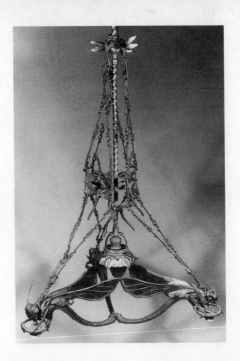

Lamp with dragonfly motif by Gaspar Homar for the Casa Lleó Morera

and Saint Paul. This was the largest of all the architectural projects of *modernisme*; its only rival in size was the church of the Sagrada Família, but Domènech finished his job and Gaudí did not; moreover, the Hospital de Sant Pau, since its completion in 1910, has done more demonstrable good for the people of Barcelona than the Sagrada Família is ever likely to. It is Domènech's masterpiece on the large scale, as the Palau de la Música Catalana is on the (relatively) small.

Barcelona in 1900 had never had an adequate general hospital. The Hospital of the Holy Cross in the Raval, off the Ramblas, dated back to the fifteenth century and had drains and services to match; it was badly damaged by fire in 1887. The impulse to create a new one came from the Catalan banker Pau Gil i Serra (1816–96), who left four million pesetas to the city for that purpose. A design competition was held, but a board of doctors turned down the winning entry (by Domènech i Estapa) because it did not meet their health and hygiene standards. Then Gil's trustees turned to Domènech i Montaner.

Domènech set out to make the enormous site—360 acres, nine full blocks of the Eixample—a garden city within the grid city. He wanted, above all, to overcome the depressing, labyrinthine character that big

Pavilions of Domènech i Montaner's Hospital de Sant Pau

general hospitals share with prisons. If the patients were to recover, they needed color, an agreeable environment, fresh air, trees, a sense of ground underfoot. Domènech hit on the brilliant idea of excavating the whole site and building all the hospital's service areas and corridors underground. Above this concealed substructure, forty-eight pavilions would rise, each one built over a basement that linked it to the service net: thirty-six for bed patients, twelve for general services and administration. Separate pavilions made it easier to isolate infectious patients and made the hospital feel like a village.

Domènech disliked, he said, "the eternal monotony of two widely separated parallel lines," and he set out to make the hospital as unlike the Eixample as possible. He aligned its plan around two avenues, each 550 yards long, crossing in the center of the site and running at a forty-five-degree angle to the Eixample's grid. The main surgery building, with its operating theaters and disinfection rooms, stood at the crossing. Smaller streets, giving open-air access to the pavilions, ran off the arms of the cross.

The hospital, then, was no mere building but a large and carefully controlled environment, and an essential part of that control was mood.

To buoy up the spirits of the patients and their families, and banish at least some of their association of hospitals with death and suffering, Domènech lavished his ingenuity on the detailing and color of each building in the Hospital de Sant Pau. The note of care is struck as soon as you come up the double ramp into the reception block, whose facade glitters with mosaic murals depicting the history of the hospital from the Middle Ages to the time of Pau Gil. Inside, octagonal columns with Domènech's signature floral capitals—originally adapted from those in the fifteenth-century cloister of the monastery of Santes Creus—bear up shallow domes sheathed, surprisingly, in dusky pink tiles; a broad staircase rises on the left toward the administration offices, and the whole space of this vestibule is bathed in golden light from a big stained-glass *claraboia*, or skylight, in the roof. The whole space is ceremonious, exciting, and optimistic. This feeling shifts down to one of intimacy once you are in the grounds of the hospital itself, among the pavilions, but the atmosphere of sedulous care remains. It shows, especially, in the upkeep of aesthetic atmosphere. Domènech seems to have believed that art was literally therapeutic. Speaking of his father's penchant for highlighting plain materials with sparks of fine decoration, Domènech i Montaner's son (who finished the hospital after his father died) pointed out that

> the material took on nobility even if it was ordinary . . . if it was joined to the use of some rich material, even in small amounts, the thing acquired a character of richness, surprisingly so in view of its real price. So it was with the Hospital of Sant Pau, in which he thought that everything that could give a feeling of well-being to the sick was also a form of therapy.

Nothing else would explain the inventive brio that Domènech put into the gay, bubbling roofscape of colored pavilion domes, or the profusion of sculpture—allegorical, symbolic, or merely decorative—that meets the eye at every turn. He put the sculpture program in the hands of two artists, Eusebi Arnau and Pau Gargallo, who in turn employed dozens of assistants. Hence the hospital pullulates with a formal imagery of saints, angels, personifications of charity and science and mercy, knights and heroes, and even distinguished Catalan doctors from Arnau de Vilanova to the late mayor of Barcelona, Dr. Bartolomeu Robert. No two pavilions are the same. They are further enriched with a profusion of ceramic motifs; lizards and snails peep from the foliage of painted orange trees; flowers—glazed, embossed, sculpted, rendered in mo-

Josep Puig i Cadafalch

saic—are everywhere, on plaques, within arches, curling around columns, or bursting from the spikes of finials like hollyhocks from their stems. The decor is a lexicon of "blossoming" and "recovery." Even the overlapping ceramic tiles on the pavilion domes, when you look at them close up, are plump, lobular, and shiny, not like ordinary flat tiles at all. The tiled interior vaults of the patients' wards are more peaceful, sheathed in cool, repetitious, mildly hypnotic patterns. Inside, rest; outside, an optimistic burgeoning, whatever the season.

After Gaudí and Domènech, the third important Catalan architect of the period was Josep Puig i Cadafalch. Puig was much younger than either—he was born in 1867, Gaudí in 1852, and Domènech in 1849. He was forced into exile in 1936, though he came back to Barcelona in 1943 and died there in 1957 at the patriarchal age of ninety. Before he fled from Falangism he hid thousands of his drawings in the attic of his house on Carrer de Provença. When this trove came to light a few years ago, it confirmed the enormous range and complexity of Puig's work, not only as an architect, but as decorator, furniture designer, archaeologist, restorer, and town planner as well. He was as much a polymath as Domènech i Montaner; projects, themes, and variations poured from his febrile imagination; the whole culture seemed to filter through him.

Puig had studied architecture under Elias Rogent at the University of Barcelona (and later, like Domènech, in Madrid). He was there from

1888 to 1891, at the peak of Rogent's influence and just as Barcelona was being transformed by the Universal Exposition. He remembered how "in class, [Rogent] would say over and over again that it was important to be a Catalanist in architecture, and that for us the Cathedral of Barcelona, Poblet and Santes Creus should be what Greek and Roman models had been for past generations." Nor did he ever forget the impact of Domènech's exposition buildings, the Café-Restaurant and the quick-building tour de force of the Hotel Internacional: one a symbol of the creative infusion of past with present, the other a dazzling proof of organizational skill.

Puig would always be a traditionalist—deeply Catalan, skeptical of claims made by international modernism that the past was only there to be fought and left behind. He resented the word *modernisme* when it was applied to his work, arguing that everything that was good in the European architecture of his day—Hoffman, Horta, Mackintosh—also sprang from local, not international, cultures: "New things have indeed come about in the field of decoration, but the *modernista* building has yet to be built," he said in 1902. *Modernista* painters like Santiago Rusinyol and writers like Jaume Brossa might rail against the past as a dead hand, conflate it with the "bourgeois" values they wanted to prick, but Puig knew right from the start that a great building is always modern because it renews itself for each generation that confronts it, whereas most of the "new" wilts into irrelevancy quite fast. He had read Ruskin on Gothic—what Catalan architect of his generation did not know Ruskin?—but his aesthetic excitement in the face of the Gothic past was instinctive, a fact of experience. In *argument*, though, he would imitate the writers—mainly Viollet-le-Duc, with his emphasis on the deep structural originality of Gothic building. "Those self-styled progressives here and elsewhere," he protested, "have no idea how truly progressive and novel Gothic art is—that mediaeval art which created the cathedral, the most intelligent structure ever built in stone, and the art most adaptable to the inventions of modern structural technology."

What Puig liked best was lacy High Gothic, the spiky organic style of the fifteenth century, with its play of stone line across dramatic voids, its almost diagrammatic resolution of thrust in structure. He was not so interested in Romanesque cave mass, although he studied Catalan Romanesque exhaustively and worked hard to record and preserve its monuments.

Puig was preeminently a draftsman, and his buildings show an illuminator's hand—moving restlessly, abhorring a vacuum, the mind racing to translate graphic effects into the solid terminology of iron, tile, wood, plaster, and brick with as little loss of spontaneity as possible. He could create fine spatial effects, mysterious passages between intimacy and breadth; there is nothing cardboardy about his best buildings. But his most striking expertise was with surfaces and materials.

We call Puig an eclectic architect, which he was; he took ideas and motifs from a wide span of sources and used them unapologetically. But some areas he was not interested in raiding. One of these was Spanish-Arabic (Mudejar) architecture. There had been quite a vogue in Barcelona for neo-Arabic detail and sometimes for whole buildings in the arabesque style. Rogent, Puig's teacher, mixed neo-Arabic and Byzantine motifs in the interiors of the University of Barcelona, with a view to making the building an anthology of references to all the early architectural styles of Spain. Gaudí's first house in Barcelona, the Casa Vicens, was partly Orientalist and contained an opulent Moorish smoking room. There was a strong Arabic influence on the architecture of the Universal Exposition. Both the bullrings of Barcelona—the Plaça de Toros Monumental by Ignasi Mas i Morell (Gran Via 749) and the Arenys by August Font (Plaça d'Espanya)—were designed in a neo-Moorish style, because the *locus classicus* of bullfighting was Andalusia, and the architecture should recall the origins of the spectacle; Font had also designed the Oriental baths in Barceloneta (1872, since demolished) as an Arabic building inside and out, for that suited the cult of the *hammam*. Perhaps the finest of all the buildings in Barcelona carrying traces of Mudejar inspiration was the house that Joan Rubio i Bellvé built between 1903 and 1913 at 31 Avinguda de Tibidabo, for the Roviralta family. Its nickname is El Frare Blanc (The White Friar), because of its stark white walls and cowled appearance. The White Friar combines the aggressive shelter imagery of the traditional *casa pairal* with the notching and corbeling of Arabic brickwork; the roof, with its huge shadowing eaves built out in laminations of thin flat brick, hangs dramatically over the double-arched opening of the top floor; the use of corbeled brick sets up a sizzling, angular rhythm across the whitewashed planes of wall.

The clue to all this profuse Arabism was not that the architects and clients wanted to be exotic, but rather the reverse: they wanted their buildings to look Spanish, to be clearly grounded in a sense of Spanish history that included Hispano-Arabic culture. To do a building evocative of Granada or Seville signaled that you were a pan-Spaniard and not a strict Catalanist. But Puig was very much the latter. The Arabs, he would no doubt have argued, had far less impact on Catalunya than on the provinces south of the Ebro; they were beaten back and left no historic structures behind them. The *absence* of a strong Moorish cultural tradition

Joan Rubió i Bellvé's The White Friar, *1903–13*

was one of the proofs of the independence of Catalunya. *Moro* might mean neighbor down south, but up here it meant hostile stranger. For Puig, Moorish motifs in architecture were alien to the spirit of Catalunya. He saw this in racial terms—Arabs may once have been great warriors and scholars, but today they were a treacherous and effete race, fit for colonization but not much else. Puig's views on this were in no way different from those of any other Catalan (or Frenchman or Englishman) of his class and time.

On the other hand, there was the north. To Puig i Cadafalch, as to the Ajuntament in the 1980s, Barcelona was "the north of the south." It was the place where Spain became European. Its territories had once spilled over the Pyrenees into France. The city had old trading links with Flanders, and cultural ones too—High Gothic Catalan painting was largely a provincial version of Flemish. It admired German culture and ideas—not only Wagner, but the Teutonic sense of destiny and industrial drive. It was traditionally Anglophile in matters of fashion. But for all that, it still comes as a surprise to see the uses to which Puig put his love of northern Europe.

Consider the building on a narrow triangular site at the intersection of the Diagonal and Carrer Rosselló (Diagonal 416–420). The Casa Terrades is known colloquially as the Casa de les Punxes, the House of Points: a cross between a Flemish guildhall and a medievalizing Mad Ludwig schloss, built by Puig in 1903–5. It has four round towers, each finishing in a witch's-hat spire, and a main tower with an elaborate lantern. The roofline is a procession of sharp gables and finials, stabbing at the sky. The plain brick walls break out into High Gothic tribunes and miradors trimmed with a profusion of detailed ornamental stone-work, mostly floral motifs, bulbous in projection and deeply undercut to read as vividly as possible. (Not for Puig the shallow incised ornament of cheap Neo-Gothic.) It is, in sum, the last structure one would expect to find in a Mediterranean city, as odd as finding a white Andalusian *finca* in Prague. And yet when its critics took aim at it, their complaint was not that the Casa de les Punxes was foreign and incongruous, but that it was too Catalanist in its detail and thus politically subversive. "THE PROPAGANDISTS OF HATRED: SEPARATISM AND ARCHITECTURE," head-lined the editor of *El Progreso* in 1907. For Puig had inserted a large ceramic plaque depicting Saint George and the dragon into the apex of the gable that looks down on Carrer Rosselló, with the legend—faintly discernible, at best, from street level—"Holy patron of Catalunya, give us back our freedom." This was not to be borne. It belonged, wrote the editor, to the sphere of "crimes against the integrity of the nation."

The best known of Puig's "northern" buildings—because of its prom-inent site as well as its spectacular appearance—is a house at 41 Passeig de Gràcia, done for a chocolate millionaire and an amateur of the arts named Amatller. When Puig started it (1898) the Casa Amatller stood alone; shortly afterward Domènech built the Casa Lleó Morera to its left, and Gaudí turned the building on its right into the Casa Batlló, thus creating the solidest group of *modernista* palaces in Barcelona: ever since, the visual argument among these three signature buildings has caused that part of Passeig de Gràcia to be known as the *mansana de la discordia*, or "block of discord." But in its original context, between two dull builders' apartment blocks from the 1870s, the Casa Amatller was a solo apparition.

It is a Catalan Gothic palace, with the same canonical plan—a flat wall to the street and a large central courtyard from which a staircase ascends to the main salon on the first floor—as the real fifteenth-century ones on Carrer Montcada. But there are big differences: the density of its decor and the sudden change of style on the facade. For two-thirds of its height, the facade wall is an ocher-and-white stucco membrane—sgraffito work, more an Italian than a Catalan decorative technique, which gives the surface the richness of damask. But then a pediment begins: an exuberant, stepped Flemish Renaissance pediment straight out of Bruges but ornamented with more polychrome tiles than any

Pediment of Puig's Casa Amatller

sober northern Renaissance burgher would have suffered to be placed on his house, blue and cream and pink, and studded with a grid of oxblood-luster florets. Its sheen and twinkle in the morning sun are astonishing. Puig's buildings show his eye in every square foot of surface, and the Casa Amatller is no exception. It would be a pity not to linger on its pseudomedieval detail: Eusebi Arnau's stone figure of Saint George transfixing the dragon on the entrance portal or especially the corbel figures in the four windows of the *pis noble* on the second floor. Here, a moustached photographer aims a stone camera, a rabbit pours molten metal from a ladle, and a monkey hammers at the forge; there an ass prints the page of a book, and a furtive-looking rat with cloak and tripod takes a photographic portrait; a pig shapes a pot, and a frog blows glass. Between them, Puig and Arnau recapture the high demotic humor of medieval grotesques, in this most "aristocratic" of town houses.

The Casa Amatller is a showcase of the fruitful relationship between the architect and the decorative arts in fin de siècle Barcelona. In the words of the historian Judith Rohrer, it was also Puig's first blow against the egalitarian uniformity of the Cerdà plan: with it, "he began the battle, soon joined by others in a spirit of bourgeois emulation, to introduce a series of privileged places meant, like colorful explosions, to destroy the uniformity imposed by the egalitarian Cerdà." The variety of Puig's

Eusebi Arnau's stone carvings on the Casa Amatller

Barcelonese buildings thus has its polemical side. Each town house is a "turn," a virtuoso exercise, whether the building in question is the Casa Macaya of 1899–1901 (Passeig de Sant Joan 106) with its ultrarefined stone detailing and lacy allover sgraffito decoration, or the Palau Quadras of 1902–4 (Diagonal 373), now the Music Museum, with the squat, bulging Ionic columns amid the Neo-Gothic excess of the main salon and, outside, the witty details of its Gothic mirador, featuring nine waterspouts in the form of water animals—newts, frogs, fish. Puig was determined to stud the Eixample with *cases pairales*, signifying the rooted and abiding values of Catalanist conservatism, partially metamorphosed into jewel boxes. In this way he would register his protest against Cerdà, whose work and ideology he so disliked. Other architects felt the same way, with the result that between 1890 and 1910 the Eixample became the site of what one could euphemistically call a dialogue between them and Cerdà.

Actually it was a rancorous disagreement. If the city plan had no hierarchies and climaxes, then the buildings themselves must provide them. If it had no quirks, they must come from architecture. The clients wanted to show off, and so did their architects. Thus the Eixample turned into a museum of individuality, eccentricity, and striking detail.

Today, the so-called Quadrat d'Or, or Golden Square, the center of the Eixample with Passeig de Gràcia running up the middle of it, contains the richest concentration of Art Nouveau structures and facade elements to be seen anywhere in Europe. It is not just the major buildings that give the effect of saturation, but the detail: the surviving shop fronts, a glitter of Byzantine-green mosaic in the curving sign above a pharmacy or of stained-glass morning glories twining through a mirador, the unexpected glimpse in a dark hallway of a spiky medieval-*modernista* electrolier, four feet across, ugly as sin, but still impressive, about half its weak bulbs still obstinately glowing.

V

The dead had an Eixample, as well as the living. Over the centuries the small local graveyards that dotted the city had been filled in and abandoned; houses and shops now stood over a fill of bones. The Middle Ages never had a cult of reverence for the corpse. A cheap shroud, a plank, an unceremonious heave-ho into the stink of the common grave, a few shovels of lime: such was the usual lot. "Man is a Noble Animal, splendid in ashes, and pompous in the grave"—Sir Thomas Browne's sentence in *Urn Burial* would have struck his seventeenth-century readers as a paradox and (if they could have read it) would have seemed nonsense to their medieval forebears. Only the very great and the very rich left clear monumental evidence of where they were buried. And not even that lasted. The bones of Wilfred the Hairy were lost for nearly a thousand years.

By the end of the eighteenth century this had begun to change. Europe's new middle classes set out to surround death with a thick carapace of ritual and ceremony. Death became industrialized and accessorized; a whole new economy of funeral goods and service businesses sprouted from the tomb. This impulse produced the immense urban necropolises of the nineteenth century, one of which is the Cementiri Nou, or New Cemetery, on the seaward side of Montjuic in Barcelona—which, hardly second to Père-Lachaise in Paris, is the most exuberant and bizarre precinct of its kind in Europe.

A new cemetery presupposes an old. Barcelona has one of these, too. The Cementiri Vell (Old Cemetery), at the end of Avinguda d'Icaria in Poble Nou, north of Barceloneta and the Citadel Park, was an artifact

Tombs in the New Cemetery, nineteenth century

of the Age of Reason. Bishop Climent founded it in 1773 to replace the old parochial cemeteries that were finally to be closed for health reasons by a military order in 1816. A neoclassical architect named Antoni Ginesi gave it a Graeco-Egyptian aspect—an entrance screen of stumpy, Piranesian Doric porches and vine-covered pyramids. In 1838 it was made a civil cemetery, and since then the Ajuntament has looked after it—abominably, to judge from the wreckage of its tombs. But it is well worth a visit, as a prelude to the necropolis of Montjuic.

The Old Cemetery is laid out like an "ideal park," in two large walled districts—the newer tombs in blocks of stacked niches, like bottle racks for the dead, near the entrance, and the older ones at the back. Between the two sectors is a flaking Doric temple with stucco wings (the flight of time) on its pediment, and behind it is a bizarre palimpsest of monuments, a medley of architectural styles crammed cheek by jowl into a space no more than five hundred feet square: Roman sarcophagi, Gothic shrines, Byzantine tombs whose mosaic panels were smashed long ago by vandals, and a legion of angels and muses and pretty neoclassical weepers wringing their hands on cracked marble coffins, staring to heaven, mourning with arms crossed over their breasts, displaying open books and pointing at the sky with imperious forefingers, their stony pathos only a little reduced by the pigeons on their heads. Here, the first wave of Barcelona's industrial-mercantile rich is buried. The cemetery wall, too, is full of small chapels that contain equally neglected and busted-up monuments. Here is the slab of a builder, José Nolla, surrounded by the tools of his business—levels, squares, a pulley, a pickax, protractors, shovels, a bricklayer's hod, coils of rope, all minutely carved in white marble bas-relief. Here is the sarcophagus of an Isabeline *indiano* who came back and put his money into the railroad and steam navigation boom of the 1840s: it bears a sextant, a compass in gimbals, and a steam-pressure gage, and above it is a marble lunette with a merchant clipper and a steam packet belching dirty stone smoke from its funnel, while the locomotive and carriages of the 1848 Barcelona–Mataró railroad chug past below them.

The intensity and elaboration of funerals grew steadily, in Barcelona as in Paris, between 1850 and 1900. The family vigil over the corpse, in a bedroom transformed by candles and black drapes into a *chapelle ardente*; the coffin, in ebony, mahogany, and ivory, with its dark bronze fittings; the black-plumed horses, shod with felt, and the hearse, like a black chapel on wheels; the mutes, the veils, the deep mourning costumes of the relatives; the solemn mass, the invocations, the prayers, the eulogies, and the long *necrologiès*, or "obituary notices," in the newspapers, which for someone important could go on for five or six black-bordered pages; the slow procession of carriages to the cemetery—all this was only a prelude to the splendors of the high-bourgeois tomb. The trouble was that such structures ate up space. By the 1870s no more big tombs could fit into the Old Cemetery. High-bourgeois Barcelona, feeling rich, wanted more and better sepulchers, tombs fit for a boom.

The New Cemetery, officially known as the Cementiri del Sud-Est, was opened in 1883 by the mayor, Rius i Taulet. It occupies the whole seaward flank of Montjuic. Nothing could show Barcelona's indifference to the sea more vividly. The dead have the best water view in the city, a perfect 180-degree arc of the Mediterranean. As you approach it, the cemetery does indeed look like a city of the dead, with all class distinctions of the city of the living inscribed on it: a common grave for paupers, high-density housing for workers (blocks of niches), and ornate, upper-crust palaces (the single tombs and family pantheons), the whole enfolded in dark stands of cypress and linked by hairpin roads that crawl up the hill.

This place is a posthumous extension of the Eixample, whose architectural fantasy it repeats. It, too, was built on virgin territory and soon became an architectural museum, with tombs that mimic or were actually designed by the owners' architects. Thus Puig i Cadafalch built a Gothic tomb with lancets, crockets, and a heavily foliated spire for the Amatller family and gave it the same stepped Dutch pediment that he had put on their house in Passeig de Gràcia. He even used the same sculptor, Eusebi Arnau. The New Cemetery contains no tomb by Gaudí or Domènech i Montaner, but there are a score of pantheons and crypts in their styles, including one that imitates the parabolic arches and slightly swollen spires of the Sagrada Família.

The exuberance, stylistic variety, and exaggeration of these bourgeois tombs are almost stifling. The late nineteenth century was the age of monuments, but in a real city they are dispersed in streets and squares: here they are impacted, jammed next to one another with nothing in between—monument overload, more delirious than any Piranesi *capriccio*, roasting white with black shadows in the Catalan sunlight. Close up, one sees the work of robbers, who have pried off the bronze incrustations, busts, escutcheons, chains, medallions, and anything else that could be sold to a melter: the forced doors of crypts hang badly ajar, emitting a smell of damp and mold from their stripped interiors: carved tomb slabs the size of Cadillacs have been levered aside to reveal slits of night beneath. In this way, the poor of Barcelona continue to take their revenge on the nineteenth-century rich.

VI

Big businessmen in nineteenth-century Barcelona believed in slavery and saw no reason to deny it. In 1862 nearly 370,000 slaves still worked on the sugar plantations of Cuba, many of them owned by Catalan companies. In 1866, when Spain passed an anti–slave trade law, its preamble stated that "slavery has to exist in the islands of Cuba and Puerto Rico as a pre-existing fact." Black Cuban workers were not freed by Spain until 1886, and even then they remained tied hand and foot to their *padrones* by lack of other work. Neither Spain in general nor Barcelona in particular felt many qualms about this. English and American zeal to abolish slavery looked hypocritical to the *gent de bé* of Barcelona. It is worth remembering this when one reflects on the way that Catalan industrialists treated their own white workers, shrugging off criticism and calls for reform. Grinding the workers was almost a patriotic act, enabling little Catalunya to survive against the foreign Goliath.

Around 1900, the lowest *jornaler*, or day worker, earned two pesetas a day; a skilled factory worker in Barcelona, five pesetas. Perhaps fifty thousand women worked in the mills there, earning half the male wage. About thirty thousand children supplemented the women's labor, at half the women's pay. A law passed at the turn of the century, forbidding the employment of children under the age of ten in factories (unless they could read) caused immense indignation in the Junta de Comerç. Was Madrid trying to strangle Barcelona? It did not matter: there were no inspectors.

The minimum workday in the city textile factories was ten hours, the usual one twelve, and in the *colonias* farther out in the country, whose operation was seasonal because rivers like the Llobregat did not have enough clear fresh water in them during the summer to fill the rinsing tanks, the workday rose to fifteen hours. A seventy-hour week was standard throughout the textile industry, and until 1904 bosses could still legally demand work from their employees on Sunday. Not until 1918 did Spanish workers win the right to have industrial tribunals; the eight-hour day was introduced only in 1919. Contracts did not exist, and job security of any kind was unknown.

The health problems of Barcelonese workers continued to be insupportable. Their factories had no more safety rules than they had had in the 1850s, and the working environment was a death trap. So was that of the home. Tuberculosis, smallpox, typhus, and anemia took their toll, and children grew up stunted with rickets and anemia if they grew at all—one child in five died before it was a year old, not counting the stillborn.

Through the 1880s and into the 1890s, no sign of relief from this appeared. "*Sanguis martyrorum*," Catholics used to say, "*semen ecclesiae*": "The blood of martyrs is the seed of the Church." The blood and tears of the Spanish working class became the seed of a very different ideology, bitterly anticlerical, yet possessing in its puritanism and millenarian hope some of the authentic attributes of religion: anarchism.

Anarchism had many fathers, including Tolstoy. But its main parentage stemmed from Proudhon, who had so greatly influenced Pi i Margall and the Spanish federalists—and, above all, from the ideas of a charismatic Russian aristocrat, Mikhail Bakunin (1814–76). Spain, however, was the only country in which anarchism, which may briefly be defined as antiauthoritarian collectivism, became a mass creed; and its particular centers of belief were among the rural workers of Andalusia and the industrial ones of Barcelona.

Bakunin argued that the authority of state and Church was the root of all evil because, by assuming that men were bad, it made them so. The state debased its citizens by coercing them; the Church debased them with its doctrine of man's fallen moral condition. Since both were enemies of freedom, both Church and state must be wiped out. In their place, let voluntary association flourish. Bakunin despised Rousseau for saying that men, alone, are given freedom by nature and that the origins of society lay in their agreement to trade off some of this primitive freedom for the sake of community. Not at all, said Bakunin: it is community that *creates* liberty. Anarchism fosters social responsibility by substituting the pressure of public opinion, the view of the tribe, for the dictates of the state. Men and women find their true nature and liberty in others and sustain it by work. But first they must destroy the institutions that imprison them, break the "mind-forg'd Manacles"—destroy, in order to create.

The difficulty was, as Bakunin clearly saw—and his rival Karl Marx did not—that the material lot of the masses of Europe could easily improve under capitalism, so that the proletariat would grow satisfied with their lot and turn into little bourgeois, thus losing whatever revolutionary zeal they had. For this reason, anarchism had to make its appeal to two other classes of people: educated and alienated youth, who would inflame the lumpen proletariat to strikes and revolts. He imagined a pattern of workers' federations linked by pacts, controlled by a secret elite.

Where were the "primitive masses" of Bakunin's dreams to be found? Not in England, or France, or Germany; rather, in Russia—and in Spain. The root cause of the quarrels between anarchists and Marxists, which led in 1872 to Bakunin's expulsion from the first Socialist International and the triumph of Marx's ideology among worker movements in northern Europe, was that anarchism was not "scientific," like Marxism. It was religious. (So was Marxism, of course, but less nakedly so than anarchism, which attracted Spanish workers largely because its mystical certainties made it a religion *à rebours*.) The historic split in Spain between Marxists and anarchists remained unhealed for sixty years; without it, Franco would have found it much harder to destroy the Second Republic.

Anarchism stepped off the train in Barcelona in January 1869 in the black-bearded person of Giuseppe Fanelli, an Italian disciple of Bakunin. He could not speak a word of Catalan or even Spanish. It did not matter; his zeal and body language did the trick. He worked on his young listeners—mostly printers, followers of Pi i Margall—like a Pentecostal preacher speaking in tongues.

From that moment, the anarchist word spread with amazing speed in both Andalusia and Barcelona. Fanelli's timing had been perfect. He had arrived at a period of utter frustration—a moment of change that, for the Spanish working masses, changed nothing at all. If people are oppressed long enough by a political system that seems to perpetuate itself through every change of government, they will stop believing in any system. If the Church deserts them, they will view all promises or achievements of ecclesiatical reform as lies. When both these things happen to a people who are intensely clannish—real believers in the redemptive, integrative powers of human society—and deeply religious, which both Spaniards in general and Catalans in particular tended to be, their last resort is an extreme form of irrational hope. Somehow, this hope says, history will be transformed by an apocalyptic act of collective will. This was the promise of anarchism. Nothing need be saved; nothing built on. Gerald Brenan, in *The Spanish Labyrinth*, supplied an unforgettable vignette of this frame of mind during the Spanish civil war:

> I was standing on a hill watching the smoke and flames of some two hundred houses in Malaga mount to the sky. An old Anarchist of my acquaintance was standing beside me.
>
> "What do you think of that?" he asked.
>
> I said: "They are burning down Malaga."

"Yes," he said: "they are burning it down. And I tell you—not one stone will be left on another stone—no, not a plant nor even a cabbage will grow there, so that there may be no more wickedness in the world."

It was the voice of Amos or Isaiah (though the old man had never read either) or of an English sectarian of the seventeenth century.

Neither the conservatives nor the *liberales* had done anything for peasants in the first half of the nineteenth century, and in its second half, they continued to do nothing for industrial workers. It is hard to say which power bloc was more flagrantly cynical in its indifference to their lot or more corrupt in its exercise of influence. On the whole, the peasants had little doubt of it: they hated the liberals more. Men had the vote by 1890, far earlier than in Great Britain, but what use was a vote when the country's entire political structure was based on caciquism, rule by local bosses who stuffed the urns and rigged the elections? Caciques ran the whole environment of a Spanish peasant's life. They lent money and controlled employment; you voted their way or starved. They handpicked all local officials from the mayor down; they worked hand in glove with the priests; and when all else failed they used thug violence and even murder to accomplish their ends. It was futile to appeal to the courts, for the caciques controlled the judges.

In the past, things had been different. There had never been a golden age of Spanish justice, but peasants once had a strong natural ally in the Church. The alliance existed because the Church owned land and was therefore in regular working contact with the men and women who farmed it. Their interests coincided, to some degree. The clergy often stepped in to get rapacious caciques off peasants' backs. The Church as the poor man's protector, however ludicrous an idea in 1900, had been true a century earlier; often, throughout the Napoleonic occupation, guerrilla priests would lead bands of peasant partisans in defense of *la pàtria* against the hated French, while nuns filled cartridges in the convent kitchens. But from the moment the Mendizábal Laws deprived the Spanish Church of its landholdings and income, it allied itself increasingly, for its own survival, with the aristocracy and the upper-middle classes, the powerful and the rich—including, in Barcelona, the industrial rich. This was the Church that created the Carlists and supported them in their murderous pursuit of a past that had never existed.

No workingman in Barcelona by the end of the century could look at the city's humid embrace of capital and piety without loathing and a sense of betrayal. Anticlericalism had been strong in Spanish popular violence for a long while now: when in doubt about a target, burn a

Paulí Pallàs throwing a bomb at Captain General Martínez Campos, September 24, 1893

convent. Those fat black beetles, fingering their pectoral crosses and smirking at the *gent de bé* in the overstuffed salons of Passeig de Gràcia as they murmured soothing words about Catalanism and Christian charity—break their heads, tear out their liver and lights, hang them by the heels! These fantasies ran deep in Barcelona; suppressed during the Glorious Revolution and the subsequent Restoration, they broke out with terrifying force in the Setmana Tragica of 1909. Through the 1890s, they made Barcelona the world capital of anarchism and inflicted on it an epidemic of bombs, made and thrown by angry young marginals determined, if need be, to go into history as martyrs.

The first of the bombs, in 1891, was flung against the offices of a powerful businessmen's association, the Foment de Treball Nacional, and did little damage. But in September 1893 the stakes increased when a young lithographer named Paulí Pallàs tossed a bomb at Arsenio Martínez Campos, captain general of Catalunya, as he was preparing to review a parade of troops at the corner of Gran Via and Carrer de Muntaner. It killed a Guardia Civil and wounded Campos slightly. Pallàs made no effort to escape; he was taken to the military prison on Montjuic, court-martialed in October, and shot. "Vengeance will be terrible!" he shouted as the firing squad leveled its guns.

It was. A couple of weeks later, his friend Santiago Salvador bought a cheap balcony ticket to the opening night of the Liceu's winter season.

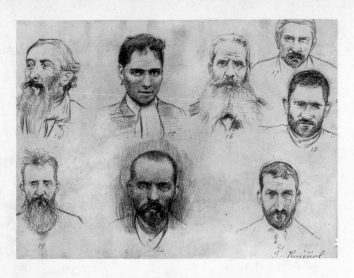

Santiago Rusinyol, sketch of anarchists prosecuted at Montjuic trial

The production was Gioacchino Rossini's five-hour opera *William Tell*, the story of patriotic Swiss resistance to a hated Austrian tyrant, set in the thirteenth century. In act 2, Tell and two friends swear an oath to free their country from the foreign yoke. Santiago Salvador, whom nobody could accuse of a lack of theatrical flair, chose this moment to stand up in the topmost balcony and produce two bombs from under his coat—polished spherical grenades studded with detonator horns, looking like miniature versions of old-fashioned naval mines. Salvador threw the first bomb into the stalls, where the rich were. It exploded in row 14 and produced carnage; twenty-two people were killed and another thirty wounded. Salvador then pitched his second bomb; it, too, landed in row 14, on the corpse of a bourgeoise whose ample flesh and folds of skirt cushioned its impact; gently, it rolled off her onto the carpet and was later found beneath a seat. Salvador then joined the crowd streaming down the staircase and vanished into the Ramblas.

The bombing of the Liceu threw Barcelona into panic. A state of siege was declared, and all constitutional guarantees suspended. Theaters had to close because no one would go to them, and women stopped wearing jewelry in public for fear of catching the eye of some enraged *descamisat*. The Barcelonese police scurried about with their usual incompetence, which rivaled that of the Keystone Kops, did a sweep of the cafés where anarchists hung out and arrested five of them more or less at random. None had any connection with Salvador or Pallàs, but that did not matter to the judge, who condemned them all to death.

Then Salvador was taken, brought to Montjuic, and shown the instruments of torture that awaited the unrepentant anarchist. He hastily made his confession to a socially prominent Jesuit named Goberna, who was eager to convert the young celebrity. What followed was farce: the aristocratic ladies of the Eixample, titillated by the thought of helping Goberna bring the handsome and wistful young monster back to Christ, started writing petitions for his reprieve as a *pobre infeliz* who had now seen the light. But to their pique, they were ignored. Salvador and the five other anarchists were executed. Their garroting was scheduled on the traditional site in the Patí dels Corders, or Ropemakers' Yard, outside the old Barcelona prison.

The city had a *botxí* or public executioner, a mild creature named Nicomedes Méndez, who each month collected his stipend and returned to live a quiet bachelor's life in a small upstairs room among his pet pigeons, rabbits, and hens. He was badly out of practice, since only one person had been garroted in Barcelona in the past thirty years. Nobody had ever taken a photo of Méndez, and when the impending executions were announced, the editor of the Barcelona daily *El Noticiero Universal* printed, as his portrait, the first photo that came to hand. It happened to be a likeness of the distinguished novelist and man of letters Narcís Oller, recent winner of the Jocs Florals. When Oller picked up a copy of next morning's *Noticiero* in his habitual café he uttered shrieks of dismay. Before the rites Méndez was introduced to the prison doctor, Font Torner i Tutau. "*Què tal*, colleague?" the doctor jovially said to the hangman, scandalizing other doctors who were present.

Despite his lack of practice, Méndez completed the job before a large and curious crowd in the dank winter dawn. At the scaffold's foot were several members of a penitent *cofradía*, terrifying in their black conical masks. Realizing that no reprieve was coming and that he had nothing to lose when the metal ring of the garrote was round his neck, Salvador pulled off his mask and shouted "Long live anarchy!" The noise of the gears that tightened the ratchet, a witness recalled, was exactly that of a bank clock being wound. At the end, the *botxí* rolled up Salvador's tongue like a small carpet and stuffed it back in his mouth.

The third and last spectacular bombing in Barcelona happened on June 7, the Feast of Corpus Christi, in 1896. A religious procession, headed by the bishop of Barcelona carrying a consecrated host and followed by the new captain General of Catalunya with a host of civic dignitaries, was passing along the Carrer dels Canvis Nous from the church of Santa Maria del Mar when someone threw a bomb at it. The unknown terrorist—it may have been a police provocateur, since he waited until all the bigwigs had passed by—killed twelve working people at the tail of the procession and wounded many more.

This set off the largest wave of police repression Barcelona had yet seen. Valerià Weyler i Nicolau, the captain general, whose name soon afterward became a byword for brutality in the Cuban war of independence, had the police round up every anarchist and anticlerical they could lay hands on and take them to the military prison on Montjuic. There, the police unrelentingly tortured them to extract confessions, with beatings, bone crushing, and applying red-hot iron to their genitals. (One writer, Pere Coromines, was saved by the intervention of Salvador Dalí's father, a lawyer.) Several died and at least one went permanently mad under torture, and five were convicted of conspiracy and garroted by the kangaroo court. Of those acquitted, sixty-one were sent to Spain's version of Devil's Island, the atrocious penal settlement of Rio de Oro. The bomber's identity was never found.

The Montjuic trials shocked the outside world. Mass protest meetings were held in London and across Europe. A young Italian anarchist named Angiolillo packed a bag and went to Madrid. He discovered that the prime minister, Antonio Cánovas, was taking the waters in a spa named Santa Agueda. He went there, drew a revolver, and shot Cánovas dead: as easy as that, to kill the most powerful man in Spain next to the king.

VII

The Corpus Christi bombing and the Montjuic trials destroyed the last hopes that clung to Bakunin's idea of "propaganda by deed." The death of working-class innocents in Carrer dels Canvis Nous stripped firebrand anarchism of most of its popular support; and while the Montjuic trials disgusted decent people throughout Europe, they certainly made young *exaltats* think twice about letting off more bombs. The affair had equally discredited anarchism and the police, showing up the bankruptcy of the revolutionaries and the corruption and cruelty of the authorities. From 1900 on, Spanish anarchists took a more reasoned course, allied to trade unionism—organization, not bombs.

Meanwhile, General Weyler had been posted off to Cuba. Having disgraced the name of justice in Spain, he would now help collapse the rest of his country's self-esteem. In 1895 Cuban separatists had revolted against colonial rule. As people thirsting for freedom from a dying tyranny sometimes will, they proved disturbingly resistant to the usual whiff of grapeshot. José Martí, leader of the nationalists' Cuban Republican party, had begun his crusade armed only with a revolver, a copy of Cicero's speeches, and an unshakable determination to convert the *isla*, the "island colony," into the *pàtria*, or "fatherland." As the insurrection gathered momentum, the sugar planters began to panic in Havana, while in Madrid the conviction grew that, to save the national honor, no effort in crushing Martí would be too great. General Martínez Campos, who had commanded the antiguerrilla campaign, was withdrawn and replaced by General Weyler. Gusts of rhetoric blew him on his way.

More than two hundred thousand soldiers were sent to Cuba, but the military campaign against Martí was a disaster. The colonial government was riddled by corruption, the army staff hopelessly inefficient, and then the United States decided to back Martí and his republicans. This was not done from a disinterested love of democracy. North America had been casting covetous eyes on Cuba ever since Thomas Jefferson's presidency. Finally, in 1898, after lodging a protest against the "uncivilized and inhumane" way in which the Spanish army was trying to crush the rebellion, President McKinley presented an ultimatum. He would give Spain three hundred million dollars for Cuba. If Spain refused, there would be war.

The American consul in Havana had asked for a show of American naval force to protect the safety of U.S. citizens in Cuba. Just before midnight on February 15, 1898, the battleship *Maine*, anchored in the port of Havana, blew up and sank with all 264 hands. The cause of the explosion remains a mystery; Washington flatly refused Madrid's suggestion that two commissions of inquiry, one American and the other Spanish, should immediately try to determine it. There is no evidence that it was done by Spanish saboteurs, but that was what McKinley wanted his country to believe. He accused Spain. Meanwhile the Spanish government had indignantly turned down the offer to purchase Cuba. The United States was swept by one of its periodic bouts of war fever, whipped up by a cynical administration. It had its casus belli for the Spanish-American War, and it struck at Spain's weakest point: its fleets, which were old, undergunned, badly manned, and largely built of wood without armor plating. In May 1898 Admiral Dewey sailed into Manila Bay and sank every ship in Spain's Pacific fleet at a total cost of eight American sailors wounded and none dead. Two months later, on July 3, 1898, another American force attacked Spain's Atlantic fleet, commanded by Admiral Cervera, off Santiago de Cuba. Few of the Spanish guns could throw a shell as far as the American ships. Four hours later all the Spanish vessels were sunk. American casualties were one dead and two wounded. Between them, Manila Bay and Santiago were the most one-sided naval disaster in modern history, and the Spanish army, cut off in Cuba, had no choice but surrender. By now this wretched force had lost two thousand men in battle and fifty-three thousand to various tropical diseases. Its sick and ragged survivors were shipped back to Spain and dumped in its ports, including Barcelona. And now the recriminations and the despair began.

The disaster of 1898 was the worst humiliation Spain had ever endured. At a time when England, France, Germany, Italy, and even little Belgium were busy carving up Africa and the East to suit their imperial designs, at the high noon of colonial acquisition by the major European powers, Spain lost the final remnants of the oldest European empire of them all, one whose origins stretched back four hundred years to Christopher Columbus. Only one of two conclusions seemed possible. The first was that Spain carried some racial flaw, some genetic streak of indolence that made it unfit, as a nation, to share the burden and challenges of modernity with other European states. The second was that the Spanish people had been sold out by its politicians and generals—a conclusion that, for anyone who saw the lines of wretched, abandoned, fever-shaken veterans begging along Barcelona's waterfront, was harder to resist.

But the pain was not just wounded pride. Spain's industry—which meant, effectively, Catalunya's—had also been stripped of its colonial markets. All during Weyler's bungled and savage attempts to suppress the Cuban revolution, Catalan industrialists had been in the van of the conservatives urging Cánovas to unrelenting war so that they could keep those markets. Now the United States had them. Of course, the disaster was everyone's fault but their own—they were the victims of Madrid's incompetence. So the familiar litany of Catalan complaints against Castile started up again: here we are, industrious but shamefully overtaxed, our money frittered away by corrupt generals and poured into grandiose but empty colonial schemes, and now we are left with no one to sell our cloth to. Thus the fallout from 1898 made big Barcelonese money somewhat less monarchist, tipping it more to the conservative Catalanist cause that, in the form of the Lliga Regionalista, was to triumph at Barcelona's polls in 1901. But Catalanism, though it had everything to do with the architecture of the day, had very little relation to a different sense of culture—mainly painting, poetry, and theater—that incubated in Barcelona under the rubric of *modernisme*.

VIII

Between 1890 and 1910, painting and sculpture in Barcelona enjoyed a revival—though a more limited one than architecture. "In the two decades of *modernisme*," wrote the art historian Cristina Mendoza, "Catalan painting experienced one of the most brilliant periods in its history." Unfortunately this is not saying much, since Catalan painting had been moribund—except at the level of folk art, ex-votos, and ceramic decoration—for the best part of three hundred years before it received some animation at the end of the nineteenth century. Once the energies of its International Gothic phase were spent and Flemish-influenced painters like Lluís Dalmau (fl. 1450) and Bernat Martorell were dead, Barcelona's painting had slipped into a long coma. The seventeenth century was the *siglo d'oro* for Castile. But in the seventeenth and eighteenth centuries, and for most of the nineteenth as well, Barcelona produced no genuinely significant painters. There was no Catalan equivalent to Velázquez, Zurbarán, Murillo, El Greco, Ribera, or Goya.

If you had asked an educated Catalan in the 1880s for a "great" living artist of Catalan extraction, he would probably have named Marià Fortuny, the painter from Reus who made a substantial career in Rome and Paris with his genre scenes of peasant life and his paintings of cardinals, done in a flickering, bravura impasto: it was to Fortuny that the city turned for the enormous panorama of General Prim routing the Arabs at the battle of Tetuán, now in the Museum of Modern Art in Barcelona. The same notional art lover might also have mentioned Catalan landscape painters, divided into two schools: one centered on the inland town of Olot, the other on the coastal fishing village of Sitges. The Olot painters, whose *chef d'école* was Joaquim Vayreda, were provincial imitators of the French Barbizon school, fond of old stone, mists, autumnal forests, rain-sogged earth, and, in general, the cultural imagery of pious rootedness and Noble Peasants that went with the Renaixença. Thus Modest Urgell (1839–1919), when painting *El Toc d'Oracio* (*The Chime of the Prayer Bell*), 1876, added a symbolic fillip to his image of a crumbling rural church: the bell in the tower swings out in the evening glow, and a barely visible bat, tiny but demonic, shies away from it in fright. The Sitges painters, led by Joan Roig i Soler and Arcadi Mas i Fontdevila (1852–1934), preferred light to mist, water to earth, and the immemorial Catalan fisherman to the equally durable Catalan *pagès*. Their clients and critics imagined they were doing something parallel to French impressionism,

Santiago Rusinyol

but actually their work was academic painting with an overlay of brightness derived from Fortuny and the Italian Macchiaioli. They sought spontaneity and painted, when possible, in the open air, but that was as far as their likeness to Monet or Pissarro went. Paris and Munich, those twin meccas for the aspiring European artist in the 1880s, were very far away from Barcelona; but Paris was closer, its gravitational field was stronger, and it was from Paris that change would come.

It came from London too: Barcelonese artists, especially Alexandre de Riquer i Inglada (1856–1920), a painter and decorative designer who had lived in England, were well aware of the Pre-Raphaelites and of the work of William Morris and his circle: the Kelmscott Press had a strong influence on Catalan *éditions de luxe*. Nevertheless the main influences on painting were Parisian, and they were transmitted through the work and ideas of two young Catalan artists in the 1890s, Santiago Rusinyol (1861–1931) and Ramón Casas i Carbó (1866–1932). They were friends throughout their entire working lives and died within a year of each other; their contribution to the sense of cultural style in Barcelona's *belle époque* was considerable. Casas was by far the better painter, but Rusinyol was an all around animator: an artist, but also a journalist, an aphorist, a playwright, a novelist, and a collector of antiquities and folk art as well. Neither, by any stretch of the imagination, could have been called an intellectual. Both were, in a general way, Catalanists, but they were also

Ramón Casas, Self-Portrait

fervent Francophiles and believers in the idea of an international culture. In 1890s Barcelona, a city of about 300,000 people (as compared with 2 million in the immense conurbation of Paris) cultural cliques lived cheek by jowl; word traveled fast; foreign art was rarely seen (there being no market for it) and quickly deferred to rather than deeply analyzed or grasped; local certainties were easily shaken by newly imported creeds; notoriety was easily attained. It was an ideal situation for a cultural entrepreneur like Rusinyol, Barcelona's chief promoter in the visual arts of the diffuse idea called *modernisme*.

He knew just how, and how far, to startle the bourgeoisie because he was one of them. Rusinyol's father employed four hundred workers in his textile factory, and though the son did not have to work there long or hard to know that he did not want to be a businessman, he was not about to turn his back on the advantages of his birth. The idea of *rejecting* the upper-middle class, the gesture of so many writers and artists of the time, never occurred to him—who would have paid his bills, if not his parents? Instead, as Josep Pla pointed out, Rusinyol thought he would "redeem" his own class by making it more open to beauty, poetry, art. His tools for this operation included satire. Rusinyol was in some ways a naïve writer, not at all deeply read, but he was a profuse and instinctive one with an ironic cutting edge. One of his fictions became a Catalan classic—a satire, *L'Auca de Senyor Esteve* (*The Tale of Mr. Es-*

teve,), 1907. The *auca* was a popular Catalan form—a kind of comic strip printed as a broadsheet, each panel illustrating a simple rhyming couplet. The hero of Rusinyol's tale is the quintessential petty bourgeois that bohemia loved to hate, with all his tics, conformist habits, timidities, blind spots, and vulgarities, owner of a haberdashery and father of a son with "artistic" pretensions. Senyor Esteve was such a Barcelonese archetype that, eighty-five years later, Rusinyol's book is still in print. It is his best-known work—involuntarily, since the fame Rusinyol most desired was as a painter.

Ramón Casas i Carbó also had the luck to be born rich. Moreover, his father was an *indiano* and hence inclined to put a certain value on risk: conservative Catalans, shopkeepers or timid craftsmen, did not as a rule take off across the Atlantic to seek their fortunes in the Caribbean but stuck to their trade and expected their sons to do the same. The father showed no prejudice and raised no obstacles when his eleven-year-old son quit school and apprenticed himself to Joan Vives, a painter and decorator in Barcelona.

The boy was precocious, though not necessarily more so than other budding artists of the time. (Artists started much younger then, in menial apprenticeship jobs, a harmless and not too exploitive form of child labor on which the studio system of Europe had depended since the days of Giotto. This should be remembered by those who believe Picasso was phenomenally precocious, which, by the standards of his time, he was not.) In his early teens Casas fell in with the group of young painters, poets, and intellectuals who put out the cultural journal *L'Avenç*, which his elder brother helped to underwrite. In 1881 his first published drawing, of a Romanesque cloister, appeared in its pages. That same year, Casas was off to Paris—an eager fifteen-year-old.

He joined the academy of Carolus-Duran, a popular and conservative teaching mill in Paris, especially hospitable to foreigners. Its most famous recent graduate was John Singer Sargent, the "American genius" whose bravura technique, admiration for Manet, and love of all things Spanish (his Parisian reputation was made with *El Jaleo*, a flamenco scene, in 1882) formed Casas's model of professional skill. Nothing suggests that Casas was interested in Monet and the other impressionists, who held their first collective show in Paris in 1882. His early work bears no trace of impressionist color, blue shadows, optical flicker. It is entirely tonal and based on Manet. He had made his own deductions about Manet's debts to Velázquez, Goya, and Ribera, but he was a Whistler enthusiast too.

In fact, Casas was so impressed by Whistler's nocturnes from the 1870s, in which the artist had finally broken with the earlier influence of Courbet's realism, that a couple of years later he raved about them to a young Australian artist he met in the Académie Gervex (where he also took classes) and now ran into again, outside Granada. Casas was bicycling with another young Catalan painter, Laureà Barrau. Tom Roberts was on foot. The year was 1884. Roberts, asked Casas, do you know about impressionism? No, said Roberts, I've never heard of it. Well, listen, said Casas eagerly, you really should: it's the latest thing in Paris, it's all done in gray, and it's mainly painted by a genius of an American called Jaume Whistler.

This impressed the future *chef d'école* of the Australian impressionists so much that, when he returned to his homeland, he began to apply Whistler's manner of silvery, tonal "impressionism" to the Australian bush. Hence the odd sensation the passing Australian has when he sees early Casas for the first time in the Museum of Modern Art in Barcelona—the painter could be an Australian doing Spanish subjects. Catalan impressionism, sired by two Americans, was to have an inspiring and decisive effect on art on the far side of the world, in a society that was even smaller than Catalunya's, without causing a ripple of interest elsewhere in Europe. Province spoke instinctively to province.

Casas was never a colorist, and indeed his preference for mono-chromes was mocked by caricaturists, one of whom in 1896 drew Casas's head emerging from a paint tube on whose label were the words "Yellow + green + blue + vermilion + white = GRAY." His work in the 1880s was sporadic (he stopped painting for two longish spells, once in Granada in 1884 to learn flamenco guitar, the second time in Barcelona in 1886 while recovering from tuberculosis), but by his midtwenties he had settled down to regular work. He and Rusinyol had grown increas-ingly irked by the narrowness of Barcelona's artistic milieu: the lack of commercial galleries—there was only one, the Sala Parès—and the pov-erty of its public and private collections. As for the climate of thought about painting, both of them found it invincibly stupid. When the twenty-year-old Casas exhibited a Manet-influenced bullfight scene in Barcelona in 1886, the critic of *La Vanguardia*, José Lázaro Galdiano, rebuked him for choosing "repugnant" subjects and pointed out that if this promising but immature talent wanted to paint the corrida he should do it as a historical painting; for instance, he might have painted the bullfight staged before Pope Calixtus III in the Colosseum in Rome.

If Barcelona could put on the International Exposition, it could have international artists too. It was time to return to the great magnet, Paris. In 1890 Rusinyol, with a large allowance from his family, leased a flat in the bohemian mecca of Montmartre—not just anywhere on that artists'

Ramón Casas and Santiago Rusinyol, painting each other, 1890

hill, but right over the top of its most famous dance hall, painted by Renoir and half the artists of Paris, the Moulin de la Galette. He invited Casas to set up house with him there, and two other Catalan artists as well: the painter Miquel Utrillo, who had been living in Paris for some years, and an engraver named Ramon Canudas, who died shortly afterward. Thus a little Catalan colony began. In time, other Barcelonese artists and cultural drifters, arriving in Paris, joined it and then drifted away; Picasso, settling in Paris in 1904, had the company of Catalan friends like Jaime Sabartès, his future secretary, and the whining, suicidal Carles Casagemas. But its original nucleus was Rusinyol's studio in the Moulin de la Galette.

Miquel Utrillo was the habitué, the man with contacts in bohemian life and on the fringes of the avant-garde. He had been living with Suzanne Valadon, a former trapeze artist who had turned to modeling for artists to support herself and little Maurice, her son by the Catalan, who later became an alcoholic painter of streetscapes. Valadon's new lover was the young composer Erik Satie, whose portrait both Rusinyol and Casas painted in 1891. Each attached the same title to his picture: *El Bohemi* (*The Bohemian*). Rusinyol's Satie is seen in his Montmartre lodgings: a frail-looking youth sitting close to the fire, a mean room with a trestle bed, posters and prints pinned to the dun-colored wall. The only spot of color is the corner of a rug, which—whether by conscious irony or not, one cannot be sure—is in red and yellow stripes, the colors of the Catalan flag.

Casas's Satie stands outside, on the street: top hat, frock coat, the pince-nez attached to a black band—a slightly ragged, dandified black profile against the misty evening backdrop of the old mill, at the violet hour, when the globes of the street lamps had just been lighted, but the pallor was not gone from the sky. This crepuscular light, learned above all from Whistler, was the favorite of Catalan *modernista* painting. Evening was vague, suggestive, nuanced, and slightly depressing. Casas reveled in it. His *Dance at the Moulin de la Galette* (1890) was very far indeed from the Dionysiac and sinister color of Toulouse-Lautrec's dance-hall scenes: in the gray light of evening, raised only a little by the gas jets, a few anemic figures bend and jerk on the dance floor, but there is more floor than clients, and even the string band seems half-asleep. This *miserablisme* had a powerful effect on Catalan critics when the painting was shown in Barcelona in 1891. *La Vanguardia* admired its rendering of "the curious and the fatigued, looking on at the wildness with indifferent melancholy, as a drunk looks at a glass of wine. . . . The soft light of the exterior penetrates through the windows diffusing itself like mist . . . [in] this most funereal scene of the dance of St Vitus." The high eyeline results in a tilting and emphasis on the floor; this, together with the brusquely "unposed," almost snapshotlike silhouettes of the figures, suggests that Casas had been looking at Degas.

Rusinyol was also absorbed by grayness. "Great Paris," he wrote in one of his articles for the Catalan press, a series entitled *Desde el Molino* ("From the Mill"), "spread itself in the pale, diaphanous background as though it were submerged in an immense silver bath. The chimney-stacks issued a thin smoke that diffused and mixed with the fog, and from this array of vapors the great domes and high steeples emerged with their pale colors." It is a scene straight from Whistler, though the article reported on a visit to a *puntillista* painter, the newest of the new, who talks to them about Seurat, "Signas" (Signac), "Gros" (presumably Cross), and Pissarro. The artist's name is not given; later, Rusinyol hinted it was Maximilian Luce. "This is the sublime hour," he tells his Catalan visitors, "this is the hour when line dies and only color rules. My golden dream will be always to live in this hour of agony, and to paint in a balloon, where I will be far, very far from the earth."

One may doubt that such words were ever uttered, but in any case neither Rusinyol nor Casas was convinced, as a painter, of the impending reign of color sensation over line. The main effect of Rusinyol's articles—they included, among their subjects, Montmartre nightlife, an itinerant photographer, an excursion to Rouen, and an unnamed "chic painter" who is amusingly guyed as a frigid, snobbish, and neurasthenic *pompier*—was to make the readers back home understand how thoroughly he and his friends were plugged into the Paris scene, with all its variety, novelty, and tantalizing hints of decadence. He wanted them to know how different it was from provincial Barcelona. "The sympathy Paris inspires as soon as one arrives there," he wrote, "does not spring from its movement, which is dizzying, nor from its immense size . . . but from the art-soaked atmosphere which everyone breathes and which spreads to everything, to architecture as much as to women's dresses, to great works and monuments as to little trifles . . . here you feel its harmony, the harmony of a colossal, well-tuned orchestra."

To have lived in such a place, navigated it, grasped its inner meanings, to be able to laugh as well as gape at it—that was to have transcended your provincial origins; it gave you authority. This has always been the expatriate's trump card—those who stay home know less; they cannot be as confident in their judgments. Thus it came about that Casas and Rusinyol, who were in fact peripheral to the newer energies of Parisian culture and, beyond their amiable dandyism, rather conservative at heart, rapidly acquired the reputation of sophisticated and even shocking innovators in their native Barcelona.

Their champion, in the pages of *L'Avenç* and elsewhere, was a young novelist and critic named Ramón Casellas, who in 1891 greeted a show of sixty-eight works by the two painters (plus a third Catalan expatriate, the sculptor Enric Clarasó) with a long article that took on the character of a manifesto of *modernista* painting, eagerly discussed, quoted, and reread in the cafés of the Ramblas. Rusinyol and Casas, complained the conservatives, painted common fragments of life—dancers, bars, lone women sitting with aperitifs in café gardens, a soldier courting a *midinette* on the Butte de Montmartre. Where was the nobility in such painting? Why didn't they do historical themes, battles or jolly cardinals, like the incomparable Fortuny? To which Casellas replied that the masters of the past had often taken "trivial" subjects: even Velázquez had painted drunks, and the Moulin de la Galette should be seen in this tradition of letting real life into the hieratic space of art. But there was another point: genre paintings became historical paintings whether you meant them to or not. "It is enough that an artist paint what he sees and do so in a very personal manner, especially when one reflects that today's paintings of life are tomorrow's history paintings." What really counted, in Ca-

sellas's view—and here he began to put his toe over the lintel of symbolism and the emphatic value it placed on feeling—is the intensity the
artist could give the image. Scenes of Barcelona were routine; scenes of
Paris brought out the empathy in Casas and Rusinyol, and in "that slice
of strange and unhealthy social life, from its ravings and sorrows to its
lack of balance" they found a world very far from *seny*, producing images
that seemed "to make the fever of that sick society of hysteria even
stronger."

One of the meanings of modernism, then, was living on one's nerves;
in the 1890s a certain cult of neurasthenia began to occupy the cultural
stage in Barcelona, as in other European capitals. It was more pertinent
to Rusinyol than to Casas. There was certainly nothing so uncontrolled
about Ramón Casas, although as he grew older he drank more heavily,
spent less thought on each picture, and relied increasingly on his fluent
manner, which before long turned into an empty, ironclad facility. Josep
Pla claimed that Casas, an amiable gastronome, took more care and
trouble making a salad than working at the easel. This did not worry
his patrons, who were American; supported by the Chicago tractor
millionaire Charles Deering, Casas became fashionable in the United
States before World War I and remained so until his death in 1932.
Little that he painted after 1900 is of any interest. But in the 1890s his
style had not yet turned into mere stylishness. He left a mark on Spanish
painting as a virtuoso performer with brush and charcoal, making political paintings that pleased his radical friends, social portraits whose
Sargentlike dash and fidelity enchanted his clients, illustrations of pretty
women that created a fashion type in Barcelona like the one Charles
Dana Gibson was constructing in New York, and posters with a wide,
vivid popular appeal. The political paintings, when they were shown in
Barcelona, caused a sensation.

The first of them was *Garotte Vil (Vile Garroting)*, 1894: the execution
of Santiago Salvador, the Liceu bomber. Casas did not witness this
execution, but he saw others, and he went to some lengths to capture
the documentary truth of the scene, painting a study of the empty Patí
dels Corders on the spot, and then using photographs as source material
for the jostling crowd of heads in the foreground, the mounted Guardia
Civil, the sinister *penitentes* in their black conical rig, and the distant,
isolated victim. Four years later he brought the same devices of jour-
nalistic immediacy to *The Corpus Christi Procession Leaving Santa Maria del
Mar*. This painting is a mere street scene unless you know about the
Corpus Christi bombing and the subsequent Montjuic trials. But since
everyone in Barcelona did know about them, the image is fiercely loaded.

Ramón Casas, Garotte Vil, *1894*

Now it takes on a different aspect: the shift and flicker of brush marks in Casas's handling of the crowd seem tinged with panic, and the indistinct white veils of the schoolgirls, like soft explosions of feathers, hint at a different and worse explosion. Casas's third political painting, *La Carga (The Charge)*, 1899, shows a mounted Guardia Civil, saber drawn, riding down a prostrate worker while in the background crowds scatter in panic; with a view to winning kudos from the Paris and Madrid salons as a historical painter, he changed its date to 1903 and its title to *Barcelona 1902* to make it into a comment on the general strike of that year. Did he want to be seen as Goya's heir, moralizing on the tragic politics of fin de siècle Barcelona? It seems more than likely, but Casas was not an artist to measure against Goya.

If Casas was prepared to make paintings about his social concerns, Rusinyol was not—he had none to speak of. He despised politics and believed in art for art's sake. "The love of Humanity," he once remarked, "is rhetorical literature. To save the life of one friend, you can let a hundred thousand Chinese be killed." Detached, sardonic, yet with irresistible charm and a talent for intimacy, Rusinyol had the strengths and weaknesses of the dandy who does not need to work and so can invent his life on his own terms; he hardly bothered to conceal his addiction to "artificial paradises," his Baudelairean term for shooting

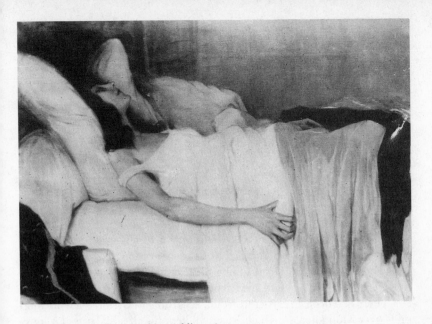

Santiago Rusinyol, The Morphine Addict, *1894*

morphine. By the mid-1890s he had an obstructive habit. Perhaps there was a family disposition to the drug: his maternal uncle, Gonçal Prats, was a dandy and a morphine addict. The cost did not matter to Rusinyol, and the drug was easily available. But stories circulated in the tiny Catalan art world about the "decadence" that Rusinyol caught like a fever in wicked Paris, thereby infecting *modernisme* with sin. Rusinyol did nothing to discourage them, and although morphine exacted its price in failures of concentration it also provided the motif for some of his more interesting work. In 1894 he exhibited a painting called *The Morphine Addict*: a girl lying in bed, her slender hand clutching at the sheet as the drug begins to take effect. This caused a scandal and solidified the idea that had been floating around Barcelona for some time—that whatever else "modernism" meant, the first thing it stood for was moral collapse. The fact that Rusinyol presented her without any symbolic condemnation made it seem all the worse.

Rusinyol liked to cultivate an air of *désinvolture*, as though the effort of painting and writing cost him nothing; that was part of the bohemian attitude, his front. In fact, as he put it later in life, "I used to be very much a Bohemian, but I always worked like a nigger and a half [*un negre i mig*]." In 1891 he started looking for a place to set up permanent house as an artist. Setting out with a friend to visit the museum created by the writer Victor Balaguer in the town of Geltru, he made a detour to spend the night in the fishing village of Sitges, some twenty-five miles south of Barcelona; he fell in love with the place and bought two adjacent houses there. They stood on a low cliff at the face of the town, an easy stroll from the beach where fishermen drew up their boats; their windows looked straight onto the sea below. This, Rusinyol decided, would be his refuge; and he would transform it into a cultural center, a private museum, a place to show old Catalan crafts—particularly forged iron-work, which he adored—and new manifestations of *modernisme* in painting, music, theater, and poetry. He spent the considerable sum of thirty thousand pesetas doing it up in an eclectic mixture of styles (Neo-Gothic with Moorish overtones) with the help of the young architect Francesc Rogent, son of Elias, the architect of the exposition. He named it the Cau Ferrat, or Den of Iron. Thus the center of gravity of *modernisme* moved, with Rusinyol and his friends, to Sitges.

There had been an earlier iron den, according to Utrillo—a workshop on Carrer Muntaner, in which Rusinyol kept his already large but inexorably growing collection of iron: armor, daggers, swords, helms, wind vanes, andirons, candelabra, braziers, locks, keys, and door knockers. But this one was far larger, a dramatic frame for Rusinyol's tireless collecting instincts. The ultramarine walls downstairs were covered with souvenirs, drawings, portraits of friends, painted tiles, lusterware dishes, and cabinets of Roman and Celtiberian antiquities; a tiled octagonal fountain, saved or stolen from some monastery, dripped meditatively in the filtered sea light, its upper basin filled with masses of maidenhair fern. The iron collection accumulated where it is today, in a hammer-beamed salon on the first floor, running the full depth of the house. In iron, Rusinyol saw the essence of the Catalan spirit, the obstinate traces of a national history, and a foretaste of modernity to come. "I think of those forges of old Barcelona as a school where instinct was set free," he said in a lecture, "Mis Hierros Viejos" ("My Old Ironwork"), that he gave in 1893 at the Barcelona Athenaeum: "There, in the darkness of those sooty workshops, under the ringing chorus of constant hammering on the anvil, I think I see springing from the fire . . . an art without esthetic rules or absurd restrictions, an art free as smoke, born from fire, and wrought in fire."

These spiky, hard-drawn, explicit objects, anonymous in their making, the result of unegotistical skill meeting the resistances of an ancient material, had another virtue: they pointed to the future. His sojourns in Paris had made Rusinyol well aware of the gathering cult of the primitive behind modern art, and he associated this with the attempt of

Rusinyol's ironwork collection at the Cau Ferrat

Catalanists of an earlier generation than his own to seek what was linguistically, culturally "pure" in the remote valleys from which his ironwork came:

> The tendency of the most modern art is to drink at primal fountains, where the water remains pure and free from all contamination. Music draws inspiration from popular song; poetry, from the muse of the village; the most modern painting from primitive artists—and if we want to find a true decorative style, we must perforce find our inspiration in this style of our inheritance, in these remains of the past.

Prophetic words, in view of the twentieth-century development of direct-welded sculpture. But Rusinyol's ideas were more modern than his art, and when he tried to imitate French symbolist painting, the results tended to be pious cliché. There were two levels of symbolist influence in Rusinyol. The first, which shows in his earlier Parisian work, was a predilection for expectant atmosphere: empty foregrounds creating a tension between the eye and the figure in the middle ground, usually a woman who seems to be waiting for something, her anticipation keyed up by an open doorway (what will come through it?) or a half-seen person in the background. These devices came out of Whistler and Degas and, within the limits of Rusinyol's draftsmanship, worked adequately. But he also greatly admired the classicist paintings of Pierre

Puvis de Chavannes, whom he had known in Paris, and his attempts to redo Puvis were bathetic. The most ambitious of them is an allegory that decorates the upper floor of the Cau Ferrat, a pseudoreligious work done on three Gothic-arch panels depicting painting, music, and poetry—the arts whose modernist revival, Rusinyol hoped, would be enacted in Sitges. "Painting" is a medieval page painting blessed damozels, in plein air, in a field of white lilies. "Music" is a particularly awkward tribute to Puvis, a nude playing a harp on the bank of a river at sunset, surrounded by blue flowers. In "Poetry," an ethereal virgin clutching a very small sheet of paper, perhaps large enough to fit a triolet on, goes into raptures beside an octagonal font. This triptych is as insipid as the worst of English Pre-Raphaelitism.

Rusinyol had grasped the rhetoric of symbolism and spoke with passion about its traits: spirituality, suggestiveness, indeterminacy, the penumbra of feeling around the thought. He felt he was arguing for a new way of experiencing things, not an "art movement":

> The growth we see today is tired of the abuses of naturalism, and seeks what is spiritual. Symbolism, decadentism, estheticism and other isms—these are only names clumsily applied to sensations, whose nature we struggle to explain: they are the murmuring of wings that spread to fly, to raise themselves above the wretched earth; they are the desires of human fantasy that flee men's prisons; they are the hopes of things to come. Today's growth partakes of the mystical, insofar as mysticism includes suffering and visions; it is anarchic, in that anarchism is an impossible fantasy . . . it includes whatever you can dream of, dreaming alone, undisturbed by the rich or the poor bourgeois, the bourgeois of art, who are all those people who do not tremble before a sunset, before a weeping woman, before a passing pink cloud . . .

Quite a number of those who, unlike their parents, felt like trembling before pink clouds made the journey to Sitges to take part in the *festes modernistes*, or "modernist festivals," that Rusinyol organized there from 1892 until 1899; they generated so much interest that special trains were arranged to bring the participants from Barcelona. The 1892 *festa* was merely an exhibition of paintings by Casas, Rusinyol, and others, but in 1893 the program expanded to include a concert conducted by the young composer Enric Morera (1865–1942) of works by himself and César Franck. There was also a production in the small local theater, directed and designed by Rusinyol, of the first foreign symbolist play ever given in Catalan—*La Intrusa* by Maurice Maeterlinck, whose theme was death: "A virginal flower of the cemetery," Rusinyol announced in a speech before the curtain, was the gift that symbolism was offering to Sitges. Maeterlinck, he went on, had sought to "extract from human life, not its direct spectacles, not its commonplace phrases, but its flashing, untrammelled, paroxysmic visions."

The star of the 1894 *festa modernista* was El Greco. From a Paris banker Rusinyol had bought, with the help of the Spanish expatriate painter Ignacio de Zuloaga, two El Grecos, a Mary Magdalene and a Saint Peter (they still hang in the Cau Ferrat), and he turned their installation into a ceremony, a reenactment of the processions of medieval homage he had read about in Vasari—the reverent portage of a Cimabue altarpiece through Florence or of Duccio's *Maestà* through Siena. El Greco's morbid mannerist figures in their *contrapposto* poses, with their pallor and ecstatic spirituality, qualified him as a forefather of symbolism; he therefore deserved the fullest homage. On November 14, 1894, he got it. Down came the train from Barcelona, carrying the two Grecos and a load of writers, painters, architects, journalists, and other local celebrities—more than sixty of them, including Casas, Joan Maragall, and the man reputed to be the worst social snob in the Eixample (a large claim in the 1890s), J. A. Riera. It was met at the station by Pere Romeu, the future manager of the café Els Quatre Gats, looking like some deranged Quixote on horseback, with an illustrator named Lluís Labarta as his Sancho Panza on foot, carrying the banner of the Cau Ferrat. Each Greco was hoisted up on a bier, carried by four artists, and the procession led by Romeu solemnly marched up the hill to deposit the paintings in the Cau Ferrat before traipsing off to a monumental lunch. For years thereafter, the people of Sitges were convinced that El Greco was a relative, an obscure cousin perhaps, of Senyor "Tiago" Rusinyol.

Rusinyol's taste for parody and *blague* also had free rein at Sitges. During one of the *festes* he announced that Loie Fuller was going to perform. Fuller was one of the half-artist, half–show biz stars of the fin de siècle, an American dancer who gained an overnight success in Paris by performing in a flesh-colored body stocking, surrounded by immense translucent veils that she flounced in the air like clouds, like wings. She, and they, were lighted by electricity (a theatrical novelty). One either loved Fuller or thought her act was kitsch, but those clouds of gauze had a big effect on Art Nouveau decoration: she was the fairy Electricity in person. Rusinyol thought she was kitsch. He hired a dancer to impersonate her on a floating platform, moored below the Cau Ferrat,

The interior of The Four Cats

equipped with battery-powered spotlights. A large crowd turned up, and the dancer did her parody of Loie Fuller for two hours; no one except Rusinyol's friends was any the wiser.

With such high jinks and the publicity they created, *modernisme* in Barcelona had the momentum of a popular fashion by 1896, and Casas and Rusinyol decided to give it a base in town. In 1897 they and Romeu rented the ground floor of a Neo-Gothic house just built by Puig i Cadafalch, the Casa Martí, and in it they proposed to put a *cerveseria*, or "beer hall." They called it Els Quatre Gats—The Four Cats.

In hindsight, The Four Cats has acquired a nostalgic aura as one of the great intellectual meeting places of fin de siècle Europe. This, like all such reputations, is exaggerated, but the place certainly played a role in Barcelona's artistic life during its six short years (1897–1903). This was due not to the food, which was mediocre and often stingy (according to Josep Pla, not servings but "an exhibition of painted plates"), but rather to the drawing power of its core clientele. The name of the place meant, in Catalan slang, "just a few people"; the "four cats" were Romeu, Casas, Utrillo, and Rusinyol. The place, Rusinyol wrote, would be something for everyone—"an inn for the disillusioned . . . a warm nook for the homesick . . . a Gothic beer-hall for lovers of the north, and an Andalusian patio for lovers of the South . . . a place to cure the ills of

Casas at the wheel of his car, with the writer Apelles Mestres in the back seat

---

our century." Casas, Rusinyol, Utrillo, and their friends created their own club and, in the tradition of French artists' estaminets with rude proprietors, got an oddity to run it.

This was Pere Romeu, a tall, gangling failed painter, whose greasy hair, pop eyes, and yellow Bugs Bunny teeth, caricatured and preserved in scores of drawings, paintings, and posters, became one of the most familiar motifs of Catalan *modernisme*. Romeu was born in the coastal village of Torredembara, south of Barcelona, around 1862. After studying art and giving it up, he went to Paris, where he gravitated toward the Catalan clique at the Moulin de la Galette and, in their favorite cabaret, developed a craze for shadow puppetry—*ombres xineses*, it was called in Catalan, "Chinese shadows." His other predilection was sport. He bicycled. He had a sports car, one of the first in Barcelona, which endeared him to Casas, who owned the very first one. (Long after The Four Cats folded, Romeu ended his days as a garage owner.) He swam in the sea every day, even in winter, a habit his bohemian friends viewed as the height of folly. He rowed, fenced, sailed, and went on long excursions in the Pyrenees. All this seemed very American, which meant *modern*. Yet despite his strength-through-joy athletic habits, he continued

Ramón Casas, Rusinyol Seated in an Iron Chandelier

to look unkempt and dingy. Ramón Casas seems to have treated Romeu partly as a friend and partly as an odd human pet. Once they had settled on the Casa Martí, Casas paid for much of the decoration, including the enormous ring chandeliers (he sketched Rusinyol sitting in one) and the ersatz medieval furniture, designed by Puig. He also contributed the painting of himself and Romeu pedaling along on a tandem bicycle. Casas, on the front seat, his face shaded by his hat, cigar stuck in its pipelike holder, is bent forward, leaning into the pedals with maximum effort. Behind him, Romeu is taking it much easier. In the upper-right corner Casas inscribed a doggerel couplet, now painted over: "*Per anar amb bicicleta, / no es pot anar amb l'esquena dreta*"—"To ride a bicycle, / you can't have a straight back." It may be a veiled reference to the financial inequality of their business relationship, whose costs Casas had to make up. Later he replaced it with another painting of the two of them in an automobile. Romeu busied himself with keeping the long room of The Four Cats up to his standards of picturesque, artists' studio

Ramón Casas, painting of himself and Pere Romeu on a tandem bicycle, done for The Four Cats

gloom—he threw screeching fits if a waiter disturbed the spiderwebs—and steered onlookers away from the main table, where the elite of bohemia drank and argued.

The Four Cats was a permanent *tertulia*; through it, the fauna of the Cau Ferrat came home to roost in Barcelona. Exhibitions were held there, and shadow-puppet shows—an excellent satirical medium, as the *gats* knew from Paris. There were also Punch-and-Judy shows for children, for whom Romeu angled on the assumption that they would bring their parents, who would spend money. New composers, including Enric Granados and Isaac Albéniz, gave recitals. The Four Cats also put on lectures and started its own eponymous magazine. Edited by Romeu, this publication lasted fifteen issues and was then replaced by a more ambitious review, *Pèl i Ploma* (*Paper and Pen*). It was antiestablishment in tone, without actually espousing anarchism or socialism. It maintained the glossy production values of French illustrated magazines like *La Plume*, printed articles and reviews from Brussels and Paris, and ran drawings by all the artists in the Four Cats circle—Casas, Utrillo, and Rusinyol, but also younger ones like Joaquim Mir, Isidre Nonell, Ricard Opisso, and the *infant prodigi* of the clientele, Pablo Picasso, who was just twenty years old in 1901 when *Pèl i Ploma* ran its first article on his work.

Top left, Santiago Rusinyol, poster for Fulls de la Vida, 1898; top right, Ramón Casas, poster for a syphilis clinic; bottom, Ramón Casas, cover of an issue of Pèl i Ploma, *1899*

Ramón Casas, Portrait of Pablo Picasso

Between them, Casas and Picasso left a detailed record of the denizens of The Four Cats in their drawings. By the 1890s Casas was well into his series of charcoal drawings of the figures of Catalan cultural life: some sketchy, others highly finished, all facile, but many of them incisive. Anyone who looked or sounded interesting, Casas drew, and the result was a gallery of hundreds of portraits whose only rival, as documentation, was Felix Nadar's photographs of the cultural lions of Paris. Bohemians and literary anarchists, Catalanists and new counts, society jewelers, architects and dandies, poets like Maragall (a weary feline face from El Greco) and musicians like Pablo Casals, the actress Réjane and the dancer Loie Fuller; even Eleonora Duse. *La Barcelona tota*, plus its visiting celebrities, were there.

The clamorous accolades that greeted Casas's drawings when they were shown at the Sala Parès in 1899 fired up Picasso's competitive instincts. In 1900, encouraged by Casas—who, happily, was secure enough to unstintingly help the gifted newcomer rather than feel threatened by him, as older artists often are by their juniors—he put up his

own show of portrait drawings on the walls of The Four Cats: likenesses
of the beer hall's younger set, students and immature dandies and café
radicals. He was then eighteen years old, and one may see in this early
show the first sign of what would become a recurrent rhythm in Picasso's
work: the habit of pitting himself against a chosen master, burrowing
into his idiom, and "Picassoizing" it before moving on to the next stage
of his work. Later, he would do so to masters like Ingres and Velázquez;
but Ramón Casas was the first artist to whom Picasso gave this canni-
balistic homage.

The younger artists at The Four Cats were the heirs of French
illustration: Daumier, Toulouse-Lautrec, Steinlen, the sardonic com-
mentators on human greed and inequality. Being poor, Picasso and Isidre
Nonell knew the life of the streets well: not the boulevard theater in
which Casas and Rusinyol moved at their ease, but the other Barcelona
of the docks and the Barri Xinó, with its whores and sailors, pimps and
gypsies, agitators and hopeless, mendicant veterans dumped there from
the troopships after the Cuban disaster. This was the place later apostrophized by Joan Maragall in his "Oda Nova a Barcelona," "New Ode
to Barcelona" (1909):

> *Tens aquest rambla que és una hermosura . . .*
> *I allí, a quatre passes, febrosa de sobres,*
> *més ampla que l'altra, la Rambla dels pobres*
> *tremola en la fosca ses llums infernals.*

> You have one Rambla, a place of delight . . .
> And there, four steps away, feverish with excess,
> broader than the other, the Rambla of the poor
> shudders in the gloom of its hellish lights.

Nonell took a sardonic pleasure in startling people with his subject
matter: it is hard to imagine how an American artist today, in our age
of "sensitivity," would embark on a series like the one Nonell produced
in 1896—drawings and watercolors of an inbred and goitrous population
of backwoods cretins who lived around the remote Catalan thermal spa
of Caldes de Boi. Before settling down to his main theme (the marginals of the Raval and the Barri Xinó, huddled in their shawls and done
in a style loosely derived from the Black Paintings of Goya), he exhibited
at The Four Cats a sequence of drawings of the 1898 veterans on the
docks, which had a strong antigovernment punch. Nonell's *miserablisme*
chimed with Picasso's and may have influenced it.

It is sometimes thought that, because Picasso made incessant sketches of the outcasts and the poor during his early years in Barcelona, he was in some way directly involved with anarchism. A recent book (1989) by Patricia Leighten argues that a current of strongly politicized anarchist belief ran right through Picasso's Barcelonese work and into cubism. No letter, recorded remark, or drawing by Picasso supports this notion. It is wishful thinking. Certainly, Picasso's early drawings of demonstrations in Madrid and beggars in Barcelona show sympathy with the down-trodden; probably, like any other young artist, he thought the anarchists were a kind of avant-garde; he may—though even this is uncertain—have been imaginatively stirred by the purity of Bakuninist "propaganda by deed." But the truth, as John Richardson's magisterial study of early Picasso has shown, is that Picasso was timorously apolitical and terrified of trouble with the authorities—especially, one may surmise, after the draconic ferocities of the Montjuic trials. He had a few anarchist friends like the writer Jaume Brossa, but such associations prove nothing; in any case, you could hardly spill a drink in The Four Cats without splashing the boots of some Bakunin-spouting kid. "Sentimental" anarchism—meaning not much more than dislike of authority and sympathy for the underdog—was commonplace in artistic circles, but active anarchists, who were now settling down to the serious work of organizing trade unions in Barcelona, viewed it with contempt. It hardly even qualified as fellow-traveling. As for the lessons of the Cuban fiasco, they inscribed themselves not so much in Catalan art as in Catalan poetry—most vividly in the work of the city's major poet, Joan Maragall, who after 1898 became the lyric and wounded voice of the desire for "regen-eration," the poetic conscience of those who felt that Spain, morally speaking, had hit rock bottom. "Listen, Spain, to the voice of a son / who speaks to you in a language that is not Castilian," Maragall cries in "Oda a l'Espanya," written soon after the disaster in 1898. Others—Castilian poets—have sung to you about your Roman origins and your heroes, victories, triumphs; this Catalan poet wants to speak *molt altra-ment*, "very differently": he has seen the boats sail away, filled with men fated to die—

> *Somrients marxaven—cap a l'atzar;*
> *i tu cantaves—vora del mar*
> *com una folla.*
> *On són els barcos?—On són els fills?*
> *Pregunta-ho al Ponent i a l'ona brava:*

Joan Maragall

---

tot ho perderes,—no tens ningú.
Espanya, Espanya,—retorna en tu . . .

Smiling they went—to the mercy of fate;
and you sang on the seashore
like a madwoman.
Where are the ships? Where are the sons?
Ask the West and the wild wave:
you have lost everything—you have nothing.
Spain, Spain, come back to yourself!

Of course, to the politicians in Madrid, the eloquence of a Maragall would have seemed impertinent—not that many of them knew about it. Who was he to lecture them on patriotism, and in Catalan at that? This well-off, German- and French-speaking internationalist, married to an Englishwoman? But Maragall's alienation from Spain was emblematic. It rose not from narrow Jocs Florals–style Catalanist convention, but from the awareness that old, imperial Spain was finished and that, to heal itself, Spain must now knit together the disjointed parts of its own classes, peoples, and body—including Catalunya. If it could not listen, it was lost: that was the real lesson of 1898, and the last two words of the ode are "*Adéu, Espanya!*"

IX

No new *modernista* institution replaced The Four Cats, after its doors closed in 1903. (Ironically, its space in the Casa Martí was later taken over by the Artistic Circle of Saint Luke, which had been founded to combat everything The Four Cats stood for—internationalism, "decadence," the relativism of modern life.) The one real institution of modern culture that rose in Barcelona during the 1890s, and prospered thereafter, was devoted to music, not painting; and it housed itself in what may seem, in retrospect, the quintessential building of Lluís Domènech i Montaner's career. This was the Orfeó Català.

The Orfeó was a choral society, set up to carry on the work of the father figure of Catalan musical revival in the 1860s, Josep Anselm Clavé. It was started by two young musicians, Lluís Millet and Amadeu Vives. Neither was old enough to have known Clavé—Millet was born in 1867, Vives in 1871. They made a contrasting pair: Millet the striding youth, tall and big handed; Vives a pallid café rat with lank, dark hair and a muscular affliction that cramped the movements of his limbs. Millet was a sailor's son whose family had fled to Barcelona to escape the Carlists. Growing up there, he showed a talent for music and gained a place in the Conservatori del Liceu. He worked for his tuition, and though he could not afford a ticket to the Liceu, he went to all the choral recitals he could reach.

Cançó popular obsessed Millet and Vives. They would carry Clavé's work and expand it by using folk music as the working public's bridge to classical music. Their choral society would mingle folk song with "the great creations of universal genius"—symphonic and choral works by Bach, Beethoven, Handel, Wagner, Haydn, Berlioz, and Mahler. Millet saw clearly that what the man in the street likes is great art, and that you cannot condescend to him. The guarantee against provincialism was a deep sense of what Millet called "universal culture." And he would even do Italian arias—now and then.

Millet and Vives had to raise money. The Café Pelayo, on the Ramblas, was their base of operations: there, they and their friends played in a quartet and wheedled money out of likely donors. They approached politicians, doctors, poets, shopkeepers, priests, and anyone else who might be presumed to have the slightest interest in music, Catalanism, workers' choirs, or preferably all three.

They also took the idea to Felip Pedrell, "the Father of Catalan Musicology," a composer who had known Clavé but was a pan-Spanish

Lluís Millet

rather than a Catalan nationalist. He was revered by younger composers in Barcelona, particularly Isaac Albéniz and Enric Granados; their imprimatur, and his, mattered greatly to Millet. Pedrell was encouraging, though mildly skeptical. On the other hand, the composer Antoni Nicolau, the man chiefly responsible for getting Wagner into the concert repertory of Barcelona only a few years before, saw the point immediately. The clincher for Millet's funding was perhaps the concerts of *cançó popular* that went with the opening of the 1888 Universal Exposition, where a monument to Anselm Clavé was also unveiled. By 1891 Millet and Vives got a government charter for the statutes of their choral society. They christened it the Orfeó Català, or Catalan Orpheum, in honor of Orpheus, the divinely inspired lyrist of Greek myth whose playing could charm animals and make rocks dance.

The new Orfeó Català gave its first recital in 1892. The next year it had 50 choristers and 62 registered supporters. By 1905 the Orfeó boasted 185 singers and 1,358 contributors. Along this path from idea to institution, its structure changed. Originally Millet and Vives thought of it as an adult, all-male affair, like the *cors de Clavé*. But taking a cue from the Russian Chapel choir, which enthralled Barcelona's audiences with its recitals in 1895, Millet decided to build the Orfeó as a "family"

The Orfeó Català, 1896

that included a choir of children, fresh young warblers who would be the basses and sopranos of the future. He also wanted to regenerate the music of the Church, which was utterly stagnant. To this end, the Orfeó sang in religious foundations all around Catalunya, and especially at its symbolic religious center, the monastery of Montserrat. It also lent singers to revive existing church choirs.

The Liceu incarnated the values of the "high" Catalan bourgeoisie; the Orfeó Català set out to find its support among the *petita burgesia* and the cultured professionals—doctors, lawyers, the backbone of the Lliga Regionalista: Catalanists, not socialists. Hence it was accused of losing Clavé's pure working-class mission. One composer who thought Millet had sold out was a sardonic, short-fused young man named Enric Morera, who in 1895 started a rival workers' choir: the Societat Coral Catalunya Nova, or New Catalunya Choral Society.

Morera exemplified the passage of Catalan music from the local ideology of the Renaixença to the international frame of *modernisme*. He had worked outside Spain, whereas Millet had not. He studied composition and musical theory at the conservatory in Brussels, where he fell in with a set of French and Belgian musicians, symbolist devotees with a shared enthusiasm for the work of César Franck, who was still (though only just) alive. Among these followers of Franck whom Morera encouraged to visit and even live in Barcelona in the 1890s were the composers Ernest Chausson and Vincent d'Indy and the conductor Matthieu Crickboom. These musicians helped turn Barcelona's ears to Franco-Belgian music and thus opened up another channel for French symbolism to infuse the avant-garde circles of Catalunya. Lluís Millet did not move in painters' circles; but Morera, in the 1890s, found common cause with Ramón Casas and Santiago Rusinyol and was in effect musical director of the *festes modernistes* at the Cau Ferrat.

Morera's rivalry with Millet came into the open in 1895, when he organized the Catalunya Nova choir at Sitges. Rusinyol painted him leading it: an intense young man with pince-nez on his beaky nose, a slight pout, and long expressive fingers. Behind him stands a choir of men in baggy clothes—workers, not professional musicians. For Morera believed that, in courting the many-headed bourgeois enemy with "masterpiece" music, the Orfeó Català had lost touch with the working class and thereby abandoned Clavé's legacy. Even the phantom of the (Italian) opera was creeping back into choral music. The blame, Morera implied in his short-lived magazine (called *Catalunya Nova*) lay with the Orfeó Català:

> Mannerism pervades all the Catalan choirs. Thanks to the virtuoso directors our muscular songs lose their Catalan character of rough ingenuity; they tart them up with borrowings from Italian music . . . they say that Clavé was no technician, because none of his works resemble the Italian ones they are devoted to. . . . They have made moribund shadows of the master's splendid poems, turning those sturdy sunbronzed fishermen and those lads with muscular shoulders into flocks of well-brought-up boys who don't dare raise their voices for fear of disturbing Papa's seraphic digestion. They haven't grasped the fact that Clavé painted from life, and when they come across passages full of the manly feeling that is so common in Clavé they have tried to invert them, festooning them with absurd sentimentality to make them sound like scraps of fatuous operas.

Morera kept Catalunya Nova going vigorously for ten years. In fact it lingered on until the civil war, still claiming to bear the only true and pure gospel of Clavé, but Morera's intransigence and socialist views kept it chronically poor. There was no contest with the Orfeó, which went on from strength to strength. Between 1891 and 1895 the Orfeó Català spawned no fewer than 145 new choral societies throughout Catalunya. Every provincial town and most large villages took part in this spectacular upsurge of organized communal singing. It became more than a musical hobby: it was a social custom deeply linked to Catalans' sense of civic and national identity, built on a broad public base with the support of

Santiago Rusinyol, Portrait of Enric Morera, *1897*

professionals and the Church, with something in its programs for everyone. And Millet was quick to bring in new material. Nowhere was this more evident than in the mania for Wagner that swept Barcelona in the 1890s.

The first performance of any Wagnerian piece in Barcelona had been given not for the posh audience of the Liceu, but in one of Clavé's summer concerts for workers in the "gardens of Euterpe" beside Passeig de Gràcia in 1862: it was the march from act 2 of *Tannhäuser*. "We have to give all of Wagner to the public," he enthused later. "How they'll rave about him!" He was right. By 1870 Barcelona had a Wagnerians society and from then on musical Catalanists saw the future, as one of them put it, in "Wagnerism, considered as an instrument and a sign of national culture." Discussion of Wagner in Barcelona became increasingly heated, especially as it became clear that first Paris, and then Italy, had been conquered by *wagnerisme*. The most enthusiastic Catalan promoter of Wagner was a young music critic and medical student named Marsillach i Lleonart (1859–83), who at the age of seventeen had actually attended the opening of the Festspielhaus at Bayreuth in 1876 and heard the whole

Ring. He was the only Catalan who had. Things came late to Catalunya, and it was not until 1882 that Barcelona saw a full Wagner production —*Lohengrin*, in Italian. But the tide of Wagner mania rose after 1888, when the Catalan tenor Francesc Vinyas sang excerpts from *Lohengrin* at the opening night of the Universal Exposition, before Queen María Cristina. This clinched Wagner's reputation among the Catalans as the supreme European musician, and from 1903 on most of his operas were translated into Catalan—an honor previously reserved for Verdi alone.

Why did the Barcelonans make such a cult of Wagner? Because they saw in him their own desire to create a myth of national identity. Wagner had never been to Catalunya, but his heroes had: Titurel and his band of Christian knights established their bulwark of Christendom against the Moors, the castle built around the hiding place of the Holy Grail from which Christ had drunk at the Last Supper, on the forested heights of Montsalvat. "My name is Parsifal, and I come from Montsalvat"— Catalunya *was* Wagnerian Spain.

But there was a more general reason. Richard Wagner framed primitive heroic legends in very advanced terms. There was an extreme contrast between the primal antiquity of his subject and characters and the daring modernity of his musical forms—a strain marvelously resolved at the higher conscious levels of his art, and skirting absurdity on the lower. This accorded perfectly with the spirit, born in the Catalan Renaixença, that now pervaded the city's most advanced architecture. Wagner meant the *Ring* cycle to be the founding epic of Bavaria, as the *Mahabharata* was of India, the *Iliad* of Greece, or the *Aeneid* of Rome. Its central theme was the identity of the German race. Likewise, the Renaixença was obsessed with establishing the mystical uniqueness, the special character, of the *raca Catalana*. It wanted to bring back an idealized, mythic past, but do it in terms that were recognizably modern. True, this past was grounded in historic time, the Middle Ages, and it would be hard to imagine any vision of the past that was less historic, more absolutely mythic, than Wagner's grandiose fable of tragic incestuous heroes, animated swords, dying gods, magic rings, warrior virgins, dragons, dwarfs, and Rhine maidens.

But the difference was merely one of degree. The very core of the Renaixença was its mixture of fable and archaisms with an exacerbated sense of modernity. Its tissue of romanticized history—the Catalan language itself, waiting for new poetic release like Siegmund's bright sword in the tree; the patriarchal values of the peasant in his *casa pairal*; the chivalry of the Catalan counts; the warrior kings and scholar monks; the four bars of Wilfred the Hairy's blood on the yellow shield; the whole stew of armorial bearings and troubadour love and elaborately self-conscious folklore—almost begged for Wagner to do it justice. The figure of Saint George melted into that of Siegfried and Parsifal, and dragons were dragons, in Catalunya as in Bavaria. Montsalvat was cousin to Montserrat, Montseny, and Montjuic, the holy mountains of the Renaixença.

It was not surprising, therefore, that Wagner's operas appealed to Catalans as a rallying point, an example of how to combine the myths of a legendary past with the supreme myth of the capitalist middle class, that of progress and innovation. He represented Germany—the industrial north, but also a culture identified with yearning and unattainable idealisms. Wagner's example encouraged them to push their romantic medievalism beyond the relatively genteel levels attained by the Pre-Raphaelite movement in England. Wagnerian ideas and motifs moved rapidly into architecture. His vision of the *totalgesamtkunstwerk*, the "global work of art," which would subsume all other art forms in its reach, had its allure for architects who were working out of a strong craft base and wanted to give full rein to painters, ceramists, bronze casters, ironsmiths, sculptors, joiners, glassmakers, mosaicists, and masons. It is likely that Wagner's power of spectacle helped to promote a taste for the relentless congestion of surface and imagery in *modernista* buildings and contributed to their expressive range. Because the anarchists burned Gaudí's archive during the civil war, Wagner's effect on Gaudí (who was fond of opera and often went to the Liceu) cannot be documented. But Gaudí's love of extremes, his belief that architecture should deal in ambiguity and gloom, exaltation and anxiety, and theatrically primal spaces—the peak and the cavern—is entirely Wagnerian. It is hard not to see his subterranean stables in the Palau Güell as a transcription, into massive squat columns and thick pads of brick, of Alberich's cavern. In general, Wagnerianism led architects and decorators to develop a pervasive imagery in which the Christian symbolism of medieval revival and the chivalric emblems of the Middle Ages were made secular and given a thick overlay of dramatic gesture, a brooding half-repressed sexuality. Generic figures influenced by characters from Wagner's operas appeared on buildings, in painting, sculpture, and every decorative art, in all materials from marble to faience, from gold to morocco leather. Rather as Loie Fuller, the American dancer with her floating, whipping veils, was a prototype of Art Nouveau woman, so Siegfried and Parsifal merged with Saint George to provide a model of *modernista* man.

X

The most Wagnerian of all buildings in Barcelona was the Palace of Catalan Music, built for the Orfeó Català by Lluís Domènech i Montaner. The Palau de la Música Catalana and Gaudí's Casa Milà are the climactic twosome of Catalan *modernisme*. They were finished at almost the same time—Domènech's building in 1908, Gaudí's in 1911. In conceptual daring, formal brilliance, and extremity of symbolism and decorative effect, nothing like them would be built in Barcelona again.

Millet had always wanted a permanent home for the Orfeó, but the task of raising funds for it passed on to a new president of the society, Joaquim Cabot (1861–1951). Cabot came from the "risen" *menestralia*. He was a jeweler and the son of a jeweler; he and his brothers ran Barcelona's equivalent of Tiffany's. A committed Catalanist, he worked for the Lliga Regionalista, helped to fund literary magazines (*Lo Gay Saber*, *La Renaixença*), underwrote luxury editions of Catalan writers such as Verdaguer, took part in the Jocs Florals (whose secretary he became in 1889), and was an enthusiastic excursionist. He immersed himself in Rusinyol's *festes modernistes* and wrote dreadful verse, about which his writer friends were carefully diplomatic. This angel kicked off the fund for the music palace with his own check for 170,000 pesetas and arranged a bond issue of 600,000 pesetas to pay for the rest of the work. As to the architect, only one man was considered: Domènech i Montaner.

By the early autumn of 1904 the Orfeó was ready to start. Cabot chose a site on the Carrer Mes Alt de Sant Pere, just off the Via Laietana. The opening of the Via Laietana—Barcelona's new main artery, cut through the Old City to link the Eixample to the port—had pumped up real-estate prices there. The Orfeó bought 15,000 square feet for 240,000 pesetas. But it was right next to the *barris* where the choristers lived, and in any case Domènech i Montaner wanted as much site as possible. He still did not get enough. Even as it stands, the Palau is cramped by the narrow streets and adjacent buildings: it is hard to take in its facades, domes, and mosaic decor as a continuous whole from street level. Domènech not only had to fit in the auditorium and all the backstage space a concert hall must have, but supply offices and archive rooms for the Orfeó itself.

He decided to put the offices and rehearsal rooms on the ground floor, separated by screen walls of wood and stained glass, and to "float" the concert hall above them like an enormous semitransparent bubble inside a box. People would reach it by a double stairway from the ground-floor foyer. And all the time they were in the building, or looking at it from the outside, they would be confronted by a Wagnerian spectacle, the global artwork, an anthology of what the great craft base of Catalan decoration and building could do.

There was not the space to stun the audience with sweeping architectonic effects: compared with the Liceu, the Palau was small. But if its first theme was to be sound, then its second one was light. The decor of the foyer, its shallow vaults sheathed in embossed pale ocher and aquamarine tiles, and of the staircase, with its squat golden-glass balusters inside each of which a twist of metal swims like an eel in amber, prepares you for the moment of entry into the auditorium; and no matter how many times one visits the Palau, that moment is always a surprise. For it is in this visually saturated concert hall that one sees the obsessive theme of Gothic architecture as treated by its revivalists, the play of light and color through stained glass, moving toward the transcendentalist ideas of color-music, of the synthesis of abstract light and equally abstract sound, that affected much early modernist art between 1915 and 1925. With Domènech, however, its parts are not abstract. They are narrative, symbolic, and heraldic.

Both the long walls of the concert hall and the upper arches of its organ loft are pink stained glass. In the ceiling a huge and spectacular stained-glass skylight swells down in the middle like an inverted bell: its radiating motif is a circle of angelic choristers, transmitting a soft pink-and-blue radiance through the roof. Domènech's effort to dematerialize the structure extends to the ring electroliers that hang around the main columns of the auditorium without touching them: with their glowing bubbles of glass set on lacy iron circles, they look like Byzantine crowns or like floating, schematic capitals. Architecture as jewelry, jewelry as architecture.

Domènech took the Gothic effort to open the wall to more and more glass membrane and pushed it a crucial step further, into the technology of steel. All the main loads of the auditorium are carried on a steel frame, so that the space becomes essentially a glass box permeated by daylight. It is a true curtain-wall building, the first in Spain and one of the first in the world.

The project was always short of money. Budgeted at 450,000 pesetas, it came in at 875,750. Work kept stopping as harassed contractors—and the Palau's richness and diversity entailed a lot of subcontracting—waited hat in hand to be paid so they could buy materials. Artists lost their temper; ceramists had fits. Cabot and his board blamed Domènech, who snapped right back at them. "Greetings to all the members of the committee," one of his letters began, "sorry I can't be there to argue with you." And again, "If you think [the contractors] are in such a big hurry to be paid, I'm in a bigger one." He had dropped his fee by 20 percent because he believed in Millet and the Orfeó's mission, but now "when we're just ready to open, I have not received . . . even the full amount I should have already got before the work had even begun!"

Domènech conceived the Palau as the summation of all his hopes of Catalanist architecture. It was to be a "speaking building," a patriotic anthology—nothing less would do justice to the memory of Clavé, for whom he and Vilaseca had designed a monument in their youth, twenty years before. It is encrusted with allegory, inside and out: a text on which the cultural values of Catalanism are written and rewritten.

The didactic note is struck, as soon as you see the Palau from the street, by Lluís Bru's mosaics on top of the facade. They show the *orfeonistes* (the men in dark jackets, the women in long sherbet-colored dresses) caroling in front of the peaks of Montserrat. A sort of festival queen presides over them, on a high throne draped with the Catalan red and yellow bars, displaying a distaff. She looks like a distant cousin of the empress Theodora in Ravenna, with overtones of English nanny. In fact she illustrates an Orfeó staple, "La Balanguera," a poem by Joan Alcover, set to music by Amadeu Vives, about the genius of Catalunya weaving the future:

> *De tradicions i d'esperances*
> *tix la senyera pel jovent,*
> *com qui fa un vel de nuviances*
> *amb caballeres d'or i argent*
> *de la infantesa qui s'enfila,*
> *de la vellura qui s'en va.*

> From traditions and hopes
> she weaves the banner for the young
> like one who makes a wedding-veil
> from the gold and silver threads
> of childhood, advancing,
> of age, passing away.

Busts of the composers who epitomized universal music stand on the balconies below: Palestrina, Bach, Beethoven, and Wagner. Folk song is represented by the main sculpture on the facade, which juts over the street corner above the carriage porch like a huge stone prow: an

Domènech's proscenium in the Palau de la Música Catalana

allegory by Miquel Blay, which rivals Llimona's monument to Dr. Bartolomeu Robert as the best public *modernista* sculpture in Barcelona. Like Llimona, Blay was an imitator of Rodin. He was also strongly influenced by Constant Meunier, the Belgian socialist sculptor who specialized in depicting miners and peasants. This *Allegory of Catalan Folksong* assembles a group of popular types—a boy and an old man, a little girl and a grandmother, a peasant, a fisherman—around the nymph clad in clinging stone veils who signifies the genius of *cançó popular*, and all are protected by Saint George, quoted from Donatello and grasping the windblown *senyera* of Catalunya.

The Palau's most spectacular sculpture, however, is the proscenium. Here, Millet wanted to set the elements of the Orfeó's musical ideology on permanent view, framing whatever took place on stage: Catalan folk song and the classical music, old and new, of northern Europe. This strange ensemble is usually but wrongly said to have been designed by Pau Gargallo (1881–1934), the sculptor who was Picasso's contemporary in Barcelona. In fact Gargallo only helped to finish it. The design was by Domènech and most of the execution was done by a sculptor named Didac Masana i Majo.

The proscenium is carved in what looks like plaster but is actually soft white pumice, supported on a hidden iron armature. Eight decades of dust have grayed it, but it still provides a startling, disjunctive contrast to the lapping and washing of colored light through the rest of the auditorium: ghost white, it brings you up with a jerk.

Eusebi Arnau and Domènech, hemicycle of ceramic music players, Palau de la Música Catalana

On the left side is *cançó popular*—a bust of Josep Anselm Clavé with a willow tree rising beside him to frame the arch. A garland of flowers drops from his pedestal and is being plaited by a young girl with flowing hair; another *donzella* gathers blossoms at her feet. The subject is Clave's own song "Els Flors de Maig," so deeply fixed in the cultural iconography of the Renaixença:

> *Sota d'un salze seguda una nina*
> *trena joiosa son ric cabell d'or;*
> *es son mirall fresca font cristallina,*
> *son sos adornos violetes de bosc . . .*

> Under a pollarded willow, a girl
> joyously plaits her rich golden hair;
> her gaze is a cool crystal fountain,
> wood-violets adorn her . . .

On the right, universal music is personified by a bust of Beethoven between two Doric columns. He is lower than Clavé, who seems to be looking over his head. This (at least, so one hopes) is due less to a fit of Catalan cultural chauvinism than to the need to make room for things happening above Beethoven. There, new music is being born. A roiling cloud of stone vapor, suggesting inspiration, starts between the columns, curls up, reemerges over the entablature and turns into Wagner's Valkyries on their winged horses, tempestuously brandishing their swords and shields. They thunder silently across the top of the arch, toward Clavé and his willow tree—the wind-borne inventiveness of new foreign

music reaching toward the unbudgeable roots of old Catalan culture.

In performance, one sees the choristers and orchestra framed in this gigantic white metaphor as a fixed reminder of the Orfeó's original meaning. Full color then resumes behind them on the back wall of the stage, a hemicycle designed by Eusebi Arnau. Domènech never meant the Palau to have sets—the building is the scenery. The hemicycle, an astonishing tour de force in ceramic, is the permanent background to the music. Its curved wall is sheathed in *trencadís*, or broken tiles, whose opulent shimmer is given by subtle inflections of color running from orange through russets and a near oxblood luster to darker umbers above. Set in this hot, rich ground are the "spirits of music," eighteen maidens playing eighteen different instruments, from zither to flute (the larger wind instruments, which would have unbecomingly distended their pretty cheeks, do not appear). Their lower bodies are flat with the wall and linked to one another with a swooping rhythm of garlands: lavishly patterned *modernista*-medieval costumes from which only their cute little feet emerge. But their heads, shoulders, and arms, along with the instruments they play, are modeled in the round and project from the wall. The effect is benignly apparitional, and without opera glasses one cannot see the broken fingers left by past *orfeonistes*, who were apt to hang their coats and clarinet cases on them during rehearsals.

The Palau was inaugurated on the afternoon of February 9, 1908, in the presence of nearly every politician, magnate, and fan who could squeeze into it. After a blessing by the archbishop and a choral "Magnificat," the choir launched into a program of Orfeó favorites—"Els

Xiquets dels Valls" by Clavé, the anthem "Els Segadors," and the Hallelujah Chorus, preceded (among tremendous diapasons from the organ) by Maragall's "El Cant de la Senyera" set to music by Lluís Millet.

There was enough oratory and banner display to satiate even the most ardent Catalan separatist. Joaquim Cabot spoke, in an emotional hush, inviting "the doubters . . . if not the pessimists" to "come, open your eyes, put out your hands, see and touch what you did not have the ability to dream of." The only conspicuous absence was the architect. Fed up with the Orfeó and its slowness with a checkbook, Domènech i Montaner stayed away.

The next day the press was ecstatic. *La Vanguardia* praised Domènech, "that master among architects," for "the proportions of the new Palace . . . the variety and daring of its lines, the novelty of its architectonic mass, the splendid fantasy of its use of materials." The *Diario de Barcelona* opined that "The place is magnificent," and went on to say how "the brilliant nuances of the majolicas that sheathe the columns, roofs, beams and friezes, the colorful windows that replace the walls and make the whole auditorium resemble an immense lantern—these give the ensemble an air of lightness, of an incomparable freedom." Even allowing for a degree of boosterism, it was quite clear that no public building in Barcelona in years had been so instant a success with critics and the public as the Palau. This was driven home when Domènech's design won the Ajuntament's prize for 1908's best new building in Barcelona. It was "a jewel of modern art," said the jury, deploying "all the materials that presently make up our industrial skills" and showing "the genius and the art characteristic of Catalunya, strong as its race, great as its history and beautiful as its incomparable sky." If you wanted to know what Catalunya could do, you consulted the Palau de la Música Catalana.

This mood was not to last, of course. The Palau was one of the last extravagances of *modernisme*, a stupendous blossom put forth by a movement at the peak of its energy, a vigor that was bound to fail. *Modernisme* in general—and Domènech's work with it—would begin its downward course into public indifference and critical revision before the next decade was up. Soon the inhabitants of the *barris* around Carrer Mes Alt de Sant Pere and the Via Laietana would be calling it the Palau de la Quincalleria Catalana, the Palace of Catalan Junk. By the late 1920s there was talk, even among architects, of demolishing it—why keep this overloaded epitome of a style that was so obviously beyond resuscitation? And there was never a shortage of complaint about its acoustic conditions—which, since its glass walls carry street noise like drum skins, have always been awful. "One of the first times I went to the Palau," recalled Josep Pla, who detested the place,

> there was a literally spellbinding concert: Beethoven by Kreisler and Pau Casals. The first sonata was interrupted again and again: first by the bell of a nearby church; then by a slow wagon going down the street, with exhausting slowness, as though it were enjoying it—a wagon so close that it seemed to be moving through the hall; then from the next floor one heard the off-key song of a maidservant doing the dishes . . . and finally one heard a cock repeatedly crowing, because the balcony roosters of Barcelona crow day and night, as everyone knows. The last part of the concert was shattered by the movement, honking, klaxon-blowing, braking and gear-changing of innumerable cars, showy but very primitive and noisy contraptions, creeping round the Palau and getting ready to take their owners away.

Pla knew what to do with the Palau—strip all the decor so that you would not have to close your eyes when listening to the music and fill in the glass with real, soundproof walls. Fortunately not everyone agreed, and in 1971 the Palau was at last declared to be a national monument. Finally, a scrupulous and brilliant restoration by Oscar Tusquets in the 1980s completed the revival of the crotchety, gaudy old *modernista* grandmother.

But the Palau had never gone into eclipse, for what saved it in the long run was not its merits as architecture, but its role as a condenser of Catalan sentiment and a nursery of musical talent. Millet and Vives wanted the Orfeó to be popular, and it always has been. That support carried the Palau through all the vicissitudes of taste and politics that have washed over Barcelona in the last eighty years. There can be few musicians who have not complained about its amenities and acoustics, but Pablo Casals was devoted to the place; the seven-year-old Alicia de Larrocha made her debut there in 1929; for fifty years a large proportion of the major orchestras and instrumental groups of Europe performed there, as did every Spanish instrumentalist or singer of real significance. True, the Palau could be a little conservative—Stravinsky, for instance, was not asked to conduct his own works there until 1933—but it always caught up in the end. Thus the Palau is the only cultural institution that managed, through thick and thin, to remain both Catalanist and international, proving that a vigorous regionalist culture does not have to be a provincial one, in Barcelona or anywhere else.

CHAPTER EIGHT

The Hermit in the Cave of Making

I

Late on the morning of June 7, 1926, an old man could be seen crossing Gran Via at the corner of Carrer Bailen, in the Eixample. He was short, with pale blue eyes and a close-cropped thatch of curly silver hair. He wore a rusty black suit. As he shuffled into the middle of Gran Via, down whose center the trolleys ran, he looked neither right nor left and did not see a line 30 tram bearing down on him. He ignored the clang of its alarm bell and the shouts. The tram ran over him.

When the police had shooed away the ring of spectators from his broken body, his pockets proved to be quite empty and no one could find out his name. He was so badly lacerated by the tram's wheels that four taxis, one after another, refused to take him to the hospital. Eventually an ambulance came. He was still breathing, but there was no alcohol on his breath; his clothes suggested poverty but not dereliction. He must have been one of the thousands of seedy old pensioners who lived alone in the boardinghouses of Barcelona. So he was taken off to the Hospital of Sant Creu, and put in an iron cot in the public ward. Not until the following day, when people came looking for him, did it emerge that this old codger was the most noted architect in Spain, Antoni Gaudí i Cornet.

His grieving friends tried to move him to a private clinic, but Gaudí did not want to go. "My place," they later reported him as saying, "is here, among the poor." Perhaps Gaudí did actually utter these words. More likely they are a pious fiction, an addition to a legend that would culminate in efforts to persuade the Vatican to make him a saint. ("What a wonderful thing it would be," one of his circle was heard to exclaim, "if Don Antoni were canonized! Then everyone would want to be an architect!") In any case, he died, at the age of seventy-four after lingering for three days and receiving extreme unction, at five in the afternoon of June 10, in the city that he had marked so indelibly with his work.

Gaudí's architecture is the delayed baroque that Barcelona never had. It is mystical, penitential, and wildly elated by turns, structurally daring and full of metaphor, obsessed with its role as *speculum mundi*, "mirror of the world." Gaudí was the greatest architect and (many would say) the greatest cultural figure of any kind that Catalunya had produced since the Middle Ages. His work dominates Barcelona as Bernini's does Rome, setting a scale of imaginative effort against which one is apt to measure everything else. And most of his best buildings are in or near the city.

The church of the Sagrada Família is still the emblem of Barcelona, as the Eiffel Tower is of Paris or the Harbor Bridge of Sydney. Gaudí's buildings have long been a tourist attraction—though not on the scale they achieved in the 1980s, especially after the Japanese latched onto them—but until recently, he was decidedly a minority taste outside Catalunya. Even Spaniards thought of him as "that mad Catalan," and in the rest of Europe and in the United States, although he certainly had his fans—and was, in any case, the only Catalan architect any foreigner could name—he did not fit a scheme of modernist architectural history whose ruling idea was functionalism and whose heroes were Le Corbusier, Mies, and Gropius.

Not that these architects rejected Gaudí themselves. When Le Corbusier visited Barcelona in the spring of 1928, he was taken on a Gaudían tour; he admired the complex geometry—hyperboloids and paraboloids —in the Sagrada Família and the attic arches of the Casa Milà, Gaudí's luxury apartment building on Passeig de Gràcia. "This man did everything he wanted to do with stone. What a formidable mastery of structure! This is the most powerful architecture of his generation." It may be that the sculptural roofscape of the Casa Milà gave Corbu inspiration for the roof of his own Unité d'Habitation in Marseilles, built four decades later.

Mies van der Rohe was silent on Gaudí, though he built one of his own most famous structures, the German pavilion for the 1929 World's Fair, in Barcelona. On the other hand Walter Gropius, in Barcelona in 1932, thought some of the Sagrada Família's wall structures had a "prophetic technical perfection." But though these Ur-modernists admired him, their followers did not, or viewed him only as an eccentric, a designer so dependent on a vanishing artisan base that he could have no practical message for the future.

There was a Gaudí cult among foreigners in the 1960s, and it came from an unlikely source: Surrealism. His work had been made known to the Surrealists by Salvador Dalí and Joan Miró, whose enthusiasm was boundless. The first mention of Gaudí in the context of French modernism was in 1933, in *Minotaure*, the Surrealists' magazine, to which Dalí contributed an article: "On the Terrifying and Edible Beauty of 'Modern Style' Architecture." In it, he rhapsodized about the organic qualities of Gaudí's work, its unceasing metamorphosis of stone into flesh and rigidity into softness; how it defied the orthogonal rules of architecture with its imagery of wrinkles, bones, stumps, stalactites; how Gaudí was the one and only architect of recent times whose work linked back to the awful fantasies of death that lurked in the penitential baroque. Gaudí and Gaudí alone, Dalí thought, supplied the alternative to the monotony of modernist fragmentation, which was not academic "whole-ness" but something absolutely natural: *dissolution*.

Thus from the 1930s on, Gaudí had two small but devoted claques. The first and most serious consisted of ultranationalistic Catalan Catholics, including some architects, who had grown up with his buildings and some of whom had actually known him. To them, Gaudí was the neglected precursor of a new age of faith: the last of the "cathedral builders," whose supreme work, the Sagrada Família, inched like Zeno's tortoise toward a finish line drawn somewhere beyond their own deaths. They took it as dogma that the Sagrada Família was his greatest building.

The second, more diffuse group was made up of foreign Gaudiphi-liacs who loved him because he had been adopted by Surrealism and seemed to share their own liking for the irrational and the subversive. For what was Gaudí but dreams in stone, soft architecture, the archi-tecture of ecstasy?

And so the Surrealists' adoption of Gaudí flowed into the 1960s counterculture. A good morning in Barcelona in 1966 was a joint on the serpentine encrusted bench of the Güell Park, and then a descent to the city to groove on the facade of the Sagrada Família, not leaving out the long, dizzying climb up the stairs inside one of the spires (there being no tourist elevator then): urban mountaineering for the stoned foreigner. Gaudí, the kids with their rucksacks thought, had been on some kind of permanent trip, and liking him was part of their craze for Art Nouveau. It declared one's freedom from the straight line, the cor-

Antoni Gaudí, lying in state

porate grid, and all that was anal repressive, programmed, and soulless
in modern architecture. His very name, one learned, was a Catalan verb
meaning "enjoy." Thus Gaudí the subversive shaded over into Gaudí
the hedonist.

But a dead artist has no control over who admires him, or why.
Antoni Gaudí i Cornet was the very opposite of a cultural subversive,
and all that side of the French Surrealists—their fantasies of revolution,
their hatred of the Church, their love of Stalin—would have disgusted
him. Nor did he think his work had the smallest connection with dreams.
It was based on structural laws, craft traditions, deep experience of
nature, piety, and sacrifice.

The last two were fundamental. Gaudí was a Catholic who believed
in papal infallibility, episcopal authority, and the perennial philosophy
of the Church. Far from being modernist in spirit, the Sagrada Família
was commissioned and designed as an ecstatically repressive building
that would atone for the sins of modernism and the "excesses" of democracy. Gaudí was convinced of the reality of both grace and divine
punishment: "Man is free to do evil, but he pays the price of his sins:
God corrects us constantly, he castigates us all the time, and we must
beg Him to punish and then console us." His imaginative life was as
much bound up with ideas of death, obedience, penance, deliverance,
and transcendence as any of the mortality-haunted Spanish geniuses of
the past: Saint Ignatius of Loyola, or Saint John of the Cross. "The idea

of death," he remarked to one of his disciples, "can never be separated from the idea of God; that's why the churches have tombs in them . . . without thinking on death there is no morally or physically good life." And again, "Everyone has to suffer. The only ones who don't suffer are the dead. He who wants an end to suffering wants to die."

II

Antoni Gaudí was born under the sign of Cancer on June 25, 1852, in Reus, a fair-sized provincial town in the Baix Camp (lower plains) west of Tarragona. He came from an artisan family. Four generations of Gaudís had been metalworkers and had married the daughters of other smiths. They made everything from candlesticks to caldrons, and specialized in sheet-copper work.

Francisco Gaudí and his wife, Antonia Cornet, had, in all, five children. Only Antoni, the youngest, lived long. Knowing that he was the inheritor, the last of the male line, probably reinforced Gaudí's growing conservatism as a man, which interwove so productively with his inventiveness as an artist. He was the first Gaudí in generations to move outside their long, deep-bedded craft tradition, which gave its name to their workshop near Reus—the Mas de la Caldera, or Caldron Maker's house.

The Baix Camp de Tarragona is archetypally Mediterranean, hard stony country where the light is bright and clear and the earth's structure shows vividly. It is prone to sudden williwaws, which blow up out of nowhere so often that a saying arose about its hardy, closemouthed, touchy folk: "*Gens de Camp, gens de llamp*"—*llamp* being "lightning bolt." Almond trees flourish in its unforgiving soil, and groves of ancient olives. In May immense drifts of wildflowers spring up, wither, and die.

When Gaudí was a boy, farming in the Baix Camp had changed little in the two thousand years since it was parceled out to Roman settlers. Growing up there, he developed a passionate curiosity about its plants and animals, birds, insects, geology, and weather. Nature, he said later, was "the Great Book, always open, that we should force ourselves to read." Everything structural or ornamental an architect could imagine was already there in natural form, in limestone grottoes or dry bones, grass shoots or a beetle's iridescent wing case, the thrust of an ancient olive or the springing of an oak's limbs from its trunk. One thinks of Osip Mandelstam's words in *Journey to Armenia*: "When I was a child . . . I would stroke the pinecones. They would bristle. They were trying to convince me of something. In their shelled tenderness, in their geometrical gaping I sensed the rudiments of architecture, the demon of which has accompanied me throughout my life."

You see Gaudí's strong liking for natural forms everywhere in his work, just as it is in the details of Gothic architecture. If you raise the ornately knotted forged-iron hammer of the door knocker on the Casa Calvet's portal, you see a flattish striking plate shaped like the back of a giant iron bedbug: it gets "squashed" every time a visitor knocks. If you look down at the pavement when strolling on Passeig de Gràcia, you notice that its hexagonal greenish-gray cement blocks by Gaudí bear an elegant design of a nautilus shell, a starfish, and a *pop*, or octopus, in low relief; these were originally designed for the courtyard of the Casa Batlló, then used in the Casa Milà, and finally spread by municipal consent over the sidewalks. He liked tortoises, too, and a sea turtle and a land tortoise serve as bases for columns on the Nativity facade of the Sagrada Família. Stone snails lurk everywhere on that temple, and Gaudí turned the helical shell into the coup d'oeil one receives when, having trudged up the dizzying staircase inside the spire on the Nativity facade, one looks down and sees a spiral shooting down in perspective beneath one's feet, diminishing as flawlessly as the rifling inside the barrel of a gun.

But his two richest sources of metaphor were plants and the human body. Sometimes his projects look like petrified woods or gardens of stone. Thirty species of plant are rendered in stone on the Sagrada Família, each native both to the Holy Land and to Catalunya. Some of them are put there to echo the imagery of the Bible—the palm, for instance, alludes to both the palms that were strewn at the feet of Christ as he entered Jerusalem on Palm Sunday, and the comparison of the bride (and hence the Virgin Mary) to a palm tree in the Song of Solomon. At the apex of this symbolic vegetation one sees the ceramic Tree of Life atop the central bay of the Nativity facade, a cedar tree swarming with white doves. Gaudí had a special liking for mushrooms, too. One of the entrance pavilions of the Güell Park sports a huge mosaic *Amanita muscaria* as its spire, and the balconies of the Casa Calvet are supported on stone fungi. The shape of mushrooms suggested the primitive origins of architecture—organic columns with capitals.

Gaudí used flowers and fruit as decoration and for their symbolism, as a link to the Bible and the Gothic past, but his architecture was "organic" in a more than symbolic way. He was fascinated by the *structure* of plants. He would photograph large cypresses and derive column designs for the Sagrada Família from their fibrous growth. The porch columns of the Güell Crypt are a grove of brick trunks, leaning and striated, sending out branches—the rib vaults—that lace into one another. Stone clusters of wisteria blossoms hang over some of the serpentine arcades at the Güell Park. The columns of these arcades mimic, in rock work, not only the natural lean of trees but also their grain and surface: the rough bark of the carob and the spiral twisting and flowing scribbles of the eucalyptus. Gaudí never ceased to draw inspiration from the tree trunk: the tree was Adam's house in Paradise, and a host of writers with whose work he may have been acquainted (as well as John Ruskin, whom he certainly read in translation) had theorized about the tree origins of both Greek and Gothic architecture.

Gaudí also knew and never forgot country building in stone, clay, and timber. Its vernacular was old beyond memory and rose from the nature of materials and of rural work. "One should work with materials from the area, used as they can be gathered by the peasants themselves in their spare time between their labors." In particular he liked the dry-stone walls common in the Baix Camp and echoed them in (for instance) the rough "rustic" colonnades of the Güell Park.

That he was the son of artisans mattered immensely to Gaudí. He thought of himself as a man of his hands, not a theoretician. He said he learned to think in terms of complex membrane surfaces—hyperboloids, helicoids, hyperbolic paraboloids, and conoids—by watching his father work metal, beating the iron and copper sheets, curving and pleating and distending them, producing the miracle of volume and enclosure from the banality of flatness, making up the forms as he went along without drawing them first. As Francisco Gaudí had been an empirical worker, so was his son. Nothing in Gaudí's work is more remarkable, once you begin to look for it, than his direct way of making the unorthodox forms he wanted, using models or on-site show-and-tell rather than drawings. Unlike Domènech or Puig i Cadafalch, Gaudí did not like to draw and did so only as a last resort. He thought entirely in terms of relief, of bulges and hollows, rather than flat planar arrangements. Some critics think that next to none of the detail sketches for Gaudí's projects were made by Gaudí himself: "They are drawings made by his assistants to understand what Gaudí wanted," wrote the Catalan historian Alexandre Cirici i Pellicer.

There is manual, empirical space, and there is conceptual, abstract space. Gaudí was at home in the former, but his professors at the School of Architecture in Barcelona, where he studied from 1873 to 1877, taught the latter in courses based on Beaux-Arts principles. They taught, as a first step, "conventional" rendering: how to cast the shadow of a cone in a niche or the shades in Doric flutes. The student moved on through basic engineering and an intensive study of Greek, Roman, and Gothic ornament to the design of imaginary and largely ceremonial structures —an assembly hall or a harbor pier. The system of design was based entirely on orthographic projection: plan, section, and elevation, producing an architecture based on the ninety-degree intersection of flat planes. Because Gaudí did not think naturally in terms of T-square architecture, he proved to be a mediocre student. His natural bent had the same relation (or lack of one) to Beaux-Arts building as the talents of a Cézanne had to the Beaux-Arts skills of a Bouguereau. Of course, no building can be fully imagined from its plans. But the spaces and volumes Gaudí eventually created in his mature buildings cannot be imagined *at all* from flat drawings. The surfaces twist and undulate; the space wriggles, flares, solemnly inflates, and then collapses again. It is haptic, not abstract, a womb with a view.

And it is full of transformations that the beaux arts system could never have endorsed. A practical dreamer, Gaudí jumped from one material to another, and years before Claes Oldenburg he used soft forms—those of fishnets, burlap, leather harnesses—in hard materials like iron. The grilles of the Güell Crypt are based on nets, the main door of the house he designed for Maria Saguès at Bellesguard (1900–1909) is an iron version of sewn cloth (ribbons, hems, flounces), and the bases of some columns on the Sagrada Família are sheathed in a parody of industrial wire mesh, complete with straps and oversize rivets.

Gaudí drew his early lessons in empiricism from the nameless vernacular of Catalan rural building but also from the Middle Ages. The lessons of both, he believed, contributed to a unique sensibility that could be pursued only in Catalunya, one that was Mediterranean in the fullest sense—neither pinched like the far Protestant north nor sensuous and lax like the deep Arabic south. "Our strength and superiority," he declared, "lies in the balance of feeling and logic, whereas the Nordic races become obsessive and smother feeling. And those of the South, blinded by the excess of color, abandon reason and produce monsters" —the last five words being, of course, a memory of Goya's *Caprichos*.

One medieval complex in particular fired young Gaudí and kept a deep emotional value for him—even before he enrolled in architecture school. It was the monastery of Santa Maria del Poblet, on the northern slope of the Prades hills outside Tarragona. Poblet's origins lay at the beginning of the Catalan Middle Ages, and it signified, for the budding architect, the splendor and independence that Catalunya must somehow

Monastery of Santa Maria del Poblet, before any restoration, photograph from 1908

regain. It had been founded in 1153 by Guernau, a Cistercian abbot, on land given to his order by Ramon Berenguer IV. Over the next three centuries the abbey rose in size and wealth. Its library was immense, its scholastic activity voluminous. Its economic dominion extended over ten neighboring towns and sixty villages. It was also the national pantheon. Beginning with Pere III (the Ceremonious) in the fourteenth century, all the kings of Aragon and Catalunya had been buried there. As architecture, Poblet was the grandest expression of the Cistercian strain in medieval Catalunya, strong, severe, and plain, with prismatic forms and daringly vaulted spaces. Its chapter house, nine vaulted square bays carried on four central columns, ranks with Santa Maria del Mar and the Saló de Tinell as one of the supreme formal utterances of Catalan Gothic. But in Gaudí's youth, Poblet was a wreck. Its economic relations with the country around had begun to disintegrate in the sixteenth century. After the wave of convent burning in 1835, when its eighty remaining Cistercian monks and lay brothers were turned out, the whole complex was left open to thieves and vandals. Over the next four decades they broke open the massive tombs that lined the walls of the royal chapel, carried off whatever paintings and carvings they could, and left a stripped shell behind. It reminded Eduardo Toda i Güell, Gaudí's boyhood friend, of the biblical City of Desolation, abandoned to the wind and to colonies of screech owls.

Toda, too, was an enthusiastic excursionist. (His passion for archaeology continued undiminished for the rest of his life; a curious

Poblet today

photograph survives of an older Toda, by 1885 the Spanish consul general in Egypt, leaning grimly on a sarcophagus in the Cairo Museum, swathed as a mummy in yards and yards of cotton and looking like a figure from Edward Gorey.) He and Gaudí visited Poblet repeatedly and came up with a plan for its restoration, not as a religious community but as a tourist attraction—an almost unheard-of idea in Spain 120 years ago.

In 1870 Toda and Gaudí, both ardent Catholic conservatives still in their teens, wrote their "Poblet Manuscript"—significantly, perhaps, on the blank backs of leaflets printed by political *liberales* in Reus the year before. It inveighed against the hated Madrid liberals whose policies had laid Poblet low. It described the monastery's buildings, their state of decay, what restoration they needed; it balanced the cost of repair (done, they hoped, by craftsmen who would live rent free and eat communally, like lay brothers) against tourist revenues; it even listed where some of its dispersed relics, manuscripts, and works of art were, in the hope that they could be brought together once more.

Toda added a poem, which extolled Poblet as the archsymbol of Catalan identity. Its fall had been Catalunya's fall, too, and its revival would herald the *pàtria*'s rebirth under the sign of the past, nobler than the present. The decay of Poblet, Toda and Gaudí thought, symbolized the abandonment of old feudal values in the revolution of 1868, an upheaval they both detested. Medieval Poblet had been "a fruitful breast of peace, love and happiness," but now even its monastery bells had

Eduardo Toda i Güell, dressed as a mummy in the Cairo Museum, 1885

been melted down to make "vile instruments of death and terror—and all in the name of peace and freedom, laws and rights." Is this freedom? Toda indignantly demanded, and went on:

> If it is to scorn
> the deeds and glories of a people
> if it is to rip up the tomb-slabs
> and violate the sepulchres of heroes
> and sow terror and death everywhere
> and disturb the ascetic's peace,
> and drag the shameless prostitute
> before the high altar of the Holy Virgin
> and smash monuments to rubble . . .
> if this is freedom, a curse on it!

The restoration of Poblet became a top priority among Catalanist conservatives in the 1890s—it was recognized as one of the shrines of national history, like Ripoll or Montserrat, and every *duro* that went into its rebuilding was also a blow aimed at anarchism and foreign decadence.

The credit for this impulse belonged, in large part, to Gaudí and Toda. The young architect's devotion to Poblet may shed light on two strands in his later work. The first was his extreme, indeed radical, religious conservatism, which he associated with the duty to preserve Catalan identity. The second was a nostalgia for monastic, or at any rate communal, life. This found its fullest expression when Gaudí, hard at work on the Sagrada Família, also helped to plan the Colonia Güell, the private mill town or industrial monastery for his patron Eusebi Güell, outside Barcelona. But it also brought him briefly into the orbit of Catalan syndicalism when he was a young man and gave him the chance to do his first building—for the oldest workers' cooperative in Spain, at Mataró, the seaside industrial town north of Barcelona.

The Mataró cooperative, run by its workers, made cotton goods and was partly managed by a friend of Gaudí's named Salvador Pagès, a union organizer of moderate anarchist views. Pagès seems to have had a maverick's reputation within the small circles of the Catalan left and was disliked by its Marxist minority because he did not believe in strikes as the workers' first line of defense against the bosses. In 1870 the Mataró commune had nearly been wrecked by a three-month strike called to express Catalan workers' solidarity with the Paris Commune; Pagès believed this had been a suicidal gesture, said so, and was expelled from the Barcelona chapter of the Marxist-led First International for saying it.

On his visits to Mataró, Gaudí was reputedly smitten by a young woman named Pepita Moreu, who taught in its co-op school with her sister Agustina. Pepita had married an *indiano*, divorced him, and then married again into a family of well-off socialist intellectuals. She was a person of independent views, and might not have been disinclined to an extramarital fling, but there is no sign that one took place: Gaudí was so shy and awkward with women, or so low in libido, that he never married and may quite possibly have died a virgin.

The Mataró cooperative showed its textiles in expositions as far afield as Paris and Philadelphia. Its emblem was a bee, that busy socialist insect, and Gaudí (whose only known schoolboy essay in Reus had been in praise of bees) made a giant bronze one as a finial for its flagstaff, whose banners he also designed. Its buildings spread over fifty acres of land. It had its own food store, a day school for children and a night school for workers, a library, a restaurant, and a social club. It even boasted one of the first electrical generators south of the Pyrenees. But it needed new buildings, and in 1878 Pagès asked Gaudí to design them. The chief ones were a bleaching room for the cotton and two residential wings for a total of thirty workers and their families. The bleaching room was simply a big barn. Gaudí raised its shallow-pitched roof on wooden catenary arches, made not from continuous pieces of timber but from short planks bolted together. A catenary is the parabolalike curve traced by a hanging chain. It has no bending moment in it, only pure tension—as in a suspension bridge—or, used upside down as an arch, pure compression. It was daring and cheap to build, the first of Gaudí's fundamentalist structures.

He also decorated the cooperative's assembly hall with anarcho-syndicalist slogans, which would have been approved by Salvador Pagès. "Nothing is more powerful than brotherhood," one read. "Comrade! Show solidarity, practice goodness," said another. And a third: "Much formality [*Els molts compliments*] shows a wrong upbringing." These could hardly be construed as the utterances of a red-hot socialist, though they suggest some general sympathy with progressive, collectivist ideas on Gaudí's part.

But how well did Pagès's avowed atheism sit with the young architect? Gaudí was certainly less religious in his youth than in his old age—though that may not be saying much, since the pope himself could hardly have been more pious than old Gaudí. Naturally, his ultra-Catholic supporters have always tried to play down whatever socialist feelings he may have had, except insofar as they coincided with Leo XIII's encyclical on labor, *Rerum Novarum*. Domènech i Montaner told the story, which was picked up by Barcelonese journalists, that young Gaudí belonged to a fiercely anticlerical *tertulia* that used to meet in the Café Pelayo on the Ramblas; worse still, he was known to heckle religious processions as they went by: "*Llanuts* [sheep, idiots]!—God will punish you!" As such conduct did not befit the future architect of the Sagrada Família, hard-core Gaudínians treat it as a vile libel on their saint, and yet it seems possible in a young man of deep, tempestuous feeling. It may, however, be only architects' gossip.

One thing was definite: after the Mataró cooperative, Gaudí wanted to do no more factories or workers' housing—there was no money in it. "As you know only too well," he wrote to a friend in Madrid, a cotton manufacturer who put such a project to him, "I live off my work and I cannot commit myself to vague or experimental projects—you yourself would never give up a sure thing for an uncertain one." From now on his politics went steadily to the right, and his work was for the rich. As he was finishing his work for Mataró, Gaudí was taken up by the man with whom his name remains forever linked: Eusebi Güell i Bacigalupi, industrialist, rising politician, and quintessential grandee of the Catalan establishment.

The future patron and the young architect met in Barcelona during the summer of 1878, when Güell was thirty-one and Gaudí twenty-six. Earlier that year, Güell had made a trip to Paris to do some business and see the Universal Exposition. In its Spanish pavilion, amid the clutter of industrial and craft products, stood an elaborate vitrine of glass and crystal, about ten feet high, with spiky wrought-iron finials on top and arched mahogany buttresses connecting its base to a marquetry plinth. This preposterous object looked like a freestanding tabernacle but merely contained a display of gloves made by the Barcelonese firm of Esteban Cornellà. Güell was enraptured by it and tracked its designer down when he got back to Barcelona. In this way the relationship between architect and client that was to transform the cultural reputation of Barcelona began.

III

Eusebi Güell i Bacigalupi was, as the Catalans say, *molt senyoral*: "very gentlemanly." Such was his reputation for a benign, aristocratic nature—and he did in fact become an aristocrat, being made the first count Güell in 1908—that by his death in 1918 there must have been many Barcelonans who, watching the immense funeral cortege, had forgotten how recent, at least by Castilian standards, the Güell family's ascent had been. "A magnificent type of Biblical character," ran one of the obituaries,

> well-proportioned, graceful in movement, with lightly curly hair, a gentle but penetrating gaze, a deep voice and distinguished manners. A great facility for grasping and explaining anything physical or meta-physical, and, like all superior men of our race, endowed with a tireless diligence—not the diligence of the Anglo-Saxon wage-slave who gets up at dawn to chop wood or load bundles of iron, as Gladstone or, they say, Theodore Roosevelt did.

No, indeed: Eusebi Güell—as all of Barcelona concurred—was of finer stuff, the perfect mercantile knight of the Restoration, prototype of the thinking, feeling capitalist. "He was diligent in the sense of over-looking nothing, of never losing a moment, of always finding the time to immerse himself in matters of art, in encouraging new constructions." Such a man "could not be more elevated. He strove to be, and in fact was, a Maecenas," and his protégés were "able to hold up his name in glory, like that of a Lorenzo de' Medici." Only a cynic would think such an encomium was in any way affected by the fact that its author, the novelist Pin i Soler, had for years been Eusebi Güell's secretary.

All Güell's thoughts of patronage were focused on Barcelona. He was not an art collector, and on his visits to Paris he took no interest in French art, not even impressionism. (None of the *gent de bé* knew or cared much about foreign painting, which is why Barcelona's museums today are rich in Catalan art and poor in everything else.)

But Güell took his civic duties very seriously and believed in the image of the capitalist-as-Medici: the enlightened patron bestowing largess on worker and artist, to the eventual contentment and glory of his city. In manners an English lord, in taste a Renaissance prince. Such was the ideal, and Eusebi Güell believed—correctly, as it turned out—that he had found his Michelozzo in Gaudí, the man who could transform his beloved city, not by further grand planning in the manner of Cerdà, but by adding exemplary buildings to it. The desire for the next building feeds on the last one.

Gaudí at this point showed little sign of the monkish austerity of his later years. He loved the boulevards, the theater (when he could afford it), and good tailoring, all of which cost money and required a patron. Above all he craved steady work. So when Güell started arranging commissions for him with his in-laws, small at first but getting larger, Gaudí responded with enthusiasm.

Güell's prepotent father-in-law, the marquis of Comillas, had a palace in his home port on the Bay of Biscay, designed by the Catalan architect Joan Martorell. In 1878 he commissioned a pantheon, or private chapel, and for this Gaudí did furniture—bulbous and spiky, all lathe work and crockets and florets and eagle finials and pointed arches, Pugin wildly mutated on the far side of the Channel: a throne, a prie-dieu, and a pew that carried, on each Gothic end, a carved wooden dragon. Comillas loved it and told Gaudí to design a pergola in his garden for an impending visit by King Alfonso XII. Gaudí had it prefabricated in lacy iron, bronze, and glass, and the marquis shipped it from Barcelona in one of his own trains. It had a profusion of crystal globes that shone in the twilight and hundreds of blown-glass wind-bells chiming in its overhanging eaves. The dinner table was a cut-crystal disk some eight feet in diameter, but a workman, straightening a wrinkle in the carpet under it a few days before the royal party arrived, accidentally bashed it with his head and broke it to shards; the man, though stunned, was unhurt. Gaudí expressed relief: one could always make a new table, he said, but not a new workman. He substituted a wooden one, covered with a damask cloth, and his workmen—voluntarily, it seems—decided to pass up a short paid vacation in Madrid at the marquis's expense in order to go straight back to Barcelona and make a new glass tabletop, which they completed and shipped in a few days.

From then on Gaudí and the Güell circle were indissolubly linked. His first design for Eusebi Güell was drawn up in 1882 but not built. It was a lodge on Güell's quail-hunting estate at Garraf, near Sitges. Garraf was to be a fantastically crenellated affair, Oriental-medieval, its main motif an octagonal tower that mingled the towers of the Royal Gate at Poblet with a touch of Hindu stupa. The walls were rustic freestone inlaid with panels, stripes, and checkers of colored tile.

Critics who have wanted to turn Gaudí into a saint of modern medievalism have tended to downplay the "pagan" Orientalism of much of his work, but in truth the Orient was a prime source of his inspiration. He loved its unfamiliar forms—the projecting arcades in the air, the ogival domes of marabouts, the Muslim prayer towers with their prismatic brick surfaces jointed by elaborate bands of carved stone or ceramic, the continuous tile decoration that turned the mosques of Isfahan or Istanbul into curving, modulated fields of color, and the fat, sculptural pinnacles of Hindu stupas. Beyond that, there was the sense of internal secrecy and luxury one could extract from Turkish or Moroccan prototypes.

Gaudí never visited the Middle or Far East, even crossed the Strait of Gibraltar to Morocco. For him, the Orient was less an actual place than a fantasy that could be ransacked for exotic motifs. In the 1880s Orientalist taste was at its peak in France and in England, propelled by novelists and painters alike. "The Orient" meant Delacroix's Riffian horsemen and Gérôme's slave merchants; it stimulated archaeological fantasy (as in *Aida* or the Carthaginian sadism of Flaubert's *Salammbô*); it evoked minarets and domes, fretted vaults, serpentine calligraphy in tile, and water trickling into shallow basins. It invited the stockbroker to dream of hashish pipes and secret interior gardens. It bore witness to the successes of empire. Spain had colonies in North Africa, and its Orientalist leanings were of course magnified by its rich Moorish heritage. The Arab conquest had left no buildings in Barcelona, but what architect could be unaware of the Generalife and the Alcázar in Granada or the Christianized mosques of Seville?

Certainly not Gaudí, whose next buildings of the 1880s were elaborately Orientalist—though his use of Arabic architectural motifs did not dispel his prejudices against Arabs. The first was the Casa Vicens

(1883–88). Then came the house at Comillas aptly nicknamed El Capricho, commissioned in 1883 by one of Comillas's rich *indiano* friends, Máximo Diáz de Quijano, lately returned from Cuba. The third, also started in 1883, was his first big job for Eusebi Güell: the pavilions and entrance gate of the Finca Güell below Pedralbes.

The Barcelona School of Architecture had a large archive of photos of "exotic" architecture: details of ceramics, stone and wood decoration, views of caliphs' palaces in North Africa, Persian towers, Indian stupas, arcaded pavilions and mosques in Cairo. Gaudí pored over these and extracted quite a few structural and decorative tropes for his own designs. The first was glazed tile, to give his buildings, inside and out, a rich colored skin. In Gaudí's work this begins with the Casa Vicens and reaches its apogee in the facade mosaics of the Casa Batlló, the chimneys and ventilators of the Casa Milà, and the serpentine benches of the Güell Park.

It made sense to use color on the Casa Vicens: the client was a tile manufacturer, Manuel Vicens i Montaner, whose firm naturally supplied the ceramics. It was to be both a house and an advertisement, built on a cramped site above the Eixample at Carrer de les Carolines 24. It has only three visible sides, and Gaudí, egged on by the enthusiastic Vicens, lavished decoration on them; one imagines long discussions about what effects Gaudí wanted and what Vicens could make, the exact color of an oxblood-luster glaze for the hall, the pigments for this leaf green or that turquoise blue.

The Casa Vicens was meant to evoke a caliph's pavilion set in an oasis. It came from the same area of Orientalist fancy that inspired Matisse in Morocco thirty years later, even down to the enormous palm tree (now gone) that Gaudí placed in its yard and the gate of forged-iron palm leaves surmounted by a tangle of wisteria. The floral ceramic decoration inside is overwrought, but the building has many witty touches, ranging from the impish little iron dragons on its window grilles to its high-camp smoking room. It is unlikely that Manuel Vicens surrendered himself there on an ottoman to the soothing fumes of hash, but the room itself is a pasha's fantasy, complete with Mudejar vaulting in many-colored gesso. The "vault" holds nothing up; it is only a suspended ceiling, designed to produce—as it certainly does—an ambience. Baudelaire, one feels, would have been crazy about Senyor Vicens's *sala de fumar*:

> *C'est l'Ennui! L'oeil chargé d'un pleure*
> *involuntaire,*

Gaudí's smoking room in the Casa Vicens

Il rêve d'échafauds en fumant son houkah—
Tu le connais, cher Lecteur, ce monstre
delicat . . .

Outside, to emphasize the movement from the second floor to the arcaded third floor, Gaudí used another Oriental motif: thin corbels, which step outward to create an overhanging upper floor. Those of the Casa Vicens are mere blades of projecting brick, like sawteeth. Gaudí used these often, as in El Capricho at Comillas, where both the roof eaves and the flared top of the watchtower are carried on corbels. The slim parabolic arches of the stables of the Finca Güell spring, with Brancusian grace, from corbeled revetments—a stutter, then flight. He got this idea from photographs of similarly corbeled houses in India.

Most telling of all was Gaudí's use of Eastern-style towers and finials. The tower of El Capricho derives from a muezzin's prayer tower in Isfahan, with the virtuoso touch of a brick baldachin that seems to hover above it on four thin metal columns, defying gravity. The ventilation towers of the Finca Güell stables clearly take off from Oriental prototypes, although they are elaborated into points and prisms in a way that

Dragon gate at the Finca Güell

recalls the dizzying solid geometries of the Czech mannerist artist Wenzel Jamnitzer (whose engravings Gaudí knew). Even the parabolic towers of the Sagrada Família resemble elongated Hindu stupas more than Gothic spires. "All styles are organisms related to nature," Gaudí said. "Some form a single block, like Greek and Roman, and others form branches and tops, like Indian architecture." This interest in "branches and tops" pervaded his work. Gaudí was out to reinvent the roof, to rescue it from its Beaux-Arts banality and invisibility. Why should the roof of a building not be as full of interest as its walls or interior? This question was answered in the amazing sculptural roofscapes of his maturity, those arrays of smoking and air-breathing totems on top of the Palau Güell and the Casa Milà.

The Palau Güell was begun in 1886 and the Finca Güell in 1884: with them, Eusebi Güell announced his wholehearted adoption of Gaudí. The Finca Güell was less a country estate than a big suburban garden with citrus orchards and a house; it stands on the slope rising toward Sarrià and the Gothic monastery of Pedralbes from the lower plain of Barcelona, and Eusebi Güell could reach it in less than an hour by carriage from his house on Rambla dels Caputxins. Gaudí designed only the main gate and its two flanking buildings, a gatekeeper's lodge and the stables; these are among the most vivid of his works and the first to have a symbolic program.

Its main image leaps at your eye at once—the "dragon gate," a masterpiece of forged iron done to Gaudí's design by the smith Vallet i Piqué. The dragon that ramps across the gate is both stylized and malignantly alive, with every iron tooth and talon, each pleat of its black wing sharp with vitality. And this sense of life is released through the nature of iron itself, bent and bashed by the smith: its ductility, its clarity of silhouette, and the strong wiriness that so lent itself to drawing lines in open space rather than enclosing volumes. Güell's dragon is not just heraldic decor but sculpture.

Why is it there? Obviously as a guardian, but for Güell and his in-laws there was more to the brute than that. It is a quotation from the national epic of the Catalanists, Verdaguer's *L'Atlàntida*; for both author and poem were bound up with the Comillas family, and Verdaguer and Gaudí were friends. Inspired by Verdaguer's voyages between Spain and Cuba on Comillas's ships, *L'Atlàntida* was dedicated to the marquis. The dragon on the gate refers to a feat of Hercules in the poem.

In the original Greek myth, the Garden of the Hesperides lay beyond the ocean at the western edge of the world. The Hesperides themselves, the daughters of Night (Nyx) and Darkness (Erebus), tended a tree that bore golden apples: it had been the earth mother Gaia's wedding present to Hera when she married Zeus, and it was guarded by Ladon, a fierce dragon. The eleventh labor of Hercules had been to kill this dragon and snatch its golden apples.

In Verdaguer's poem, Hercules arrives at the Garden of the Hesperides by way of Barcelona and Cádiz. In Cádiz he meets the shepherd Geryon, who tells him of the garden, the magic tree (which, this being Spain, becomes an orange, not an apple, tree), and the widowed Queen Hesperis, who can be won by a hero bold enough to kill its guardian reptile and take the fruit. Hercules crosses the Atlantic, approaches the tree, and, when the dragon leaps on him, gives it the death blow. "Bloody poison glitters on the flowers, and the dragon's fierce eyes slowly fade like light in a dry crucible."

The Güell-Comillas circle had no difficulty interpreting this. For the gardens at the western edge of the world, read Cuba; for the golden fruit, profits; for Hercules' valor, the go-getter business habits of the *indiano*. It was a perfect, flattering allegory for them, and especially for Comillas, whose *pubilla* would now have her garden in the Finca Güell.

Hyperbolic arches and limestone pillars at the Palau Güell

So the iron dragon is not Saint George's adversary, but Hercules'; and Gaudí set a carved effigy of the Hesperides' orange tree as a finial on the gatepost, above the monogram *G* for Güell.

Meanwhile, he was also designing a palace for Eusebi Güell.

His father's house on the Ramblas, designed by Joan Martorell i Montells, was of small architectural distinction; but Eusebi wanted to be near it, and instead of building a house in the Eixample he bought a smallish lot of about five hundred square yards on Carrer Nou de la Rambla, behind his father's house. In 1885 Güell was approaching forty, and he wanted something altogether more grand and original than Martorell's design. Gaudí gave it to him.

With the Palau Güell, Gaudí's maturity as an architect truly began. It was the first building to show him at full stretch—he was 34 when he began the designs in 1886—and Eusebi Güell had made it clear that there would be no crimps in the budget. The final cost of the *palau* is not known, but it was certainly enormous, especially for a building that was to stand empty for so much of its life—Güell used it for only sixteen years, removing to a hermitlike retreat in the Güell Park in 1906. Gaudí gave Güell the most elaborate wrought iron; the best joinery in ebony, palisander, and rare Brazilian woods; the finest carving and polishing of stone both common and rare; the most luxurious inlays.

While it was under construction, one of Güell's secretaries, a poet named Pico Campamar, showed his boss a sheaf of bills and begged him to tell Gaudí to economize. Güell leafed through them. "Is *that* all he spent?" asked the patron airily. For his part, Gaudí refused to cut any corners at all. As the palace was nearing completion in 1889, the head joiner proudly showed him a wardrobe he had made, finished in *faux-marbre*, and invited the architect to rap it. On hearing the hollow sound of wood, Gaudí congratulated the man on his skill and then delivered a little sermon on the impropriety of deception: "Art is a very serious business," he concluded, and stalked away.

It was Gaudí's showplace. He took infinite pains over the design, doing at least three complete versions of the facade before settling on the one he built, Venetian in feeling even though the entrance and exit arches that rise two stories above pavement level are parabolas. The wrought iron, such as the wildly snaking tympana, their iron lines tense as springs, that fill in the upper part of the arches and the massive shield of Catalunya that sits between them, with four bars surmounted by a helmet and an iron eagle, had to be modeled in plaster to full scale by the smith Joan Oños before he started work. There was not going to be a routine element anywhere. From the window latches to the wooden louvers that sheathe the tribune on the back facade in a curved membrane like the scales of an armadillo—everything bears the mark of an insatiable, self-critical inventiveness.

And yet it strikes one as a lugubrious building now—partly, of course, because no one has lived in it for decades. It was stripped of its furniture, which Gaudí also designed, long ago. (A few pieces, including the *condesa*'s wonderfully eccentric vanity desk, are preserved in the museum of the Güell Park; some early Gaudí chairs with lion's-head arms recently turned up beneath a clutter of theatrical props in the basement.) In the civil war it was badly vandalized by anarchists. It now serves as Barcelona's theater museum, and this fits its character of dramatic melancholy. The note is struck first in the basement, where Güell stabled his horses—they were unhitched from the carriages in the porte cochere and led down a circular ramp, the predecessor of the spiral ramps of the Casa Milà. Its low vaults spring from squat, thick brick

The grand salon of the Palau Güell

---

columns with widely splayed capitals that corbel out a quarter of a brick's width per course—funguslike pads of cooked earth. Some, engaged in the walls, are polygonal in section; the freestanding columns in the middle are circular. It is astoundingly dramatic architecture, this crypt. It could be a set for the *Ring*; all it needs is Alberich and a chorus of dwarfs. A huge green papier-mâché stage dragon stored under one of the vaults looks quite at home in the dust and troglodytic gloom. But for Gaudí, the Catalan associations of the cave ran back to the Pyrenees as well as forward to Wagner. Clearly, he and Güell shared a taste for morbid, penitential rhetoric, and in the Palau Güell it comes into its own with an intensity unique in Gaudí's work at least until the construction of the Güell Crypt in 1908.

Naturally, the main salons are less archaic than the basement, but they are still closer to the fanatic melancholy of the Escurial than to the bright mayflower medievalism of the Catalan Renaixença. It is a self-consciously princely building, not a bourgeois one. The core of the palace is a high salon capped by an elongated parabolic dome that fits inside the central spire—a continuous rise of three stories from the *pis noble* to the roof. It is encased in two stories of galleries and halls, some with miradors that look out on Carrer Nou de la Rambla in front and over the terrace at the back. Gaudí's fascination with Mudejar architecture, already set free in the Casa Vicens and the Finca Güell, was still strong. This salon is based on the central hall of a Moorish *hammam*. Its light is filtered, coming mainly through internal windows on the second and third floors and through parabolic windows between the pendentives of the dome; the light reaches these from skylights in the attic and is filtered through a crazy paving design of tinted glass. There are also small holes for natural light in the dome itself. But nothing is direct. Thus one moves in dimness, a foggy light pierced by glare from electroliers and spots of brightness high up in the dome. All it needs, you think at first, is steam and some naked Arabs.

But no. Güell and Gaudí wanted a pious space, not a sensuous one. The salon was for concerts and religious worship. Its materials are somber. The wall sheathing and columns are gray, polished Garraf limestone, with the metallic sheen of a gun barrel—this at least was free, since Güell's cement company owned the quarry. There is some relief of color in reddish-orange inset panels of a rare Pyrenean onyx, but these have darkened over time and it is hard to say how bright they originally were. The corners of the cornice, where the archivolts begin, are bound with sinuous, carceral strips of iron. The balustrade and staircase screens are ebony, black, and bristling, inset with ivory.

The pièce de résistance—at least until you reach the roof—is Eusebi Güell's private chapel, built into the south wall of the salon. This is an enormous cupboard with doors sixteen feet high, framed in some rare, pale South American hardwood, inlaid with ivory, their recessed panels sheathed—a touch of quite crushing sumptuousness—with bookmatched plates of creamy-white Caribbean turtle shell. Better not to guess how many of these harmless, now-rare animals gave up their lives to produce nearly two hundred square feet of shell for the glory of God, Güell, and Gaudí. Today, when the doors open they reveal, rather anticlimactically, a couple of aluminum ladders and a janitor's bucket. The chapel was trashed in the civil war and so was everything in it— the organ, the Madonna, the cordovan-leather wall coverings, and the altar.

In some ways the interior of the Palau Güell is hard on the nerves. Not only are its discomfort and pietism grating, but most of the wood paneling in the vestibules and gallery halls, though admirably joined and carved, is kitsch—a Catalan's parody of Scots Baronial, which clashes hideously with the Hispano-Moresque elements elsewhere. Moreover it is clear that neither Gaudí nor Eusebi Güell cared a fig for the art of painting, so that the religious murals on the theme of charity are somewhere below ghastly and the family portraits, if anything, worse.

And yet, in the very midst of this mélange, one finds the most perfect and inventive architectural detailing in the columns and capitals that support the screens in the miradors. Cut and polished from the metallic Garraf stone, they look as radically new as Brancusi's sculpture. Their fairing and subtle concavities, their purity of line, seem to owe very little to either Mozarabic or Western sources, though probably their inspiration came from the thirteenth-century capitals in the refectory of the monastery of Poblet.

And then there is the roof of the Palau Güell. It is now closed to visitors—in a pinch, it can be seen fairly close up from the top floor of the Hotel Gaudí directly across the street. Nevertheless the resolute Gaudíphile must wangle his or her way up to the roof, because only the overused word will do: it is a masterpiece.

One should think of it as an elevated mesa set in a plain of roofs. What one sees from it, the skyline of the Raval and of the Barri Gòtic, is little changed (except for the low scrub of television aerials) since Gaudí's day. This domestic averageness, with bright washing on clotheslines amid the dun-colored attics, is the background to Gaudí's acropolis of chimneys and ventilators, dominated by the conical spire that contains the high slender dome of the main salon.

There are twenty chimneys, all roughly the same shape: an obelisk or cone, mounted on a shaft, which sits on a base, the whole form sheathed in fragments of tile or glass. This fragmented tile work is known as *trencadis*, *trencar* being the Catalan verb "to break." The art of *trencadis* originated with the Arabs in Spain, but Gaudí was the first architect to revive it. It is especially useful because it can cover curved surfaces without the need to cast and fire custom-shaped ceramics. And cheap, too: the tile or glass can be scrap. But above all, *trencadis* can be wonderfully varied in their beauty. Gaudí used them over and over again, because he was clearly fascinated by the way the mosaic fragmentation of *trencadis*, their quick shifts of color and pattern, could play against the stable mass of an architectural form—breaking it up, even seeming to dissolve it under some conditions of light. The artist Ellsworth Kelly, in 1990, piercingly observed that no history of fragmentation in modern art could possibly be complete without considering the effects of Gaudí's *trencadis* on the young Picasso, who must have seen them—years before painting his first cubist pictures—when he was living in Barcelona in a room just down the Carrer Nou de la Rambla from Palau Güell.

No two chimneys or ventilators of the Palau Güell roof are the same. They all look organic—like morels, or stiff pricks—but the variety of shape and finish bespeaks the studious inventiveness of Gaudí's imagination: he was making a demonstration piece, a pre-Picassian virtuoso show of how many variations he could run on a basic form, aided by the plasticity of *trencadí*-sheathed surfaces. The purest chimney (also the latest, probably added after 1900) is all white. On one of its porcelain chips you will eventually see a small green stamp—the maker's mark of Limoges: it seems that Eusebi Güell had a white Limoges dinner service he no longer wanted and let Gaudí smash it.

This roof is perhaps the most beautiful permanent sculptural installation in Barcelona; its only rival is Gaudí's other roof, on the Casa Milà. The climax of this array of totems is the spire. Most descriptions say it is sheathed in tile, but it is not. Its nubbly, rocklike surface—a precursor, in its matte roughness, of the dry-stone arcades of the Güell Park—is made of Triassic limestone that had once been used to line the inside of limekilns on Güell's properties around Garraf. This stone, originally reddish, had acquired a blue-gray vitrified surface from repeated firings of the kiln. After thirty or so firings the stone would start to break down, and the lime burners would abandon the oven and build another. (If one kept reusing the kiln its lining would burn to a black coke, porous and twisted, which Gaudí also used—on the outside of the crypt of the Colonia Güell.) Crushed down to the size of pebbles, this substance covers the spire. The lower third of the spire is a web of parabolic windows, and a ring of larger parabolic arches runs around its midsection, thus letting light into the dome within. Gaudí topped off the whole affair with a finial that serves both as weather vane and lightning conductor, featuring a gilded wind rose, an iron bat with mesh wings three feet across, and a Greek cross. Delicate and sinister, the bat is the best flourish: it seems to be flapping off toward the horizon, exorcised from the gloomy thoughts of Eusebi Güell.

IV

Through the 1890s Gaudí kept himself aloof from the pagan currents of *modernisme*. He ignored Casas and Rusiñol—significantly enough, Gaudí is the one prominent figure in Barcelona's aesthetic life of whom no sketch by Casas exists. He never visited Sitges, and avoided The Four Cats. This was a moral decision; he thought internationalism pernicious. He was not alone. Conservatism, in fin de siècle Barcelona, was not necessarily the refuge of the mediocre: there were a few talented and many weak artists on both sides. After he reached his forties, Gaudí helped to found an aggressively conservative and religious society of artists, sculptors, architects, and decorators, the Artistic Circle of Saint Luke, that played at least as large a part in shaping Catalan middle-class taste as the goings-on at the Cau Ferrat and The Four Cats.

Apart from Gaudí, the chief figures among the "Lukes" were the Llimona brothers—Josep (1864–1934), a sculptor, and Joan (1860–1926), a painter who had married the sister of the composer Enric Granados and specialized in frescoes for religious foundations. They were joined by Alexandre de Riquer, the Anglophile imitator of the Pre-Raphaelites, who wanted to see a renaissance of religious stained glass in Barcelona. These, and perhaps a dozen others, founded the circle in 1893.

There is some dispute about how the Artistic Circle of Saint Luke started. One version is that the more devout Catholic artists seceded from the rest of Catalan bohemia after some "indecent" goings-on at a costume ball in 1892. Another has Joan and Josep Llimona attending a celebration thrown in a Montjuic inn by Rusinyol and Casas to mark the success of their show at the Sala Parès in February 1893. Everyone got drunk and the dinner turned, as such events were apt to do, into a torrent of dirty songs, republican anthems, anticlerical jokes, and blasphemies. The Llimonas were scandalized and resolved to found an artists' society whose members would never behave like that. Josep Llimona, a red-faced giant of a man whom the poet Josep Carner compared to a "clumsily molded archangel," once toppled a newsstand on the Ramblas in his zeal to destroy a foreign magazine with a caricature of Christ and the pope on its cover. The Lukes were so worried about sexual morality that, for the first dozen years after they set up their headquarters in Barcelona, which had a teaching studio attached, their governing committee refused to allow a nude female model to pose in it. Women artists were excluded from the circle until 1920, when they were grudgingly admitted on condition that they did not draw from the naked male model. These prohibitions may not have mattered greatly, since the only artist in the circle who made a regular practice of working from the naked figure was Josep Llimona. Nudes seldom appeared anywhere in fin de siècle Catalan art, religious or not. The fashion, among Lukes and modernists alike, was for draped ladies in "spiritual," unrevealing costumes, flourishing their garlands or swooning over founts but rarely showing flesh. The body was more diaphanous than the clothes, which may have had some appeal to the patrons of the textile industry.

The Lukes thought they were re-creating the guild past. Joan Lli-mona, proud that the Artistic Circle had marched with its own banner in the Corpus Christi procession, called it "a Society that sets out to revive the splendours of the ancient guilds, abolished in an evil hour by modern liberal centralism—the guilds, sons of the Catholic Church." They were also intensely regionalist; the only modern French artist they admired seems to have been Rodin.

To show their agreement with conservative Catalan ideology, the Lukes invited Torras i Bages to become their religious adviser. He accepted. His inaugural address in March 1894 struck the main theme: art for art's sake is a parody of religion. But if its claims to spirituality are bogus, the opposite idea of a materialist art is impossible: "materialism and Art are mutually contradictory ideas, like night and day." The "neurotic" art of the fin de siècle—Art Nouveau, symbolism, call it what you will—is only a twisted response to the failure of materialism. And so, "The two newest currents . . . in Art, naturalism and surrender to the Unknown, which pretend to herald a new age of Beauty, converge towards the same point; and in the name of a purely human civilization they unmake Man . . ."

Torras's special bête noire was Nietzsche, "great prophet of artistic anarchy, twin brother of social anarchism." "Law is dead," Nietzsche had cried. Take away law from art and the ancient consensus of image, custom, meaning, and authority that leads men to God is shattered. You then have war: a struggling mass of avant-gardes, "ridiculous vanity, misshapen extremes of romanticism or modernism." And you no longer have even the possibility of an organic regional culture. "Decadence is a display, not of high spiritual activity, but of pure passivity, impressions, nervous reflexes, scattered and confused echoes."

In sum, Torras i Bages's attitudes to cultural change remind one of what is often forgotten a hundred years later, now that the cultural issues of the fin de siècle are as remote from us as the French Revolution was from him. We are apt to ascribe the opposition to modernism—however one defines its spirit—as coming from "academic" interests within the art world, as though it were an in-house fight between artists over which style would end up on top. But the struggle was far deeper than that. It lay in the moral domain. Torras i Bages's anxieties came out of an encyclopedic sense of loss whose result, he feared, might be the loss of God Himself. About that, Torras was certainly not deceived. One may ridicule him point by point, though he got a few things right: who could deny that the art of the French Rosicrucians, in all its sickly "mysticism," *was* decadent in comparison with the virile spirituality of the nave of Santa Maria del Mar or the portal of Ripoll? Many people today would agree with Torras's verdict that "the simplest works, those an artist painted with the most disinterestedness, like a hermit's *retaules* meant to be contemplated by a few peasants . . . speak to us in a franker language of love than the paintings in the Paris Salons." He was not a highly visual man, but the crisis he saw was real. A chasm had opened under the pillars of the Church, beneath the very idea of a regional, theocratic culture. His first mistake was to imagine that this could be repaired by a collective act of local will. "All the great artistic epochs have had a certain collectivism," he wrote, not realizing that this was true of the late nineteenth century as well. But his second mistake was to volley anathemas at the heralds who brought the news of crack-up: Nietzsche, Ibsen, Wagner, Maeterlinck, Baudelaire, Mallarmé, even Emerson and Thoreau—the outriders of a transnational culture of early modernism. The only "modern" thing about Torras i Bages was the anxiety behind his lofty cultural rage. But that was modern in itself—if not *modernista*.

Because of its links to the business and religious establishments of Barcelona, therefore, the Artistic Circle of Saint Luke was rather more than the gaggle of out-of-step nostalgists that some writers today assume it to have been. If you were an artist you could make a career without it, but if you wanted to do public works and enjoy some degree of patronage, especially from the Church, you had to join it. The Catalan clergy rarely seems to have hired an artist or an architect for a major job without first talking to Torras i Bages. It was Torras who, in his capacity as bishop of Vic in 1900, gave the young Josep-Marià Sert— the future Tiepolo of the dictatorships, decorator of Rockefeller Center, and *arbiter elegantiarum* of the transatlantic set in the 1930s—his first big mural project, the frescoes in the cathedral of Vic.

Consequently, a lot of architects, painters, and sculptors became Lukes for reasons not necessarily connected with piety. Even Joan Miró joined, briefly; the architect Puig i Cadafalch enrolled (though not Domènech i Montaner), as did Gaudí's associate Josep Marià Jujol. Joan Rubió i Bellvé, architect of the White Friar, and the busy architect Enric Sagnier, who probably designed more houses in the Eixample than anyone else during the *modernista* period, were Lukes as well. And of the important decorative programs done by sculptors, muralists, and mosaicists for new buildings in Barcelona through the 1890s and 1900s, the lion's share went to Lukes, for whom the Artistic Circle did function with the exclusiveness of a guild.

Josep Llimona

Josep Llimona and his brother Joan had been raised, in a general way, as Catholics, but they both experienced a deep and emotional access of faith in their twenties. By then Josep Llimona had completed his art training with a scholarship to Rome, and he went to Paris. The Rodin sculptures he saw there were to form his own mature work. He was particularly struck by one of the earliest of Rodin's *non-finito* marble carvings, in which the figure, in homage to Michelangelo's *Slaves*, is only partly detached from the rough block of stone from which it emerges. This was the *Danaid* (1888). It is clearly the origin of the best known of Llimona's public sculptures, *El Desconsol* (*Despair*), 1907—the young marble woman, head averted and hands lightly wrung in grief, who until recently sprawled on her block in the middle of the oval pond of the Citadel Park outside the Museum of Modern Art. (She has been replaced by a copy.) Llimona had mastered the combination of generalized, almost impressionistic shape—the hair—and suave, light-responsive nuances of modeling that tended to escape most of Rodin's imitators, try as they might to mimic it. *El Desconsol* is a very Catholic nude, in that it wants to be two things at once: sexy and moral. It is the woman as delicious victim, the flower beneath the foot—the granddaughter of the slave girl on the tyrant's bed in Delacroix's *Death of Sardanapalus*, a painting Lli-

Llimona's El Desconsol, 1907

mona undoubtedly knew. It is also a secular version of a long line of penitent Magdalens meant to evoke pity of a libidinous kind.

If sex is the undertheme of *El Desconsol*, its overt message is idealistic and moralizing. Llimona's figure is, literally, a fallen woman, collapsed and helpless under the weight of guilt, awaiting redemption. There is no indication of why she despairs (that would have made her too specific), but sexual transgression is implied. She is unthreatening—not a bit like Beardsley's fatal women, still less the raffish whores that Ramón Casas drew to warn Catalans against syphilis. She is an ideal public sculpture for a society whose politer members believed in private charity, Catholic trade unions, and the morbid effects of Vice.

To see Llimona at full stretch, however, one must visit his largest public sculpture, the monument to Dr. Bartolomeu Robert, the first Catalanist mayor of Barcelona. Bartolomeu Robert i Yarzábal (1842–1902) was born in Mexico, the son of an émigré Catalan doctor who soon afterward returned to Barcelona with his Mexican wife. The boy studied medicine at the University of Barcelona, made a brilliant career as a doctor, and, by his early forties, was president of the Barcelona Academy of Medicine and Surgery. He entered politics on the conservative ticket in the Ajuntament, brandishing a Catalanist policy: most Catalan voters, he later told a Madrid reporter, would be satisfied with tax concessions and other decentralizing measures, but he and his allies wanted more—"the total triumph of a regional solution; we demand for Catalunya her language, her laws, her customs, even her theater."

Dr. Bartolomeu Robert, mayor of Barcelona, 1899–1902

On becoming mayor of Barcelona in 1899, Dr. Robert purged the city's electoral rolls of twenty-seven thousand phony names put there by caciquism and gave official sanction to a strike—not of workers, but of banks. In 1899 the minister of finance in Madrid, Fernández Villaverde, eager to reduce the looming deficit caused by the disaster of 1898, decreed an increase in profit taxes. Predictably, the Catalan bankers saw no reason to pay for what they saw as Madrid's failures. Instead of paying up, the banks of Barcelona closed down and, with them, hundreds of businesses all over the city. Bartolomeu Robert enthusiastically supported this Tancament de Caixes, as it was called. But Madrid was in earnest, and, amid general amazement, it declared war on Catalunya. No troops actually moved; Robert and the two Catalan ministers saved the day by resigning, the taxes were paid, and business resumed. Nevertheless the episode made a hero of Robert, at least among conservatives, and when he died in 1902 the *bones famílies* set about raising money for a monument to him, which Josep Llimona was commissioned to make. Considering that the good doctor had lasted less than a year in office, the result was (to put it mildly) lavish. Actually, it is less about Robert as mayor than Catalan self-congratulation in general.

The Robert monument is Barcelona's quintessential *modernista* public sculpture, a masterpiece of its genre. It was set up in front of the university in 1907. After the civil war, Franco's officials decreed that so pugnacious a souvenir of Catalan nationalist sentiment should not stay on public view, so it was dismantled and stored, undamaged. In the 1980s, with the Caudillo safely dead, the Ajuntament reerected it, this time in Plaça de Tetuán. Antoni Gaudí seems, on stylistic evidence, to have designed the base. Llimona sculpted the eighteen figures. The result is a curious *concetto* indeed—an encyclopedia of Catalanist virtue as promoted by Torras i Bages and the Artistic Circle of Saint Luke.

The base is no ordinary socle, but a sculpture in its own right—a kind of hill with grottoes from which Llimona's figures rise. Its undulations and surface treatment (stone, pecked matte with chisels), are exactly like those of the building Gaudí was designing at the time on Passeig de Gràcia, the Casa Milà. And since, as we shall see, Gaudí wanted the Casa Milà to be the base for an enormous figure of the Virgin, one may view the Robert monument with its surge of secular figures as a sketch for that gigantic and unachieved emblem of piety.

Gaudí's base is meant to evoke the "sacred mountains" of Catalunya—Montseny, Montserrat, and Montjuic (from whose stone it is carved). It contains fountains of water from which you can drink: an emanation of the Catalan spirit. The taps look like bronze nipples; and drawing back a little, you see that they *are* nipples, and that the stone bulges to which they are fixed are in fact large, handsomely formed breasts, swelling from the stone wall of the grottoes. The image of nurture, Catalunya as motherland, *genetrix Catalanorum*, takes on an almost Surrealist intensity here. No wonder Dalí was so crazy about Gaudí.

Llimona's figures continue the allegory in a more explicit vein. Not very specific—there is no top-hatted bronze banker with a key to symbolize the Tancament de Caixes—but clear enough. On top, there is a stone herm of Dr. Robert, grave and mustached, with the (female) genius of Catalunya whispering directives in his ear. Below, in front, bronze Rodinesque figures rise from the stone mountain. The males on the right—a peasant in his floppy *barretina*, a cloaked savant showing the book of old Catalan laws to a shirtless worker—are particularly indebted to the burghers of Calais. The conservative tone of Robert's (and Llimona's) Catalanism is embodied in the man with the sickle, another archetype of folk culture from the time of the Reapers' War. He is ready to start cutting—*bon cop de falç!*—but another man prudently restrains him. To their left, Truth handsomely unveils herself, and above them all is another genius of Catalunya, androgynous, holding up an oak twig, symbol of the Ur-Pyrenean forests, at the side of a young man in Regency dress who grips the staff of a huge national flag and is probably the poet

Gaudí and Llimona, the Robert monument

Aribau. The flag wraps around the top of the monument and emerges above another group, this time in stone, at the back—five compassionate citizens watching Mercy attend to a helpless girl, while a mother stands by with her baby. It might be said that, with this work, Llimona hit all the buttons of conservative Catalanism.

Torras's formidable certainty about the unchanging *philosophia perennis* of the Church impressed figures whose works have lasted far better than his own. The poet Joan Maragall, for instance, admired him very much and found refuge in Torras's conservatism when his own romantic and relativist instincts as a poet left him feeling too exposed. Nietzsche, Ibsen, and Emerson spoke to Maragall the poet, but Torras spoke to Maragall the patriarch, the middle-class rentier with thirteen children, a private income, and a deep Catholic education, tormented by the crisis of Spanish identity that came in the wake of 1898. He and Torras were partners in the same "obsession," Maragall wrote to the bishop in 1911, "the work of revival which seems fundamentally needed by our people; they are agitated with formulas on the surface, whilst all is left dying inside."

Gaudí felt the same way, but more so. Torras i Bages was the only intellectual mentor he ever completely accepted. They were friends for nearly thirty years. In the Catalanist counterreformation that Torras wished to spearhead, Gaudí was destined to play the role of Bernini. His surviving remarks—written down by Gaudí's disciples—reflect the opinions of the conservative Thomist of Vic. "There is no freedom in Heaven, because if one knows the whole Truth one completely submits to it. Liberty is a temporal, passing thing." That was Gaudí echoing Torras glossing Dante's version of Aquinas on the contingent nature of free will, a gift from God that becomes irrelevant once one reaches heaven: "*In la sua voluntate e nostra pace.*" He was not by any means indifferent to his fees, but he agreed with Torras that higher art was disinterested and entailed a willing suspension of ego: "Productive things are not made for money; yet we know that nothing bears fruit without sacrifice, and sacrifice is the shrivelling of the ego without reward."

Gaudí became more authoritarian as he matured, lamenting the revolution of 1868 and the expulsion of Isabel II, and viewing all federalist and democratic ideas as fraudulent: "Democracy is the rule of ignorance and stupidity." He would tolerate disciples (the more submissive the better) but not *argument* about his work, which explains his lifelong aversion to theory and publicity. Flaubert said that the artist should be like God in his work, present everywhere but invisible; and like the Deity, Gaudí would have added, incontrovertible as well. "The man in charge," he said of architects—but not, one suspects, them alone—"should never enter into discussions, because he loses authority by debate. No light is shed by argument. . . . The architect is a governor in the highest sense of the word, which is that he does not find the constitution made, but makes it himself. Hence people call governors constructors of societies [*constructores de pueblos*]." Gaudí was eager to present his work as the outcome, not of fantasy, but of natural law.

And this, as some of his contemporaries saw, was the biggest fantasy of all, for the humility that his more pious disciples were always droning about, as though Gaudí were Saint Francis with buildings instead of birds, had another side. In Gaudí one sees flourishing the egotism achieved by those who think they have stepped beyond the bounds of the mere ego and identified themselves with nature, becoming God's humble servant but copying their employer. "His personality," said Rafael Puget, whose memories Josep Pla transcribed in *Un Senyor de Barcelona*, and who claimed to have known Gaudí quite well, "was shot through by a morbid, insoluble pride and vanity. In a country where most things remain to be done and the little that has been done is always in danger of being torn down or left unfinished, our architect was born unique and worked as though architecture itself had begun at the precise moment when he made his appearance on earth." Gaudí's aim, Puget thought, was not to make an architecture "of arbitrary forms suited to human life"; it was "an imitation of cosmic life, inside which people would pass a mystical-troglodytic existence. . . . He is neither a Roman nor a Catholic in the sense these words normally have in our culture. He is a primitive Christian of the woods. . . . Talking about Gaudí's 'taste' is like discussing the 'taste' of whales."

The poet Joan Maragall, in a letter to the critic Josep Pijoán in 1903, recounted a conversation he had just had with Gaudí while strolling through the unfinished Güell Park. The architect kept talking about his idea of "southern decoration," but then

we went deeper, deeper, and we got to a point where we could somehow understand one another. In his work, in his struggle to make ideas material, he sees the law of *punishment*, and he revels in it. I can't conceal my repugnance at such a negative sense of life, and we discussed a tiny bit, very little, why I constantly find that we can't grasp one another's ideas. I, who think of myself as so basically Catholic!

I come to see that it's he who represents the tradition of Catholic dogmatism, and that in the orthodox sense he's in the strong position; that compared to him, I'm a dilettante, riddled with heterodoxies.

And then what? If you want to call work, suffering and human struggle "punishment," that is a question of words. But isn't it true that the word seems to pollute human life at its very source?

It seems to me that, the stronger one feels the reign of God on earth to be . . . then if you take a slightly less backward view you can't be sure that everything is meant to be a punishment, because you are transfixed by the glory that stands before you and the love you feel inside it.

The mild and self-absorbed facade behind which these penitential impulses burned became, of course, the stuff of legend: Don Antoni, the hermit of the Eixample, a character out of Dostoyevski. Gaudí did not go out in society—he did not need to, because in Güell he had his patron already. He could be glimpsed on the street, stoop shouldered, timid, white haired, and blue eyed, dressed invariably in a baggy dark suit and slippers, munching an orange or a dry crust of bread as he shuffled along. One did not speak to him. Like Torras, his spiritual mentor, Gaudí often prayed to Saint Anthony of Alexandria, remarking that the saint "went into the desert and sowed and planted to get salads and fruit to eat; this is real asceticism. Physical exercise and moderation in food, drink and sleep are mortifications of the flesh. They fight lust, beastliness, drunkenness and sloth." Gaudí's dietary habits seemed odd to the gluttonous Catalans: he was a vegetarian, eschewing meat, thick soups, fried food, and all fat except olive oil, which, as he pointed out with a trace of topological pedantry, ought to be eaten with lettuce and escarole, "which are thirsty for oil and present a combination of small volume with great surface extension." He preferred water to wine and counseled his juniors always to wear two pairs of socks. He opposed wearing spectacles on the grounds that they weakened the eyes: one should strengthen them with exercise and a morning splash of cold water and not tax them by reading too much. He never married, and from his thirties on no rumor of erotic entanglement seems to have touched his quiet, solitary life. He kept a prie-dieu in his bedroom and in his later years took to sleeping in a narrow four-poster, hemmed in by worktables and plaster models, in a temporary house on the site of the Sagrada Família. "Elegance," he said, "is the sister of poverty; so one should not confuse poverty with misery." This commendable sentiment did nothing to lower the ambition of his buildings, their exorbitant cost, or Gaudí's own fees, as the few clients he had apart from Eusebi Güell would in due course find out.

V

In the meanwhile there were two more projects to do for Eusebi Güell, neither destined to be finished. They were a small mill town and a large park.

Güell was an "enlightened" industrialist. It was in his interest to reduce the class friction between workers and management. He thought this could be done through paternalist control. In spiritual matters, Güell took his cues from Torras i Bages, and in secular ones, as we have seen, he looked to Prat de la Riba. Hence his decision to found a self-contained *colonia* in the village of Santa Coloma del Cervelló, on the banks of the Llobregat River, for making cotton goods and corduroy. It would resemble worker-run cooperatives like the one in Mataró, with a clinic and an infirmary, a choir hall, a library, a small theater, and even its own football club. However, it would be run by Güell. The mill itself, and the brick houses for its workers, were designed by Gaudí's assistants,

Count Güell showing church prelates a loom at the Colonia Güell

Francesc Berenguer i Mestres and Joan Rubio i Bellvé, and managed by his right-hand man, the engineer Fernando Alsina y Parellada.

Gaudí's contribution to the *colonia* was its church. A small chapel had been attached to the original *masia* on the property, but it could hardly meet the ritual needs of a whole factory. Gaudí started thinking about the design of the church in 1898. The first stone was laid ten years later, but the church was never finished because, after Eusebi Güell's death in 1918, his sons were not prepared to sink great sums in it, and by then its construction had got no further than the crypt. A few surviving sketches show Gaudí's ideas of a large, vague, Wagnerian edifice with parabolic spires that would have been absurdly out of place in the country setting. Nevertheless, fragment though it is, the crypt of the Colonia Güell is one of Gaudí's masterworks, a building that looks wild and "expressive" at first—until one grasps the sublimely empirical logic of construction that removes it from the world of mere fantasy and creates, on a quite small scale, one of the greatest architectural spaces in Europe.

The crypt was not, and could not have been, designed with flat drawings in plan, section, and elevation. Gaudí thought of it in terms of the angles and planes generated by a web of compressive and tensile forces with the absolute minimum of bending moment, using brick and stone without any steel in it. This means that the crypt contains hardly one right angle. It is an intimidatingly complex web of funicular polygons, designed not from the ground up, but from the roof down.

The crypt for the chapel at Colonia Güell

Gaudí's design method was an inspired piece of inverted modeling with string and weights. Drawing out the ground plan of the crypt, he hung a string from each point where a column would stand and transmit the thrust of the structure into the foundations. Then he joined the hanging strings with cross strings to simulate arches and vaults, attaching to each string a little cotton bag of bird shot, carefully weighted to mimic the compressive load on each column, arch, and vault. (The load scale was 1:100,000, or a tenth of a gram of lead, a fraction of a single pellet of partridge shot, to the kilo.) Naturally, none of the strings in these complicated cats' cradles hung vertically. All the loads in them were pure tension—the only way string, which has zero resistance to bending, knows how to hang. Gaudí then photographed the string model from all angles *and turned the photos upside down*. Tension became compression. He could measure the compound angles and—given the superior quality of Catalan workmanship—build the right scaffolding and forms.

No one in the history of architecture had gone about designing a building in this way. The photos of the string models one sees in the little gallery of the Güell Crypt may look odd and old-fashioned, like a dotty aunt's dream of chandeliers, but they point forward three-quarters of a century to an idea of designing that only computer modeling would make possible (though, alas, when the computer did become part of architectural practice, there was no new Gaudí).

The Güell Crypt is perhaps the most vivid illustration of how the imagination of this great conservative inventor worked. Gaudí wanted to imagine a "new" kind of space that would, at the same time, be deeply archaic: buildings that did not have the abstract regularity of Renaissance architecture, but which in their visceral and theatrical qualities recalled the Ur-forms of shelter, the cave, the ledge, the den, the tree. One recalls Rafael Puget's words to Pla: "Not an architect of houses, but an architect of grottoes; not an architect of temples, but an architect of forests."

This urge to speculate about the origins of culture was strongly felt by artists in other fields; primitivism was one of the root projects of modernism. But because architecture is supremely a "cooked" art, dependent on social consensus, the desire for the primitive and the chthonic rarely got a chance to show itself in building. Architects might talk about primitivism, as Walter Gropius did about the *volkisch* log huts of the German forests, but they seldom displayed it in their actual buildings. Gaudí, enjoying the support of Eusebi Güell (the King Ludwig, so to speak, of mercantile Catalunya), was the exception. And, of course, his own architecture is very "cooked" indeed. He made fantastically advanced, painstaking calculations, pushed far beyond normal engineering procedures, in order to design something that traditional masons could build in a brick-stone technology that excluded structural steel and had not changed since the thirteenth century. Moreover, he was doing this for the biggest concrete manufacturer and one of the biggest machine capitalists in Spain. What Gaudí wanted you to think about in the Güell Crypt—apart from the incarnated presence of God in the Eucharist, which loomed larger for him than for most visitors today—was caves and the Gothic past.

The imagery of both is plain. The main columns of the crypt are rough black basalt organ pipes, taken unworked from a quarry outside Castellfollit near Girona. Gaudí had these massive stone crystals, roughly hexagonal in section, set up leaning against the thrust of the roof on lead pads. They suggest the pillars of the volcanic earth—pre-Gothic, even pre-Romanesque: the refuge culture of Old Catalunya, the church as the ark or cave in which Christianity finds shelter from the Moors or, by extension, from heresy in general. Had the church been built above this crypt, the way Gaudí meant it to be, this image of subterranean refuge for menaced truth would have been even more vivid.

The forms of the brick vaults and wall surfaces are based on Gaudí's favorite geometrical shape, the hyperbolic paraboloid, and mark the first appearance of this shape in his work. However, it is done through the

most traditional of means—shallow Catalan vaulting and diaphragm ribs
that refer back to Gothic structural systems—hence the impression of
an ancient building that has been dramatically deformed. Space flows
in the Güell Crypt; it winds around the leaning walls, expands and
contracts, and seems to breathe, making the visitor feel like Jonah in the
belly of the brick whale.

VI

The Güell Park was not conceived as the great recreational gardens of
the nineteenth century were—Central Park in New York, for instance.
In fact it is less a park than a failed high-income housing project that
was left to the city of Barcelona by its developer, Eusebi Güell. In terms
of gardening and planting, it is fairly banal and probably always was.
But its open space and the view it affords over the packed city below
are precious to Barcelonans, who flock there on weekends and holidays
to jog, take the air, stroll around on the great plaza with its serpentine
ceramic benches, and enjoy the works of Gaudí. It has acquired a durable
populist fizz.

Originally it consisted of two adjacent farms on Mont Pelat, or Bald
Mountain, part of the hills behind Barcelona. Güell bought one in 1899
and the other in 1902, meaning to develop them as an expensive housing
project by setting up some amenities—a grand entrance with lodges, a
staircase up to a covered market where the residents could shop, a communal plaza, and some elaborate formal terracing, with carriage roads
going up to the lots above. He asked Gaudí to design these.

The standard sales contract for building sites in the park was long
and detailed, and it strongly suggests that Güell was thinking of the kind
of ideal planned community or garden city that had been in the air
among English planners since William Morris first proposed it in the
1870s. (The Garden Cities and Town-Planning Association was set up
in England in 1898, but there is no evidence that Gaudí was influenced
by any of the garden cities—Letchworth, Bourneville, Welwyn, Hamp-
stead Garden Suburb—that sprouted in England before he did the Güell
Park.) Güell proposed to furnish sewers, aqueducts, and electricity lines,
along with maintenance staff, gardeners, and night watchmen. On pur-
chasers of house lots he imposed a fixed relation between the size of the
lot and the size of the house. He contracted to maintain "natural" forest

areas and to plant trees, and the buyer agreed not to fell any existing tree if it had a trunk thicker than six inches, on pain of a fine of fifty pesetas per tree. Though the houses did not have to be designed by Gaudí, their design had to be approved by Güell. There were strict clauses governing height, setbacks, the pitch of approach roads, and, above all, residential use. No owner, the contract said, could use his site for

> factories, workshops, brick or bread ovens, forges, hospitals, clinics, sanatoriums, hotels, inns, restaurants, cafés, chocolate-houses, snack-bars, groceries, stores for drugs or explosive substances, warehouses, or in general for the pursuit of any industry, trade or profession that might prejudice or inconvenience the owners of Park property or clash with the special planning whose permanent character we seek to maintain.

The sites were expensive and, if they had been fully subscribed, would have given Güell a handsome profit. Unfortunately only two buyers signed up. Perhaps Gaudí's reputation for eccentricity scared clients away. More likely, the park was too far out of town for people who wanted to live within reach of Barcelona, but not far enough for those who wished to escape to the country.

For his part, Gaudí does not seem to have been unduly concerned with the salability of lots on Mont Pelat. He had other fish to fry. He saw his work on the park as a chance to make an elaborate statement about his second religion—Catalan nationalism.

The first decade of the twentieth century was the high tide of Catalanism. Prat de la Riba's successes as head of the Lliga Regionalista kept up their momentum after 1901, carried by the general resentment of Madrid and the military that had been provoked by 1898. Prat now had his own newspaper, *La Veu de Catalunya*. In the 1905 municipal elections, the Lliga won a majority. The pro-Lliga satirical paper *Cu-Cut!* ran a cartoon showing an army officer and a civilian outside a restaurant where the Catalanists were celebrating. "Why are there so many people?" asks the fat man. "The victory banquet," the officer answers. "Victory? Oh, then, they must be civilians." This thrust infuriated Barcelona's garrison officers in their fort up on Montjuic. They sent a squad of troops to trash the offices of both *Cu-Cut!* and *La Veu de Catalunya*. As if this intrusion were not enough, the Madrid parliament shortly after passed a bill giving army courts-martial the right to try people for spoken and written libels against "the unity of the Nation

Gaudí, 1910   *Josep Marià Jujol, 1929*

and the honor of its armed forces and their symbols." This imbecilic piece of legislation united Barcelona as nothing else could have done. In the 1900s working-class Catalanism had begun to emerge, and the "law of jurisdictions" brought these together with the conservatives of the Lliga in a new coalition called Solidaritat Catalana. In May 1906 some two hundred thousand supporters of Solidaritat flooded into the concourse below Vilaseca's Arch of Triumph, outside the Palace of Justice, to demonstrate against the law and the army. The national elections of 1907 brought a record turnout of 50 percent at the Catalan polls and a landslide victory for Solidaritat—forty-one out of forty-four seats available to Catalunya in the Madrid legislature and nine out of ten seats in the provincial government. In May 1906 Prat de la Riba had also published his most widely read book, *Catalan Nationality*, in which he set forth a framework for the Mancomunitat (autonomous regional government) of Catalunya—a Catalan state within the Spanish one, uniting the four provincial administrations of Barcelona, Girona, Tarragona, and Lleida and responsible for such matters as public health, culture, communications, transport, finance, and education. In 1914 Madrid at last gave its assent to the Mancomunitat, with Prat de la Riba at its head.

This upsurge of Catalanism would seem to have formed the background to the design of the Güell Park. Güell and Gaudí, *catalanistes* both, consulted closely on the imagery for it, some of which came from

Güell himself. The park's *concetto* had largely been ignored by scholars until it was dug up and reassembled in 1986 by Eduardo Rojo Albarrán's book *El Parc Güell*. One does not need to accept all Albarrán's interpretations to agree with the general thrust of his argument.

Gaudi was fifty when he started work on the Güell Park. He was set in his ways and his *catalanisme* was not in doubt. Indeed it was so extreme that when presented to King Alfonso XIII, he had refused to speak Castilian and addressed the puzzled monarch in Catalan. He loathed Madrid centralism and believed that Catalans were so fundamentally different from other Spaniards that there could be no common ground between them—culturally, politically, none. "Central government," he once declared,

> goes from violence (when it acts collectively) to penny-pinching (in individuals). Its art goes from rhetorical didacticism to abject naturalism. . . . Its business runs from monopoly to usury. And so government is always unjust, art for art's sake does not exist, and instead of wealth, daughter of commerce, there is misery.
>
> We Catalans are the middle term, with our qualities that become defects . . . as a people of *seny* we are open to all solutions, including violent ones (which is a quality and a defect, both). Our instinctive desire is to trade, to make money; this often leads us into avarice (though not to usury).
>
> And so our qualities are not those of the people of the center—and neither are our faults. We can never unite with them.

To Gaudí, the rest of Spain looked merely "abstract"; Catalunya alone was "concrete." Drawing on the Roman past, in which Catalunya, or Hispania Citerior, had been the first "civilized" part of Spain, he opined that in fact Catalunya could not reject the idea of Spain or Spanishness because it *was* that idea—it, and not Castile or Andalusia, adulterated as they were by long Arab occupation, was the "*ser autentic*" of the peninsula. "We cannot say 'Death to Spain,' because we *are* Spain (Hispania Citerior, or Tarraconense); those of the Center are outside of Spain, they are of the Ulterior. The name is *ours*."

Consequently the Güell Park is loaded with emblems of Catalan patriotism. Yet that is not all of its metaphoric content: the two entrance pavilions, for a start, are linked to Catalunya only indirectly. With their big ceramic windows, their looping curves, their luscious *trencadi*-sheathed surfaces, they look like polychrome gingerbread houses. Which,

The Güell Park entrance pavilions

in fact, they may be. One of the hits of the Barcelona Liceu's 1900–1
opera season—when work was beginning at the Park—was a production
of Engelbert Humperdinck's *Hänsel und Gretel*, translated into Catalan
as *Ton i Guida* by Gaudí's friend Joan Maragall. Probably Gaudí knew
Humperdinck, who had been professor of music at the Conservatori del
Liceu in 1886. But certainly he, like everyone else in those circles, would
have known Humperdinck had collaborated on *Parsifal* with the divine
Richard Wagner, who had set the hiding place of the Holy Grail in
Catalunya. Güell and Gaudí shared a Wagnerian enthusiasm. Indeed,
the high dome in Palau Güell was seen, by Güell's friends, as a realization
of the dome of Montsalvat, the castle of Wagner's Christian knights
where the Grail reposed. Did Humperdinck give Gaudí the cue for an
odd, semipop reference? There are two houses in *Hänsel und Gretel*—the
children's own home and the wicked witch's. The "sinister" character
of the pavilion on the right of the Güell Park entrance (looking in toward
the park) is attested to by a ceramic *fong*, a poisonous, hallucinogenic
mushroom that rises from its roof: *Amanita muscaria*, a fine emblem for
a sorceress. But the spire of the left-hand pavilion is crowned with a
cross and ornamented with blue and white checkers, the colors of the
Bavarian flag and so, perhaps, a reference to Wagner's patron, Ludwig
II. Here, all is virtue. It is Hänsel and Gretel's (or, if you prefer, Ton
and Guida's) *casa pairal*, home of their father, the virtuous old broom

The trencadis *serpent in the Güell Park*

---

maker. Between the good house and the bad, one begins one's journey to the forests of the Güell Park.

Maybe. Since no word has survived from Gaudí on his intentions, one cannot know. But Albarrán's plot is certainly intriguing, and so is his unraveling of other elements of the park. The priest Pere Miquel de Esplugues, who had been Güell's lifelong friend and quondam chaplain, had no doubt that Güell wanted the park to be an allegory of Catalanism: "This Park," he wrote in a posthumous memoir (1921), "responded to a mass of ideals that were dear to Güell's heart. In the Park, there are memorable explosions of high Catalan ideals . . . [Güell] ordained the use of the Park for the enlargement of the Catalan spirit."

The shield of Catalunya on the lower fountain on the steps is no problem, but what of the ceramic reptile, glittering handsomely in its many-hued *trencadis*, that clings like a gecko to the upper fountain? Albarrán argues that this derives from the old Calvinist shield of the French city of Nîmes, whose heraldic emblem was a crocodile with a palm. Why Nîmes? Because it represented the northern limit of Old Catalunya in the days of the Frankish kings and was the twin city of Barcelona; because, like Barcelona, it was a great textile center; and because Eusebi Güell lived and studied there for a time in his youth and often visited its public gardens, the Parc de la Fontaine. The main emblematic sculpture in this park was a crocodile between two palm

Gaudí and Jujol, the Greek temple in the Güell Park

trees. Presumably Güell told Gaudí to do his own version of this: an early photo of the park stairway from 1905 shows two palms (now gone) flanking the lizard fountain.

If the stairway fountains refer to the ancient extent of Catalunya, the cavern to which the stair leads is an emblem of their Roman origins. It is a reinvention of a classical temple in the form of a vast grotto. Its roof is carried on eighty-six Doric columns connected by shallow dome vaults, whose surfaces are richly embroidered in *trencadis* designed by Gaudí's assistant, the architect Josep Marià Jujol. This was to have been a covered market for the convenience of residents, but it is hard to imagine people selling chickens, lettuces, and *butifarra* in so grand and eccentric a space; perhaps Gaudí, who was not without his sly ironies, was thinking of the biblical episode of the merchants and moneylenders in the temple. In any case, he and Güell clearly felt that a big, vivid Roman reference was justified, since they thought the original Roman road south to Tarragona—the road that, in ancient times, bypassed Barcelona—ran just below the site of the park.

If Roman Catalunya gets its symbol here, Romanesque Catalunya is evoked in the gloom and rough grandeur of the dry-stone porticoes and arcades—though no Romanesque architect ever came up with anything like Gaudí's famous arcade in the Güell Park, its pillars leaning in toward the hill so that walking along it is like moving under a curling wave of rock. If sometimes in the rock gardens one feels stranded in a surreal landscape, that is because the place had such a powerful effect on Salvador Dalí: its upper pathways, lined by strange "trees" of rock with aloes bushing out wildly from them, filled him with "unforgettable anguish" in his youth. The other Surrealist artist influenced by the Güell Park was Joan Miró, who doted on the serpentine benches, sheathed in ceramic, that wiggle entrancingly around the perimeter of the great plaza on top of the Roman temple. These, like much of Gaudí's other ceramic work, were mainly done by his assistant, the architect Josep Marià Jujol (1879–1949).

In the summer of 1905 a writer for a satirical weekly passed by the entrance of the Güell Park and noticed "about thirty laborers breaking tiles and recombining their fragments again as pieces of decoration. A bystander remarked, 'What a weird sight! Thirty men breaking things and still more of them putting them back together again! Hanged if I can understand it!' " All the workers on Casa Milà, Sagrada Família, and the Güell Park were told to pick up whatever tiles, plates, or bottles they could find in the street and bring them to a depot, from which they were carted uphill to Jujol. (Gaudí had a particular liking for the deep blue glass of rosewater bottles, much of which is still to be seen in the mosaic ceiling of the temple-market.) Under Jujol's direction, the *trencadís* of the Güell Park benches became a panoramic design hundreds of yards long, filled with curlicues, emblems, words, and ravishing passages of abstract design—a kind of demotic rococo on the grand scale, with patterns and objects embedded in its surface. Insofar as one can point to the "first" anything in art history, this is the first collage: the earliest attempt to make a work of art by transposing independent objects into a new matrix where their original identity remains visible, but where their meaning is changed by proximity to others. It far predates cubism. It is a freak. No wonder the wandering calligraphy and isolated words on the Güell Park benches were such an inspiration to Miró.

Twenty years ago Jujol tended to be seen as a mere epigone of Gaudí, an idea that cannot survive a visit to the village of Sant Joan Despí outside Barcelona, which contains some of the best of his independent buildings—the villa made of five mosaic-domed cylinders known as the Torre de la Creu (1913) and the extraordinary Can Negre, a riotously polychromed conversion of a *casa pairal* carried out in 1917. Jujol was the rococo to Gaudí's baroque, and like the older man he was a Luke and a devout Catholic: most of the words on the Güell Park benches are fragments from a litany of devotion to the Virgin. But in Barcelona itself, at least until the 1920s, Jujol worked mainly as Gaudí's assistant, called in to lend his brilliant talents as a colorist to the design of mosaics and *trencadis*. His best collaboration with Gaudí, apart from the park, is the mosaic facade of the Casa Batlló.

VII

The Casa Batlló (1904–6) was not built from scratch; it was a drastic conversion of an existing apartment building put up in 1877 and bought by the textile mogul Josep Batlló i Casanovas. Gaudí enlarged the entrance lobby, redid the whole interior well and the inner walls of the apartments, and altered the form of every room with his sweeping curves: there is hardly a squared-off corner in the whole plan, and the ceiling of the drawing room whirls toward the center into a vortex. Evelyn Waugh, when he visited Barcelona in 1930, thought it very fitting that the Casa Batlló, with its "stalactites of colored porcelain" like a "clumsily iced cake," should have held—as it then did—the offices of the Turkish consulate.

Almost nothing survives of the original house except its floor levels. The central light well is a marvel of sympathetic design. Gaudí wanted to avoid the usual impression of a top-lighted well—glare above, gloom below—and he did so by sheathing it in ceramic plaques, some flat and others in relief, while increasing the size of the internal windows as they went down, so that the largest ones are at the ground and the smallest at the top. Under the skylight where they take the most light, the skin of the internal walls is flat, a cobalt blue. The walls get lighter in color and develop a ripple of texture (to catch the light falling from above) as they descend from floor to floor. They pass from cobalt to sky blue, and thence to pearly gray, before becoming white at street level for maximum reflection. When you look down the well from the top floor, its walls seem quite uniform in color, eliminating the impression of a dark pit. The effect is so discreet as to be almost subliminal.

Gaudí and Jujol collaborated on the new facade on Passeig de Gràcia, with its undulating band of stone-framed windows on the first floor and its mosaic-covered wall, which rises five stories above the *pis noble* to

Interior, Casa Batlló

culminate in the scaly serpent back of a roof. This plane of mosaic looks both visionary and embedded in its time. Claude Monet was still alive, and the Casa Batlló's facade is an architectural equivalent to the shifting, luminous crusts of airy and watery color in Monet's water-lily paintings. All its surface is covered with little blue, green, gray, and white mosaic tiles, punctuated here and there with more than two hundred larger, round ceramic plaques. These pop out of the surface as highlights, and the whole wall takes on different hues as the light strikes it. On a gray day it looks subaqueous; in bright light—especially the floodlights that sometimes come on at night—it seems irreal, a jewel-box fantasy. This, one realizes, is symbolist architecture, as Monet's *Nymphéas* are symbolist painting: vague, almost oceanic, responsive to the beautiful nuance and the self-sufficient passage of light.

Nevertheless the Batlló facade is not, or not only, meant to be a work of abstract evocation. Gaudí intended the house to be a religious and patriotic symbol. Or so one gathers from one of the few people to whom he explained his intent, the architect Joan Martorell, who as a child had been introduced to Gaudí by the priest of the Sagrada Família, Monsignor Gil Parès. Gaudí, by Martorell's account, wanted the Casa Batlló to be read as a symbolic paean to the legend of Saint George, patron saint of Catalunya, in his victory over the dragon. The building

Exterior, Casa Batlló

"represents" the dragon, its lair, its victims, and the triumph of Saint George, all in one. The ridged roof, with its interlocking glossy scales, is the monster's back. Below, the curving iron balconies of the intermediate floors, pierced with holes like eye sockets, look like masks and represent the skulls of the dragon's victims. The tribune windows of the first floor are framed in Montjuic limestone carved like bones and tendons—more spare parts from the dragon's larder, with the curved gape of the windows themselves suggesting the open maw of the beast. (Bones went inside the building too: Gaudí designed a suite of benches, settees, love seats, and chairs in flowing carved wooden forms reminiscent of tibiae and femurs. They were meant for Batlló's dining room and are now in the Gaudí Museum.) Finally, the half-round tower set in the facade culminates in a form like a garlic bulb surmounted by a cross: it is Saint George's lance, with a tip inscribed with the names of Jesus, Mary, and Joseph that catches the rising sun. So it is a work of ostentatious piety as well as luxury—a conjunction that Batlló clearly approved of, since he also had an *oratori*, or private shrine, with a Holy Family painted by Josep Llimona installed behind a screen in the main salon.

Casa Milà

Despite its quality as spectacle, the Casa Batlló was not meant to interfere with its neighbor building, the Casa Amatller designed by the younger Puig i Cadafalch. Gaudí took care to respect the roof line of the Casa Amatller where it joined his own facade and abandoned his first idea of putting the "lance" tower up the middle in case it made an awkward rhyme with Puig's symmetrical housefront. But still, the Casa Batlló was seen, from the outset, as an extravagant signature building —not rivaling the Palau Güell, perhaps, but certainly with a more extroverted facade. In 1906 it was the new wonder of Passeig de Gràcia, which was why one of Batlló's friends promptly commissioned Gaudí to build a newer prodigy to eclipse it, on the other side of the street.

Pere Milà i Camps was a developer who had married a widow somewhat older and far richer than himself, Roser Guardiola. Her previous husband, José Guardiola i Grau, had been an *indiano* who, dying in 1901, left her an estate that included a big block of land at the corner of Passeig de Gràcia and Carrer de Provença. With his dandified and dashing air, which extended to pearl-gray suits with black piping and one of the earliest cars in Barcelona, Milà swept her off her feet and they were married in 1903. At the time it was said that Milà was less interested in *la viuda de Guardiola* (Guardiola's widow) than *la guardiola de la Viuda* (the widow's money box). But in the first flush of conjugal bliss the couple decided to build the most spectacular apartment block on Gràcia, on the inherited site just uphill from the block where Domènech's Casa Lleó Morera was soon to join Puig's Casa Amatller and the Casa Batlló, cheek by jowl in radiant incongruity. They called on Gaudí to outdo himself and the others. If he had achieved such results with a renovation in the Casa Batlló, what might he not do if he built from the ground up? The result was the Casa Milà (1906–10), known to generations of Barcelonans since as La Pedrera (The Stone Quarry).

The Casa Milà is a sea cliff with caves in it for people. Its forged-iron balconies, with their wreathing and flopping tracery, are based on kelp and coral incrustation. Various writers have tried to pinpoint the geological features Gaudí may have been remembering: perhaps the inland rock ledges at Sant Miquel del Fai, perhaps the so-called Portals Vells (Ancient Gates) in Andratx, or the contorted and lowering cliffs framing the beach of Pareis in northern Majorca. Such efforts are too literal.

Its interior layout seems to have risen from Gaudí's studies of medieval fortresses: some, he noted, had ramps, and the Giralda in Seville had one instead of a staircase, so that carts and wheeled guns could move in and out. "Ramps ought to be double," he reflected, "one to go up, the other to go down." He then came up with the idea, visionary for 1905, of such a double ramp winding around the empty light well of an apartment building, so that residents could drive their cars directly to their doors. The automobile was a novelty in Barcelona then—the painter Ramón Casas is thought to have been the first resident to own one, in 1903—and Gaudí was the first Spanish architect to think about its possible effect on design. Doubtless he discussed the idea with Milà i Camps, his car-owning client. But it was impractical; the grade of the ramps would have been too steep for safety, and their double helix would have eaten up too much space, space that Milà needed for the floors of luxury apartments on a limited site. So Gaudí opted for a spiral pedestrian ramp and put in a separate elevator (not, as was normally the case at the time, inside an existing stairwell) so that the residents' and servants' access to the flats would be quite distinct and the *senyors* would not risk bumping into their staff on the way to their apartments. He also built an underground parking lot in the basement, the first in any of Barcelona's buildings.

Chimneys and ventilators on the Casa Milà

But Gaudí's mental image of the medieval castle remained, though changed by metaphoric fantasy. The Casa Milà's nickname, La Pedrera, fits it well. Rearing in its folds of stone over Passeig de Gràcia—a pale honey-colored limestone from the Montjuic quarry, sparrow pecked to render its surface matte—it evokes the primitive idea of the *roca*, a word meaning both "fortress" and "cliff." This military image is softened by the organic curves of the facade but then reinforced by the chimneys and stairway exits on the roof, like the helmets of armed and staring sentinels.

Combining the fortress image with that of maternal protection—the cave wall, the soft undulation of the facades—La Pedrera is a strikingly hermaphroditic building, but its "masculine" and "feminine" aspects do not clash. The roofscape of chimneys and ventilators cannot be seen from street level; from the roof, the facades are invisible. And no visit to La Pedrera is complete without its top. For there they are, the guardians, the extraordinary totemic presences that Gaudí produced out of the banal necessity to air the building, carry off the smoke from its apartments, and reach the roof. Some of the chimneys are in the form of centurions, with

Contemporary cartoon about the Casa Milà

slit eyes in their helmets. The stair exits are bulbous white structures like salt licks, surmounted by thick mosaic crosses. Long before the idea of environmental sculpture arose in modern art, Gaudí produced one of its masterpieces—though an incomplete one, as we shall see.

The construction of La Pedrera was daring, but it would not have pleased a purist forty years ago. It is not a curtain-wall building but a curtain-rock one. The mighty folds and trunks of stone, which look so formidably solid, are more like a stage grotto of papier-mâché and wire: they are supported on a complicated steel armature, designed by Josep Bayo i Font (1878–1971), Gaudí's engineer on the Casa Batlló. When the reinforcement was going up, the wags and wits on Passeig de Gràcia thought the whole thing looked like a train smash that had occurred, with notable loss of life, near Riudecanyes a year before. A cartoonist also compared it to the results of a severe earthquake that struck Andalusia in the 1900s. It required, in those precomputer days, enormous efforts of calculation: Gaudí and Font spent weeks cudgeling their brains over the stresses on the radiating steel floor beams and their shallow Catalan vaults of interlaced brick. Nevertheless, both men liked to work directly, if they could; when designing the exquisitely elegant catenary arches to support the attic roof, all of different curvatures due to the

Contemporary cartoon about the Casa Milà

wavy wall, Font simply hung chains between the columns on site and traced their curve to make the framing.

The stone is a skin and not, like true masonry, self-supporting. (Thus quite a few of the columns of La Pedrera are not continuous between the upper and lower floors.) In calling this a skin, of course, one must acknowledge that there is no relation at all between the mingy veneering of today's "lite" architecture—stone sliced so thin that it might as well be the Formica it resembles—and Gaudí's robust plasticity: La Pedrera's skin has body behind it, and the whole surface of the building is intensely muscular and organic, with its prognathous eyebrows that swell out to shade the balconies and its elephantine feet rooted in the pavement.

There were problems with use: for instance, one of the internal columns had to be moved because a resident could not swing his long-hooded Rolls-Royce past it to get into the underground garage. Building inspectors objected to some details. One of the elephant's foot pillars was found to stick out beyond the datum line of the site, and a man from the Ajuntament warned Bayo to trim it. The engineer said he would speak to Gaudí about it. Gaudí replied that if the Ajuntament really wanted him to cut the column "as though it were a cheese," then he would—and he would also smooth the face of the stump and carve an inscription on it that read "Column mutilated by order of the Ajuntament." The column stayed. He was no more amenable with the owners of apartments in the Casa Milà after it was finished. The fate of one of its inhabitants, Mrs. Comes i Abril, was described by the poet Josep Carner in "Auca d'una Resposta del Senyor Gaudí," "The Tale of Mr. Gaudí's Answer." The lady, it seems, had just been given a fine Erard piano and asked the great man where, in her salon devoid of straight walls, it could be put.

En Gaudí mira el saló	Gaudí looks at the salon
amb aquella atenció.	with that attention of his.
Resseigueix tots els indrets	He looks in every corner
i mesura les parets.	and measures the walls.
D'un brocat alça les gires	He lifts the folds of a brocade
i separa cinc cadires.	and separates five chairs.
I aleshores somrient	And now he smiles
ell que mou el cap d'argent.	nodding his silvery head.
¡Tanmateix senyor Gaudí!	Well then, Mr. Gaudí!
Digui digui, ja pot dir.	Tell me, tell me, do!
Don Antoni amb la mà dreta	Don Antoni scratches his beard
es rascava la barbeta.	with his left hand.
¿És voste—diu molt atent—	Is it you, he says gravely,
qui es dedica a l'instrument?	who plays the instrument?
La senyora que li explica:	The lady explains:
O, veurà, toco una mica.	Oh, look, I play a little.
I va fer el senyor Gaudí:	And Gaudí says:
—Miri, toqui el violí.	"Look, take up the violin."

Santiago Rusinyol quipped that nobody who lived in La Pedrera could keep a dog for a pet; it would have to be a snake. In the same vein the French statesman Georges Clemenceau joked after a visit to Barcelona that the Catalans were so preoccupied with the legend of Saint George that they built houses for dragons. And of course the cartoons were many. One of them showed La Pedrera as a garage for blimps and airships—soft things like polyps, stuck in holes in its aerial reef. Another had a real-estate agent trying to let an apartment to a couple, who gaze in dismay at the fantastic accumulation of iron sea forms in the balcony: No, it's fine, but no . . . where could we hang the laundry?

Carles Mani, The Degenerates

VIII

La Pedrera, singular though it is, was less than Gaudí's original idea. Its roofscape was not merely the landscape of a dream. The centurions and figures were to combine with a devotional sculpture: having created one metaphor of religion in the Casa Batlló, he wanted to make a further leap by crowning the Casa Milà with a sculptural allegory of the holy rosary (Rosario being Mrs. Milà's name) in the form of a bronze medallion of the Mother of God, some twelve feet (four meters) tall, gazing down across Barcelona to the port. Joan Martorell, to whom Gaudí explained the Casa Batlló when he was a child, said that the architect meant it to convey "the calming of the storms of life at the feet of the Mother of God," thus evoking Mary in her traditional Catalan form of Star of the Sea and Protector of Mariners. The sculptor was to have been Carles Mani i Roig (1868–1911). Gaudí had seen and liked a large plaster model of Mani's called *The Degenerates* (two pinheaded figures waving oversized hands: Max Stirner's ideas of "racial degeneration" were in the air then, in Catalunya as in Paris and Berlin) and commissioned a maquette from him. Milà, the client, said it reminded him of a huddle of sheep and goats, and he disliked Mani's scruffiness, which was extreme: once, visiting the sculptor's studio, Gaudí to his horror found armies of fleas marching up his legs. But the project went ahead until, after the ferocious church burnings that took place in the Setmana Tragica of 1909, Milà figured that any apartment block with a large Virgin on it would be a target for popular wrath and prudently canceled it.

The Setmana Tragica, in its suddenness and violence, shattered Barcelona. The city had been volatile and strike ridden through the preceding decade, but no outbreak like this had occurred since the Burning of the Convents more than sixty years before. It was set off by yet another political blunder in Madrid.

Spain still had colonial territory in Morocco in 1909, and it had never succeeded in "pacifying" (as the euphemism went) the Arabs of the Rif. Near a district of Morocco called Melilla were some iron mines that had recently been acquired by the powerful Madrid politician, Alváro de Figueroa y Torres, the count of Romanones. Romanones wanted to secure them from hostile Arabs, and in July 1909 he arranged for a column of troops to march out of Melilla to the mines. The Spaniards were attacked by a smaller Arab force and decimated. Romanones then persuaded the war office to call up the reserves in Catalunya and send them to Morocco—forty thousand men, most of them married with children, all working class. The ships on which they were to sail belonged to Romanones's friend Claudi López Bru, the second marquis of Comillas, who also owned a slice of the company that owned the mines. The marquise of Comillas and her friends showed their charitable concern for the troops by descending to the docks on the day they filed on board her husband's ships to go off and die in the Rif Mountains and giving out rosaries, scapulars, holy medals, and tobacco. The next day, July 26, the whole city—almost unanimously pacifist since 1898—rose against the "Bankers' War," with a general strike and riots.

The fuse of this rising had been lighted long before. In the first place, the workers of Barcelona were far better knit than they had been in the heyday of 1890s anarchism. The anarchists had dug in after the Montjuic trials and concentrated on strikes and organization, not bombs. The eventual result was the CNT (Confederació Nacional del Treball), a strong anarcho-syndicalist trade union founded in 1907 and now extended throughout Spain, with its main membership base in Barcelona.

Second, since the formation of Solidaritat Catalana, the city had become jittery: another wave had apparently been directed against Catalanist factory owners and businessmen, with some two thousand bombs exploded. But nearly all of them, it turned out, were thrown by agents provocateurs in the pay of the police, who hoped to discredit the Catalanist cause.

Third, there was Alejandro Lerroux, the real key to the Tragic Week. Lerroux (1864–1949) was an ex-journalist with an iron throat and a gift for whipping up crowds to explosions of anger. He was a left-wing, anticlerical, republican demagogue, but also violently anti-Catalanist; Madrid was prepared to overlook the former in gratitude for the latter. Much of his constituency lay with Barcelona's migrant workers, who hated Catalanists. Lerroux was elected a deputy for the first time in 1901, and the size of his following earned him the nickname the Emperor of the Parallel—the Parallel being the slum quarter of the city then. His followers called themselves the Jovens Barbars (Young Barbarians), and he exhorted them to wreck "this unhappy country . . . destroy its temples, finish off its gods, tear the veil from its novices and raise them up to be mothers to civilize the species."

Lerroux's Young Barbarians ran amok in the streets and thousands joined them. But the Tragic Week would certainly have happened without them. It was a pure jacquerie, spontaneous and leaderless, with no group—not even the anarchists—behind it. (Lerroux himself prudently stayed out of the way once it started.) And as such violence habitually did in Spain, it rapidly devolved into an orgy of anticlericalism. About eighty churches, monasteries, convents, and religious schools were sacked and burned, many to the ground. Macabre scenes were witnessed as rioters broke into monastic crypts and dragged out the ragged, half-mummified corpses of priests and nuns, propping them up in grisly tableaux in cloisters or dancing wildly with them in the streets. The government sent in the troops, but the city, under its mounting pall of smoke, did not reach the calm of exhaustion until August 1; then it was time to bury the dead and choose scapegoats. The man selected for this role by Antonio Maura's government was an anarcho-syndicalist schoolmaster named Francesc Ferrer, who had not been in Barcelona during the Tragic Week. Nevertheless he was arrested and, after a perfunctory show trial, executed—thus supplying the anarcho-syndicalists with a martyr whose name would be brandished right up to, and through, the Spanish civil war.

IX

For thoughtful and moderate Catalans like Joan Maragall, the Tragic Week was anguish. However, it inspired some of his finest writing, including the "New Ode to Barcelona," his vision of the city divided against itself, and "The Burned-Out Church," an essay (much cut by the censors) reflecting on a mass among the ruins the day after:

I had never heard a Mass like that one . . . all of us who were present at the Sacrifice celebrated on that simple deal table, before the injured crucifix which was its only ornament, among the dust and the debris and the sun and wind which entered from outside, and feeling still around us the trail of destruction and blasphemy which had so recently passed through that very air. . . . I am certain that we all heard it as never before, and that it filled us with a new, active virtue, as only the first Christians could have experienced it, persecuted and hiding in a corner of the catacombs, delighting above all . . . in the beginnings of the mystery of redemption.

The ruins were the image of blasphemy; the symbol of rebirth and transcendence, for Maragall, was his friend Gaudí's immense project, the Sagrada Família. It rises as the life-giving image in the "New Ode to Barcelona":

> *A la part de Levant, mistic exemple,*
> *com una flor gegant floreix un temple*
> *meravellat d'haver nascut acquí,*
> *entremig d'una gent tan sorruda i dolenta,*
> *que s'en riu i flastoma i es baralla i s'esventa*
> *contra tot lo humà i lo diví.*
> *Mes, enmig la misèria i la ràbia i fumera,*
> *el temple (tant se val!) s'alça i prospera*
> *esperant uns fidels que han de venir.*

> In the east, mystical example,
> like a giant flower, a temple blossoms,
> amazing to be born here
> amid such a coarse and wicked people
> who laugh at it, blaspheme, brawl, vent their scorn
> against everything human and divine.
> Yet amid misery, madness and smoke
> the temple (so precious!) rises and flourishes
> waiting for the faithful who must come.

Gaudí had been intermittently at work on the Sagrada Família for a quarter of a century when the Tragic Week struck Barcelona. He was terrified that the rioters would attack it, but they did not. Except for the Sagrada Família and the last stages of the Casa Milà, which he brought to completion in 1911, Gaudí—now the most famous architect in Barcelona—was out of work. From 1911 on he busied himself with a scatter of minor projects, but the Sagrada Famìlia remained the obsession of his last years.

I have left this building until last because Gaudí did—not by choice, but by necessity. As everyone knows, he did not finish it. As everyone also knows, others are now finishing it, to designs that only guess at Gaudí's intentions and in materials—reinforced concrete and resin-bonded finishes instead of stone—that have nothing whatsoever to do with the parts of the building done in his lifetime. The most enthusiastic backers of the project are Japanese corporations, who have poured millions of dollars in cash and technological backup into the Sagrada Famìlia (for who knows more about design simulation and architectural pastiche than the Japanese, except Mike Eisner at Disneyland?) as a public-relations gesture, to promote their image as patrons of *le beau et le bien*. The Japanese are nuts about Gaudí-san. They think of him as the van Gogh of architecture. His struggles to complete the Sagrada Famìlia strike a plangent chord in a culture that has traditionally placed great emphasis on the nobility of failure. Can it be that Gaudí going from door to door with his begging bowl, asking for contributions for the temple (which, late in life, he persistently did) has fused, in Japan, with the image of the heroic, impoverished samurai-monk? Yes, it can. In the late eighties an exhibition of Gaudí material in Osaka— furniture, metalwork, photos, drawings—was seen by 1.4 million people, nearly twice as many as visited the 1981 Picasso retrospective at the Museum of Modern Art in New York. Antoni Gonzalez, the architect in charge of the Ajuntament's brilliant and respectful restoration of the Palau Güell, thinks that half its original window latches and knobs have vanished into the capacious Vuitton handbags of Japanese tourists over the last few years. Because they strip the tiles without compunction, all tourists have been banned from the roofscapes of Palau Güell and the Casa Milà. The bases of the Gaudí iron street lamps on Passeig de Gràcia, which are sheathed in white *trencadis*, keep losing their ceramic surface because the Japanese pry off the chips to take them home as relics—unaware that these bases are not by Gaudí at all, but only in his manner. The Casa Batlló is on the market at an asking price of $100 million, which (it is assumed) only a Japanese can pay. Nobody in Barcelona is quite sure why the Japanese have fixed on Gaudí in this way—he is the one great modern architect whose work has absolutely nothing to do with classical Japanese architecture, which may in fact be the reason—but it seems unwise to probe too closely, lest their benign mania vanish like fairy gold. One thing is sure: the Sagrada Famìlia is the first Catholic temple whose bacon was ever saved by Shinto tourism. Not even Gaudí, who believed in miracles, could have foreseen that.

But money also comes from Catalan Catholics—and indeed from Catholics all over Spain; and for the first time since the civil war it now seems quite possible that the building will be completed, and within the next twenty years at that: certainly well before the centenary of Gaudí's death. This prospect continues to cause sharp disagreement in Barcelona, between the majority of architects, critics, and intellectuals, who despise the "new" Sagrada Família as inauthentic kitsch, and those faithful to the project, headed by the architect Jordí Bonet and the sculptor Josep Subirachs, who view it as a sacred mission. But the critics are impotent: nothing can be done to arrest the rise of the building, since the Sagrada Família is the property of neither the Ajuntament nor the Generalitat, nor even the Church. It belongs to a private religious foundation, which exists only to finish the temple and is by now completely impervious to criticism or lobbying.

The project that became Gaudí's Sagrada Família goes back more than a century. It started in 1866, among a group of fervent right-wing Catholics representing the most reactionary and pious elements of lay life in Catalunya. This was a moment of crisis for the Spanish Church. Garibaldi's victory in Italy had stripped the pope of most of his temporal power and confined him to a ministate within Rome: Vatican City. (We see the very existence of Vatican City as a sign of the power of the papacy; in the 1860s, it was viewed as proof of an unprecedented weakness.) Now, the same kind of prospect was looming on the religious horizons of Spain, in the form of the man who, especially in Catalunya, seemed to incarnate the liberal threat to the Church—General Prim. In 1868 the liberal revolution thrust the Bourbon queen, Isabel II, into exile. Spain's first republican government was voted in. Pi i Margall and the federalists came to power. Civil war broke out. It looked as though the Church would soon be fighting for its life in Spain; and in Rome, a pope of fiercely reactionary convictions, Pius IX, sat on the Fisherman's Chair, issuing one encyclical after another to damn everything that smelled of liberalism, democracy, freedom of individual conscience—the pollution of the modern world. A new Counter-Reformation was needed. Among its weapons would be the definition, as mandatory dogma, of papal infallibility and the Immaculate Conception. But for the present, the pope and his bishops called for new levels of faith, an increase of cultish devotion to Mary, Joseph, and Jesus—the Holy Family, the *Sagrada Família.*

Josep Marià Bocabella i Verdaguer in 1920

Lay associations sprang up to propagate this cult. The chief one in Catalunya called itself the Spiritual Association for Devotion to Saint Joseph—for short, the Josephines. The Josephines first met at Montserrat, the holy mountain of the Black Virgin, in 1866, with the declared object of "beseeching God, through the intercession of St. Joseph, for the triumph of the Church in the difficult and perilous conditions that pervade the world in general and our Catholic Spain in particular." They published a religious magazine called *El Propagador de la Devociòn a San José.* They chose as honorary patrons Pius IX, Queen María Christina, the future king Alfonso XIII, and the priest Antoni Maria Claret, who was soon to be beatified. A more reactionary quartet than this would have been hard to pick. Their actual leader was a bookseller and amateur flutist named Josep Marià Bocabella i Verdaguer. Bocabella was such a palaeo-conservative that he even refused to eat French food, since its recipes came from the land of Voltaire and Napoleon. He persuaded the Josephines that Barcelona needed a permanent church devoted to Joseph, his virgin spouse, and their Son. There, men and women could go in contrition to pray and do penance for the sins of modernism. Hence its name: the Expiatory Temple of the Holy

The church of the Sagrada Família, under construction, 1904

Family. It was never meant to be a cathedral—Barcelona already had one of those. It would be Spain's great emblem of antimodernism, loaded with political as well as religious meaning: *la casa pairal de Déu*, "God's patriarchal house."

Before long the Josephines had raised 150,000 pesetas and bought a site in an unfashionable part of the Eixample. (Flocks of goats were still grazing around the foundations of the Sagrada Família in the 1890s.) Then they chose an architect named Villar, a man of more piety than talent who produced a singularly ugly Gothic Revival design. In March 1882 its first stone was laid. But Villar quit the next year, and in 1884 the Josephines chose a new architect: Antoni Gaudí.

Why did this archconservative sodality select Gaudí, who at this stage of his career had built so little? The reason usually given is his own piety—he convinced the Josephines that he was more Catholic than the pope. Undoubtedly his secular patrons, the Comillas and Güell families, put in a word for him. However, Josep Pijoan, the éminence grise of Catalan art history, told Josep Pla another and more peculiar story before he died. Pijoan knew Bocabella. "He was a little shopkeeper. I don't mean to criticise him. I simply mean that in sensibility, ideas, conception of things and in terms of religious depth, Bocabella was the

Gaudí with Bishop Reig and Prat de la Riba inspecting the church of the Sagrada Família

---

diametric opposite of Gaudí." But Bocabella had had a religious vision: the Temple of the Sagrada Família would be built by a true Aryan, a man with blue eyes. When he met Gaudí for the first time, in the office of the architect Martorell, Bocabella and his Josephine colleagues were struck by the young designer's eyes: clear, frank, piercing, and blue. "This young man," announced Bocabella suddenly, "will be the architect of the Sagrada Família."

Se non e vero e ben trovato. What is incontestably true is that Gaudí, from the moment the Josephines hired him, had a free hand. Nobody seems to have interfered with his plans or offered any criticism of them; the more grandiose they got, the better. The Josephines had before their eyes the model of the Gothic cathedrals; and like the Church itself, they felt, they had time.

At first they had money, too; in the early stages of excavation and construction, at least three hundred laborers were employed on the site. (Probably the Sagrada Família was spared in the 1909 riots because it provided jobs.) The Josephines kept public interest up by organizing processions, festivals, and formal visits by bishops and even cardinals, to whom Gaudí would expatiate on the Great Work. It would revive the lost impulses of the Gothic world, he told them, by marrying them

The church of the Sagrada Família, 1906, with goats

to the light and clarity of the Mediterranean. The Sagrada Família would be an immense palace of Christian memory in which every column and niche and spire would stand for its own dogma or New Testament event; a book, encrusted with sculpture, in which the entire iconography of Catholicism would be set forth. He took them patiently through the structural system: the paraboloid arches, the inclined columns that would surpass the conventions of Gothic by transmitting the loads straight to earth without outward thrust, thus eliminating the need for buttresses. Gaudí even sent an exhibition of models and drawings of the Sagrada Família to Paris and showed them at the Universal Exposition of 1900, in the hope of raising money from French Catholics. This was by no means a wild bet: after all, the French themselves had had their ecstasies of lugubrious piety in the 1880s and 1890s, resulting in the cult of Bernadette at Lourdes and the construction of the Sacré-Coeur in Montmartre. Gaudí was a little too late. Making the models and shipping them in huge cases to Paris cost thousands of pesetas— paid for, luckily, by Eusebi Güell. But the show was a flop. Neither the public nor the press, nor even the clergy, and least of all other French architects, showed the smallest interest in Gaudí's *totalgesamtkunstwerk*. It looked to them all like a ridiculously inflated hermit's grotto. This Gallic notion of Gaudí would persist: as late as the 1960s, one could still read French critics who had no idea of his profundity as an architect treating him as a Hispanic cousin to Fernand Cheval, the Douanier Rousseau of architecture, an obsessively pottering postman admired by the Surrealists, who created a *palais idéal* in his garden at Hauterives out of bricks, oyster shells, tiles, and other salvage that he picked up on his rounds.

Moreover, by 1910 the impetus of radical-conservative Catholicism in Barcelona itself had begun to wear down. The cult of the Holy Family, as a remedy for modernist heresies and an icon of the ideal Catalan state, was losing ground. Contributions dwindled. Even the sale of holy medals and devotional postcards at the site declined. Thus the tempo of work on the cash-eating monster slackened and went into longer and longer comas during which nothing was done. Gaudí, according to Josep Pla, managed to interpret these intervals—which were enough to discourage any architect—as a sign of God's intention. "Submitting himself completely to the will of divine Providence, Gaudí always believed that these delays were absolutely normal and of a higher order, of an order that ordinary human reason could not unravel—in sum, that they favored the true development of the Temple." They gave him time to think, to plan, to let the vast conception stew and expand in his mind. After the Casa Milà, Gaudí had no more outside work anyway, except for the Güell Park—where he lived in a house that is now the Gaudí Museum, with his ailing father and his niece Rosa. His father died, and then Rosa; once a week, some Carmelite nuns would come and clean house for him. He began to sell whatever he had and give it to the Sagrada Família, starting with the family house at Riudoms. He had ceased going to the theater or to cafés long ago; now he gave up restaurants and contented himself with a nibble of bread and some vegetables on the site. He adopted a penitential diet, much stricter than his normal vegetarian ways, which he had read about in the works of a German priest named Kneipp. His skin, once ruddy, became pallid from ingrained plaster dust and long hours at the drafting table and the prie-dieu. He let his hair and beard grow for months until, reluctantly, he would let a nun trim them. As Gaudí entered his seventh decade, his once sturdy peasant frame shriveled so much that the pants of his rusty suits would hardly stay up.

His spiritual mentor, Torras i Bages, died in 1916; Eusebi Güell died two years later and was buried with immense pomp and ceremony, leaving Gaudí with no more than a few old friends to talk to, his work-

Gaudí receiving communion

men, and some junior collaborators. He plunged ever more deeply into his iconographic obsessions, his structural researches, his religious exercises. Nothing remained in his life but the Expiatory Temple. He never stopped begging for money for it. He knocked on doors in the street. Five pesetas would do, or one. But from the rich he expected more. The architect Martorell, Pla recounted, once saw Gaudí at work on a prospective donor.

"Make this sacrifice!" he said imperiously, with a thousand-yard stare from those blue eyes.

"With pleasure," said the man, "it's no sacrifice at all."

"Then give me enough for it to *be* a sacrifice," Gaudí insisted. "Charity that doesn't amount to sacrifice is not charity at all. Often it's merely vanity."

It is not altogether surprising that members of the *bones families* used to cross the street when they saw the emaciated old genius heading their way.

Through the first quarter of the twentieth century, which was also the last third of Gaudí's life, the Expiatory Temple of the Holy Family rose so slowly and fitfully that Gaudí only saw one of its facades, that of the Nativity, go up as far as its rose window; and only one of the spires on the Nativity facade, that of Saint Barnabas, would be finished before his death, being capped off with its ceramic-sheathed finial in

January 1926. The sculptures of the Nativity facade continued to be made and installed, a pullulating mass of them, from the adoring shepherds to the Virgin, from the plants of the Holy Land to a figure of an anarchist about to throw a bomb. By 1920 most Catalans—practical and unmystical by nature, shopkeepers to the marrow—were bored by the daily sight of this unfinishable temple in an obsolete style. Let the Church pay for it! But the Church had no intention of doing that. The Josephines remained saddled with the responsibility. Their magazine *El Propagador* continued to appear, forlorn and stubborn in its fund-raising efforts. Barcelona, neutral during World War I and bursting with money, reveling in a second *febre d'or* created by selling uniform cloth, foodstuffs, and other staples to the belligerents, might have paid for it—but it saw no reason to.

The culture of the city had altered. Romantic Catalanism and the extravaganzas of Art Nouveau were on the way out; in their place came a movement toward the classic imagery of the Mediterranean, called by its adherents *noucentisme*—denoting attachment to the twentieth century, as the Italian word *quattrocento* means "fifteenth century." The change was signaled by a didactic novel written by Eugeni d'Ors (1881–1954) under his pseudonym, Xènius, and published in 1912: *La Ben Plantada* (*The Well-Planted One*, or perhaps *The Woman Standing Strong*). Teresa, she of the title, is a peasant prophetess, the emanation of memory and *seny*; she stands for all that is classic and immemorial, Mediterranean, in Catalunya. (Salvador Dalí claimed that d'Ors had based her on his nurse in Cadaqués.) "I have not come to set up a new law," she tells the narrator,

> but to restore the old one. I do not bring you revolution, but continuity. Your Race, Xenius, is prostrated by much evil today. Long centuries of servitude have extinguished the ancient virtues. There is the corruption of the arts, mother of worse outrages. There are enraged men who perpetuate anarchy. There are frenetic decorators, who have turned your eyes from all harmony . . . but all that is ashes and dust . . . it will all pass away, and soon.

The graphic artist Xavier Nogués i Casas (1873–1941) etched a memorable image of *La Ben Plantada*, tall as a tree, mysterious and vatic in her shawl, surrounded by capering and cursing dwarfs—capitalists, anarchists, a caricatural Jew: the Catalan self, in short, assailed by various forms of the Other.

D'Or's voluble earth-mother image was a parallel to others in Europe. *Noucentisme* was an early form of a general recoil from modernist fragmentation that gathered strength in France and Italy after World War I, but actually predated the conflict. *Noucentisme* could walk all over *modernisme* because it promised a relief, not just from the elitism of Art Nouveau architecture and decoration, but from the aura of social decadence that undeniably clung to them by 1914. And by 1920, *modernisme* seemed to be the style of a dead world. If you were going to feel nostalgic for anything old, especially after World War I, it would have to be something immemorial, not the corpse of a departed fashion. To evoke the classic rural order of the Mediterranean coast—a premodern world, that of Lucretius and Virgil's *Georgics*—was a healing act. It evoked what all southern European countries had in common, not what kept them apart. "The good patriot loves his country," d'Ors wrote in one of the many essays he contributed in 1906–20 to Prat de la Riba's paper, *La Veu de Catalunya*—"but its frontiers, even more."

Ruined temples, goatherds with panpipes, sturdy *ben plantadas* picking grapes, nudes with baskets on their heads, melons, a view of the sea: and behind these, a common Graeco-Roman heritage. *Noucentisme* wished to remind its readers that stern Rome had been the father of Barcelona, a fact ignored by the *modernistes*. This attitude underwrote the biggest city-planning project actually achieved in Barcelona at the time, the construction of the Via Laietana, which slashed through the Old City and abolished a score of streets and hundreds of buildings. Augustus would not have hesitated to open such an incision in Rome; why should we be fainthearted about it?

Eugeni d'Ors was a highly recognizable type, the intellectual journalist as ringmaster. *Noucentisme* could be what he said it was. In his 1911 *Almanach dels Noucentistes* and in other writing, he nominated the artists who seemed appropriate to it, and they were a mixed bag, ranging from Picasso—who had left Barcelona years before, and now, unbeknownst to Xènius, was on the verge of cubism—to the flamboyant international muralist Josep-Mariá Sert. But the core *noucentista* artists were the sculptors Pau Gargallo, Josep Clarà, Manolo Hugué, and Enric Casanovas, and the painters Joaquín Torres Garcia and Joaquím Sunyer. The sculpture tended to follow the lead of Maillol—massive in volume, *ben plantat*, full of archaizing images of peasant nudes, utterly unlike the floral urban maidens of *modernisme* and without the Catholic guilt of Josep Llimona. The painting, influenced equally by Puvis de Chavannes and Cézanne (in his role as heir of Poussin and son of the Provençal soil), was timid, lyrical, and bucolic: emblematic nudes in Arcadian landscapes. Joan Maragall, shortly before his death in 1911, purchased

Xavier Nogués, La Ben Plantada

Sunyer's *Pastoral* and wrote a rhapsodic passage on it that suggested his belief in the healing powers of *noucentisme*:

> I seem to stand at an intersection in our mountains, those mountains that are so typical of Catalunya, at once rugged and undulating, as lean and harsh as our souls. . . . Consider the woman in Sunyer's *Pastoral* —she is the embodiment of the landscape; she is the landscape which, in coming to life, has assumed flesh. That woman is not there by chance; she is destiny. She represents the whole history of creation. . . . The woman and the landscape are stages of one and the same thing.

There was no *noucentista* architecture—at least not at the beginning. When it came, it was predictably classicist: the classicism of banker and dictator, perhaps a little more florid than its equivalents in Rome and Paris but not essentially different from them. Ample examples of it survive around Plaça de Catalunya (which Puig i Cadafalch, entering a second career as a *noucentista* classicist, helped redesign) and down the Via Laietana. But Gaudí was not spared the heavy hand of *noucentista* displeasure, and after 1911 Maragall was not alive to defend him. Gaudí's encyclopedic Gothicism now began to seem as repugnant as it was old

Sagrada Família, 1934

hat. It is scarcely an exaggeration that *noucentisme* set out to bury the hermit of the Sagrada Família alive; from its stylistic viewpoint, the Sagrada Família was a grotesque, overwrought mess.

Thus Gaudí became marginalized by the 1920s. Furthermore, the Catalanism he believed in suffered what appeared at the time to be terminal defeat in 1923, when Miguel Primo de Rivera became dictator of Spain. Primo despised Catalanism as the irrelevant hobby of Barcelonese professors. It had no part in a unified Spain. Once again, the wheel turned on the Madrid axle: he suppressed Catalunya's autonomous administrative body, the Mancomunitat, along with *sardanas* and the Catalan flag. Primo had no particular interest in architectural style, but the buildings of the World's Fair held in Barcelona on his orders in 1929 were eloquent enough: led off by the enormous neobaroque Palau Nacional on the heights of Montjuic, they were done in a heavy, pan-Hispanic manner with scarcely any Catalan references at all. The epitome of this hovered halfway between architecture and fairground—the Poble Espanyol, also on Montjuic, an "ideal village" designed, with great skill, to incorporate all the styles of Spanish architecture. "Spainland" had come to Barcelona, while, a little farther down the hill, there was Mies van der Rohe's German pavilion, its polemical purity announcing the advent of an international modernism that, in time and through its influence on Catalan followers of Mies and Le Corbusier, would serve to push Gaudí's work further back into the past.

X

Gaudí did not live to see this. He had already walked under the line 30 tram, three years before. He drew as many mourners as Verdaguer: ten thousand people followed his coffin to its burial place in a chapel of the crypt of the Sagrada Família, next to the tombs of Bocabella and his family. The work limped on, under the direction of his assistant Domenech Sugranes i Gras, who had helped with the design of the Casa Milà. In 1927, the spire of Saint Simon was finished; in 1929, that of Saint Judas Thaddeus; in 1930, the cranes got the finial onto the spire of Saint Matthew and installed the ceramic Tree of Life, a green cypress with white doves, above the rose window of the Nativity facade. By 1935 the two gables above the flanking portals, the Door of Faith and the Door of Hope, were in place. And then the civil war broke out.

If there is one idea that propagandists for the Sagrada Família have always harped on, one essential component of its public myth, it is that Gaudí's project was and remains "the last of the Gothic cathedrals," raised by the collective desire and faith of a whole people, high and low, working in harmony toward the achievement of a shared symbol. This is pious nonsense, created by the religious right and believed only by them and by tourists. In fact, the Sagrada Família, very much unlike Santa Maria del Mar, has never been a popular church in Barcelona. If it is becoming one now, it is largely (or so the skeptic might think) because Catalans know on which side their bread is buttered: it is the city's logo—even Cobi, the mascot figure of the 1992 Olympics, is seen on posters carrying it under his arm like a multiple baguette—and it brings in hundreds of millions of tourist pesetas. In the 1920s and even more in the 1930s, most workers in Barcelona regarded it with indifference or outright hostility as a gloomy, excessive symbol of the ideology of their bosses and of the clergy who served them. With a few significant exceptions, the Catalan intelligentsia has never liked it. The Catalan anarchists in particular loathed it.

It is hardly surprising, therefore, that when the arsonist furies of the civil war were unleashed on Barcelona's churches, not sparing even Santa Maria del Mar, the anarchists tried to make sure the Sagrada Família would never be finished by attacking the crypt, the site workshops, and (as far as possible, since they were long dead) the donors and the architect. On June 20, 1936, a mob broke into the crypt, opened the Bocabella tombs, dragged out the skeletons, and dumped them on the street. Gaudí's tomb was opened too, but his coffin was not violated—though Salvador Dalí would later recount that a friend had seen children dragging Gaudí's body down the streets by a rope around its neck, this seems to be untrue. However, the anarchists burned the plaster models and every scrap of paper that could be found—esquisses, calculations, working drawings, accounts, letters, in fact the entire archive relating to the Sagrada Família. They set fire to the studio-workshops and the crypt and departed.

The result of this hecatomb (inspired by a faith hardly less absolute than Gaudí's own) was that nobody, to this day, knows exactly how Gaudí would have gone about finishing the Sagrada Família, or what it would have looked like if he *had* finished it. All the successive architects and work teams have been able to do since 1936 is reconstruct the plaster models as well as they could, partly on the basis of photographs, and then make the best guesses they can about Gaudí's intentions. It was Gaudí's invariable habit to make his buildings up as their construction advanced, not rigidly planning everything. This room for maneuver, this spontaneity, were essential parts of the inventive genius that lies behind the Güell Crypt or the Casa Milà, giving them much of their vitality. It is absent from the last half century of work on the Sagrada Família, with the result that the building seems to die as it advances. In detail, in ornamental texture, and even in material—for it is being finished largely with synthetic stone, which has the same relation or lack of it to the original material of the Nativity facade as Sculpstone has to marble—the new work is becoming little more than a huge simulacrum, an inert copy of a nonexistent "original." It also begins to look less inventive as a building: its structure adds nothing except size to the brilliance of Gaudí's investigations in the Güell Crypt and is in fact somewhat less adventurous.

Defenders of the project say that one should think of it as a medieval cathedral, begun by some hands and finished by others, with all authorial egotism submerged in the final collective work *ad majorem Dei gloriam*. But this will not wash, for two reasons. First, because Gaudí, beneath the image of poverty, humility, and self-abnegation, was one of the most relentlessly willful and egotistical geniuses that ever lived: like it or not, everything he touched is stamped by his own impress, and his many collaborators served essentially as conduits for his ideas—including, of course, the idea of collaboration under a medieval-style *mestre d'obres*, which was itself so much an artifact of his own personality and time. He is not a man you can collaborate with posthumously.

The architect now in charge of the Sagrada Família, Jordí Bonet, claims that Gaudí published enough detailed drawings during his lifetime—that is to say, before 1926—to make it possible to know exactly what his intentions for every part of the temple were. This seems, to put it politely, excessively optimistic: neither the general nor the architectural press, in Gaudí's time, printed more than general plans, sections and elevations of the building. Bonet also seems to think that one can intuit Gaudí's intentions for the temple from a broad system of proportion the great man used, based on a module of fifteen units—but this, again, is too vague to help excavate an "authentic" Gaudian design from infinite possible variations.

On visiting the unfinished pile in 1930 and noting how its construction depended entirely on private contributions, Evelyn Waugh lamented that "unless some eccentric millionaire is moved to interpose in the near future, in spite of the great sums that have already been squandered upon it, the project will have to be abandoned. . . . It would be a pity to allow this astonishing curiosity to decay. I feel it would be a graceful action on the part of someone who was a little wrong in the head to pay for its completion." That task is now, of course, beyond any private purse. But contributions do come in, and not only from tourists: in 1990, according to Bonet, when a group of Catalan artists and architects and historians got up a manifesto against what the Barcelona College of Architects' definitive guide to Barcelona architecture calls the "progressive distortion" of the work, an anonymous Catalan donor sent in a check for 75 million pesetas (about three-quarters of a million dollars) as an expression of faith in the project.

And yet, on esthetic grounds, one cannot contemplate the progress of this work without a sinking heart. From the costume-jewelry finials of the Facade of the Passion to the sculptures by Josep Subirachs, almost everything that has been added to it in the seventies and eighties is rampant kitsch—almost as bad, in its way, as the eye-grating vulgarity of the church above the funfair at Tibidabo. It could have been done by Mormons, not Catholics. Subirachs is the official artist of the Sagrada Família, and the results of his long labors, which adorn the portal of the growing Facade of the Passion and will in time proliferate over other parts of the building, must be seen to be believed. Admittedly, the contrast between Subirachs's work and the devotional figures on the Nativity facade is not as absolute as some critics, for convenience, have supposed. There is hardly a figure among the "old" sculptures that would survive aesthetically if you put it in a museum. They are all devotional cliché, no better than the *bondieuserie* Christs and Madonnas that are exported in the thousands to Latin America from the Catalan manufacturing town of Olot. Many of them are simply pointed up—carbon copied into carved stone—from plaster casts of live human figures. But they look good in photos, at least when scanned inattentively, and they give the Nativity facade its rippling texture in slanting light. Not even that can be claimed for Subirachs's work, which from its faceless Christ to its ludicrous Darth Vader centurions—copied, of course, from the chimneys on the Casa Milà—is the most blatant mass of half-digested modernist clichés to be plunked on a notable building within living memory. It is sincere in the way that only the worst art can be: which is to say, utterly so. Art historians of the future will point to it, no doubt, as the precise moment when the public religious art of Catholic Europe died for want of anything better to do, almost exactly two thousand years after it began.

Nothing can be done about the Sagrada Família. It cannot be torn down. It cannot very well be left as it is, the biggest *non-finito* relic of the early twentieth century—although this view certainly has had its proponents in Catalunya, including Dalí, who thought it should be put under a glass geodesic dome and left as it was at Gaudí's death. It can only be finished—preferably as soon as possible—at this level of taste and left to the avid chittering of massed Nikons. It will be a giant eyesore in many respects, but it will have its devotees, not all of them Japanese. The more it is criticized, the more defensive its defenders will get. "*Pulchrum est quod visum placet*," said "the Angelic Doctor"—"Beauty is that which causes pleasure when seen." And Aquinas begat Torras i Bages, who was the doctrinal and aesthetic mentor of Gaudí, whose successor Josep Subirachs takes himself to be. In Catalunya as elsewhere in the world, it is rarely wise to overestimate the taste of the churchgoing public. "Poverty preserves and keeps things," Antoni Gaudí once observed. "Many monuments have been saved from the ravages of the 'academics' through lack of money." He was griping, probably, about the abusive restoration of places like Ripoll by men like Elias Rogent. He could not have foreseen how dramatically true this would become of his own sacrificial monument. And yet if any single building can be said to epitomize Barcelona, it is still the Sagrada Família. The divisions it continues to provoke, the fanaticism it engenders as a project—so

uncharacteristic of the Catalans' belief in their own *seny*—are very Barcelonan. It stands for the immense, often irrational ambitions of the city;
its way, regularly displayed since Gothic times, of making leaps of civic
and architectural faith against all the odds, and winning. It will always
be a divisive building, but for most of its life Barcelona has been a divided
city. "You are boastful and treacherous and vulgar," cried Joan Maragall,
in the last lines of his ode. But then: "Barcelona! and with your sins,
ours, ours! Our Barcelona, the great enchantress!" There is still truth
in this.

BIBLIOGRAPHY

All works were published in Barcelona unless otherwise noted.

Ajuntament de Barcelona. *Barcelona Sub: El Clavegueram de Barcelona.* 1989.

————. *Ordinance for the Protection of the Historico-Artistic Architectural Heritage of the City of Barcelona.* N.d.

————. Quadern Central series from *Barcelona: Metròpolis Mediterrànea*:
No. 8. *La Circulació, Conflicte i Repte.*
No. 9. *La Barcelona de 1993.*
No. 10. *La Exposición de 1888 y Barcelona del Fin de Siglo.*
No. 11. *Crònica i Crítica de la Música a Barcelona.*
No. 16. *Barcelona i la Passió Modernista.*
No. 18. *Ciutat Vella: L'Hora Decisiva.*

Albarrán, Eduardo Rojo. *El Park Guell.* 1986.

Albet, Montserrat. *Mil Anys de Música Catalana.* 1991.

Alcolea, Santiago. "La Renaixença i el seus reflexos en l'Art català." *La Renaixença.* 1986.

————. *El Saló de Cent.* 1968.

Alier, Roger. "L'ambient musical a Barcelona." *La Renaixença.* 1986.

————. "La música al temps del Modernisme." *El temps del Modernisme.* 1985.

Amades, Joan. *Folklore de Catalunya.* 3 vols. 1951–69.

Aramon i Serra, R. "Els Origens de la llengua Catalana," in *L'Epoca Mediaeval a Catalunya.* 1989.

Ardit, Manuel, with Albert Balcells and Núria Sales. *Història dels Països Catalans.* 1980.

Artís, Andreu A. *Retrats de Ramón Casas.* 1971.

——. *Sonata a la Rambla.* 1961.

Balaguer, Victor. *Les Calles de Barcelona.* 1865.

Balcells, Albert. *Cataluña Contemporánea I (Siglo XIX) / II (1900–1939).* 1977.

——. *Historia Contemporánea de Catalunya.* 1980.

——. *El problema agrari a Catalunya, La questió rabassaire 1890–1936.* 1968.

——, with Ramon Canals, Joan Culla, Jesus Mestre, Conxita Mir, Eugènia Salvador, Rosa Toran, and Rosa Virós. *Les Eleccions Legislatives i Municipals a Barcelona 1810–1986: Context polític i resultats electorals.* 1989.

Balil Illana, Alberto. *Colonia Iulia Augusta Paterna Faventia Barcino.* Madrid, 1964.

Bancells, Consol. *Sant Pau, Hospital Modernista.* N.d.

Barey, André. *Barcelona: De la Ciutat Pre-Industrial al Fenomen Modernists.* N.d.

Barrut Roma, Jose Maria. *L'Exposicio Universal de Barcelona de 1888.* 1976.

Bassegoda Nonell, Juan. *El Gran Gaudí.* N.d.

——, and Roberto Pane. *Antoní Gaudi.* 1989.

Benet, Josep, and Casimir Martí. *Barcelona a mitjan segle XIX. El moviment obrer durant el Bienni Progressista, 1854–56.* 2 vols. 1976.

Bilbeny, Norbert. *La ideologia nacionalista a Catalunya.* 1988.

Blasco i Bardas, Anna María. *La pintura Romanica sobre fusta.* 1984.

Bofarull, Antonio de. *Guia-Cicerone de Barcelona.* 1847.

Bohigas i Guardiola, Oriol, and Manuel de Sola-Morales. *Inicis de la Urbanística Municipal de Barcelona: Mostra dels Fons Municipals dels Plans i Projectes d'Urbanisme 1750–1930.* 1985.

——, and Josep Acebillo. *Plans i Projectes per a Barcelona, 1981–82.* 1982.

——. *Reseña y católogo de la arquitectura modernista.* 2 vols. 3rd ed. 1983.

Bohigas, Pere. "Ausiàs March," in *L'Epoca Mediaeval a Catalunya.* 1989.

——. "Francesc Eiximinis," in *L'Epoca Mediaeval a Catalunya.* 1989.

Brenan, Gerald. *The Spanish Labyrinth: An Account of the Social and Political Background of the Spanish Civil War.* Cambridge, 1943.

Caballé i Clos, Tomás. *Barcelona de antano: memorias de un viejo reportero*. Madrid, 1944.

Caballero, Oscar, ed. *Barcelone Baroque et Moderne: L'Exuberance Catalane*. Paris, 1986.

Cadena, Josep M. *Dia a Dia: Calendari de Fets Històrics Catalans*. 1983.

————. "Xavier Nogués i altres dibuixants noucentistes," in *El Noucentisme*. 1987.

Capmany y de Montpalau, Antonio de. *Memorias históricas sobre la Marina, Comercio y Artes de la antigua Cuidad de Barcelona*. 4 vols. Madrid, 1779–1792.

Carandell, Josep Maria. *L'Eixample de Barcelona*. 1982.

————. *Guia secreta de Barcelona*. Madrid, 1974.

Carner, Josep. *Obres Completes*. 1968.

————. *Poems*. Trans. Pearse Hutchinson. Oxford, 1962.

Carr, Raymond. *Modern Spain 1875–1980*. Oxford, 1980.

————. *Spain, 1808–1939*. Oxford, 1966.

Carrera Pujal, J. *Història política de Catalunya en el sigle XIX*. Vols. 5–7. 1958.

Casanova, Eudald, et al. *Introducció a la Història de Catalunya*. 1989.

Casanovas i Canut, Sebastià. *Memoriès d'un pagès del segle XVIII*. 1978.

Castellanos, Jordi. *Aspectes de les relacions entre intel.lectuals i anarquistes a Catalunya al segle XIX*. "Els Marges," no. 6. 1978.

————. "El Noucentisme: Ideologia i estètica." *El Noucentisme*. 1987.

————. *Raimon Casellas i el Modernisme*. 1983.

————, ed. *Antologia de la poesia modernista*. 1990.

Castellet, J. M., and J. Molas, eds. *Antologia General de la Poesia Catalana*. 1972.

Català i Roca, Pere. *Comentaris a Castells Catalans*. 1990.

Cerdà, Ildefonso. *Teoría General de la urbanización y aplicación de sus principios y doctrinas a la reforma y ensanche de Barcelona. Monografía estadística de la clase obrera de Barcelona en 1856. Vida y obra de Ildefonso Derdà por Fabiàn Estapé*. 3 vols. Madrid, 1868–71.

Cirici i Pellicer, Alexandre. "L'arquitectura al temps del Modernisme," in *El Temps del Modernisme*. 1985.

————. "L'Arquitectura Gòtica," in *L'Epoca Mediaeval a Catalunya*. 1989.

————. *Barcelona Step by Step.* 1974.

Coll i Alentorn, Miquel. *Guifré el Pelós en la historiografia i en la llegenda.* 1990.

Collins, George R. *Antoni Gaudí.* 1961.

Colomer i Pous, Eusebi. "Pensament Català Mediaeval," in *L'Epoca Mediaeval a Catalunya.* 1989.

Comes, Pau. "La situació econòmica a l'època del Modernisme," in *El Temps del Modernisme.* 1985.

Corredor Matheos, J., and J. M. Montaner. *Arquitectura industrial a Catalunya.* 1984.

Cruells, Manuel. *Els no Catalans i nosaltres.* 1965.

Cucurull, Fèlix. *Panoràmica del nacionalisme català.* Vols. 2 and 3. Paris, 1975.

Dalí, Salvador. *The Secret Life of Salvador Dalí.* London, 1968.

Dalrymple, William. *Travels through Spain and Portugal in 1774.* Dublin, 1777.

Deaux, George. *The Black Death, 1347.* London, 1969.

Desclot, Bernard. *Crònica.* Ed. Miquel Coll i Alentorn, 1992.

Duran i Albareda, Montserrat. *Josep Marià Jujol a Sant Joan Despí: Projectes i Obra 1913–1949.* 1988.

Duran i Sanpere, Augustí. *Felip V i la cuitat de Cervera.* 1963.

Elliott, J. H. *Imperial Spain, 1469–1716.* London, 1963.

————. *The Revolt of the Catalans: A study in the decline of Spain, 1598–1640.* London, 1968.

Espuche, Albert Garcia. *El Quadrat d'Or: Centro de la Barcelona Modernista.* 1990.

Fabre, Jaume, and Josep M. Huertas. *Barcelona, La Construcció d'Una Ciutat.* 1989.

Fàbregas i Barri, Esteve. *Dos segles de marina catalana.* 1961.

Farré i Sanpera, M. Carme, ed. *L'Arquitectura en la Història de Catalunya.* 1987.

Fernández-Armesto, Felipe. *Barcelona: A Thousand Years of the City's Past.* London, 1991.

Ferraté, Joan, ed. *Les poesies d'Ausiàs March.* 1979.

Figueras, Lourdes, et al. *Lluís Domènech i Montaner i el Director d'Orquestra.* 1989.

Fontana Lázaro, Josep. *La revolució de 1820 a Catalunya.* 1961.

————. *La revolución liberal. Política y Hacienda, 1833–1845.* Madrid, 1977.

Fort i Cogul, Eufemià. *Aspectes de la desamortització.* 1968.

————. *Catalunya i la Inquisició.* 1973.

————. *Gaudí i la restauració de Poblet.* 1976.

Fuster, Joan. *Contra el Noucentisme.* 1977.

————. *Literatura Catalana Contemporània.* 1988.

Galofré, Jordi, ed. *Documents de Catalunya: Recull de Testos Històrics.* Vols. 1 and 2. 1990.

Garcia-Martín, Manuel. *Benvolgut Palau de la Música Catalana.* 1987.

Garrut, Josep M. "L'escultura al temps del Modernisme." *El temps del Modernisme.* 1985.

Generalitat de Catalunya. *Els Cent-cinquanta anys de la Renaixença, Edició commemorativa de la publicació de "La Patria" de Bonaventura Carles Aribau.* 1983.

Gilbert, Josep. *La Masia Catalana.* 1947.

Giner, Salvador. *The Social Structure of Catalunya.* Sheffield, 1980.

Goldston, Robert. *Barcelona, the Civic Stage.* New York, 1969.

González, Antonio. "Gaudí, Constructor: La Materialización de una Arquitectura Singular." *Informes de la Construcción.* July/August 1990.

————. "El Palau Guell de Barcelona: La construcción de una idea espacial. *Informes de la Construcción.* July/August 1990.

————, and P. Carbó. "La Azotea Fantástica (La Cubierta del Palau Guell). *Informes de la Construcción.* July/August 1990.

Grau, Ramon, and Marina López, *Exposició Universal de Barcelona: Llibre del Centenari, 1888–1988.* 1988.

Griñó, David. *Oficis que es perden.* 1981.

Hernandez-Cros, J. Emili, with Gabriel Mora and Xavier Pouplana. *Arquitectura de Barcelona.* 5th ed. 1990.

Hobsbawm, E. J., ed. *The Invention of Tradition.* Cambridge, 1983.

————. *Nations and Nationalism since 1780: Programme, Myth, Reality.* Cambridge, 1990.

Izard, Miquel. *Revolució industrial i obrerisme. Les Tres Classes de Vapor a Catalunya.* 1970.

Jardí, Enric. *La ciutat de les bombes: El terrorisme anarquistas a Barcelona.* 1964.

————. *Eugeni D'Ors: Obra i vida*. 1966, 1980.

————. *Història de "Els Quatre Gats."* 1972.

————. *Història del Cercle Artístic de Sant Lluc*. 1975.

————. "La pintura al temps del Modernisme," in *El temps del Modernisme*. 1985.

Jaume I. *Crònica, o Llibre dels Feits*. Ed. Ferran Soldevila. 1982.

Keay, S. J. *Roman Spain*. London, 1988.

La Rosa, Tristán. *España contemporánea, siglo XIX*. 1972.

Leighten, Patricia. *Re-Ordering the Universe: Picasso and Anarchism 1897–1914*. Princeton, N.J., 1989.

Leiz, Juliet, and Ricardo Feriche. *Barcelona Design Guide*. 1990.

Lewis, Archibald. *The Development of Southern French and Catalan Society, 718–1050*. London, 1965.

Llanas, Albert. *Trenta anys de teatre*. 1975.

Lleonart, Jordi, and Josep Camarasa, eds. *La Pesca a Catalunya el 1722, Segons un manuscrit de Joan Salvador i Riera*. 1987.

Llovet, Jordi, with A. Espadeler, A. Carbonell, and A. Tayadella. *Litteratura Catalana, dels Inicis als nostres dies*. 1989.

Lubar, Robert S. "Miró Before 'The Farm': A Cultural Perspective." Essay in catalog to "Joan Miró: A Retrospective," Solomon Guggenheim Museum. New York, 1987.

Mackay, David. *L'Arquitectura Moderna a Barcelona (1854–1939)*. 1989.

McCully, Marilyn. *Els Quatre Gats: Art in Barcelona around 1900*. Princeton, N.J., 1978.

————. "Ramon Casas, *Modernista* Painting, and the Critical Evaluation of Provincial Art." Unpub. MS. 1987.

————, ed. Catalog to "Homage to Barcelona: The City and Its Art, 1888–1936." London, 1985.

McDonogh, Gary Wray. *Good Families of Barcelona*. Princeton, N.J., 1986.

Mainar, J. *El moble català*. 1976.

Manent, A. *Tres escritores catalanes: Carner, Riba, Pla*. 1973.

Maragall, Joan. *Obres Completes (obra Catalana)*. 1981.

Marfany, Joan Lluís. *Aspectes del Modernisme*. 1975.

Martorell, Joanot. *Tirant lo Blanc*. Trans. David H. Rosenthal. New York, 1984.

Martorell Portas, Vicente. *Historia del urbanisme en Barcelona: Del plan Cerdà al area metropolitana*. 1970.

Masriera, Lluís. *Mis memorias*. 1954.

Mendoza, Cristina and Eduardo. *Barcelona Modernista*. 1989.

Mendoza, Eduardo. *City of Marvels*. London, 1988.

Menéndez Pidal, Ramón. *Historia de España*. Madrid, 1956.

Mercader i Riba, Joan. *Felip V i Catalunya*. 1969.

Miracle, Josep. *Estudis sobre Jacint Verdaguer*. 1989.

———. *La restauració dels Jocs Florals*. 1987.

Monjo i Pons, Joan. *Sofriments morals que m'ha causat "L'Ictineo."* Facsimile of 1869 MS. 1987.

Montalbán, Manuel Vásquez. *Barcelones*. 1987.

Mora, Josep Ferrater. *Les Formes de la Vida Catalana, i altres assaigs*. 1980.

Morris, C. B. *Surrealism and Spain, 1920–1936*. Cambridge, 1972.

Oller, Narcis. *Obres Completes*. 2nd ed. 1985.

Ors i Rovira, Eugeni d'. *La Ben Plantada*. 1912.

———. *Glosari* (selected essays). 1982.

Panyella, Vinyet, *Epistolari del Cau Ferrat, 1889–1930*. Sitges, 1981.

Parés, Fina. *Els ex-vots pintats*. N.d.

Pelegri i Partegas, Joan, ed. *Fidelitat a Catalunya*. 1986.

Pérez-Cors, Empar, ed. *Versos Bruts: Pomell de poesies escatalògiques*. 1989.

Permanyer, Lluís. *Història de l'Eixample*. 1990.

Pestana, Angel. *Terrorismo en Barcelona*. 1979.

Pijoan, Josep. *Política i Cultura*. Ed. Castellanos, Jordi. 1990.

Piqué i Padró, Jordi. *Anarco-Col.lectivisme i anarco-comunisme: L'oposició de dues postures en el moviment anarquista català (1881–1891)*. 1989.

Pla, Josep. *Barcelona, Una Discussió Entranyable*.

———. *Guia fondamentada i popular del Monestir de Poblet*.

————. *Homenots*. 4 vols.

————. *Joan Maragall*.

————. *El Quadern Gris*.

————. "Santiago Rusinyol i el seu temps," in *Tres Artistes*.

————. *Un Senyor de Barcelona*.

Planes, R. *El Modernisme a Sitges*. 1969.

Poblet, Josep Maria. *Catalunya, 1833–1913: Una Panoràmica amb el teatre i els Jocs Florals*. 1969.

Prats, Llorenç L. *El Mite de la Tradició Popular*. 1988.

Puig y Alfonso, F. (Jordi de Bellpuig). *Curiositats Barcelonines*. 3 vols. 1920.

Ràfols, J. F. *Modernisme i Modernistes*. 1949.

Richardson, J. S. *Hispaniae: Spain and the Development of Roman Imperialism, 218–82 B.C.* Cambridge, 1986.

Richardson, John. *A Life of Picasso: Volume 1, 1881–1906*. New York, 1991.

Riera, C. *Els cementiris de Barcelona*. 1981.

de Riquer, Borja. "La societat catalana," in *El Temps del Modernisme*. 1985.

Rohrer, Judith, and Ignasi de Solà-Morales. Catalog to "Josep Puig i Cadafalch: L'Aquitectura entre la casa i la ciutat." 1989.

Romeu i Figueras, Josep. "La lirica catalana des del segon quart del segle XIV a Ausiàs March," in *L'Epoca Mediaeval a Catalunya*. 1989.

Rossich, Albert, ed. *Poesia eròtica i pornogràfica catalana del segle XVII*. 1985.

Rubio i Balaguer, Jorge. *La Cultura Catalana del Renaixement a la Decadència*. 1964.

Ruiz i Calonja, Joan, ed. *Retaule de la vida medieval: Textos catalans coetanis*. 1990.

Sabat, Antonio. *Palau de la Musica Catalana*. 1984.

Sagarra, J. M. de. *Memories*. 2 vols. 1981.

Sanpera, M. Carme Farré. *El Museo de Arte de Cataluña*. 1983.

Sobrequés i Callicó, Jaume, with Maria Aurèlia Capmany and Lluís Pewrmanyer. *Reencontrar Barcelona*. 1986.

Sola i Dachs, Lluís. *Història dels diarís en Catala: Barcelona 1879–1976*. 1979.

Solà-Morales, Ignasi. *Gaudí*. 1983.

————. "Sobre Noucentisme i Aquitectura. Notes per a una història de l'arquitectura moderna a Catalunya." *El Noucentisme*. 1987.

Soldevilla, Carlos. *Figures de Catalunya*. 1955.

Sòria i Ràfols, Ramon, ed. *Diccionari Barcanova d'Història de Catalunya*. 1989.

Subirachs i Burgaya, Judit. *L'Esculture Commemorativa a Barcelona, Fins al 1936*. 1986.

Tarracó, Emilia. *El Monasterio de Santa Maria de Ripoll*. León, n.d.

Toda i Guell, Eduardo. *La Destrucció de Poblet*. Poblet, 1935.

Tomás, Margalida. "Consideracions entorn dels Jocs Florals de Barcelona," in *La Renaixença*. 1986.

Torras i Bages, Josep. *La Tradició Catalana* (1892). In *Obres Completes* (7 vols.) Vol. 1, 1984.

Torrents, Ricard. "Verdaguer, culminació i contradicció de la Renaixença." *La Renaixença*. 1986.

Tort i Mitjans, Francesc. *Santa Maria del Mar, Cathedral of the Ribera*. 1990.

Townsend, Arthur. *A journey through Spain in the years 1786 and 1787*. 3 vols. London, 1791.

Trenc Ballester, E. *Les arts gràfiques de l'epoca modernista a Barcelona*. 1977.

Triás Vejerano, J. J. *Almirall y los orígines del catalanismo*. Madrid, 1975.

Utrillo, Miquel. *Història Anecdòtica del Cau Ferrat*. Sitges, 1989.

Valentí, E. *El primer modernismo literario catalán y sus fundamentos ideológicos*. 1973.

Varela, Andreu, et al. *Història de Catalunya*. 1989.

Verdaguer, Jacint. *Obres completes*. 1974.

Vicens Vives, Jaume, and Montserrat Llorens. *Industrials i polítics del segle XIX*. 1958.

Vila, R. "El Uso del Hierro en la Casa Milá de Barcelona." *Informes de la Construcción*. July/August 1990.

Vila-Grau, Joan. *Els vitrallers de la Barcelona modernista*. 1982.

Vilanova, Mercedes. *España en Maragall*. 1968.

Vilar, Pierre. *Catalunya dins l'Espanya Moderna*. 2 vols. 1964–68.

Waugh, Evelyn. "Barcelona." *Architectural Review*. June 1930.

Wheelen, Guy. *Miró*. Trans. Robert Wolf. New York, 1989.

Woolard, Kathryn. *Double Talk: Bilingualism and the Politics of Ethnicity in Catalonia*. Stanford, Calif., 1989.

Young, Arthur. "A Tour in Catalonia." *Annals of Agriculture*, vol. 8. London, 1787.

Ziegler, Philip. *The Black Death*. London, 1969.

INDEX

Note: Page numbers in *italics* refer to illustrations

Puig and, 404–6
Universal Exposition and, 364
University of Barcelona designed by,
346–7, *347*, 406
Rohrer, Judith, 409
Roig, Jaume, 123–4, 135–6
Roig i Soler, Joan, 359–60, *359*, 425–6
Roís de Cornella, Joan, 133–4
Romance languages, affinities between
Catalan and, 58–9
Roman Empire and Romans, 55–69, 85–91
Barcelona and, *see* Barcelona, Roman
Catalunya settled by, 58–62
Laietani destroyed by, 55
religion of, 68–9
Spain occupied by, 56–7
Visigoth occupation of, 72
walls built around Barcelona by, 140–1
war between Carthage and, 56–7
Romanesque style, 405, 511
frescoes in, 88–93, *90–3*
of Santa Maria de Ripoll, 85–7
of Sant Joan de les Abadesses, 87–8
Romanones, Alváro de Figueroa y Torres,
Count of, 522
Romantic poetry, 239–50
Romeu, Pere:
Casas's painting of, *443*
The Four Cats and, 439–43
Romulus Augustulus, Emperor of Rome,
71
Rossini, Gioacchino, 420
Rovira, Joan, 263
Rovira i Trias, Antoni:
Eixample design of, 281–3
Mercat de Sant Antoni designed by, 343,
345
Royal Chapel of Saint Agatha, seizure and
auction of, 221–2
Rubio i Bellvé, Joan, 393, 492
Colonia Güell structures designed by,
501
The White Friar designed by, 406, *407*
Rubió i Ors, Joaquim, 239, 300
and re-creation of Jocs Florals, 299
works of, 242–4, 248
Ruis i Taulet, Francesc de Paula, 35
beard of, 390
cartoons of, *363*, 372
Columbus monument and, 365, 367
New Cemetery and, 414
Universal Exposition and, 362–4, 371–3
Rusinyol, Santiago, 348–9, 405, *420*,
426–44, *426*, *435*, 456
background of, 427
on Casa Milà, 520
Casas's portraits of, *430*, 442, *442*
drug addiction of, 434–5

festes modernistes organized by, 438–40
The Four Cats and, 440–2
Gaudí and, 489
ironwork collections of, 159, 436–7, *437*
modernisme and, 432–3, 435, 438–40
Morera's portrait painted by, 452, *453*
in Paris, 429–33, 435
posters of, *444*
symbolist influence in, 437–8
writings of, 427–8, 431–2
Rusinyol Seated in an Iron Chandelier (Casas),
442, *442*
Ruskin, John, 405

Safont, Jaume, 122
Safont, Marc, 119, *120*
Sagarra, Josep de, 245
Sagasta, Práxedes, 371
Sagnier, Enric, 492
Sagrada Família, 3, 6–7, 43–4, 465–7,
469–71, 482, 524–33, 536–41, *536*
background of, 526–8
Barcelona epitomized by, 540–1
columns of, 470–1
completion of, 525–6, 537–40
construction of, *528*, 530–1
financing of, 525–6, 529–32, 539
Gaudí, Reig, and Prat inspecting, *529*
with goats, *530*
Nativity facade of, 469, 532–3, 538, 540
Sagrera, Guillem, 146
Saint Bonaventure, College of, razing of,
222
Saint George, chapel of, 120
Saint John's Night, 26
Saint-Simon, Henri de, 230
Salarich, Jaume, 257
Saldoni, Baltasar, 290
Saló de Cent (Room of the Hundred),
122–3
Saló del Tinell, 123, *144*
description of, 143–4
Salses, siege of, 177–8
Salvador, Santiago, 419–20
Salvador i Riera, Joan, 162
Santa Caterina, convent of, sacking and
burning of, *218*, 222
Santa Coloma, Count of, 177–9
Santa Madrona, convent of, razing of,
209
Santa Maria d'Aneu, frescoes of, 91–2, *91–2*
Santa Maria del Mar, 143, 145, *151*
carving of stevedores in, 148, *148*
description of, 147–50
fishermen's and sailors' visits to, 166–7
monument to resisters of Bourbons next
to, 186

ILLUSTRATION CREDITS

Grateful acknowledgment is made to the following for permission to reprint illustrations appearing on the pages indicated:

Arxiu Fotografica, Biblioteca de L'Orfeó Català: 451

Arxiu Fotografica de Museus, Barcelona: 292, 347, 359, 420, 444, 459

Robert Hughes: 66, 80, 84, 90, 91, 92, 100, 118, 183, 224, 226, 227, 345, 366, 368, 396, 402, 407, 409, 410, 473, 482, 509, 514, 515

Institut Amatller de Arte Hispanico, Barcelona: 223, 420, 459, 460, 461, 472, 481, 484, 517, 528, 535

Institut Municipal d'Historia, Barcelona: 64, 67, 68, 72, 78, 79, 86, 88, 106, 109, 110, 114, 116, 121, 126, 144, 148, 151, 152, 157, 170, 174, 177, 182, 190, 192, 199, 200, 202, 203, 214, 215, 216, 218, 229, 231, 232, 238, 245, 256, 258, 259, 261, 265, 266, 273, 274, 275, 276, 277, 281, 282, 286, 296, 301, 303, 308, 314, 318, 321, 324, 328, 329, 331, 342, 344, 349, 356, 360, 363, 365, 373, 377, 380, 382, 384, 387, 398, 400, 404, 419, 426, 437, 440, 441, 450, 467, 474, 486, 493, 497, 501, 502, 506, 510, 518, 519, 521, 527, 529, 530, 532, 536

Museo Español de Arte Contemporáneo, Madrid: 434

Museu Cau Ferrat, Sitges: 430, 435, 442, 453

Museu d'Art Modern, Barcelona: 401, 427, 443, 444, 445, 494

Museu de l'Historia de la Ciutat, Barcelona: 156, 196, 207, 219, 234, 287, 338

Museu Marítim, Barcelona: 160, 163

Does he have an idea about price?